BEDIUZZAMAN SAID NURSI

Bediuzzaman Said Nursi
Author of the Risale-i Nur

Şükran Vahide

Islamic Book Trust
Kuala Lumpur

© Şükran Vahide 2011

All rights reserved. No part of this publication may be produced, stored in a retrieval system, or transmitted, in any form or by any means, electronic, mechanical, photocopying, recording or otherwise without the prior permission of the publisher.

Published by
Islamic Book Trust
607 Mutiara Majestic
Jalan Othman
46000 Petaling Jaya
Selangor, Malaysia
www.ibtbooks.com

Islamic Book Trust is affiliated with The Other Press.

Perpustakaan Negara Malaysia   Cataloguing-in-Publication Data

Vahide, Sukran
    Bediuzzaman Said Nursi : the author of the risale-i nur / Sukran Vahide.
    Includes index
    Bibliography: p. 493
    ISBN 978-967-5062-86-5
    1. Nursi, Said, 1873-1960. 2. Muslim scholars--Biography. I. Title.
    297.092

Printed by
Academe Art & Printing Services Sdn. Bhd.
No. 7, Jalan Rajawali 1A
Bandar Baru Puchong
Batu 8, Jalan Puchong
47100 Selangor

Contents

Foreword		vii
Abbreviations		xiii
Part I: The Old Said		
1	Childhood and Youth	3
2	Istanbul before Freedom	40
3	Freedom and Constitutionalism	64
4	Bediuzzaman and the Thirty-First of March Incident	86
5	"The Future shall be Islam's, and Islam's Alone"	105
6	The Medresetü'z-Zehrâ	127
7	War and Captivity	135
8	Return and Appointment to the Darü'l-Hikmeti'l-İslamiye	158
9	The Supremacy of the Qur'an and Birth of the New Said	178
10	Opposition to the British and Move to Ankara	195
Part II: The New Said		
11	Van	215
12	Barla	234
13	Eskişehir	274
14	Kastamonu	291
15	Denizli	333

16 Emirdağ 351
17 Afyon 372
Part III: The Third Said
18 The Third Said 401
Conclusion 467
Selections from the *Risale-i Nur* 473
Bibliography 493
Index 499

Foreword

Similar to the author's introduction to Bediuzzaman Said Nursi's official biography, written in the last years of his life, the first thing to state about the present biography is that it by no means describes comprehensively this unique figure whose importance is increasingly being understood. His life, works, and approach to the problems facing the Islamic world, and indeed all humanity are becoming better known.

One reason the present work may best be described as an introduction to Bediuzzaman's life is the diversity of his character and the exceptional nature of his abilities, all of which he developed to the highest degree. He was a religious scholar of the highest standing who, unusually among such scholars, had a wide knowledge of modern science and many areas of modern life and learning. He was a great *mujāhid*; he fought for the defence of Islam and the Ottoman Empire on the battlefield. He strove with his pen, producing many works, writing for newspapers and journals. He gave sermons and speeches and addressed gatherings large and small. He was a famous debater, and was able to solve complex problems. And while engaging in these active and scholarly struggles in the cause of Islam, he was by nature a lover of solitude; he would retire into seclusion to devote himself to worship and contemplation of his Maker. Foremost, Bediuzzaman was the last of the great saints, a spiritual figure of the greatest stature who takes his place in Islam alongside Imam Ghazālī, 'Abd al-Qādir al-Jīlānī and Imam Rabbānī. Indeed, he was their heir, carrying forward their legacy inherited from Prophet Muḥammad (ṣ) and presenting it to the people of this age and the future.

Another reason this biography may best be described as an introduction was the length of Bediuzzaman's life and the variety of the periods through which he lived: under the Ottoman Empire, he saw the absolutist rule of Sultan Abdulhamid, and the Constitutional Revolution of 1908 and ascendancy of the Committee of Union and Progress, which came to an end with the collapse of the Empire following the First World War, then the War of Independence and birth of the modern Republic of Turkey, in each of which he was actively involved. This was the period he called the Old Said. The second main period of his life, that of the New Said, began in the years following the First World War. It coincided with the founding of the Republic and coming to power of the new regime, the chief objective of which was the westernization of Turkey, and the next twenty-five years were ones of exile, imprisonment, and oppression for Bediuzzaman. They were followed in 1950 by an easing of conditions and the emergence of a Third Said. These last ten years of his life, from 1950-1960, differed from the previous period in so far as he once again took a keener interest in social and political matters.

Another factor limiting the present biography is the paucity of information about a number of areas of Bediuzzaman's life, particularly the early period. When his official biography was being written, he instructed his close students who were preparing it to cut out the majority of passages describing himself and his personal achievements and adventures—for indeed his life reads like an adventure story—and to include only parts which looked to the "the fruit" of his life, the *Risale-i Nur* and its service of belief and the Qur'an.

As the conditions of the times required, the Old Said's struggles for the cause of Islam were largely in the public domain and in the realm of politics. But on the emergence of the New Said,

Bediuzzaman virtually discounted this colourful early period of his life and, withdrawing from social and political life, concentrated on the struggle to save and strengthen belief in God and the other truths of faith, which were then under threat. It was during this period and for this purpose that he wrote—rather, was inspired to write—the *Risale-i Nur*. In spite of attempts to suppress the work, Bediuzzaman developed a method of blending science and the truths of religion in order to address the mentality of modern man. It had unparalleled success in strengthening belief and combating atheism and materialist philosophy, so that by the 1950s it had many thousands of students in Turkey and beyond.

Bediuzzaman wrote that his life was "a seed" out of which in His mercy, Almighty God had created "the tree of the *Risale-i Nur*." Thus, when his biography was being prepared, he wanted attention to be directed towards this work for the cause of religious belief, rather than towards his own self and personality. For this reason there are many blank spots in the early period of his life. He himself never illuminated them and it is largely due to the research of Necmeddin Şahiner and his indefatigable tracking down and interviewing of anyone who met, saw, or heard of Bediuzzaman in this period and later, that a fuller picture of these years has emerged. The two main sources in addition to these are Bediuzzaman's own works and his official biography. His early years in this work are taken from the biography written by his nephew, Abdurrahman, which was first published in 1919. The official archives and other materials relating to this period remain largely unexplored.

A further point that should be borne in mind while reading the first part of this biography concerns the Old Said's insistence that, in apparent contradiction to the dire situation into which the Ottoman Empire and Islamic world had fallen, the Qur'an and Islamic civilization would dominate in the near future. In later years he explained that these repeated and insistent predictions of the Old Said were not in error, but in need of closer interpretation.

He wrote that "in order to dispel despair" at that time, the Old Said frequently stated that "he saw a light in the future", and along with others he had striven for its achievement in the field of politics and social life. This light had proved to be the *Risale-i Nur*. His predictions of a turn in the fortunes of the Islamic world had been correct, but his interpretation of them had not been correct. And in the 1950s he wrote that "the certain good tidings" he had given in his sermon in Damascus in 1911 of the supremacy of Islam, which he had said would occur in the near future, had been "delayed by the two World Wars and twenty-five years of despotism"; there were then signs of them being realised. Thus, through reasoning and "premonition", the Old Said had foretold the resurgence of Islam and rise of the Islamic world that began in the 1950s and continues at the present time and in which the *Risale-i Nur* plays an increasingly important part.

All of Bediuzzaman's endeavours throughout his long life were for the advancement and prosperity of Muslims and the Islamic world, and their happiness in this world and the next, as well as for all humanity. These he believed to lie in the Qur'an. In his search to find a way of relating its truths to modern man, he was inspired to write the *Risale-i Nur*, which expounds and explains in a unique way the Qur'an's teachings concerning belief in God and other truths of faith. He believed that the root of man's problems lied in weakness of belief in these truths, and that the problems facing the Islamic world in particular would be solved only through renewal of belief. Thus he turned his back on politics and dedicated all his efforts to this end. With his profound knowledge of both the religious and modern sciences, the new way to the truth that he opened up with the *Risale-i Nur* was so successful in the renewing and strengthening of belief that it is accepted by many to be the Regenerator of Religion promised each century in the well-known *ḥadīth*. Now, thirty years after Bediuzzaman departed this life, the *Risale-i Nur* continues to find thousands of new students within Turkey, particularly among the young, and so too it continues to

Foreword   xi

spread rapidly throughout the Islamic world, where it is acclaimed by the scholars of al-Azhar and elsewhere.

Bediuzzaman shunned acclaim and wanted all attention to be directed away from himself to the *Risale-i Nur*. He embodied the Islamic virtues of courage, enterprise, self-sacrifice, compassion, humility, and unbending resolve in the face of enemies to such a high degree, reflecting in his life the practices of Prophet Muḥammad (ṣ) to a degree rarely achieved. Whatever the deficiencies of this work, and there are bound to be many, they should be attributed to the author. *Wa mā tawfīqī illā billāh.*

Abbreviations

The following abbreviations are used in the notes:

Aydınlar Konuşuyor—N. Şahiner, *Said Nursî ve Nurculuk Hakkında Aydınlar Konuşuyor.*
Cemal Kutay, *Bediüzzaman*—*Çağımızda Bir Asr-ı Saadet Müslümanı Bediüzzaman Said Nursî.*
Ott. edn.—Ottoman edition.
Şahiner, *Said Nursî*—*Bilinmeyen Taraflariyle Bediüzzaman Said Nursî, Kronolojik Hayatı* (unless otherwise stated, 6th edition, 1988).
Son Şahitler, i-v—N. Şahiner, *Son Şahitler Bediüzzaman Said Nursî'yi Anlatıyor, Vols. 1-5.*
Tarihçe—(Bediuzzaman's 'official' biography, prepared during his life time) *Risale-i-Nur Külliyatı Müellifi Bediüzzaman Said Nursî*—*Hayatı, Mesleki, Tercüme-i Hâli.*

Part I
The Old Said

1
Childhood and Youth

Birth and Early Childhood

Bediuzzaman Said Nursi was born early one spring morning in the village of Nurs, a small hamlet in the province of Bitlis in eastern Turkey. The year was 1293 according to the Rumi calendar then in use in the Ottoman Empire, that is, 1877.[1] The circumstances into which he was born were humble; the house, of sun-dried brick, one of twenty or so built against the south-facing slope of a valley in the towering Taurus Mountains to the south of Lake Van.

Even at his birth the child displayed signs of being exceptional. It is said that on coming into the world he peered around attentively, his look fairly frightening those present. It was as if he was going to speak. He did not cry, just clenched his fists. Then they chanted the call to prayer in his ears, and named him Said.[2]

Said's mother was called Nuriye, and his father, a villager with a small holding of land, was Mirza. They were a Kurdish family. Said was the fourth of seven children. The two eldest were girls, Dürriye and Hanım, then came his elder brother, 'Abdullah. Said was followed by two more boys, Mehmed and Abdülmecid, (pronounced Abdulmejid) and last was a girl, Mercan (pronounced Merjan).

Mirza's forbears had come originally from Jizre on the Tigris.[3] Also known as Sufi Mirza, he died in the 1920's and was buried in the graveyard at Nurs. At the head of his grave stands a rough uncut stone with simply the name Mirza etched on it. Nuriye,

Said's mother, was from the village of Bilkan, three hours distant from Nurs.[4] Like her husband, she was devout and virtuous. She died during the First World War and was also buried in Nurs. In later years, Said was to say: "From my mother I learnt compassion, and from my father, orderliness and regularity."[5]

Said passed his early years with his family in Nurs, long winters in the village, short summers in the higher pastures or in the gardens and fields along the river banks in the valley bottom. A short growing season, but sufficient to meet the villagers' needs. It was a life close to the natural world, in harmony with its rhythms and cycles, full of wonders for an aware and responsive child like Said. He was unusually intelligent, always investigating things, questioning and seeking answers. Years later, when explaining how scholarly metaphors may degenerate into superstition "when they fall into the hands of the ignorant", he himself described an occasion which illustrates this.

One night, on hearing tin cans being clashed together and a rifle being fired, the family rushed out of the house to find it was an eclipse of the moon. Said asked his mother: "Why has the moon gone like that?" She replied:

"A snake has swallowed it." So Said asked:

"Then why can it still be seen?"

"The snakes in the sky are like glass; they show what they have inside them."[6]

Said was only to learn the true answer when studying astronomy a few years later.

Whenever the opportunity arose, and especially in the long winter evenings, Said would go and listen to any discussions being held by students and teachers of the *madrasahs*, that is, the religious schools, or by religious figures. These discussions, often about the famous scholars, saints, and spiritual leaders of the past, usually took the form of contest and debate. If any of the students or scholars displayed more intelligence than the others, or was

Childhood and Youth

victorious in debate, he was made much of by the others, and was held in great esteem.[7] This appealed to the young Said, too.

In addition, more than being merely independent-minded, it was as though from his very earliest years, Said was reaching for or was being driven to discover a way other than that which those around him followed, as the following, written by some of his students, shows:

"Our Master himself said: 'When I was eight or nine years old, contrary to my family and everyone else in the vicinity, who were attached to the Naqshbandī *ṭarīqah* and used to seek assistance from a famous figure called Ghawth Hizan, I used to say: 'O Ghawth Jīlānī!' Since I was a child, if some insignificant thing like a walnut got lost, [I would say] 'O Shaykh! I'll say a Fātiḥah for you and you find this thing for me!' It is strange and yet I swear that a thousand times the venerable Shaykh came to my assistance through his prayers and saintly influence. Therefore, however many Fātiḥahs and supplications I have uttered in general in my life, after the person of the Prophet (ṣ), they have been offered for Shaykh Jīlānī. While I am a Naqshbandī in three or four respects, the Qādirī way and love of it prevail in me involuntarily. But preoccupation [with study of the religious sciences] prevented my becoming involved with the *ṭarīqah*.'"[8] Although, as is stated here, Said never joined a *ṭarīqah* or followed the Sufi path—he was later to describe Sufism as being inappropriate for the needs of the modern age—his close relationship with Shaykh 'Abd al-Qādir al-Jīlānī continued throughout his life; on many occasions throughout his life Said received guidance and assistance through his saintly influence.

Said Begins His Studies

Said started his studies at the age of nine. He appears now as a pugnacious child, prone to quarrelling with both his peers and his elders. But this sprang not from any innate fault, but from the frustration at bearing within him a great and brilliant spirit.

It was his elder brother Mullah[9] 'Abdullah who first prompted the young Said to start studying. He had noticed how he had benefited from his studies. 'Abdullah had gradually improved and progressed so that when Said saw him together with his friends from the village who had not studied his self-evident superiority awoke in Said a strong urge to study himself. With this intention, he set off with him for Mullah Mehmed Emin Efendi's *madrasah* in the village of Tağ, near İsparit. However, he fought with another student called Mehmed, and did not stay there long.

For the young Said also held himself in great esteem. He could not endure even the smallest word spoken to him in a commanding tone, or to be dominated in any way. So he returned to his own village, where he told his father that he would not attend any more *madrasahs* until he was older, because the other students were all bigger than him. Due to its small size, Nurs had no *madrasah*, so Said's lessons were then restricted to the one day a week that his elder brother, 'Abdullah, returned.[10]

Let us see how in later years Bediuzzaman described himself at this age.

> When I was ten years old, I had great pride in myself, which sometimes even took the form of boasting and self-praise; although I myself did not want to, I used to assume the air of one undertaking some great work and mighty act of heroism. I used to say to myself: "You are not worth tuppence, what is the reason for this excessive showing-off and boasting, especially when it comes to courage?" I did not know, and used to wonder at it. Then, a month or two ago [1944] the question was answered: the *Risale-i Nur* was making itself felt before it was written: "Although you were a seed like a common chip of wood, you had a presentiment of those fruits of Paradise as though they were actually your own property, and used to boast and praise yourself."[11]

About a year passed in this way. Then, once again, Said set off to continue his studies full-time. But his needs were not to be answered by any of the teachers or *madrasahs* he visited. He

Childhood and Youth

went first to the village of Pirmis, and then to the summer pastures of the Hizan Shaykh, the Naqshbandī Sayyid Nur Muhammad. There, his independent spirit and the fact that he could not endure being dominated in any way made him fall out with four other students in particular. They would join forces and harass him constantly. So, one day Said went to Sayyid Nur Muhammad and said: "Shaykh Efendi! Please tell them that when they fight me to come two at a time and not all four at once." This courage on the part of the ten-year-old Said pleased the Shaykh greatly, who smiled and said: "You are my student, no one shall bother you!" And from then on Said was known as 'the Shaykh's student'.[12]

Visit to Nurs

Shaykh Nur Muhammad was intrigued by Said's ability and courage, and one day set out together with him and some others of his students on the six or seven hour journey to Nurs in order to meet his parents. A short time after arriving, Mirza appeared, driving before him two cows and two oxen with their mouths bound. After the introductions, Said's teacher asked him the reason for this. Mirza replied in a modest manner:

> Sir, our fields are a fair way off. On the way, I pass through the fields and gardens of many other people. If these animals' mouths were not tied, it is possible they would eat their produce. I tie them up so that there is nothing unlawful in our food.

Having seen how upright Said's father was, Shaykh Nur Muhammad asked how his mother had brought up Said. Nuriye Hanım replied;

> When I was pregnant with Said, I never set a foot on the ground without being purified with ablutions. And when he came into the world, there was not a day when I did not suckle him without being purified by ablutions.

Said's teacher had now discovered what he had come to learn. Of course such parents should expect to have such a son. They spent that night in Nurs and returned the following morning to Hizan.¹³

"One of the Nurs students will revive the religion of Islam"

After remaining a while longer with Sayyid Nur Muhammad, Said went together with his elder brother, 'Abdullah, to the village of Nurşin. Since it was summer, they left the village together with the villagers and other students for the high pastures of Şeyhan. Once there, Said quarrelled with his elder brother, and they fell out. The teacher of the Tağ *madrasah*, Mehmed Emin Efendi, was angry with Said and asked him why he opposed his elder brother. But Said did not recognise the teacher's authority either, and told him that since the *madrasah* where they were at the time belonged to the famous Shaykh Tağı, he was a student like himself and did not have the right to act as a teacher. Then he left the *madrasah* immediately for Nurşin, passing through a dense forest that was difficult to penetrate even by day.¹⁴

It was later related from Bediuzzaman himself that the owner of the Tağ *madrasah*, Shaykh Tağı, used to show a close interest in the students from Nurs, rising at night during the winter to make sure they were all covered and would not catch cold. Moreover, he used to say to the older students:

> Look after these students from Nurs well, one of them will revive the religion of Islam, but which of them it will be I do not know at present.¹⁵

Young Said's Independence

At that time in eastern Anatolia any scholar who had completed the course of study in a *madrasah* and could demonstrate his mastery of the subjects obtained his diploma (*ijāzah*), and could then open a *madrasah* in a village of his choice. If he was able, he would himself meet the needs of the students, such as food, heating and clothing, and if he was not able, they were met by the villagers either through *zakāh* or some other way. The teacher asked for no payment for his teaching.

Young Said would in no way accept *zakāh* or alms. To accept assistance meant becoming obliged to others, and he felt that would be an unbearable burden on his spirit.

One day, his fellow students went to the neighbouring villages to collect *zakāh*, but Said did not accompany them. The villagers were impressed by this and appreciative of his independence so they collected a sum of money and tried to give it to him. Said thanked them and refused it. So they gave it to Mullah 'Abdullah in the hope that he would persuade him to accept it. The following exchange then ensued:

Said said: "Buy me a rifle with the money!"

Mullah 'Abdullah: "No, that is not possible."

"Well, in that case, get me a revolver."

"No, that is not possible, either."

So, smiling, Said said: "Well, get me a dagger, then."

At which his elder brother laughed and said: "No, nor is that possible. I'll only buy you some grapes; then we will make sure the matter remains sweet!"[16]

Said Dreams of the Prophet (ṣ)

Said spent that winter in Nurs. In the course of it, he had a powerful dream which impelled him to return to his studies. It was like this: it was the Last Day and the Resurrection was taking place. Said felt a desire to visit Prophet Muḥammad (ṣ). While wondering how he could achieve this, it occurred to him to go and sit by the Bridge of Sirāṭ, because everyone has to pass over it. While the Prophet is passing, he thought, I shall meet him and kiss his hand. So he went and sat by the Bridge and there met with all the prophets and kissed their hands. Finally, Prophet Muḥammad (ṣ) came. Said kissed his hand and asked for knowledge from him. The Prophet said: "Knowledge of the Qur'an will be given to you on the condition you ask no questions of any of my community."

Upon this Said awoke in a state of great excitement.¹⁷ And indeed, he thereafter made it a personal rule never to ask questions of other scholars. Even when he went to Istanbul, he adhered to it; he only answered questions put to him.

So following the dream, Bediuzzaman left Nurs going first to the village of Arvas and from there to Shaykh Emin Efendi's *madrasah* in Bitlis.¹⁸ Because of Said's tender years, the Shaykh did not teach Said himself, saying he would appoint one of his students to do so. This wounded Said's self-esteem. One day while Shaykh Emin was teaching in the mosque, Said rose to his feet objecting to what he was saying with the words: "Sir! You are wrong, it is not like that!" The Shaykh and his students looked at the young Said in amazement. Then, Said remembered that the Shaykh did not even condescend to teach him.

Shortly after this Said set off for the Mir Hasan Veli *madrasah* at Müküs [Bahçeseray], the principal of which was Mullah Abdülkerim. When he saw that the new, lower grade students were given no importance, he ignored the first seven books, which should have been studied in sequence and announced he would study the eighth. He remained there only a few days then went to Vastan [Gevaş] near Van. After a month in Gevaş, he set off with a companion called Mullah Mehmed for [Doğu] Bayezit, a small town in the province of Erzurum and it was here that his real studies commenced. Until this time, he had only studied the principles of Arabic grammar and syntax.¹⁹

Bayezit

Said's period of study in the Bayezit *madrasah* under Shaykh Muḥammad Jalālī lasted only three months, but it was to provide him with the foundations of religious sciences on which his later thought and works would be based. Also, it once again showed what he had instinctively displayed from the very beginning of his studies, namely, his dissatisfaction with the existing education system and his awareness of the urgent need for its reform. Moreover, the astonishing number of works that Said read, memorised and digested in this short period of time was to demonstrate his remarkable power of memory, and exceptional intelligence and understanding, both of which were developed to a degree far exceeding the average for boys of his age. He was fourteen years old.

During his time in Bayezit, Said completed the entire course of study then current in *madrasahs*. The works studied were heavily annotated, with commentaries, commentaries on commentaries, and even commentaries on those commentaries and further expositions. To complete the course under normal conditions took the average student fifteen to twenty years. The method was to completely master one book and one subject before passing onto the next.

Said began from 'Mullah Jami',[20] and completed all the works in the course in turn. This he did by ignoring all the commentaries and expositions, and by concentrating on only a certain number of sections in each work. On being asked by a displeased Shaykh Muḥammad Jalālī why he was studying in this way, Said answered thus:

> I am not able to read and understand this many books. But they are caskets of jewels, treasure chests, and the key is with you. I only implore you to show me what is in them so I can understand what these books are discussing, and then I shall study those that are suitable for me.

Said's aim in replying thus was to point out the need for reform in *madrasah* education and to prevent time being wasted through the inclusion of so many commentaries, annotations and expositions. And in answer to his master's question: "Which subject, which of the sciences studied is suitable for you?", Said replied:

> I cannot distinguish these sciences one from the other. I either know all of them or none of them.

Whichever of the books Said studied, he would understand it without seeking anyone's assistance. He was able to study and master the most difficult works of two hundred pages or more, like *Jamʿ al-Jawāmiʿ*, *Sharḥ al-Mawāqif*, and *Ibn Ḥajar* in twenty-four hours. He gave himself over to studying to such a degree that all his ties with the outside world were cut. On whichever subject he was questioned, he would give the answer correctly and without hesitation.[21]

While in Beyazit, Said passed much of his time, and even the nights, in the mausoleum of the Kurdish saint and literary figure Ahmad Khānī, so that the people said he was specially privileged with Ahmad Khānī's spiritual radiance. One night Said's friends from the *madrasah* missed him and started searching for him. Finally they looked in the mausoleum and found him there studying by the light of a candle. But he rebuked them saying: "Why are you disturbing me in this way?"[22] On the one hand Said plunged himself into studying, while on the other he started to follow the way of the Illuminist (*Ishrāqiyyūn*) philosophers and to practise extreme self-discipline and asceticism. The Illuminists had accustomed their bodies to such practices gradually, but Said ignored the necessary period of adjustment and suddenly undertook the most rigorous ascetic exercises. His body could not support it and he grew progressively weaker. He would make one piece of bread last three days, trying to emulate the Illuminists in their practice of the theory that 'asceticism serves to expand the mind'.

Not being content with this, he followed Imam Ghazālī's Sufistic interpretation of the Ḥadīth, "Give up what you are doubtful about for that about which you have no doubts" from *Iḥyā' 'Ulūm al-Dīn*, and for a time gave up eating bread, even, and existed on grass and plants. Furthermore, he rarely spoke.[23]

At the end of three months, Said obtained his diploma from Shaykh Muḥammad Jalālī, the Principal of the Beyazit *madrasah*, and was then known as Mullah Said. Having received it, he donned the simple garb of a dervish and set out for Baghdad, intending to visit its famous religious scholars and the tomb of Shaykh ʿAbd al-

Qādir al-Jīlānī. Avoiding roads, travelling at night over mountains and through forests, he arrived after some time in Bitlis. There, for two days he attended the lectures of Shaykh Mehmed Emin Efendi. The Shaykh proposed that he wear the dress of a scholar. In eastern Anatolia at that time the turban and scholar's robe were not worn by students, but only presented when the diploma (*ijāzah*) was obtained. The scholar's dress was the right only of teachers (*mudarris*). But Mullah Said did not accept the Shaykh's proposal, answering that since he was not yet mature, he did not think it was fitting for him to wear the dress of a respected teacher. How could he be a teacher while still a child? And he put the gown and turban away in a corner of the mosque.[24]

Şirvan

Mullah Said then travelled on to Şirvan to his elder brother, Mullah 'Abdullah. The following exchange took place at their first meeting:

Mullah 'Abdullah: "I have finished *Sharḥ Shamsī* since you were here. What have you read?"

Mullah Said: "I have read eighty books."

"What do you mean?"

"Yes, I have finished eighty books. And I have read a lot of books not included in the syllabus."

Mullah 'Abdullah found it hard to believe that his brother had read so many books in such a short time and wanted to test him. Mullah Said agreed so 'Abdullah tested him and was left in admiration and astonishment. Then hiding it from his own students, he accepted his younger brother as his master who only eight months before had been his student, and started to take lessons from him. But peering through the keyhole, 'Abdullah's students finally discovered him being taught by Mullah Said. However, in order not to let them learn the truth, he told them that he was doing so in order to avert the evil eye.[25]

Siirt

Mullah Said remained with his brother a while longer and then made his way to Siirt. It was here that Said was challenged by the local *'ulamā'* for the first time and was successful in debating with them and answering all their questions. His reputation now became firmly established. On his arrival in Siirt, he went to the *madrasah* of the famous Mullah Fethullah Efendi, who was to experience the same astonishment as Mullah 'Abdullah at the number of books Said had read and learnt. He also examined Mullah Said, who again gave perfect answers. So he then decided to test Said's memory and handed him a work called the *al-Maqāmāt al-Ḥarīriyyah*.[26] Mullah Said read one page once, memorised it, then repeated it by heart. Mullah Fethullah expressed his amazement by saying: "For this degree of memory and intelligence to be combined in one person is indeed rare."

While there, Mullah Said memorised the whole of a work on the principles of jurisprudence of the four schools of Islam by the Shāfi'ī scholar Ibn al-Subkī, the *Jam' al-Jawāmi'*, by reading it for one or two hours every day for a week. Whereupon Mullah Fethullah wrote in the book, in Arabic, "He memorised the whole of the *Jam' al-Jawāmi'* in a week".

From a letter written by Bediuzzaman in 1946 while in exile in Emirdağ, it is learned that it was as a result of these feats of learning that he was first given the name of Bediuzzaman— Wonder of the Age—and by Mullah Fethullah Efendi. He wrote to one of his important students:

> My Curious Brother, Re'fet Bey, you want information about Bedi'uzzaman Hamadani's duty and written works in the 3rd century [Hijrī]. I only know that he had an extraordinary intelligence and power of memory.
>
> Fifty-five years ago one of my first masters, the late Mullah Fethullah of Siirt, likened the Old Said to him and gave him his name.[27]

News of these events spread around Siirt and on hearing it, the *'ulamā'* of the area gathered together and invited Said to a debate

Childhood and Youth

and to answer their questions. Said accepted, and not only defeated them in debate but was successful in answering all their questions. Those present were full of praise and admiration for him and when the people of Siirt came to hear of it, they regarded Mullah Said as something of a *walī* or saint. However, all this aroused the jealousy of the lesser scholars and students in the area who, since they were unable to defeat him in argument or in learning, tried to do so by force. They set upon him one day, but the people intervened and prevented any harm from coming to Said, who told the gendarmes who arrived on the scene, having been sent by the Governor:

> We are students; we fight and make it up again. It is better if no one outside our profession interferes. The fault was mine.

Said answered in this way out of his extreme respect for the learned profession, which he felt would be slighted by the interference of the ignorant and uneducated, although it would have been to assist him.

After this incident, Said always carried a short dagger with him in order to deter those tempted to fight him. He was strong and agile and now came to be known as Said-i Meşhur, Said the Famous. He challenged all the *'ulamā'* and students in Siirt to debates, letting it be known that he never asked questions, but answered anyone who chose to put questions to him.[28] He also competed in sports and physical feats, and demonstrated his superiority in these too. One day in Siirt, he challenged a friend, Mullah Jalāl, to jump a water canal. He himself cleared the broad canal successfully, then stood back to watch his friend. Mullah Jalāl took a running jump, but alas, not being as athletic as Said, landed in the mud at the edge of it.[29]

Bitlis

Mullah Said remained some while in Siirt, then, rather than continuing his journey to Baghdad, returned to Bitlis and the *madrasah* of Shaykh Emin. There, as before, the Shaykh dismissed

Said as too young to understand anything. Unable to endure being treated in this way, Mullah Said requested once again that he be given the opportunity to prove himself.

So Shaykh Emin asked him sixteen questions on difficult subjects, all of which Mullah Said answered correctly and without hesitation. The Shaykh then set him a literary riddle in the form of three letters from the Arabic alphabet written without diacritical points thus: [فمل] Said had to compose a twelve-word sentence using only letters of those shapes and adding the points. They contain a total of ten possibilities with regard to the points distinguishing the different letters, and twelve with regard to the vowels, making a total in all of one hundred and twenty. Mullah Said found all those possibilities within three days and composed the sentence accordingly, proving once again his intelligence.[30] He then went to the Quraysh mosque and began to preach to the people.

Said became very popular, drawing a large number of the people of Bitlis to listen to him. But it resulted in two factions forming in the town; those who supported him and those who supported Shaykh Emin. To forestall any trouble arising from this situation, the Governor expelled Mullah Said from Bitlis, and he made his way from there to Şirvan.[31]

Şirvan

As Said's fame grew so did his difficulties. Some teachers and lesser scholars whom he had previously defeated in debate constantly sought opportunities to reduce his prestige in the eyes of the people. They had him watched and followed, and one day when he missed the time for the morning-prayer and performed it late, they started a rumour among the people saying: "Mullah Said has given up performing the obligatory prayers." When asked the meaning of this, Said said:

> Something that has no basis does not spread among the people so quickly. The fault was mine, and I suffered two punishments: one was God's reprimand, the other insinuations against me by

Childhood and Youth

the people. The true reason for this was as follows: I gave up the prayers I was in the habit of reciting at night. If the world's spirit perceived this fact, it made them describe it wrongly, because they did not grasp the matter entirely.

While in Şirvan, someone came to him from the Siirt area saying that a fifteen-year-old youth had silenced in argument all the *'ulamā'* of the region and that he had come in order to invite Mullah Said to come and challenge this youth to a debate. Mullah Said responded favourably to this request, made some preparations for the journey, and they set out together. After some two hours on the road, Said asked the description of this youth, his dress, behaviour, and such matters. The man from Siirt said:

> I do not know his name, but when he first arrived he was wearing the dress of a dervish with a sheepskin over his shoulders. Then later he put on student's dress and silenced in argument all the learned men of Siirt.

On listening to this, Said realised that the man was talking about him and that news of the events of the previous year had now spread around all the surrounding villages. He turned back the way they had come and did not accept the invitation.[32]

Tillo

After some time, Mullah Said went to the town of Tillo, in the district of Siirt. Outside the town on a hill stands a small domed building of stone. Said confined himself in this Kubbe-i Hasiye as it was known, and there memorised an Arabic lexicon, the *Qāmūs al-Uqyānūs*, as far as the fourteenth letter of the alphabet, *Sīn*.[33]

While here, his younger brother, Mehmed, used to bring Said's food each day. And Said, dipping his bread in the soup would eat it and give the crumbs to the ants around the building. When asked the reason for this, he would say:

I have observed that they have a social life, and work together diligently and conscientiously, and I want to help them as a reward for their republicanism.[34]

Although it was not until subsequently to this, in Mardin as we shall see, that Said stated that he was first "awakened politically", it is clear from this story of the ants that he had already at this stage acquired the beliefs that he would adhere to throughout his life. Since these are described below and in detail in a later chapter, suffice it to say here that the basis of his political ideas, based on Islamic practice as is clear in the footnote below, was a system based on the principles of freedom, justice, consultation, and the rule of law.

It was also while he was in Tillo that Mullah Said had the dream in response to which he first started to work among the tribes as a conciliator and a man of religion. He dreamt that Shaykh 'Abd al-Qādir al-Jīlānī appeared to him and ordered him to go to Mustafa Pasha, the head of the Miran tribe,[35] "and summon him to the way of guidance." He was to desist from oppression, perform the obligatory prayers, and enjoin what was lawful. Otherwise Said was to kill him.[36]

This was a challenging task for Mullah Said, who can still have been little more than sixteen years old. The Miran tribe was powerful and numerous, and despite being a commander in one of the Hamidiye regiments,[37] its chief, Mustafa Pasha—entitled Pasha because of this appointment— engaged in brigandage and oppression. Nevertheless, Said immediately gathered together his belongings and made his way south to the area of Jizre on the Tigris. Said's relations with the tyrannical chief there illustrate one of his most striking and enduring characteristics, namely his courage and absolute lack of fear, especially in the face of tyrants and the powerful. Rather, it was a disdain for fear of anything other than his Maker.

Mullah Said and Mustafa Pasha

On approaching Mustafa Pasha's tent, Said learnt that he was elsewhere and took the opportunity to rest. A while later

Childhood and Youth

Mustafa Pasha returned to the encampment and entered his tent whereupon all those present rose to their feet, except Mullah Said, who did not so much as stir. This attracted Mustafa Pasha's attention, and he enquired who it was from Fettah Bey, a major in the militia. He informed him that it was the Famous Mullah Said. Now, Mustafa Pasha did not care at all for the *'ulamā'*, but he thought it wise to suppress his anger, and asked why he had come there. Mullah Said replied as ordered in his dream:

> I have come to guide you to the right path. Either you give up your tyranny and start performing the obligatory prayers, or else I shall kill you!

Mustafa Pasha was doubtless taken by surprise with this reply and left the tent to consider the situation. He returned after a while and again asked why he had come. Said repeated what he had said. After further exchanges, Mustafa Pasha thought of a solution; he would set up a contest between Mullah Said and "his" religious scholars in Jizre. If Mullah Said was victorious, he would do as he said. Otherwise he would throw him in the river. Said was quite unperturbed. He told Mustafa Pasha:

> Just as it is beyond my power to silence all the *'ulamā'*, so also is it beyond your power to throw me into the river. But on my answering them, I want one thing from you, and that is a Mauser rifle. And if you do not stick to your word, I shall kill you with it!

After this exchange had taken place, they mounted their horses and rode down to Jizre from the high grazing grounds. Mustafa Pasha would in no way speak to Mullah Said on the way. When they came to the place known as Bani Han on the banks of the Tigris, Said slept, entirely confident about his forthcoming trial. When he awoke, he saw that the scholars of the area had foregathered and were waiting books in hand. After introductions, tea was served. These *'ulamā'* had heard of the Famous Mullah Said, and as they prepared their questions in a state of some trepidation, Said drank not only his own tea, but some of their's as well. Mustafa Pasha noticed this and informed the scholars he was of the opinion that they would be defeated.

Mullah Said told the Jizre scholars that he had taken a vow and asked no questions of anyone, but that he was ready for theirs. Whereupon they presented him with about forty questions, all of which Said answered satisfactorily. Except for one, which they did not realise was incorrect, and accepted. As the gathering was dispersing, Mullah Said recalled this, and hurried back to inform them and give the correct answer, upon which they admitted that they were well and truly defeated, and a number of them started to study under Mullah Said. Mustafa Pasha also presented him with the promised rifle, and began to perform the obligatory prayers.[38]

Mullah Said was physically fit and strong, just as he was intellectually. He particularly enjoyed wrestling, and used to wrestle with all the students in the *madrasahs*. And neither were they able to defeat him.

One day, he and Mustafa Pasha went out to race each other on horseback. Mustafa Pasha had ordered that an unbroken, uncontrollable horse be prepared, which he gave to Mullah Said to ride. Mullah Said wanted to gallop the rebellious horse after walking it round for a bit. Given some rein, the horse galloped off away from the direction it had been pointed. Said tried to stop it with all his strength; he could not. Finally the horse careered towards a group of children. The son of one of the Jizre tribal leaders was standing right in its path. The horse reared up and struck the child between the shoulders with its forelegs. The child fell to the ground under the horse's hooves and began to struggle desperately. After some minutes, those watching reached them. When they saw the child, by then motionless as though dead, they wanted to kill Mullah Said. On the tribal leader's servants pulling out their daggers, Mullah Said immediately drew his revolver, and said to them:

"If you look at the reality of the matter, Allah killed the child. If you look at the cause, Kel Mustafa killed him, because it was he who gave me this horse. Wait, let me come and look at the child. If

Childhood and Youth 21

he is dead, we can fight it out later." And dismounting, he picked up the child. When he saw no signs of life in him, he plunged him into cold water and immediately pulled him out. The child opened his eyes and smiled. All the people who had poured onto the spot to watch were dumbfounded.

Mullah Said stayed a short time longer in Jizre after this strange incident. Then he set off with one of his students for some desert country and its nomadic Arab tribes. He had not been there long when he heard that Mustafa Pasha had reverted to his former evil ways, and he returned to advise him to give them up. But it was more than Mustafa Pasha could bear to be dictated to in this way, and it was only on his son's intervention that he refrained from assaulting Mullah Said, who then left at the son's request and returned to the Biro desert, this time alone.

Said was attacked twice by bandit nomads in the desert. The second time he would have met his end, but they recognised him and, regretting their attack, offered him their protection on the dangerous parts of the road. Mullah Said rejected their offers of assistance, and continued on his way alone until several days later when he reached Mardin.[39]

Mardin

Besides his continuing success in scholarly debate, and in all his contests with the Mardin *'ulamā'*, Mullah Said's stay in Mardin was significant in several respects. But firstly an anecdote which illustrates Said's characteristic daring and courage.

While in Mardin, Mullah Said stayed as a guest in the house of Shaykh Eyyub Ensari, a descendant of Prophet Ayyūb [Job], and began to teach in the Şehide Mosque, answering the questions of all those who came to visit him. One of the notables of the town, Hüseyin Çelebi Pasha, was so impressed by Said's knowledge and skill at debating that he offered him numerous gifts. But in keeping with his usual practice, Said refused them all, except for a good quality rifle, a repeater.

One day, Mullah Said went out with a friend named Kasım, and suggested they climb the minaret of the Ulu Mosque to see the view. They went and climbed it. Then Mullah Said suddenly jumped up onto the parapet of the gallery of the minaret, which was only about four centimetres in width. There he spread his arms wide and started to walk around the minaret. Kasım shut his eyes out of fear. Appearing from around the other side of the minaret, Said shouted out: "Kasım! Kasım! Come on, let's walk around the minaret together!" But shaking at the knees, Kasım descended the minaret and joined the people who had gathered to watch from below, in wonder at the boldness of this intrepid young mullah.[40]

It was at his time, however, that Mullah Said was, in his own words, "awakened" politically, and became aware of the wider issues facing the Islamic world. In a work entitled *Münâzarat, Debates*, first published in 1913, Bediuzzaman wrote: "Sixteen years before the [Constitutional] Revolution [of 1908], I encountered in the region of Mardin a person who guided me to the truth; he showed me the just and equitable way in politics. Also at that time, I was awakened by the Famous Kemal's Dream."[41]

The Famous Kemal mentioned here is Namık Kemal, one of the leading figures of the 19th century Young Ottoman Movement, the main aims of which are reflected in this work of Kemal which Mullah Said came across at that time, *The Dream*. It is written in the form of an address to the nation by a heavenly representative of Freedom. This beautiful, fairy-like symbol of Freedom, which has slipped through the clouds, urges liberation from despotism, struggle in the way of the nation, progress, and the prosperity of the fatherland (*watan*). Following this, it outlines the picture of a society and country of the future, which is free, based on the sovereignty of the people, whose citizens are educated, and in which the rights of all and justice are established.[42]

In another place in *Münâzarat*, Bediuzzaman described himself as "Someone who for twenty years has followed it [Freedom] in

Childhood and Youth 23

his dreams even, and has abandoned everything because of that passion."⁴³

Thus, it was at this time in Mardin that Mullah Said first became aware of the struggle for Freedom and constitutional government which the Young Ottomans had been pursuing since the 1860's. As we shall see in the following chapter, this Freedom was not only enjoined by Islam, but was also the key to progress, and the answer to the question: "How can this State be saved?" Despotism and absolutist government were among the major causes of the dire condition, internal and external, of the Ottoman Empire and Islamic world. Mullah Said was to be a champion of Freedom, constitutional government, and the rule of law throughout his life.

Also while in Mardin, Mullah Said met two students who were instrumental in broadening his ideas. One was a follower of Jamāl al-Dīn al-Afghānī, (1255/1839-1315/1897), who in the summer of 1892 was brought to Istanbul by Sultan Abdulhamid in order to use him in furthering his Pan-Islamic policies. And the second was a member of the Sanūsī *ṭarīqah*, which played such an important role against the colonial expansion in North Africa.

Mullah Said was also to be a great defender and advocate of *Ittihad-i Islam*, that is, Islamic Unity or Pan-Islam, and he later wrote: "My predecessors in this matter [of Islamic Unity] are Jamāl al-Dīn al-Afghānī, Ali Suavi Efendi and Hoja Tahsin Efendi, [Namık] Kemal Bey, and Sultan Selim."⁴⁴

It is recorded that it was during this stay in Mardin that Mullah Said first engaged in politics. Although it is not clear precisely what is meant by this, the above probably provide the clue, especially when considered in the light of Bediuzzaman's later activities in Istanbul. In any event, the Governor, Mutasarrıf Nadir Bey, saw fit to intervene, and expelled him from the town, sending him to Bitlis under armed guard.⁴⁵

The task was to be an unusual one for the two gendarmes, Savurlu Mehmed Fatih and his friend İbrahim, assigned to deliver

Mullah Said to the Governor of Bitlis. The story of it became well-known in the region. They set out on the journey, Said riding with both his hands and feet bound with iron fetters. While they were in the vicinity of a village called Ahmedî, the time for the obligatory prayers came in. Said asked the gendarmes to unfasten his bonds so that he could pray, but they refused, frightened he would try to escape. Whereupon, Said the Famous undid the fetters, dismounted from his horse, took his ablutions at a stream, and performed the prayers under the astonished gazes of the two gendarmes. Recognizing his unusual powers, they said to him when he had finished: "Up to now we were your guards, but from now on we shall be your servants." But Mullah Said merely requested them to do their duty.

When asked at a later date how this had occurred, he replied: "I myself do not know, but at the most it was a miracle of the prayers."[46]

And on another occasion Bediuzzaman replied: "I am not a sorcerer, I am not a conjuror. I was someone who had taken the Holy Qur'an as his guide and had turned toward God. In truth such an event happened to me. I faced the *qiblah*, uttered a prayer, and then looked: the manacles had opened. When I handed them to the gendarme, he was frightened."[47]

Mullah Said was indeed famous, and news of his exploits spread throughout the region, reaching also the village of Nurs. In later years he described his parents' reactions to what they heard:

> In the old days, my father and mother used to be told of my strange doings in that eventful and rough and ready life. When they heard news like, your son is dead, or, he has been wounded, or, he is in prison, my father used to laugh and enjoy it immensely. He would say: "*Māshā' Allāh*! My son is doing something of importance again, he is demonstrating his courage and daring; that is why everyone is talking about him." My mother would weep unhappily in the face of his pleasure. But then time would very often prove my father to be right.[48]

Bitlis

Mullah Said was to stay two years in Bitlis on the insistence of the governor, Ömer Pasha, in whose residence he stayed. It was his fearless defence of right that earned him the Governor's respect and the invitation to stay there.

Mullah Said had heard one day that the governor and some officials were having a drinking session. Finding it unacceptable that government representatives should behave in such a way, he went and interrupted them. And reading out a Ḥadīth about the drinking of alcohol, he rebuked them in strong terms. The governor evidently suppressed the anger he had felt on being addressed in this way, and did nothing. When leaving, the governor's aide-de-camp asked Mullah Said why had had acted in such a way, which would normally have led to being executed. But Said merely replied:

> Being executed did not occur to me, I was thinking of prison or exile. Anyway, if I die repulsing a denier of God's law, what harm is there in it?

And when, a couple of hours later, two policemen sent by the governor brought him back, the governor rose to his feet when Said entered his office and treated him with great respect, saying: "Everyone has a spiritual guide; you shall be mine and you shall stay with me."[49]

During the next two years, Mullah Said was able to greatly extend his knowledge of the Islamic sciences. We are told that until about this time all Said's knowledge had been of the sort called *sunūḥāt*. That is to say, he had understood the subjects he had studied without much thought; understanding had come to him as a sort of inspiration without his exercising his reasoning faculty unduly. Because of this, he had not found it necessary to study the subjects at great length. But whether due to his increasing maturity or because he had become involved in politics, this former ability now slowly began to disappear. And so, in order both to preserve his position among the *'ulamā'*, and especially to refute the works of Western orientalists on Islam and answer the doubts they had raised, Mullah Said embarked on a comprehensive study of all the Islamic sciences. These included those that can be thought of as 'instrumental', such as logic and Arabic grammar and syntax, as well as the main sciences of Qur'anic exegesis (*tafsīr*), traditions of the Prophet (*ḥadīth*), and jurisprudence (*fiqh*). He committed to memory around forty books in two years, including works on theology (*kalām*), like the *Matāli'* and *Mawāqif*, and the work of Ḥanafī *fiqh*, *Mirqāt*. It used to take him three months to go through them all, reciting a part of each from memory each day.

Mullah Said was subject to two conflicting states of mind. The first was one of expansion when there was nothing he could not understand. The second was when his mind contracted; then it was not only studying, but he preferred not to even speak. When he was young, the former state was prevalent. But once he passed the age of twenty, the hours when his mind contracted increased, and the times of its expansion started to decrease until they were about half and half.

During his time in Bitlis, Mullah Said began to memorise the Qur'an, by reading one or two *juz'*[50] each day. He learned the greater part in this way, but did not complete it. There were two reasons for this. Firstly, he wanted to avoid being disrespectful to the Qur'an, and it had occurred to him that to read the Qur'an at great speed was to lack respect for the Book. And secondly, it occurred to him that the more urgent need was to learn the truths that the Qur'an was teaching. In the following two years, therefore, he learned by heart the forty or so works noted above on the Islamic sciences and philosophy which would be the key to the Qur'anic truths, and which would preserve those truths by answering the doubts that had been raised concerning them.[51] The governor's residence in Bitlis provided a favourable environment to pursue this programme.

Ömer Pasha's wife was dead, and he had six daughters. One day, one of these girls wanted to go into Mullah Said's room to

Childhood and Youth

clean it, or for some such innocent reason. However, Mullah Said scolded her, and brusquely shut the door in her face. The girl was taken aback and upset at this.

The same day while in his office, someone who was trying to make trouble for Said, no doubt jealous of him, whispered in the Governor's ear: "How can you leave Mullah Said in the house all day? Your daughters are not married and you have no wife, and he is a vigorous young man. How can you do such a thing?", thus sowing seeds of doubt in his mind about Said.

That evening when he returned to his family, Ömer Pasha was met by his disconsolate daughter who immediately complained to her father: "That Said you have given the room to is mad. He just tells us off and never leaves it." Feeling remorse for his suspicions, Ömer Pasha went straight to Mullah Said's room and treated him with great courtesy and kindness.

In a later work, Bediuzzaman explained his attitude as follows:

> When I was twenty or so, I stayed for two years in the residence of the governor of Bitlis, Ömer Pasha, on his insistence and because of his extreme respect for learning. He had six daughters. Three of them were small, and three of them were older. Although I stayed in the same house as them for two years, I could not tell the three older ones apart. I paid them so little attention, how could I have done? Another scholar came and stayed together with me as a guest, and within two days he knew them and could tell them one from the other. They were all perplexed at my attitude, and asked me: "Why do you not look at them?" I replied: "Preserving the dignity of learning does not allow me to look at them."[52]

The last time Mullah Said received a lesson and was taught by anyone was while he was in Bitlis, from one of its leading shaykhs, Shaykh Muḥammad Kufrawī (d. 1313/1895-6). Then one night following this, he dreamt of the Shaykh, who said to him in his dream: "Mullah Said, come and visit me. I am leaving." So Said immediately went to him, and when he saw that the Shaykh had already gone, he awoke. He looked at his watch; it was one o'clock in the morning. He went back to sleep again. When in the morning he heard the sound of mourning and weeping coming from the direction of the Shaykh's house, he hurried there to find that the Shaykh had died at one o'clock the night before. Uttering a prayer for him, Said returned home sadly.

Mullah Said had tremendous love for the great Naqshbandī/ Khālidī shaykhs of eastern Anatolia, such as Sayyid Nur Muhammad, Shaykh 'Abdurrahman Taği, Shaykh Fehim and Shaykh Muḥammad Kufrawī, from each of whom he had received lessons and instructions in different aspects of the spiritual life. And so also did he greatly love the leading *'ulamā'* such as Shaykh Emin Efendi, Mullah Fethullah, and Shaykh Fethullah Efendi, who had taught him.[53]

Van

While Bitlis was a religious centre with many *'ulamā'*, there were no well-known *'ulamā'* in Van at that time. Thus, when Mullah Said received an invitation from Hasan Pasha, he left Bitlis for Van. He was to stay there off and on studying and teaching, and travelling among the tribes as a conciliator and man of religion until he left for Istanbul at the end of 1907. He was around nineteen or twenty years of age when he moved there.

While in Van, Mullah Said stayed first with Hasan Pasha, and then, after İşkodrali Tahir Pasha was appointed governor, for a long period in the governor's residence. Tahir Pasha was a distinguished official much respected by Sultan Abdulhamid II. He served as governor in both Mosul and Bitlis, in addition to the many years he was in Van, and among other things led the delegation which presented Abdulhamid's gifts to the Russian Czar Nicholas in 1902, in Lidvadya.[54] Tahir Pasha was a patron of learning, and also followed developments in modern science and owned an extensive library. He was the first state official to perceive Bediuzzaman's great talent and potential, and continued to encourage and support him till his death in 1913.

Staying in the governor's residence, Bediuzzaman had the opportunity to mix with the government officials and took up reading the newspapers and journals provided for the governor's office. As he gained more knowledge of the broader issues and problems facing Ottoman society and the Islamic world generally, he realised that the traditional form of Islamic theology was inadequate for answering the doubts that had been raised concerning Islam and that study of modern science was also necessary. Therefore, taking advantage of the facilities, he himself took up the study of the modern sciences, including history, geography, mathematics, geology, physics, chemistry, astronomy, and philosophy.

Said did not have a teacher for these subjects; studying books, he taught himself. For example, on one occasion he got into a discussion on geography with a teacher of that subject. The discussion became prolonged and they decided to continue the following day. Within twenty-four hours, therefore, Mullah Said memorised a geography book he was able to obtain, and when they met again, silenced the geography teacher in his own subject. And on a second occasion, Mullah Said silenced a chemistry teacher, having mastered the principles of inorganic chemistry in five days.[55]

Mullah Said's quickness and brilliant intelligence demonstrated itself particularly in mathematics. He could solve the most difficult problems mentally and almost instantaneously. He wrote a treatise on algebraic equations, which unfortunately was subsequently destroyed by fire in Van. On occasion, different calculations would become the subject of discussion in Tahir Pasha's presence. Whatever the calculations, Mullah Said would find the solution before any of the others were able to do so, even the most skilful scribes. They would often hold competitions, and Mullah Said always came first, beating everyone else.[56]

Mullah Said continued to memorise those works he considered essential, approximately ninety during the years he was in Van, endeavouring to go through the entire list reciting each book by heart once every three months. On one occasion while passing the door of Said's room, Tahir Pasha heard what he thought was the sound of prayers and invocations being recited softly; it was Mullah Said repeating his books by heart. Years later, he told Mustafa Sungur, one of his closest students:

> I used to repeat by heart the eighty to ninety books I had memorised. They were the steps by which to ascend to the truths of the Qur'an. Some time later, I ascended to those truths and I saw that each verse of the Qur'an encompasses the universe. No need then remained for anything else, the Qur'an alone was sufficient for me.[57]

It was at this time that, as a result of these feats of learning and the prodigious amounts of knowledge he was acquiring, Mullah Said now became widely known as Bediuzzaman or the Wonder of the Age.[58]

Although Mullah Said, or Bediuzzaman as we shall now call him, also used this title himself, it was not out of vanity. In an article entitled, "To Dispel Any Fears" (*Reddü'l-Evham*), which appeared in the newspaper *Volkan* dated 31 March 1909, Bediuzzaman replied as follows to the question: "You sometimes sign yourself Bediuzzaman. Does such a name not point to self-praise?"

> It is not for self-praise. I present my faults, excuses and apologies with the title, because *Badī'* means strange. Like my style, my manner of expression and dress are strange, they are different. Through the tongue of this title, I am requesting that the opinions and customs generally held and practised are not made the criteria for judging mine.[59]

While in a later work he stated that he used the name "in order to make known a divine bounty." He wrote:

> I now realise that the name Bediuzzaman, which was given to me many years ago although I was not worthy of it, was not mine anyway. It was rather a name of the *Risale-i Nur*. It had been attached to the *Risale-i Nur*'s apparent translator temporarily and as a trust.[60]

Bediuzzaman had his own *madrasah* in Van, at the foot of the citadel, called the Horhor *madrasah*, with sometimes as many as sixty students,[61] and it was during his stay in Van that Bediuzzaman developed his ideas on educational reform and created his own particular method of teaching. He developed this through examining the principles of all he had studied together with his experience of teaching religious and scientific subjects, then considering them in relation to the needs of the times. The basis of this method was to "combine" the religious sciences and modern sciences, with the result that the positive sciences would corroborate and strengthen the truths of religion. Bediuzzaman now followed this method when teaching his students.[62]

Bediuzzaman's greatest aim at this time was to establish a university in eastern Anatolia where this method would be practised; that is, where modern science would be taught side by side with the religious sciences and his other ideas put into practice. This university he called the Medresetü'z-Zehra after the Azhar University in Cairo, as it was to be its sister university in the centre of the eastern Islamic world. Having travelled throughout eastern Anatolia, Bediuzzaman had seen that such an educational establishment was essential not only for combating the widespread ignorance and backwardness of the region, but also as a solution for its other social and political problems. Bediuzzaman's ideas concerning education are discussed in greater detail in a subsequent chapter.

As a patron of learning, Tahir Pasha's residence was a place where learned discussions in all fields were held. On one such occasion, Tahir Pasha said with the intention of slighting the Mālikī school of law, "Dogs (*kalb*) are considered unclean the same as pigs, are they not?" Mullah Said replied:

> According to the Mālikī school, dogs are clean (*kelb tahir-dir*). But Tahir is not a dog (*Tahir kelb değildir*)." Thus with a witty pun, he was able to both gently rebuke Tahir Pasha and conciliate him. As for Tahir Pasha, he was delighted with both the explanation and the '*fatwā*'.[63]

Tahir Pasha used to study scholarly books from Europe and prepare questions to ask Bediuzzaman. Despite the fact that it was only now that Bediuzzaman was learning Turkish, he would give the answers unhesitatingly. If he saw some books on a table or somewhere, he understood that Tahir Pasha was compiling some questions, and would quickly read the books and learn their contents.[64]

Bediuzzaman used to spend the summer months in the high pastures of Başid, Feraşin, and Beytüşşebab. On a previous occasion he had told Tahir Pasha that there was snow on these mountains even in July. Tahir Pasha had objected, declaring that there was definitely no snow there in July. Recalling this exchange while up in the mountains, Bediuzzaman wrote his first letter in Turkish to Tahir Pasha:

> Pasha! There is snow on the mountain tops at Başid. You should not deny what you have not seen! Everything is not restricted to what you know! *Vesselam*!

During these summer months in the mountains, besides acting as a conciliator in tribal disputes, Bediuzzaman would roam the mountains and forests, reading the book of the universe, and pondering over its meaning and messages as directed by the Qur'an. In respect of this Bediuzzaman greatly loved and respected the natural world—and particularly his mountainous and wild native land—and had a close affinity with its creatures. They also felt an affinity with him. Of the stories illustrating this is one for which we also have the date: 1321, that is, 1905. On this occasion Bediuzzaman was high up on Mount Başid, alone, and was sitting on a rock in contemplation having performed the evening prayers when a great wolf appeared. But this "lion of the mountain" merely came to him "like a friend", then passed on its way doing nothing.[65]

When news of any dispute between the tribes reached Bediuzzaman, he would intervene, and pointing out the just way, would reconcile the two parties. He was even successful where the government had failed in making peace between Şeker Ağa and Mustafa Pasha, the chief of the Miran tribe mentioned earlier. Where personal courage was the most highly prized quality, Bediuzzaman was held in awe by all the tribes of the area. Mustafa Pasha was still persisting in his lawlessness and oppression, and this time tried to placate Bediuzzaman by giving him money and a horse as gifts. But following his usual practice, Bediuzzaman refused them, and pointing out that above all he could never accept money from a wrongdoer like himself, told him that if indeed he had gone back on his word to give up all oppression and wrongdoing, he would not reach Jizre, for which he was headed. And indeed, they heard later that Mustafa Pasha had died on the road, and had never reached Jizre.[66]

One day while in the governor's residence in Van, they came to Bediuzzaman and said there was a simply-dressed villager waiting to see him at the door. He immediately went down to find his father, Sufi Mirza, who had ridden over to Van from Nurs. Bediuzzaman kissed his hand and brought him into the house. Feeling abashed, Mirza implored his son not to say that he was his father. Bediuzzaman took him to the room where the governor and other notables were gathered, and Sufi Mirza sat himself down as inconspicuously as possible in a place near the door. However, Bediuzzaman introduced him to all present, saying: "This is my father, Sufi Mirza Efendi!", and seated him at the top of the room next to Tahir Pasha.[67]

Bediuzzaman's dress was distinctive. With a large dagger and pistol at his waist and a bandolier slung across his chest, baggy trousers, and on his head a shawl wound round a conical hat, it resembled the dress of a tribal chief rather than that of a scholar.

One of his friends, Malazgirtli Acem Ağa, said to him one day:

> Seyda! Why don't you dress in accordance with your learning, in a manner that befits it? Bediuzzaman replied:
>
> What are you saying, Acem Ağa? Ömer Pasha wanted to give me a villa, a thousand gold liras, and one of his daughters so that I would change my dress, and I still would not change it for all that.[68]

As we shall learn later, of the reasons Bediuzzaman did not consent to forsake the local dress of eastern Anatolia, was his desire to draw attention to the region and its problems, to stress the importance of provincial development in maintaining the unity of the Empire, and, by publicizing local industry so as to create a demand for it.[69] That is to say, he wore this striking dress not for self-advertisement, but to serve the cause of the Empire and its unity and progress.

One day, Bediuzzaman fell out with Tahir Pasha during a discussion, and he left the governor's residence and barricaded himself in his *madrasah*, together with a few of his students. When they came to get him, he put two conditions to them. Firstly, they were not to arrest him in his *madrasah*, as it would slight its honour and reputation, but could do so in the market place. And secondly, that if he was to be exiled, they should allow him his firearms. The governor accepted these conditions and exiled him to Bitlis. From there he moved to Hizan, then Bulanık, followed by Erciş, continuing to debate with the *'ulamā'* in each place. He finally decided to go to Iran, but Tahir Pasha heard of this and invited him back to Van.[70]

Another incident is recorded that occurred during Bediuzzaman's years in Van. He wrote:

> My old students who are still living know that [we were in] the citadel of Van which is simply a great monolith the size of a mountain and the height of two minarets, we were going to a secret door which was like a chamber dating from ancient times. The shoes slid from my feet and my two feet slipped suddenly. The danger [of falling] was one hundred per cent. Although there was nothing on which to support myself, I was hurled in a three metre arc to the door of the cave as though I had been standing on something broad. Both myself and my friends who were there with me considered that it was only due to Divine protection and some miraculous unseen assistance that my time had not come.[71]

Childhood and Youth 35

Bediuzzaman read the newspapers regularly while in Van, particularly the articles concerning Islam and the Islamic world. One day, Tahir Pasha pointed out an item that evoked an overpowering response in him. It was the report of a speech made in the British House of Commons by the Secretary for the Colonies. Bediuzzaman described it as follows:

> Round about the year 1316,[72] the author of the *Risale-i Nur* underwent a radical change in regard to his ideas. It was as follows:
>
> Up to that time, he had only been interested in, and had studied and taught, the various sciences; it was only through theoretical knowledge that he had sought enlightenment. Then at that date, he suddenly learned through the late Governor, Tahir Pasha, of Europe's dire intentions towards the Qur'an. He heard that a British Secretary for the Colonies had even said in a newspaper:
>
> "So long as the Muslims have the Qur'an, we shall be unable to dominate them. We must either take it from them, or make them lose their love of it."
>
> He was filled with zeal. Heeding the decree of, "So turn away from them" (Qur'an, 6:68), the numerical value of which is 1316, it overturned his ideas and changed the direction of his interest. He understood that he should make all the various sciences he had learned steps by which to understand the Qur'an and prove its truths, and that the Qur'an alone should be his aim, the purpose of his learning, and the object of his life. Thus, the Qur'an's miraculousness became his guide, teacher, and master. But unfortunately, due to many deceiving obstacles in that period of youth, he did not in fact take up the duty. It was a while later that he awoke with the clash and clamour of war. Then that constant idea sprang to life; it began to emerge and be realised."[73]

Thus, as this passage states, the explicit threats of the British Colonial Secretary to the Qur'an and Islamic world caused a revolution in Bediuzzaman's ideas, clarifying them and setting him in the direction he would now follow. The threats caused him to declare: "I shall prove and demonstrate to the world that the Qur'an is an undying, inextinguishable Sun!"[74] Using the knowledge he had acquired to prove its truths, he would defend the Qur'an against the deliberate efforts to discredit it and corrupt the Muslim community. In a letter he wrote in 1955, Bediuzzaman stated that he found two means of doing this, one was the *Medresetü'z-Zehra*, his eastern university which took him to Istanbul and even to Sultan Abdulhamid's court, and the second was the *Risale-i Nur*.[75] But this second means only became realised with the emergence of the New Said subsequent to the First World War. Until that time, Bediuzzaman was both actively involved with the compelling events of the times and for the most part served the cause of Islam through active participation in social and political matters, and also, as shall be described in a later chapter, he was preoccupied with "human" science and philosophy, and hoped to follow his aim through them.

Notes

1. While a variety of dates for Bediuzzaman's birth are given in available sources, the majority give it as 1293 Rumi.
2. Eşref Edip, *Said Nursi, Hayatı, Eserleri, Mesleği*, 17.
3. N. Şahiner, *Nurs Yolu*, 68.
4. Şahiner, *Said Nursi*, 45.
5. N. Şahiner, *Nurs Yolu*, 69.
6. Şahiner, *Said Nursi*, 46; Nursi, *The Flashes Collection* (Eng. tr.) 128-9; Nursi, *Muhâkemat*, 22-3.
7. Şahiner, *Said Nursi*, 47; Nursi, *Emirdağ Lahikası*, i, 53.
8. Nursi, *Sikke-i Tasdik-i Gaybi*, 116.
9. Mullah: a title denoting that a certain level of knowledge had been reached in the religious sciences—a teacher.
10. *Tarihçe*, 31; Şahiner, *Said Nursi*, 47-8.
11. Nursi, *Emirdağ Lahikası*, i, 52.
12. *Tarihçe*, 31-2.
13. Şahiner, *Said Nursi*, 49-50.
14. *Ibid.*, 50; *Tarihçe*, 49-50.
15. Şahiner, *Said Nursi*, 51.
16. *Ibid.*, 51-2.
17. *Ibid.*, 52; *Tarihçe*, 32.

Childhood and Youth 37

18. Shaykh Emin Efendi was a famous scholar whose *madrasah* was in the Kızılmescit quarter of Bitlis. He was the teacher of many notable people, including Reşid Akif Pasha, at one time Governor of Sivas. He went to Istanbul in 1900 where he was greeted with a formal ceremony and had a private conversation with Sultan Abdulhamid II. The Sultan offered him the post of Şeyhü'l-İslam, which he did not accept. He returned to Bitlis in 1903, and died there in 1908 at the age of seventy. See, Şahiner, *Said Nursi*, 53.
19. *Ibid.*, 52-3; *Tarihçe*, 33.
20. That is, the famous poet and scholar Nūr al-Dīn 'Abd al-Rahmān Jāmī, who lived in Herat 817/1414-898/1492. Of his numerous works, the one known as 'Mullah Jami' was a commentary on a work on Arabic syntax called *Kāfiyah* by Ibn Ḥājib, and formed part of the *madrasah* syllabus until recent times.
21. *Tarihçe*, 33-4; Şahiner, *Said Nursi*, 53-5.
22. *Ibid.*, 55.
23. *Tarihçe*, 34-5.
24. *Ibid.*, 35.
25. *Ibid.*, 35-6; Şahiner, *Said Nursi*, 55-6.
26. By the famous poet and literary figure, 'Ali Ḥarīrī, d. 665 A.H.
27. Nursi, *Emirdağ Lahikası* (Ott. edn.), 383.
28. *Tarihçe*, 36-7; Şahiner, *Said Nursi*, 56-8.
29. *Ibid.*, (8th edn.), 52-3; "Şeyh Celal Efendi," in *Son Şahitler*, ii, 259.
30. Şahiner, *Said Nursi*, 58.
31. *Tarihçe*, 38.
32. *Ibid.*, 38.
33. The *Qāmūs al-Uqyānūs* was written by Abū Ṭāhir Fīrūzābādī, born in Kazerun in Fīrūzābād in 729/1328-9. He died in 817/1414-15 at an advanced age. In one edition the chapter *Sīn* starts on page 204 of the second volume. The first volume is of 410 pages, so Said memorised approximately 614 pages. In this edition the volumes are large with twenty-four lines on each page.
34. While being tried for hostility towards the Republic in Eskişehir Criminal Court in 1935, Bediuzzaman was asked his opinion of republicanism. He replied: "As my biography which you have in your hands proves, I was a religious republican before any of you, with the exception of the President of the Court, was born", and related the above story of the ants. He went on to say that each of the four Rightly-Guided Caliphs had been both Caliph (that is, successor to the Prophet) and President of the Republic, and that this had not been some meaningless title; they had been presidents of a religious republic in which true justice and freedom prevailed. See, *Tarihçe*, 39.

35. See, Şahiner, *Son Şahitler*, iv, 198-201.
36. *Tarihçe*, 39.
37. The Hamidiye militia, or cavalry, had been set up by Sultan Abdulhamid II in 1891 as a force against Russian encroachments, as a means of controlling the Kurdish and Turcoman tribes of which it was composed, and also to combat Armenian terrorism in eastern Anatolia. It was commanded by both tribal chiefs and regular officers. See, Shaw and Shaw, *History*, ii, 246.
38. *Tarihçe*, 39-41.
39. *Ibid.*, 41-2.
40. Şahiner, *Said Nursi*, 63-4.
41. Nursi, *Münâzarat* (Ott. edn.), in *Asar-ı Bedi'iyye*, 462.
42. Vasfi Mahir Kocatürk, *Büyük Türk Edebiyatı Tarihi*, Ankara 1970, 662.
43. Nursi, *Münâzarat*, 15.
44. Nursi, *Divan-ı Harb-i Örfî*, 19.
45. *Tarihçe*, 42.
46. *Ibid.*, 42; Şahiner, *Said Nursi*, 64-5.
47. Mustafa Sevilen, in *Son Şahitler*, ii, 42. Şahiner, *Said Nursi*, 65, also gives the event as related by Bediuzzaman's brother, Abdülmecid Nursi, in his memoirs, which is the first-hand account of the gendarme Ibrahim.
48. *Ibid.*, 65-6; Nursi, *Emirdağ Lahikası*, i, 135.
49. *Tarihçe*, 42-3.
50. A *juz'* is one thirtieth of the Qur'an.
51. *Tarihçe*, 43-4.
52. Şahiner, *Said Nursi*, 52-3; Nursi, *Emirdağ Lahikası*, i, 257.
53. *Tarihçe*, 44.
54. Cemal Kutay, *Bediüzzaman*, 136-7; Şahiner, *Son Şahitler*, iii, 16-20.
55. *Tarihçe*, 44-5. In fact, many years later while describing his years of study in Van to one of his students, Muhsin Alev, Bediuzzaman said that he had studied and mastered all sciences with the exception of organic chemistry; that was the only one he had not been able to master completely. See, *Son Şahitler*, i, 227.
56. *Tarihçe*, 46.
57. Şahiner, *Said Nursi*, 70; Mustafa Sungur, in N. Şahiner, *Aydınlar Konuşuyor*, 395.
58. *Tarihçe*, 45.
59. Şahiner, Said Nursi, 68-9; Nursi, *Hutbe-i Şamiye*, 90.
60. Şahiner, Said Nursi, 69; Nursi, *Şualar*, 629.
61. Nursi, *Emirdağ Lahikası*, ii, 187.
62. *Tarihçe*, 45.
63. Şahiner, *Said Nursi*, 69-70.

64. *Tarihçe*, 46.
65. Nursi, *Lem'alar* (Ott. edn.), 648.
66. *Tarihçe*, 46.
67. Şahiner, *Said Nursi*, 71.
68. *Ibid.*, 71.
69. *Ibid.*, 91.
70. *Ibid.*, 72.
71. Nursi, *Sikke-i Tasdik-i Gaybî*, 126.
72. That is, around the turn of the century.
73. Nursi, *Sikke-i Tasdik-i Gaybî*, 76.
74. *Tarihçe*, 47.
75. Nursi, *Emirdağ Lahikası*, ii, 195.

2
Istanbul before Freedom

Foreword

In November 1907, Bediuzzaman set off for Istanbul with the intention of obtaining official support and backing for his Islamic university, the Medresetü'z-Zehra. He was now around thirty years of age. From his humble beginnings in the village of Nurs, he had established his reputation among the *'ulamā'* of Kurdistan, and was a figure well-known not only for his unbeaten record in debate, extensive learning, and extraordinary abilities, but also for his pursuit of justice and defence of right, and his absolute fearlessness before anyone save his Maker. His ambitions matched his ability. This had marked him out from his earliest years. He had never been content with the status-quo; something within himself had perpetually pushed him to seek fresh, new, better paths. As his horizons expanded, this path became clear. As is described in the previous chapter, besides the continuing process of his study, two key events may be seen as being decisive in giving him direction. One was his realization of the extremely severe nature of the threats to the Qur'an by Islam's perennial enemies, and that, through his learning he should make the defence of it the aim of his life. The second were the acquaintances he made in Mardin in 1892, and his learning through them of the struggle for freedom and constitutionalism, and of the movement for Islamic Unity and other issues concerning the Islamic world. Until the beginning of the First World War, it was with these issues that Bediuzzaman was chiefly concerned.

The Constitutional Movement

What was the struggle for Freedom and constitutional government? What were the issues involved? Why should a young religious scholar from the remote eastern provinces of the Ottoman Empire have embraced the struggle with such conviction? Primarily these questions find their answer in a further question, one that had been asked with increasing urgency as the power of the Ottoman Empire waned in the face of Europe's development and expansion in the 18th, 19th, and early 20th centuries: how can this state be saved? *Bu devlet nasıl kurtarılabilir*? The great debate revolved around this question, and around the causes of the decline of the Empire and Islamic world.

The struggle for Freedom emerged as the response of a group of intellectuals and literary figures, namely Namık Kemal and the Young Ottomans, to the solutions to the above question offered by the Ottoman rulers. The late 18th and 19th century sultans had sought to reverse the Empire's decline by a series of reforms, concentrating firstly on the army, then between 1839 and 1876 in the period known as the Tanzimat, on virtually every area of government, together with education and many areas of Ottoman life. The models for the reforms were all imported from the West, and were introduced largely under European pressure and advice.

Furthermore, the Europeans pressed on the Ottomans the idea that the only civilization was European civilization, and that it was only through espousing it that they could raise the Empire out of its state of relative backwardness. This false idea came to be accepted more and more by the Ottoman educated classes.[1]

Namık Kemal and Young Ottomans were not anti-Western *per se*, nor were they opposed to progress and reform. On the contrary, they opposed the Tanzimat reforms as being obstacles to progress and counterproductive in combating the disintegration of the Empire. One of the main reasons for this was the increase, rather than decrease, in the autocratic authority of the Sultan as the result of the reforms, and thus of arbitrary and absolutist government.[2]

The Young Ottomans were the first to propose constitutional and parliamentary government as the means of solving the Empire's problems, Namık Kemal, in particular, pointing out its compatibility with the Sharī'ah, and demonstrating the parallels between such a system and the form of government practised by Prophet Muḥammad (ṣ) and his immediate successors.

The struggle was continued after Sultan Abdulhamid II's accession to the throne in 1876. Despite substantial losses of territory, Abdulhamid, a master politician, succeeded in holding the Empire together for the thirty-three years of his reign by playing off against one another the Great Powers and opposing interests of those bent on its destruction. But the price was high. His successful foreign policies were paid for by internal repression of considerable severity. In the face of the lack of unity in the first parliament, elected following the Proclamation of the First Constitution on 23 December, 1876, and many of the members representing the minorities, that is, Armenians, Greeks, Jews, Bulgars, Serbs, and others, pursuing interests other than those of the Empire, Abdulhamid was left with little alternative but to dissolve it, though the Constitution was not abrogated. Following this, the Sultan ruled as a despot from Yıldız Palace, supported by far-reaching intelligence networks, rigorous censorship, denunciations, and the like.[3]

It should be stressed, however, that this was not a bloody despotism. And it was not from the ordinary people that opposition came, but from the intellectuals, students educated in the new educational establishments, and particularly from army cadets in the military academies. Despite his vigorous criticisms of Abdulhamid's absolutist government and its consequences, Bediuzzaman referred to him as "compassionate". In the thirty-three years of his reign, he only signed the death-warrant for three or four criminals, pardoning even those who made attempts on his life, including the Armenians who placed a bomb in his carriage. Others he sent into exile, rather than spilling their blood.[4]

The Young Turk movement emerged at this time. Its members, which included former Young Ottomans, represented a wide spectrum of ideas, and were united only in their common opposition to Abdulhamid's internal despotism and their desire to see fundamental social and political reforms and the restoration of the Constitution. The Committee of Union and Progress, which led the Constitutional Revolution of 1908, formed one group within the movement. They saw representative government and freedom from despotism to be the essential conditions for preserving the unity of the Empire, particularly in the face of the nationalist aspirations of the minorities, and for securing its material progress. So long as the CUP adhered to these aims, they continued to enjoy Bediuzzaman's support, as they did in continuing to pursue Abdulhamid's Pan-Islamic policies, but when, as they progressively gained tighter control over the government, they created a worse tyranny than the one preceding it, Bediuzzaman did not hesitate to oppose them. In a newspaper article which appeared in April 1909, in reply to the question: "In Salonica you co-operated with the Committee of Union and Progress, why did you part from them?" he wrote: "I did not part from them; it was some of them that parted. I am still in agreement with people like Niyazi Bey and Enver Bey. But some of them parted from us. They strayed from the path and headed for the swamp."[5]

As we examine Bediuzzaman's writings and activities, it will become clear that not only did he see tyranny and despotism to be a root cause of the Ottoman Empire's decline and material backwardness relative to the West, and also to be in no way compatible with Islam, but also did he demonstrate the solutions for its recovery and progress to all lie within Islam. He pointed out the dynamic nature of the Sharī'ah and Islam's predisposition for progress, both materially, and morally and spiritually, an important element of which is the fact that Islam enjoins the exercise of basic liberties and rights, without which progress is not possible. Further to this, at that time of defeat and disintegration for the Islamic world, he saw the future—the age of science, technology, and reason—to be nothing less than a golden age of Islamic civilization. For him the achievement of this was the logical consequence of the comprehensive, universal nature of the revealed religion of Islam and of the trend of events in the world, that is, the decline of Western civilization.

Maintaining unity within the Empire was one of the major problems of the time. Bediuzzaman argued also that Constitutionalism and Freedom within the framework of Islam was the way to preserve unity, just as it created suitable conditions for strengthening Islamic Unity and brotherhood. However, "Unity cannot occur through ignorance. Unity is the fusion of ideas, and the fusion of ideas occurs through the electric rays of knowledge."[6] Thus, education was an area in which Bediuzzarnan expended great effort, particularly for his native Kurdistan. Quite contrary to the accusations of his enemies subsequently that he was a Kurdish nationalist, the aim of all Bediuzzaman's endeavours for the reform and spread of education in Kurdistan, and for its material and cultural development, was the strengthening of the Ottoman Empire and Islamic world. It was with this intention that he had set out a second time for the Ottoman capital in November, 1907.

Let us now return to 1907, and Bediuzzaman's arrival in Istanbul.

Tahir Pasha's Letter

The Governor of Van and Bitlis, Tahir Pasha, who had provided Bediuzzaman with so much encouragement and support, now wrote him a letter of introduction to the Palace, pointing out Bediuzzaman's fame and position among the 'ulamā' of eastern Anatolia, and requesting the Sultan's favour and assistance in securing medical treatment. This treatment was for a form of mental exhaustion brought about by his extreme mental exertion over a long period of time. Bediuzzaman's nephew, Abdurrahman, notes that it was the competitive solving of mathematical problems

Istanbul before Freedom

in particular that had exhausted his brain, and that for a period of some three years during his stay in Van, he virtually gave up debating of this kind and would only speak when necessary.[7] The following is a translation of Tahir Pasha's letter:

> A request from His most humble servant.
> Since Mullah Said, who is famous among the *'ulamā'* of Kurdistan for his brilliant intelligence, is in need of medical treatment, seeking refuge in the compassion and kindness of His Excellency the Shelter of the Caliphate, he has set out at this time for His Exalted Excellency.
>
> Although the above-mentioned is a person to whom everyone in these regions has recourse for solving problems concerning knowledge and learning, since he considers himself to be a student, he has not as yet consented to change his dress.
>
> Together with his being a faithful and sincere servant of His Excellency the Supreme Benefactor, the above-mentioned is by nature gentlemanly and satisfied with little, and in the opinion of this most humble servant, whether in regard to good moral qualities or loyalty and worshipfulness towards His Excellency the Shelter of the Caliphate, among the Kurdish *'ulamā'* who up to this time have had the good fortune to go to Dersaadet [Istanbul], is a person distinguished for his devoutness and is most worthy of benevolence. It is therefore boldly submitted that if he is made the object of special favour and facility in the matter of receiving treatment, it will be considered by all the students of Kurdistan to be an eternally unforgettable gracious kindness of the dynasty of His Excellency the Sultan.
>
> In this and in every matter the command belongs unto him to whom all commanding belongs.
>   3 Teşrin-i Sani 1323 (16 November, 1907)
>   "The Governor of Bitlis, Tahir[8]

The 'Şekerci Han'

There is no record of this letter having evoked the desired response. In any event, Bediuzzaman's first task when he arrived in Istanbul was to establish himself among the Istanbul *'ulamā'* to attract attention towards the problems of the Eastern Provinces, and publicise his ideas on educational reform. Indeed, by way of spurring him on, Tahir Pasha had said to him: "You can defeat in argument all the *'ulamā'* of eastern Anatolia, but you could not go to Istanbul and challenge all the big fishes in that sea," knowing that he could not let such a challenge remain unanswered.[9] Thus, on his arrival, Bediuzzaman established himself in the religious centre of Istanbul, Fatih, in a large building known as the Şekerci (Sweetmakers') Han, which served as a hostel for many of the leading intellectual figures of the time. The poet Mehmet Akif, and Fatin Hoca, the Director of the Observatory, were among its inhabitants. There are many contemporary descriptions of Bediuzzaman. The following, written by Ahmad Ramiz Efendi, owner of the İctihad Publishing House, describes his arrival:

> It was in 1323 (1907) that the news spread around that a person of flashing brilliance—a rarity of creation—called Said-i Kurdi,[10] having risen like the sun over the rugged, precipitous mountains of the East, had appeared on the horizons of Istanbul....
>
> Said said: "I have come here to open schools in my native land, I have no other aim. I want this, nothing else." In other words, Bediuzzaman wanted two things, to open educational establishments in every part of the Eastern Provinces, and to receive nothing in return.[11]

Bediuzzaman cut a striking figure in Istanbul. On the door of his room in the Şekerci Han he hung a sign which read:

Here all questions are answered, all problems solved, but no questions are asked.

The following are the impressions of some of his visitors to the Han and those who saw him at that time. The first is the account of Hasan Fehmi Başoğlu, later a member of the Consultative Committee of the Department of Religious Affairs.

> About the time the Second Constitution was proclaimed I was studying in the Fatih *madrasah*. I heard that a young man called Bediuzzaman had come to Istanbul and had settled in a *han*, and that he had even hung a notice on his door which said: "Here every problem is solved, all questions are answered, but

no questions are asked." I thought that someone who made such a claim could only be mad. But hearing nothing but praise and good opinions concerning Bediuzzaman, and learning of the astonishment of the many groups of *'ulamā'* and students who were visiting him, it awoke in me the desire to visit him myself. I decided that I would prepare some questions on the most difficult and abstruse matters to ask him. At that time I was considered to be one of the foremost members of the *madrasah*. Finally one night I selected a number of subjects from several of the most profound books on the theological sciences, and put them into question form. The following day I went to visit him, and I put my questions to him. The answers I received were quite astonishing and extraordinary. He answered my questions precisely, as though we had been together the previous evening and had looked at the books together. I was completely satisfied, and understood with certainty that his knowledge was not 'acquired' (*kasbī*) like ours, it was 'innate' (*wahbī*).

Afterwards he got out a map, and explained the necessity of opening a university in the Eastern Provinces, pointing out its importance. At that time there were Hamidiye regiments in the Eastern Provinces, it was being administered in that way. He explained to us convincingly the deficiencies of this form of administration, and that the region had to be awakened from the point of view of education, industry and science. He explained that he had come to Istanbul to realise this aim, and he said: "The conscience is illuminated by the religious sciences, and the mind is illuminated by the sciences of civilization."[12]

And another account, that of Ali Himmet Berki, a former president of the Court of Appeal:

During those years I was a student in the Medresetü'l-Kuzat [Law Faculty]. I was ahead of the other students. Bediuzzaman's name and fame had spread throughout Istanbul; everyone was talking about him in all the scholarly circles. We heard reports that he was staying as a guest in a *han* in Fatih, and that he answered every sort of question that anyone put to him. I decided to go with some fellow students, and we went to visit this famous person.

That day we heard he was in a teahouse answering questions. We went there immediately. There was quite a crowd, and he was wearing unusual clothes. He was wearing not the dress of a scholar, but the local dress of eastern Anatolia.

When we got close to him, Bediuzzaman was answering the questions being asked him. He was surrounded by scholars who were listening to him in rapt silence and wonder. Everyone was satisfied and pleased with the answers they received. He was replying to the assertions and ideas of the Sophist philosophers. He demolished their views with rational proofs.

That was the first time I saw and met him. What I gathered about him was this: he knew all the dictionaries. Whatever word you asked him from the Arabic dictionaries, he would answer immediately and give its meaning. Then in theology there was no one superior to him. In these two sciences his knowledge was endless. He knew Arabic literature, Persian literature, Eastern and Western literature. And there was another piece of information about him that was well-known: as a man of religion he did not accept gifts, money, etc., from anyone. He could have owned lots of things if he had wanted. He did not own a stick in the world.[13]

Abdullah Enver Efendi, known as the Walking Library, gave the following account in an interview with Necmeddin Şahiner:

> Harbizade Tavaslı Hasan Efendi, a teacher in the Fatih *madrasah*, was a scholarly and respected figure. He lived into his nineties, teaching right up until his last days. He was someone who never missed a day at his duties; there was not one day in his whole teaching life that he did not go to teach. But that day Hasan Efendi said to his students: 'I cannot come to teach today, because someone from eastern Anatolia called Bediuzzaman has arrived, and I am going to visit him.' He left the *madrasah* and went to visit Bediuzzaman in the Şekerci Han. On his return, he expressed the astonishment and love he felt, saying to his students: 'Never has such a person been seen, he is a rarity of creation. The like of him has yet to appear.'[14]

Forty years later Bediuzzaman himself recalled in a defence speech in court how the Istanbul *'ulamā'* had sought his assistance. He said: "Forty years ago and the year before the proclamation of the Constitution I went to Istanbul. At that time, the Japanese

Istanbul before Freedom 49

Commander-in-Chief [of the Army] had asked the Muslim *'ulamā'* a number of questions concerning religion. The Istanbul *'ulamā'* asked me about them. And they questioned me about many things in connection with them."[15]

And finally, an anecdote from Haji Hafız Efendi, who used also to be present in the discussions held in the Fatih *madrasah* at that time of lively and vital debate. It was recorded by Necmeddin Şahiner exactly as related by Haji Hafız's son, Visali Bey, from his father's memoirs.

> One day, some *'ulamā'* were debating a subject in the courtyard of Fatih Mosque, but they could in no way convince one another and solve the question. The subject did not become clear and evident at all. The debate continued. At that point, Bediuzzaman appeared dressed in simple and humble clothes, with a shawl, and fur cap on his head. I recognised him and knew of his knowledge on scholarly matters, so I observed the situation, and listened.
>
> Bediuzzaman said to the scholars: "What is this matter you are discussing? May I know? Would you please tell me?"
>
> Seeing his humble dress, the scholars replied: "See here, shepherd efendi! You would not understand these matters. Off with you and attend to your own business!"
>
> Bediuzzaman was not the least offended at this. He learnt what the matter was, then explained and solved it so beautifully with verses from the Qur'an and Ḥadīths that everyone's mouths dropped open in amazement. All those religious scholars were completely convinced of the subject. He explained the verses so masterfully that it was as though he had been at the Prophet's (ṣ) side when they had been revealed. And the scholars declared: "Your years are few, but your knowledge is great. Allow us to kiss your hand."
>
> Bediuzzaman replied: 'There is need for that', and took his leave in a most modest and unobtrusive manner.[16]

Proposals for Educational Reform

Some months after arriving in Istanbul Bediuzzaman was successful in presenting a petition setting out his ideas for educational reform in the Eastern Provinces to the court of Sultan

Abdulhamid. The text was later printed in *The East and Kurdistan Gazette*, dated 19 November, 1908. However, as the paper's introduction to the article points out, Bediuzzaman's initiative was to have unhappy consequences. In the short time he had been in Istanbul, he had attracted a lot of attention, both favourable, and as far as the authorities were concerned, adverse. As was inevitable during those repressive times, being such a controversial figure, he was kept under close surveillance.[17] He had also attracted the enmity of others in the same profession, jealous at his learning and fame. Bediuzzaman, however, had one aim: to serve the cause of Islam and the Empire, and he knew no fear in doing this. It is not known what passed between him and the pashas of the Palace Secretariat, but his implied criticism of the Sultan's educational policies[18] must also have provoked their unfavourable reaction.

The text of the petition was as follows. It is preceded by a few introductory words by the newspaper:

> We are proud to include the exact text of the proposal which Bediuzzaman Mullah Said Efendi presented to the Palace, and as a result became the target of many misfortunes.
>
> While, in order to be in harmony in progress like the other brothers in this world of civilization and age of progress and competition, the founding and construction of schools has been ordered as a government service in the towns and villages of Kurdistan—and this has been witnessed with thanks—only children who know Turkish can benefit from them. Since Kurdish children who have not learned Turkish consider the only mines of perfection to be the *madrasahs* [traditional religious schools], and the teachers in the *maktabs* [new secular schools] do not know the local language, these children continue to be deprived of education. Their resulting uncivilized behaviour and disorder invites the West to rejoice at our misfortune. Moreover, since the people remain in a primitive state, uncivilized and blindly imitating, they become prey to doubts and suspicions. And it is as though these three points are preparing a ghastly blow against the Kurds in the future, and have caused suffering to those with insight.

The remedy for this: three educational establishments should be set up in different areas of Kurdistan as examples to be followed, and as encouragement and stimulation: one in Beytüşşebab, which is the centre of the Ertuşi tribes; another in the middle of the Mutkan, Belkan and Sasun tribes; and one in Van itself, which is in the middle of the Haydar and Sipkan tribes. These should be known by the familiar name of *madrasah*, and should teach both the religious and modern sciences. Each should have at least fifty students, and their means of subsistence should be provided by the illustrious government. Also, the revitalization of a number of other *madrasahs* would be an important means of securing the future life—both material, and moral and spiritual—of Kurdistan. In this way, the basis of education would be established, and together with making over to the government this huge force which is now being dissipated in internal conflict, it would cause it to be expended outwardly. And it would demonstrate that they are thoroughly deserving of justice, and capable of being civilized, as well as displaying their natural ability.[19]

Thus, Bediuzzaman was finally successful in presenting to the Palace an outline of his proposals, the fruit of his own experience over many years. And, pointing out some of the damaging results of the system as it then was, he with foresight predicted problems of great magnitude in the future.

Bediuzzaman's ideas on educational reform were far-reaching and innovative. They are in part described above and in his 'Conversation with the Doctor' following this section. But due to their importance we include a summary of them in their entirety.

The heart of his proposals lay in reconciling "the three main branches" of the educational system, the *madrasahs* or traditional religious schools, the *maktabs* or new secular schools, and the *takiyyahs* or Sufi establishments, and the disciplines they represented. The embodiment of this rapprochement was the Medresetü'z-Zehra, which has been mentioned earlier. Bediuzzaman attached the greatest importance to establishing this university where the religious sciences and modern sciences would be taught side by side and "combined", and pursued it till the end of his days.

The second main area of his proposals concerned the complete restructuring of *madrasah* education. The proposals were extremely modern in their approach and consisted of what might be described as the democratization of the *madrasah* system, and its diversification so that "the rule of the division of labour" could be applied.

A third area concerned the preachers, who "guided the general public".

While the role the Medresetü'z-Zehra was to play was seen by Bediuzzaman to be vital for securing the future of Kurdistan and unity of the Empire as well as acting as an important centre for the eastern Islamic world, the general principles it represented were applicable to all *madrasahs*. Several of the conditions Bediuzzaman considered to be essential were mentioned in the petition: the Medresetü'z-Zehra and its two sister establishments should be known by the familiar name of *madrasah* and the instruction should be in a language known by potential students. In another work, *Münâzarat*, Bediuzzaman stated that they should be tri-lingual, with Arabic being "compulsory", Kurdish "permissible", and Turkish "necessary".[20] In the same work, he also stated that Kurdish scholars who were trusted by Turk and Kurd should be selected as teachers, as well as those who knew the local languages, and that it was necessary to take into account the capacity and cultural level of the community they were to serve. Also these *madrasahs* should be on an equal footing with the official secular schools, and like them, their examinations should be recognised. The basis of the system Bediuzzaman was proposing, however, was the combined teaching of the religious and modern sciences.

In the course of time, the *madrasah* syllabi had become narrow and sterile, with modern developments in science being rejected altogether. So that at the beginning of the twentieth century, the *madrasahs* were producing *'ulamā'* who believed, together with the Europeans, that there was a clash and contradiction between certain "externals" of Islam and certain matters of science— matters as basic as the Earth being round. This false idea had caused feelings of hopelessness and despair, and had shut the door of progress and civilization. "Whereas", pointed out Bediuzzaman, "Islam is the master and guide of the sciences, and the chief and father of all true knowledge."[21]

On a human level, Bediuzzaman saw religion as representing the heart and conscience, and science, and reason; both were necessary for true progress to be attained. He explained it as follows: "The religious sciences are the light of the conscience, and the modern sciences are the light of the reason. The truth becomes manifest through the combining of the two. The students' endeavour will take flight on these two wings. When they are separated it gives rise to bigotry in the one, and wiles and scepticism in the other."[22]

On a wider scale, the Medresetü'z-Zehra would unite the three traditions in the educational system by representing "the most superior *maktab* by the reason, the very best *madrasah* by the heart, and the most sacred *zāwiyah* by the conscience."[23] As a result of its unique value for the Islamic world, it would in time gain financial independence by reason of the donations and pious bequests it would receive.

The benefits of such a system would be manifold: just as it would ensure the future of the *'ulamā'* in the eastern provinces, at the same time it would be a step towards the unification and reform of the general system; so would it deliver Islam from the bigotry, superstitions, and false beliefs which had encrusted parts of it over the centuries; and, importantly, would be a means of introducing modern learning into the *madrasahs* in a way which would allay the *'ulamā'* suspicions concerning modern science. Also, it would "open the door to spreading the beneficial aspects of constitutionalism."[24]

Bediuzzaman wished for Islam to function like a consultative council, that is to say, through the mutual consultation (*shūrah*) of "the three divisions of the army of Islamic education", those of the *madrasahs*, the *maktabs*, and the *takiyyahs*, so that "each would complete the deficiencies of the other". His aim was for the Medresetü'z-Zehra to be such an embodiment.[25]

According to Bediuzzaman, transforming the *madrasahs* from being single-faculty institutions into being multi-faculty and putting into practice "the rule of division of labour" was in accordance with wisdom and the laws of creation. The failure to practise it in previous centuries had led to despotism and the exploitation of learning in the *madrasahs*, and the teaching being undertaken by those not qualified to do so. It had pointed the *madrasahs* towards their destruction.[26]

In many places, Bediuzzaman stresses the need for students to specialise in a subject for which they have an aptitude, and in addition only study subjects that complement it. Since it is described in some detail in his 'Conversation with the Doctor', together with the need for creative study, debate, and a return to the study of the essential religious sciences by the students, we shall leave the description there. Nevertheless, it should be pointed out that specialization in particular represented a radical break with traditional methods.

Finally, a further point which could be considered radical was Bediuzzaman's view that "public opinion" should prevail among both the *'ulamā'* and the students. That is to say, he believed that it was "scholastic despotism", an offspring of political despotism, "which has opened the way to blind imitation (*taqlīd*), and barred the way to searching for the truth." For the problems of the modern age to be grappled with and progress to be secured, "constitutionalism among the *'ulamā'* should be established "in the *'ulamā'* state." In the same way, among the students, "public opinion" or the prevalent ideas emerging from debate and the exchange of ideas between students of varying disciplines should be taken as master. Bediuzzaman predicted that this would provide a strong stimulation and incentive for progress. Thus, "Just as public opinion predominates in the state, so too should the prevailing opinions of the *'ulamā'* be mufti, and the prevailing opinions of the students be master and teacher."[27]

Years later, Bediuzzaman wrote: "Born in the village of Nurs in the province of Bitlis, as a student I entered into contests with all the scholars I encountered, and continuing through Divine Grace to defeat in scholarly debate all who challenged me, I continued the contests in this calamitous fame, and as a result of the incitements of my rivals, on orders from Sultan Hamid, was dragged as far as the mental hospital."[28]

Toptaşı and the 'Conversation with the Doctor'

How long Bediuzzaman's tribulations in the mental hospital continued is not known, but finally he was released on the strength of the doctor's report, which stated: "If there is the tiniest trace of madness in Bediuzzaman, there is not a sane person in the world."

Of the doubtless many examinations which Bediuzzaman had to undergo in the hospital, the following is the text of his conversation with the doctor which contributed directly to the favourable report. In it he explains with clarity and logic his aims and intentions, and why he has aroused opposition in Istanbul.

First of all Bediuzzaman points out to the doctor four points he should take into account while making his diagnosis. Firstly is his background, for "the prevalent virtues in Kurdistan are courage, self-respect, strength of religion, and the agreement of heart and tongue. Matters which are considered to be polite and refined in civilization are considered by them to be flattery."

Secondly, the doctor should not make his judgement superficially according to current deviant norms, but should realise that Bediuzzaman takes Islam as the criterion for his actions through which he intends to serve the nation, state, and religion. Thirdly, Bediuzzaman points out that some of those in authority could not stomach him because he provided answers to a number of the hitherto insoluble problems of the time, and their only recourse was to declare him mad. And fourthly, he has for fifteen years been pursuing Islamic Freedom, that is, "the Freedom which is in accordance with the Sharī'ah", and now that it is close to being realised he is prevented from seeing what is going on, how should he not be angry? And he adds: "And it is only one in a thousand who is not afflicted by this temporary madness."

He then goes onto expand these points and explain them in greater detail, stressing that he is not prepared to sacrifice any of his sacred aims and principles, which are for the common good, for his own personal benefit or so that he should be better accepted.

Firstly, his aim was for the strengthening and progress of the Ottoman Empire through the development and progress— educational, material, and cultural—of its component parts. By retaining the dress of his native region and professing his love for it, he wanted to stress in the Empire's capital the importance of provincial development, and create demand for local industries. And by declaring that he had offered allegiance to Sultan Selim, that is, Yavuz Selim, known in the West as Selim the Grim (1512-1520), Bediuzzaman was stating that he was dedicated to the same aim as Selim, that is, unity. Reforms aimed at the development of the provinces would serve to strengthen the unity of the Empire, thereby strengthening Islamic Unity.

Secondly, Bediuzzaman had aroused opposition through his practice of debating with the *'ulamā'*. He now explains to the doctor that by doing so he wanted to offer a practical example for a solution to the stagnation in the *madrasahs*. He was recommending more active participation in the process of study on the part of the students. A second reason he gives for their backwardness is that the instrumental sciences [grammar, syntax, logic] had been emphasised in place of the sacred sciences [Qur'anic exegesis (*tafsīr*), Ḥadīth, theology (*kalām*), and the like]. Thus, firstly,

Bediuzzaman is stressing the need for lively debate and the role of competition in revitalizing the *madrasahs*, and secondly, the importance of the fundamental sacred sciences. He then goes on to emphasise the need for specialization. It was through taking one science as a basis and in addition only studying further subjects in so far as they would complement the main subject, that the students could study in sufficient depth and penetrate the subject as required.

In the Third Point, Bediuzzaman examines the reasons for the divergence and differences between the various branches of the educational system, which he states are a major cause of the backwardness of Islamic civilization, which constitutes true civilization, in relation to modern civilization. He says: "Those in the *madrasahs* accuse those in the *maktabs* of weakness in belief because of their literalist interpretation of certain matters, whereas those in the *maktabs* consider the former to be ignorant and unreliable because they have no knowledge of modern science. While those in the *madrasahs* look at those in the *takiyyahs* as though they were following innovations…" While recognizing the differences in their ways, he stresses that the barriers between them should be broken down and by way of a remedy modern science be taught in the *madrasahs* "in place of obsolete ancient philosophy", religious sciences be taught "fully" in the secular schools, and scholars from the *madrasahs*, "some of the most learned *'ulamā'*", be present in the Sufi *takiyyahs*. He then goes on to analyse the reasons for the ineffectiveness of the preachers, who played such a vital role in educating the mass of the people. He gives three "causes", which we quote in full:

> The First Cause: by comparing the present to the past, they merely represent what they claim in glittering terms. In former times ease of mind and blind imitation of the *'ulamā'* prevailed, and for these proof was not necessary. But now an urge to investigate the truth has emerged in everyone. In the face of this, embroidering a claim has no effect. For it to be effective, it is necessary to prove what is claimed, and to convince.

The Second Cause: by deterring from one thing and encouraging another, they reduce the value of something else more important. For example, they say that to perform two *rak'ahs* of prayers at night is like circumambulating the Ka'bah, or that if someone indulges in backbiting, it is as though he has committed fornication.

The Third Cause: they do not speak conformably with the demands of the situation and necessities of the time, which is the requirement of eloquence. It is as if they draw people into the corners of former times, then speak to them. That is to say, I want preachers to be both searching scholars, so that they can prove what they claim, and subtle philosophers so that they do not spoil the balance of the Sharī'ah, and to be eloquent and convincing. It is essential that they are thus.

Bediuzzaman completed addressing the doctor as follows:

The Fourth Point: I said that my mind was confused, but my intention from all this is to point to the forgetfulness in my memory, the distress in my mind, and the foreignness in my nature. Since no one who is mad says they are mad, how can it be a proof of my madness? Also, I said that I had three months study after *Izhār*.[29] This invites doubt in two respects. Either it is untrue…whereas most of Kurdistan knows that it is true. Or although it is true…like you said, O Doctor, things like pride and self-praise would indicate my madness.

That is to say, it is our doctors' understanding that is sick, and their reports which are mad, and the Minister of Public Security is mad, because he was angry. Hey, doctor! You are a good doctor, cure those unfortunates first, then me![30]

It became plain to the doctor, then, that Bediuzzaman was in no way deranged[31] and he prepared his report accordingly; whatever the reasons were for his being sent to the mental hospital, they were not medical, and the doctor did not concern himself with them. Of course, it was for political reasons that Bediuzzaman had been incarcerated, and on his release he was still held in custody. The Palace then embarked on a new tactic to silence him; they tried to buy him off. But to no avail. Just as Bediuzzaman did not know the meaning of fear, and could not be cowed or scared into abandoning the path he knew to be right, so too he had no desire for wealth or position, throughout his life one of his most salient characteristics was his refusal to accept any personal benefits, material or otherwise; there was no way he could be bought. If the Islamic world was to progress and be revitalized, it would be through Freedom and constitutionalism; he could not be made to renounce the cause. The proposals were put to him by Şefik Pasha, the Minister of Public Security, and the exchange between him and Bediuzzaman went as follows:

The Minister: "The Sultan sends you greetings. He has assigned you a thousand kuruş as a salary. He said that later, when you return to the East, he will make it twenty to thirty liras. And he sent you these gold liras as a royal gift."

The Reply: "I am not a beggar after a salary; I could not accept it even if it were a thousand liras. I did not come to Istanbul for myself, I came for my people. Also this bribe that you want to give me is hush-money."

The Minister: "You are rejecting an imperial decree. An imperial decree cannot be rejected."

The Reply: "I am rejecting it, so that the Sultan will be annoyed and will summon me, and I can tell him the truth."

The Minister: "The result will be disastrous."

The Reply: "Even if results in the sea, it will be a spacious grave. If I am executed, I shall rest in the heart of a nation. Also when I came to Istanbul, I brought my life as a bribe; do whatever you like. And I say seriously that I want to give a practical warning to my fellow-countrymen that if one forms a connection with the State, it should be to serve it, not to grab a salary. And someone like me serves the nation and State through advising and admonishing. And that is through making a good impression. And that is through expecting nothing in return. And that is through being unprejudiced, which is through being without ulterior motives, which is through renouncing all personal benefits. As a consequence, I am excused from not accepting a salary."

The Minister: "Your aim of spreading education in Kurdistan is being discussed by the Cabinet."

The Reply: "According to what rule do you delay education and speed up salaries? Why do you prefer my personal benefits to the general benefit of the nation?"

The Minister became angry.

Bediuzzaman: "I have been free. I grew up in the mountains of Kurdistan, which is the place of absolute freedom. There is no point in getting angry; do not tire yourself for nothing. Send me into exile; be it Fizan or Yemen, I do not mind. I will be saved from falling from a height."

The Minister: "What do you want to say?"

Bediuzzaman: "You have drawn a veil as thin as a cigarette paper over everyone in the face of all these ideas and emotions which are boiling over, and called it law and order. Underneath everyone is groaning at your oppression like moving corpses. I was inexperienced, I did not go in under the veil, I remained on top of it. Then one time it was rent in the Palace. I was in an Armenian's house in Şişli; it was rent there. I was in the Sweetmakers' Han; it was rent there, too. I was in the mental hospital. And now I am in this place of custody.

"In short, you do so much patching up that I am annoyed as well. I was well-acquainted with you while I was in Kurdistan. And now the above-mentioned events have taught me your secrets well. Especially the mental hospital, it explained these texts to me clearly. So I thank you for these events, because I used always to think favourably, instead of distrusting."[32]

And finally, a newspaper article on the subject written later by the journalist and writer Eşref Edip, who was a close associate of Bediuzzaman and played an active role in the constitutional movement with his writings and the magazine, *Sırat-ı Müstakim*, later called *Sebilürreşad*, which he owned:

No one, not even the Sultan, could at any time agree that there was even the smallest amount of disloyalty in him. They appreciated his excellence, his zeal.

He had come to Istanbul in order to open schools in the Eastern Provinces, to revive education. He was a great cherisher of Freedom, he had great courage and civilization. Think of the conditions of the time. What was the attitude of the Palace towards the Namık Kemals, the Ziya Pashas, and other supporters of Freedom? Bediuzzaman was far ahead of them as regards courage and fearlessness, patriotism, and love of Freedom. The Palace displayed great tolerance towards this struggle of his for Freedom out of respect for his learning and virtue. But it was not possible to curtail his striving. His youth, his overflowing brilliant intelligence, his love of Freedom, his combative spirit could not save him from the consequences to which the other supporters of Freedom were subject.

He displayed such a degree of courage and boldness in the struggle for Freedom at a time when everyone was frightened to open their mouths and only hinted and made allusions that it was incomprehensible to them. It was only natural that for someone to arrive from the Eastern Provinces and display so much boldness at a time when the Palace and Pashas were sovereign and held absolute power would be met with astonishment and surprise. The despotic Pashas, who considered the people to be their slaves, could see no other way of ridding themselves of him and regaining their comfort apart from saying: 'To display this much courage is not conformable with sanity', and putting him in the mental hospital. That was why he was sent there.

What he said to the doctor in the mental hospital left the doctor in amazement, he was amazed at his intelligence and knowledge, courage and bravery. He understood why he had been sent there, and reminded Bediuzzaman of the refined manners of the age. He advised moderation, then begged his pardon.

Yes, this is the man they said was mad, this mad lion![33]

Notes

1. B. Lewis, *The Emergence of Modern Turkey*, London 1968, 124.
2. *Ibid.*, 171.
3. Y. Bahadıroğlu, *Osmanlı Padişahları Ansiklopedisi*, iii, 722.
4. Y. Bahadıroğlu, *Bediüzzaman Said Nursi*, i, 67-8.
5. Nursi, "Lemean-ı Hakikat ve İzale-i Şübehat," *Volkan*, No. 101, 29 Mart 1325/11 April 1909, in *Asar-ı Bedi'iyye*, 392-3.
6. Nursi, *Münâzarat*, 61.

7. Abdurrahman, *Bediüzzaman'ın Tarihçe-i Hayatı*, 33-4; *Son Şahitler*, iii, 20.
8. Şahiner, *Son Şahitler*, iii, 17-18 (Istanbul Başvekalet Arşivi).
9. *Tarihçe*, 48-9.
10. In this period, until following the First World War, Bediuzzaman was mostly known by this name. Subsequently, he was called 'Nursî', after the village of his birth.
11. Şahiner, *Said Nursi*, 78; Nursi, *Divan-ı Harb-i Örfi*, 5-6.
12. H. Fehmi Başoğlu, "Bir Hatira," *Uhuvvet Gazetesi*, 11 December 1964, as quoted in Şahiner, *Said Nursi*, 82-3.
13. Ali Himmet Berki, in *Son Şahitler*, ii, 12.
14. Şahiner, *Said Nursi*, 84.
15. Nursi, *The Rays Collection* (Eng. tr.), 380-1.
16. Şahiner, *Son Şahitler*, iv, 356.
17. Ali Riza Sağman, in *Son Şahitler*, iv, 294-5.
18. In a newspaper article published in March 1909, Bediuzzaman suggested to the Sultan in an imaginary conversation how he should act as Caliph in the new age of constitutionalism: "Since despotism has left no blood in Istanbul, the heart of the Muslim countries, show that your intention is good and make Yıldız Palace, which is now abhorred, beloved of hearts in the way you compassionately accepted constitutionalism with no bloodshed: raise Yıldız Palace to the Pleiades by filling it with leading *'ulamā'* like angels of mercy in place of the former demons of hell, and by making it like a university and reviving the Islamic sciences, and by promoting the offices of Şeyhü'l-İslam and the Caliphate to their rightful positions, and by curing with your wealth and power the weakness in religion which is the nation's heart disease and the ignorance which is the disease of its head. Then the Ottoman dynasty may scatter the rays of justice in the constellation of the Caliphate.", "Bediüzzaman Kürdi'nin Fihriste-i Makasıdı ve Efkârının Programı", *Volkan*, Nos. 83-4, 11-12 Mart 1325/23-4 March 1909, as in *Asar-ı Bedi'iyye*, 375-6.
19. Nursi, *Asar-ı Bedi'iyye*, 366-7; Şahiner, *Said Nursi*, 85-7.
20. Nursi, *Münâzarat*, 71.
21. Nursi, *Muhâkemat*, 8.
22. Nursi, *Münâzarat*, 72.
23. *Ibid.*, 74.
24. *Ibid.*, 74-6.
25. *Ibid.*, 76.
26. Nursi, *Muhâkemat*, 46-7.
27. Nursi, "Bediüzzaman Kürdi'nin Fihriste-i Makasıdı ve Efkarının Programı," *Volkan*, Nos. 83-4, in *Asar-ı Bedi'iyye*, 374.
28. Nursi, *The Rays Collection* (Eng. tr.), 493.

29. *Iẓhār al-Asrār*: a book in the *madrasah* syllabus.
30. Nursi, *Asar-ı Bedi'iyye*, 324-9; Şahiner, *Said Nursi*, 89-95.
31. Two other accounts may be referred to, showing that other doctors reached similar conclusions. See, N. Şahiner, *Türk ve Dünya Aydınları Gözüyle Nurculuk Nedir*, 142-3; N. Şahiner, *Said Nursi* (8th edn.), 106-7.
32. Nursi, *Asar-ı Bedi'iyye*, 330-1; Şahiner, *Said Nursi*, 95-7.
33. Eşref Edip, "Islam Düşmanlarının Tertiplerini Ortaya Çıkarmak Vazifemizdir," *Yeni Istiklal Gazetesi*, No. 241, 23 March 1966, as quoted in Şahiner, *Said Nursi*, 97-8.

3
Freedom and Constitutionalism

Salonica

How Bediuzzaman was saved from his place of custody in Istanbul is not known. According to one account, he escaped and was taken secretly to Salonica¹ where he stayed as a guest in the house of Manyasizade Refik Bey, who was to be Minister of Justice in the first Cabinet following the proclamation of the Constitution, and was at that time Chairman of the Central Committee of the Committee of Union and Progress in Salonica. Through him Bediuzzaman made the acquaintance of the leading figures of the CUP.²

As was mentioned above, the CUP was one group within the Young Turk movement, which formed the main focus of opposition to Sultan Abdulhamid, and had members both within Turkey and Europe. In Turkey, the movement was well suppressed, but conditions favoured its growth, particularly among army officers, the composition of whom was changing as a result of the reforms. It was in Salonica, a place open to diverse influences, that a group of officers and other people founded a revolutionary secret society in 1906, and subsequently establishing relations with one of the groups of Young Turks in Paris, adopted their name of the Committee of Union and Progress.³

It is important at this point to clarify Bediuzzaman's attitude towards politics generally, and towards the Young Turks in particular. We can make two main points. Firstly, his involvement with politics was always with the aim of making politics serve religion, to point out Islamic principles and give direction to those in power. He was never involved in politics for their own sake, or for power, prestige or position. The members of the Committee of Union and Progress in Salonica were a 'mixed bunch' and what unified them was their patriotism and desire to save the crumbling Empire. The majority of them being army officers, they had little experience in politics and political administration and even when they forced the proclamation of the Constitution, they had no political plan or programme.[4] For the most part, their attitude towards Islam was positive; and not only as the main politically unifying factor of the Empire. Even the secular theorists from among the Young Turks such as Ahmed Rıza and Abdullah Cevdet accepted the positive function of Islam in society.[5] Bediuzzaman himself later wrote: "At the beginning of the Constitutional Period I saw that there were atheists who had infiltrated the CUP who accepted that Islam and the Sharī'ah of Muḥammad (ṣ) contained exalted principles extremely beneficial and valuable for the life of society and particularly Ottoman policies and who supported the Sharī'ah with all their strength."[6] But while a majority of them were not hostile to Islam, due to their secular backgrounds and education, they had been influenced in varying degrees by European ideas; many were uninformed about their religion and were lax in the practice of it. An important reason, therefore, in Bediuzzaman associating with the Young Turks before the Constitution was proclaimed was to persuade them that, for the Empire's future progress and well-being, Freedom must be established on the Sharī'ah as well as for himself to be able to serve this end. But again it must be stressed that while he continued to support those Young Turks who shared this end, he became a strenuous opponent of those of them who deviated from it. For their part, the leading members of the CUP in Salonica were impressed by the calibre of this famous young scholar, and, as a man of religion and an unswerving supporter of Freedom, were keen to employ him in the propagation of his ideas on Freedom.

The second point to make about Bediuzzaman and politics will perhaps illuminate this further. He was a realist; he accepted the current situation, and looking to the future, sought ways of directing the trend of events into Islamic channels. For example, subsequent to the French Revolution, the ideas of liberty, equality, justice, and the rule of law had been universally accepted as preferable to despotism and arbitrary rule; the trend towards representative government was inevitable and unavoidable in the Ottoman Empire as well as in Europe. Bediuzzaman accepted the trend, and through pointing out that these luminous concepts were not the exclusive property of the West as the Europeans would have it but were fundamental to Islam, showed the way towards developing a truly Islamic form of government. This demonstrating that consultation, equality before the law, justice, freedom, and brotherhood were enjoined by Islam and were practised by Prophet Muḥammad (ṣ) and his immediate successors, and that despotism was contrary to Islam, was a genuine statement of fact, and was, furthermore, a recognition of the dynamic nature of the Sharī'ah.

Bediuzzaman's success in spreading these ideas in Salonica caused him to be looked on very favourably by the Committee of Union and Progress. A figure of some fame, or notoriety, got to hear of Bediuzzaman and his activities, and that was Emanuel Karaso, later the Jewish deputy for Salonica, and Grand Master of the Macedonia Risorta Masons' Lodge. No doubt wanting to find a way of influencing such a talent and using it for his own purposes, he sought a meeting with Bediuzzaman. He agreed, but the Grand Master left abruptly half way through the conversation and confessed to those waiting for him outside: "If I had stayed any longer, he would have made a Muslim of me!"[7]

In July 1908, the events in Macedonia leading to the proclamation of the Constitution followed on one after the other. Mutiny, assassinations, and ultimatums demanding the restoration of the Constitution culminated in its reinstatement by the Sultan

Freedom and Constitutionalism 67

on 23rd July. It was met with joy as news spread through out the Empire, with the people spilling onto the streets to celebrate their deliverance from despotism and express their optimism at the future—emotions doubtless shared by Bediuzzaman. He was concerned however that these unfamiliar concepts should be properly understood.

In the speech he gave, firstly impromptu in Beyazit in Istanbul immediately following the proclamation of the Constitution and subsequently in Freedom Square in Salonica, he explained to the people the meaning of constitutionalism, and how they should regard it, and that if the Sharī'ah was made the source of it, "This oppressed nation will progress a thousand times further than in former times."

'Address to Freedom'

The text of the speech, entitled Address to Freedom, is too long to include here in its entirety, so we shall briefly point out the main ideas it describes and include parts of it by way of illustration. But first it is worth noting the importance Bediuzzaman attached to illuminating and mobilizing the ordinary people and community of believers in the struggle for progress, as is illustrated by the few introductory sentences to the Address. For while the proclamation of the Constitution was greeted with jubilation it was still believed by many that the new government was irreligious and that it was not permissible to obey it, a belief that was clearly open to exploitation by its opponents.[8]

In addition, in regard to politics, the fundamental ideas that Bediuzzaman adhered to were that all the community should participate in the political process, and that the government should reflect the nation's will and that, furthermore, government based on these principles was enjoined by Islam. Following the proclamation of the Constitution, therefore, he expended much effort addressing the ordinary people, and especially his fellows Kurds, who had been subject to negative propaganda about the Constitution and were deeply suspicious of it, in order to explain to them its meaning, and their own rights and responsibilities towards it. And so, in an introductory passage to the Address to Freedom, Bediuzzaman addresses his audience directly and asks them to participate mentally in what he is going to discuss. Let their hearts be open..."For there is work to do for your zeal, religious feeling, and endeavour; they are going to discuss certain matters; they are going to kindle a light from the dark corners of the heart."[9]

Rather than being merely an ode in praise of Freedom, the Address to Freedom[10] is primarily an exhortation to adhere to Islam and its morality in the new era. With the advent of Freedom, the Ottoman nation has been given the opportunity to progress and establish true civilization as in former times, but this will only be achieved if they make the Sharī'ah the foundation of Freedom.[11] It points out the detrimental effects of despotism on the one hand, and the possibilities for progress that Freedom provides on the other. Together with this, it constitutes a programme of what must be achieved and what must be avoided in order to preserve Freedom and secure progress. In doing this it describes some of the causes of the Ottoman decline.

> O Freedom!...I convey these glad tidings to you, that if you make the Sharī'ah, which is life itself, the source of life, and if you grow in that paradise, this oppressed nation will progress a thousand times further than in former times if, that is, it takes you as its guide in all matters and does not besmirch you through harbouring personal enmity and thoughts of revenge... Freedom has exhumed us from the grave of desolation and despotism, and summoned us to the paradise of unity and love of nation...
>
> ...The doors of a suffering-free paradise of progress and civilization have been opened to us...The Constitution, which is in accordance with the Sharī'ah, is the introduction to the sovereignty of the nation and invites us to enter like the treasury-guard of Paradise. O my oppressed compatriots! Let us go and enter!

So, having pointed out that sovereignty will now lie with the nation, Bediuzzaman goes on to describe "five doors" that have to be entered, or five principles to which the state should be bound so that this paradise might be attained. The first is "the union of hearts". This has been described as preserving the consciousness of the Ottoman state's unity and wholeness, especially in the face of the nationalist and separatist movements of the minorities. The second door is "love of the nation;" that is, the individuals who make up the nation being aware of their nationhood and nurturing love for one another, remembering that "the foundation and spirit of our true nationhood is Islam."[12] The third is "education", which refers to the cultural and educational level of the nation being raised to a satisfactory point. The fourth is "human endeavour"; that is, everyone being guaranteed work and receiving fair recompense for their labour. And the fifth door is "the giving up of dissipation", which is understood as the giving up of ostentation and extravagance, both on an individual level and as a society, which caused discord, and were malaises afflicting state officials in particular at that time.[13]

Bediuzzaman points out the harmful effects of the vice and immorality that result from despotism, material as well as moral, while "The voice of Freedom and justice…raises to life our emotions, hopes, exalted national aspirations, and fine Islamic character and morality, all of which were dead."

After immediately warning against killing these again "through dissipation and carelessness in religion", he predicts that unity, adherence to Islamic morality together with the successful functioning of the constitutional government and genuine practice of the Islamic principle of consultation will result in the Ottoman nation soon "competing neck and neck with the civilized nations." The metaphors for progress he uses in the passage demonstrate his own belief in science and technology.

Bediuzzaman lays great stress on the need to adhere to Islamic morality for true progress and civilization to be achieved, and next voices his constant fear that if Freedom is understood as licence, it will be lost and will result in a return to despotism, "for Freedom flourishes and is realised through the observance of the ordinances and conduct of the Sharī'ah, and good morals."

Bediuzzaman next warns against acquiring "the sins and evils of civilization" and abandoning its virtues. The Ottomans should imitate the Japanese in taking from Western civilization what will assist them in progress, while preserving their own national customs:

> We shall take with pleasure the points of Europe—like technology and industry—that will assist us in progress and civilization. However,...we shall forbid the sins and evils of civilization from entering the bounds of Freedom and our civilization with the sword of the Sharī'ah, so that the young people in our civilization will be protected by the pure, cold spring of life of the Sharī'ah. We must imitate the Japanese in acquiring civilization, for in taking only the virtues of civilization from Europe they preserved their national customs, which are the leaven of every nation's continuance. Since our national customs grew up within Islam, they should be clung on to in two respects.

By contrasting conditions under the old and new regimes, he goes on to describe five indestructible truths on which Freedom will be established. They are as follows: the First Truth is unity, the Second, science, learning, and civilization. The Third Truth is a new generation of able and enlightened men to lead and administer the nation. Bediuzzaman describes how with "the rain of Freedom", the abilities and potentialities of everyone, even common villagers, will develop and be expanded so that "the vigorous field of Asia and Rumelia will produce the crops" of the brilliant and superior men so badly needed. "And the East will be to the West what dawn is to sunset. If, that is, they do not wither up through the languor of idleness and the poison of malice."

The Fourth Truth is the Sharī'ah. Bediuzzaman explains: "Since the Illustrious Sharī'ah has come from the Pre-Eternal Word of God, it will go to Post-Eternity." The Sharī'ah adapts and expands in relation to man's development. It comprises equality, justice, and true freedom with all its relations and requirements. The initial period of Islam is proof of this. Therefore, he says, their present unfortunate condition results from four causes: failure to observe the Sharī'ah, arbitrary and erroneous interpretations of it, bigotry on the part of certain "ignorant literalist scholars", and fourthly, "abandoning through ill-fortune and bad choice, the virtues of Europe, which are difficult to acquire, and imitating like parrots or children the sins and evils of civilization, which are agreeable to man's base appetites."

The Fifth Truth is the Parliament, and the Islamic principle of mutual consultation. In this complex modern age, it is only through a constituent assembly, consultation, and freedom of thought that the state can be upheld, administered, and guided.

Bediuzzaman completes the Address with three "warnings". Firstly, state officials who are prepared to adapt to the new regime must be treated with respect and their experience must be benefited from. Secondly, he points out that the sickness afflicting the Empire has spread from the centre of the Caliphate, from Istanbul, and goes on to urge reconciliation between "the three main branches of the 'public guide'", the scholars of the *madrasahs*, those of secular schools, and the Sufis in the *takiyyahs*. This point was discussed above, as was the following third warning, which concerns the preachers. Again, he is urging them to renew their ideas and methods, and speak conformably with the needs of the times.

Bediuzzaman's Ideas on Freedom and Constitutionalism

What, then, was the relationship between constitutionalism and Islam? For in this speech, and in all his speeches and writings of the time, Bediuzzaman was at pains to make clear to the people that the Constitution, which was the 1876 Constitution, was in no way contrary to the Sharī'ah. He describes it as the "*Kanun-u Şer'î*",[14] or Islamic Constitution, and "the Constitution which is founded on the Sharī'ah."[15] "Constitutionalism and the Constitution about which you have heard," explained Bediuzzaman, "consists of true justice and consultation enjoined by the Sharī'ah."[16]

He very often gives clear definitions of constitutionalism by contrasting it with despotism:

> Despotism is oppression. It is dealing with others in an arbitrary fashion. It is compulsion relying on force. It is the opinion of one person. It provides extremely favourable ground for exploitation. It is the basis of tyranny. It annihilates humanity. It is despotism which reduces man to the most abject valleys of abasement, has caused the Islamic world to sink into abjection and degradation, which arouses animosity and malice, has poisoned Islam—and in fact sows its poison everywhere by contagion, and has caused endless conflict within Islam by giving rise to its deviant sects like the Mu'tazilah, Jabriyyah, and Murji'ah.[17]

Constitutionalism, on the other hand, is "the manifestation of the Qur'anic verses 'And consult them in affairs [of public concern]' (Qur'an, 3:159), and 'Whose rule is consultation among themselves' (Qur'an, 42:38). It is the consultation enjoined by the Sharī'ah. This luminous body's life is truth, in place of force. Its heart is knowledge, its tongue, love. Its mind is the law, not an individual. Indeed, constitutionalism is the sovereignty of the nation."[18] And again, "...the real meaning of constitutionalism is that power lies in the law."[19]

On another occasion Bediuzzaman stated: "I expounded and commented in detail on the authentic connection between the Sharī'ah and constitutionalism in numerous speeches. And I explained that despotism has no connection with the Sharī'ah. For according to the meaning of the Ḥadīth, 'A nation's ruler is its servant', the Sharī'ah came to the world in order to extirpate oppression and despotic tyranny...And I said that essentially, the true way of the Sharī'ah is the reality of constitutionalism in accordance with the Sharī'ah. That is to say, I accepted constitutionalism on proofs from the Sharī'ah."[20] "I claimed that it is possible to deduce the truths of constitutionalism explicitly, implicitly, permissibly, from the Four Schools of Islamic Law."[21]

Freedom and Constitutionalism

A further argument was: "The consensus of the community constitutes a certain proof in the Sharī'ah. The opinion of the mass of the people forms a fundamental principle in the Sharī'ah. The public wish is esteemed and respected in the Sharī'ah."[22]

On the question, "Some people say [constitutionalism] is contrary to the Sharī'ah?" being put to him, Bediuzzaman replied: "The spirit of constitutionalism is from the Sharī'ah. And its life is from it. But under force of circumstance it may be that some details fall temporarily contrary to it. Also, all situations that arise during the constitutional period do not necessarily arise from constitutionalism. And what is there that conforms to the Sharī'ah in every respect?"[23]

Thus, Bediuzzaman's approach can be seen to be realistic. While in essence constitutionalism did not differ from Islamic principles, the extremely difficult circumstances of the time demanded a measured and balanced approach. It was a question of "making constitutionalism conform to the Sharī'ah meticulously and in a balanced manner taking into account what is required."[24]

As for consultation, which, as is shown above, is enjoined by Islam, he frequently stressed it as a constituent of constitutionalism. He described it as "the key to the good fortune, felicity, and sovereignty of Islam."[25] For due to the nature of constitutionalism, consultation is practised in all areas of the state and society. "Yes, this is the time of constitutionalism; consultation rules in everything."[26] That is to say when constitutionalism is adopted by a government, it spreads throughout the state and manifests itself as consultation, the supremacy of public opinion and consensus. These and their accompanying unity, co-operation, and brotherhood are fundamental to progress:

> When constitutionalism falls to the lot of a government, the idea of freedom awakens constitutionalism in every respect. It gives birth to a sort of constitutionalism in every area and walk of life, according to the calling of each. It results in a sort of constitutionalism among the *'ulamā'*, in the *madrasahs*, and among the students. Indeed, it inspires a particular

constitutionalism and renewal in all walks of life. It is flashes of consultation, then, hinting of the sun of happiness, and inspiring desire, mutual attraction, and harmony, that have caused me to love the Constitutional Government so much.[27]

Bediuzzaman also describes scientific progress in terms of 'historical consultation', and stresses its importance:

> Just as the consultation of the ages and centuries that mankind has practised by means of history, a 'conjunction of ideas' or 'meeting of minds', formed the basis of the progress and sciences of all mankind, so too one reason for the backwardness of Asia, the largest continent, was the failure to practise that true consultation. The key and discloser of the continent of Asia and its future is mutual consultation. That is to say, just as individuals should consult with one another, so must nations and continents also practise consultation.[28]

As regards Freedom, as is clear from the Address to Freedom, it could only be the source of progress if the Sharī'ah was taken as it's basis. It did not consist of absolute freedom or licence. While technology and industry could be imported from Europe, which in any case were not the property of the West, the Ottomans stood in no need of their culture, morals, and "the evils of civilization".

> I declare with all my strength," said Bediuzzaman, "that our progress will only occur through the progress of Islam, which is our nationality, and through the manifestation of the truths of the Sharī'ah. Otherwise we shall confirm the saying, 'he abandoned his own way of walking, and did not learn anyone else's.'[29]

Bediuzzaman defined Freedom as follows:

> Delicate Freedom is instructed and adorned by the good manners of the Sharī'ah. Freedom to be dissolute and behave scandalously is not Freedom, it is animality. It is the tyranny of the Devil. It is to be the slave of the evil-commanding soul. General Freedom is the product of the portions of individual Freedom. The characteristic of Freedom is that one harms neither oneself, nor others.[30]

> Freedom is this: apart from the law of justice and punishment, no one can dominate over anyone else. Everybody's rights are protected. In their legitimate actions, everyone is royally free. The prohibition: 'Take not one from among yourselves as Lord over you apart from God' is manifest.[31]

That is to say, "Freedom springs from belief in God." For "belief requires not degrading others through tyranny and oppression, and abasing them, and not abasing oneself before oppressors. Someone who is a true slave of God cannot be a slave to others."[32] "That is to say, however perfected belief is, Freedom will shine to that degree."[33]

Bediuzzaman says that Freedom is not to be absolved from all the ties of social life and civilization; "Rather, what shines like the sun is the beloved of every soul, and is the equal of the essence of humanity. Freedom is seated in the felicitous palace of civilization and is adorned with knowledge, virtue, and the good manners and raiment of Islam."[34]

The positive results of Freedom with regard to progress were in part noted above in the Address to Freedom: unity, love of the nation, the end to "personal enmity and thoughts of revenge", and also to extravagance and vice; the elimination of the chains on human thought; the rearing of a new generation of able men to run the country. In another work he says it is Islamic Freedom "which teaches mankind exalted aims in the form of competition for exalted things, and causes them to strive in that way; which shatters despotism; and excites exalted emotions and destroys jealousy, envy, malice, and rivalry, and is furnished with true awakening, the eagerness of competition, the tendency towards renewal, and the predisposition for civilization…It has been fitted with the inclination and desire for the highest accomplishments worthy of humanity."[35]

Indeed, Freedom was the means of "the progress of Islam". Bediuzzaman declared that "Freedom is the only way of delivering the three hundred and seventy million strong Islam from captivity."[36] And that: "The Ottomans' Freedom is the discloser of mighty Asia's good fortune. It is the key to the prosperity of Islam. It is the foundation of the ramparts of Islamic unity."[37]

Bediuzzaman explains this in terms of a reawakening of the consciousness of "Islamic nationhood" among individual Muslims. That is to say, as a result of Freedom, sovereignty now lies with the nation, or Islamic community, and "each individual Muslim possesses an actual part of the sovereignty."[38] His use of scientific language and metaphors in the first of the following passages shows that he wanted to demonstrate that this was the first step on the road to scientific advancement and civilization:

> Freedom has made manifest nationhood. The luminous jewel of Islam within the shell of nationhood has begun to appear. It has given news of Islam's stirring and motion [showing] that each Muslim is not independent like an atom, but is part of a compound, interconnected and ascending. Each is united with all the other parts through the general attraction of Islam.[39] And:
> Islamic Freedom and the consultation enjoined by the Sharī'ah have made manifest the sovereignty of our true nationhood. The foundation and spirit of our true nationhood is Islam...Thus, through the bond of this sacred nationhood, all the people of Islam become like a single tribe...They assist one another morally and if necessary, materially.[40]

A further point Bediuzzaman frequently stressed was that in this modern age material progress was the most effective way of 'upholding the Word of God', with which every believer is charged. In other words, it was a fundamental duty of all Ottomans and Muslims to work for progress.

> Each believer is charged with 'upholding the Word of God'. In this age, the chief means of this is to progress materially, for the Europeans are morally crushing us under their tyranny with the weapons of science and industry. We, therefore, shall wage holy war with the weapons of science and industry on the greatest enemies of 'upholding the Word of God', which are ignorance, poverty, and conflicting ideas. And we shall refer external holy war to the diamond sword of the certain proofs of the illustrious

Sharī'ah. For the civilized are to be conquered through persuasion and being convinced, not through compulsion as though they were savages who understand nothing.⁴¹

For Bediuzzaman, then, "Constitutionalism within the sphere of the Sharī'ah" was "the means of upholding the might of Islam and exalting the Word of God."⁴²

Bediuzzaman Combats Disunity and Secularism

There followed after the proclamation of the Constitution a period of open and vigorous debate made possible by the new freedom of thought and expression. Bediuzzaman took every advantage of this, endeavouring to further the cause of Islam and unity through every means possible. He gave speeches, addressed gatherings, and published articles in many of the newspapers and journals that appeared with the advent of Freedom, together with publishing a number of independent works.

Although the debate centred on the old questions of how progress could be secured and the Empire saved, the tension created by external and internal pressures caused a polarization and hardening of ideas. There were three main answers: westernization, Islam, and increasingly, in reaction to the separatist activities of the minorities, Turkish nationalism. These did not necessarily run parallel to the political parties that developed, and adherents to all three currents were to be found within the Committee of Union and Progress, though the image it acquired was predominantly secular and Western. Following the Revolution the CUP remained in the background with its headquarters in Salonica, largely making its presence felt through established figures.

The proclamation of the Constitution had been met with widespread rejoicing and optimism; it was seen to be the cure for all the many and serious ills afflicting the Empire. But those high and fervent hopes were soon to be dashed. Almost immediately there were substantial losses of territory, and rather than serving unity, the first parliament opened five months later, intensified division. In pursuing its aim of holding the Empire together through its strong centralist policies, the CUP increasingly resorted to force. The 31st of March Incident provided it with the opportunity to disband the opposition parties and restrict political freedom. Though the opposition reformed, within five years the CUP had set up the military dictatorship that was to lead the Empire to its final collapse in 1918.

In the first months of Freedom, opposition to the CUP was centered in the Liberals, or *Ahrār*, who, with hasty preparations, were the only party to challenge the new regime in the first elections at the end of 1908. Their leader was Prince Sabahaddin Bey, a nephew of Sultan Abdulhamid and rival in their days of exile in Paris to Ahmed Rıza, who became one of the main ideologues of the CUP. While the CUP were committed to a policy of strong central government, following a different school of French philosophers, Sabahaddin Bey had developed what he believed would be the solution for the Empire based on the totally opposite principles of 'Personal Initiative and Decentralization'. These ideas, which involved a devolvement of power from the Government to the various *millahs* and religious and ethnic minorities, aroused extreme opposition.

Included in Bediuzzaman's first work, *Nutuk*, (Speech) published in 1910, is an open letter to Sabahaddin Bey entitled, Reply to Prince Sabahaddin Bey's Good but Misunderstood Idea.[43]

In it Bediuzzaman points out that a federal system for the Ottoman Empire was theoretically acceptable but because the level of development of the different *millahs* and groups varied greatly, it was not practicable at that time. "Life lies in unity", he wrote. It is interesting to note that at that time of mudslinging, intimidation, and political violence, Sabahaddin Bey himself commented on Bediuzzaman's "intellectual excellence", describing his manner of address as "the very model of polite discourse."[44]

Bediuzzaman likened "love of the nation" to the attraction between particles; just as the latter caused the formation of a mass, so did "love of the nation" result in the formation of a cohesive whole. It was through strengthening these bonds of unity and awareness and love of the nation that a harmony of progress could be achieved. He did not believe that national differences should be erased, on the contrary as we have seen, it was his view that the government should be working to raise all the elements of the Empire to the same level through programmes geared to "the intellectual capacity and national customs of each." This would result in healthy competition.

Quite correctly as it turned out, Bediuzzaman warned Sabahaddin Bey that the idea of decentralization and "its nephews" the political clubs and organizations of the various minorities, would lead to autonomy, and "rending the veil of Ottomanism and constitutionalism" to independence and an army of small states. He could not equate the breaking up of the Empire, stirring up of discord, and destruction of the future with the patriotism and nobility of such a gifted and highly-educated person. As believers in God's Unity, they were charged with establishing unity and cultivating love of the nation. Islam was sufficient. Solutions should be sought within the framework of Islam.[45]

Reflecting the attitude of many of the CUP and their followers in this period, there was a general air of laxity, excess, and carelessness in matters of religion. In the face of the circulation of many new ideas from Europe, this was coupled with uncertainty and confusion as to religion and its role. It is in this light that Bediuzzaman's enormous concern to address the intellectuals and to educate as many people as he could reach from all levels of society about the true meaning of Freedom, constitutionalism, and the vital role of Islam in progress should be seen.

"Europe is pregnant with Islam"

In the autumn of 1908, one of the leading members of the famous al-Azhar University in Cairo, and at one time Grand Mufti of Egypt, Shaykh Muḥammad Bakhīt[46] visited Istanbul. The Istanbul *'ulamā'*, who themselves had been unable to better Bediuzzaman in argument and debate, asked Shaykh Bakhīt if he would be prepared to meet him. The shaykh accepted, and an opportunity was found one day after the prayers in Aya Sophia. Bediuzzaman was seated in a tea-house. Other *'ulamā'* also being present, Shaykh Bakhīt approached Bediuzzaman, and put the following question to him:

> What is your opinion concerning Freedom and the Ottoman State, and European civilization?

Bediuzzaman's unhesitating reply revealed his realism and insight.

> The Ottoman State is pregnant with Europe, and it will give birth to a European state one day. And Europe is pregnant with Islam; one day it will give birth to an Islamic state.

Shaykh Bakhīt applauded this answer:

> "One cannot argue with this young man", he said. "I am of the same opinion myself. But only Bediuzzaman could express it so succinctly and eloquently."⁴⁷

Bediuzzaman Maintains Public Order

As the great effusion of optimism at the coming of Freedom was transformed into disillusion and views and parties became more polarized, the situation generally became increasingly volatile and unstable. Thus, so that constitutionalism could become established and its benefits be obtained, Bediuzzaman did whatever he could to maintain public order and harmony. There are many examples, such as the following.

The first major blows to the Empire under the new regime occurred soon after the Constitution was proclaimed. On 5 October, 1908, Austria annexed Bosnia-Herzogovina, and Bulgaria proclaimed independence, while on the 6th, Greece annexed Crete. In response to this, on the 10th October, the people of Istanbul declared a boycott on all Austrian goods and the places where they were sold. The commercial life of Istanbul depended on the twenty thousand or more Kurdish porters who prepared to go on strike. Fearing that the whole business might get out of hand, Bediuzzaman went immediately to the tea-houses and places the porters frequented and persuaded them to avoid any extreme action.

An occasion he played a similar role was at a lecture given by the well-known owner of the *Mizan* newspaper, Mizancı Murad Bey, in the Ferah Theatre in Şehzadebaşı in Istanbul. The subject of the lecture was the rise and fall of the Roman Empire, and as the lecture progressed it became clear that Murad Bey, who had previously represented the 'Islamist' group of the Young Turks, was comparing the Committee of Union and Progress and the government to the Roman state. His comparisons became more explicit, and the CUP supporters among the audience started muttering and grumbling. Murad Bey continued with his criticisms unperturbed, not wavering even when threatened by a man with a revolver. But when the muttering developed into shouting and stamping, his opponents had their way and he was unable to continue. He withdrew into the wings, and the curtain was lowered. But the hubbub did not abate. On the contrary, the audience, now divided into two camps, started pushing and shoving and flinging insults and abuse at each other. No one attempted to leave, and no one attempted to intervene.

Suddenly, someone sprang nimbly onto his seat and shouted above the din: "O you Muslims one and all!" It was Bediuzzaman. Having commanded the attention of the whole audience, he pointed out that freedom of speech had to be respected; it was shameful for members of a nation that had just proclaimed Freedom and constitutionalism to exceed the bounds of good behaviour and prevent a speaker from lecturing in this way. The religion of Islam also commanded that ideas be respected. He supported what he said with verses from the Qur'an and Ḥadīths, gave examples from Islamic history, and told them of how Prophet Muḥammad (ṣ) used to consult the ideas of others and related his teachings and words, then advised them all to disperse quietly and go on their way.

Bediuzzaman spoke so well and convincingly that no one objected. Even the roughs and rowdies who a few minutes earlier had been hurling invective and abuse said nothing. Everyone left the theatre thoroughly subdued and contrite.[48]

The writer of the work from which the description of the above event is taken, Münir Süleyman Çapanoğlu, had further memories from that time, which he told Necmeddin Şahiner in an interview in 1972. He said:

> ...Certainly, he [Bediuzzaman] was someone who knew his theories well and could defend them well. He began way back at that time, in the Constitutional Period. He went at the same tempo, at the same speed, in the same direction, and defended the same ideas...They were frightened of him at that time the same as in this period, because whenever he came out onto the street, he was immediately surrounded by a crowd.

On being asked if these were his own students who flocked round him, Münir Çapanoğlu continued:

> Both his students and the ordinary people, but mostly the people; they wanted to see him, they wanted to hear him speak. I myself witnessed this many times. He spoke beautifully. He spoke persuasively.[49]

We learn from one of his works that on the Constitution being proclaimed, Bediuzzaman sent fifty to sixty telegrams to the Eastern Provinces through the Grand Vizier's Office urging all the tribes to accept it, saying: "Constitutionalism and the Constitution about which you have heard consists of true justice and the consultation enjoined by the Sharī'ah. Consider it favourably and work to preserve it, for our worldly happiness lies in constitutionalism. And we have suffered more than anyone from despotism."[50]

The Constitution was not without opponents, particularly in the East where those whose interests were threatened were seeking to turn all the tribes against it with negative propaganda. While Bediuzzaman spent several months in the summer of 1910 travelling among them explaining its vital importance both for the

Kurds and the Empire and Islamic world, as we shall see, at this point his efforts were confined to the written word.

In Istanbul, too, profiting from their ignorance and naivity, opponents of constitutionalism were trying to provoke the Kurdish porters against the Constitution. In response, Bediuzzaman took every opportunity to combat this negative propaganda and illuminate them concerning it. The text of one of his addresses to them is included in *Nutuk*. In this speech it is unity that Bediuzzaman is most insistent on. He told them that they had three enemies that were destroying them: "poverty, ignorance, and internal conflict", but that they now had to procure "three diamond swords" so as to rout the three enemies and preserve themselves. These were "national unity, human endeavour, and love of the nation".

That is to say, first the Kurds had to achieve unity among themselves, then making over the resulting "mighty force" to the government and expanding it outwardly, they would make themselves worthy of justice, and in return for it would demand justice and their rights from the government: "The Turks are our intelligence, and we are their strength, together we make a whole person. We shall not resist them, nor rebel against them. With this resolution of ours, we shall be a good example to the other minority peoples [elements] of the Empire...If we obeyed [the government] 'to the degree of one *batman*' during the time of despotism, now 'ten *batman's* worth' of obedience and unity are necessary. For we shall see only benefits, because the Constitutional Government is in truth government based on the Sharī'ah...In unity lies strength; in union, life; in brotherhood, happiness; in obedience to the government, well-being. It is vital to hold fast to the strong rope of unity and bond of love."[51]

On another occasion Bediuzzaman calmed a tense situation was at a mass protest organised by the *madrasah* students in Beyazid in Istanbul in February 1909. Traditionally, students of the religious schools were exempt from military service of any kind, but following the proclamation of the Constitution the government had decided to introduce an examination on the pretext that the privilege was being abused. Students who passed the examination were to be exempt from military service, while for those who failed it military service would be compulsory. The students had organised the meeting ostensibly to protest the very short time they had been given to prepare for the examination.

The meeting was becoming fairly turbulent by the time Bediuzzaman reached it. Well known to the students, he addressed them explaining the authentic relationship between the Sharī'ah and constitutionalism and pointing out that despotism could in no way be associated with the Sharī'ah. In a short time he calmed the situation and prevented any serious disturbance occurring.[52]

Notes

1. Cemal Kutay, *Bediüzzaman*, 186
2. *Ibid.*, 310; Şahiner, *Said Nursi*, 98.
3. Shaw and Shaw, *History*, ii, 264-5.
4. *Ibid.*, 274.
5. Şerif Mardin, *Continuity and Change in the Ideas of the Young Turks*, Istanbul 1969, 23.
6. Nursi, *Barla Lahikası*, 191.
7. Şahiner, *Said Nursi*, 99-100.
8. A. Vehbi Vakkasoğlu, *Bediüzzaman Said Nursî'den Siyasi Tesbitler*, Istanbul 1977, 17.
9. Nursi, *Asar-ı Bedi'iyye*, 347.
10. *Ibid.*, 347-356; Nursi, *Divan-ı Harb-i Örfî*, 56-70.
11. The term Sharī'ah should be understood as signifying not only the injunctions and prohibitions of the Law in a narrow sense, but the entire body of Islamic teaching. Bediuzzaman's arguments demonstrating the conformity of constitutionalism with the Sharī'ah are given following the speech.
12. Nursi, *Hutbe-i Şamiye*, 47 (Eng. tr.: *The Damascus Sermon*. Istanbul, 2001, 51).
13. Safa Mürsel, *Bediüzzaman Said Nursi ve Devlet Felsefesi*, 249-252; Kutay, *Tarih Sohbetleri*, i, 207.
14. Nursi, 'Hürriyet'e Hitab,' in *Asar-ı Bedi'iyye*, 348; Nursi, *Divan-ı Harb-i Örfî*, 57.
15. *Op. cit.* 349, and, 59.

16. Nursı, *Divan-ı Harb-i Örfî*, 12.
17. Nursi, *Münâzarat* (Ott. edn.), in *Asar-ı Bedi'iyye*, 406.
18. Nursi, *Münâzarat* (Ott. edn.) in *Asar-ı Bedi'iyye*, 407.
19. *Ibid.*, 415.
20. Nursi, *Divan-ı Harb-i Örfî*, 13.
21. *Ibid.*, 16.
22. Nursi, *Münâzarat* (Ott. edn.), in *Asar-ı Bedi'iyye*, 417.
23. *Ibid.*, 416.
24. *Ibid.*, 417.
25. Nursi, *Divan-ı Harb-i Örfî*, 41.
26. Nursi, *Muhâkemat*, 20.
27. Nursi, *Münâzarat* (Ott. edn.), in *Asar-ı Bedi'iyye*, 411.
28. Nursi, *Hutbe-i Şamiye*, 52-3.
29. Nursi, *Divan-ı Harb-i Örfî*, 34.
30. Nursi, *Münâzarat*, 15-16.
31. *Ibid.*, 17.
32. Nursi, *Hutbe-i Şamiye*, 53 (Eng. tr.: *Damascus Sermon*, 57).
33. Nursi, *Münâzarat*, 19.
34. *Ibid.*, 18.
35. Nursi, *Hutbe-i Şamiye*, 29-30 (Eng. tr.: *Damascus Sermon*, 37).
36. Nursi, *Divan-ı Harb-i Örfî*, 41.
37. Nursi, *Münâzarat*, 21.
38. Nursi, *Divan-ı Harb-i Örfî*, 41.
39. Nursi, *Münâzarat*, 23.
40. Nursi *Hutbe-i Şamiye*, 47 (Eng. tr.: *Damascus Sermon*, 51).
41. Nursi, "Hakikat," *Volkan*, No. 70, 26 Şubat 1325/5 March 1909, in *Asar-ı Bedi'iyye*, 368.
42. Nursi, "Lemean-i Hakikat ve Izale-i Şübehat," *Volkan*, No. 101, 29 Mart 1325/11April 1909, in *Asar-ı Bedi'iyye*, 393.
43. Nursi, *Asar-ı Bedi'iyye*, 356.
44. Cemal Kutay, "Hakikat Pırlantıları," *Köprü Magazine*, No. 36, March 1980, 33.
45. See also, Şahiner, *Said Nursi*, 114-115; Kutay, *Bediüzzaman*, 199-211; Kutay, *Tarih Sohbetleri*, iv, 224.
46. For further biographical details of Shaykh Bakhīt, d. 1935, see Şahiner, *Son Şahitler*, iv, 363-4.
47. *Tarihçe*, 49-50; Nursi, *Emirdağ Lahikası*, i, 108; Şahiner, *Said Nursi*, 105-6.
48. Münir Süleyman Çapanoğlu, *Türkiye'de Sosyalizm Hareketleri ve Sosyalist Hilmi*, as in Şahiner, *Said Nursi*, 110-111.
49. N. Şahiner, *Nurs Yolu*, 131.
50. Nursi, *Divan-ı Harb-i Örfî*, 12-13.
51. Nursi, *Asar-ı Bedi'iyye*, 358-9; Şahiner, *Said Nursi*, 112-113.
52. *Ibid.*, 115-116; Nursi, *Divan-ı Harb-i Örfî*, 17.

4
Bediuzzaman and the Thirty-First of March Incident

Introduction

*A*fter nine months of CUP rule, increasing discontent found expression in the famous Thirty-First of March Incident.[1] Many aspects of this revolt, which started with certain sections of the Army in Istanbul mutinying and continuing for eleven days, have still not been brought to light.

Bediuzzaman played no part in the revolt. On the contrary as far as he could, he used his influence and reputation to persuade the rebelling soldiers to obey their officers and return to barracks. He was somewhat successful in this. Nevertheless, when order was restored on the arrival of the Operation Army from Salonica, he was arrested along with many hundreds of others and sent before one of the military courts. The reason for this was his involvement with the *İttihad-ı Muhammedî Cemiyeti* or Society for Muslim Unity, which was accused of inciting the revolt. In any event, he was acquitted in one hearing. His defence speech, which was also instrumental in forty to fifty other prisoners being released, was published in 1911 entitled *The Testimonial of Two Schools of Misfortune* or *The Court Martial*.

The Society for Muslim Unity

The Society for Muslim Unity had been founded on 5 February 1909,[2] though the full versions of its manifesto and code of rules did not appear in the *Volkan* newspaper until 16 March 1909.³ The ceremony to mark its founding took the form of a *Mawlid*⁴ and was held at the later date of 3 April, to coincide with Prophet Muḥammad's birthday (12 Rabīʿ al-Awwal 1327). Bediuzzaman played a prominent role in the *mawlid*, which was held in Aya Sophia, giving a sermon that lasted two hours. But before describing it, let us learn from his address to the Court Martial his reasons for joining the Society, and how he viewed it.

"I heard," said Bediuzzaman, "that a society had been formed called the Society for Muslim Unity (*İttihad-ı Muhammedî*). I was frightened to the utmost degree that certain people would act in error under this blessed name. Then I heard that some sound people like Süheyl Pasha and Shaykh Sadık had joined so as to make their actions more apt to follow the Exalted Sunnah of the Prophet (ṣ). They had transferred from that political society [CUP] and cut their relations with it, and they were not going to interfere in politics. But again I was afraid, I said: 'This name is the right of everyone, it cannot be appropriated or restricted.' As for me, just as I belonged in some respect to seven societies because I saw that their aims were the same, so too I joined this blessed name. However, I define the Society for Muslim Unity I belong to as follows:

> It is a circle bound with a luminous chain stretching from east to west, and from north to south. Those within it number more than three hundred million at this time. The point of unity of this Society and what binds it is Divine Unity. Its oath and its promise is belief in God. Its members are all believers, belonging from the time of God's covenant with man. Its register is the Preserved Tablet. The Society's means of communication are all Islamic books. Its daily newspapers are all religious newspapers that aim to 'uphold the Word of God'. Its clubs and councils are the mosques, religious schools, and Sufi *takiyyahs*. Its centre is the two sacred cities [Makkah and Madīnah]. Its head is the Glory of the World [Prophet Muḥammad (ṣ)]. Its way is the struggle of each person with his own soul; that is, to assume the morality of Prophet Muḥammad (ṣ), to give new vigour to his

practices, and to cultivate love for others and, if it is not harmful, offer them advice. The regulations of this Society are the Practices of the Prophet (ṣ), and its code of laws, the injunctions and prohibitions of the Sharī'ah. Its swords are clear proofs, for the civilized are to be conquered through persuasion, not compulsion. Investigating the truth is with love, while enmity is for savagery and bigotry. Its aim and purpose is 'Upholding the Word of God'. And ninety-nine per cent of the Sharī'ah is concerned with morality, worship, the Hereafter, and virtue. One per cent is concerned with politics; let our rulers think of that.

Bediuzzaman then continued: "Our aim now is to urge everyone towards the *ka'bah* of achievement and perfections on the way of progress with an eagerness and desire of the conscience by making that luminous chain vibrate. Because at this time the chief means of upholding the Word of God is material progress.

> Thus, I am a member of this Society. I am one of those working for this Society's manifestation. I do not belong to the parties and groups which cause dissension.[5]

Bediuzzaman, then, was firstly concerned to prevent a society bearing the name of the Prophet (ṣ) being appropriated by any group, and being exploited for political ends, becoming a source of dissension and disunity. Rather, the Society for Muslim Unity embraced all believers and formed a barrier to the serious differences which had developed between the various societies and political parties in the months of CUP rule—differences so bitter that it was to this that Bediuzzaman ascribed what he called "the great disaster", that is, the 31st of March Incident.[6]

In a newspaper article Bediuzzaman wrote: "Our Society's way is love towards love, and enmity towards enmity. That is, to assist love among Muslims and defeat the forces of enmity."[7] In fact, he described the *İttihad-ı Muhammedî* as *İttihad-ı İslam*, or Islamic Unity, that is, "the unity that exists either potentially or in fact among all believers."[8] The unity and brotherhood of Muslims were "like hidden veins of gold in half the globe", and the Society in Turkey was "a new flame which had appeared in one corner of it and gave the good news of that mighty reality being wholly revealed." It had emerged from the potential to the actual and now sought to awaken other believers and urge them towards the way of progress through the drive of the conscience. Muslims had not realised that vast potential. Due to neglect, the luminous chain of unity which had bound the centres of Islam together had become inert. It had not been benefited from. Now it had to be brought to life and made to vibrate.[9]

The foundation of unity and progress and of the strengthening and liberation of the Islamic world was moral renewal. Bediuzzaman saw the Society as spearheading a more widespread movement for moral rearmament by putting new energy into observing the Sharī'ah and following the Practices of the Prophet (ṣ). He stated: "The reason for our worldly decline was failure to observe our religion. Also, we are more in need of moral improvement than government reform."[10]

In these articles Bediuzzaman explained in great detail the aims of the Society for Muslim Unity as they appeared in the Society's Manifesto and Code of Rules. The Manifesto also pointed out that societies and parties of every shade had been organised in different parts of the world, and stated that just as it was not injurious for a Muslim not to belong to the Society, so also belonging to it did not form an obstacle to belonging to other societies, whether religious or political. Societies were necessary, because "the desired fruits can never be plucked from Constitutionalism without parties and societies." The Society recognised the fact that under the Constitution all citizens, that is, non-Muslims as well as Muslims, were equal before the law. Furthermore, the Manifesto was at pains to point out that all its activities, and the activities it aimed to promote among Muslims, were to be within the law.[11]

The *Mawlid* in Aya Sophia

That a *Mawlid* was being organised by the Society in Aya Sophia to coincide with the Prophet's birthday was announced in the *Volkan* on 18 Mart 1325/31 March 1909. It stated that the Society "had entered a new era of tranquillity and progress having successfully surmounted all the attacks to which it had been subject, and the crises arising from those attacks." The *Mawlid* was to be "a gift to Muhammad's pure and unstained spirit."[12]

The news of the *Mawlid* evoked a tremendous response among the population of Istanbul, and around one hundred thousand people gathered on the specified day. Never before had there been such a throng in the area surrounding Aya Sophia. However, despite the numbers, no untoward incidents occurred either before or after the *Mawlid*, and the whole occasion was most orderly; "a display of Islamic brotherhood and decorum." Dervis Vahdetî described Bediuzzaman's arrival and address as follows:

> Round about ten o'clock Bediuzzaman Said Kurdi Hazretleri arrived at the head of the Society for Students of the Religious Sciences. We greeted him at the outer doors, where we were meeting all who arrived...The turbans on the students' heads were white like light and enspiriting like flowers. But more than anything, it was the religious education they had received which gave the students an exceptional quality.
>
> Since it was requested of him, 'Our *Hazret*', that is, the Wonder of the World of Islam [Bediuzzaman], mounted the pulpit with that famous Kurdish dress and heroic manner of his and like always with a dagger at his waist, and standing, delivered an eloquent address.[13]

Bediuzzaman began the address with the words: "The truth has risen naked from the grave of the heart. Let those for whom it is prohibited not gaze on it." And mentioning all the important political, social, and religious subjects of the time, he continued for two hours. In the words of one of those present: "The sermon he delivered standing in the pulpit was a masterpiece."[14]

Derviş Vahdetî

Bediuzzaman was one of the twenty-six members of the Governing Board of the Istanbul Central Committee of the Society for Muslim Unity.¹⁵ It functioned from the offices of the *Volkan* newspaper, the owner of which was Hafız Derviş Vahdetî, and it was Derviş Vahdetî who had first founded the Society.

Derviş Vahdetî continues to this day to be something of an unknown quantity. According to the official histories, he has been portrayed as a radical reactionary opposed to Constitutionalism and even as a subversive and British agent. However recent research has shown these accusations to be false. He now appears more as a victim of circumstance who was made the symbol of the Revolt and who suffered the consequences.¹⁶ From the first issue of the *Volkan*, which appeared on 28 Teşrin-i Sani 1324/11 December 1908, Vahdetî used it to answer the attacks on the Sharī'ah and Islamic traditions and morality made by the newspapers supporting the CUP. As Vahdetî himself put it, the *Volkan* was "very small but active", "moderation" was its "way", "however, when truth and right are attacked, it is not possible for the Volkan not to erupt."¹⁷ Nevertheless, it supported the Constitution and the rule of law. Its aim was to promote the interests of Muslims and to further the cause of Islam and the Qur'an in the face of the increasing despotism and unlawfulness of the CUP and their supporters.

The apprehension expressed by Bediuzzaman on hearing that "certain people" had founded a society called the Society for Muslim Unity mentioned above refers to his anxiety that a society bearing the name of Prophet Muḥammad (ṣ) should become involved in politics or be limited to one group, rather than referring to Derviş Vahdetî. Nevertheless, however much he shared the views expressed by the newspaper it is probably fair to say that he wished Derviş Vahdetî to personally adhere to the moderation which was its way. For Bediuzzaman was severely critical of the divisive role of the press in that period and on several occasions published articles pointing out how the newspapers should conduct themselves. At the end of two long articles of the fifteen of his that appeared in the *Volkan*, Bediuzzaman wrote a brief reminder to Vahdetî advising him of his responsibility to act moderately as Islam requires:

> My Brother, Derviş Vahdetî Bey!
>
> Writers should be mannerly. And their manners should be moulded by the manners of Islam. Let the sense of religion in the conscience order the Press Regulations, for this Islamic revolution has shown that what rules in all consciences is Islamic zeal, the light of lights. Also, it has been understood that the Society for Muslim Unity includes all the people of Islam. There is no one outside it.[18]

Articles written by Bediuzzaman appeared in most of the leading newspapers of the day, including *İkdam, Serbesti, Mizan, Misbah*, and the *Şark ve Kürdistan Gazetesi*, not only in the *Volkan*. He defended the same ideas in all of them.[19] Along with the *Mizan* and other papers, the *Volkan* had taken an open position against the CUP. It was itself, and the Society for Muslim Unity for which it spoke, the object of much criticism. In his articles, therefore, in the most moderate and reasonable tone, Bediuzzaman particularly sought to allay fears about the Society, explaining it in the terms described above. Three of his later articles, appearing between 31 March 1909 and 15 April, specifically answered criticisms, misgivings, and questions concerning it. The final two instalments of the third, Dispelling Doubts in the Light of the Truth, appeared after the 31st March Incident had broken out, and this article was given as a further reason for his being arrested and sent before the Court Martial. As for Derviş Vahdetî, he was accused and found guilty of inciting the rebellion, and was hanged along with twelve others on 19 July 1909.[20] Indeed, the Committee of Union and Progress truly took their revenge: the total numbers executed were two hundred and thirty-seven.[21]

Background to the Revolt

The CUP considered the 31st of March Incident to be a reactionary movement and held Sultan Abdulhamid responsible for it. But on the contrary, all the evidence points to the opposite being true, that the CUP at least had a finger in it.²² It is beyond the scope of this book to examine the Incident in detail, but since both it and Bediuzzaman's role in it have been consistently misrepresented, we shall attempt to give a clearer perspective by including the following brief outline of its main causes and the course of events.

When the high hopes and expectations engendered by the proclamation of the Constitution were not realised, there was widespread disappointment and dissatisfaction, particularly among Muslims who received few benefits but saw the minorities using the new freedom to pursue their own interests at the expense of the Empire. Disenchantment with the CUP increased daily as its true colours became more and more evident.

Remaining in the background, the CUP was neither an official political party, nor were its members responsible to anyone. They were in power, but indirectly. Furthermore, in contrast with Abdulhamid, they were inexperienced and their refusal to admit to this contributed directly to the immediate loss of territory and the speedy demise of the Empire. Censorship was abolished. The CUP began a relentless attack on the Sultan in the press. Claiming constitutionalism as their own, they tried to force their views on the people. But the more they showed their true colours, the more mistrusted and unpopular they became. And the battles between the parties and societies became fiercer. The press became the field of battle. In response, the CUP resorted to covert and illegal methods to establish itself more firmly, increasingly using force to eliminate opponents.

This intimidation and political violence created an atmosphere of terror, and those prompting it remained in the background. On 15 December 1908, one of the Sultan's men, İsmail Mahir Pasha, was murdered. His murder was followed by others, including prominent journalists, one of which was Hasan Fehmi Bey. He was the editor of the *Serbesti*, one of the loudest voices of opposition to the CUP. His assassination on 6 April 1909 resulted in widespread, unanswered calls for justice. It was a return to despotism in a form worse than before.[23]

At the same time, the CUP started a drive to weed out government officials and replace them with their own supporters, whether experienced or not. There were substantial numbers involved. The same policy was followed in the Army. The officers were of two kinds, those risen from the ranks on their merit and experience, and those trained in the new military academies. The CUP started to replace the former with the latter, who were mostly CUP supporters. Nearly 8000 were expelled from all sections of the Army. Many of the new officers were inexperienced, and the CUP supporters from among them mocked the religion of Islam and tried to prevent the ordinary soldiers from carrying out their religious duties. Thus, dissatisfaction within the army grew to serious proportions, while the expelled officials and officers formed a significant body ready to rebel against the Government.

Also, there was a general feeling of affront and distrust among the people due to the CUP's lax attitude towards religion. Freedom had accelerated the import of Western culture, manners and morality, and had led to a decline in moral standards.

And finally there resulted extreme partisanship amongst the different parties and societies. The excessive and bitter 'war' between the newspapers representing the CUP and their opponents exacerbated the situation. Derviş Vahdetî could not be altogether exonerated from this.

The Revolt

The revolt broke out among one of the Light Infantry battalions which only a few weeks previously had been brought to Istanbul from Salonica as the Defenders of Freedom. It started in the middle of the night of 12-13 April. Locking their officers in their rooms, the soldiers took control of the barracks and poured out into the streets. There, as they made their way to Aya Sophia and the parliament building, the throng increased in magnitude as they were joined by other soldiers, *madrasah* students, and members of the public. The shout was for the Sharī'ah. It was daytime by the time they reached Aya Sophia. They surrounded the Parliament and presented their demands. These included the dismissal of the Grand Vizier, the War Minister, and Commander of the Imperial Guards, the removal of Ahmed Rıza who had acted as Speaker of the Parliament since the Proclamation of the Constitution, the application in full of the Sharī'ah, the reinstatement of their expelled officers, and a guarantee that the soldiers who had taken part in the rebellion would not be punished.

In the meantime, the rebels had murdered one of the deputies on the mistaken supposition that he was the leading CUP journalist Hüseyin Cahid, together with the Justice Minister supposing him to be the Grand Vizier.

The government resigned, and the Sultan appointed a new Grand Vizier and Minister of War. The rebellion continued; there was looting and some bloodshed. The offices of the CUP and their main press organs were sacked. Rather than attempting to quell the disturbance—it was not supported by anyone of authority either military or civil—the CUP chose to send for forces from Salonica.

News of the uprising provoked a strong reaction in Salonica, which was still the centre of the CUP. Spreading the news that Freedom itself was threatened, the CUP had no difficulty in forming a force of volunteers consisting largely of bands of Serbs, Bulgars, Greeks, Macedonians, and Albanians. Regular units were in a small minority in this Operation Army. They were armed, and entrained for Istanbul. The force gathered at Yeşilköy several kilometres outside the city, where Mahmud Şevket Pasha took command of it. On 24 April, they took possession of the city, and the following day proclaimed martial law. On the 27th, Sultan Abdulhamid was deposed. It was Tal'at Bey who with great insistence managed to obtain the *fatwā* authorizing the dethronement from two religious notables—having failed to extract it from the Şeyhü'l-İslam,²⁴ just as it was due to Tal'at Bey's influence that having moved to Yeşilköy in order to declare their support for the Operation Army, members of the Parliament and Upper House had taken the secret decision to depose the Sultan even though they had published a declaration saying their purpose was to save him.²⁵

It is worth mentioning briefly that the 31st of March Incident should also be seen in the broader perspective of the Great Powers and their rivalry and ambitions concerning the Ottoman Empire. Particularly as far as the British were concerned, Abdulhamid and his Caliphate policy and successful diplomatic manoeuvring formed one of the greatest barriers to their designs on the area, including the establishment of a Jewish state. Also, among the CUP were Masons and those representing interests opposed to the Empire, although the great majority of their supporters in the Parliament were patriotic and well disposed towards Islam, if uncertain as to what its role should be. When answering questions on this subject put to him by the tribes in eastern Anatolia the following year, Bediuzzaman said:

> I observed a situation similar to this in the 31st of March Incident. For Islam's constitutionalism-cherishing and patriotic devotees were suggesting ways of applying certain details in order to adapt to the Sharī'ah the divine bounty of constitutionalism, which they knew to be the very essence of life, and direct those involved in government towards the *qiblah* in the prayer of justice, to uphold the sacred Sharī'ah with the strength of constitutionalism, and perpetuate constitutionalism with the strength of the Sharī'ah, and to impute all the former evils to opposition to the Sharī'ah. Then supposing, God forbid, the Sharī'ah to be conducive to despotism, those who could not distinguish right from left started saying: 'We want the Sharī'ah!' like parrots and in that situation the real purpose could not be understood. In any case, the plans had been laid. So then a number of villains who had donned masks of false patriotism attacked the sacred name [the Sharī'ah]…²⁶

That is to say, Bediuzzaman is saying that plans had been laid to incite just such a revolt, and when the 31st of March Incident broke out, it was exploited to the full in order to attack the Sharī'ah, and reduce the power of Islam within the State. Indeed, the historian Cemal Kutay described the military courts set up afterwards as "a cleansing operation", and their purpose not to carry out justice, but "to eliminate a mentality and a system."[27]

Bediuzzaman Calls for Order

We learn of Bediuzzaman's own movements during the revolt and how he did all he could to reestablish order within the Army from his defence speech to the court martial. He told the court:

> I watched the fearful activity on the day of the 31st of March for two or three minutes from a distance. I heard numerous demands...I understood the matter was bad; obedience was spoilt, advice would have been ineffective. Otherwise like always I would have attempted to quench the fire. But the people were many, my fellow-countrymen heedless and naive, and I would have been conspicuous because of my undeserved fame. I left after three minutes, and went to Bakirköy so that those who knew me would not join it. And I advised those who just happened to be there not to take part. If I had been involved to even the tiniest degree, my clothes would have shown me up, my unwanted fame would have pointed me out to everyone. I would have appeared very significant in the matter. Indeed, even if alone as far as Ayastefanos [Yeşilköy], I would have put in an appearance confronting the Operation Army. I would have died manfully. Then my involvement would have been plain; it would not have been necessary to prove it.
>
> On the second day I asked about obedience in the Army, which is the source of our life. They said: "The officers have put on soldiers' uniforms and discipline is not spoilt too much." Again I asked how many officers had been shot. They deceived me and said: "Only four. And they were tyrants. Also, procedure and punishment will be according to the Sharī'ah."
>
> Also, I looked at the newspapers. They too described the uprising as though it was lawful. And in one way I was pleased,

because my most sacred aim is for the Sharī'ah's rulings to be applied and enacted in full. But I felt infinitely hopeless and saddened because harm had come to discipline in the army. So I addressed the soldiers through all the newspapers saying:

"O Soldiers! If your officers are wronging themselves with some transgressions, you are in one respect wronging thirty million Ottomans and three hundred million Muslims and infringing on their rights through this insubordination. For the honour, happiness, and banner of Divine Unity of all Islam and all Ottomans is at this time in some respect dependent on your obedience.

"And you want the Sharī'ah, but with your disobedience you are opposing the Sharī'ah."

I flattered their action and courage, because the newspapers—those lying interpreters of public opinion—showed their action to be lawful. To a degree I made my advice effective by showing appreciation. And to a degree I quelled the rebellion. Otherwise it would not have been put down so easily.

On Friday, together with other *'ulamā'*, I went in among the soldiers who were around the War Ministry. I induced eight battalions to submit and obey orders. My exhortations showed their effect later.

Bediuzzaman then quoted his speech to them, which began similarly to the few sentences from his newspaper address to the rebelling soldiers quoted above, and pointed out that they were threatening Islamic Unity and brotherhood through their insubordination. He continued:

You should know that the army corps resembles a huge, orderly factory. If one machine rebels, it throws the whole factory into turmoil. Private soldiers should not meddle in politics. The Janisseries testify to that. You say you want the Sharī'ah, but you are opposing the Sharī'ah, and besmirching it. It is established by the Sharī'ah, and the Qur'an, and Ḥadīth, and wisdom and experience that it is obligatory to obey trustworthy, religious, and just rulers. Your rulers are your instructors and officers."
Bediuzzaman then went on to say that they should obey the officers who had come from the new military academies even if their conduct was in part unlawful. Just as if a doctor or

engineer committed wrongdoing it did not necessarily harm their professional activities, the same was true for these officers. The banner of Divine Unity was in the hand of the soldiers' courage, and the strength of that hand lay in obedience and order. A thousand regular, obedient soldiers were equal to a hundred thousand irregular troops. He concluded the speech:

"I proclaim to you the Glory of the World's decree that obedience is obligatory. Do not rebel against your officers! Long live the army! Long live the Islamic Constitution!"[28]

The Court Martial

If further illustration is needed of Bediuzzaman's unwavering fidelity to the cause he knew to be the only path of salvation for both the Ottomans and the Islamic world, and his extraordinary boldness and courage in furthering it, his defence speech to the court martial provides it. It is a restatement of his ideas and at the same time forms a stinging condemnation both of the CUP and the new despotism they were creating in the name of constitutionalism, and of the military courts that had been set up in the name of justice following the 31st of March Incident. Bediuzzaman had been held in prison before being sent before the court martial, which he described as a place of torture; it was this together with his experience of the mental hospital which prompted him to deliver this attack on the CUP's betrayal of constitutionalism and gave the name to the speech when it appeared in book form. The basic lesson he had learnt from these Two Schools of Misfortune was "compassion for the weak and an intense detestation of tyranny."[29]

The military courts were fairly awesome affairs with the pashas and officers who were acting as judges haughty and autocratic and holding absolute power of life and death over those brought before them. Formalities were of the most summary nature, and the sentences and executions carried out immediately. The day Bediuzzaman was brought before the court in Bayezit, the corpses of fifteen of its victims could be seen hanging in the square beyond the windows.

At the beginning of the hearing, Bediuzzaman was asked a number of questions put to all the accused. One of these, asked by Hurşid Pasha, the President of the Court, was: "Did you want the Sharī'ah? Those wanting the Sharī'ah are hanged like those out there." Bediuzzaman replied:

> If I had a thousand lives, I would be ready to sacrifice all of them for one truth of the Sharī'ah, for the Sharī'ah is the source of prosperity and happiness, pure justice, and virtue. But not like those who revolted want it.

Then he was asked: "Are you a member of the Society for Muslim Unity?" To which he replied:

> With pride. I am one of its most insignificant members, but in the way that I define it. Show me someone apart from those without religion who is not a member.

Bediuzzaman told the court:

> Pashas and officers! By way of introduction I say: the manly and brave do not stoop to crime. And if they are accused of it, they do not fear the punishment. If I am executed unjustly, I shall gain the reward of two martyrs. And if I remain in prison, it is probably the most comfortable place of a tyrannical government whose freedom consists thus only of the word. To die oppressed is better than to live as oppressor.[30]

The main part of Bediuzzaman's long defence took the form of describing the eleven and a half "crimes" for which he had been imprisoned. These were his main activities in the nine months of Freedom, and were all in the cause of Islam and the Constitution. They have mostly been described above, including his reasons for joining the Society for Muslim Unity and how he viewed it, and his movements during the revolt. Bediuzzaman then said: "I have done one good thing in place of all these bad deeds. I shall tell you:

> I opposed this branch of despotism here, which has destroyed everyone's enthusiasm and extinguished their joy, awakened feelings of hatred and partisanship, and given rise to the formation of racialist societies, whose name is constitutionalism and meaning is despotism, and who has besmirched the

name of unity and progress...Since I am pledged to true constitutionalism based on the Sharī'ah, whatever form despotism takes, even if it clothes itself in constitutionalism and calls itself that, I shall strike it wherever I encounter it. I think the enemies of constitutionalism are those who multiply the enemies of mutual consultation by showing constitutionalism to be tyrannical, ugly, and contrary to the Sharī'ah.

O you who command! I had a good name and I would have served the nation of Islam with it; you have destroyed it. I had an undeserved fame and I used to make my words of advice to the people effective with it; I am pleased to say you have razed it. Now I have a frail life of which I am weary. May I be damned if I begrudge the gallows. May I not be a man if I do not go laughing to my death....You put me to the touchstone. I wonder how many of those you call the pure party would emerge sound if you put them to the touchstone. If constitutionalism consists of one party's despotism, and it acts contrary to the Sharī'ah, let all the world, men and jinn, bear witness that I am a reactionary."[31]

Bediuzzaman also wanted to set the record straight concerning the 31st of March Incident, discipline in the Army, and the Sharī'ah and its role, which from the start had been misinterpreted and misrepresented by newspapers of both sides. The seven main reasons he put forward for the revolt were substantially the same as those given above. Then saying to the court: "Pashas and officers! Now I want the punishment for my 'crimes' and the answers to my questions", he put to them eleven and a half questions which pointed out that the majority of those involved were not blameworthy and suggested that injustices arising from CUP rule were the cause. These questions resulted in between forty and fifty prisoners being released.[32]

Towards the end of his address, he told the court that he was absolutely insistent on everything he had written in all his newspaper articles. Whether he was summoned to a court in the Era of the Prophet (ṣ), or to one three hundred years hence, his case, "dressed according to how the fashion of the time required", would be exactly the same. "The truth does not change; the truth is the truth."[33]

Bediuzzaman expected to be hanged by this court martial, which for its evidence had relied chiefly on informers and denouncers. Indeed, he had asked the court: "The detectives now are worse than the ones before, how can their word be relied on? How can justice be built on what they say?"[34] On learning that the court's unanimous decision was for his acquittal, Bediuzzaman expressed no gratitude. He turned and left the court on being released, then walked from Bayezit to Sultan Ahmet at the head of the large crowd that had gathered, shouting: "Long live Hell for all tyrants! Long live Hell for all tyrants!"[35]

The 31st of March Incident was indeed as Bediuzzaman described it, "The Great Disaster". Whatever the CUP's role in it, it provided them with the opportunity they had been seeking. Firstly, they realised their long-held ambition to depose Sultan Abdulhamid. Immediately preceding the revolt, they had come out into the open and proclaimed themselves an official party. Then following it, they disbanded the opposition parties and a little later further reduced the powers of the Sultan, and gained tighter control over the State. The same year they introduced a number of measures that restricted freedom to a greater degree than under Abdulhamid. The Society for Muslim Unity was closed and disbanded; indeed, many of its leading members had met their end in the gallows of the military courts.

Bediuzzaman felt profound disillusion with Istanbul and its deceptively civilized exterior after what he had experienced in the short time he had been there. His gaze now returned to his native East. He wrote: "If civilization provides such a favourable ground for honour-destroying aggression and dissension-causing slander, cruel thoughts of revenge, satanic sophistry, and carelessness in matters of religion, let everyone witness that in place of this seat of malice known as the felicitous palace of civilization I prefer the wild nomad tents of the high mountains of Kurdistan, the place of absolute freedom...I thought that writers' conduct should be worthy of literature. But I see some ill-mannered newspapers disseminating hatred. If that is how manners should be, and if public opinion is thus confused, bear witness that I have renounced such literature. I shall have no part in it. In place of the newspapers, I shall study the heavenly bodies and tableaux of the world in the high mountains of my native land.

> Yes, I prefer the wild life to civilization which is thus mixed with despotism, depravity, and degradation. This civilization makes individuals impoverished, dissolute, and immoral, whereas true civilization serves mankind's progress and development and the realization of man's potential. In this regard, therefore, to want civilization is to want humanity...
> Long live Islamic Constitutionalism! Long live the shining Freedom which has learnt a thorough lesson from the instruction of the reality of the Sharī'ah!"[36]

Notes

1. The revolt is named according to the Rumi calendar then in use in the Ottoman Empire. 31 March 1325 corresponded to 13 April 1909 on the Gregorian calendar.
2. M. Ertuğrul Düzdağ, (ed.), *Volkan Gazetesi*, (No. 36), Istanbul 1992, 168.
3. *Ibid.*, (No. 75), 362-4; Sadık Albayrak, *31 Mart Vak'asi, Gerici Bir Hareket Mi?* Istanbul 1987, 166-175; T.Z. Tunaya, *Türkiye'de Siyasal Partiler*, i, 199-203.
4. A *Mawlid* is a recitation by special singers of the long poem depicting the birth of Prophet Muḥammad (ṣ) written by Süleyman Çelebi, who died in Bursa 780 A.H./1378.
5. Nursi, *Divan-ı Harb-i Örfî*, 17-19.
6. *Ibid.*, 20.
7. Nursi, "Yaşasin Şeriat-ı Ahmedî," *Volkan*, No. 77, 5 Mart 1325/18 March 1909, in *Asar-ı Bedi'iyye*, 371; Nursi, *Hutbe-i Şamiye*, 76 (Eng. tr.: *Damascus Sermon*, 76).
8. Nursi, "Reddü'l-Evham," *Volkan*, Nos. 90-1, 18-19 Mart 1325/ 31 March-1 April 1909, in *Asar-ı Bedi'iyye*, 380; Nursi, *Hutbe-i Şamiye*, 84.
9. Nursi, "Lemean-ı Hakikat ve İzale-i Şübehat," *Volkan*, Nos. 101, 102, 103,105, in *Asar-ı Bedi'iyye*, 388.
10. *Op. cit., Asar-ı Bedi'iyye*, 387.

11. T.Z. Tunaya, *Türkiye'de Siyasal Partiler*, i, 199-200, from *Volkan*, No.75.
12. S. Albayrak, *31 Mart*, 212-214, quoted from *Volkan*, No. 90.
13. S. Albayrak, *31 Mart*, 220, quoted from *Volkan*, No. 95; Şahiner, *Said Nursi*, 116.
14. *Ibid.*, 116-7, quoted from Hafız Ali Sağman, *Mevlid Nasil Okunur ve Mevlithanlar,* Istanbul 1951.
15. S. Albayrak, *31 Mart*, 174, from Volkan No. 75; also, Tunaya, *Siyasal Partiler*, i, 182.
16. See, M.E. Düzdağ, *Volkan*, ix.
17. *Ibid., Volkan*, No.1, 1; No.4, 20.
18. Nursi, "Lemean-ı Hakikat ve İzale-i Şübehat," in *Asar-ı Bedi'iyye*, 394; Şahiner, *Said Nursi*, 118.
19. *Ibid.*, 118.
20. S. Albayrak, S. *31 Mart*, 118.
21. Cemal Kutay, *31 Mart Ihtilalinde Abdülhamid*, Istanbul 1977, 59.
22. Y. Bahadıroğlu, *Osmanlı Padişahları Ansiklopedisi*, iii, 746.
23. Danişmend, *İzahlı*, iv, 371.
24. M. Müftüoğlu, *Her Yönüyle Sultan İkinci Abdülhamid*, Istanbul 1985, 340-1, 350-1.
25. Y. Bahadıroğlu, *Osmanlı Padişahları Ansiklopedisi*, iii, 747.
26. 27. Nursi, *Münâzarat*, 35-6.
27. Cemal Kutay, in Şahiner, *Aydınlar Konuşuyor*, 345.
28. Nursi, *Divan-ı Harb-i Örfî*, 21-5.
29. *Ibid.*, 39.
30. *Ibid.*, 11-12.
31. *Ibid.*, 28-30.
32. *Ibid.*, 35-7.
33. *Ibid.*, 37-8.
34. *Ibid.*, 12.
35. *Tarihçe*, 57.
36. Nursi, *Divan-i Harb-i Örfî*, 39-40.

5
"The Future shall be Islam's, and Islam's Alone"

Bediuzzaman Heads East

Bediuzzaman did not remain long in Istanbul after his acquittal. He set off for the East by way of the Black Sea accompanied by two of his students. It was the spring of 1910. It is recorded that on the way, the boat stopped off at İnebolu, and on visiting the town Bediuzzaman had a warm reception from its leading religious figure, Haji Ziya, and others, and on leaving, was accompanied as far as the boat by a large crowd.[1] And he himself related the following incident which occurred in Tiflis, the capital city of Georgia, while he was making his way from Batum to Van.

He had climbed a prominent hill known as Shaykh Sanan Tepesi, which has a commanding view of the city of Tiflis and the valley of the River Kura which is situated together with the surrounding countryside. He was gazing at the view plunged in thought when approached by a Russian policeman. The following exchange ensued, which began with the policeman asking:

"Why are you studying the land with such attention?"
Bediuzzaman replied: "I am planning my *madrasah*."
"Where are you from?"
"I'm from Bitlis."
"But this is Tiflis!"
"Bitlis is one of Tiflis' brothers."
The policeman was bewildered: "What do you mean?"
Bediuzzaman explained: "Three lights are beginning to be revealed one after the other in Asia and the world of Islam.

While with you three layers of darkness will start to recede one over the other. This veil of despotism shall be rent; it will shrink back, and I shall come and build my *madrasah* here."²

This only increased the policeman's bewilderment. "I'm sorry for you," he said. "I'm astonished that you should entertain such a hope."

"And I am astonished at your not understanding!" replied Bediuzzaman. "Do you think it possible that this winter will continue? Every winter is followed by spring, and every night by day."

"But the Islamic world is all broken up and fragmented."

"They have gone to study. It is like this: India is an able son of Islam; it is studying in the high school of the British. Egypt is a clever son of Islam; it is taking lessons in the British school for civil servants. Caucasia and Turkestan are two valiant sons of Islam; they are training in the Russian war academy. And so on.

"You see, having received their diplomas, each of these noble sons of Islam will lead a continent, and waving the banner of Islam, their just and mighty father, on the horizons of attainment and perfection, they will proclaim the mystery of pre-eternal wisdom inherent in mankind in the view of pre-eternal divine determining and in the face of obstinate fate."³

This short anecdote gives the note for Bediuzzaman's main message for the tribes of eastern Anatolia, and of his celebrated sermon in Damascus early the following year; namely, encouragement and hope for the future. That is to say, despite his disillusion with developments in Istanbul, Bediuzzaman was unwavering in his conviction that constitutionalism was the way to further the cause of Islam and preserve the Empire by securing progress and unity. Indeed, as we shall see when examining the Sermon, he predicted that according to all the signs, Islam and Islamic—or, true—civilization would prevail in the future, and that the majority of mankind would accept and join the religion of Islam. He said: "In the future when reason, science and technology hold sway, that will surely be the time the Qur'an will gain ascendancy, which relies on rational proofs and makes the reason confirm its pronouncements."⁴

Among the Tribes of Eastern Anatolia

Bediuzzaman spent the summer of 1910 travelling throughout the Eastern Provinces. "Making a *madrasah* of mountain and plain," he wrote, "I gave lessons on constitutionalism." He found that the general understanding of the subject was "extremely odd" and confused, and therefore suggested the people ask the questions, which he then answered. He afterwards made a compilation of these and published it in Turkish in 1913 under the title, *Münâzarat*, or Debates. He also prepared an Arabic version with the title *Rachata al-'Awāmm*, Prescription for the Common People.⁵

The questions cover a number of subjects related to Freedom and the new regime, and its consequences for the tribespeople and their leaders. The answers constitute one of the main sources for Bediuzzaman's ideas on the subject and form a substantial and fascinating work which space does not allow us to examine in detail. Those relating specifically to constitutionalism and Freedom have been described in some detail above; here we shall mention a few additional points which explain further how, through the people "awakening" and becoming conscious, as autonomous, enterprising, self-sacrificing individuals, of their being members of the "the nation of Islam", the new order would secure the progress—in this instance—of the Kurds, and the unity of Islamic world and the Empire. But first it should not go unnoticed that Bediuzzaman did not spare himself in this struggle, nor did he restrict it to the pen or to the theoretical. He had pursued it as far as Istanbul, publicizing in particular the needs of the East and doing what he could to further his plans for educational reform. Now he had returned to his native country and proceeded to travel all over that wild, mountainous, backward and impoverished region. And it was primarily the ordinary people he was seeking to address, the ordinary people who through the adoption of the Constitution had been raised to the rank of "sovereign", and were the builders of the future.

On giving definitions of despotism and constitutionalism in response to the people's questions, Bediuzzaman was asked by them why they had not seen the great benefits he described. He replied that it was problems associated with the area such as ignorance, poverty, internal enmity and lack of civilization that was preventing it. What he wanted to make plain was that the onus lay with them, but added that he only pointed out their faults "to deliver them from laziness." "If you want constitutionalism to come quickly, build a railway out of learning and virtue so that it can mount the train of attainment and achievement called civilization, and riding on the seeds of progress, surmount the obstacles in a short time and greet you. However quickly you build the railway, it will come with the same speed."[6]

It is appropriate here to relate the following anecdote: during his travels through the region, Bediuzzaman had arrived at Urfa from Diyarbakır. He then set out to make a tour of the surrounding area and returning to Urfa, addressed a large gathering in the courtyard of the Yusuf Pasha Mosque. He began his address by describing how in one of the places he had visited, a villager he had questioned on the state of local agriculture had replied: "Our *ağa* [feudal landlord or tribal chief] knows" to whatever he had been asked. Bediuzzaman had told him: "Well, in that case, I shall talk with your intelligence which is in your *ağa*'s pocket!", and had proceeded to explain that he should not refer everything to the *ağa* but should be enterprising and have initiative, and himself be informed about all the matters concerning the village. He made this the basis of his address.[7]

It can be seen from these examples that Bediuzzaman wanted to impress on the people that the way forward now lay in their own hands. The sovereignty of the nation was this. When asked about the position of their chiefs and leaders, for traditionally tribal society had been dominated by the chiefs, elders and religious figures, he replied as follows:

> Each era has its own rule and ruler. According to your terminology, an *ağa* was necessary to make the machinery of the former era run. Thus, the era of despotism's immaterial rule was force. Whoever had a sharp sword and hard heart rose. But the era of constitutionalism's spring, spirit, force, ruler, and *ağa* is truth; it is reason, knowledge, the law and public opinion. Whoever has a sharp mind and luminous heart will rise, and only he. Since knowledge increases as it advances in years and force decreases, medieval governments, which rely on force, are condemned to extinction. But since the governments of the modern age rely on science, they shall manifest immortal life.

Bediuzzaman was not attacking the chiefs and elders as such by speaking like this, but describing the path the modern world was taking, and the path they, too, had to take if they were not to remain outside the stream of time. Under the new order, leaders were the servants of the people and the nation. He continued:

> O Kurds! If through relying on force their swords are sharp, your *beys* and *ağas*, and even your shaykhs, will of necessity fall. And they will deserve it. But if, relying on reason in place of compulsion, they employ love and make the emotions subject to the mind, they will not fall; indeed, they will rise.[8]

In another place in the work we learn of the main criticism Bediuzzaman was levelling at the chiefs, though here he specifies that it is at the former chiefs that he is "throwing his stone", and describes it as another of "the evils of despotism". This was that "certain chiefs, and some imposters who posed as patriots sacrificing themselves for the nation, and certain unqualified, phoney shaykhs who claimed exceptional spiritual powers" had drained the nation of material and moral resources, thereby extinguishing the sense of nationhood, and breaking up and destroying the collectivity of the nation.[9] This idea of the collectivity, or the "collective personality" or "corporate identity" (*şahs-ı ma'nawī*) of a nation or social body, is frequently encountered in Bediuzzaman's writings. He described the modern age as "the age of the group or social body (T. *cemaat*; Ar. *jamā'ah*)...If the collective personality, which is the spirit of a social body, is righteous, it is more brilliant and complete [than that of an individual]. But if it is bad, it is exceedingly bad." That is to say, he is explaining to the people of eastern Anatolia that what falls to them now is to transcend their narrow traditional interests and loyalties, expand their ideas, and develop, or rather regain, a consciousness of Islamic nationhood. He told them:

> If only those who hold their lives in little account for some benefit, or minor matter of reputation, or imaginary glory, or to hear the words: 'So and so's a brave hero', or to uphold the honour of their *ağas* were to awake, would they not hold their lives in little account, and thousands of souls too if they possessed them, for the nation of Islam, which is worth treasuries; that is, the nation of Islam which gains them the brotherhood and moral assistance of three hundred million Muslims?

Bediuzzaman went on to say that the willingness to sacrifice one's life for the nation was essentially part of the high morality of Islam, and a requirement of it, which had been stolen from them by non-Muslims. It was the foundation of modern progress. He continued: "We must declare with our spirits, lives, consciences, minds, and all our strength: 'If we die, Islam, which is our nation, lives; it will live for ever. Let my nation be strong and well. Reward in the Hereafter is enough for me. My life as part of the nation will make me live; it will make me happy in the world above.'"[10]

Thus, to recapitulate, with "the destruction of the barrier of despotism", constitutionalism and the idea of Freedom had spread throughout the Islamic world and had caused a thorough awakening, and had brought about progress in ideas and great changes. This was because it had "showed up the existence of the nation," and in turn, "the luminous jewel of Islam within the shell of nationhood had begun to be manifest." Islam was vibrating, stirring to life. This had made it clear to all Muslims that each was not isolated and disjoined, but connected to all the others through shared interest and fellow-feeling. The whole Islamic world was bound together like a single tribe. This vibrating was also making Muslims aware that they had at their disposal a source of great strength and support. This had given birth to hope, which had revived their morale, previously destroyed by despair.[11]

It may be seen from this why Bediuzzaman was insistent on the present regime, despite the objections that could legitimately be raised concerning the CUP. He answered the uncertainties and objections put to him by the tribesmen, pointing out that it was "the lesser of two evils" and that "if consultation now deviates from the Sharī'ah one finger, formerly it did so one hundred yards."[12] Also through explaining it in this way, he allayed their fears concerning religion, which they had understood to be under threat by the Revolution. On the contrary, constitutionalism was the way to protect Islam. The feeling for Islam and sense of religion which lay behind the public opinion of the nation was a much surer, more effective, and exalted way to protect religion than leaving it to "an unhappy, defeated Sultan, or sycophantic officials, or a few unreasonable policemen."[13]

Questions on Minority Rights

As is to be expected, the tribesmen asked a number of questions concerning the Armenians, and non-Muslims generally, and the conformity with the Sharī'ah of their gaining equality of rights under the Constitution. Because both of the universal relevance of the matter, and how it further makes plain Bediuzzaman's enlightened and realistic views, we include a few of the main points.

First, however, to put the questions in context it should be remembered that although the Armenians in their *millah* had been contented to be part of the Ottoman Empire for centuries, and many of them continued to be loyal to it despite the rise of nationalist sentiments, following the Russo-Turkish War of 1877-78 the Russians, supported by the British, intensified their policy of inciting the Armenians to revolutionary acts of terrorism against the Ottoman State as a way of further dismembering it. The acts of terrorism and slaughter were carried out primarily for propaganda purposes: by provoking retaliatory attacks by the Muslims, the Armenians intended to portray themselves as innocent victims and thus to ignite European feeling against the Turks and gain support for the setting up of an Armenian state in eastern Anatolia, even to force Russia and Britain to intervene in their support.[14]

After listening to Bediuzzaman's definitions of Freedom, the tribesmen accepted it as a good thing, but said that the Greeks' and Armenians' freedom seemed to them to be "ugly" and made them think. They wanted to learn Bediuzzaman's opinion. His reply was in two parts:

> Firstly, their freedom consists of leaving them in peace and not oppressing them. And this is what the Sharī'ah enjoins. More than this is their aggression in the face of your bad points and craziness, their benefiting from your ignorance.[15]

It may be understood from this that again Bediuzzaman is impressing on the Kurds that their real enemy is the situation into which they had fallen: "Also, our enemy and what is destroying us is *Ağa* Ignorance, and his son, Poverty Efendi, and grandson, Enmity Bey. Even if the Armenians have opposed us in hatred, they have done so under the commandership of these three corrupters."[16]

In the second part of his answer to the question, Bediuzzaman pointed out that even if the Armenians' freedom was as bad as they thought, Muslims still do not cause harm. The Armenians and the total number of non-Muslims in the Empire were relatively few compared with the whole Muslim nation of more than three hundred million. And these three hundred million had been bound with "three dreadful fetters of despotism" and were being "crushed, captive under the Europeans' tyranny." "Thus," continued Bediuzzaman, "the non-Muslims' freedom, which is one branch of our freedom, is the bribe for [the price of] the freedom of all our nation [the Islamic world]. It is the repeller of that despotism and the key to those fetters. It is the raiser of the dreadful tyranny the Europeans have made descend on us." He considered they could afford this price, for as we have seen, "the Ottomans' freedom is the discloser of mighty Asia's good fortune. It is the key to Islam's prosperity. It is the foundation of the ramparts of Islamic Unity."[17]

Bediuzzaman Addresses the Generations of the Future

Bediuzzaman's eyes were on the future. It was a time of defeat for the Islamic world, a period of regression and darkness. But he knew the spring would come, and a golden age would dawn bringing true happiness, progress, and civilization for mankind. This return to life had begun. Flashes of light, signs of life could be seen. Bediuzzaman's view was so clear, he became impatient with the reluctance of the tribesmen to grasp it; rather, he expressed his impatience with his contemporaries generally:

> Why should the world be the world of progress for everyone else, and the world of decline and retrogression only for us? Is that the case? See, I shall not speak to you, I am turning this way; I shall speak to the people of the future:
>
> O you Said's, Hamza's, Ömer's, Osman's, Tahir's, Yusuf's, Ahmad's and the rest of you who are hidden behind the high age of three centuries hence, and listening silently to my words, watch us with a secret, unseen gaze! I am addressing you! Raise your heads and say: "You are right!" And it should be incumbent on you to say it. Let these contemporaries of mine not listen if they do not wish. I am speaking to you over the wireless telegraph that stretches from the valleys of the past called history to your elevated future. What should I do? I was hasty, I came in winter, but you will come in a paradise-like spring. The seeds of light sown now will open as flowers in your

ground. And we await this from you as the recompense for our service that when you come to go to the past, pass by my grave, and place a few of those gifts of spring by the citadel of Van, which is the gravestone of my *madrasah* and houses my bones, and is the custodian of the Horhor's earth. We shall warn the custodian; call, and you will hear the cry: 'Good health to you!'

If they wish, let the children who have sucked milk together with us at the breast of this age and whose eyes look behind them at the past, and whose imaginings are disloyal and alienated like themselves fancy the truths of this book to be delusions. Because I know that with you the matters in this book will prove to be true.

O my listeners! I am indeed shouting, for I am standing at the top of the minaret of the thirteenth century [of the Hijrah], and calling to the mosque those who in ideas are in the deepest valleys of the past.

O you miserable two-footed mobile mausoleums who have left Islam, which is like the spirit of the two lives! Do not stop at the door of the generation that is coming. The grave awaits you. Retreat into it and let the new generation come forth, which will wave the reality of Islam over the universe in earnest![18]

The Damascus Sermon

In the autumn of 1910, Bediuzzaman moved south and until the following spring, made "a winter journey through the Arab lands," continuing "to give lessons on constitutionalism."[19] He visited Damascus in early 1911, where he stayed as a guest in the Ṣāliḥiyah district. It was during this stay that, on the insistence of the Damascus *'ulamā'*, he gave his famous sermon in the Umayyad Mosque. Bediuzzaman's fame must have been considerable, for close to ten thousand people, including one hundred *'ulamā'*, packed into the historic building to listen to him.[20] The text of the sermon was afterwards printed twice in one week.

If one considers the backwardness of the Islamic world at that time in relation to the West and its resulting subjection to the European Powers, and the accompanying feelings of hopelessness and helplessness on the part of the educated Muslims in particular, it is not difficult to see why Bediuzzaman's message of hope and certain predictions supported by argument of the future supremacy of the Qur'an and Islamic civilization met with the enthusiastic response that they did. The Sermon is in the form of "Six Words" taken from "the pharmacy of the Qur'an", which constitute the cure or medicine for the "six dire sicknesses" which Bediuzzaman had diagnosed as having arrested the development of the Islamic world. He described it as follows:

> In the conditions of the present time in these lands, I have learnt a lesson in the school of mankind's social life and I have realized that what has allowed Europeans to fly towards the future on progress while it arrested us and kept us, in respect of material development, in the Middle Ages are six dire sicknesses. The sicknesses are these:
>
> Firstly, the coming to life and rise of despair and hopelessness in social life. Secondly, the death of truthfulness in social and political life. Thirdly, love of enmity. Fourthly, not knowing the luminous bonds that bind the believers to one another. Fifthly, despotism, which spreads like various contagious diseases. And sixthly, restricting endeavour to what is personally beneficial.[21]

Bediuzzaman had started by quoting the verse: "Do not despair of God's mercy" (Qur'an, 39:53), and the Ḥadīth: "I came to perfect good moral qualities", which provide the theme of the six Words of which the Sermon is composed. The First Word is Hope, and we shall describe it in some detail for in it he sets forth the reasons for his optimism concerning the future of the Islamic world. It consists of "one and a half preliminary arguments" to support his "firm conviction" that "the future shall be Islam's, and Islam's alone, and the truths of the Qur'an and belief shall be sovereign." The premises of his arguments are that "the truths of Islam are able to progress both materially, and in moral and non-material matters, and possess a perfect capacity to do so."[22] The first aspect is progress in moral and non-material matters, and contains five or six main points.

Quoting the commander-in-chief of the Japanese army, who in 1905 had defeated Russia at war, Bediuzzaman begins by making this point:

> History shows that the Muslims increased in civilization and progressed in relation to the strength of the truths of Islam; that is, to the degree that they acted in accordance with that strength. And history also shows that they fell into savagery and decline, and disaster and defeat amidst utter confusion to the degree of their weakness in adhering to the truths of Islam. He then points out:
>
> As for other religions, it is quite to the contrary. That is to say, history shows that just as they increased in civilization and progressed in relation to their weakness in adhering to their religions and bigotry, so were they subject to decline and revolution to the degree of their strength in adhering to them.

Thus, in contradistinction to other religions, Islam has the capacity to progress and holds everything necessary to achieve true civilization. It is significant that this acute observation was made not only by a non-Muslim, but a Japanese. For the Japanese were held up by many supporters of constitutionalism as an example to be followed in their taking only science and technology from the West in their drive for progress and civilization while retaining their own culture and morality. Following this, Bediuzzaman continues his argument by stating that history presents no evidence for any Muslims having embraced other religions on the strength of reason, whereas as a result of "reasoned argument and certain proofs", the followers of other religions are "gradually drawing close to and entering Islam." He then lays this challenge before the believers:

> If we were to display through our actions the perfections of the moral qualities of Islam and the truths of belief, without doubt the followers of other religions would enter Islam in whole communities; indeed, some entire regions and states on the globe of the earth would take refuge in Islam.

Next, he describes modern man's search for true religion. He says that developments in science together with the terrible wars and events of the twentieth century have aroused in man a desire to seek the truth. Man has been awakened by these, and has understood "the true nature of humanity and his own comprehensive disposition." He has thus realised his need for religion, for "the only true support for impotent men in the face of the innumerable disasters and the external and internal enemies that plague them, and the only point from which they may seek help and assistance in the face of the innumerable needs with which they are afflicted and their desires which stretch to eternity despite their utter want and poverty is in recognizing the world's Maker, in faith, and in believing and affirming the Hereafter. There is no other help for awakened mankind apart from this." And he goes on to say that, like a human being, countries and states have also now begun to realise "this intense need of mankind."

For the next stage in his argument, he points out that the Qur'an repeatedly "refers man to his reason", telling him to use his intelligence, and ponder over and take lessons from his own life and the events of past ages. Advising his listeners to heed these warnings of the Qur'an, Bediuzzaman concludes that it will prevail in the future:

> We Muslims, who are students of the Qur'an, follow proof; we approach the truths of belief through reason, thought, and our hearts. We do not abandon proof in favour of blind obedience and imitation of the clergy like some adherents of other religions. Therefore, in the future, when reason, science and technology prevail, that will surely be the time that the Qur'an will gain ascendancy, which relies on rational proofs and invites the reason to confirm its pronouncements.

To complete this First Aspect, Bediuzzaman describes "eight serious obstacles" which "prevented the truths of Islam from completely conquering the past", but which are now dispersing, and follows this with quoting the testimony to the truth of Islam of two "enemies" by way of proof of his argument.

Before describing the obstacles, Bediuzzaman says that "the veils which eclipse the sun of Islam…and prevent it from illuminating mankind have begun to disperse." The signs of dawn were appearing then, in 1911. He later added that the true dawn began in 1371, that is, 1951, when a number of Islamic countries were gaining their independence.²³ Or even if that was the false dawn, the true dawn would break in forty to fifty years' time. He was absolutely insistent on it. The obstacles were as follows:

The first three obstacles were "the Europeans' ignorance, their barbarity at that time, and their bigotry in their religion. These three obstacles have been destroyed by the virtues of knowledge and civilization, and they have begun to disperse."

The fourth and the fifth were "the domination and arbitrary power of the clergy and religious leaders, and the fact that the Europeans obeyed and followed them blindly. These two obstacles have also started to disappear with the rise among mankind of the idea of freedom and the desire to search for the truth."

The sixth and seventh obstacles were "the despotism that oppressed us, and our immorality and degeneracy that arose from opposing the Sharī'ah...The fact that the separate despotic power residing in a single individual is now declining indicates that the fearful despotism of larger sections of society and of revolutionary groups will also decline in thirty to forty years time. And the great upsurge in Islamic zeal together with the fact that the ugly results of immorality are becoming apparent show that these two obstacles are about to diminish; rather, that they have begun to do so. God willing, they will completely disappear in the future."

The eighth obstacle was that "since certain positive matters of modern science were imagined to oppose and be contrary to some apparent meanings of the truths of Islam, it prevented, to an extent, their prevailing in the past." That is to say, scientists and philosophers opposed Islam because they did not understand its true meaning, but, "after learning the truth, even the most opinionated philosopher is compelled to submit to it."

Bediuzzaman concludes the First Aspect of his argument by quoting a few short passages from the 19th century Scottish philosopher Thomas Carlyle, and from the famous Prussian, Prince Bismarck (1815-1898). They testify to the truth of Islam and the Qur'an's being the revealed word of God. On the strength of their testimony, Bediuzzaman repeated the prediction he had made previously to Shaykh Bakhīt in Istanbul:

> Europe and America are pregnant with Islam. One day, they will give birth to an Islamic state. Just as the Ottomans were pregnant with Europe and gave birth to a European state. He then concluded:
>
> O my brothers who are here in the Umayyad Mosque and those who are in the mosque of the world of Islam half a century later! Do the introductory remarks, that is, those made up to here, not point to the conclusion that it is only Islam that will provide true and moral and spiritual rule in the future, and will urge mankind to happiness in this world and the Hereafter? And that true Christianity, stripping off superstition and corrupted belief, will be transformed into Islam; following the Qur'an, it will unite with Islam?[24]

The Second Aspect of Bediuzzaman's argument "offers strong proofs for Islam's material progress and supremacy in the future." These proofs he describes in the form of "five extremely powerful, unbreakable Strengths", which having "blended and fused", "are established in the heart of the Islamic world's 'collective personality'." But before describing them he makes the very important and interesting point that the Qur'an instructs man in progress and urges him towards it. By mentioning the miracles of the prophets, he says, "the Qur'an is informing mankind that events similar to those miracles will come into existence in the future through progress and is urging them to achieve them, saying: 'Come on, work! Show examples of these miracles! Like Prophet Solomon, cover a journey of two months in a day! Like Prophet Jesus, work to discover the cure for the most frightful diseases!'", and cites further miracles as examples.

Of the Five Strengths, the first is "reality of Islam", the second is "an intense need, which is the real master of civilization and industry" together with "utter, back-breaking poverty", while the third is "the Freedom which is in accordance with the Sharī'ah". The fourth Strength is the "courage" or "valour of belief", and the fifth, "the pride of Islam, which proclaims and upholds the Word of God." And, as we have seen, "in this age, proclaiming the Word of God is contingent on material progress."

Bediuzzaman then infers that it was because in the drive for modernization so far pursued in the Ottoman Empire it was not the beneficial aspects of civilization that had been taken but its "evils and iniquities" which had been "imitated", that the empire had been reduced to the state of defeat it was then in. And it was also because the iniquities of civilization had prevailed over its benefits that mankind had suffered the bloody and calamitous wars of this century. "God willing," he said, "through the strength of Islam in the future, the virtues of civilization will predominate, the face of the earth will be cleansed of filth, and universal peace be secured."

Continuing, he says: "Powerful indications and means" to the future supremacy of Asian civilization are the facts that European civilization is founded on the negative virtues of "lust and passion, rivalry and oppression," rather than virtue and guidance, that its evils have predominated over its virtues, and that "it has been infiltrated by revolutionary societies like a worm-eaten tree."[25]

And so, Bediuzzaman asks his audience: "How is it that while there are such powerful and unshakeable ways and means for the material and moral progress for the believers and people of Islam, and the road to future happiness has been opened up like a railway, you despair and fall into hopelessness in the face of the future and destroy the morale of the Islamic world?…Since the inclination to seek perfection has been included in man's essential nature…in the future truth and equity will show the way to a worldly happiness in the world of Islam, God willing, in which there will be atonement for the former errors of mankind.

Indeed, consider this: time does not run in a straight line so that its beginning and end draw apart from one another; it rather moves in a circle like the motion of the globe of the earth. Sometimes it displays the seasons of spring and summer as progress, and sometimes the seasons of storms and winter as decline. Just as every winter is followed by spring and every night by morning, mankind too shall have a morning and a spring, God willing. You may expect from Divine Mercy to see true civilization within universal peace brought about through the sun of the truth of Islam."[26]

The remaining five 'Words' of the Sermon point out how this true civilization will be achieved and the morning and springtime for mankind brought about. They are concerned mainly with morality.

In the Second Word, Bediuzzaman points out some of the destructive results of despair, which he describes as "a most grievous sickness" which "has entered the heart of the world of Islam." He says that it was despair that had destroyed the morale of Muslims, so that the Europeans had been able to dominate them and make them their captives for the preceding four hundred years. And it was despair that had killed their high morality, and caused them to abandon the public good for personal benefit. And despair had even caused them to use "the indifference and despondence of others" as "an excuse for their own laziness," and "to abandon the courageousness of belief, and neglect their Islamic duties." He says that despair "is the quality and pretext of cowards, the base, and the impotent." It cannot be the quality of the Arabs in particular, who are famous for their tenacity. He concludes the Word with a call to the Arabs to give up despair and stand in "true solidarity and concord" with the Turks, and "unfurl the banner of the Qur'an in every part of the world."[27]

The Third Word is Truthfulness. This, says Bediuzzaman, is the basis and foundation of Islam. Truthfulness and honesty are the principles of Islam's social life. Hypocrisy, flattery and artifice, duplicity and double-dealing are all forms of lying. Unbelief in all its varieties is lying and falsehood, while belief is truthfulness and honesty. For this reason, there is a limitless distance between truth and falsehood. Like fire and light, they should not enter one another. But politics and propaganda have mixed and confused them, and as a result have confused man's achievements.

Bediuzzaman points out that this has happened in the course of time and that during the Era of Bliss, that is, the time of Prophet Muḥammad (ṣ), truthfulness and lying were as distant from one another as belief and unbelief. They have gradually drawn closer to each other, and now evil and lying have to some degree taken the stage. Salvation, he told them, is only to be found in honesty. Sometimes in the past lying may have been permissible, but since it was abused, now there are only two ways, not three: "Either truthfulness or silence."[28]

The Fourth Word is a call to Love and Brotherhood. Bediuzzaman says that "the thing most worthy of love is love, and the quality most deserving of enmity is enmity." For it is love that guarantees man's social life and ensures his happiness, while enmity and hatred have overturned his social life, and more than anything deserve to be loathed and shunned. The awesome evil and destruction of the two World Wars[29] show that the time for enmity and hostility is finished, so that enemies, even, so long as they are not aggressive, should not attract the enmity of Muslims. Hell and Divine punishment are enough for them.

As for believers, he says that sometimes arrogance or self-worship may cause a fellow-believer to be unjustly hostile towards them without realizing it. But this is to slight powerful causes of love, like belief, Islam, nationality, and humanity. If the causes of enmity are personal matters, these are like small stones; to nurture enmity towards a Muslim is a great error; it is like scorning the causes of love, which are as great as a mountain.[30]

In the Fifth Word, Bediuzzaman is urging the Arabs to take up their positions alongside the Turks as sentries of the sacred citadel of Islamic nationhood. We have already seen how Freedom and constitutionalism were serving and would serve to develop awareness of the sense of Islamic nationhood among Muslims. Here we learn more of why this was vital for the Islamic world. With his knowledge of the modern world and extraordinarily clear vision of the way it would take, Bediuzzaman explained to his listeners that at this time man's actions, either good or bad, very often do not remain with the doer, but have widespread consequences; one sin may become a hundred sins, and one good deed, a thousand good deeds. He explained it in the following way:

> Thus, through the bond of this sacred nationhood, all the people of Islam are like a single tribe. Like the members of a tribe, the groups and peoples of Islam are connected to one another through Islamic brotherhood. They assist one another morally, and, if necessary, materially. It is as if all the groups of Islam are bound to each other with a luminous chain.
>
> If a member of a tribe commits a crime, all its members are guilty in the eyes of another, enemy, tribe. It is as though each member of the tribe had committed the crime so that the enemy becomes the enemy of all of them. That single crime becomes like thousands of crimes. And if a member of the tribe performs a good act which is the cause of pride affecting the heart of the tribe, all its members take pride in it. It is as if each person in the tribe feels proud at having done that good deed.
>
> It is due to this fact that at this time, and particularly in forty to fifty years' time, evil and bad deeds will not remain with the perpetrator, but will transgress the rights of millions of Muslims. Numerous examples of this shall be seen in forty to fifty years' time.

Then, having pointed out the damage caused by laziness and indifference, he says that since at this time good deeds also do not remain with the doer but "may be beneficial to millions of believers", "it is not the time to cast oneself on the bed of idleness."

Bediuzzaman goes on to remind the Arabs of their responsibility as teachers and leaders towards the other, smaller Muslim groups and peoples, a responsibility they were neglecting due to laziness. At the same time their good deeds are also great, he says, and predicts that in forty or fifty years' time, the different Arab peoples would "enter upon exalted circumstances...like those of the United States of America", and would be "successful in establishing Islamic rule in half the globe...If some fearful calamity does not soon erupt, the coming generation shall see it, God willing."

However, he immediately continues: "Beware, my brothers! Do not fancy or imagine that I am urging you with these words to busy yourselves with politics. God forbid! The truth of Islam is above all politics. All politics may serve it, but no politics can make Islam a tool for itself."

And then: "With my faulty understanding, I imagine Islamic society at this time in the form of a factory containing many machines and cog-wheels. Should one wheel fall behind or encroach on another, which is its fellow, the whole mechanism ceases to function. Thus, this marks the beginning of Islamic Unity. And this necessitates not paying attention to one another's faults."

That is to say, he is saying that Islamic supremacy will be won through the material and technological progress achieved through the unity and co-operation of all the different components, that is, the groups and peoples that make up the Islamic world.

As we saw when looking at Bediuzzaman's *Debates* with the Kurdish tribes, he considered that the Europeans had taken from the Muslims some of their high moral values and made them the means of their progress, while giving them their own corrupt morals in return. The willingness to sacrifice everything, even one's life, for one's nation was among these. He says it was "the firmest foundation in their progress." He then points out that through the idea of nationhood, "an individual becomes as valuable as a nation. For a person's value is relative to his endeavour. If a person's endeavour is for his nation, that person forms a miniature nation on his own." Whereas, "Because of the heedlessness of some of us and the Europeans' damaging characteristics that we have acquired and, despite our strong and sacred Islamic nationhood, through everyone saying: 'Me! Me!'

and considering personal benefits and not the nation's benefits, a thousand men have fallen to become like one man."[31]

The Sixth Word or sixth constituent of the cure Bediuzzaman is prescribing for the Islamic world is mutual consultation, as enjoined by the verse, "Whose rule is consultation among themselves" (Qur'an, 42:38). We have already discussed this "fundamental principle" in some detail; here, he describes it as "the key to Muslims' happiness in Islamic social life", and stresses its importance as the basis of progress and scientific development, adding that one reason for Asia's backwardness was the failure to practise consultation. He then says it is "the key and discloser of the continent of Asia and its future," and that, "just as individuals should consult one another, so also must nations and continents practise consultation." This is because, as we have also seen, it was Freedom in accordance with the Sharī'ah—which is born of the consultation enjoined by the Sharī'ah—that would liberate Islam from the various forms of tyranny to which it was subjected, and "cast out the evils of dissolute Western civilization."

To conclude, Bediuzzaman explains that it is the sincerity and solidarity that result from consultation which make it the means of life and progress. For, "three men between whom there is true solidarity may benefit the nation as much as a hundred men. Many historical events inform us that as a result of true sincerity, solidarity, and consultation, ten men may perform the work of a thousand men."[32]

Notes

1. Nursi, *Kastamonu Lahikası*, 121; Şahiner, *Said Nursi*, 132.
2. Thus in 1910 Bediuzzaman foretold the lifting of "the three darknesses" which would descend on the peoples of Caucasia and Turkestan, the last of which we are now seeing in 1991-2. They may be seen as the collapse of Czarist Russia, the collapse of communism, and the Muslim states of the area gaining their independence with the falling apart of the Soviet Union. Indeed, in Abdurrahman's

biography, he quotes the Russian policeman as saying, "Freedom will cause you [the Ottoman Empire] to break up." To which Bediuzzaman replied: "It is you it will cause to break up, and I'll come and build my *madrasah* here." [*Bediüzzaman'ın Tarihçe-i Hayatı*, 34-5] Also, in 1990, Bitlis and Tiflis were proclaimed twin towns.

3. Nursi, *Sünûhat*, 63-4; *Tarihçe*, 72-3; Şahiner, *Said Nursi*, 133-4.
4. Nursi, *Hutbe-i Şamiye*, 23 (Eng. tr.: *Damascus Sermon*, 32).
5. Şahiner, *Said Nursi*, 134.
6. Nursi, *Münâzarat* (Ott. edn.), in *Asar-ı Bedi'iyye*, 410-411.
7. Şahiner, *Said Nursi*, 136.
8. Nursi, *Münâzarat* (Ott. edn.), in *Asar-ı Bedi'iyye*, 412.
9. Nursi, *Münâzarat*, 46-7.
10. Nursi, *Münâzarat*, 50-1.
11. *Ibid.*, 22-3; 55.
12. Nursi, *Münâzarat* (Ott. edn.), in *Asar-ı Bedi'iyye*, 416.
13. Nursi, *Münâzarat*, 7-8.
14. Shaw and Shaw, *History*, ii, 202.
15. Nursi, *Münâzarat*, 20.
16. Nursi, *Münâzarat* (Ott. edn.), in *Asar-ı Bedi'iyye*, 433.
17. *Ibid.*, 20-1.
18. Nursi, *Münâzarat*, 39-41.
19. *Ibid.* (Ott. edn.), in *Asar-ı Bedi'iyye*, 404.
20. Şahiner, *Said Nursi*, 136-7; *Tarihçe*, 81.
21. Nursi, *Hutbe-i Şamiye*, 16-17 (Eng. tr.: *Damascus Sermon*, 26-7).
22. Nursi, *Hutbe-i Şamiye*, 18 (Eng. tr.: *Damascus Sermon*, 28).
23. The passages quoted and paraphrased from the Damascus Sermon here are translated from the Turkish edition of the work. This was translated by Bediuzzaman himself from the original Arabic in the 1950's, and contains a number of additions and alterations to the original text; hence the references to dates and events subsequent to 1911.
24. Nursi, *Hutbe-i Şamiye*, 19-28 (Eng. tr.: *Damascus Sermon*, 28-36).
25. Bediuzzaman's comparative analysis of Islamic civilization and Western civilization is examined in greater detail in Chapter Nine.
26. Nursi, *Hutbe-i Şamiye*, 28-32 (Eng. tr.: *Damascus Sermon*, 36-9).
27. *Ibid.*,, 37-9 (Eng. tr.: *Damascus Sermon*, 43-5).
28. *Ibid.*, 39-44 (Eng. tr.: *Damascus Sermon*, 45-9).
29. See note 25 of this chapter.
30. Nursi, *Hutbe-i Şamiye*, 44-6 (Eng. tr.: *Damascus Sermon*, 49-51).
31. *Ibid.*, 47-51 (Eng. tr.: *Damascus Sermon*, 51-5).
32. Nursi, *Hutbe-i Şamiye*, 52-4 (Eng. tr.: *Damascus Sermon*, 56-8).

6
The Medresetü'z-Zehrâ

Return to Istanbul

Soon after giving his Sermon, Bediuzzaman left Damascus for Beirut and from there took the boat for Izmir and Istanbul. His intention in returning to Istanbul was to renew his efforts to found the Medresetü'z-Zehra or Eastern University. The last part of *Münâzarat* is devoted to this ideal of Bediuzzaman, and he many years later described it as "the spirit and foundation" of the work.[1] Thus, after his long travels through the region he resolved to get official support and backing for the construction of the university, reaffirmed in his conviction that it was the most comprehensive and far-reaching solution for the region's problems. And this time he was to have success, though the tide of events finally prevented the realization of his project.

The Rumelia Journey

On 5 June 1911, Sultan Mehmed Reşad set out with a large retinue on his famous Rumelia Journey. It was to be the last time an Ottoman sultan visited the European provinces, for soon they were all to be lost to the Empire. The previous year had seen the first Albanian uprising. The purpose of the Sultan's journey was to reawaken feelings of patriotism and solidarity among the various peoples of Macedonia and Albania in the face of the upsurge of nationalism, and to secure social calm. Bediuzzaman joined those accompanying the Sultan as the representative of the Eastern Provinces.

Travelling by sea to Salonica, the Sultan and his party stayed there two days and then continued their journey by train, arriving at Skopje on 11 June. In the same compartment as Bediuzzaman on the train were two school teachers who had studied modern science. A discussion of great relevance started between the three on their asking Bediuzzaman: "Which is more necessary and should be stronger, religious zeal or national zeal?" The gist of his answer was that "With us Muslims religion and nationality are united, although there is a theoretical, apparent, and incidental difference between them...Religious zeal and Islamic nationhood have completely fused in Turk and Arab and may not now be separated." And by means of a comparison in which Muslims were represented by a six-year-old child and Europeans or unbelievers by the heroes Hercules and Rustam, he demonstrated the unassailable strength of belief in Divine Unity.[2] Related from some elderly inhabitants of Skopje who recalled the visit was the following description of Bediuzzaman:

> Bediuzzaman was wearing boots. His moustaches were short and his eyes brilliant. He was a handsome, imposing young man with a darkish complexion. He carried a Circassian, gold tula-work whip and at his waist was an ivory-handled dagger. Within a short time he was known in Skopje as 'Bediuzzaman Mullah Said Efendi.' The Skopje *'ulamā'* came group by group to visit him and put their questions to him.
>
> Bediuzzaman was immediately next to Sultan Reşad while the Sultan was greeting the people from the balcony of the High School in Skopje, which was later destroyed by an earthquake. Thousands of Skopjans gave them the most enthusiastic reception.[3]

On 16 June, the Sultan and his retinue arrived in Kosova from Priştina, and in the large open space where the tomb of Sultan Murad Hudavendigar is situated, they performed the Friday prayers, a congregation of two hundred thousand. It was an unforgettable and nostalgic occasion.[4]

The Medresetü'z-Zehrâ 129

While in Kosova, there was much talk of a large university they were attempting to found there, doubtless for reasons similar to Bediuzzaman's Medresetü'z-Zehra. It provided him with just the opportunity he had been waiting for. He suggested to Sultan Reşad and the CUP leaders who were accompanying him that the East was in greater need of such a university, for it was like a centre of the Islamic world. They accepted his arguments and promised that a university would be opened in the Eastern Provinces. At the end of the following year, the Balkan War broke out and Kosova was lost to the Empire, whereupon Bediuzzaman applied for the nineteen thousand gold liras allotted to its proposed university. His application was accepted. He then returned to Van and on a site on the shores of Lake Van at Edremit, finally laid the foundations of the Medresetü'z-Zehra. But it was not to be. With the outbreak of the First World War shortly afterwards, the construction was halted and never resumed.[5]

Sultan Reşad and his accompanying party completed their visit to Rumelia on returning to Salonica. There they once again boarded the warship Barbaros and attendant vessels, and, being greeted by a cannon-salute at Çanakkale, retraced their path to Istanbul. There, on 26 June, they were met by large welcoming crowds. The trip had lasted three weeks.[6]

The tide that was flowing against the Ottomans was running too strongly by this time, however, to be stemmed by such gestures, despite the Sultan's enthusiastic reception on the trip and the large demonstrations of loyalty. The nationalists and separatists continued to receive support from the foreign powers, but more than anything it was CUP misrule that exacerbated the already volatile situation and led finally to the end of Turkey in Europe with the Balkan Wars of 1912 and 1913. Also in late 1911 the Tripolitanian War broke out: Italy attacked Tripoli and Benghazi, modern-day Libya, and they too were lost to the Empire. The Italians went on to occupy the Dodacanese Islands and bombard the entrance to the Dardanelles. And with the outbreak of the

Balkan War in November 1912, Greece seized the Aegean Islands, and Salonica was also lost. The deposed Sultan Abdulhamid was hurriedly removed from his place of exile and taken to Beylerbeyi Palace in Istanbul. The unexpected occupation of Tripoli added to the other events caused a political crisis in Istanbul and the CUP were ousted from power for a period of some six months, from July 1912 until the famous Raid on the Sublime Porte in January 1913 led by Enver Pasha. After the liberation of Edirne in July 1913, Enver was made Minister of War, and it was he who set up the alliance with Germany the following year which brought Turkey into the First World War on the side of the Central Powers.

Return to Van—1913

At some point Bediuzzaman had returned to Van, for it was at that time that he laid the foundations for the Medresetü'z-Zehra. His old patron and friend Tahir Pasha,[7] the governor of Van, was present at the ceremony, and both he and Bediuzzaman gave speeches. The occasion was marked by further celebrations and a banquet.[8]

During his research in the Ottoman archives of the Prime Minister's Office in Istanbul, Necmeddin Şahiner has unearthed twenty or so documents related to this matter, most of which bear the seal and signature of Tahsin Bey, the governor of Van, and are addressed to the Palace and Sultan Reşad. Şahiner writes that Sultan Reşad was well-informed of the progress of the project. In the letter he quotes, dated 4 Haziran 1329 (17 June 1913), the governor writes to the Grand Vizier's Office that all the 'ulamā', notables, and tribal chiefs of the area were requesting the speedy payment of sufficient money "from the Imperial pocket"—only a small amount had been paid up to that time due to the financial straits of the government—to begin the construction of an Islamic university for eighty students in Van, the plans and preliminaries of which had already been completed. It was hoped the running costs would be met by the imperial estates. He writes it would be an important point of support for the continued existence of Islam and the Ottomans [in the region] in the face of daily increasing Shī'ī propaganda and the ignorance of the Kurdish people. It would strengthen feeling for Islam and remove every sort of misunderstanding, and would be most beneficial and effective.[9]

While in Van, Bediuzzaman spent much of his time teaching his students in his *madrasah*, the Horhor, which took its onomatopoeic name from the spring that rose at its side. A young visitor to the *madrasah* described it as follows: "There was a green-covered table in Bediuzzaman's *madrasah* in Horhor on which he had written out in thumb-tacks the Ḥadīth: 'Seek knowledge from the cradle to the grave.' He himself taught the students when they had finished studying. His students were all selected. He taught about twenty-five of them. He was very fond of me and never called me by my name; he used to call me 'nephew'. Before the War he used to stay in Nurşin and Hüsrev Pasha Mosques."[10]

It was also during this visit to the East that what was known as the Bitlis Incident occurred, when, in July 1913, rebelling against the irreligious behaviour of some of the military commanders of the Government, Shaykh Selim of Hizan occupied the town for a week.[11] The shaykh had first approached Bediuzzaman seeking his support, but as on numerous occasions including the much larger Shaykh Said revolt in 1925, he declined, refusing to draw his sword against fellow Muslims. He told the shaykh:

"Those bad things and that irreligious behaviour are peculiar to commanders like them; the Army is not responsible for them. There are perhaps a hundred thousand saints in the Ottoman Army; I will not draw my sword against it. I will not join you." He continued: "Those people left me, drew their swords, and the futile Bitlis Incident occurred. A short time later the First World War broke out, and the army took part in it in the name of religion, it undertook the *jihad*. A hundred thousand martyrs from the army attained the rank of sainthood, and confirming what I had said, signed their diplomas of sainthood with their blood."[12]

"Arms and Books Side by Side"

As conditions deteriorated and hostilities became inevitable, Bediuzzaman bought "five or six Mauser rifles". Quoting one of two friends from Doğubayezit who attended the *madrasah*, Necmeddin Şahiner describes how for military training, Bediuzzaman used to take his recruits up Mount Sübhan and set up eggs for target practice. He would give whoever hit an egg a *mecidiye* [a silver coin] as a reward. The students he was thus training became so proficient and bold that when they came to the mountain for training, the Armenian revolutionaries would make themselves scarce and go elsewhere.[13]

With his charismatic character and ability to inspire great love and devotion in his students and followers, which manifested itself particularly under those harsh and testing wartime conditions, Bediuzzaman was able to infuse them with something of his own absolute fearlessness and powers of endurance, and move them to acts of great bravery. The following is a contemporary account of Bediuzzaman and his *madrasah*; but first, two short descriptions of his activities against the Armenians, the first by himself:

> Since at that time years ago the Old Said's students' devotion to their Master was such that they would have sacrificed everything for him, [he] never rested in the face of the Armenian Taşnak revolutionary societies, and was able to silence them to a degree although they were very active. He found Mauser rifles for his students, and for a time his *madrasah* was like a barracks with arms and books side by side.[14]
>
> In 1331 (1915), the Armenian and Russian savages were in no way successful in killing Bediuzzaman, although they used to attack him from every quarter and tried to do so. As for Bediuzzaman and his followers, they used to pursue the Armenians mercilessly, who used to flee as hard as they could.[15]

Now a description of a visit to Bediuzzaman's *madrasah*-barracks given to Necmeddin Şahiner by Nureddin Burak, who related it exactly as told by his father, Zeyneddin Burak:

The Medresetü'z-Zehrâ

At that time in the East, studying in the *madrasahs* was like this: the *hoja* (teacher) taught for nothing; in fact, through the mediation of the *hoja*, the people provided the students' livelihood. So there was no material reason preventing study. The choice of teacher was made only through his standing in regard to learning. So if someone was known as a great scholar, he would have many students; everyone would want to be taught by him. At that time, I and a few friends gathered together and began to search for a good teacher. We were told of Said the Famous in Van, in a *madrasah* called the Horhor.

Three of us went there. Hoja Efendi was not present when we arrived at the *madrasah*. Someone called Mullah Habib met us and invited us inside. He told us to wait saying the Hoja would come soon. At this point, the *madrasah*'s walls caught our attention. Hung up on them in rows were Mauser rifles and various weapons, swords, daggers, and cartridge-belts. There were also books on reading-stands. In truth, we were astonished.

In a short while they said: "Hoja Efendi is coming." We straightened ourselves up. He entered, and said: "Welcome!", then asked us why we had come.

The second thing that caught our attention and astonished us was the Hoja's manner and dress, because we did not see the customary dress of a teacher, which we knew and had expected. With a conical hat on his head, boots on his feet, dagger at his waist, and firm step, he reminded us of a soldier or high-ranking officer rather than a *hoja*. In fact, because of his youth, we thought to ourselves: "I wonder if he is learned." But then Mullah Habib, the most advanced student, was studying books like *Mullah Cami*. He was like the students' sergeant.

We said we had come to study under him. So he told us: "Fine, but I have conditions. You can on condition you comply with them." Then he added: "There is no possibility of going back for someone who starts with me. He remains with me to the end of his life." He then said: "And do not think you can accept and give your word today, then leave later if you get fed up or for any other reason, because the governor of Van is my close friend. I could have you brought back here through him. Tonight you are my guests. Stay here and think it over, then make your decision in the morning."

We were bewildered and did not know what to say to the proposal. We consulted with Mullah Habib. We asked him: "Do you stay with the Hoja under these conditions?" "Yes," he replied. "We gave our word once and undertook the matter. It is true it is not all that easy, but his learning is truly extraordinary. But you know best, do whatever seems right for you." We bowed our heads in shame, and saying we could not accept, left.[16]

Notes

1. Nursi, *Kastamonu Lahikası*, 46.
2. Nursi, *Hutbe-i Şamiye*, 56-65 (Eng. tr.: *Damascus Sermon*, 59-66).
3. Şahiner, *Said Nursi*, 141.
4. Cemal Kutay, "Avrupa Topraklarinda Son Padişah," in *Tarih Sohbetleri*, v, 226.
5. *Tarihçe*, 95.
6. Şahiner, *Said Nursi*, 142-5.
7. Tahir Pasha, who was ill, returned to Istanbul around the beginning of 1913, where he died in November of that year. See *Son Şahitler*, iii, 16-20. He was succeeded by Tahsin (Üzer) Bey, also a friend and supporter of Bediuzzaman.
8. Nuh Polatoğlu, in *Son Şahitler*, i, 90.
9. Şahiner, *Said Nursi* (8th edn.), 161-2.
10. Abdülbaki Arvasi, in *Son Şahitler*, i, 99-100.
11. Şerif Mardin, *Religion and Social Change in Modern Turkey, The Case of Bediuzzaman Said Nursi*, New York, 1989, 88.
12. Nursi, *Şualar*, 302 (Eng. tr.: *The Rays Collection*, Istanbul: Sözler Publications, 2002, 383).
13. Şahiner, *Said Nursi*, 156.
14. Nursi, *Şualar*, 439-440 (Eng.tr.: *Rays*, 518).
15. Şahiner, *Said Nursi*, 158.
16. *Ibid.*, 156-8.

7
War and Captivity

Bediuzzaman and the War

For Bediuzzaman, the War may be seen as a watershed. At some point he was appointed by Enver Pasha, the Minister of War, to raise and command a volunteer militia force. This he did, making his students the centre of the force. It was a *jihād*, and Bediuzzaman performed this bounden duty of Muslims on two fronts. In addition to raising the militia, training it to the very highest standards, and personally leading his men in bold and courageous actions, he continued to teach his students and to write his celebrated commentary on the Qur'an. Wielding both sword and pen, he was like a figure from the golden age of Islam, a model Muslim. When Bitlis fell to the Russians in early March 1916, he was captured and spent the next two years in various prisoner-of-war camps in Kosturma in Russia. He escaped, and travelling across Russia safely, came to Warsaw and Berlin, and arrived back in Istanbul in June 1918. But the rigours of his captivity had taken their toll on his health, and his outlook, too, had changed. The dreadful period of defeat and foreign occupation following the War was one of inner turmoil for Bediuzzaman, despite his worldly position and success, but from it the New Said was to emerge.

Events on the Eastern Front

The first shots of the War had been fired when Russia invaded north-eastern Anatolia on 31 October 1914. On this occasion,

Russia was not successful, and the invasion was repulsed by the Ottoman army under Enver Pasha. But he was only successful in this after leading the disastrous counter-offensive at Sarikamış in the arctic conditions of December and January as a result of which sixty-thousand out of his one hundred-thousand-strong army perished. The Russian army retreated, and Grand Duke Nicholas spent the following year completing preparations for the final invasion of Anatolia. He began this operation on 13 January 1916. Defeating the Ottomans at Pasinler with an army three times the size, the Russians entered Erzurum on 16 February.[1]

The Russians had long been inciting the Armenians to acts of terrorism against the Ottoman state, and providing material and moral support for their revolutionary societies. Now, in pursuit of an independent state in eastern Anatolia, the Armenians collaborated with the Russians on a large scale, many entering the Russian army. Armenian officers had played a prominent role in the 1877 invasion of north-eastern Anatolia. Distorted and exaggerated accounts by Armenian separatists of the events of 1915 were seized on by the Entente Powers and used in their propaganda war against the Turks, as they had been doing for years. Indeed, the same propaganda is still being used presently. Since Bediuzzaman was present and actively engaged in the defence of the Empire against the Russians and Armenians, we include the following facts concerning those events, all of which are taken from the second volume of *History of the Ottoman Empire and Modern Turkey* by the American historians S.J. and E.K. Shaw. Indeed, both his nephew's biography and other contemporary sources describe his humanitarian efforts, both during the fall of Van and, subsequently to save from certain slaughter, Armenian women and children along with Muslim ones.[2] Some are mentioned later in this chapter.

Upon the Russian withdrawal in January 1915, the Ottomans ordered the evacuation of all Armenians from the provinces of Van, Bitlis, and Erzurum as part of their preparations for the inevitable second invasion. It was arranged that they should settle in the Mosul area of northern Iraq. A special commission was set up to record the Armenians' property, all of which was to be handed back on their return after the War. The army was specifically instructed to protect and provide the needs of the deportees on their journey. Armenian propagandists claimed that over one million Armenians were massacred in the War. But according to the Ottoman census, the population was 1,300,000, not 2.5 million as claimed. And the number of those transported was no more than 400,000. The figure that died was probably around 200,000, "and not only of transportation, but of war, famine, and disease that killed 2 million Muslims at the same time." In April 1915, the Armenians staged a revolt in Van. In May, the Russians reached the city and a massacre of Muslims followed. An Armenian state was proclaimed under Russian protection, and by July some 250,000 Armenians had crowded into the area. Early the same month, the Ottomans were successful in pushing back the Russo-Armenian Army, together with which were some 200,000 refugees. Of these, some 40,000 perished, not because they were deliberately massacred, but from conditions of war.[3]

The Front

On the declaration of war Bediuzzaman had enlisted in the army together with his student Mullah Habib as a voluntary regimental mufti or religious functionary. They were posted to the Van Division and sent to the front at Erzurum.[4] At the front the fighting was fierce, cold and intense. The Ottomans were greatly outnumbered. To boost the volunteers' morale in those arduous conditions, Bediuzzaman rarely entered the trenches, but moved around the front lines on his horse, always to the fore of the fighting. He later wrote:

> On the Pasinler Front during the Great War, the late Mullah Habib and I were moving forward with the intention of

attacking the enemy. Their artillery fired three shells at us at one or two minute intervals. The three shells passed right over our heads two metres high, and although our soldiers were concealed in the ravine behind us and could not be seen, they retreated. By way of a test I said: "What do you say, Mullah Habib, I'm not going to hide myself from the shells of these infidels?" And he replied: "I'm not going to fall back either, I'll stay behind you." A further shell fell very close to us. Certain that Divine succour would preserve us, I said to Mullah Habib: "Forward! These infidels' shells can't kill us. We won't deign to draw back!"[5]

Of several accounts Necmeddin Şahiner has collected from soldiers present at Pasinler, all describe Bediuzzaman's moving about the trenches on horseback in this way, in complete disdain of the Russian shells. The following account mentions particularly the severity of the shelling:

It was snowing and everywhere was white. We were defending our beloved country against the Russians. We could not raise our heads above the trenches because of the bullets which were falling like rain. We were fighting under shells that fell like rain. It was just as though shrapnel was raining from the skies. The thing we were most powerless before was this shrapnel, which exploded in the air. It was destroying us and our losses were heavy. The shrapnel which exploded in the air was scattered to right and left in fragments.

Just as this was going on, Mullah Said the Famous was touring the trenches. He was moving up and down the valley on horseback. Then some people emerged from their trenches, and they were hit and killed.

I wanted both to see Mullah Said and to kiss his hands, but I was frightened of being hit. I had heard the name before, but I was seeing this great person for the first time at the bloody front at Pasinler. Then I saw he had come level with me. I heard him say:

"Fight for Allah! Allah is our helper!"[6]

Another soldier who fought under Bediuzzaman at Pasinler, Mustafa Yalçın, recalled him like this:

They suddenly took us from Çanakkale, and sent us to the Eastern Front. We were in the Eighth Division in Kars, and at our head was Mullah Said. Bands of Russians and Armenians were attacking us ceaselessly.

At that time, Mullah Said used to teach us concerning religious matters. Every night he used to teach us. At Hasankale [Pasinler] we fought against the Russians mercilessly with Mullah Said. Before, the Hoja used to wear a turban, but while fighting he would wear what we called a 'felt hat'.

At that point I was wounded at Hasankale and drew back. I received this shrapnel wound on my hip, look, it is still open. I would have died long before but Mullah Said wrote out a prayer for each of us. We hung them round our necks, and no bullets hit us. At that time there were a hundred infidels firing on one Muslim. In the end I was wounded and they took me back. Mullah Said continued to fight. They treated me in Konya then sent me to the Western, Austrian, Carpathian, and Galician Fronts.

Mullah Said was a heroic person. At the front, he used to lead the attacks on horseback. He was a good shot. He did not go into the trenches. Once, Mullah Said was told that some units were about to break up. He immediately removed the cause of their differences, and made sure that they did not disperse. He explained things wonderfully well; it was as though he could cast a spell on people.

Then during that hell-like war he was writing a book. His students used to write down what he dictated. He was an excellent horseman. They used to heave out great rocks and roll them down on the Russians. He used to say to us: 'Don't be frightened of anything; a Muslim's belief is stronger than any power.' Every night he used to read to us from the books he had written. I could not understand much because I am not educated, but whenever I saw Mullah Said, my courage soared. He was a formidable person, but he acted most kindly towards us.[7]

"*Signs of Miraculousness*"

The book Mustafa Yalçın describes Bediuzzaman as writing here was his commentary on the Qur'an, *Signs of Miraculousness*

(*Ishārāt al-I'jāz fī Maẓānn al-Ījāz*), and it was Mullah Habib who used to act as his scribe. Written on horseback, in the trenches and the skirmishing lines, this Arabic commentary, only the first section of which was completed, was later acclaimed by the *'ulamā'* in Damascus and Baghdad, while Ali Rıza Efendi, the head of the office for issuing *fatwās* in Istanbul (*fetva emini*), described it as: "As powerful and valuable as a thousand other commentaries."[8] In the work, Bediuzzaman described its purpose as follows:

> Our aim from these indications is a commentary on a number of the symbols of the Qur'an's word-order, for [one aspect of] its miraculousness is manifested in its word order. Indeed, the embroidery of its word-order is its most brilliant [form of] miraculousness.[9]

In addition, in the preface,[10] setting out the method by which Qur'anic commentaries should be written in the modern age, he explains further his purpose in writing it. He first explains the nature of the Qur'an as Divine speech which addresses all men in every age then points out that it also encompasses the sciences which make known the physical world. Indeed, the Qur'an's truths become manifest through the discoveries of science. Thus, in the modern age when the cosmos is being opened up and its workings are being revealed by science, commentaries on the Qur'an must keep pace with the giant strides science is taking. It is beyond the capacity of an individual or even a small group to be familiar with all the sciences, and a commentary should therefore be written by a committee of scholars who are specialists in a number of sciences, both religious and modern. It will be recalled that among his proposals for educational reform were the combining and joint teaching of the religious and modern sciences, specialization, and the application of the principle of mutual consultation.

When he understood that some great catastrophe was going to occur—he gave repeated warnings of it in the years preceding the First War as many of his students testified, he began to write *Signs of Miraculousness* on his own. It was because he realised its extreme urgency and importance that he continued to write it in the unfavourable conditions of the front. In fact, he had had a dream or vision around the beginning of the War that had corroborated his premonitions and confirmed his intention to write the commentary.[11] Thus, he presents the work as a model or example that could be followed by a committee of scholars such as he had described at some point in the future.

Bediuzzaman and His Militia Move South

When the Russians began their second invasion in January 1916, Bediuzzaman and his militia moved to the front at Pasinler near Erzurum.[12] A second Russian force moved south down the eastern side of Lake Van. The Ottomans were unable to halt the enemy advance in north-east Anatolia and retreated as the Russians moved on to take Erzurum. Bediuzzaman and his militia withdrew to Van to join its defence against the second major Russian force, though it is not known at precisely what point. There, as the city was being evacuated in the face of the Russian attack, he and a number of his students decided to hold out to the end in the citadel. Unwilling to lose such a valuable figure in that way, the governor of Van, Cevdet Bey—who was the son of Tahir Pasha the old Governor—insisted that they withdraw to Gevaş, on the road to Bitlis. For it was to Bitlis that all the officials, the army, and people of the area were retreating.

There are many incidents recorded of the heroic actions of Bediuzzaman and his volunteers at this stage of the bitter fight to save eastern Anatolia from the Russians and Armenians. At Gevaş, as the mass exodus from Van was in progress, a Cossack cavalry regiment staged an attack. Bediuzzaman together with about forty men made a stand against the attack in order to prevent the people and their possessions falling into the hands of the enemy. Climbing a mountain, they attacked the Cossacks at night from above, and deceived them into thinking a large number of reinforcements had arrived. In this way, Bediuzzaman and his force threw the

Cossacks into sufficient disarray to allow the people to move on to safety, and Gevaş too was saved.[13]

Many of Bediuzzaman's students and volunteers fell at this time. Mullah Habib also was killed at Gevaş, having successfully conveyed news of the enemy's movements to Halil Pasha at the Iranian Front.[14]

On one occasion when the Ottomans were retreating, the Felt Hats lured the Russians and Armenians—filled with false confidence—into an enclosed valley, and opening fire on them, wiped out the entire force.[15]

On another occasion, Bediuzzaman and his volunteers were able to recapture thirty large guns from the Russians by surprising them at night. And using them to delay the Russian advance, they allowed all the women and children of the area to be evacuated. Necmeddin Şahiner notes that all these exploits appear in the contemporary military records of the militia forces. Bediuzzaman's students, too, were famous for their daring and bravery. One of them called Mir Mahey actually crossed into the Russian units several times, and killing as many as ten to fifteen of the enemy, returned to his own lines.[16]

The owner of the newspaper *Hür Adam*, Sinan Omur, had these memories of Bediuzzaman and the militia, which he related to Necmeddin Şahiner in an interview.

> I was a student in the teachers' training college in Istanbul when the First World War broke out. I was eighteen years old at the time, so they took me into the Army. I first saw Bediuzzaman in August 1331 (1915) on Mount Sübhan. He was on a white horse. Galloping up and down, he was raising the soldiers' morale. He was commander of the militia forces at that time. He had a turban on his head, and epaulets on his shoulders. He was continually moving in among the volunteers on horseback to give them courage. Enver Pasha had appointed Bediuzzaman to the militia forces. They had long been friends. So Bediuzzaman formed a militia in the East; it consisted of around four to five thousand men.

The militia forces did not obtain their weapons and provisions from us, but provided everything for themselves. They always went in front of the Army and always fought in the front lines. They were known as the Felt Hats. The Russians did not know where to flee when they heard: "The Felt Hats are coming!"; they did not know what had hit them. At that time our swords were only for prodding, but they used to use them on horseback and would hit whatever they struck. They used to wear white capes so as to blend in with the snow-covered ground and not be detected by the enemy. They would throw the horses reins over one arm, or attach them to the horse's neck and leave the animal completely free. Then, galloping at speed, they would fire their rifles uninterruptedly. They were extremely accurate shots. While the commanders addressed the volunteers in order to encourage them to fight, in their excitement, the volunteers would not remain in their places squatting on the ground; as soon as the order to move was given: "Tention! Tention!", they would spring up and flying onto their horses, would gallop off against the enemy.[17]

Bediuzzaman's actions were cited in both Ottoman and foreign records. One of the latter, quoted by Necmeddin Şahiner, is the French *Documents Sur Les Atrocités Arméno-Russes*, a copy of which is in Istanbul's Municipal Library. The following is a translation of just one page:

Yusuf and Abdurrahman, sons of Mehmed, said the following under oath:

Our family comes from Nurs, Vavink, And, and Mezraa-i And, the summer pastures of the district of İsparit in the sub-province of Hizan. After the sub-province of Çatak had been occupied by the Russians, the Armenians of the neighbouring villages of Livar, Yukari Kutis, Aşağı Kutis, Çaçuan, Sikuar, and Yukari Adr came to the village of Yukari Kutis under the leadership of Lato, also known as Mihran, and Kazar Dilo, both of whom had infiltrated into Anatolia from Russia. They presented three written proposals to the notables there. Among the notables was Mullah Said, who was well-known under the name of Bediuzzaman. Was he taken prisoner, or was he killed? I do not know. These were the proposals:

1. Surrender.
2. Evacuate the district.
3. Fight.

Nine hours after the enemy arrived, a force of six hundred attacked the village. The enemy soldiers were wearing uniforms and caps. We could not discover whether or not there were Russian soldiers among them. The number of those who looked destitute in the enemy army was extremely high. These could have been Russians or Armenians from Russia.

The enemy took all the people of our village to Mezraa-i And. Abdurrahman, the son of Hurşid Bey, one of the notables, was also present together with his son and wife. The following day, thirty-three men and boys, and around eighty women, young women, and girls were moved to Müküs in separate convoys. The women's convoy was left at Çaçuan, but at night all the men were put to the sword. I was saved from the slaughter because I had been assigned a duty. When they gave me the duty, they said this:

"We promise to give you money. Go to Mullah Said, and tell him to hand over to us the Armenians who remain there. Tell him there is no benefit in having them killed unnecessarily. The country is just about entirely occupied. The Russians have reached as far as Aleppo. Armenia has been set up. Bring us information about the numbers and strength of the Turkish Army there."

This was said to me by Dilo. I set out immediately. When I reached Çaçuan, I saw that our forces, which were formed of gendarmes and Kurds, had arrived there together with our mayor and Mullah Said. Our forces under the command of Bediuzzaman Said Efendi were successful in saving the women's convoy after five hours of fierce fighting. The state of the women was really pitiful. They did not have the strength to walk. Most of the children had been trodden underfoot. And of the thirty-three men, only two of us survived.[18]

When the Armenians massacred the Muslim women and children as well as the men, Armenian children would sometimes be killed in retaliation. To a degree Bediuzzaman was able to put a stop to this barbaric practice through his exemplary Islamic conduct, and was able to bring some humanity to the chaos of war. One time, thousands of Armenian women and children had been gathered together in the place where Bediuzzaman was. He issued an order that none of them were to be touched. Then later he released them and they returned to their families in Russian-held territory. The Armenians were so impressed by this example of Muslim morality that from then on they themselves refrained from slaughtering Muslim children. In this way, many innocent lives were saved.[19]

The Fall of Bitlis and Capture of Bediuzzaman

Having taken Van to the east of Lake Van and Muş to the west, the Russians moved south with three divisions to attack Bitlis. Their advance was halted for a time by the fierce resistance they met from the Turkish and volunteer forces at the defence line at Mount Dideban. In the appalling February conditions of eastern Anatolia with snow lying to a depth of three to four metres the important centre of Bitlis was evacuated. Once again the women and children, the sick and the lame, the government officials and dignitaries retreated before the advancing enemy. The Russians were unable to break the Ottoman lines, and it was only through the treachery of the Armenians, who opened up the way for them by capturing Mount Dideban, and setting up machine-guns at crucial points and gunning down many people, that they were finally able to enter the town. Bediuzzaman was in the town with what remained of his volunteers and fought a fierce hand to hand battle with the enemy cavalry. With one of his legs broken, Bediuzzaman hid with his four surviving students in an underground water conduit. After thirty hours they surrendered to the Russians. We have a description of this from Bediuzzaman's own pen:

> Although in one minute three bullets hit me in vital spots, they had no effect. When Bitlis fell, a number of my students and myself found ourselves in the middle of a battalion of Russians.

They surrounded us and there was firing on every side. All my friends were killed with the exception of four. Then we broke through the four lines of the battalion and hid. But they were still there. Although they were above us and all around us and could hear our voices and coughs, they did not see us. We remained thirty hours in that way in the mud with me wounded; I was preserved with a tranquil heart by Divine succour.[20]

Finally, since their lives were in danger from loss of blood and extreme cold, one of them went and informed the Russians of their whereabouts. The Russians came and took them prisoner.

One of those four surviving students of Bediuzzaman's was Ali Aras from the village of Çoravanis near Van. Also known as Ali Çavuş, he wrote down his memories of Bediuzzaman at the fall of Bitlis, and they were published in the newspaper *İttihad* six years after his death in April 1971. They also gave a lively account of Bediuzzaman and his Russian captors after they had been taken prisoner.

The Russians occupied Muş before we reached it. The people who had evacuated the town said when we met them on the road that all the ammunition together with fourteen heavy guns had remained there. Ustādh Bediuzzaman divided up the three-hundred-man force according to the fourteen guns and assigned a six-man squad to capture the ammunition. We captured the guns and ammunition and handed them over to a regular regiment which was posted on the Bitlis-Tatvan road. At this point the Russians began to attack from three sides and left us cut off in the Bitlis valley. The defence against the Russians continued day and night for seven days. Three shells hit Ustādh. One of these hit the handle of his dagger, another his cigarette case, and the third his right shoulder. Kel Ali, the commander of the regular troops, witnessed this and said to Ustādh:

"Bullets have no effect on you either, Bediuzzaman!" To which Bediuzzaman replied: "If Allah protects a person, even the shells of a heavy gun cannot kill him!"

War and Captivity

At the end of a week's fierce resistance, the Russians still could not enter Bitlis, so they evacuated the Papşin Han on the Tatvin road and withdrew. Then it was seen that, guided by the Armenians, they had skirted round the south of Bitlis by the Güzeldere road by way of Simek, had cut the Bitlis-Siirt road, and were holding the Arab Bridge. After midnight they started the attack on Bitlis. There was very fierce fighting. At this point Ustādh's nephew, Ubeyd,[21] whom he was very fond of, and many of his students, and our friends, were killed.

Although the Russians had taken the town's three bridges, Ustādh wanted to get to the other side of town. We jumped down from the top of a conduit which passed beneath a large building next to what is now Kazımpaşa Primary School. Because the water was entirely covered by snow and it was also night-time, we could not estimate the ground, and Ustādh hit his leg on a stone and broke it. Showing me a more suitable place underneath the conduit, he said: "Get me in there, Ali. Then go. I give you permission. God willing, you will get away." I got him in there and sat him down. He continued to insist that I go, but when I said that I was not going and that I wanted to remain and die as a martyr alongside him, he stroked my head with his hand, and said: "Fate has made us prisoners." I declared that I too had surrendered to fate.

We remained in the water for about thirty-six hours. The Russians had occupied the building over the conduit and their voices could be heard from below. We were busy planning how we could get out of there when a squad of fifty Russians soldiers arrived. They pulled us all out and took us to a building which was a hotel beneath and in which the Russian Second Army was billeted. They placed us in a room.

A regimental commander met us. They brought a chicken for Ustādh to eat. Two Russian commanders started to speak with Ustādh. It was clear they were talking about the War. Ustādh was talking to them standing on one leg. It was as though Ustādh was the commander and the two Russian commanders were prisoners. Ustādh did not take them seriously at all. They realised that his leg was broken, and called a health orderly who put it in plaster. After about two and a half hours there, we were taken to the Government Building by a detachment of soldiers.

A Tatar officer, who we later learnt was a Muslim, took pity on us, and taking us inside, put us in the governor's room.

It was during the first week of our stay in Government House that an aide-de-camp arrived. He asked for Ustādh then said the general had summoned him. They took Ustādh to the place the general was staying in Mahallebaşı by stretcher, because his leg was broken. Ustādh went in. The general asked a number of questions. These were centred on someone well-known called Abdülmecid, who had gone to Iran and was planning to go from there to the Caucasus to organise the Muslims there to fight against the Russians. They wanted information about him from Ustādh. Ustādh answered the questions as required. The general's questioning and the coming and going continued for about two weeks. Since we waited in the room outside, we could hear them speaking. We would hear Ustādh's terse answers and sharp retorts, and from time to time the sound of a fist being thumped on the table. We would get worried and shudder at the possibility of being lined up and shot, and when from time to time Ustādh emerged from the room, we did not neglect to reproach him because of these sharp exchanges.

On the twenty-seventh day of our stay in Government House they took us to what was then the gendarme station and is now the courthouse. They had brought there around twenty-five captured officers and government officials, most of whom were high-ranking. Then the general's aide-de-camp came again, and said to Ustādh: 'Take one of your students, we are sending you away now.' Ustādh took a student called Said. We did not want to part from him. To console us he said to the police chief, İrfan Bey, who was also a prisoner: "I entrust my students to you. Show them the police there."

Before leaving the gendarme station, he said as a prayer: "I am hopeful that, God willing, you will return, but I cannot say the same for Said." And in fact, the student he took with him called Said was killed while fighting the Russians in Turkestan. They separated us from Ustādh and sent us to Russia. Ustādh told me on his return from captivity that they had made him wait an additional month because his leg was in plaster.

A month later, they sent Ustādh to Van, and from there on to Khuy in Iran, from where he was put on a train for Russia. We remained in Russia thirty months as prisoners. On the communist revolution, we got away to Rumania by way of Hungary and handed ourselves over to a Turkish division there. As for Ustādh, I read in the newspapers in Rumania that he had gotten to Berlin by way of Warsaw, the capital of Poland, and from there had returned to Istanbul.

The 15th Division in Rumania was formed into the North Caucasus Corps with some reinforcements, and I served an additional fourteen months in it before being demobilized after the Treaty of Sèvres, when I returned to Van.[22]

The heroism of Bediuzzaman and his students in defending the east against the Russians and Armenians became legendary among the people of the area. They told also of how the Russians had tried to kill Bediuzzaman on his surrendering to them, and how this desire had been transformed into wonder at this courage, since Bediuzzaman did not so much as wince when they handled his broken leg.[23] Also one of his students who fought alongside him tells of Bediuzzaman's anger on learning, when being questioned by the Russians, that the Armenian interpreter was misinterpreting what they said. So the Russians brought a Tatar interpreter who explained his rejection of the Russians' proposals that he should write letters to all the tribes calling on them to surrender their arms.[24]

Subsequent documents which have recently come to light in the archives of the Prime Minister's Office in Istanbul show that in September 1916, Bediuzzaman was still in Tiflis in Georgia, presumably receiving treatment for his leg. The first, dated 9 August 1332 (22 August 1916) is from Memduh, the deputy governor of Bitlis, to the Ministry of Internal Affairs in Istanbul. It states that the officials held as prisoners-of-war in Tiflis required their salaries to be sent to them. Also in need of money there was Bediuzzaman Said-i Kürdî, who had saved eight large guns from Muş during the fall of Bitlis and had gathered together volunteers.

The second, dated 7 Eylül 1332 (20 September 1916), is from the Interior Minister, Tal'at Bey, to the director of the Ottoman Red Crescent Society, Besim Ömer Pasha, requesting him to send sixty lira to Bediuzzaman in Tiflis by special courier. And the third is Besim Ömer Pasha's reply, dated three days later, informing Tal'at Pasha that the sixty liras had been changed into 1254 marks and despatched as requested.[25]

The Prisoner-of-War Camps

Bediuzzaman was sent to the province of Kosturma in north-western Russia. Firstly, to the town of Kologrif, and then—according to one source, after a period in a large camp further into the northern wastes—to a camp in the town of Kosturma on the River Volga. It was here that a large part of his two years of captivity was spent. There are various accounts of him and his activities in the camp from a number of his fellow prisoners. As the commanding officer of a regiment, he was in a position of authority. This he used to ensure the prisoners' freedom to practise their religious duties. He won the right for them to perform the five daily prayers, which he led, and secured a room for use as a mosque. Also, as a commander he received a salary which he spent almost entirely on the mosque and things beneficial for the other prisoners. He was in a group of ninety or so officers, to whom he would give *dars* or religious instruction. Conditions were hard in the camp, and the winters long and dark and extremely cold. In this way he endeavoured to boost the prisoners' morale.

Mustafa Yalçın, whose description of Bediuzzaman at the Pasinler Front is quoted above, was already at the camp when one day to his amazement he saw that Bediuzzaman had been brought there. Among his recollections, he says:

> On our arriving there, they said that some prisoners had arrived from the Eastern Front. We all gathered outside in the camp with interest. There were a lot of prisoners, but there were two they were bringing from the other side and keeping a close eye

on. I looked and suddenly saw that these were Mullah Said and one of his students, whom we called İznikli Osman. He was carrying something like a trunk; it had Ustādh's books in it. He did not allow anyone other than Osman to be with him. Osman saw to his needs. He was wounded. He had been wounded in the leg. They treated it there. They put him in a dormitory.

It was terribly cold. You could not tell day from night. [In the summer] the sun did not set. And there as well, Mullah Said Efendi was not idle at night; he used to go to other camps and read to them, although it was forbidden. He himself used to lead the prayers for us during the day. First of all they intervened and did not let us perform them. Then Ustādh spoke to them and they allowed us a bit more freedom. They did not want too many of us to gather together at the same time. We used to call Bediuzzaman 'Head of Religious Affairs'. He used to explain religion even to the Russian guards. The Russian officers would harass those of them who listened. Mullah Said Efendi always boosted our morale. "Do not worry", he used to say. "We shall be saved." I never knew him to sleep at night there. He always read and took notes. He would say to us: "These will be Muslims too, in the future, but they do not know it now." We were never frightened or distressed so long as he was with us.

Mustafa Yalçın went on to describe how one night he escaped along with a group of seventeen other prisoners. Bediuzzaman declined to join them, but among the group was a major who had been trained by him. He acted as their guide, finding the way "from everything from the stars to the moss on the trees." He continued:

Mullah Said was completely fearless. Night and day he strove for Islam. He always used to say: "It is belief in God that is necessary," and, "Belief in God is worth everything".[26]

Another fellow prisoner, Dr M. Asaf Dişçi, recalled that he first saw Bediuzzaman in the town of Kologrif. They were together there for about six months and then Bediuzzaman was sent to another large prison camp further into the interior. In Kologrif they were held in a cinema, and he divided part of it and made it into a mosque. Dr Asaf Dişçi went on to say:

> Because he was the commander of a regiment, the other prisoners used to be very respectful towards him, but he used to say: "I am a *hoja* [teacher]"...He lived very frugally. He would make do with two eggs and a slice of bread a day...His time was always full. He would read his commentary on the Qur'an and teach the prisoners. The officers and men were all extremely deferential towards him...he commanded respect.[27]

Mustafa Bolay, a prisoner who spent six months in the Kosturma camp with Bediuzzaman, stated that the Russians wanted to kill him and that it was the military high command that had specified his being sent to that camp. Bediuzzaman's nephew, Abdurrahman, who wrote a short biography of his uncle, corroborated this claim. He wrote:

> They sent my uncle to Kosturma by way of Van, Julfa, Tiflis, and Kologrif. I wanted to describe in detail all the dangers to which he had been subject at this time—the Russian officers had even wanted to kill him on several occasions, then record that he had committed suicide—but he would not permit it, so I just wrote it briefly.[28]

Both Mustafa Bolay and Mustafa Yalçın also corroborate an event Bediuzzaman was involved in that happened in the prisoner-of-war camp and doubtless contributed to the awe in which he was held by captors and captives alike. It is described in Bediuzzaman's biography, and Necmeddin Şahiner gives a longer version of it from an article by Abdürrahim Zapsu in the magazine *Ehl-i Sünnet*, which is what we give here:

On one occasion, Nicola Nicolayavich, the Czar's uncle who at the same time was commander-in-chief of the Russian forces at the Caucasian Front, came on an inspection of the camp. While on his tour of it, he passed by Bediuzzaman, who was seated. Bediuzzaman paid him no attention and did not so much as stir. The general noticed him, and finding some excuse, passed in front of him a second time. Bediuzzaman still did not rise to his feet. So he passed by him a third time then stopped. He said to him through an interpreter:

War and Captivity

"Do you not know who I am?"

"Yes, I know," replied Bediuzzaman, and told him.

"So why do you insult me?" asked the general.

"Forgive me, but I have not insulted you. I only did as my beliefs commanded me."

"What do your beliefs command?"

"I am a Muslim scholar. There is faith in my heart. A person with faith is superior to a person without. If I had risen to my feet, it would have been disrespectful to my beliefs. Therefore, I did not."

"In which case, you are saying that I am without faith, and you are insulting both myself, and the army of which I am a member, and my nation, and the Czar. A court martial will be set up immediately, and you will be questioned."

A court martial was set up as the general decreed. The Turkish, German, and Austrian officers all came to the headquarters and tried to persuade Bediuzzaman to apologise to the general, but he told them:

> I am eager to travel to the realm of the Hereafter and enter the presence of God's Prophet, and I have to have a passport. I cannot act contrary to my beliefs.

Unable to dispute this reply, they awaited the court's verdict. The examination was completed. Then the decision was given for Bediuzzaman's execution on the grounds of insulting the Czar and the Russian Army.

When the squad arrived to carry out the sentence, Bediuzzaman requested fifteen minutes "to perform his duty." This was to take his ablutions and perform two *rak'ahs* of prayers. The Russian general arrived on the scene while Bediuzzaman was doing this. He suddenly realised his mistake and said to him when he had finished praying:

> Forgive me! I thought you behaved as you did in order to insult me and I acted accordingly. Now I realise you were merely acting as your beliefs required. Your sentence is quashed. You

should be commended for your firmness of belief. Once again, I apologise.²⁹

Bediuzzaman mentioned this incident, which demonstrates his extraordinary personal qualities, in a letter to one of his students written when being held in another prison, Afyon, in 1949. The story had appeared in the newspapers. He wrote:

> The incident which happened while I was a prisoner-of-war is basically true, but I did not describe it in detail because I had no witnesses. I did not know [at first] that the squad had come to execute me; I understood later. And I did not know that the Russian commander had said some things in Russian by way of an apology. That is to say, the Muslim captain who was present and told the newspapers of the incident understood that the commander had said repeatedly: "Forgive me! Forgive me!"³⁰

In the spring of 1918, Bediuzzaman found a way to escape amid the confusion following the Bolshevik Revolution. In later years, he wrote an evocative description of his "temporary awakening" in the winter darkness of the days preceding his escape, and the almost miraculous ease with which it was accomplished. The following is a translation of part of the piece, which forms a section of the Twenty-Sixth Flash.

> In the First World War, I was a prisoner in the distant province of Kosturma in Northern Russia. There was a small mosque belonging to the Tatars beside the famous River Volga. I used to become wearied among my friends, the other officers. I craved solitude, yet I could not wander about outside without permission. Then they took me on bail to the Tatar quarter, to that small mosque on the banks of the Volga. I used to sleep there alone. Spring was close. I used to be very wakeful during the long, long nights of that northern land; the sad plashing of the Volga and the mirthless patter of the rain and the melancholy sighing of the wind of those dark nights in that dark exile had temporarily roused me from a deep sleep of heedlessness. I did not yet consider myself old, but all those who had experienced the Great War had become old. For there were days that, as though manifesting the verse: "A day that will turn

the hair of children grey" (Qur'an, 73:17), made even children old. While I was forty years old, I felt myself to be eighty. In those long, dark nights of sorrowful exile and melancholic state, I despaired of life and of my homeland. I looked at my powerlessness and aloneness, and my hope failed.

Then, while in that state, succour arrived from the All-Wise Qur'an; my tongue said: "God is enough for us; and how excellent a guardian is He" (Qur'an, 3:173).

And weeping, my heart cried out: "I am a stranger, I am alone, I am weak, I am powerless: I seek mercy, I seek forgiveness, I seek help from You, O my God!"

And, thinking of my old friends in my homeland, and imagining myself dying in exile there, like Niyazi Misri, my spirit poured forth these lines:

Fleeing the world's grief,
Taking flight with ardour and longing,
Opening my wings to the void,
Crying with each breath, Friend! Friend!
It was searching for its friends.

Anyway, my weakness and impotence became such potent intercessors and means at the Divine Court on that melancholy, pitiful, separation-afflicted, long night in exile that I still wonder at it. For several days later I escaped in the most unexpected manner, on my own, not knowing Russian, across a distance that would have taken a year on foot. I was saved in a wondrous fashion through Divine favour, which was bestowed as a consequence of my weakness and impotence. Then, passing through Warsaw and Austria, I reached Istanbul, so that to be saved in this way so easily was quite extraordinary. I completed the long flight with an ease and facility that even the boldest and most cunning Russian-speakers could not have accomplished.

That night in the mosque on the banks of the Volga made me decide to pass the rest of my life in caves. Enough now of mixing in this social life of people! Since finally I would enter the grave alone, I said that from now on I would choose solitude in order to become accustomed to it.

But, regretfully, things of no consequence like my many and serious friends in Istanbul, and the glittering worldly life there, and in particular the fame and honour granted me, which were far greater than my due, made me temporarily forget my decision. It was as though that night in exile was a luminous blackness in my life's eye, and the glittering white daytime of Istanbul, a lightless white in it. It could not see ahead, it still slumbered. Until two years later, Ghawth al-Jīlānī opened my eyes once more with his book *Futūḥ al-Ghayb*.[31]

Notes

1. Danişmend, iv, 420, 427, 431.
2. Abdurrahman, *Tarihçe*, 36.
3. Shaw and Shaw, *History*, ii, 315-317.
4. According to a *curriculum vitae* while a member of the *Darü'l-Hikmeti'l-İslamiye* in October 1921, Bediuzzaman "first joined the Imperial Army as a regimental mufti," and secondly as a regimental commander. See, S. Albayrak, unpaged Appendix to *Son Devrin İslam Akademisi*, Istanbul 1973.
5. Nursi, *Emirdağ Lahikası*, ii, 13; Şahiner, *Said Nursi*, 160-1.
6. Ahlatlı İsmail Hakkı Arslan, in *Son Şahitler*, v, 236-7.
7. Mustafa Yalçın, in *Son Sahitler*, ii, 21-22.
8. *Tarihçe*, 99.
9. *Ishārāt al-I'jāz*, 11 (Eng. tr. *Signs of Miraculousness. The Inimitability of the Qur'an's Conciseness*. Istanbul: Sözler Publications, 2004, 19).
10. Ibid., 7-8 (Eng. tr.: *Signs of Miraculousness*, 14-15); *Tarihçe*, 99-100.
11. See, Nursi, *Mektûbat*, 343 (Eng. tr. *Letters 1928-1932*. New edn. Istanbul: Sözler Publications, forthcoming 2009, 424); Şahiner, *Said Nursi*, 73; *Tarihçe*, 48.
12. Recent research suggests that Bediuzzaman fought at the Pasinler front for six months or so from the time of the first Russian invasion in October 1914, moving south and arriving in Van around the time of the Armenian revolt in April 1915. At the time of the second invasion he was fighting with his force in the Bitlis and Hizan area.
13. *Tarihçe*, 98; Şahiner, *Said Nursi*, 161.
14. *Tarihçe*, 101; Şahiner, *Said Nursi*, 161.
15. *Ibid.*, 162.
16. *Ibid.*, 162.
17. *Ibid.*, 158-9.
18. *Ibid.*, 162-4.
19. *Tarihçe*, 101.
20. Nursi, *Sikke-i Tasdik-i Gaybî*, 124; Şahiner, *Said Nursi*, 168.
21. Ubeyd was the son of Bediuzzaman's eldest sister, Dürriye.

22. Ali Çavuş, "Erek Dağında Bir İslam Mücahidi," *İttihad Gazetesi*, No. 181, 20 Nisan (April) 1971, as quoted in Şahiner, *Said Nursi*, 169-174.
23. Sıddık Alp, in *Son Şahitler*, iv, 347.
24. Molla Münevver, in *Son Şahitler*, i, 80-1.
25. Şahiner, article in *Zaman Gazetesi*, 28 Ocak 1992, p.12.
26. Mustafa Yalçın, in *Son Şahitler*, ii, 23-4.
27. Dr M. Asaf Dişçi, in *Son Şahitler*, i, 189-190.
28. Şahiner, *Son Şahitler*, i, 78-9; Abdurrahman, *Tarihçe*, 38.
29. Abdürrahim Zapsu, in *Ehl-i Sünnet Mecmuası*, vol. 2, No. 46, 15 Teşrin-i Evvel (October) 1948, quoted in, Nursi, *Şualar*, 442-3 (Eng. tr.: *Rays*, 521); Şahiner, *Said Nursi*, 174-5; *Tarihçe*, 103-4.
30. Nursi, *Şualar*, 441 (Eng. tr.: *Rays*, 520).
31. Nursi, *Lem'alar*, 224-5 (Eng. tr.: *Flashes*, 299-301); Şahiner, *Said Nursi*, 181-2; *Tarihçe*, 107-8.

8
Return and Appointment to the Darü'l-Hikmeti'l-İslamiye

The Escape and Return Journey

*B*ediuzzaman never described in detail either the manner of his escape or his journey back to Istanbul, nor did he permit his nephew to write it. He travelled by way of Vienna and Sofya, and certainly the last part of the journey was by train. In Sofya he was given a passport by the Military Attaché, which is dated 17 June 1918. It gives these details on the front face:

Name: Said Mirza Efendi
Rank: Honorary Lt Colonel
Detachment: Volunteer Kurdish Cavalry Regiment
Nationality: Ottoman
Point of Departure: Sofya
Destination: Istanbul (Dersaadet)
Reason for journey: Returning from captivity
Date: 17 June 1918

The back of the passport bears a copy of the photograph taken by the German authorities, and states that the train fare is to be charged to the army's account.[1]

Bediuzzaman's arrival in Istanbul was announced in several of the newspapers. The *Tanin* dated 25 June 1918 carried this short announcement:

> Bediuzzaman Said-i Kürdi Efendi, one of the Kurdistan *'ulamā'* who fought in the War on the Caucasian Front together with his students and fell prisoner to the Russians, has recently arrived back in our city.[2]

Istanbul

Bediuzzaman was given a hero's welcome on his return to Istanbul. Enver Pasha introduced him to the leading military personnel in the War Ministry saying: "Do you see this *hoja*? This was the person who withstood the Russian Cossacks in the East!" He received invitations from prominent pashas and dignitaries and was also visited by them. He was offered various positions and honours and was awarded a War Medal. Mullah Süleyman, one of his students, recounted the following exchange:

> I read of Bediuzzaman's return in the *Tanin*, and visited him in Sultan Ahmet and kissed his hand. Later Enver Pasha, the Minister of War, invited him to visit the War Ministry. He said to him there: "How are you? What are you doing these days, hoja?" Bediuzzaman replied: "If you are offering me work for some worldly gain, I do not want it. But if any duties related to knowledge and learning fall to me, that would be different. But for now I am in need of rest, for I received much harsh treatment and suffered great hardship while I was a prisoner."[3]

Also at this time Bediuzzaman was endeavouring to have his commentary on the Qur'an, *Signs of the Miraculous*, published. Wanting to show his appreciation of the work and of Bediuzzaman's service in the War, Enver Pasha offered to publish it for him. So Bediuzzaman suggested he might get the paper. Not easy to find in war-time Turkey. Thus, Enver Pasha provided the paper for *Signs of the Miraculous*, and Bediuzzaman had it published.[4]

Bediuzzaman was given no opportunity to rest and regain his strength. On 12 August 1918, the Darü'l-Hikmeti'l-İslamiye, a learned council or Islamic academy, was set up in association with the Şeyhü'l-İslam's Office, and without his knowledge Bediuzzaman was appointed as the nominee of the Army. However, in order to understand better the problems this institution faced and Bediuzzaman's attitude towards it, and indeed all his thought and activities at this time, we include here a brief outline of the main events of these difficult years.

An Outline of Events from 1918 to 1922

By bringing the Ottoman Empire into the War on the side of the Central Powers, the leaders of the Committee of Union and Progress had secured its final demise. For on its defeat the victors and Britain in particular were able to realise their long-cherished designs of finally breaking up the Ottoman Empire and vanquishing their ancient foe, the Turk. On hearing the terms of the Mudros Armistice, signed by Turkey and Britain on 30 October 1918, the Sultan was heard to murmur: "This is not an armistice; it is an unconditional surrender."[5] The day following its signature, the leading members of the CUP fled the country for Berlin. On 13 November a fleet of fifty-five ships belonging to the victors anchored off Istanbul, including four Greek warships, which was contrary to the agreement, and on 8 December, a military administration was set up. While there could have been nothing more galling for the Muslim Turks to see than the Allied forces enter Istanbul as conquerors, the Ottoman Greeks, Jews, and Armenians of the city greeted them rapturously. The French General, Franchet Despérey even rode through the streets of Istanbul to the French Embassy on a white horse, in the style of some conquering king or emperor.[6]

A number of secret war-time agreements had been signed by the Entente Powers concerning the partition of the Ottoman Empire.[7] When Russia renounced her claims following the Bolshevik Revolution in 1917, her place was taken by Italy. And when, in a timely move, the Greek Prime Minister, Venizelos, brought his country into the War the same year, it was for the promise of Izmir and a portion of Aegean Turkey. The same area had, incidentally, already been promised to the Italians.

Thus, on the signing of the Armistice, the French occupied parts of southern and south-eastern Turkey, while in February 1919, their troops entered Istanbul as mentioned above. On 29 April, Italian troops landed at Antalya. The British held the Dardanelles and other places of strategic importance. Plans had

Return and Appointment to the Darü'l-Hikmeti'l-İslamiye 161

been made to set up a Kurdish state in eastern Anatolia. And the Armenians prepared to set up an Armenian state in the north-east of the country, while the Greeks of the Black Sea region aimed to resurrect the Greek state of Pontus. Indeed, the ultimate aim of Venizelos and many Greeks was to recreate a Greater Byzantine Empire based in Istanbul—the ancient capital of Constantinople. And when on 15 May 1919 the Greek Army landed at Izmir with the assistance of French, British, and American warships, it provided the spark that ignited the Muslim inhabitants of Anatolia to resist the invaders[8] and finally after more than two years of struggle and war, to rid their country of all aggressors.

But there was no united front in the face of the occupation. While various groups were based and fighting in Anatolia, the National Forces had many supporters in Istanbul, among whom was Bediuzzaman, many of the Deputies in the Parliament, the Sultan[9] and a number of prominent statesmen and *'ulamā'* who opposed it, believing the interests of the Ottoman State would be best served by co-operation and collaboration with the occupying Powers. The supporters of the National Forces gaining strength in Istanbul, notably in the new parliament opened in January 1920, led to a reoccupation of the city by British troops in March, followed by large-scale arrests and deportations. Under considerable pressure from the British, the Sultan dissolved the parliament the following month, and a *fatwā* was extracted from a specially installed Şeyhü'l-İslam declaring the nationalists to be rebels and the killing of them a duty.[10] An army was then formed to fight them.

In Ankara, which became the centre of the national movement, a new representative assembly was formed, and on 23 April 1920, the Turkish Grand National Assembly had its formal opening. But it was only upon the Istanbul government's agreeing to sign the Treaty of Sèvres in August 1920 that the nationalist cause obtained the almost total support of the Turkish people. Enraged by the signature of this ill-gotten and vengeful document, which purported to legitimise the carving up of Turkey itself between the Powers mentioned above, they determined to liberate their country from its foreign invaders.[11]

It is beyond the scope of this book to describe the course of the War of Independence, but it may be noted that up to the Armistice, the Turks had been engaged in various wars since 1909, and by 1920 were exhausted and impoverished, with the male population decimated. On their defeat the Ottoman army had been disarmed and disbanded by the victors. Against the heaviest odds, inspired and sustained by their faith in God and the religion of Islam, the Turks won a truly remarkable victory. Indeed, religion and men of religion played a role of great importance in the war, which was proclaimed a *jihād*. One of the main aims was considered by all, including the Ankara government, to be the saving of the Caliph and Sultan from enemy hands.[12] Their victory was recognised by the Mudanya Armistice, signed by Britain and Turkey on 11 October 1922, and received international recognition in the Treaty of Lausanne, signed 24 July 1923.

The Turkish victory in the War of Independence was not simply the thwarting of the imperialist designs of a number of European Powers. As has already been suggested, the matter must be seen from a much wider perspective: for a thousand years the Turks had been "the standard-bearers of the Islamic World" against the Christian West. The word Turk was synonymous with Islam. When they were victorious against the West, it was in the name of Islam, and when they suffered defeat, it was at Islam, which they represented, that the blows had very often been directed. And so, when the Ottomans failed to match the material progress of the West and as a result became progressively subject to it, this was interpreted by Christian Europe as being proof of the superiority of Western civilization. And it was also seen as a kind of justification for their greed, as they vied with one another over the disposal of "the sick man of Europe's" estate.

British imperialism considered Islam as the greatest obstacle. British efforts to conquer, subdue, and divide the Islamic world had been countered with some success by the Ottomans' caliphate policy and movement for Islamic Unity. The revolt of the Arabs against the Ottomans during the First World War and the subsequent setting up of separate Arab states was one result of Britain's sustained and intense espionage and propaganda campaign against the Ottomans.

Thus, the defeat of the Ottomans in 1918 was seen by the victors as the final triumph of the West over Islam, of Western civilization over Islamic civilization, of the cross over the crescent. It is in this light that the occupation of Istanbul should be seen,[13] and also the extremely harsh terms of the peace treaties which were far harsher than those imposed on the other defeated nations.[14]

But the desire of the British and French in particular to exact revenge on their ancient foe did not stop there. Appointing officials to oversee the various ministries, the government itself was no more than a puppet. And having for many years spurred on the Christian minorities to rebel against the Ottoman state, they now proceeded to encourage them to take over all positions of authority in local government and state officialdom. This discrimination against Muslim Turks in their own country went so far that only Christian children could attend state schools. The Armenians and Greeks also massacred thousands of Muslims, while the occupying forces turned a blind eye.[15]

The problems associated with the occupation of foreign armies are many. But in this case the situation was exacerbated by these deep-seated attitudes of the victors. Here it was not only the gall of defeat and excesses of occupying troops relaxing in "the flesh-pots of Constantinople" that had to be tolerated. An insidious policy of Christianization through attempts to discredit Islam had been implemented. Also attempts to sap the moral fibre of the Turks through the deliberate encouragement of immorality, the drinking of alcohol, and other "evils of civilization" had to be combated. As Bediuzzaman later told the deputies in the Ankara National Assembly: "Although for a long time the Western world has been attacking the Islamic world with its civilization, philosophy, sciences, missionaries, and all the means at its disposal and has conquered it materially, it has not been able to conquer it in religion."[16] Now, it seemed, the stage was set for it to pursue this inauspicious and unachievable aim.

Bediuzzaman and the Darü'l-Hikmeti'l-İslamiye

It may be seen from the above description how great the need was for a learned body with the authority of the Darü'l-Hikmet. The bill proposing its establishment had been introduced in Parliament at the beginning of the year, and it was envisaged that it would perform various functions. Just as it was to find solutions for problems confronting the Islamic world, so was it to answer in a scholarly manner the attacks made on it, combating attempts to discredit the religion of Islam. It was to have the power to refer the open flouting of Islamic morality to the relevant authorities. Furthermore, it was to serve the Muslim people of Turkey, answering questions, supplying information about internal and external dangers, and generally meeting religious needs with various publications. To this end, branches were opened in all provinces and major towns. At any one time, it was composed of nine members, a principal, and various officers. Mehmed Akif was appointed as its first secretary (*Başkâtip*). The members, all of whom were prominent '*ulamā*', were divided into three committees: jurisprudence (*fiqh*), ethics (*akhlāq*), and theology (*kalām*).[17] Bediuzzaman remained as a member of the Darü'l-Hikmet for the four years of its short existence. It was closed in November 1922 when the Sultanate was abolished by the Ankara Government. However, as we shall see, despite the great need for the Darü'l-Hikmet, and the efforts of its members, the situation did not allow for the full accomplishment of its aims.

A number of Darü'l-Hikmet documents concerning Bediuzzaman are still extant. Below are the Şeyhü'l-İslam's memo concerning his appointment to the rank of *Mahrec*,[18] and the Caliph's edict ratifying the appointment. Firstly is the War Ministry's request that he be appointed, signed by Enver Pasha, referred to in the Şeyhü'l-İslam's memo.

> Exalted permission is requested that, on account of his patriotic efforts in mobilizing the tribes to fight and his distinguished and witnessed public-spirited services to the fatherland, Bediuzzaman Said Efendi, who took part in the fight against

the Russians at Bitlis, was taken prisoner, and has recently returned, be appointed to a rank in the religious establishment conformable with the dignity of his learning.

> 10 Ağustos 1334 (10 August 1918)
> Deputy of the Commander-in-Chief
> and Minister of War,
> Enver[19]

The Office of the Şeyhü'l-İslam
212

Honoured Sir,
It has been made known by the Illustrious Ministry of War that Bediuzzaman Said-i Kurdi, who took part in the battle with the Russians at Bitlis, was taken prisoner, and has recently returned, has been honoured with a grade in the religious establishment on account of his patriotic efforts in mobilizing the tribes to fight and his distinguished and witnessed public-spirited services to the fatherland. The Imperial Rescript considering it suitable that the above-mentioned, who has recently been appointed to the Darü'l-Hikmeti'l-İslamiye, be honoured with the rank of *Mahrec*, has been set out and presented. In whatever way, therefore, the Caliph's Imperial Decree is concerned with the matter, it is evident, Sir, haste will be made to carry it out.

> 17 Zi'l-Ka'de 1336/24 Ağustos 1334 (24 August 1918)
> Şeyhü'l-İslam
> Musa Kazım

The Office of the Şeyhü'l-İslam Mehmed Vahiduddin

Bediuzzaman Said Efendi, a member of the Darü'l-Hikmeti'l-İslamiye, has been awarded the rank of *Mahrec*.

The Office of the Şeyhü'l-İslam is charged with carrying out this Imperial Decree.

> 18 Zi'l-Qa'de 1336/25 Ağustos 1334
> Şeyhü'l-İslam
> Musa Kazım[20]

On his return to Istanbul, Bediuzzaman had been joined by his nephew, Abdurrahman. Born in 1903 in Nurs the son of Bediuzzaman's elder brother Mullah Abdullah, he was very intelligent and able. He was described by Bediuzzaman as a student, an assistant, a friend and a spiritual son. He remained with his uncle for a number of years, whose biography he wrote during this time. It is forty-five pages in length and forms the main source for his early life. It was published in Istanbul in 1919.[21] The following is a passage from an appendix to it describing Bediuzzaman's appointment to the Darü'l-Hikmet, and something of his attitude towards it and his resulting activities.

> I have described the life of my uncle, Said-i Kurdi, the author of the *Lemeât Collection*, briefly in an independent work. But for the past two and a half years they have burdened him with the duty of the Darü'l-Hikmeti'l-İslamiye. He used to say: "I would have given it up, but I want to render an account to the nation." And now I am writing a few words about how my uncle wanted to render an account through his duties in the Darü'l-Hikmeti'l-İslamiye.
>
> It was two years ago in 1334 (1918) that without his consent, my uncle was appointed as a member of the Darü'l-Hikmeti'l-İslamiye. But because he was very shaken by his captivity, he obtained leave not to take up his duty. In fact, he tried to resign on many occasions, but his friends would not let him. So he continued, and now it has been two and a half years.
>
> From the beginning I noticed that he did not spend anything on himself over and above what was necessary. In reply to those who asked him: "Why do you live so frugally?", he would say: "I want to follow the majority of Muslims. The majority can only obtain this much. I do not want to follow the extravagant minority." And after putting aside the minimum amount from his salary from the Darü'l-Hikmet, he would give me the remainder, saying: "Look after this!" But, relying on my uncle's kindness towards me and his contempt for possessions, I spent all of the money which had been left over in a year without telling him. So he said to me: "It was not appropriate for us to spend that money, it belonged to the nation. Why did you

spend it? But since this is how the matter stands, I dismiss you from the post of Deputy for Expenditure and I appoint myself!" After this, he put aside twenty liras a month for me, and fifteen for himself. But other expenses were included in his fifteen. That is to say, ten or twelve liras used to remain over for him per month. He used to put aside any money that remained over and above this.

Some time passed and it occurred to him to have twelve of his works printed in the name of religion. He gave the money which had accumulated, about one hundred liras, to cover the expense of having the works printed. Then with the exception of only one or two small ones, he had them distributed free. I asked him why he had not had them sold, and he said to me: "It is permissible for me to take only just enough to live on out of the salary. Anything more than that is the property of the nation. In this way I am returning it."

His service in the Darü'l-Hikmeti'l-İslamiye was all in the form of personal enterprises like that, for he perceived certain obstacles in working together with the others there. People who were acquainted with him knew that he had donned his shroud and was risking his life. It was for this reason that he resisted and stood firm as a rock in the Darü'l-Hikmeti'l-İslamiye. He would not let the foreigners' influence make the Darü'l-Hikmet a tool for itself. He held out against the wrong *fatwās* and opposed them. When a current harmful to Islam appeared, he used to publish a work to destroy it.[22]

As may be seen from this, Bediuzzaman's main service in the Darü'l-Hikmet—and indeed the greater part of his activities in this period—was countering the divisive and corrupting influence of the occupying forces, for the situation in Istanbul under occupation did not permit the Darü'l-Hikmet to fulfil its important functions properly. There were several reasons for this. On being asked on one occasion why he had nothing to do with politics during this period, he replied: "I take refuge with God from Satan and politics. Yes, Istanbul politics are like Spanish flu; they make a person delirious. We do not act of our own accord, but at the agency of another. Europe puffs, and we dance."[23] That is to say, at a time when the British were using every means to utilise all areas of power and influence in Istanbul for their own ends, Bediuzzaman worked to neutralise their influence as far as the Darü'l-Hikmet was concerned, even if it lessened the effectiveness of the institution itself. And in another work he pointed out that it was because it lacked any real power that the Darü'l-Hikmet could not put an end to serious wrongs such as immoral conduct, the drinking of alcohol and gambling, whereas the Government in Anatolia stopped them with one command.[24]

Another reason Bediuzzaman gave for the Darü'l-Hikmet being unable to perform its duties adequately was lack of harmony between its members. Their personal qualities prevented "a communal spirit" from emerging. The "I's" did not become a "We".[25] In fact, Bediuzzaman had long favoured the setting-up of a learned body such as the Darü'l-Hikmet, made up of specialists in different fields and based on the principle of consultation, to tackle the problems facing not only the Ottoman Empire, but the Islamic world as well. In *Sünûhat*, published in 1919-20, he discussed this in connection with the Caliphate, a subject of urgent debate at the time. Briefly, having stated that the Sultanate and Caliphate were inseparable, and that the Office of Grand Vizier represented the former and the Office of Şeyhü'l-İslam the latter, he pointed out that in modern, complex society and in the face of the myriad problems facing the Islamic world, it was beyond the capacity of a single individual to perform the duty of Şeyhü'l-İslam effectively. A voice of such strength and authority was required at that time that it could only be supplied by a learned council such as one described above. He suggested that with the addition of further *'ulamā'*, both Ottoman and from other parts of the Islamic world, an up-graded Darü'l-Hikmeti'l-İslamiye could form its basis.[26]

Bediuzzaman's efforts, and success, in preventing the Darü'l-Hikmet from being subverted and becoming a mere puppet in the hands of the British should not be underestimated. For it should be remembered that the British were all-powerful in Istanbul and exerted overwhelming pressure on the Sultan and those in positions of authority to have their will carried out. Also, there were severe differences of opinion among Turks—including the *'ulamā'*—as to solutions to Turkey's predicament. These ranged from acceptance of the partition of Turkey, through various mandates or protectorates, to national sovereignty and independence. Furthermore, manipulation of the Caliphate played an important part in Britain's imperialist games. That Bediuzzaman was held in the greatest respect by other *'ulamā'* is attested to in the recollections of Professor Ali Nihad Tarlan, who visited him on several occasions during these years, here one night in the Medresetü'l-Mütehassisin in Yavuz Selim:

> Bediuzzaman was wearing grey. He spoke of many matters that night, scholarly and religious. I'll tell you how he greeted me there; he met me saying: "Welcome, my dear brother!" He was always thinking, always reflecting. He was a superhuman person. Babanzade Ahmed Naim Bey said of him: "Whenever Bediuzzaman started to speak in the Darü'l-Hikmet, we used to just listen to him in wonder."[27]

Fatwā and Counter-*Fatwā*

As was mentioned when describing the outline of events above, following their reoccupation of Istanbul in March 1920, the British forced Şeyhü'l-İslam Dürrizade Abdullah Efendi—installed after his predecessor, Haydarizade İbrahim Efendi had resigned rather than sign it—to issue a *fatwā* declaring the various nationalist groups in Anatolia to be rebels and the killing of them the bounden duty of Muslims. In his book on the fundamental role of religion and men of religion in the national struggle, which includes a short section on Bediuzzaman, Kadir Mısıroğlu describes both the coercion by which the *fatwā* was extracted by the British, and in some detail the counter-*fatwā* signed by 84 muftis in Anatolia, and a further 68 *'ulamā'*, of whom 11 were deputies in the Ankara Assembly. This counter-*fatwā* stated that a *fatwā* issued under enemy duress was null and void, and declared the national struggle to be a *jihād*, a Holy War.²⁸

Bediuzzaman also opposed the Şeyhü'l-İslam's *fatwā*, and said:

> A *fatwā* issued by a government and Şeyhü'l-İslam's Office in a country under enemy occupation and under the command and constraint of the British is defective, and should not be heeded. Those operating against the enemy invasion are not rebels. The *fatwā* must be rescinded.²⁹

In addition, Bediuzzaman opposed it on the learned grounds that since it comprised a legal judgement, the claims of both parties should have been considered before judgement had been passed. He wrote:

> It is not only a *fatwā* that it might be justified; it is a *fatwā* that comprises a legal judgement. The difference between a *fatwā* and a legal judgement is that its subject is general, not specific, nor is it binding. But a legal judgement is both specific and binding. As for this *fatwā*, it is both specific—whoever looks at it will necessarily understand its purpose, and it is binding, because its ultimate cause is to impel the mass of Muslims against them [the National Forces].
>
> This *fatwā* comprises a legal judgement, but in a legal judgement it is imperative that the enemies [both sides] hear it. Anatolia should also have been made to speak. The *fatwā* could have been issued after judgement had been passed on the assertions and counterclaims by a committee of politicians and *'ulamā'* taking into account the interests of Islam. In fact, a number of things are being reversed these days. Opposites are changing their names and being substituted for each other; tyranny is being called justice; *jihād*, insurrection; and captivity, freedom.³⁰

Green Crescent Society and Madrasah Teachers' Association

Bediuzzaman was involved with other organizations and societies at this time, one of which was the Green Crescent Society, founded on 5 March 1920. He was a founder member of this non-political society, set up specifically to combat the spread of alcoholic consumption and other harmful addictions, which were being deliberately encouraged by the occupying forces. Other members were the Şeyhü'l-İslam, Haydarizade İbrahim Efendi, Dr Tevfik Rüştü Aras, Eşref Edip and Fahreddin Kerim Gökay.[31] Answering questions put to him in 1975 by Necmeddin Şahiner, Fahreddin Gökay quoted some minutes taken at a meeting of the Society in which "Said Efendi" [Bediuzzaman] suggested giving priority to the writing and free distribution of articles and pamphlets.[32]

Another society with which Bediuzzaman was involved was the Madrasah Teachers' Association (*Cemiyet-i Müderrisîn*), founded 15 February 1335/1919. Its main aims were "to undertake the necessary enterprises for raising the teaching profession to the high level that is in keeping with the the Islamic nation (*millah*) and civilization,...to produce students for the *'ulamā'* profession who would be thoroughly informed of the Islamic sciences and have knowledge of the modern sciences sufficient for the needs of the times...To instil the truths of religion and elevated conduct of Islam in Muslims' spirits, strengthen bonds of brotherhood, encourage personal enterprise, and to protect the rights of *madrasah* teachers." This society was subsequently transformed into the Society for the Advancement of Islam [24 November, 1919], with which Bediuzzaman did not appear to have been connected, as opposed to many of the initial members.[33] A number of the leading *'ulamā'* of the time belonged to the Madrasah Teachers' Association, including Mustafa Safvet Efendi, Mustafa Sabri—twice Şeyhü'l-İslam, and Mehmet Atıf Efendi. The last two undertook together with Bediuzzaman the task of replying to articles attacking Islam that appeared in the press. Bediuzzaman included some of his replies on such subjects as polygamy, slavery, the position of women, and the representation of the human form in some of his subsequent works.[34] They are most reasonable and convincing, and by way of example we include here a short reply concerning polygamy and slavery:

The ordinances of Islam are of two sorts: the first consists of those on which the Sharī'ah is based. This sort is pure good. The other is the modified Sharī'ah; that is, it takes matters that are cruel and savage, and as the lesser of two evils, rectifies them and makes them practicable and conformable with human nature. It puts them in a form that is consonant with time and place, thus making it possible to move on to pure good. For it would necessitate reversing human nature to suddenly do away with a matter that governs it. Thus, the Sharī'ah did not impose slavery; it modified it so that it ceased being of a savage form and made it one that would lead to complete freedom; it adjusted and rectified it. Also, the Sharī'ah did not raise the number of wives from one to four—although polygamy is conformable with nature, reason and wisdom. It rather reduced the number to four from eight or nine. And regarding polygamy, it imposed such conditions that it can cause no harm at all in being practised. Even if there is some bad in it, it is the lesser of two evils, and the lesser of two evils is relative justice. Alas, every situation in this world cannot be pure good![35]

Bediuzzaman's Ill-Health

As his nephew described above, it was only with reluctance that Bediuzzaman had taken up his position in the Darü'l-Hikmet. He had been severely shaken by the War, but because of his sense of responsibility towards "the nation", he undertook the duties imposed on him as a way of serving it. Abdurrahman wrote that he asked his uncle why he had been shaken to such a great extent, and Bediuzzaman replied:

> I can bear my own sorrows, but the sorrows arising from Islam's grief have crushed me. I feel each blow delivered at the world of Islam to be delivered first at my own heart. That is why I have been so shaken. But I see a light; it will cause those sorrows to be forgotten, God willing.[36]

Among the extant documents of the Darü'l-Hikmet are two requests for leave of absence on grounds of ill-health. We include them here together with an identity paper dated 26 September

1921, and Bediuzzaman's answers to an official questionnaire dated 17 October 1921. They are all included in the appendix of Sadık Albayrak's book on the Darü'l-Hikmet.

> To the Illustrious Şeyhü'l-İslam
> A Petition:
> The nervous debility with which I am afflicted as a result of both the searing difficulties I endured day and night for two years on the Caucasian Front in the present War in defence of religion and country, and the intolerable hardships I suffered in two and a half years of captivity, and the regretful conditions which we witness at the present time, has turned into neurasthenia.
>
> As required in accordance with the attached report giving the results of the doctors' examination stating that five to six months' change of air is imperative, I request the permission of the Illustrious Şeyhü'l-İslam for leave for about six months' change of air.
>
> And the command belongs...
>
> 19 Nisan 1335 (19 April 1919)
Bediuzzaman Said
Member of the Darü'l-Hikmet [37]

> Member Said Efendi's request, corroborated by a doctor's report, for five months' leave of absence for a change of air on account of his having neurasthenia has been accepted. Since there is no obstacle in his leaving his post for that period, his petition has been noted accordingly. 17 Receb 1337 / 19 Nisan 1335 (19 April 1919)"
>
> To the Illustrious Şeyhü'l-İslam
> Illustrious and Munificent Excellency,
> Since, as the attached report makes clear, the illness from which I suffered earlier has returned and I am at present undergoing treatment by a specialist doctor in Sarıyer, I request that permission be granted for three months leave of absence for treatment and a change of air as the report requires.
>
> 13 Eylül 1337 (13 September 1921)
Said
Member of the Darü'l-Hikmeti'l-İslamiye

Document Concerning the *Curriculum Vitae* of Officials, Clerks, and Employees of the Ottoman State

Price ten *kuruş*

1. My name is Said, I am known as Bediuzzaman, my father's name was Mirza. I am not connected to any well-known family. I belong to the Shafi'i school of law. I am a subject of the Ottoman State.
2. My date of birth was 1293 (1877). My place of birth was the village of Nurs in the district of İsparit, attached to the district of Hizan in the province of Bitlis.
3. I made my preliminary studies under my brother for about two years in the above-mentioned sub-district of İsparit. Later I completed the customary course of study in the study-circle of Shaykh Muhammad Celali in the town of [Doğu] Bayezit in the province of Erzurum. Later on I started to study in Van. For about fifteen years I was occupied with studying various sciences. I took part in the recent War on its declaration as a volunteer and regimental commander. I was taken prisoner by the Russians at Bitlis. I escaped from captivity and returned to Istanbul. I have been a member of the Darü'l-Hikmeti'l-İslamiye since it was first founded. I lost the diploma I received from the above-mentioned Muhammad Celali Efendi while I was a prisoner-of-war. I am the author of seventeen works. Firstly, in Arabic, are the Qur'anic commentary *Ishārāt al-I'jāz*, the treatises on logic called *Ta'līqāt* and *Kızıl İjāz*, and *al-Khuṭba al-Shāmiyya*. And I have such written works in Turkish as *Nokta, Şuaat, Sünûhat, Münâzarat, Muhâkemat, Tulu'at, Leme'ât, Rumûz, İşârât, Hutuvat-ı Sitte, İki [Mekteb-i] Musibetin Şehadetnamesi* and *Hakikat Çekirdekleri*. Most of my works are written as admonishments for the guidance of Muslims and to awaken the heedless. Just as I speak Turkish and Kurdish, so I also read and write Arabic and Persian. No copies remain of *Rumûz, İşârât, Hutuvat-i Sitte, İki [Mekteb-i] Musibetin Şehadetnamesi, al-Khuṭba al-Shāmiyya, Münâzarat,*

Muhâkemat, and *Ta'līqāt*. I have no certificate or diploma in science or other subjects.

4. On the declaration of the Great War, I joined the Army for the honour of it as a volunteer, first as a regimental *müfti*, and secondly as a regimental commander. While performing this duty, I was taken prisoner by the Russians at Bitlis. All these duties were undertaken as a volunteer. On my return to Istanbul from captivity, as a gratuity, the Ministry of War gave me fifty liras a month for three months making a total of one hundred and fifty liras. I have one War Medal. I have no other rank or decoration. I have no foreign decorations or medals. I was appointed to the Darü'l-Hikmeti'l-İslamiye on a salary of five thousand *kuruş* in accordance with the Imperial Rescript dated 26 Shawwāl 1336, and as required by the Imperial Decree dated 18 Dhī al-Qa'dah 1336, I was honoured with the rank of *Mahrec*....

17 Teşrin-i Evvel 1337 (17 October 1921)
Bediuzzaman Said
Member of the Darü'l-Hikmeti'l-İslamiye[38]

A Memorandum of the Ottoman State

Name: Bediuzzaman Said Efendi
Father's name and place of residence: The late Mirza Efendi
Mother's Name: The late Nuriye Hanım
Date and place of birth: 1295 (AH) and 1293 (Rumi) (1877-8), the village of Nurs in the sub-district of Hizan.
Religion (*millah*): Muslim
Profession, title, and eligibility to vote: a member of the Darü'l-Hikmeti'l-İslamiye.
Civil state: single

Features and Place Where Registered

Height: average
Eyes: hazel

Complexion: dark
Distinguishing marks: none
Vilayet: Istanbul
District: Beyoğlu, European Bosphorus
Quarter: Sarıyer
Street: Fıstıklı Bağlar
Number of residence: 18/11
Type of residence: foreigner [not local]. Originally registered in the province of Bitlis, District of Hizan, village of Nurs.

Bediuzzaman Said Efendi whose name, state, and description is written above is a national of the Ottoman Empire, and this document showing that he is recorded on the register of births is duly delivered.

26 Eylül 1337 (26 September 1921)
Ministry of Internal Affairs.

Notes

1. *Tarihçe*, 105-6; Şahiner, *Said Nursi*, 177-8.
2. *Ibid.*, 179-180.
3. Şahiner, *Said Nursi*, 182-3.
4. *Ibid.*, 183; *Şualar*, 385 (Eng. tr.: *Rays*, 453).
5. Y. Bahadıroğlu, *Osmanlı Padişahları Ansiklopedisi*, iii, 783.
6. İbnü'l-Emin İnal, *Son Sadrıazamlar*, iv, 1717-8.
7. Shaw and Shaw, *History*, ii, 320.
8. B. Lewis, *Emergence*, 241-2.
9. Writers sympathetic to the Ottoman dynasty disclaim the official view that Sultan Vahideddin was "a base traitor" and state that on the contrary, he laid the foundations of the War of Independence and used every means at this disposal to further its cause. See, Kadir Mısıroğlu, *Sarıklı Mücahitler*, Istanbul 1980, 40 ff.
10. *Ibid.*, 297-8.
11. Y. Bahadıroğlu, *Osmanlı Padişahları Ansiklopedisi*, iii, 778.
12. Niyazi Berkes, *Türkiye'de Çağdaşlaşma*, Istanbul, 465; B. Lewis, *Emergence*, 251.
13. Shaw and Shaw, *History*, ii, 329.
14. T.Z. Tunaya, *Türkiye'de Siyasal Partiler*, ii, 27.
15. Shaw and Shaw, *History*, ii, 329-330.

16. *Tarihçe*, 126.
17. Sadık Albayrak, *Son Devrin İslam Akademisi, Dar-ül Hikmet-il İslamiye*, İstanbul 1973, 7-9.
18. *Mahrec*: One of the ranks of the *'ulamā'* or religious establishment, it was also known as *Mahrec Mevleviyeti*. *Mahrec Mevleviyeti* was higher than *Kibar-ı Müderrisin*, and lower than *Bilad-ı Hamse Mevlevieyeti*. *Mahrec* was the equivalent of the civil ranks of *Saniye Sınıf-ı Sanisi* and *Mirü'l-Ümeralık*, and of the military rank of *Kaymakamlık*. [Şahiner, *Said Nursi*, 185].
19. S. Albayrak, *Yürüyenler ve Sürünenler* (4th edn.), Istanbul 1989, 148-9.
20. Şahiner, *Said Nursi*, 185-7; S. Albayrak, *Son Devrin*, appendix n.p.
21. Şahiner, *Said Nursi*, 190, 194.
22. Abdurrahman, *Tarihçe-i Hayatin Zeyli*, n.p.
23. Nursi, *Sünûhat*, 48-9.
24. Nursi, "Tuluât," in *Asar-ı Bedi'iyye*, 105.
25. *Ibid.*, 110.
26. Nursi, *Sünûhat*, 36-40; Safa Mürsel, *Bediüzzaman Said Nursi ve Devlet Felsefesi*, 197-8.
27. Ali Nihad Tarlan, in Şahiner, *Aydınlar Konuşuyor*, 162.
28. Kadir Mısıroğlu, *Kurtuluş Savaşında Sarıklı Mücahitler*, Istanbul 1980, 297-307.
29. Şahiner, *Said Nursi*, 238, quoted from Eşref Edip, *Risale-i Nur Muarızları Yazarların İsnadları Hakkında İlmi Bir Tahlil*, Istanbul 1952.
30. Nursi, "Tulu'at," in *Asar-ı Bedi'iyye*, 105-6.
31. Şahiner, *Said Nursi*, 213-214.
32. Prof. Fahreddin Kerim Gökay, in Şahiner, *Aydınlar Konuşuyor*, 158-9.
33. Sadık Albayrak, *Meşrutiyet İslamcılığı ve Siyonizm*, Istanbul 1990, 124-33. See also, Tunaya, *Siyasal Partiler*, ii, 382-3.
34. Şahiner, *Said Nursi*, 227-230.
35. *Ibid.*, 232; Nursi, "Tuluât," in *Asar-ı Bedi'iyye*, 109.
36. Abdurrahman, *Appendix to Bediüzzaman'ın Tarihçe-i Hayatı*, n.p.
37. Also in, Şahiner, *Said Nursi*, 184-5;
38. See also, Şahiner, *Said Nursi*, 188-190.

9

The Supremacy of the Qur'an and Birth of the New Said

"The Strongest Voice will be Islam's"

In the September of 1919 Bediuzzaman had a "true dream" or vision, which he subsequently recorded and included in *Sünûhat*.[1] He tells us that he was greatly distressed at the course of events and was "searching for a light in the dense darkness." In his dream, he was summoned by "a great assembly" made up of representatives of the leading figures of Islam from each century and called upon to give an account of the present state of Islam. Contrary to what might be expected, Bediuzzaman's reply pointed out positive aspects of the defeat, including the strengthening of Islamic brotherhood and the Ottomans being saved from being carried away to a greater extent on "the tyrannical current" of capitalism. Then, in order to show why Islam rejects modern Western civilization, which was epitomised by the ugly and exploitative capitalism and aggressive imperialism of the time, he made a comparison of the principles on which Western and Islamic civilizations are based and their results. This extremely interesting and original exposition was greeted with approval by the Assembly in the dream, and one of the deputies declared:

> Yes, be hopeful! The loudest and strongest voice in the coming upheavals and changes will be that of Islam!

The same comparison of Western and Islamic civilizations appears in different contexts in a number of Bediuzzaman's works of the period. From these and other references to the same subject, we see in greater detail his views on the subject, and also the reasons for the optimism and hope for the future engendered by the dream.

It should be noted firstly that Bediuzzaman frequently pointed out that just as modern civilization was not the product or property of Christianity, neither was decline and retrogression in keeping with Islam: "To consider civilization to be the property of Christianity, which it is not, and to show decline, which is the enemy of Islam, to be its friend, is to suggest that the firmament is revolving in the opposite direction."[2] As we have already seen, Islam enjoins progress and comprises all the necessities of civilization: "I declare with all my strength that there is nothing which is in reality good in civilization that is itself, or what is better than it, not guaranteed either explicitly or implicitly by Islam."[3] And in another work he wrote: "The things known as the virtues of civilization are each a transformed matter of the Sharī'ah."[4] Further to this, Bediuzzaman pointed out that Islam had played a fundamental and significant role in the development of modern civilization:

> I cannot deny this: there are numerous virtues in [modern] civilization, but they are neither the property of Christianity nor the creation of Europe, nor the work of this century; they are everyone's property. They arise from the combined thought of mankind, the laws of the revealed religions, innate need, and in particular from the Islamic revolution brought about by the Sharī'ah of Muḥammad (ṣ)."[5] And in another work he put it in even stronger terms: "The good things and great industrial progress to be seen in Western civilization are entirely reflected and derived from Islamic civilization, the guidance of the Qur'an, and the [other] revealed religions.[6]

However, in the West, the evils of civilization had come to dominate over its beneficial aspects. Bediuzzaman gave two reasons for this. The first was the permissive attitude of Western civilization towards "dissipation" and "the appetites of the flesh", which arose from "not making religion and virtue the principles of civilization." The second was "the appalling inequality in the means of livelihood", which also ultimately resulted from lack of religion. These would eventually lead to its destruction.[7]

Thus, Bediuzzaman predicted that because Western civilization had become distant from true Christianity and was based not on the principles of revealed religion, but on those of Greek and, primarily, Roman philosophy, it would eventually "be dispersed" and "change its form", and make way for the emergence of Islamic civilization. His comparisons, then, are between the "positive" principles and results of revelation, and the "negative" principles and results of philosophy, or between divine guidance (*hudā*) and genius, meaning reason (*dahā'*), as he sometimes calls them. Western civilization he describes as follows:

> It takes as its point of support force, which shows itself as aggression. Its aim and purpose is benefit and self-interest, after which everyone jostles and pushes without restraint. Its principle in life is conflict, which is manifested as contention and discord. The tie between different groups is racialism and negative nationalism, which thrives on devouring others and which manifests itself in ghastly clashes. Its alluring service is encouraging lust and passion, satisfying desires, and facilitating the attainment of whims, and as for these, they make man descend from the level of the angels to that of a dog. They cause him to become a beast.

The principles on which Islamic civilization is based, on the other hand, are the reverse of these:

> Its point of support is truth instead of force, which is manifested as justice and equity. Its aims are virtue and God's pleasure in place of benefit and self-interest, which are manifested as love and friendly competition. Its means of unity are the bonds of religion, country, and class instead of racialism and nationalism, which are shown as sincere brotherhood and reconciliation, and co-operation in only defending against outside aggression. The principle in life is that of mutual assistance and co-operation instead of conflict, which is manifested as unity and mutual

support. In place of lust is guidance, which appears as progress for humanity and being perfected spiritually. It restricts the passions, and instead of facilitating the base desires of the carnal soul, it gratifies the high sentiments of the spirit.[8]

Of the various aspects of civilization in which are more detailed comparisons in Bediuzzaman's works, we shall briefly mention two. The first of these is literature.

In a piece on the subject in *Lemeât*, a collection of writings in free verse on various subjects which was published in Istanbul, probably in 1921, he makes a comparison between the Qur'an as literature and European literature. This literature is represented by the novel, for which there had been a strong vogue among Europeanized Ottomans since the time of Abdulhamid. He states that there are three areas of literature. These are concerned with love and beauty, heroism and valour, and thirdly, the depiction of reality. As regards European literature, he says that in the first sort it does not know the meaning of true love, and merely excites the carnal appetites—though it purports to be high-minded and condemn such things as unfitting for man, while in the second, it does not favour right and justice, but exalts the concept of force.

In the depiction of reality, Bediuzzaman describes the Western view in greater detail. He points out that since European literature regards the universe not as Divine art but from the point of view of nature, it prompts materialism and the worship of nature. And the novel, whether in book form, or as theatre or cinema, is the only remedy it has been able to find for the distress of the spirit arising from this misguidance. He goes on to say that both produce feelings of sadness, but while the sadness produced by the Qur'an is of a lofty and elevated nature, that caused by European literature offers no hope. This again springs from the view of existence it expresses. The world is a wild and ownerless place; what inspires the sorrow is "deaf nature" and "blind force". It is the pathetic woe of an orphan, of the lack of friends, rather than their absence. And while both give pleasure and stir the emotions, where the Qur'an stirs the spirit and moves the higher emotions, European literature stimulates man's animal appetites and affords pleasure to his lower nature only.[9]

The second aspect to be considered here is of a socio-economic nature. It concerns the injustice inherent in Western civilization and the remedy for its grievous consequences provided by Islam.

Bediuzzaman summarizes the root cause of the great social upheavals man has suffered, particularly this century, in two phrases. One is: "So long as I'm full, what is it to me if others die of hunger." And the other: "You struggle and labour so that I can live in ease and comfort." And he demonstrates that if they are to be eradicated, it will be through applying the Qur'anic injunction of almsgiving and prohibition on usury and interest. His argument is as follows:

By urging the wealthy classes to act in a cruel, oppressive, and arrogant manner towards the poor, the first phrase has been the cause of such sedition and strife that it has come close to overturning humanity. And the second phrase, by driving the poor to harbour hatred and envy towards the rich, has for several centuries destroyed public order and peace, and this century, due to the struggle between capital and labour, has given rise to disaster and disorder on a vast scale. The role of *zakāh* and the prohibition on usury in rectifying this situation is this:

> The most important factor in maintaining the order of society as a whole is not allowing an unbridgeable gulf to develop between the various classes. The upper classes and the rich should not become so far removed from the lower classes and the poor that the lines of communication are broken, as happened in European civilization. "Despite all its societies for good works, all its establishments for the teaching of ethics, all its severe discipline and regulations", it could neither reconcile those two classes, nor heal the two wounds in human life caused by the two phrases above. However, through making the payment of *zakāh* obligatory and prohibiting usury, Islam establishes relations between rich and poor, and forges links of respect and sympathy between them. By not allowing the classes to draw far apart, it

maintains order and balance in society. It "uproots" the two phrases and heals the wounds they have caused in mankind.[10]

How is it then that while Islam comprises true civilization, it was materially defeated by Western civilization? In his dream, Bediuzzaman was questioned concerning this. He was asked by one of the deputies in the Assembly: "With which of your actions did you issue a *fatwā* to Divine Determining so that it ordered this disaster for you?" He replied that it was their neglect of three of the 'pillars of Islam'—the prescribed prayers, fasting in Ramaḍān, and payment of *zakāh*—that had brought it upon them.[11] And he afterwards added a note to this, including neglect of the Hajj.

The Absolute Sovereignty of the Qur'an

Many reasons have been touched upon so far in describing Bediuzzaman's thought and works on the decline of the Islamic world and the Ottomans in particular. Broadly speaking they can be classed under two main headings. One is despotism and the other is religion, or rather the failure to adhere to its principles in various areas. The two are interconnected. Despotism has already been discussed in some detail. With regard to religion, many areas of decline may be included under this heading. For example, the decline in the field of learning and *madrasah* education, and the solutions he put forward for this which would also heal the deep rifts that had developed between the *'ulamā'*, the Sufi community, and those with a secular, Western educational background; the negligent attitude towards the pillars of Islam mentioned in the dream above; and the various "sicknesses" in the social life of Muslims, and in the field of morality, and the "remedies" offered in his sermon in Damascus. However, rather than attempting a comprehensive analysis of all the reasons Bediuzzaman put forward for the decline and relative backwardness of the Islamic world, we shall just make the following points.

In *Muhâkemat*, a work written to establish the principles of Qur'anic exegesis and published in 1911, he attributes the decline to the fact that the heart or true meaning of the teachings of Islam had been abandoned for its externals. He wrote:

> Abandoning the essence and kernel of Islam, we fixed our gazes on its exterior and shell. And due to misapprehension and ill-manners, we did not afford Islam its right nor pay it the respect it was due. So in disgust, it swathed itself in clouds of illusion and delusion, and concealed itself. And it had the right, for we mixed *isrā'īliyyāt*[12] with the fundamentals of belief, and stories with the tenets of faith, and metaphors with the truths of belief, and did not appreciate its value. So to punish us in this world, it left us in abasement and penury. And what will save us is again its mercy.[13]

Later in the same work, Bediuzzaman expands on this, explaining how some *isrā'īliyyāt* and a portion of Greek philosophy had been incorporated into Islam, and "appearing in the apparel of religion", had thrown minds into disarray. Explaining how this happened, he concludes that when commenting on the Qur'an, some literalist *'ulamā'* had expounded certain of its verses (*naqliyāt*) by making them fit the *isrā'īliyyāt*. He wrote. "What will explain and expound the Qur'an is again the Qur'an, and sound Ḥadīths. Not the Gospels and the Torah, whose ordinances have been superseded, just as their stories are corrupted."

As for Greek philosophy, it had sprung from fables and superstitions, and just as it had caused confusion, so it also opened up a way for mere imitation (*taqlīd*) in place of investigative and dynamic scholarship. Supposing there to be points of similarity and agreement between philosophy and matters of the Qur'an which demand the use of reason (*'aqliyāt*), externalist scholars explained these verses in terms of philosophy and adapted them to it. Bediuzzaman then said:

> God forbid!...For the criterion of the Book of Miraculous Exposition is its miraculousness. Its expounder and commentator are its parts. Its meaning is within it. Its shell, too, is of pearl, not clods.[14]

The Supremacy of the Qur'an and Birth of the New Said

In *Sünûhat*, published in 1919-20, there is a piece concerned with the Qur'an and the decline of Islam entitled 'The Absolute Sovereignty of the Qur'an'. It describes what Bediuzzaman considered to be "the most important cause of the Islamic community displaying carelessness and negligence in the precepts of religion."

The gist of his argument is that while it is the sacredness (*qudsiyyāt*) of the Qur'an, rather than reasoning, that drives the mass of ordinary believers to conform to the precepts of religion, the way Qur'anic commentaries and books on the Sharī'ah have developed in the course of time is that they have come to act as a veil to the Qur'an's sacredness.

In his argument, Bediuzzaman states that the fundamentals of belief and pillars of Islam, which are the "personal" property of the Qur'an and the Sunnah of the Prophet (ṣ), form ninety per cent of the religion. Controversial matters which are open to interpretation (*ijtihād*) form only ten per cent. In the course of time the former have been "placed under the patronage" of the latter and have become subordinate to them.

Then, while "the books of those qualified to interpret the law (*mujtahid*) should be like means and display the Qur'an as though they were glass; they should neither act on its behalf nor obscure it", it is on these books that the attention of the mass of believers became focused. They have only thought of the Qur'an in a hazy sort of way. They have read these books in order to understand not what the Qur'an says, but what the authors say. As a result the ordinary believer's conscience "has become accustomed to being indifferent, and has become lifeless and unresponsive." However, he continues:

> If the Qur'an had been shown directly in the fundamentals of religion, the mind would have naturally perceived its sacredness, which urges conformity [to the precepts of religion], is the rouser of the conscience, and is [the Qur'an's] inherent property. In this way the heart would have become sensitive towards it, and would not have remained deaf to the admonitions of belief.

Bediuzzaman then states that there are three ways to direct the attention of the mass of believers towards the Qur'an—"the exemplification of the Pre-Eternal Address, which shimmers with the attraction of miraculousness, has a halo of sacredness, and constantly stirs the conscience through belief." The first he describes as dangerous, the second as needing time, while the third is to remove the veils obscuring the Qur'an and display it directly to the ordinary believers; to seek its "pure, unmixed property" from itself alone, and only its secondary (*bilvasita*) decrees from the means.

The fundamentals and essentials, which as we saw form ninety per cent, should be sought from the Qur'an itself and from the Sunnah, while matters of secondary importance, which are open to interpretation and form ten per cent, sought from the works of those qualified to interpret them, that is, the *mujtahids*. If that had been the case, the demand shown for these truly numerous commentaries and books on the Sharī'ah and divided up between them would have been directed towards the Qur'an itself. And in that way the Qur'an would have been dominant and influential in its full meaning over the Muslim community.

Bediuzzaman had a significant dream shortly after writing this piece, and included it at the end. We also include it:

> One night shortly after writing this matter, I dreamt of the Prophet (ṣ). I was in a *madrasah* in his blessed presence; he was going to instruct me on the Qur'an. On their bringing the Qur'an, the Prophet (ṣ) rose to his feet out of respect. It occurred to me at that moment that he rose in order to guide his community.
>
> Finally I related this dream to a righteous member of his community, and he interpreted it in this way: "It is a powerful sign and certain good news that the Qur'an of Mighty Stature will acquire the exalted position of which it is worthy throughout the world."[15]

Birth of the New Said

Some two years after his return to Istanbul from the prisoner-of-war camp in Russia, Bediuzzaman underwent a radical interior change, "a strange revolution of the spirit", and out of this inner turmoil, the New Said was born. Indeed, it is clear from Abdurrahman's biography and from his own requests for leaves of absence from the Darü'l-Hikmet that since his return he suffered certain difficulties. The strains of war and harsh conditions of his captivity had taken their toll on his health, while the Ottoman defeat and foreign occupation were sources of great distress. However, as we saw at the end of the piece describing his "awakening" in the little mosque beside the River Volga, he considered the first two years of his return to be a period of heedlessness during which his fame and the acclaim he received made him temporarily forget his decision to withdraw from social life and concentrate on the inner life. He described the major turning-point that which occurred in some detail in various places in his works, and we shall chart its course from there.

It seems that a few flashes of realization restarted the process of "spiritual awakening". These occurred on high vantage points overlooking the city of Istanbul and took the form of realizing the stark realities of death and separation, old age and the transitory nature of things. Bediuzzaman says that, before anything, he tried to find consolation and a ray of light in his learning and the things he had studied for so many years. But rather than providing this, he found that they had "dirtied his spirit" and had been an obstacle to his spiritual progress.[16]

Up to this time, he had "filled his brain with philosophical and Islamic sciences", for he thought that "the philosophical sciences were the means to spiritual progress and enlightenment." In addition, he was of the opinion that European science and philosophy could be used to "reinforce" and "strengthen" Islam. He described it like this:

"The Old Said together with a group of thinkers accepted in part the principles of human philosophy [as opposed to revealed knowledge] and European science, and fought them with their own weapons; they admitted them to a degree. They accepted unshakeably some of their principles in the form of the positive sciences, and thus could not demonstrate the true value of Islam. Simply, they supposed philosophy's roots to be extremely deep and grafted Islam with its branches, as though they were strengthening it. But since the victories were few and it depreciated Islam, I gave up that way. And I demonstrated [in the *Risale-i Nur*] that Islam's principles are so profound that those of philosophy cannot reach them; indeed, they remain superficial beside them."[17]

And, now, when overwhelmed by the realization of his own increasing years and the fleeting nature of everything to which he was attached, Bediuzzaman's learning afforded him no light, no hope. "The spiritual darkness arising from the sciences of philosophy plunged my spirit into the universe, suffocating it. Whichever way I looked seeking light, I could find no light in those matters, I could not breathe."[18]

His spiritual crisis prompted him to withdraw from the society of men and seek solitude in places removed from Istanbul life. He retreated to *Yuşa Tepesi*,[19] a high hill on the Asian side of the Bosphorus near its junction with the Black Sea. Here, he tells us, he would not permit Abdurrahman even to attend to his essential needs.[20] Following this he took a house in Sarıyer, on the European side, and it was here in this old wooden house which is still standing that Bediuzzaman's crisis was resolved and he found what he was searching for.

It was Gawth al-A'zam, 'Abd al-Qādir al-Jīlānī, who came first to Bediuzzaman's aid. A copy of his *Futūḥ al-Ghayb* came into Bediuzzaman's possession "by a happy coincidence", and on opening the pages at random to take an omen from it, these lines came up:

Anta fī dāril-ḥikmati fa'ṭlub ṭabīban yudāwī qalbak[21]

or, as Bediuzzaman interpreted them:

"O you unfortunate! As a member of the Darü'l-Hikmeti'l-İslamiye, you are like a supposed doctor curing the spiritual sicknesses of the people of Islam, whereas it is you who is sicker than anyone. You first of all should find a doctor for yourself, then try to cure others!" He continued:

> So I said to the Shaykh: "You be my doctor!" And I took him as my doctor and read the book as though it were addressing me. But it was most severe. It smashed my pride in the most fearsome manner. It carried out the most drastic surgery on my soul. I could not stand it. I read half of it as though it were addressing me, but did not have the strength and endurance to finish it. I put the book back on the shelf. Then a week later the pain of that curative operation subsided and pleasure came in its place. I again opened the book and read it right through; I benefited a lot from that book of my first master. I listened to his prayers and supplications, and profited abundantly.[22]

The second work which was instrumental in transforming the Old Said into the New Said was the *Maktūbāt* of Shaykh Aḥmad Sirhindī, Imam Rabbānī. Some time after his "cure" through the mediation of Gawth al-Aʿẓam, Bediuzzaman opened Imam Rabbānī's *Maktūbāt* to take an omen from it as well. He wrote:

> It is strange but in the whole of *Maktūbāt*, the word *Bediuzzaman* appears only twice. And those two letters fell open for me at once. I saw that written at the head of them was: *Letter to Mirza Bediuzzaman*, and my father's name was Mirza. Glory be to God! I exclaimed, these letters are addressing me. At that time the Old Said was also known as Bediuzzaman. Apart from Badīʿuz-Zamān Hamādānī, I knew of no one else in the last three hundred years who was famous with the name. Whereas, in the Imam's time, there was such a person and he wrote him these two letters. This person's state must have been similar to mine, for I found these letters to be the cure for my ills. Only the Imam persistently recommended in many of his letters what he wrote in these two, which was: 'Make your *qiblah* one.' That is, take one person as your master and follow him; do not concern yourself with anyone else.'[23]

Bediuzzaman wrote that this most important piece of advice seemed inappropriate for his state of mind, and he was bewildered as whom to follow. In the Introduction to the *Mesnevi-i Nuriye*, he explained this in greater detail:

Since the Old Said proceeded more in the rational and philosophical sciences, he started to look for a way to the essence of reality like that of the Sufi's (*ehl-i tarikat*) and the mystics (*ehl-i hakikat*). But he was not content to proceed with the heart only like the Sufis, for his intellect and thought were to a degree wounded by philosophy; a cure was needed. Then, he wanted to follow some of the great mystics, who approached reality with both the heart and the mind. He looked, and each of them had different points of attraction. He was bewildered as to which of them to follow.[24] None of the great figures, such as Imam Ghazālī, Mawlānā Jalāl al-Dīn al-Rūmī, or Imam Rabbānī, answered all of his needs.

While in this state, "it was imparted to the Old Said's much wounded heart" that the one true master was the Holy Qur'an. It occurred to him "through Divine Mercy" that "the head of these various ways and the source of these streams and the sun of these planets is the All-Wise Qur'an; the true single *qiblah* is to be found in it. In which case, it is also the most elevated guide and most holy master. So I clasped it with both hands and clung on to it."[25]

Thus, we can say that Bediuzzaman's enlightenment occurred in three stages. Firstly, he realised the deficiency of the "human philosophy" he had studied and how it had been an obstacle to his enlightenment and progress. Secondly, as he himself confessed, through the "bitter medicine" of Shaykh 'Abd al-Qādir al-Jīlānī's *Futūḥ al-Ghayb*: "I understood my faults, perceived my wounds, and my pride was to a degree destroyed."[26] Then to complete the process of his transformation into the New Said, he understood through the *Maktūbāt* of Imam Rabbānī that he should take the Qur'an as his sole master. The instruction in Divine Unity he then received from the Qur'an through the phrase "*There is no god but God*" was "a most brilliant light" scattering the darkness in which he had been plunged and allowing him to breathe easily. Bediuzzaman describes how the Devil and his evil-commanding soul would not brook this, and "relying on what they had learnt from philosophers and the people of misguidance, attacked his mind and his heart", but that the ensuing debate resulted in "the heart's victory."²⁷

He notes that he now proceeded "through an alliance of mind and heart". That is, through the guidance of the Qur'an he found a way to the essence of reality through employing both the heart and mind. And since it employed both heart and mind, he found that before anything it cured his wounded spirit and heart, and silencing Satan and his evil-commanding soul, rescued him from doubts and scepticism. This then was the way of the New Said. It was also to be the way of the *Risale-i Nur*. In fact, the first work the New Said wrote was a collection of eleven or so treatises in Arabic called *al-Mathnawī al-'Arabī al-Nūrī*, which he described as "a kind of seed of the *Risale-i Nur*", and as "the seedbed" and the *Risale-i Nur* as "its garden."²⁸

As will be recalled, Bediuzzaman had undergone "a radical change in his ideas" at the turn of the century on learning of the explicit threats to the Qur'an and Islamic world made by the British Colonial Secretary, and had understood that he should dedicate his life to the defence of them with his learning. However events and his youth had served as "obstacles", preventing him "taking up the duty."²⁹ From his own accounts of his transformation into the New Said quoted above it is seen that his first realization was of the deficiency of "human philosophy" as opposed to revealed knowledge. And so, in addition to the other "obstacles" which had prevented his "taking up his duty to defend the Qur'an and Islam" was his preoccupation with "philosophy". Now some twenty years later at the age of forty-three, through what was clearly an overwhelming mental and spiritual upheaval, he had found what he had been searching for. Near the end of his life, he described this search in the presence of his close student, Mustafa Sungur:

> Sixty years ago, I was searching for a way to reach the truth and reality at the present time. That is, I was searching for a short way to obtain firm faith and belief and a complete understanding of Islam which would not be shaken by the attacks of the numerous negative and damaging currents.

Firstly, I had recourse to the way of the philosophers; I wanted to reach the truth with reason alone. I reached it only twice and with extreme difficulty. I looked and saw that even the greatest geniuses of mankind had gone only half the way, only one or two had been able to reach the truth by means of reason alone. Then I said: 'A way which even the greatest geniuses had been unable to take cannot be made general for everyone', and I gave up. For numerous philosophers, even Ibn Sīnā [Avicenna], Fārābī, Aristotle and others had only gotten half way. I saw that only one or two had been able to rise to the truth. Then I understood that a path and way by which not even the great geniuses had been able to rise could not be the way for everyone. Then I had recourse to the way of Sufism and studied it. I saw that it was most luminous and effulgent, but that it needed the greatest caution. Only the highest of the elite could take that way. So saying, this way cannot be a general way at this time either, I sought help from the Qur'an. And thanks be to God, the *Risale-i Nur* was bestowed on me, which is a sound and short way to the Qur'an for the believers.[30]

Notes

1. Nursi, *Sünûhat*, 41-47.
2. *Ibid.*, 60-61; Nursi, *Mektûbat*, 445 (Eng. tr. *Letters*, 534).
3. Nursi, "Bediüzzaman Kürdi'nin Fihriste-i Makasıdı," *Volkan*, Nos. 83-84, in *Asar-ı Bedi'iyye*, 373.
4. Nursi, *Muhâkemat*, 39.
5. Nursi, *Sözler*, 666-7 (Eng. tr.; *Words*, 748).
6. Nursi, "Hubab," in *Mesnevi-i Nuriye*, 81.
7. Nursi, *Muhâkemat*, 37-38.
8. Nursi, *Sünûhat*, 44; *Sözler*, 664, 119, 379 (Eng. tr.: *Words*, 745-6); *Mektûbat*, 445-6 (Eng. tr.: *Letters*, 548).
9. Nursi, *Sözler*, 686-8 (Eng. tr.: *Words*, 775); see also, *Sözler*, 382 (*Words*, 423-4).
10. Nursi, *İşârâtü'l-İ'caz* (Turk. tr.), 47-9, (Eng. tr.: *Signs of Miraculousness*, 53); *Sözler*, 380, (Eng. tr.: *Words*, 421-2).
11. Nursi, *Sünûhat*, 47-8; *Sözler*, 667 (Eng. tr.: *Words*, 748).
12. *Isrā'īliyyāt*: teachings and stories which with time had been corrupted and become superstitions and were introduced into Islam

by scholars of the People of the Book on their becoming Muslim in the early period of Islam.
13. Nursi, *Muhâkemat*, 7.
14. *Ibid.*, 16-18.
15. Nursi, *Sünûhat*, 31-5.
16. Nursi, *Lem'alar*, 226-228 (Eng. tr.: *Flashes*, 305).
17. Nursi, *Mektûbat*, 413 (Eng. tr.: *Letters*, 516).
18. Nursi, *Lem'alar*, 229 (Eng. tr.: *Flashes*, 306).
19. A point of interest which should be mentioned here was recorded by Bediuzzaman's student of later years, İbrahim Fakazlı, from one of Bediuzzaman's Van students, Seyyid Şefik, who joined him in Istanbul on his return from captivity in Russia. Seyyid Şefik Efendi, who was subsequently Imam of Sultan Ahmad Mosque in Istanbul, related to İbrahim Fakazlı how Said Halim Pasha, in the period following his resignation from the office of *Sadrıazam* (Prime Minister) in 1917, and "before going abroad", had decided to make over to Bediuzzaman an estate on the Bosphorus containing woods and a number of fine buildings for the purpose of founding an Islamic university, since he had no heir. However, at this point Bediuzzaman had disappeared from the scene for a month. When it was learnt he was on Yuşa Tepesi, word was sent to him that he had only to present himself at the Land-Registry Office for the transaction to be completed. Bediuzzaman requested twenty-four hours' grace to seek guidance, whereupon the two 'Levhas', or tables in verse, beginning "Don't call me to the world!" occurred to him, and he turned down the offer. That is to say, he had already taken the decision "to abandon the world", and on the strength of the two pieces, which he later included in the *Risale-i Nur* in the Seventeenth Word, did not go back on his decision (See, *Sözler*, 203-4; *Words*, 231-2). This event, which shows the esteem in which Bediuzzaman was held by the highest members of the Ottoman establishment, makes it probable that the process of his transformation into the New Said began at an early date and continued for some period of time. For, as a member of the CUP Government which had taken Turkey into the First World War, Said Halim Pasha was arrested in early March 1919, and together with 66 others, sent into exile in Malta on a British ship on 28 May 1919 (See, İbnü'l-Emin İnal, *Son Sadrıazamlar*, iv, 1909-12). Also, the extant documents show Bediuzzaman as resident in Sarıyer in September, 1921.
20. Nursi, *Şualar*, 446 (Eng. tr.: *Rays*, 523).
21. The original reads: "*Yā 'ibāda'llāh antum fī dāri'l-ḥikmati; lābuda min al-wāsiṭah, aṭlubū min ma'būdikum ṭabīban; yuṭibbu amrāḍ qulūbikum mudāwiyan yudāwīkum...*" It is in the 62nd. Meclis, p.

245, of Shaykh Jīlānī's work, *al-Fatḥ al-Rabbānī*, which in a printed edition of uncertain date was bound together with *Futūḥ al-Ghayb* under that title.
22. Nursi, *Mektûbat*, 330 (Eng. tr.: *Letters*, 418-9); Nursi, *Sikke-i Tasdik-i Gaybî*, 116-7.
23. Nursi, *Mektûbat*, 330-1 (Eng. tr.: *Letters*, 419).
24. Nursi, *Mesnevi-i Nuriye*, 7.
25. Nursi, *Mektûbat*, 331 (Eng. tr.: *Letters*, 419).
26. Nursi, *Sikke-i Tasdik-i Gaybî*, 117.
27. Nursi, *Lem'alar*, 229 (Eng. tr.: *Flashes*, 306).
28. Nursi, *Mesnevi-i Nuriye* (Turkish tr.), 7-8.
29. Nursi, *Sikke-i Tasdik-i Gaybî*, 76.
30. Mustafa Sungur, in Şahiner, *Aydınlar Konuşuyor*, 399.

10
Opposition to the British and Move to Ankara

Bediuzzaman's Dagger

*B*efore continuing with the story of Bediuzzaman's life, it is appropriate to relate the following story of his dagger, which he gave at this time to Gazi Ahmet Muhtar Pasha. Having first been compelled to carry a dagger when attacked by fellow students jealous of his fame and success in scholarly debate in Siirt in 1309 Rumi/1891, Bediuzzaman had followed this local custom ever since. The writer and historian İbrahim Hakkı Konyalı described to Necmeddin Şahiner how he came across the ivory-handled dagger:

> There are many mementos of great value, old and new, in the Military Museum, and among them I found an ivory-handled dagger while classifying the weapons. It had the name Said-i Kurdi engraved on it. I made enquiries as to how and when it had come to the Museum. Formerly known as Said-i Kurdi, Said Nursi had been appointed as a member of the Darü'l-Hikmeti'l-İslamiye in the years following the Great War. I knew him personally. He used to go around in the vicinity of Şehzadebaşi and wore a turban wound round a long cap and the local dress of eastern Anatolia with a dagger at his waist. According to what I learnt, the great scholar and historian and second founder and curator of the Military Museum, Ahmed Muhtar Pasha, had got to know Said Nursi and had acquired great respect for his learning. Thus, he had taken his dagger for the Museum as a memento, and had numbered it and put it away.[1]

Bediuzzaman Opposes an Autonomous Kurdistan

Bediuzzaman's undergoing great inner changes at this time did not prevent him from combating the British occupying forces in whatever ways he could. Described above are some of his activities related to this in the Darü'l-Hikmet, the area of learning, and in various other fields. In addition, he opposed them openly in the press, above all warning against their intrigues in the field of politics and efforts to sow discord among the *'ulamā'*. Before looking at this more closely though, another relevant subject concerning the British should be mentioned with which he was also concerned, and this was the question of Kurdistan.

It will be remembered that when allotting the spoils of the Ottoman Empire, Britain—and also France—had laid claim to the geographical region of Kurdistan and the oil-fields of Mesopotamia. In order to further its interests in the area, British plans included the setting-up of an autonomous Kurdistan, and provision for this was contained in the Treaty of Sèvres. And so, following the war, the promise of autonomy was used by the British as a means of instigating the inhabitants of the area to rebel against Ottoman authority, and also, incidentally, to hamper the National Forces. A number of political societies with the same aim were founded at the same time, one of which was the Society for the Advancement of Kurdistan (*Kürdistan Teâli Cemiyeti*).[2] Bediuzzaman was again approached in the hope of gaining his support and access to his considerable influence, but as before and after, he refused absolutely and condemned any action which would damage unity with the Turks. One of those who approached him was Seyyid Abdülkadir, the president of the above society. Bediuzzaman is reported to have given him this reply:

> Almighty God says in the Holy Qur'an: "God shall produce a people whom He will love as they will love Him" (Qur'an, 5:54). I pondered over this Divine declaration and I understood that the people mentioned is the Turkish nation, which for a thousand years acted as the standard-bearer of the Islamic world. I shall not follow a few brainless racialists rather than

Opposition to the British and Move to Ankara 197

serving this heroic nation, in place of four hundred and fifty million true Muslim brothers.³

Necmeddin Şahiner quotes another passage from the same work which, since it includes a firsthand description of Bediuzzaman illustrating further the point in question, we give it in full. It is related by Konsolidçi Asaf Bey, a well-known writer:

> One day while sitting in the printing office a man entered. He was wearing a strange outfit and had some sort of long cap on his head. On seeing him, Mevlânzâde rose to his feet and pointed to me. He said:
>
> "This is our leader-writer, Konsolidçi Asaf." Then addressing me, he said:
>
> "This is Bediuzzaman Said Efendi, one of our greatest religious scholars." So from that point I started to have conversations with Bediuzzaman, and truly I benefited enormously from his knowledgeable conversation. After this he used to come frequently to our press and we would talk. Sometimes we would even go out together and go round the town.
>
> I do not know how long it was after this, Said Nursi left Istanbul. I cannot remember now whether he went to his home region or some other place. Anyway, Germany and its allies had met with a crushing defeat. The country was divided up and they started to create new states in every corner of it. Armenia was one of these. One day, Mevlânzâde Rifat Bey said to me:
>
> "They are setting up an Armenian state. So, since the Empire is falling apart, we ought to set up a Kurdish one."
>
> When I looked at him in astonishment, he said to me:
>
> "I am not a traitor. And it is not me who broke up the mighty Ottoman Empire. God curse those who did destroy it; they have all fled like thieves. For sure there are the National Forces, but they do not offer much hope. We are not living in the age of miracles. I'm going to write to Bediuzzaman about the matter, because he is very influential. He is thought a lot of, so I shall write to him and ask him to join us."
>
> Mevlânzâde wrote and sent the letter. Then, about ten days or two weeks later we were sitting in the printing office with some guests. There was Cakalı Hamdi Pasha, who was Minister of the Navy at the time, and also the Chief of the Military Court.

We were talking of this and that when the postman came in, left a letter, and went. Rifat Bey's face darkened as he read the letter, it was clear he was angry. After reading it through, he flung it at me, saying:

"Read this and see. Bediuzzaman rejects my proposal and says he does not support my idea."

It would have been rude to read the letter to myself, so I began to read it out loud. Cakalı Hamdi Bey and Mustafa Pasha, the Chief of the Military Court, listened. Although I do not remember exactly how the letter went, Bediuzzaman rejected Mevlânzâde's proposal to set up [an independent state of] Kurdistan, and said: 'Rifat Bey, let's not set up Kurdistan, let's revive the Ottoman Empire. If you accept to do this, I am willing to sacrifice even my life for it.

After listening to this, Mustafa Pasha turned to Mevlânzâde and said:

"You are wrong, Rifat Bey, and Bediuzzaman is right. It is not Kurdistan that should be formed, but the Ottoman Empire that should be re-formed and revived."[4]

Indeed, Bediuzzaman continued to support any attempts to strengthen unity between the Kurds and the rest of "the nation". As before, this was particularly in the area of education. In 1919 a society was founded to this end of which he was one of the fifteen founder members. Called The Society for the Propagation of Education among Kurds (*Kürd Neşr-i Ma'arif Cemiyeti*), it was non-political, independent, and concerned solely with education. It aimed initially to set up one primary school for Kurdish children in Istanbul, who, "of all the sons of the fatherland, were the ones most deprived of the bounty of education", and later as funds permitted to found others in areas where Kurds formed the majority of the inhabitants.[5] He was also going to be successful in securing further funds from the Ankara Government for the Medresetü'z-Zehra, his university-level *madrasah* in the East, as we shall see.

Bediuzzaman Combats the British

During this time, the Şeyhü'l-İslam's Office was presented with a questionnaire on the religion of Islam by the Church of England authorities, and as a member of the Darü'l-Hikmet, Bediuzzaman was asked to prepare the answers. Outraged at this insolence on the part of the British, he wrote a few succinct words which bore the meaning of insults rather than answers. His intention was to protect the honour of Islam. He later described the affair as follows:

> One time, when the British had destroyed the guns on the Bosphorus and had invaded Istanbul, the chief cleric of the Anglican Church, which is that country's highest religious authority, asked the Şeyhü'l-İslam's Office six questions about religion. I was a member of the Darü'l-Hikmeti'l-İslamiye at the time and they said to me: "You answer them!" They wanted a six-hundred-word reply to the six questions. I said: "I shall answer not with six hundred words, nor with six words, and not even with one word, but with a mouthful of spit! Because, you can see, the moment they stepped ashore here, their chief cleric arrogantly started asking us questions."[6] And in *Rumuz*, Signs, a work he published at the time, Bediuzzaman included the following piece entitled, Answer to a Scheming Cleric Who Wanted to Pour Scorn on Us:
>
> "Someone has thrown you down into the mud and is killing you. Although he is pressing his foot on your throat, he asks mockingly what school of law you follow. The silencing answer to this is to feel the offence, be silent, and spit in his face. So not to him, but in the name of the truth:
>
> 1. Q. What does the religion of Muḥammad consist of?
>   A. The Qur'an.
> 2. Q. What has it given to life and thought?
>   A. Divine Unity and moderation.
> 3. Q. What is the remedy for man's troubles?
>   A. The prohibition of interest and usury and the obligatory payment of *zakāh*.
> 4. Q. What does it say concerning the present upheavals?
>   A. 'Man has nought save that which he strives' (Qur'an, 53:39). 'And those who amass gold and silver and do not spend it in the way of God; announce to them a most grievous punishment' (Qur'an, 9:34)."[7]

Bediuzzaman's most effective work at this time, however, was a short work called *The Six Steps*, in which he pointed out six ways in which the British, and the Greeks, sowed discord and dissension in the Muslim community. It has at its head the verse: "And do not follow in the footsteps of Satan" (Qur'an, 2:168), and Bediuzzaman later described it as having "turned the Istanbul *'ulamā's* opinions against the British and in favour of the national movement",[8] and as having "spoilt the fearsome plan of the commander of the British forces occupying Istanbul." This plan was "to prepare the ground for the defeat of the National Forces and victory of Greeks by sowing strife among Muslims, and even deceiving the Şeyhü'l-İslam and some of the *'ulamā'* and inciting them against each other, and by making the supporters of the two main political groupings contend with each other [that is, those of the by then disbanded Committee of Union and Progress and those of the Freedom and Accord Party]."[9]

To illuminate this further, it should be mentioned that the source of the conflict lay in the fact that, according to the official account, Sultan Vahideddin,[10] the Istanbul government, some of the *'ulamā'*, and others, opposed the national movement in Anatolia absolutely. They considered those involved in it to be either members of the Committee of Union and Progress or people of a like kind, that is to say, bandits, whom they held responsible for entering Turkey into the War, and for its defeat which had dealt the death-blow to the Empire. Although it never came to power, the old rivals of the CUP and now dominant political party, the Freedom and Accord Party, also considered the people involved in the national movement to be the chief enemy rather than the foreign aggressors.[11]

In addition, many Western-inclined intellectuals opposed the nationalists, and their distorted writings combined with the propaganda of the British aiming to widen and play on divisions, were a cause of confusion among the people, shaking their faith even, and weakening their resolve to withstand the enemy. Thus, in his writings, Bediuzzaman pointed out the distortions, and in *The Six Steps* in particular showed with his usual clarity how the British were playing on their differences and answered their insidious suggestions so summarily and witheringly that it both illuminated its readers and heartened them.

Bediuzzaman also severely condemned those who disparaged their own nation and thought that "the interests and ambitions of the British nation were consistent with the interests and dignity of Islam" and accepted British protection.[12] When asked which society or grouping he belonged to and why he was severely critical of the opposition, that is, the Freedom and Accord Party, he replied:

> I belong to the society of martyrs. It is inauspicious to either deny or belittle a single saint. So it is the most inauspicious of all inauspiciousness to deny two million martyrs who are saints, and to consider their blood to have spilt in vain. Because the opposition say that we were wrong to enter the [First World] War, and that our enemies were right; that it was not a *jihād*. Thus, such a judgement is to deny the martyrdom of two million martyrs. In my opinion the prayer we should utter most is: O God, do not put harm amongst us!
>
> There is a fact before which the most uncivilized and even the most savage bow their heads in submission and respect, and that is, when confronted by an external enemy, two hostile clans of a tribe lay aside their own enmity instinctively. It is astonishing therefore that people who are considered to be civilized and enlightened are far inferior to those savages; when faced with external hostility they intensify internal enmity. If civilization and science are thus, then man's happiness lies in savagery and ignorance![13]

The Six Steps was published shortly before the reoccupation of Istanbul by the British in March 1920, and as they came to realise Bediuzzaman's effectiveness in opposing them, the British authorities determined to get rid of him. However, they were told that if they attempted to assassinate him, the inhabitants and tribes of eastern Anatolia would never forgive the British, and it would earn them their eternal enmity. There are various sources which corroborate the fact that the British wanted to do away with this vehement enemy who so persistently and successfully foiled their attempts to annihilate Islam and the Turkish nation through their plots and propaganda. One such incident was related by Bediuzzaman's student, Mullah Süleyman:

> We set off in the direction of the Divanyolu, and Mısırlı Said Mullah was there. He was the second president of The Friends of England Association. He had no religion, and whether he was a Mason or what he was, I do not know. This man used to inform on Bediuzzaman to the British; he used to tell them about his appearance, features, dress, and where he lived. This was because Bediuzzaman used to make dreadful attacks on them in the press. He used to publish articles in the *Tanin* and other newspapers which said things like: "You dogs, who are more basely and utterly dog-like than any dog!"
>
> Then one day, soldiers of the occupying forces were waiting for Bediuzzaman in the square by Aya Sophia, they were going to seize him. I was terrified and he said to me: "You follow close behind me, Süleyman, and don't fall behind." Then he recited the verse from Sūrah Yā Sīn: "And We have put a bar in front of them and a bar behind them, and further, We have covered them; so that they cannot see" (Qur'an, 36:9), and they did not see us. We passed right by them and came to the house. I knocked on the door, and when it was slow in opening, I said to my friend inside: 'Come on open it quickly; Bediuzzaman is with me!' He opened it immediately and we went in. Bediuzzaman sat down on the divan, and I pulled off his boots. Then he asked me:
>
> "What did you understand from all that?"
>
> "I do not know", I replied. So he said:
>
> "They had received the order to shoot me, and I did as I did in order to save you. I pitied you because you had no weapon. Otherwise I would have lined up ten of them and taken my aim. I would have killed at least ten of them before being killed myself."[14]

Another account of Bediuzzaman at this time has been given by Tevfik Demiroğlu, who later served as the Deputy for Van for many years. He provides a number of details concerning Bediuzzaman's life, and recalls particularly his own adventures with Abdurrahman when distributing *The Six Steps* secretly under the noses of the British. The work was printed secretly "through the efforts of Eşref Edip."[15] Tevfik Demiroğlu also notes that Bediuzzaman was closely associated with Eşref Edip, and with Mehmet Akif and the magazine *Sebilürreşad*, and that they used to meet for long conversations in the Yusuf Izzeddin Pasha Pavilion in Çamlıca, where Bediuzzaman stayed for some time. He also describes his adventures in stealing breech-blocks from the arsenals so as to make the British heavy guns unusable, while others would steal rifles and other weapons.[16]

Bediuzzaman's enemies were not restricted to the British. Some thirty years later he wrote in a letter that a fellow member of the Darü'l-Hikmet, Seyyid Sadeddin Pasha, had warned him of another plot to kill him. The Pasha had told him: "I have learnt via certain means that an aggressive atheistic organization which is here but whose roots are abroad has read one of your works, and has declared that so long as its author remains in this world, they shall be unable to impose their ideas of irreligion on this nation, and that he shall have to be eliminated. So guard yourself well!" Bediuzzaman wrote that in reply he said to Sadeddin Pasha: "I place my trust in God! Death only comes once and the time of its coming cannot be changed."[17]

Ankara

In recognition in these services to the national cause, and particularly through *The Six Steps*, the national leaders in Ankara invited Bediuzzaman to join them there. However he declined to "flee" from Istanbul.[18] Mustafa Kemal Pasha himself, who had been elected as President of the Grand National Assembly, sent three messages in cipher summoning him. These were repeated on numerous occasions by various people including Marshal Fevzi Çakmak; this is corroborated by National Defence Imam and

Regimental Mufti, Osman Nuri Efendi.[19] But Bediuzzaman told them:

> I want to fight where it is dangerous; I do not like fighting behind trenches. I consider here to be more dangerous than Anatolia.

On these insistent demands, Bediuzzaman sent three of his students, Tevfik Demiroğlu, Mullah Süleyman, and Major Refik Bey to offer their support to the National Government. He himself finally went on being invited by his old friend, the Deputy and former Governor of Van, Tahsin Bey.[20]

The War of Independence was reaching its climax, and on 22 August there began what became known as the Great Offensive, which by 29 September had resulted in the Turkish victory and liberation of Anatolia. In October, the Mudanya Armistice was signed.[21] These were also the last days of the Ottoman Empire. The Armistice had been signed with the Ankara Government, but the Sultan's government was still nominally functioning in Istanbul. So to solve the problem, on 1 November 1922, at the prompting of Mustafa Kemal, the Grand National Assembly voted to abolish the Sultanate and retain only the Caliphate. The right to choose the Caliph would rest with the Assembly. The deposed Sultan Vahiddedin left the country on a British warship on 16 November, and his cousin Abdülmecid was appointed as Caliph by the Assembly.[22] The Caliphate was finally abolished on 3 March 1924 after being held for 407 years by the Ottoman House.[23]

With all these momentous events, it was not till 9 November 1922, that Bediuzzaman was given an official welcoming in the Assembly. The ceremony was recorded as follows in the minutes of that day:

> Welcome for the religious scholar Bediuzzaman Said Efendi Hazretleri.
>
> *Speaker*: The Deputy for Bitlis, Arif Bey, and his friends have a motion.

> We propose to the Illustrious Presidency that a welcome is given to Bediuzzaman Mullah Said Efendi Hazretleri, one of the well-known *'ulamā'* of the Eastern Provinces, who has come here from Istanbul in order to visit the *ghazis* of Anatolia and this Exalted Assembly and is at present in the Visitors' Gallery.
>
> | Bitlis | Bitlis | Muş | Muş | Siirt | Bitlis | Ergani |
> |---|---|---|---|---|---|---|
> | Arif | Derviş | Kasım | İlyas Sami | Salih | Resul | Hakkı |
>
> (Applause)
>
> *Rasih Efendi* (Antalya): We request him to honour the platform and offer prayers.[24]

Whereupon Bediuzzaman mounted the platform, congratulated the veterans of the War of Independence, and offered prayers.

Despite the warm reception he was given and the rejoicing at the triumph of Islam and the Turks over their enemies, Bediuzzaman was dismayed to find a lax and indifferent attitude towards Islam and their religious duties among many of the deputies in the Assembly. His intention in coming to Ankara had been to encourage those in power to set up a form of government based on the Qur'an and the Sharī'ah. Through Divine assistance, the Turks had totally defeated those who had wanted to destroy Islam and themselves. It was the beginning of a new era and exactly the time to marshal their forces to make the new republic the means for bringing about a renaissance of Islam and Islamic civilization, and make it a centre and source of support for the Islamic world.[25] But rather than this, in addition to an indifference towards religion, he found that atheistic ideas were being propagated. He described it like this:

> When I went to Ankara in 1922, the morale of the people of belief was extremely high as a result of the victory of the army of Islam over the Greeks. But I saw that an abominable current of atheism was treacherously trying to subvert, poison, and destroy their minds. "Oh God!", I said, "This monster is going to harm the pillars of belief."[26]

That is to say, once the victory had been won, the old differences came to the fore once again. Up to the final victory it would have been considered traitorous of any deputy in the Assembly to assume any position opposed to Islam, but once it was secured those who favoured Westernization and the abandoning of religion, began to show their true colours. Indeed, since its inception there had been various opposing groups in the National Assembly. In the summer of 1922 a group was formed which opposed the autocracy of Mustafa Kemal.[27] But with the victory he was to increase his dictatorial powers, and aimed to gain total control of the Assembly. The position of the 'religious' group was progressively weakened until, in the elections of June 1923, before which Bediuzzaman had left Ankara, he was able to have elected a docile Assembly that would present him with no serious opposition.

In the face of the laxity and "current of atheism" which he found, Bediuzzaman wrote a work in Arabic disproving atheism called *Zeylü'l-Zeyl*, and another called *Hubab*. He noted however that, "Alas, those who knew Arabic were few and those who considered it seriously were rare, also its argument was in an extremely concise and abbreviated form. As a result, the treatise did not have the effect it should have had, and sadly, the current of atheism both swelled and gained strength."[28] Bediuzzaman's main concern in Ankara, however, was urging the deputies to adhere to Islam and perform their religious duties at this crucial time. In regard to this he published a ten point circular which he had distributed to all the deputies. It was read to Mustafa Kemal by Kazım Karabekir Pasha.[29]

The circular, dated 19 January 1923, stresses in particular the necessity of performing the prescribed prayers and is of some length, so rather than giving the whole text, we shall include a translation of the last part. Firstly, Bediuzzaman is pointing out here the harm to the nation if its leaders and representatives do not perform their religious duties, and says that in truth such people are not fit to govern:

What excuse can be found for the neglect and giving up of the religious obligations, which causes harm to matters of both religion and the world? How can patriotism permit it? Especially these *mujāhidīn* commanders and this Grand Assembly, for they are held as examples. The nation will either imitate their faults or criticise them, and both are harmful. That is to say their religious duties concern public rights. True and serious work will not be performed by those who, comprising the meaning of consensus and agreement, do not heed innumerable warnings and indications, and accept delusions arising from the sophistry of the soul and the whisperings of Satan. The foundation stones of this mighty revolution have to be firm.

Bediuzzaman then states that due to the power invested in it by the nation, the Assembly now represents the Sultanate. It has also to represent the Caliphate, but to do this it has to both fulfil its religious obligations and see that they are fulfilled by the nation, and answer the nation's religious needs. If it does not do these things, out of need, the nation will compel it to "give meaning" to the "name" of the Caliphate, which in effect it had undertaken as mentioned above, and will also invest the Assembly with the power to carry out the Caliphate's functions. However, he says, if due to its members' negligence and laxity in performing their religious duties the Assembly does not have the ability to do this, it will give rise to discord and disunion, which is contrary to the verse, "And hold fast all together to the Rope of God" (Qur'an, 49:10).

Bediuzzaman goes on to make a point which is fundamental to his ideas and that has been mentioned in several places in the present work so far. This is that the modern age is the age of the masses. Communities give rise to collective personalities or spirits. In the case of government or authority, in this complex modern age, they can only function adequately by means of collective personalities of this sort. He mentions this here in regard to the Caliphate.

The present is the time of community. The collective personality of a community, which is its spirit, is firmer and more capable of carrying out the ordinances of the Sharī'ah. The person of the Caliph can only undertake his duties through relying on [such a collective personality]. If a collective personality, the spirit of a community, is righteous, it is more brilliant and perfect [than that of an individual]. But if it is bad, it is exceedingly bad. Both the goodness and badness of an individual are limited, but those of a community are unlimited. Do not spoil the goodness you have gained in the face of external [enemies] through internal badness. You know that your perpetual enemies and opponents and foes are destroying the practices and marks of Islam. Therefore, your essential duty is to revive and preserve them. Otherwise, unconsciously you will be helping the conscious enemy. Contempt for the practices and marks of Islam shows weakness of nationhood, and as for weakness, it does not arrest the enemy, it encourages him.

"God is enough for us, and how excellent a Guardian is He" (Qur'an, 3:173).[30]

This exhortation had a considerable effect; it added around sixty to the number of deputies who performed the prayer regularly and the room used as a mosque had to be changed for larger one. However, it drew an unfavourable reaction from the president of the Assembly. One day in the presence of a large number of deputies in the Assembly, he shouted angrily at Bediuzzaman:

"We are in need of heroic *hojas* like you. We called you here in order to benefit from your elevated ideas, but you came here and immediately started writing things about the prayers, and have caused differences amongst us." Bediuzzaman countered this with a few words, then himself in anger, he jabbed his fingers and said:

"Pasha! Pasha! After belief, the most elevated truth in Islam is the obligatory prayers. Those who do not perform the prayers are traitors, and the opinions of traitors are to be rejected."[31]

In saying these words, Bediuzzaman had, in his own words, "smashed an appalling idol". Those present feared for him, certain that he would be made to suffer for his words. But Mustafa Kemal suppressed his anger and in effect apologised, for two days later he had a two hour meeting with Bediuzzaman in his office.

Just as with the pashas in the court martial and Grand Duke Nicholas in Kosturma, Bediuzzaman did not bow before Mustafa Kemal. He took the opportunity to admonish him on the great harm to the nation, country, and Islamic world in attacking Islam and trying to eradicate its practices in the hope of gaining a reputation among their enemies. If a revolution had to be brought about, it had to be achieved through making the Qur'an the basis of it. He dwelt particularly on the great error of trying to find favour with the enemies of Islam and the Turks by attacking Islam in order to satisfy ambition and the desire for fame and position. Mustafa Kemal apparently took no offence at these words which "wounded all his sensibilities and principles".[32] On the contrary, he tried to placate him and win him over so as to take advantage of his influence. He offered Bediuzzaman Shaykh Sanusi's post of General Preacher in the Eastern Provinces with a salary of 300 liras, a deputyship in the Assembly, and a post equivalent to that he had held in the Darü'l-Hikmeti'l-İslamiye, together with such perks as a residence.[33] Bediuzzaman did not accept, and before examining the reasons, it may also be mentioned that Mustafa Kemal was also one of the 163 deputies who endorsed the allotting of 150,000 liras for Bediuzzaman's Medresetü'z-Zehra.[34]

Throughout the time Bediuzzaman was in Ankara, he pursued the matter of founding this university in the East. There were three points in particular that he impressed on the deputies in regard to it, many of whom were of the belief that the religious sciences should be dispensed with and that general education should be in the Western style and concentrate on the modern sciences. Firstly was the geographical location of the Eastern Provinces; since they were like a centre of the Islamic world, it was essential to teach the religious sciences together with modern science. Secondly, the fact that most of the prophets had appeared in the East and most of the great philosophers in the West showed that the East would only be aroused by religion. Progress therefore, was dependent on religion. And thirdly was the most important point that religion and the teaching of it was the only way to maintain unity. If religion was not taken as the basis, the non-Turkish Muslims of the region "would not feel true brotherhood for the Turks", and the need for co-operation and solidarity at that time was great. Of two hundred deputies addressed on this question, 163 endorsed the decision to set aside 150,000 liras for the project.[35]

One reason Bediuzzaman gave for declining the offers was the change that had come about in himself. As he wrote: "Their conduct and the way they were going did not accord with my own feelings of old age." And he quoted himself as telling them: "The New Said wants to work for the next world and cannot work with you, but he will not interfere with you either."[36] However, the main reason was that Bediuzzaman had perceived the course that would be taken and understood that he could not work alongside the new leaders. In a later work he wrote:

> So I was compelled to leave those most important posts. And saying that nothing can be gained from working with or responding to those people, I abandoned the world and politics and social life, and spent all of my time on the way of saving belief.[37]

Indeed, Bediuzzaman had understood that it would be followers of the Qur'an that would combat them, and that they would be defeated not in the realm of politics but with the "immaterial sword" of the Qur'an's miraculousness. Thus, he refused to work together with the new leaders and left Ankara for Van, where he retired into a life of solitude.[38]

When leaving, Bediuzzaman was escorted to the station by a number of deputies and friends. Mustafa Kemal Pasha also, who at the time was living by the station, joined the group. It is recorded that they had a conversation about statues, and that on the Pasha asking Bediuzzaman his opinion on them, he replied sharply: "The Qur'an's attacks are all at statues and idols. The statues of Muslims are monuments like hospitals, schools, orphanages, mosques, and roads."[39] The date on Bediuzzaman's ticket—the ticket which took the Old Said to the New Said—shows that it was issued on 17/4/39; that is, 17 April 1923, which was the first day of Ramaḍān 1341.

Notes

1. Şahiner, *Said Nursi*, 212-213; İbrahim Hakkı Konyalı, in Şahiner, *Aydınlar Konuşuyor*, 316.
2. See, T.Z. Tunaya, *Türkiye'de Siyasal Partiler*, ii, 186-229.
3. Şahiner, *Said Nursi*, 216, quoted from Mustafa Polat, *Mülakat*, 37.
4. Şahiner, *Said Nursi*, 214-6, quoted from Mustafa Polat, *Mülakat*, 31-4.
5. T.Z. Tunaya, *Türkiye'de Siyasal Partiler*, ii, 188, 214-5.
6. Nursi, *Mektûbat*, 390 (Eng. tr.: *Letters*, 488).
7. Nursi, "Rumûz," in *Asar-ı Bedi'iyye*, 85.
8. Nursi, *Şualar*, 385 (Eng. tr.: *Rays*, 453).
9. Nursi, *Şualar*, 379 (Eng. tr.: *Rays*, 445).
10. See Chapter 8, note 9.
11. Tunaya, *Türkiye'de Siyasal Partiler*, i, 29-30, 34-5.
12. Or the idea of a British Protectorate. Nursi, "Hutuvat-i Sitte," in *Asar-ı Bedi'iyye*, 117-118.
13. Nursi, "Işârât," in *Asar-ı Bedi'iyye*, 96-7.
14. Şahiner, *Said Nursi*, 218-219.
15. Nursi, *Şualar*, 379 (Eng. tr.: *Rays*, 445).
16. Tevfik Demiroğlu, in *Son Şahitler*, i, 229-231.
17. Nursi, *Emirdağ Lahikası*, i, 189-90.
18. Nursi, *Şualar*, 379 (Eng. tr.: *Rays*, 445).
19. Mehmet Süleyman Teymuroğlu, "Muhterem Said Nursi'nin Doldurduğu Boşluk," *Hilal Dergisi*, No.13, Şubat 1969; see, Şahiner, *Said Nursi*, 239-40.
20. *Tarihçe*, 124; Şahiner, *Said Nursi*, 239-40.
21. Shaw and Shaw, *History*, ii, 362-4.
22. B. Lewis, *Emergence*, 259.
23. Danişmend, iv, 470.
24. TBMM Zabit Ceridesi, Vol. XXIV, p. 457, as in Şahiner, *Said Nursi*, 241.
25. *Tarihçe*, 129.
26. Nursi, *Lem'alar*, 170 (Eng. tr.: *Flashes*, 233).
27. B. Lewis, *Emergence*, 381.
28. Nursi, *Lem'alar*, 170 (Eng. tr.: *Flashes*, 233).

29. *Tarihçe*, 124.
30. *Tarihçe*, 125-7; Şahiner, *Said Nursi*, 242-8; Nursi, "Hubab," in *Mesnevi-i Nuriye*, 92-3.
31. *Tarihçe*, 128.
32. Nursi, *Emirdağ Lahikası*, i, 242.
33. *Tarihçe*, 131; Nursi, *Şualar*, 301 (Eng. tr.: *Rays*, 381-2).
34. Nursi, *Emirdağ Lahikası*, ii, 196.
35. *Tarihçe*, 128.
36. *Ibid.*, 195.
37. Nursi, *Şualar*, 300-1 (Eng. tr.: *Rays*, 381-2).
38. *Tarihçe*, 131.
39. Şahiner, *Said Nursi*, 250; Av. Hulusi Bitlisi Aktürk, "Defence Speech in Afyon Court," in Nursi, *Müdâfaalar*, 447.

Part II
The New Said

11
Van

On arriving in Van, Bediuzzaman stayed with his younger brother, Abdülmecid, a teacher of Arabic, in the Toprakkale district of the town. But we learn from Abdülmecid's wife Rabia that his well-wishers and visitors were so numerous he was obliged to move to Nurşin Mosque. This then became Bediuzzaman's base in Van in place of his *madrasah*, the Horhor, which had been razed in the general destruction of the city wrought by the Armenians and occupying Russians during the War. Nurşin Mosque became a centre of learning, with large numbers of religious scholars and shaykhs coming to visit Bediuzzaman to pay him their respects and seek his advice. He again attracted many students and began to teach them, in addition to speaking with his many visitors. This busy life however weighed on him and impinged on his inner life. So as soon as the weather became sufficiently warm, taking a small number of his students with him, he withdrew from Van to Mount Erek, a mountain among jagged peaks to the east of the town. Here he was able to devote himself entirely to prayer and contemplation.

That he was the New Said was clear to everyone in Van. Most of the recorded memories of him at this time mention some aspect of the changes that had come about in him. The most apparent of these is that he had abandoned the colourful local dress of the area for clothes of a more sober nature.[1] Indeed, on first seeing his destroyed *madrasah* and the sacked and burnt city of Van, he was to relive the harrowing events of war and the deaths of so many of his students that had been instrumental in bringing about the New Said. Then too they mention that he had altogether turned his back on politics and the world, and people who heard him speak learnt of the way of the New Said, that of saving belief, which would form the basis of renewal and reconstruction.

For the next two years Bediuzzaman stayed on the mountain, inhabiting a cave near the source of the river Zernabad and returning to Van only for the coldest months of the winter. It was also his practice to go down to the town on Fridays, to give the sermon in Nurşin Mosque. From what has been recorded of these sermons and what he taught his students, they too were entirely in accordance with the way of the New Said. That is to say, Bediuzzaman concentrated on explaining and teaching the fundamentals of belief, the basic tenets of faith, such subjects as Divine Unity and the resurrection of the dead and the hereafter. He told one of his students on this being questioned, for his treatment of these subjects was new and different in addition to his congregations being unaccustomed to hearing these basic matters:

> My aim is to construct firmly the foundations of belief. If the foundations are sound, they cannot be destroyed by any upheavals.[2]

The same student, Mullah Hamid, has also quoted Bediuzzaman as saying in connection with this:

> Honoured sirs, the Old Said is dead; you still think of me as the Old Said. This is the New Said you see before you. Almighty God has granted limitless blessings to the New Said...Ten months of the New Said's teaching may be the equivalent of what the Old Said taught in ten years, and sufficient.[3]

The New Said was to find total manifestation in the *Risale-i Nur* and the three years till the spring of 1926 when he was inspired to write the first parts may be seen as a time of preparation and waiting for Divine guidance. It may also be noted that just as the first writings of the New Said, the *Mesnevi-i Nuriye*, were the

Van

"seedbed" of the *Risale-i Nur*, so too at this time in Van, some of the *dars* Bediuzzaman gave or subjects he taught were later included in the *Risale-i Nur*. Another student, İsmail Perihanoğlu, has recorded two instances of this, which we include here:

> Another day, Mullah Resul, Kopanisli Mullah Yusuf and I went together with Ustādh to Zeve, the people of which had been entirely wiped out in the Armenian massacres. Ustādh paused, and said:
> "This is the resting-place of martyrs. My brother Mullah Ahmad-i Cano lies here also." And unable to hold back his tears, he wept with great sorrow.
> Mullah Ahmad-i Cano had studied with Ustādh.
> Later Ustādh taught us concerning the levels of life as described in the First Letter.[4] And we afterwards wrote out this *dars* and duplicated it.[5]

On another occasion they climbed to the top of the citadel in Van, and as was Bediuzzaman's practice, he climbed to the very highest point and spread out his prayer-rug there. Looking down on the ruins of his *madrasah* at the foot of the citadel, he spoke of the signs of the end of the world. Then shifting his gaze to Lake Van, he explained the story of Jonah and the whale. He made a comparison of Jonah's situation and that of modern man, and explained how his moral and spiritual state resembles that of Jonah in the belly of the whale. Bediuzzaman later incorporated this into the *Risale-i Nur* as the First Flash.[6],[7]

Bediuzzaman's absorption in worship has also been commented on by many of those connected with him at this time. His sister-in-law, Rabia, notes that he never slept at night while staying with them; from his room came the continuous sound of prayer and supplication.[8] İsmail Perihanoğlu notes how he preferred to perform his worship, an important element of which was contemplation [*tafakkur*], in high places and elevated spots. Besides describing him climbing to the highest point in the citadel of Van, mentioned above, he tells of another occasion when he found Bediuzzaman on the roof of the mosque plunged in thought.⁹ While Mullah Hamid, who spent the most time with him on Mount Erek, states that he was never idle for a moment but always occupied, mostly in prayer and supplication. He spent hours on his knees, so that his toes became raw. When one of his students suggested he sit in a more comfortable position like themselves, he replied:

> We have to win eternal life in this brief life and fleeting world. Both sit comfortably and claim Paradise—that's not possible! I'm not so bold as to sit comfortably!¹⁰

Bediuzzaman and his students transformed a ruined monastery on the mountain into a mosque, and in a thicket of trees by the source of the Zernabad, they built a small platform on the interwoven branches for Bediuzzaman, which he found conducive to study, prayer, and contemplation. These tree-houses became a mark of the New Said and after he had been exiled to western Anatolia, he had a number made in spots favourable for reading "the book of the universe".

Mullah Hamid also relates many anecdotes illustrating Bediuzzaman's kindness towards animals and his respect for them as creatures, and his affinity with them and power over them. The following is an example showing the latter, that is, illustrating his *karāmāt*, or spiritual powers.

A number of people arrived one day on the mountain to visit Bediuzzaman, and when it became apparent they were to stay overnight, Mullah Hamid was sent down to a neighbouring village to get some quilts. He was frightened of meeting wolves, dogs, or other wild animals, of which there were many, and cut himself a stout stick. But Bediuzzaman would not allow this. "The dogs won't harm you", he told him.

Mullah Hamid set off and on approaching the village he encountered a flock of sheep or goats guarded by dogs. He saw that a great brute of a dog lay across the path, blocking it. Remembering Bediuzzaman's words, he approached the animal; it rose to its feet and moved off making way for him. On reaching the village, the villagers expressed their astonishment, saying that they could not approach the herd even as a group armed with clubs, for the dogs were fed on sheep's milk to make them sufficiently ferocious to ward off the wolves. Whereupon Mullah Hamid told them he had been sent by Bediuzzaman. "Ah," they said. "We can accept it then!"

Mullah Hamid took the quilts and retraced his steps. He was met by Bediuzzaman when he arrived, who asked him if he had been attacked by dogs on the way. On hearing that he had not, he told him:

Have courage! Don't be scared!

It had been a lesson in courage for Mullah Hamid.[11]

Mullah Hamid also related this 'lesson' which Bediuzzaman gave him. In answer to an unasked question about looking at what is forbidden, Bediuzzaman struck himself angrily on the knee, and said:

"I am not satisfied with the Old Said, I'm only happy at three things about him." Then he added: "At a glittering time in Istanbul, I used to change my dress once a week, splendid clothes. I used to go to the most brilliant places in Istanbul. Then my *Hoja* friends appointed one of themselves as observer and got him to follow me, to see where I went and what I did. Three days later while talking with these friends they said to me: 'Said, whatever you do is right. Where you are going is right, and you will be successful in it.' When I asked them why they said this, they told me: 'We have had you followed for three days to see if you did anything contrary to Islam and we saw that you are not concerned with anything apart from your own business. Therefore you will achieve your aims.' Just as a small flame thrown into a forest will by degrees destroy the whole forest, a believer who lowers himself to look at what is forbidden will day by day eat up his actions and destroy them. I am frightened of such a person having a bad end." Then he added:

"The Old Said stayed in Istanbul for ten years during his youth, and he did not look at a woman once."[12]

The Shaykh Said Revolt

Although it was known by everyone that Bediuzzaman had given up all political concerns and gone into retreat, the tribal leaders and those with power still wished to benefit from his enormous influence in the eastern provinces. Thus among his visitors were chiefs and tribal leaders, besides those who came to him purely as a man of religion. The problems of the area had found no solution. Among the Kurds were many who favoured independence or autonomy, especially since the abolition of the Sultanate and Caliphate and the establishment of what many of them saw as the godless Republic. It also provided fertile ground for the British to pursue their ambitions in the area. By early 1925 unrest was widespread, and the tribal chiefs tried to gain Bediuzzaman's support for a full-scale uprising against the Government. As before, Bediuzzaman did all he could to persuade them against such a move. A number complied with his wishes. Thus many thousands of lives were saved when what was to be known as the Shaykh Said Revolt finally broke out on 13 February, 1925, so-called as it was led by a Naqshbandī shaykh called Shaykh Said of Palu. He too had tried to gain Bediuzzaman's support in a letter Bediuzzaman's reply to which is still extant and is given below. The revolt, which was only put down after two months or so, was to have far-reaching results both for Bediuzzaman, who was sent into exile entirely unjustly along with many hundreds of others, and for the area, and not least for the future of the country as a whole. It set the course for the new regime. The Government in Ankara used the revolt as a pretext for rushing through the Law for the Maintenance of Order, passed 4 March 1925, which empowered it to set up the notorious Independence Tribunals and gave them dictatorial powers to pursue their policies without opposition.[13]

Among the tribal leaders who visited Bediuzzaman on several occasions was Kör Hüseyin Pasha. One time he was accompanied by Abdülbaki, the son of the Mufti of Van, Shaykh Masum, a close friend of Bediuzzaman. This visit Abdülbaki describes in some detail, telling of the extremely ascetic conditions under which Bediuzzaman lived on Mount Erek. He also records that during the visit Bediuzzaman foretold the great difficulties they would undergo in the future, but that they should not be unduly dismayed for Allah would send someone to protect and revive His religion of Islam.[14] Interestingly, there is another record of his foretelling the difficulties of the future. On this occasion he told his students to "seek refuge with Almighty God...dire things are going to happen." When they asked for an explanation of this, he merely told them that he was not permitted to say anything further at present.[15]

During the same visit, Kör Hüseyin Pasha tried to give Bediuzzaman money, something he never accepted under any circumstances. Mullah Hamid describes a similar occasion, noting Bediuzzaman's anger at the offer and his refusal. Their exchange continued with Hüseyin Pasha saying:

I want to consult you. My soldiers, horses, weapons and ammunition are all ready. We only await your command.
What do you mean? Whom do you want to fight?
Mustafa Kemal.
And who are Mustafa Kemal's soldiers?
I don't know...soldiers.

So Bediuzzaman told him: "Those soldiers are the sons of this land. They are my kith and kin and your kith and kin. Whom will you kill? And whom will they kill? Think! Use your head! Are you going to make Ahmad kill Mehmed, and Hasan kill Hüseyin?"[16]

Kör Hüseyin Pasha also approached Bediuzzaman on the question on a further occasion, this time in Nurşin Mosque after the Friday prayers and in the company of several other tribal leaders and notables. Ali Çavuş describes how together with the Deputy for Çaldiran, Hasan Bey, and three others he again tried to obtain Bediuzzaman's support. The Governor of Van was alarmed by the visit of these chiefs and on the pretext of a burial service also attended the prayers at the mosque. But his alarm turned out to be needless, for on them admitting to their intention of joining the revolt, Bediuzzaman told them:

> Where has the idea of serving this cause come from, I wonder? I ask you. Is it the Sharī'ah you want? But such an action is absolutely opposed to the Sharī'ah. There is very great likelihood of its being exploited by the foreigners and their provocations. The Sharī'ah can't be contravened by making it a tool and saying: "We want the Sharī'ah." The Sharī'ah can't be demanded like that. The key to it is with me. Now, all of you return to your own homes and places!

When he had finished speaking, Bediuzzaman rose to his feet and returned to Mount Erek. As for Kör Hüseyin Pasha and the tribal leaders, they heeded his warnings and did not join the revolt, which meant too that Van and its people were not forced to join it and thousands of lives were thus saved.[17] Many others testify to this fact.[18]

As was mentioned above, Shaykh Said wrote in person to Bediuzzaman requesting him to join the movement, for if he did so they would be "victorious". Bediuzzaman replied as follows:

> The Turkish nation has acted as the standard-bearer of Islam for centuries. It has produced many saints and given many martyrs. The sword may not be drawn against the sons of such a nation. We are Muslims, we are their brothers, we may not make brother fight brother. It is not permissible according to the Sharī'ah. The sword is to be drawn against external enemies, it may not be used internally. Our only salvation at this time is to offer illumination and guidance through the truths of the Qur'an and belief; it is to get rid of our greatest enemy, ignorance. Give up this attempt of yours, for it will be fruitless. Thousands of innocent men and women may perish on account of a few bandits.[19]

The Journey to Exile

Towards the end of the revolt, the authorities started to round up all the influential religious and tribal leaders in the province of Van, although they had not taken part in the revolt, and send them into exile in western Anatolia. Rumours began to circulate that Bediuzzaman also was going to be exiled. There were moves to persuade him to leave the area for Iran or Arabia. But he declined the offers, saying that should he go to Anatolia, it would be of his own consent. First Shaykh Masum, the Mufti of Van, was arrested, then a squad of three gendarmes and a captain were seen climbing the lower slopes of Mount Erek; they were going towards the source of the Zernabad and Bediuzzaman's cave.

Bediuzzaman was uninformed of this squad and its orders, and on being surprised in his retreat and ordered in peremptory and overbearing fashion by the captain to accompany them, he responded with the boldness that had always marked his response to such behaviour. A tense and electric situation was suddenly created. In the meanwhile, his students and a number of people from the nearest villages had gathered. They awaited his orders to act; it would have been simple for them to get him away from the area and out of the country. However, Bediuzzaman prevented them attempting action of any sort and permitted the gendarmes to take him to Van.[20]

Those arrested and awaiting exile were held in a secondary school in Van. Besides Bediuzzaman and Shaykh Masum were Kör Hüseyin Pasha, the Mufti of Gevaş, Hasan Efendi, Küfecizade Shaykh Abdülbaki Efendi, and Abdullah Efendi, the son of Shaykh Hami Pasha, in addition to hundreds of others including the elderly, women, and children. It was the month of Ramaḍān when they started their long trek, just as it had been in Ramaḍān that Bediuzzaman had returned to Van almost exactly two years previously. That year, 1925, it began on 25 March. It was still bitterly cold and the whole land covered in snow. They set off from Van, some seventy to eighty sledges drawn by oxen or horses, with many also on foot or on horseback. The whole caravan stretched for about a kilometre. To start with Bediuzzaman was handcuffed to Shaykh Masum. According to

Haydar Süphandağlı, Kör Hüseyin Pasha's son, unlike all the others being exiled, who were leaving their homes and native land amid tears and in trepidation like a retreating army, Bediuzzaman was entirely calm and resigned at the turn of events. He also stated that the caravan stopped for three to four days in Patnos, one night in Ağrı, and a week in Erzurum, from where they continued in horse-drawn carts. At Trabzon, where they stayed some twenty days, they boarded a ship for the week-long journey to Istanbul. Here Bediuzzaman stayed some twenty to twenty-five days before travelling on with other exiles to Izmir and Antalya in the same boat. From there he was sent on to Burdur in south-western Anatolia, his destination.[21]

Kinyas Kartal, who as a young man of twenty-five or so was sent into exile in the same group, related that when they were leaving Van, villagers, the rich, many people from the surrounding area collected together a considerable sum of money and gold in order to give it to Bediuzzaman. But he would not even look at it. He would accept presents, charity, or money from no one.[22] Among his own memories of the journey he tells also how "Seyda" did not sleep at night in their first stopping-place, spending it in prayer. After this he requested a room to himself, so as not to disturb the others.[23] That Bediuzzaman received special treatment on the journey is attested to by the gendarme assigned to guard him, Mustafa Ağralı. He gives a detailed description of him, the caravan, and some of the villages in which they stayed. He said:

> All the other sledges were loaded up with people and belongings, but there was nothing on Bediuzzaman's at all. He was all alone. He was being given special treatment. Wound round his head was a long, twisted turban of white printed muslin material. He had thick black moustaches, and no beard...

Mustafa Ağralı described also the hospitality they received from the Kurdish villagers in the places where they stopped for the night. He notes however that in the first place Bediuzzaman refused all offers of food pleading illness. And after spending the night in prayer and performing together with him the morning prayers, he got out a kettle from the small basket which contained his belongings, then proceeded to boil himself an egg on the stove. It was the first food he had eaten since leaving Van.[24]

Of the details given by Münir Bakan when the caravan stayed two or three days in his village of Koruçuk near Erzurum, is the fact that there were officers assigned to write down whatever Bediuzzaman said. As he told Necmeddin Şahiner, "Of course, they weren't writing down these notes out of 'sincerity', but for 'capital'." One of the things he said to Münir Bakan was:

> Don't be afraid, my brother, these disasters that are being visited on us are temporary. Only there is one point you should take careful note of and be afraid of: make your children study, otherwise this religion will be lost to you in no time at all.[25]

By the time the exiles boarded the ship for Istanbul in Trabzon, it was spring and approaching summer in the warmer western climate. Two independent witnesses have told of how Bediuzzaman insisted on remaining on deck in the ship, defying the captain when he tried to force him to go below to join the other exiles.[26]

In Istanbul, he stayed in the Barley Sellers Mosque in Sirkeci, in the Hidayet Mosque, and with his student Tevfik Demiroğlu. His fears had been justified, for the attempts to uproot Islam and expunge Turkey's Islamic past and identity had already begun, and he saw here some of the results. He described one of these as follows:

> When I was brought to Istanbul on my way to exile, I asked what had happened to the Şeyhü'l-İslam's Office, for I was connected with it having worked and served the Qur'an in the Darü'l-Hikmeti'l-İslamiye, which was attached to it. Alas! I received such an answer that my spirit, heart, and mind all trembled and wept. The man I asked said: 'The Office, which for hundreds of years shone with the lights of the Shari'ah, is now a girls' high school and playground.' I was seized by such a mental state that it was as though the world had collapsed on my head.

I had no power, no strength. Uttering sighs of anguish in sheer despair, I turned to the Divine Court, and the feverish sighs of many others whose hearts were burning like mine combined with my sighs. I cannot remember whether or not I sought the assistance of Shaykh Jīlānī's prayers and saintly power for our supplications; I do not know. But in any event it was his prayers and influence that set fire to the sighs of those like me in order to save from darkness a place which for so long had been a place of light. For that night the Şeyhü'l-İslam's Office was in part burnt down. Everyone said, What a pity! But I, and those who were burning like me, declared, All praise and thanks be to God![27]

According to Tahsin Tandoğan, who was a Chief Superintendent of Police in Istanbul in 1925, Bediuzzaman also stayed in Süleymaniye near the old Şeyhü'l-İslam's Office. His recollections have been recorded by Necmeddin Şahiner and provide both added proof of Bediuzzaman's innocence and further interesting details of his stay in Istanbul. Tahsin Bey himself arrested those ring-leaders of the Shaykh Said Revolt who were in Istanbul and took their statements. Namely, Palulu Sadi, Seyyid Abdülkadir, his son Mehmed Bey, and Nazif Bey. He was also ordered by his Chief, Ziya Bey, to go to Süleymaniye to the Şeyhü'l-İslam's Office, in order to bring Bediuzzaman to the Police Headquarters and take his statement. The Police Chief told Chief Superintendent Tahsin Bey: "It is the famous Said-i Kürdi, but he is not in touch with these here involved in the Revolt. We could not establish any connection between them at all." Tahsin Bey continued in his conversation with Necmeddin Şahiner:

> They had recently brought him [Bediuzzaman] from the East. He was staying in Süleymaniye. He had one of his students with him called Bitlisli Kürt Hakkı, who attended to his needs. I myself went to Süleymaniye to get him and bring him to the Special Branch. I had his file. It was me who took the file to the Police Chief and to the Governor [of Istanbul] to have it signed. I myself took his statements. Said Nursi said:

"I have no connection with this revolt whatsoever. I would have nothing to do with a negative movement such as that and know nothing of it. I would not have my brothers' blood on my hands. Such movements are the cause of the blood of brothers being spilt."

Tahsin Bey went on to describe how he took the other four to Diyarbakır to the Independence Tribunal, where three were condemned to death and executed, and one, Nazif Bey, was acquitted. He then went on to say that the enquiries continued for fifteen days, after which they let Bediuzzaman go. Both Seyyid Abdülkadir and Palulu Sadi testified that Said Nursi had no connection with them at all. Tahsin Bey described his impressions of Bediuzzaman like this:

> Bediuzzaman was an extremely intelligent person. I have never seen such an intelligent person. Thousands of guilty people have passed though my hands, and I understand what they are from their faces. What eyes he had! Like a motor, sparking, turning. I have never in my life seen such eyes. They sent him to Isparta as a precautionary measure, he was ordered to reside there. I am of the opinion that he was not the sort of man to be involved in simple revolts such as that; he was a most intelligent person.[28]

After some three weeks, the greater part of which thus passed in helping the police with their enquiries, Bediuzzaman again boarded the ship, which set sail for Antalya having called at Izmir to disembark a number of the other exiles. A considerable crowd of friends and well-wishers gathered on the Galata Bridge to make known their sorrow at his leaving them and bid him farewell. From Antalya he was taken inland to the small town of Burdur.

Burdur

Thus unjustly began twenty-five years of exile for Bediuzzaman. And the injustice was to continue. For rather than merely compulsory residence, he was to be held under the most oppressive conditions, constantly under supervision and subject to arbitrary and unlawful treatment by government officials. He arrived in Burdur in the mulberry season, that is, June, and stayed in the Haji Abdullah Mosque in the Değirmenler district of the town. We learn from another neighbour that he used to hold *dars*, or teach, every day in the mosque after the afternoon prayers, and that this attracted many people.[29] It is probable that as material for these he used what was later entitled *The First Door of the Risale-i Nur (Nur'un İlk Kapısı)*. This was a collection of thirteen short sections, called "dars", which he wrote while in Burdur and had put together secretly into book form. This was then duplicated by hand by people who felt the need for the basic truths of belief that it teaches. Bediuzzaman described it as "an index, list, and seed of the *Risale-i Nur*" and as "the Qur'an's first lesson to the New Said."[30]

Of those who came to visit Bediuzzaman in Burdur was A. Hamdi Kasaboğlu, a member of the Consultative Council of the Department of Religious Affairs. He related the following to Necmeddin Şahiner:

> One day, I went to visit Bediuzzaman in Burdur. I took a page of Arabic with me wondering if he knew the language. During the visit, I requested, "Would you read this for me, please?", and I handed it to him. He took it, cast an eye over it, and handed it back to me. And saying, "Now let's see if I can remember it", he read by heart the whole page.[31]

Field Marshal Fevzi Çakmak, the head of General Staff, came to Burdur while Bediuzzaman was there. He knew him of old, and when the governor complained to him about Bediuzzaman, saying that he, and a number of his students, declined to report to the police station every evening as was required of them, and that he was giving religious instruction to those who came to him, Fevzi Pasha told him: "No harm will come from Bediuzzaman. Treat him with respect and don't bother him."[32]

Isparta

However, Bediuzzaman's activities were contrary to what those inimical to religion had expected when he had been exiled to this small Anatolian town, and they began to raise anxieties among the authorities concerning him. And so in January 1926, Bediuzzaman was taken from Burdur and sent to the centre of Isparta. There he stayed in the Müftü Tahsin Efendi Madrasah and at once again began to teach and attract many students. The Governor of the town felt consternation at this. According to one eye witness who visited the *madrasah*, when he went there it was full to overflowing and he was only able to sit in the doorway.[33] So the authorities determined to send Bediuzzaman away to some tiny and remote place where he would not attract attention, and where deprived of all company and civilization, he would just fade away and be forgotten. The place they chose was the village of Barla, a tiny hamlet in the mountains near the north-western shore of Lake Eğridir. After some twenty days in Isparta, Bediuzzaman was taken there.

Always severely self-critical and interpreting events according to their inner or true meaning, Bediuzzaman gave the following reasons for his being exiled to the three places we have described:

> This concerns this unfortunate Said: whenever I have flagged in my duties, and saying "what is it to me", have become preoccupied with own private affairs, I have received a slap.
>
> For example, so long as this unfortunate Said was busy teaching the truths of the Qur'an in Van at the time of the Shaykh Said events, the suspicious government did not and could not interfere with me. Then when I said 'What is it to me?' and thinking of myself withdrew into a ruined cave on Mount Erek in order to save my life in the hereafter, they took me without cause and exiled me. And I was brought to Burdur.
>
> There, again so long as I was serving the Qur'an—at that time all the exiles were watched very closely, and although I was supposed to report to the police in person every evening, my sincere students and myself remained as exceptions [we did not comply]. The governor there complained to Fevzi Pasha when he came. But Fevzi Pasha said: "Don't interfere with him; treat him with respect." What made him say that was the sacred nature of service to the Qur'an. But whenever I have been

overcome by the idea of saving myself and thought only of my life in the hereafter, and there has been a temporary slackening in my serving the Qur'an, I have received a slap contrary to my intentions. That is to say, I was sent from one place of exile to another. I was sent to Isparta.

In Isparta I took up my duties once again. After twenty days, a number of cowardly people said by way of a warning: "Perhaps the government won't look favourably on this situation. It would be better if you go a bit cautiously." Again I began to think only of myself and I said: "Don't let the people come!" And again I was taken from that place of exile and sent to a third, to Barla.

And in Barla whenever I have felt a slackness and the idea of thinking of myself only has gained strength, one of these serpents and two-faced hypocrites from among those concerned only with this world has been set to pester me.[34]

Thus, after his short stay in his second place of exile, Isparta, Bediuzzaman was sent to the village of Barla. At that time the easiest way to travel there through that mountainous country was by way of Lake Eğridir. The gendarme who accompanied him from the village of Eğridir to Barla, Şevket Demiray, described their journey as follows:

> The morning after market day in Eğridir, they called me to the Town Hall. I went, and the head official of the district, the gendarme commander, members of the Town Council, and an imposing-looking man of around forty years[35] of age wearing turban and gown were there. The gendarme commander said to me: "Look here, son, you've got to take this Hoja Efendi to Barla. He is the famous Bediuzzaman Said Efendi. It is a very important task for you. When you hand him over to the police station there, get these documents signed and then report back here." I said: "Right away, Sir!", and undertook the duty. I went out from there with the Hoja Efendi, and said to him on the way: "You are my superior, forgive me, but what can I do, it is my duty." We arrived at the jetty and there agreed on a price with a boatman. He accepted to take us for fifty *kuruş*. Bediuzzaman Efendi got out the money for the boat and paid him. Then he gave a further ten *kuruş* and got them to buy a kilo

of seedless raisins. When boarding the boat he had in his hand a basket containing his belongings: a teapot and kettle, a few glasses, and a prayer-rug. In his other hand was a Qur'an. With the two boatmen, a friend of the boatmen's, and the two of us, we were five in the boat. It was afternoon. The weather was cold. It was round about the time when the first signs of spring were appearing. The lake was iced over in places. The front boatman broke the ice with a long pole he had in his hand opening a way for the sailing boat. Bediuzzaman offered each of us raisins and pieces of dried pressed fruit from the East on the way. I was watching him carefully; he was completely calm and steady. He was looking at the lake and surrounding mountains. His fingers were long and thin. He was shining as though electricity was burning inside him. He was wearing a silver ring set with a stone, and on his back was a garment of very high quality cloth.

It was the time for the afternoon prayers since the days were short. He wanted to perform them in the boat. We turned the boat towards the *qiblah* then I heard the sound of '*Allāhu akbar*'. The first time I heard the words uttered in this awe-inspiring and solemn way was from him. He declared the words '*Allāhu akbar*', 'God is Most Great', in such a fashion that we all shivered. His manner did not resemble that of any other *hoja*. We were trying not to let the boat veer away from the direction of the *qiblah*. Bediuzzaman offered the words of peace and completed the prayers, then turned to us and said: 'Yes, brother, that was a bother for you.' He was a most polite and gentlemanly person. We arrived at the Barla jetty after a voyage of some two hours. The forester Burhan was wandering up and down on the jetty. I called out to him: "Hey, son, come here!" He came immediately. We took the *hoja's* basket and sheepskin from him and put them on the donkey.

At this point, the boatman Mehmed took the forester's rifle intending to shoot partridges with it, but Bediuzzaman prevented him saying: "The spring is close now and their mating season. It's a shame, give up the idea if you like." He stopped him shooting them. And the partridges took off and started to fly over our heads following us.

I slung my rifle over my left shoulder and took Hoja Efendi's left arm. We climbed the hill slowly and after walking for about an hour came to Barla. The partridges which had taken off from the shore remained above us as far as Barla. They kept flying round above us.

Evening had drawn close. We stopped at the police station beside the Ak Mescid in Barla. The head official of the district, Bahri Baba, and the chief of the police station were there. I handed Bediuzzaman Efendi over to them and got them to sign the papers. After spending the night there I returned to Eğridir in the morning.[36]

Notes

1. Abdullah Ekinci, in *Son Şahitler*, i, 192.
2. Hamid Ekinci, in *Son Şahitler*, i, 200.
3. *Ibid.*, 198-9.
4. See, Nursi, *Mektûbat*, 5-7 (Eng. tr.: *Letters*, 21-9).
5. İsmail Perihanoğlu, in *Son Şahitler*, ii, 26-7.
6. See, Nursi, *Lem'alar*, 5-7 (Eng. tr.: *Flashes*, 18-20).
7. İsmail Perihanoğlu, in *Son Şahitler*, ii, 27.
8. Rabia Ünlükul, in *Son Şahitler*, i, 63.
9. İsmail Perihanoğlu, in *Son Şahitler*, ii, 27.
10. Hamid Ekinci, in *Son Şahitler*, i, 209.
11. Hamid Ekinci, in *Son Şahitler*, i, 205-6.
12. N. Şahiner, *Said Nursi*, 252-3.
13. *Türkiye Tarihi*, iv, Istanbul 1989, 101-2.
14. Abdülbaki Arvasi, in *Son Şahitler*, i, 100.
15. İsmail Perihanoğlu, in *Son Şahitler*, ii, 29.
16. Şahiner, *Said Nursi*, 253-4.
17. *Ibid.*, 255-7.
18. For example, the one-time deputy for Van and president of the Grand National Assembly, Kinyas Kartal. See, *Son Şahitler*, ii, 17.
19. Şahiner, *Said Nursi*, 254-5, quoted from the personal notes of Zübeyir Gündüzalp, one of Bediuzzaman's closest and most influential students in the last ten years of his life.
20. *Ibid.*, 257-9.
21. Haydar Süphandağlı, in *Son Şahitler*, ii, 95-6.
22. Abdullah Ekinci, in *Son Şahitler*, i, 193.
23. Kinyas Kartal, in *Son Şahitler*, ii, 17.
24. Mustafa Ağralı, in *Son Şahitler*, i, 104-7.
25. H. Münir Bakan, in *Son Şahitler*, iv, 371-2.

26. Ahmet Alpaslan, in *Son Şahitler*, i, 98, and, Said Şamil, in Şahiner, *Nurś Yolu*, 133-5.
27. Nursi, *Sikke-i Tasdik-i Gaybî*, 130; Şahiner, *Said Nursi*, 259-60.
28. Tahsin Tandoğan, in *Aydınlar Konuşuyor*, 165-7.
29. Nasuhizade Shaykh Mehmed Balkır, in *Son Şahitler*, iv, 212-3.
30. Nursi, *Nur'un İlk Kapısı*, 6-7.
31. Şahiner, *Said Nursi*, 261.
32. Nursi, *Lem'alar*, 40 (Eng. tr.: *Flashes*, 70); *Tarihçe*, 135-6; Şahiner, *Said Nursi*, 260-1.
33. Mehmed Sözer, in *Son Şahitler*, ii, 211-2.
34. Nursi, *Lem'alar*, 40 (Eng. tr.: *Flashes*, 70-1).
35. Bediuzzaman was actually nearly fifty years old.
36. Şahiner, *Said Nursi*, 262-4.

12

Barla

Isolation in Barla

Barla, Ankara had indeed found a remote spot removed from easy contact with the outside world. With its low, red-rooved houses nestling on a hillside among the green-sprinkled mountains to the west of Lake Eğridir, this small village could only be reached on foot, horse or donkey; there was no motor road. The road was to come to Barla in later years, as was the telephone and electricity. The authorities in Ankara were not to know, however, that in unjustly exiling Bediuzzaman to this distant spot that they were serving the very cause they were intending to extirpate. They were not to know that their injustice in not only exiling him, but in imposing these conditions of isolation on him would be "transformed into a divine mercy". They allowed him only the occasional visitor, and spreading rumours and slander about him in the area of Barla they frightened off the local people and tried to prevent them approaching him; they had him watched, followed, and harassed continuously; and when after a time the government granted an amnesty to those exiled with him, they denied him this right. But these repressive measures were merely serving the purposes of divine wisdom. For in this way Bediuzzaman was isolated from all distraction and his mind was kept clear, so that he could "freely receive the effulgence of the Qur'an" and be employed to a greater degree by his "Compassionate Sustainer in its service."[1] He was to remain nearly eight and a half years in the gardens and mountains of Barla, and during this time he wrote the greater part of the one hundred and thirty parts of the *Risale-i Nur*. Barla became the centre from which radiated the lights of the truths of belief at a time when the darkness of unbelief was gathering force to stifle the Islamic faith of the people of Anatolia.

The Attempt to Uproot Islam

Indeed, 1925 had seen the start of twenty-five years of an absolute despotism which descended on Anatolia at the very moment of its liberation. By supreme effort its people had driven out the enemies who had seized their land and threatened their existence. Now it was becoming clear that one of those who had led them in that struggle and subsequently established himself as the nation's leader in Ankara intended to uproot the very values they had sacrificed themselves to preserve, their religion, Islam, and replace it with those of their eternal enemies. This could only be done by force. His purpose was to make Turkey into a Western-style state, so he had to uproot one way of life together with everything that made it what it was, and impose an alien one. For centuries the Turkish people had carried the banner of the Islamic world. To be a Turk was to be a Muslim. Every corner of Anatolia bore the traces of their forefather's religion, every part of its soil had been watered by their blood. Now, in order to remove all obstacles to Westernization, the intention was to distance them from Islam, to make them forget their religion, to sever all their links with the past. How could this be done other than by force, by despotism, by rooting out the very heart of the Turkish nation?

The drive to bring this about began soon after the victory in the War of Independence, and proceeded on all fronts. One after an other the institutions and marks of Islam were abolished or banned, and replaced by imported Western models. First, the power of the *'ulamā'*, still considerable, which also constituted a possible threat, was removed. The Caliphate, the Office of Şeyhü'l-İslam, and Ministry of the Sharī'ah were all abolished; and the religious schools, the *madrasahs*, were closed. This all occurred in 1924 before Bediuzzaman visited Istanbul on his way to exile.

Following the Shaykh Said Revolt in 1925, with the new dictatorial powers afforded the government by the Law for the Maintenance of Order mentioned above, a law was passed providing for the closure of all dervish lodges, Sufi convents, and tombs of saints, and for the disbanding of the Sufi orders, in addition to banning their meetings and special dress.[2]

Later the same year it was announced that the people of Anatolia should dress in a "civilized" manner, that is, according to Western fashion. Religious dress was banned, and the famous Hat Act of November 1925 stated that all men should wear European-style hats making the wearing of all other headgear a criminal offence. These decrees provoked outraged reactions and were imposed only by means of the Independence Tribunals and not a few executions.[3] Many hundreds of people were arrested in efforts to enforce this law, men of religion being the main targets and victims. Characteristically, Bediuzzaman resolutely refused to discard his turban and gown, and persisted in defying attempts to make him do so till the end of his days, even making his court appearances in them. "This turban comes off with this head!", he told Nevzat Tandoğan, the governor of Ankara, in 1943 after a very sharp exchange. He was taken from the governor's office and transported to prison in Denizli.[4]

The traditional calendars and forms of time-keeping were the next to go. The Western Gregorian calendar and twenty-four hour clock were introduced with effect from 1 January, 1926. Then came the final blow to the *'ulamā'* and Islamic establishment: the adoption of European codes of law. The adoption of the Swiss Civil Code removed the last areas where the Sharī'ah was still in force, personal and family law, and the remaining areas of competence of its lawyers.

These changes were not without opponents, even at the highest level, and a conspiracy against Mustafa Kemal in June 1926 provided him with the pretext to do away with many of them. The Independence Tribunals went into action following the discovery of the plot and many were sent to the gallows, whether implicated or not.

By 1928, Mustafa Kemal felt sufficiently secure to adopt Western numerals, and then the Latin alphabet. The New Turkish Letters were officially adopted in accordance with a law passed on 3 November 1928, and the Arabic alphabet, the script of the Qur'an and mark of Islam, was declared banned after the end of that year. A more effective way of cutting off an entire nation from its religion, its roots, and its past could not have been devised. The *Risale-i Nur* was to play an important role in keeping the Qur'anic script alive in Turkey.

Having Turkified the alphabet the next logical step was to Turkify Islam itself. The Arabic letters had been done away with, now the language itself had to be substituted by Turkish. To retain the Arabic language was considered incompatible with the principle of nationalism, one of the six basic principles of Kemalism, and the decision was taken to substitute it with Turkish. Thus from the end of January, 1932, the glorious Arabic words of the call to prayer, the great mark and symbol of Islam, were banned and a Turkish version was provided to take its place. This, which according to one historian "caused more widespread popular resentment than any of the other secularist measures",[5] remained in use till the Democrat Government repealed the law in June, 1950, as one of its first pieces of legislation.[6]

All these 'revolutions' were carried out in the cause of secularism, one of the most important of the Kemalist principles. The meaning of this concept, *laiklik*, taken from the French, laicism, was and continues to be a subject of fierce debate. Suffice it to say here that during the twenty-five years of Republican People's Party (RPP) rule, its implementation was seen as the means of destroying most of the outward signs of the religion of Islam in Turkish life. It shall be discussed in greater detail in a subsequent chapter. Indeed, it was the alleged infringement of this principle that was used as the pretext for Bediuzzaman's arrest and imprisonment on a number of occasions.

In the early 1930's the RPP, the party Mustafa Kemal had founded, merged with the state, thereby gaining absolute control over it and its resources. Its six principles were written into the Turkish Constitution in 1937. Having obtained an absolute monopoly of power, the RPP embarked on a programme of mass education in the principles of the Kemalist Revolution. Opening thousands of People's Houses, People's Rooms, and later Village Institutes in every corner of the country, these were the means of instilling the six principles, particularly secularism, nationalism, and Western culture into the Turkish people at grass roots level. The Qur'an and traditional Islamic culture were to go, everybody had to identify with the new order. Eyes had to be turned from the Islamic past to a Godless future. If they could not impose their atheistic principles on many of the people of mature years, the young and the generations of the future could be made to accept them. It is said that the underlying intention of these programmes was the eventual establishment of communism or socialism in Turkey.

This has been a brief description of the main course of the Kemalist revolutions, and prevailing atmosphere and conditions in Turkey during the twenty-five years of Bediuzzaman's exile, first in Barla and then in other places. And while it does not adequately express the tyranny, oppression, and injustice which accompanied these changes, it is hoped that as the story of Bediuzzaman's struggle in the face of them unfolds, the magnitude of that struggle and his success through the *Risale-i Nur* in overcoming these ill-conceived designs on the Qur'an and Islam will become clear.

The *Risale-i Nur*

Within a month or two of arriving in Barla, Bediuzzaman wrote a treatise proving the resurrection of the dead and existence of the hereafter; it was the first part of the *Risale-i Nur* to be written. This was followed by a succession of others, one of the most significant being *The Miraculousness of the Qur'an*, which proves the very points by which its enemies had attempted to discredit the Qur'an to be the sources of its "eloquence" and "miraculousness". By 1929 the first collection of the treatises, thirty-two in number, was completed, the thirty-third was added later, and Bediuzzaman gave it the name of *Sözler, The Words*. Thus began Bediuzzaman's silent struggle against the forces of irreligion.

The way the *Risale-i Nur* was composed was unique, just as its form and manner of exposition are unique. It was inspired directly by the Qur'an at this time when the Qur'an faced severe threats, and the greater part of the Islamic world too was under foreign domination and suffering. Bediuzzaman wrote:

> Unlike other works, the *Risale-i Nur* was not taken from the sciences and branches of learning or from other books; it has no source other than the Qur'an; it has no master other than the Qur'an; it has no authority other than the Qur'an. Its author had no other book with him when it was written. It was directly inspired by the effulgence of the Qur'an, and descended and was revealed from the skies of the Qur'an and the stars of its verses.[7]

The *Risale-i Nur* is a commentary (*tafsīr*) on the Qur'an that expounds it not according to the order of the verses and the immediate causes for its revelation, but explains those verses which concern the truths of belief. Commentaries on the Qur'an are of various sorts. As the Pre-Eternal Word of God, the Qur'an addresses all people of every age; it has a face that looks to each century and age, and speaks according to the conditions and needs peculiar to each. The *Risale-i Nur* expounds that face which looks to the modern age, and by virtue of its source possesses certain characteristics which uniquely qualify it to address contemporary man and his needs.

Firstly, it is almost entirely concerned with expounding the truths of belief, as opposed to verses concerning social and *fiqh* or *shar'ī* matters; it explains and proves the pillars of faith, like the existence and unity of God, the resurrection of the dead, the hereafter, and prophethood, together with such questions as the true nature of man and the universe. For while in the past these were secure, now these very bases of faith were under attack. The method it employs to do this is reasoned argument and logical proof—since they had been attacked in the name of reason, and also in the manner of the Qur'an, through the use of comparison and allegory. That is to say, the *Risale-i Nur* answers the attacks made on the Qur'an and belief in the name of science and Western philosophy and civilization, and through comparisons of the two demonstrates the rationality of belief and logical absurdity of materialist philosophy, and that man's happiness and salvation lie only in the former.

Furthermore, with these comparisons it explains matters from the simplest to the most profound and abstruse in such a manner that everyone can grasp them in accordance with their level of understanding. This last point is of fundamental importance: the *Risale-i Nur* is populist. That is to say, just as the Old Said had striven to make his message heard to ordinary people and to involve them in the great movement of the time, so too the New Said in his new struggle strove to reach the ordinary people and to renew and strengthen their belief. The *Risale-i Nur* makes available in this age of mass communication the truths of belief, and even the most profound aspects of them which were hitherto available only to the few, to the whole community of believers, so that all may gain firm and true belief. For it is only through true belief that the assaults of the various forms of misguidance at the present time may be withstood. The many further points about the *Risale-i Nur* and the new way to the truth that it opened up will become clear in later chapters. Before examining the Tenth Word, the Treatise on Resurrection and the Hereafter, which illustrates many of the points made above, let us return briefly to Bediuzzaman and his life in Barla.

Bediuzzaman lived the life of a recluse in Barla, thinking and writing. The first week he spent as a guest of one of the villagers,

Muhajir Hafız Ahmed, who together with his family was later to perform great services for Bediuzzaman and the *Risale-i Nur*.⁸ On Bediuzzaman's request for somewhere quieter and less-frequented, a small, two-roomed house was suggested, that had formerly served as the village meeting-house. This humble dwelling was more suitable to Bediuzzaman's needs and he stayed there for the next eight years. In his own words it became his "first Nur *Madrasah*", that is, "*Risale-i Nur* School". Beneath it ran a stream, summer and winter, and in front stood a truly majestic plane tree. Among its great boughs Bediuzzaman had made a small tree-house, which in spring and summer he used as a place for contemplation and prayer. His students and the people of Barla used to say that he would remain there all night, neither rising nor sleeping, and at dawn the birds would fly round the tree as though drawn by the sound of his supplications and join their songs to his prayers.⁹

Barla's situation is one of great beauty. Mountains rise up behind it, and before it the land falls away to Lake Eğridir, with orchards and fields along the curve of its valley. Bediuzzaman spent much of his time walking through this country and down along the lake. High above the lake some four hours' distance from Barla is Çam Dağı, Pine Mountain. Here Bediuzzaman spent much time, particularly after 1930, staying weeks on end in complete solitude. Here too he had tree-houses made, two of them, one in a pine tree and one in a cedar, where he would write and also correct the handwritten copies of *The Words*, and other parts of the *Risale-i Nur*, which by that time were becoming increasingly numerous as it became better known and more widespread.

The way the *Risale-i Nur* was written and disseminated was another of its unique aspects. Together with his extraordinary learning and abilities, Bediuzzaman himself had very poor handwriting, so that he described himself as "semi-literate". He interpreted this as a Divine bounty, however, because in consequence of this need, Almighty God sent him students who were "heroes of the pen".[10] He would dictate at speed to these scribes, who would write down what he dictated with equal speed. The actual act of writing, therefore, was very fast, so that some of the parts of the *Risale-i Nur* were written in an incredibly short space of time, like one or two hours. This shall be discussed at greater length later. And Bediuzzaman himself was busy with the actual writing for only an hour or two each day. Copies of the original were written out by hand, and distributed. These then were copied and passed on to others who would write out further copies. In this way *The Words* passed from village to village, and in the course of time, from town to town, and throughout Turkey, as we shall see.

'Resurrection and the Hereafter'

Since the New Said had emerged from the Old Said in the years following the First World War, Bediuzzaman had immersed himself in the Qur'an in his search for a new way to reach and relate its truths in the fast-changing conditions of the times. He had withdrawn from public life of every sort and given himself over to an intense inner life of worship, thought, and contemplation. Thus, what was to be known as the Tenth Word, the Treatise on Resurrection and the Hereafter, was the first fruit of those five or six years of inner search, the answer to his prayers and supplications.

On revisiting Barla in 1954 with some of his students, Bediuzzaman described to them how it was written. They had gone to the fields and orchards on the slopes to the east of Barla down towards Lake Eğridir when Bediuzzaman rose to his feet and pointing to the orchards, told them:

> My brothers! It was about thirty years ago and just this same season. I was walking through these orchards and the almond trees were in blossom. Suddenly the verse, *"So think on the signs of God's Mercy, how He gives life to the earth after its death; indeed, He it is Who will give life to the dead, and He is powerful over all things"*[11] came to mind. It became clear to me that day. I

was both walking and repeating that verse over and over again at the top of my voice. I recited it forty times. Then in the evening I returned and together with Şamlı Hafız Tevfik wrote the Tenth Word. That is, I dictated and Hafız Tevfik wrote it down.[12]

Unlike most subsequent parts of the *Risale-i Nur* when they were first written, Bediuzzaman was able to have the Tenth Word printed. Immediately after it was written, a local merchant, Bekir Dikmen, took the manuscript to Istanbul and gave it to one of Bediuzzaman's old students from the East, Müküslü Hamza Efendi, who had a thousand copies printed. When the sixty-three-page books were ready, Bekir Dikmen brought them back to Eğridir, from where they were taken by boat to Barla, and there handed over to Bediuzzaman. He then corrected each copy and had them distributed.[13]

A number of these copies Bediuzzaman had sent to Ankara and distributed among the Deputies in the National Assembly and top government officials. It happened that this coincided with moves in government circles to officially inculcate ideas denying bodily resurrection in the Turkish people.[14] Bediuzzaman later described this as follows:

> The Council for Education had met in Ankara in order to discuss their programme for uprooting religious ideas and imposing their atheistic views on school children and students. They decided that this should be carried out through the teaching of philosophy and denial of the resurrection of the dead. A short time after this meeting, one of the members of the council encountered a deputy who had with him a copy of Bediuzzaman's treatise at the door of the Assembly. He spotted the book and told the deputy: "Said Nursi is receiving information about our work and is writing works to counteract it." Kazım Karabekir Pasha informed him of this. But Bediuzzaman explained it like this:
>
> "I had received no such information that the Council for Education had taken that decision. Almighty God bestowed the Treatise on Resurrection on me on account of their decision. I did not write it out of my own desire or at my own whim. It was written as a consequence of need."[15]

This was an instance of an extraordinary property associated with the Qur'an and which was manifested particularly in the Tenth Word, and in other parts of the *Risale-i Nur*, which may be mentioned briefly at this point, and that is what is known as *tevâfük* (Ar. *tawāfuq*), that is, coinciding or agreement. This consists of the coinciding of events or more usually of certain letters or words in written copies of these works. The most well-known is the Divine Name of Allah in copies of the Qur'an written according to the pagination of Hafız Osman, which on some pages takes up positions forming vertical lines or other patterns. It is a most striking and clear indication of its miraculous nature. In regard to the *Risale-i Nur*, Bediuzzaman wrote:

> My brothers! We are in need of truly great moral strength in the face of misguidance and heedlessness at this time. But regrettably, I personally am extremely weak and bankrupt, I do not possess any wonderful spiritual powers with which to prove these truths, nor do I have any saintly powers with which to attract hearts. I do not possess an elevated genius with which to subjugate minds. I am like a suppliant servant at the court of the All-Wise Qur'an. Sometimes I seek help from the All-Wise Qur'an's mysteries in order to smash the obduracy of the stubborn people of misguidance and make them see things fairly. I perceived a Divine favour in this 'coinciding', as instances of the miraculous power of the Qur'an, and I embraced it with both hands.[16]

In the Tenth Word, this appeared both in the timing of its being written, and in hand-written copies of the work in particular, written by Bediuzzaman's students, where, in a manner entirely outside their will, the letter *alif*, the first letter of the word Allah, displayed this coinciding to such a degree that it could in no way be attributed to chance. Examples in other parts of the *Risale-i Nur* will be given later.

Bediuzzaman attached the greatest importance to this treatise, which, as he said, "explained to ordinary people, and even to children", truths of belief which even a genius of philosophy like Ibn Sīnā (Avicenna) had confessed his impotence before. Ibn Sīnā had declared that 'resurrection cannot be understood by rational criteria.'[17] Bediuzzaman wrote also in a letter in the early 1930's that its "value had not been fully appreciated." And that he himself had "studied it perhaps fifty times, and each time I have received pleasure from it and felt the need to reread it."[18]

What form then does the Treatise on Resurrection take that it is able to prove such difficult matters so simply and clearly? He himself described it like this:

> Each [of the Twelve Truths of which the main part of the work is composed] proves three things at the same time. Each proves both the existence of the Necessarily Existent One, and His Names and attributes then it constructs the resurrection of the dead on these and proves it. Bediuzzaman then continues: Everyone from the most obdurate unbeliever to the most sincere believer can take his share from each Truth, because in each the gaze is turned towards beings, works. Each says: 'There are well-ordered acts in these, and a well-ordered act cannot be without an author, in which case it has an author. And since the act has been carried out with order and balance, its author must be wise and just. Since he is wise, he does nothing in vain. And since he acts with justice, he does not permit rights to be violated. There will therefore be a great gathering, a supreme tribunal.' The Truths have been tackled in this way. They are succinct, and thus prove the three things at once.[19]

At the end of the conclusion of the Tenth Word itself, this is enlarged upon. Bediuzzaman explains that the proofs for resurrection rest on Divine works in the universe which proceed from the manifestation of the Greatest Divine Name and the greatest degree of manifestation of the other Names and are therefore vast and immense. He writes:

> Since the resurrection and Great Gathering occur through the manifestation of the Greatest Name, they are to be proved as easily as the spring, and submitted to with certainty, and believed in firmly, through seeing and demonstrating the immense acts which are apparent through the manifestation of God Almighty's Greatest Name and the greatest degree of all His names.[20]

Thus, Bediuzzaman explains that it is because of this great breadth and profundity that the matter of resurrection is difficult to comprehend rationally. But he adds that thanks should be offered that the way had been shown by the Qur'an where man's reason on its own had remained impotent.

Life in Barla

Barla's spring and summer rains are famous. The sunny skies suddenly cloud over, the thunder crashes, the lightning flashes, and the heavens open. Then the air is filled with the sweet smell of the soaked earth.

On one of the early days of the first summer he was in Barla, Bediuzzaman was walking alone in the surrounding country when the skies darkened and just such rain started to fall. Finding nowhere to shelter in the mountains, he made his way back to Barla drenched to the skin. On entering the village, he slowly climbed the narrow streets to the common water tap with his by now ripped black rubber shoes in his hand and white woollen stockings soaked in mud. There, a group of the villagers were gathered together chatting. One of them, seeing "the Hoja" in this sorry and lonely state, parted from the group and came up behind him.

Sensing there was someone behind him, Bediuzzaman turned and seeing Süleyman as he was called, said to him: "Come, my brother!" Süleyman hurried forward, and taking the torn and muddy shoes, washed them in the trough, then together they climbed on up the hill to Bediuzzaman's house. This Süleyman attended to Bediuzzaman's needs with complete willingness and faithfulness for the next eight years. Bediuzzaman called him 'Sıddık Süleyman', Süleyman the True. The Twenty-Eighth Word, about Paradise, was written in his garden. To this day it is known as the Paradise Garden.[21]

Bediuzzaman continued to suffer from bad health all the time he was in Barla. It was also his habit to eat just enough to keep body and soul together. This had always been his practice and had often been noted by those who knew him, generally a small bowl of soup and a small piece of bread. The first four years he was in Barla, his soup came from Muhajir Hafız Ahmed's house, brought by his seven and eight year old children, who were *huffāz*[22] of the Qur'an like himself. Bediuzzaman would always without fail give them the price of the soup in return, ten kuruş in those days. The four years following this it was provided by another of the villagers, Abdullah Çavuş.[23]

For the first years Bediuzzaman was in Barla, he was very much alone, and he described this isolation in several letters, two of which are given below. However he also raised a lot of interest in the area, and on occasion received visits from local people from all walks of life. One of these was by a local District Official called İhsan Üstündağ, who visited Bediuzzaman together with the District Doctor, the Finance Officer, and a chemist, sometime between 1926 and 1930. As a firsthand account as well as because of its interest, his description of the visit is included here:

> While on the way to Barla in the boat, a conversation started up on religious matters. The chemist had little religious belief, and he said to us: "You say God exists, so why did He create evil?", denying God. We could in no way convince him. So we spoke to him of Bediuzzaman and told him: "Don't say anything else or we'll throw you in the lake! We're going to Barla, so ask the Hoja Efendi there; he'll give you your answer." We went to the District Chief's house and before drinking our coffee even, sent word that we wanted to go to Bediuzzaman. He received us gladly, greeting us standing. "While it should have been I that visited you, you have come to visit me", he said, and before we could ask any questions, opened the subject of good and evil. He continued: "Now I'll explain to you how evil can be good." We gasped in amazement. He gave this example: "Cutting off an arm infected with gangrene is not evil, it is good, because if it isn't cut off, the body would go. That means Allah created that evil for good." Then he turned to the doctor and the chemist, and said: "You are a doctor and a chemist, you know this better

than I do." On hearing this, the chemist turned as white as chalk. He was completely tongue-tied. [They had not said who they were.] Hoja Efendi then gave an additional example: "If a number of eggs are put under a turkey and nothing comes of some of them, but from the others chicks hatch, can it be said that this is evil, because each chick that hatches is worth five hundred eggs?" Finally he described the heart from the medical point of view, giving a lot of scientific facts. Several days later, Dr Kemal Bey said to me: "I had never before heard such a fine scientific exposition of the heart even from professors!"[24]

The following are extracts from the two letters describing Bediuzzaman's solitude. All his letters begin with the words, "In His Name, be He glorified", and are followed by the verse: "And there is nothing but glorifies Him with praise."[25]

> My Dear Brothers!
> I am now on a high peak on Pine Mountain, at the top of a mighty pine tree in a tree-house. In lonely solitude far from men, I have grown accustomed to this isolation. When I wish for conversation with men, I imagine you to be here with me, and I talk with you and find consolation. If there is nothing to prevent it, I would like to remain alone here for one or two months. If I return to Barla, I shall search for an opportunity for the verbal conversation with you I so long for, if you would like it. For now I am writing two or three things which come to mind here in this pine tree.
>
> *The First*: this is somewhat confidential, but no secrets are concealed from you. It is thus:
>
> Some of the people of truth manifest the the Divine Name of Loving One, and with that manifestation at a maximum degree look to the Necessarily Existent One through the windows of beings. In the same way, but just when he is employed in service of the Qur'an and is the herald of its infinite treasuries, this brother of yours who is nothing, but nothing, has been given a state that is the means to manifesting the Divine Names of All-Compassionate and All-Wise. God willing, *The Words* manifest the meaning of the verse: "He who has been given wisdom, has been given great good" (Qur'an, 2:269).

The Second: This saying about the Naqshbandī *ṭarīqah* suddenly occurred to me: "On the Naqshbandī way one must abandon four things: the world, the hereafter, existence, and abandoning itself." It brought following to mind:

On the way of impotence four things are necessary: absolute poverty, absolute impotence, absolute thanks, and absolute ardour, my friend.[26]

Another example is Bediuzzaman's famous *Gurbet* letter. There is no direct equivalent for the word *gurbet* in English; it denotes the idea of being away from home, exile, and strangeness, and has long been a theme in the literatures of the Islamic lands. After starting in his customary way, he writes:

My hard-working brothers, zealous friends, and means of consolation in these lands of exile known as the world!

These last two or three months I have been very much alone. Sometimes once every two or three weeks I have a guest with me, the rest of the time I am alone. And for nearly three weeks now there has been no one working in the mountains near me; all have dispersed...

One night in these strange mountains, silent and alone amid the mournful sighing of the trees, I saw myself in five exiles of different hues.

The first: due to old age, I was alone and a stranger far from the great majority of my friends, relations, and those close to me; I felt a sad exile at their having left me and departed for the Intermediate Realm [the grave]. Then another sphere of exile was opened within this one: I felt a sad sense of separation and exile at most of the beings to which I was attached, like last spring, having left me and departed. And a further sphere of exile opened up within this, which was that I found myself far from my native land and relations, and was alone. I felt a sense of separation and exile arising from this too. Then through that, the lonesomeness of the night and the mountains made me feel another pitiable exile. And then I saw my spirit in an overwhelming exile, which had been prepared to journey to eternity both from this exile and from the transitory guest-house of this world. I said to myself suddenly, My God, how can these exiles and layers of darkness be borne? My heart cried out:

"My Lord! I am a stranger, I have no one, I am weak,
I am powerless, I am impotent, I am old;
I am without will; I seek recourse, I seek forgiveness,
I seek help from Your Court, O God!"

Suddenly the light of belief, the effulgence of the Qur'an, and the grace of the Most Merciful came to my aid. They transformed those five dark exiles into five luminous and familiar spheres. My tongue said:

"God is enough for us, and He is the best disposer of affairs" (Qur'an, 3:173).

While my heart recited the verse:

"And if they turn away, say: God is enough for me, there is no god but He; in Him do I place my my trust, for He is the Lord of the Mighty Throne" (Qur'an, 9:129).

Bediuzzaman goes on to quote lines of poetry, and concludes that: "through impotence and reliance on God, and poverty and seeking refuge with Him, the door of light is opened and the layers of darkness dispersed." "What does the one who finds God lose? And what does the one who loses Him find?"[27]

And in another letter Bediuzzaman wrote: "I have understood and believe firmly that this world is a guesthouse undergoing rapid change. It is not, therefore, the true homeland and everywhere is the same...Since everywhere is a guesthouse, if the mercy of the guesthouse's Owner befriends one, everyone is a friend and everywhere is friendly. If it does not befriend one, everywhere is a load on the heart and everyone an enemy."[28]

Abdurrahman's Death and Bediuzzaman's Students

These letters were written to Hulûsi Yahyagil,[29] "the first student of the *Risale-i Nur*". Then serving as a captain in the army stationed at Eğridir, he first visited Bediuzzaman in the spring of 1929. From Elazığ in eastern Turkey, he was to perform enormous services for the *Risale-i Nur* when he returned there eighteen months later. He formed a very close bond with Bediuzzaman identifying completely with *The Words*, and "his zeal and seriousness were

Barla

the most important reason the last of *The Words* (*Sözler*) and most of the *Letters* (*Mektubat*) were written."[30] More than this, Bediuzzaman considered him to be the successor to his nephew, Abdurrahman.[31]

Yes, together with all the other hardships he suffered at this time, Bediuzzaman was struck by this heavy blow: the death of his spiritual son, companion, and helper, Abdurrahman. Let us hear it from his own pen:

> One time I was being held in the district of Barla in the province of Isparta in a distressing captivity called exile, in a truly wretched state suffering both illness and old age, and absence from home, and in a village alone and with no one, barred from all social intercourse and communication. Then, in His perfect mercy, Almighty God bestowed a light on me concerning the subtle points and mysteries of the All-Wise Qur'an which was a means of consolation for me. With it, I tried to forget my pitiful, grievous, sad state. I was able to forget my native land, my friends and relations, but, alas, there was one person I could not forget, and that was Abdurrahman, who was both my nephew, and my spiritual son, and my most devoted student, and my bravest friend. He had parted from me six or seven years previously. Then, out of the blue someone gave me a letter. I opened it, and saw that it was from Abdurrahman, written in a way showing his true self. It made me weep, and it still makes me weep. The late Abdurrahman wrote in the letter seriously and sincerely that he was disgusted with the pleasures of this world and that his greatest desire was to reach me and look to my needs in my old age just as I had looked to his when he was young. He also wanted to help me with his capable pen in spreading the mysteries of the Qur'an, my true duty in this world. He even wrote in his letter: "Send me twenty or thirty treatises and I'll write twenty or thirty copies of each and get others to write them."...
>
> He had obtained a copy of the Tenth Word on belief in the Hereafter before writing the letter. It was as if the treatise had been a remedy for him curing all the spiritual wounds he had received during those six or seven years. He then wrote the letter to me as if he was awaiting his death with a truly strong and

shining belief. One or two months later while thinking of once again passing a happy worldly life thanks to Abdurrahman, alas, I suddenly received news of his death. I was so shaken by the news that five years later I am still under the effect of it. Half of my private world had died with the death of my mother, and now with Abdurrahman's death, the other half died. My ties with the world were now completely cut.[32]

Once again Bediuzzaman found consolation through the Qur'an, this time through the meaning of the verse: "Everything shall perish save His countenance; His is the command, and to Him shall you return" (Qur'an, 28:88), and the phrase, "The Eternal One, He is the Eternal One". And Bediuzzaman completes this piece, taken from his *Treatise for the Elderly*, by saying that Almighty God gave him thirty Abdurrahman's in place of the one He had taken.

The most important of these new students was Hulûsi Yahyagil, who first visited Bediuzzaman a year or so after Abdurrahman's death. Another was Kuleönlü Mustafa, whom Bediuzzaman found waiting for him when he returned home to Barla after hearing the news.[33] There were also a number of army officers, besides Hulûsi Bey. One of these was Re'fet Bey,[34] a retired captain, another was Binbaşı Asım Bey,[35] who died under interrogation in Isparta in 1935 when Bediuzzaman and over a hundred of his students were rounded up and arrested. There was also Santral Sabri,[36] the 'jetty keeper' at the village of Bedre on Lake Eğridir, who played a central role in distributing the parts of the *Risale-i Nur* to the surrounding villages. He was the prayer-leader in the village mosque, and shared with Bediuzzaman a "seal of brotherhood", in the form of the second and third toes of one foot being webbed. And Hüsrev[37] from Isparta, who had very fine handwriting and devoted himself entirely to writing out copies of the *Risale-i Nur* and to its service.

Bediuzzaman's relations with his students were quite unlike the usual formal, distant relations between teacher and students or shaykh and followers. He considered himself to be a student of the *Risale-i Nur* the same as them, and besides having close personal relations with them—true to his belief in consultation—consulted them concerning all matters to do with the writing and dissemination of the *Risale-i Nur*. And just as he was awe-inspiring and utterly uncompromising in the face of unbelief and the enemies of religion, towards those who served the truth he was most kind and compassionate. Bediuzzaman was also extremely modest and courteous with his students, and personally would accept no superior position, praise or adulation. "I don't like myself", he used to say, "and I don't like those who like me!" He would only accept praise in so far as it belonged to the *Risale-i Nur* or the Qur'an. Bediuzzaman also kept in constant touch with his students and an unceasing flow of letters passed between them. These thousands of letters were gathered together and form a substantial part of the *Risale-i Nur*. The following is part of a letter, from the collection of those written while Bediuzzaman was in Barla.

> My brothers Hüsrev, Lütfi, and Rüştü,
> In one respect—beyond my due—you are my students, and in one respect you are my fellow students, and in one respect you are my assistants and consultants.
> My dear brothers! Your Ustādh [Master] is not infallible. It is an error to suppose him to be free of error. One rotten apple in an orchard does not harm the orchard. And one worn coin in a treasury does not negate the treasury's value. If good points are reckoned as ten and bad points as one, it is fair in the face of the good points not to upset the heart and object because of the one bad point and error...
> Understand this, my brothers and fellow students! I shall be happy if you tell me freely when you see a fault in me. If you hit me over the head with it even, I shall say, May God be pleased with you! Other sakes should not be considered in preserving the sake of the truth. I will accept it immediately because of the egotism of the evil-commanding soul, not to defend a truth which I did not know was for the sake of the truth. Understand that at this time, this duty of serving belief is most important. It should not be loaded on a wretch who is weak and whose

> thought is dispersed in numerous directions; assistance should be given as far as it is possible. Yes, the absolute and succinct truths emerge and I am the apparent means, and the ordering and clarifying and giving of form are up to my valuable and capable fellow students.
>
> You know that in summer the heedlessness of this world prevails. Most of my fellow students become slack and are compelled to cease from their occupations. They cannot be fully occupied with serious truths. In His perfect Mercy for two years now Almighty God has granted a favour to our minds with the subtle coincidences, which are like fruits in relation to the serious truths; He has given joy to our minds. In His perfect compassion, through the fruits of those subtle coincidences, He has driven our minds to a serious Qur'anic truth, and made those fruits food and sustenance for our spirits. Like dates, they have been both fruit and basic sustenance.[38]

It is important to continuously bear in mind when reading these pages the extremely difficult conditions under which Bediuzzaman and his students were working at this time. It will be recalled that the plans had been laid to entirely root out Islam from the fabric of Turkish society, and that these plans were being progressively and forceably, put into practice. First the *madrasahs* and Sufi *takiyyahs* had been closed. Then a final stop had been effectively put to the teaching of religion with the banning of the Arabic alphabet in 1928 and its substitution by the Latin letters. Subsequent to this those caught teaching or reading books in the old alphabet were treated as criminals and very often suffered imprisonment, exile, or even death as a consequence. This was also true for the Qur'an. The teaching and learning of it were carried on in secrecy. Imprisonment and torture were the lot of the persecuted *hojas* caught teaching it. It was a nightmare for the people of Anatolia, so bound to the religion of their fathers. This official terror and persecution increased in severity throughout the 1930's and 40's.

In reading the letters of those who were introduced to the *Risale-i Nur* at this time, it becomes clear how greatly they benefited from it. Their belief became firm and strengthened as they read its treatises and they gained great strength and courage. They also had the example of Bediuzzaman and his proverbial courage and persistence, so that they bore all the hardships, attached no importance to the persecution, and like him devoted themselves entirely to writing out copies of the treatises of the *Risale-i Nur* and passing them on to others. The following are two examples of letters to Bediuzzaman from his students. The first is from Hüsrev of the "graceful pen", who for years wrote innumerable copies of the *Risale-i Nur*.

> My Dear and Respected Master!
> Each of your *Words*, that is, your treatises, is a mighty cure. I receive great blessings from your *Words*. So much so that the more I read them the more I want to read them. And I can't describe the sublime delight I feel each time I read them. I am certain that one who takes, not all, but even one of your *Words* and reads it fairly will be obliged to submit to the truth; and if he is a denier, he will be obliged to give up the way he has taken; and if he is a sinner, he will be obliged to repent.[39]

The second is from Kuleönlü Mustafa, who as mentioned above visited Bediuzzaman after he had received news of Abdurrahman's death, and was a forerunner of the many hardworking students who were to devote themselves to the *Risale-i Nur* in place of Abdurrahman. Included here are only several extracts of his long letter, which is interesting in that it describes both how he himself found his "guide" in the *Risale-i Nur*, and how others like him responded to it in the same way and found how it "cured their wounds", and also how the *hojas*, not known for their readiness to accept anything new, recognised its unique value. This letter also makes the important point that at the time that the *madrasahs* had been closed and the people were deprived of any opportunity of learning Arabic, the language in which all teaching of religion had been carried out, the *Risale-i Nur* took the place of the *madrasahs*, teaching the truths of belief and the Qur'an both in Turkish and in a way suitable for their needs.

My Revered Master!

My spirit was searching for a perfect guide, and while searching it was imparted to me, 'You are seeking the guide far away, while close by there is Bediuzzaman. His *Risale-i Nur* is like a regenerator. It is both the spiritual pole, and the Dhū al-Qarnayn, and the deputy of Jesus (upon whom be peace), who is to come at the end of time; that is to say, it brings the good news of him.' So I approached the respected Master. He gave me the order to write out the treatises. So I wrote out fifteen or so of *The Words* and I am reading them...I began to benefit from them immensely...Eventually young people gathered around me...

My Esteemed Master! The treatises cure the material and spiritual wounds of these hundred friends of mine.. Sometimes even those from far off are submerged in doubts and they come here; if this impotent student of yours reads a treatise to them, their doubts are dispelled and disappear...

This impotent student of yours never studied Arabic or saw the inside of a *madrasah*. He used to read books in Turkish written long ago and could find no remedy to cure his material and spiritual wounds...[But] just as Almighty God creates a Paradise-like time in a Hell-like time, and creates solutions appropriate for each time and bestows remedies appropriate for each wound, so too in this time of ours which lacks *madrasah*s He is causing the treatises [of the *Risale-i Nur*] to be written by means of our Esteemed Master, in Turkish, for those wounded like us....Countless and innumerable thanks be to Almighty God, and may He give our Esteemed Master success in the service of the Qur'an and exalt him in this world and the next. Amen! Although I received no education in Arabic or had ten to fifteen years' *madrasah* education and have only written out the treatises of the *Risale-i Nur* and studied them seriously, I imagine myself to have studied in a *madrasah* for twenty years. The reason is this: many Arabic *hojas* now come to this impotent, humble wretch and are in wonder at what he has studied. Those who have previously received training from perfect guides come and are captivated by the words they hear from me. Many *hojas* come in all humility and get me to read the *Risale-i Nur*. If my voice was sufficiently powerful I would shout with all my strength to the young people on the earth: "Writing and studying the *Risale-i Nur* seriously is superior to studying in a *madrasah* for twenty years and more beneficial![40]

The *Risale-i Nur* Spreads

By degrees the *Risale-i Nur* was disseminated as the writing of it became more widespread. Particularly in the area of Isparta, there were eventually thousands of students of the *Risale-i Nur*, men and women, young and old, who devoted themselves to writing out copies of it. Of these students, there were some who did not emerge from their houses for seven or eight years. In the village of Sav, which came to be known as the Nur School, the treatises of the *Risale-i Nur* were duplicated by literally a thousand pens. And this continued for a considerable number of years. A duplicating machine was first used continuously in İnebolu in 1946 and '47,[41] while it was not till 1956 that it was possible to print the whole *Risale-i Nur* Collection in the new script.[42] The number given for handwritten copies of the various parts of the *Risale-i Nur* is six hundred thousand.

Radiating out from Bediuzzaman himself through these students of the *Risale-i Nur* was a courage and hope which countered the pervading air of defeat and despair engendered by the pressure, propaganda, and terror directed against Islam and those who practised it. This courage and hope were contagious and generated a positive movement which eventually spread through the whole country. The students were undaunted by the intimidation and official efforts to prevent them. They suffered every sort of persecution. They lived under the constant threat of having their houses raided and searched for copies of the *Risale-i Nur*. Many were taken time and again from their houses to police stations, where they suffered imprisonment, torture, and the bastinado.

The women too played a vital and heroic role in this extraordinary movement. Some took on their husband's work to leave them free to either write or serve the *Risale-i Nur* in some other way, others assisting their husbands in writing. Many wrote out copies by simply tracing the letters. Many others now learnt to read and write for the first time and wrote out copies of the treatises themselves. Others read the *Risale-i Nur* themselves and then read it to other women in the vicinity. Undaunted like their husbands at the intimidation, they found their strength from the firm belief they obtained through reading and listening to the "lessons" of the *Risale-i Nur*. Children too played an important part in writing out the treatises.[43]

It may be seen from this how the *Risale-i Nur* contributed to preserving the Qur'anic script in Turkey when the authorities were attempting to abolish it entirely. And more than this, in the face of the so-called language reforms which followed in the 1930's aiming at removing all loan-words of Arabic and Persian origin, it played a truly important role in maintaining and even reinvigorating traditional, Islamic, culture. It may even be said that the *Risale-i Nur* movement contributed significantly to increasing the literacy rate and raising the cultural level of thousands of people, quite apart from its duty of preserving and renewing the Islamic faith. In connection with this Bediuzzaman wrote: "Just as the *Risale-i Nur* works to protect the truths of belief against atheism, so also one of its duties is to preserve the letters and script of the Qur'an against innovations."[44]

What was it about the *Risale-i Nur* that attracted these people to it, causing them to undertake so many risks and hardships and very often leave aside their own concerns so as to devote themselves to its service? What was the source of its power to strengthen their belief in this way? Or was it in fact Bediuzzaman that attracted them and infused them with this zeal? Or did the the *Risale-i Nur* itself possess some attractive power that drew them and held them? First we can say that Bediuzzaman always directed attention away from his own personality and self towards the *Risale-i Nur*, shunning any sort of adulation that would damage the absolute sincerity he considered necessary for the task to which he had been appointed. Also, he considered that all of himself had gone into the *Risale-i Nur*. And as was mentioned before, he saw himself not as the source of the *Risale-i Nur*, but merely as its "translator", as the means of its being written. He said of himself: "Just as an ordinary private can announce the commands of a field marshal, and a bankrupt can shout out the wares of a shop full of priceless jewels and diamonds, so I announce the wares of the sacred shop of the Qur'an."[45] He also wrote: "I do not say about *The Words* out of modesty but to state a fact, that the truths and perfections in *The Words* are not mine, they are the Qur'an's, and have issued from the Qur'an."[46] Thus, it may be said that it was the lights of the Qur'an shining through the *Risale-i Nur* that were attracting and illuminating ever-increasing numbers of people.

"Divine Favours" Associated with the Writing of the *Risale-i Nur*

As a form of thanks and also in order to encourage his students in their work in the difficult conditions of the time, Bediuzzaman dedicated a long section of one of his letters to describing a number of "divine favours" associated with the writing of the *Risale-i Nur* which strengthen this claim. He told them that without their knowledge and beyond their will, someone was employing them in these important matters. And his evidence for this was these favours and the fact that things were made easy for them. He then enumerated some of them, calling them Indications.[47]

Firstly was the question of the coincidences, mentioned above in connection with the Tenth Word. Here Bediuzzaman takes the Nineteenth Letter as an example, which in certain handwritten copies displayed some truly extraordinary examples of these agreements or coincidences. He also used it as an example for others of the points, including the great ease and speed with which most of the *Risale-i Nur* was written, for the most part when he was suffering most from illness and the torments of the authorities. Briefly, the Nineteenth Letter, entitled *The*

Miracles of Muhammad (ṣ), describes more than three hundred of the Prophet's miracles, very often citing the narrators of the Ḥadīths quoted. Despite being over a hundred pages long, it was written entirely from memory, without recourse to any books for reference, outside in the countryside, and within the space of three or four days working only for two or three hours each day, thus making a total of about twelve hours. When the first copies were made, it was before they knew about these 'coincidences', and in copies written by eight different, inexperienced, scribes who were in different places and did not communicate with each other, the alignments and positioning of the phrase "the Most Noble Prophet, Upon whom be blessings and peace," turned out to be so clear and well-ordered that it was impossible to attribute them to chance. As though positioned by an unseen hand, this arrangement of the phrase was itself a sort of miracle or wonder of the Miracles of Muhammad (ṣ).[48]

The Second Indication was "the brothers, each of whose pens were like diamond swords", whom Almighty God had bestowed on Bediuzzaman as helpers. They themselves formed a sort of coincidence, and the fact that they dedicated themselves to serving the cause of the Qur'an through the *Risale-i Nur*, "never flagging and with total enthusiasm and enterprise, at that time when the alphabet had been changed and there were no printing-presses and everyone was in need of the lights of belief, and there were many things to destroy their enthusiasm, was itself a sort of miracle of the Qur'an and a clear Divine favour."

A further Indication was that the *Risale-i Nur* proved all the most important truths of belief and the Qur'an in clear fashion, and Bediuzzaman cited a number by way of example. For instance, the Tenth Word, about the resurrection of the dead and the hereafter, before which, as we have seen, even Ibn Sīnā had confessed his impotence. Another is the Twenty-Sixth Word, which solves the problem of Divine Determining, sometimes called fate or destiny, and human will, in a manner that everyone may understand. Others are the Twenty-Fourth Letter, and the Twenty-Ninth Word, which is a brilliant exposition on the angels, the immortality of man's spirit, and the resurrection of the dead, and the Thirtieth Word, on the human 'I' or ego, and the transformations of minute particles, all of which "uncover and explain the talisman of the astonishing activity in the universe, the riddle of the creation or the world and its end, and the mystery of the wisdom in the motion of minute particles."

The Fourth Indication of the Divine favours associated with the writing of the *Risale-i Nur*, Bediuzzaman writes modestly, was that the various parts of it explain by means of comparisons the most profound and inaccessible truths of belief to even the common people in a way beyond his own abilities and outside of what the conditions of the time allowed. These comparisons, which are an important feature of the *Risale-i Nur* and are "reflections" and "similitudes" of the comparisons in the Qur'an, "bring the most distant truths close and teach them to the most ordinary person." So also, although the *Risale-i Nur* had by then become widespread, its treatises had not been the object of criticism by religious scholars or anyone else, and everyone from religious scholars and those who followed the *ṭarīqahs* to atheistically-minded philosophers and the ordinary people had benefited from it according to their degree; it addressed everyone according to their level.

The Sixth Indication is very significant, and it shall be mentioned again later; it was that Bediuzzaman's whole life had been as though in preparation for the *Risale-i Nur*. He wrote: "I am now certain that my life has passed in such a way, beyond my will and power, consciousness and planning and has been given so strange a course, so that it would yield the result of these treatises to serve the All-Wise Qur'an. It is quite simply as though all my scholarly life has been an introduction to them and in preparation of them. It has passed in such a way that the displaying of the Qur'an's miraculousness through *The Words* [the *Risale-i Nur*] would be its result." And now his isolation in Barla and the persecution he suffered from the authorities, not even being allowed his books for study, had concentrated all his attention on the Qur'an and the writing of the *Risale-i Nur*.

Furthermore "almost all the treatises had been bestowed on the spur of the moment and instantaneously due to some need arising out of [Bediuzzaman's] spirit, without any external cause." After they had been read by others, he learnt from them that the treatises met the needs of the times and were a cure for its ailments.

And a final indication of the Divine favour directed towards them was the ease and assistance they experienced in all matters concerned with the writing, copying, and disseminating of the *Risale-i Nur*. Bediuzzaman described this as being "extraordinary", and said that he had no doubt it emanated from the Qur'an. So also they found that they received an ease and plenty in their livelihoods as a result of serving the *Risale-i Nur*.

The Authorities Increase Their Pressure on Bediuzzaman

As the *Risale-i Nur* became more widespread and it became clear to the authorities that they had failed to stifle Bediuzzaman's endeavours in the cause of Islam, they stepped up their pressure on him. The aim was to constantly needle him—unlawfully—to provoke a reaction which would provide them with the excuse to further curtail his freedom. With this aim, two officials were posted to Barla in 1931; one was a new Chief District Officer, while the other was a teacher. Although these two were a constant thorn in his flesh, they failed in their attempts to provoke him. Even when they arranged for his small mosque to be raided while he and a few others were worshipping, and then closed it, Bediuzzaman contained his righteous wrath. They had anyway previously barred him from it on occasion in their efforts to make his isolation total, as well as preventing him from holding his *dars* or readings with one or two of his students in his own room.

When Bediuzzaman had first come to Barla, he had repaired a small mosque which had fallen into disuse, and thereafter, on the strength of his certificate which dated from before his exile, acted as imam or prayer-leader to a small congregation of three or four people. Thus these two officials staged a raid on the mosque making the new law imposing the Turkish call to prayer the pretext.

According to Cemal Can, the District Chief, when Bediuzzaman refused to have the call to prayer and the preliminary prayer given in anything other than Arabic in his mosque, he received repeated directives from Ankara on the subject and finally arranged the raid.[49] On 18 July 1932, then, gendarmes were concealed in various dark corners of the mosque and on the Arabic words being uttered, sprang into view with bayonets fixed surrounding Bediuzzaman and his small congregation of innocent villagers. Four of these were then arrested and marched off to Eğridir. They were, however, released after questioning and being ill-treated. Bediuzzaman described the affair like this:

> "The aggression of the heretics behind the scenes recently has taken on a most ugly form; they have assaulted the people of belief in a most tyrannical and irreligious manner. During the private and unofficial worship of myself and one or two friends in the mosque I myself repaired for my own use, they intervened in the call to prayer and *kamet*. 'Why are you saying the *kamet* and call to prayer secretly in Arabic?', they demanded." He then went on to make a verbal attack, not on "those lacking conscience" who planned the raid, whom he said were not worth addressing, but on "the heretics and innovators" who were the instigators of these moves in the name of Turkish nationalism, "the heads of the committees who, following the path of pharaoh, are playing in arbitrary and tyrannical fashion with the nation's destiny."[50]

Tevfik Tığlı, the teacher, said of Cemal Can that he made every effort to have Bediuzzaman moved from Barla. And he too took it on himself to pester and harass him. However, as very often happened with those whose intention was to harm Bediuzzaman, the Chief District Official received a blow from the Almighty: totally unexpectedly, he was arrested in connection with some quite different matter and was sent to prison for two and half years.[51]

In regard to the changes to the call to prayer, Bediuzzaman supported his adamant opposition to Turkifying the practices of Islam with various reasoned arguments. Particularly in regard to the Qur'an, when the authorities announced it was to be translated in the early thirties, he wrote various letters and treatises arguing the impossibility of translating it, and pointed out the evil intentions of those who were urging it.

For example, some people said that words of the Qur'an and those used by the Prophet (ṣ) in various prayers and supplications illuminate man's inner faculties and are spiritual sustenance for him. The words alone are not enough if their meaning is not known. The words are like clothes; if they are changed, would that not be more beneficial? To which Bediuzzaman replied:

> The words of the Qur'an and those of the glorifications of the Prophet (ṣ) are not lifeless clothes; they are like the living skin of a body. Indeed, with the passage of time, they have become the skin. Clothes can be changed, but if skin is changed it is harmful to the body. Indeed, the blessed words like those in the prescribed prayers and in the call to prayer, for example, have become the signs and marks of their accepted meanings. And as for signs and names, they cannot be changed. He then goes on to say that whenever they are repeated, each of man's subtle inner senses takes its share from these phrases, whereas if they are in a language other than the revealed Arabic of the Qur'an, man's spirit remains in darkness, and he becomes heedless of the Divine presence. So also Bediuzzaman provides arguments stating it to be contrary to the Sharī'ah to change these 'marks of Islam'.[52]

In another letter after pointing out that it was blind imitation of Europe that was the source of these attempts to change the marks of Islam, as in all bad things, Bediuzzaman stressed the importance of an environment which constantly reminds Muslims of the meanings of these sacred phrases, and instructs them in them[53]—these phrases which are "each a seed of the pillars of belief."[54]

Bediuzzaman said that when the proposal was first made to translate the Qur'an, it was part of a conspiracy against it and was made with the direct intention of discrediting it. "But," he wrote, "The irrefutable arguments of the *Risale-i Nur* have proved that a true translation of the Qur'an is not possible. No other language can preserve the subtle points and fine qualities of the Qur'an in place of the grammatical language of Arabic. The trite and partial translations of man cannot hold the place of the miraculous and comprehensive expressions of the words of the Qur'an, each letter of which affords from ten to a thousand rewards; [such translations] may not be read in mosques."[55] While some aspect of this fact is shown to be true in many places in the *Risale-i Nur*, it is chiefly the Twenty-Fifth Word,[56] called *The Miraculousness of the Qur'an*, which in demonstrating forty aspects of the Qur'an's miraculousness proves this to be the case. This remarkable treatise, which demonstrates Bediuzzaman's profound and extensive knowledge of the Qur'an shows its miraculousness in respect of the eloquence of its word-order, meanings, styles, manner of exposition, the comprehensiveness of its words, meanings, subjects, styles and conciseness; its giving news of the Unseen, preserving its youth, and addressing all classes and levels of men, and in various other respects.

The more they increased the pressure on Bediuzzaman with their arbitrary and unlawful oppression, the greater was his endeavour and the more the *Risale-i Nur* spread. Just as by unjustly exiling him, and unlawfully isolating him and preventing him from all social intercourse, the authorities in Ankara had unwittingly served the cause of the Qur'an, now too in Barla their persecution of him served only to "make the lights of the Qur'an shine brighter." Indeed, the same was true for the next twenty years; the spread and successes of the *Risale-i Nur* were in direct proportion to the continual increase in the severity of the treatment meted out to Bediuzzaman and his students. Bediuzzaman points this out in the conclusion to the following letter, describing some of the injustices he received in Barla.

> The treatment I have received this seven years has been purely arbitrary and outside the law. For the laws concerning exiles and prisoners are clear. By law, they can meet with their relations and they are not prevented from mixing with others. In every nation and state worship and prayer are immune from interference. People like me stayed together with their friends and relations in towns. They were prevented neither from mixing with others, nor from communicating, nor from moving about freely. I was prevented. Then even my mosque was raided. And while it is *Sunna* to repeat the words, There is no god but God in the prayers following the prescribed prayers according to the Shafi'i school, they tried to make me give them up. Even, one of the old exiles in Burdur, an illiterate called Şebab and his mother-in-law, came here for a change of air. They came to me because we come from the same place. They were summoned from the mosque by three armed gendarmes. The official then tried to hide that he had made a mistake and acted unlawfully, and apologized, saying: "Don't be angry, it was my duty." Then he gave them permission and told them to go. If other things and treatment are compared to this event, it is understood that the treatment accorded to me is purely arbitrary, and that they inflict vipers and curs on me. But I don't condescend to bother with them. I refer it to Almighty God to ward off their evil. In fact, those who instigated the event that was the cause of the exile are now back in their own lands, and powerful chiefs are back at the heads of their tribes. Everyone has been discharged, but they put me in a village and set those with the least conscience on me. And just as I have only been able to go to another village twenty minutes away twice in six years, so they did not give me permission to go there for a few days' change of air, crushing me even more under their tyranny. Whereas whatever the government, the law is the same for all. There cannot be different laws for villages and for individuals.

That is to say, the law as far as I am concerned is unlawfulness. The officials here utilize the government influence for their own personal interests. But I offer a hundred thousand thanks to Almighty God, and by way of making known His bounties, I say this: "All this oppression and tyranny of theirs is like pieces of wood for the fire of ardour and endeavour which illuminates the lights of the Qur'an; it makes them flare up and shine. And those lights of the Qur'an, which have suffered that persecution of theirs and have spread with the heat of endeavour, have made this province, indeed, most of the country, like a *madrasah* in place of Barla. They supposed me to be a prisoner in a village. On the contrary, in spite of the atheists, Barla has become the teaching desk, and many places, like Isparta, have become like the *madrasah*."[57]

Bediuzzaman's Relations with the World and the Worldly

In early February 1934, Bediuzzaman wrote this letter to Re'fet Bey in Isparta:

> My Dear, Loyal, Meticulous, and Ardent Brother, Re'fet Bey!
> However much you want to talk with me, I probably want to talk with you more. But unfortunately, I am in a distressing situation afflicted with numerous difficulties. When I find the opportunity, I try to write seven or eight letters in the space of an hour or two. Galib too, who used to come from time to time, has been prevented. Only poor Şamlı remains, and he cannot come all the time. Also they wound these vipers and make them attack us like savage beasts. They try to cause annoyance at every opportunity....And because they have made me think of the world, the ideas that come to me have ceased. Let it be the end of them, thinking of the worldlys' world is poison for me... I implore Almighty God to bestow on me firm patience and to abstract my mind so I do not think of it.[58]

The New Said had withdrawn from the world and politics. The Ankara Government had aimed to isolate him from all contacts with the world beyond the village of Barla, and indeed within it too, but this was also what the New Said had chosen. It was after all from the cave in Mount Erek near Van that he had been taken to exile. But now the authorities would not leave him in peace. They would not leave him alone. They could not pin anything on him, he did not break any of their laws, yet the religious treatises he was writing were being duplicated in hundreds of homes in the province of Isparta and beyond at a time when the production of books and writings on Islam had been suppressed virtually entirely. They were extremely agitated by Bediuzzaman and the *Risale-i Nur*, interpreting his writings only in political terms. According to their way of thinking—Bediuzzaman calls them "*ehl-i dünya*", the worldly whose view is restricted solely to the life of this world—the *Risale-i Nur* was being written as a means to political ends, hence their constant provocation and harassment of him and his students. Bediuzzaman answered these suspicions of the politicians and the authorities in several letters, stating clearly that he was compelled to explain the matter to them "in the tongue of the Old Said, not that of the New Said", in order to save not himself, but his friends and the *Risale-i Nur* from "the unfounded suspicions and torments of the worldly."[59] In the Sixteenth Letter, Bediuzzaman made clear his attitude towards politics like this:

> The New Said flees from politics so vehemently so as to not sacrifice for one or two years of dubious worldly life…, [or] his working for and gaining eternal life, which lasts millions of years, and so also to serve belief and the Qur'an, which is the most important and necessary, the most sincere and loyal duty. For he says, I am getting old, I don't know how much longer I shall live. For me the most important matter, therefore, has to be working for eternal life. And the first means of gaining eternal life and the key to eternal happiness is belief in God, so one has to strive for them. But because I am bound by the Shari'ah to be beneficial to others in regard to learning, I want to perform that duty. Therefore, I gave up the other way and chose the way of serving belief, which is the most important, the most necessary, and the soundest….
>
> But if you ask: "Why does service to the Qur'an and belief bar you [from politics]?", I would reply: Since the truths of belief and the Qur'an are each like diamonds, if I was polluted

by politics, the ordinary people, who can be deceived, might wonder: 'Isn't he making political propaganda in order to win supporters?', and they might look at those diamonds as though they were common glass. Then I would be wronging those diamonds by being in contact with politics, and would be as though reducing their value.[60]

A passage in the Thirteenth Letter[61] enlarges on this, pointing out that politics were not the way to bring the guidance of the Qur'an to the majority of people at that time, in fact, they formed an obstacle. It shows Bediuzzaman's acute awareness of the state of Turkish society and its needs. In the face of the misguidance that had permeated all aspects of life, most people were not opposed to the truth, they were confused and uncertain; what they needed was to be drawn to the truth through the lights of the Qur'an, whereas politics frightened them off. Only a minority embraced misguidance, but all the attention was focussed on them, while the "bewildered" majority remained deprived of the guidance of which they were in need. Bediuzzaman's concern was for this majority. He also pointed out that there were supporters of the truth in all the political currents; thus, one showing the truths of the Qur'an had to remain outside all partisanship, so that the Qur'an should not be left open to attack by his political opponents.

Isparta

In the summer of 1934 Bediuzzaman wrote to one of his students in Isparta, a calligrapher called Tenekeci Mehmed, saying that things had become intolerable in Barla. He wrote:

> My brother, the torments of the teacher and Chief District Officer here have made my situation unbearable. They discomfort me incredibly. I can't even go out into the countryside. I live in my damp room as though living in the grave.

This student took the letter immediately to the Governor, Mehmed Fevzi Daldal, and the next day, 25 July, Bediuzzaman was collected and taken to Isparta. He was to remain there till the following April, staying first in the *madrasah* he had used before being sent to Barla. He moved then to a two-storey house set amid gardens where his student Re'fet Barutçu was staying, and afterwards rented a wooden house belonging to another student, Şükrü İçhan.[62]

During these months in Isparta, Bediuzzaman was held under very close surveillance. Police were permanently posted on his door and in the vicinity. One particularly obnoxious police officer has found his place in history, called Dündar. He used to make whatever trouble he could for Bediuzzaman and his students. Often Bediuzzaman's students could not approach him, he was kept under such strict surveillance. For a time just one, called Mehmed Gülirmak, was permitted to remain with him to attend to his needs. He also acted as 'Nur Postman', collecting or distributing the *Risale-i Nur* as required. In Isparta, Bediuzzaman wrote several more parts of *Lem'alar*, *The Flashes*, the third collection of the *Risale-i Nur*. When completed, *The Flashes* numbered thirty treatises, and the complete *Risale-i Nur*, one hundred and thirty. He loved the province of Isparta, as the centre from which the *Risale-i Nur* irradiated by means of his numerous students. He expressed this to a number of them sometime later: "...Because of you, I love Isparta and the surrounding country together with its very stones and soil. I can even say that if the Isparta authorities were to impose a prison sentence on me and another province was to acquit me, I would still choose Isparta."[63]

Some of Bediuzzaman's closest students such as Hüsrev and Re'fet Bey were in the town of Isparta. They remained with him as far as they were able now that he had been moved there, principally acting as his scribes and writing out copies of the *Risale-i Nur*. Among Re'fet Bey's reminiscences of this time were these:

> Hüsrev and I were writing out copies of the Risale. Ustādh was in the upstairs room. Suddenly the door clicked and opened, and what did we see but Ustādh entering with a tray and two glasses

of tea. We were overcome with confusion and embarrassment and sprang to our feet wanting to take the tray from him. But he lifted his hand and said, "No, no. It's me that has to serve you." My goodness, and he added "has to". What modesty! What courtesy! I never saw such courtesy and modesty anywhere...

We were studying the truths of the Qur'an and writing them. We were benefiting enormously. To tell him this one day, we said to him: "What would we have done, Ustādh, if we had not found you?" And again with that tremendous modesty he replied to us: "What would I have done if I had not found you? If you are happy once over that you found me, I should be happy a thousand times that I found you."[64]

Of the three parts of the *Risale-i Nur* written here, the Nineteenth, Twenty-Fifth, and Twenty-Sixth Flashes, called the treatises On Frugality, Message for the Sick, and For the Elderly, respectively, Re'fet Bey recalled the following about the writing of the Treatise for the Elderly. In the event, only the first thirteen 'Hopes' were written due to their being taken into custody by the authorities:

One day Ustādh called us, and saying: "The Twenty-Sixth Flash is about the elderly. It consists of twenty-six Hopes. The First Hope...", he began to dictate.

He dictated five or six Hopes, and it stopped at that. Some time passed and certain parts of other treatises were written in the interval. Then one day he called us, and without asking, without saying something like, "Where did we stop, just read out a bit', he continued to dictate from where we had left off." That is to say, it was still fresh in Bediuzzaman's mind as though they had broken off five minutes earlier. Re'fet Bey then went on:

I used to go to him early, to assist him. One day I was a bit late. When I arrived, he said to me, 'Brother! If only you had come a bit earlier, what I have just told this person (indicating the Kadı Zeynel Efendi beside him) would have made an excellent addendum to the treatise on Divine Determining.' He had answered the Kadı's questions about Divine Determining and taught him on the subject of fate. We understood from all this that his works were born in his heart through Divine inspiration. And he would write at that time only.[65]

Notes

1. *Tarihçe*, 155; Nursi, *Mektûbat*, 43-4 (Eng. tr.: *Letters*, 66).
2. B. Lewis, *Emergence of Modern Turkey*, 266.
3. *Türkiye Tarihi*, iv, 111.
4. Şahiner, *Said Nursi*, 323-4; Nursi, *Emirdağ Lahikası*, ii, 19.
5. B. Lewis, *Emergence of Modern Turkey*. 416.
6. *Türkiye Tarihi*, iv, 178.
7. Nursi, *Şualar*, 598.
8. Muhacir Hafız Ahmed, in *Son Şahitler*, ii, 101-2.
9. *Tarihçe*, 147-8.
10. Nursi, *Barla Lahikası*, 178.
11. Qur'an, 30:50.
12. Mustafa Sungur, in *Aydınlar Konuşuyor*, 395.
13. N. Şahiner, *Said Nursi*, 272-3.
14. Nursi, *Barla Lahikası*, 171.
15. Ahmet Gümüş, in *Son Şahitler*, i, 324.
16. Nursi, *Barla Lahikası*, 99.
17. *Sözler*, 85 (Eng. tr.: *Words*, 106).
18. Nursi, *Barla Lahikası*, 169.
19. *Ibid.*, 160.
20. *Sözler*, 85 (Eng. tr.: *Words*, 106-7).
21. Şahiner, *Said Nursi*, 278-9.
22. pl. of *ḥāfiẓ*.
23. Şahiner, *Said Nursi*, 281.
24. İhsan Üstündağ, in *Son Şahitler*, iv, 300.
25. Bediuzzaman explained his reason for heading his letters with this verse as follows: "This was the first door opened to me from the sacred treasuries of the All-Wise Qur'an. Of the Divine truths of the Qur'an, it was first the truth of this verse that became clear to me and it is this truth which pervades most parts of the *Risale-i Nur*. Another reason is that the masters in whom I have confidence used it at the head of their letters." See, Şahiner, *Said Nursi*, 285, and, Nursi, *Barla Lahikası*, 179.
26. Nursi, *Mektûbat*, 27 (Eng. tr.: *Letters*, 37-8).
27. *Mektûbat*, 22-4 (Eng. tr.: *Letters*, 42-4).
28. *Ibid.*, 68.
29. Hacı Hulûsi Yahyagil, in *Son Şahitler*, i, 33-55.
30. *Barla Lahikası*, 18.
31. Abdurrahman had remained in Ankara when Bediuzzaman left it for Van in 1923, finding himself a position as a scribe in the National Assembly. He married and had one son, called Vahdet. He died in Ankara in 1928, and is buried in what was at that time the village of

Barla

Solfasol (*Zü'l-Fazl*) near Ankara. See, Şahiner, *Said Nursi* (8th edn.), 202; (6th edn.), 190 fn. 1.
32. *Lem'alar*, 232-5 (Eng. tr.: *Flashes*, 310-2).
33. *Lem'alar*, 235 (Eng. tr.: *Flashes*, 312).
34. Şahiner, *Nurs Yolu*, 89-97.
35. Ahmed Asım Önerdem, in *Son Şahitler*, iv, 144-6.
36. Sabri Arseven, in *Son Şahitler*, ii, 112-4.
37. Hüsrev Altınbaşak, in *Son Şahitler*, ii, 196-8.
38. Nursi, *Barla Lahikası*, 98-9.
39. *Tarihçe*, 184.
40. Nursi, *Barla Lahikası*, 100-6.
41. See Chapter 6 below.
42. Şahiner, *Said Nursi*, 389-391.
43. *Tarihçe*, 144-6.
44. Nursi, *Kastamonu Lahikası*, 48.
45. Nursi, *Mektûbat*, 329 (Eng. tr.: *Letters*, 417).
46. *Ibid.*, 344 (Eng. tr.: *Letters*, 434).
47. *Ibid.*, 345-50.
48. *Ibid.*, 81.
49. Cemal Can, in *Son Şahitler*, i, 212.
50. Nursi, *Mektûbat*, 402 (Eng. tr.: *Letters*, 502.
51. *Ibid.*, 314 (Eng. tr., 398); *Son Şahitler*, i, 212-3.
52. Nursi, *Mektûbat*, 316 (Eng. tr.: *Letters*, 400). See also, 370-1 (464).
53. *Ibid.*, 405-6 (Eng. tr.: *Letters*, 506-7).
54. Nursi, *Asâ-yi Mûsa*, 48.
55. *Sözler*, 430 (Eng. tr.: *Words*, 474-5).
56. See, *Sözler*, 338-431 (Eng. tr.: *Words*, 375-458).
57. *Mektûbat*, 337-8 (Eng. tr.: *Letters*, 426-7).
58. Nursi, *Barla Lahikası*, 181.
59. Nursi, *Mektûbat*, 57 (Eng. tr.: *Letters*, 83).
60. Nursi, *Mektûbat*, 58-9 (Eng. tr.: *Letters*, 84-5).
61. See, Nursi, *Mektûbat*, 45-6 (Eng. tr.: *Letters*, 69-70).
62. Şahiner, *Son Şahitler*, i, 83.
63. Nursi, *Şualar*, 248 (Eng. tr.: *Rays*, 320).
64. Re'fet Bey, in Şahiner, *Nurs Yolu*, 93.
65. *Ibid.*, 95-6.

13
Eskişehir

The Arrests Start

On 25 April, 1935, a number of Bediuzzaman's students were taken from their homes and places of work and held in custody. Two days later Bediuzzaman himself and another group were arrested. It was the start of an event which very often bordered on the ridiculous, despite its seriousness. It was another example of the lengths the government went to in order to reduce the standing of influential religious figures and to scare the population away from religion.

According to Süleyman Rüşdü, the affair began when Bediuzzaman went to attend the Friday prayers and thousands of people poured into the streets to see him. The town's Governor and administrators took fright at this, and when a copy of the Tenth Word, Bediuzzaman's treatise on resurrection and the hereafter, was found on the Governor's desk, they panicked and sent urgent wires to Ankara saying, "Bediuzzaman and his students have taken to the streets. They are storming the Government Building."[1] In fact, this was part of the 'plan' of the authorities to provoke 'an incident', as we shall see. The houses of anyone known to have had any connection with Bediuzzaman were then searched and the arrests began.

Tenekeci Mehmed tells how someone sent word to him that this was happening and he took all the parts of the *Risale-i Nur* he had in his house together with any other books to do with Islam or religion and buried them in the garden. At that point no less than eighteen police came and searched the house. Despite their thoroughness they found nothing, and he was one of the few not arrested.² Besides Isparta and its province, suspects were arrested in Milas, Antalya, Bolvadin, Aydın, Van, and other places. They had been denounced to the authorities as reactionaries (*mürteci*), and were charged under Article 163 of the Criminal Code, which among other things prohibited the exploitation of religion and religious sentiments in any way damaging to the security of the state, and the formation of political associations on the basis of religion. There was questioning and statements were taken, and it was while this was in progress that Colonel Asım Bey died. He had to make the choice between saying something that could be harmful to Bediuzzaman, and telling a lie, which his honour would not allow. So he uttered a prayer: "Lord! Take my spirit!", and indeed, the Almighty did take his spirit, and he attained the rank of what Bediuzzaman called "an integrity martyr".

Meanwhile, a furore was started in the press startling the country with stories of a "network of reactionaries" which had been uncovered. And as if to quell some major unrest which threatened the foundations of the state, the Minister of Internal Affairs, Şükrü Kaya, the commander-in-chief of the gendarmerie, Kazım Orbay, and the chief of police travelled together to Isparta at the head of a detachment of gendarmes. Isparta and the surrounding region were put under the control of military units, and cavalry was posted along the road all the way from Isparta to Afyon. Rumours were spread throughout the region that Bediuzzaman and his students were going to be executed and a general atmosphere of terror was generated. At the same time, in order to forestall any uprising in eastern Turkey that Bediuzzaman's being put in prison might provoke, İnönü, the head of that despotic government, set off on a tour of the Eastern Provinces.³

On around 12 May, Bediuzzaman and thirty-one of his students were handcuffed in pairs as though they were dangerous criminals and bundled into lorries at the point of bayonets. Unknown to them, they were to be taken to the prison at Eskişehir, some three hundred and thirty kilometres to the north. Thousands of the local people gathered when they were leaving, weeping families of those arrested, all the people weeping to see them being taken away in this pitiable state.[4] One of the gendarmes sent from Ankara to escort them related this and the journey, first telling how they had been fitted out with new equipment and how Bediuzzaman had been described to them in the most unfavourable terms, Şükrü Kaya, the Home Affairs Minister, calling him in derogatory fashion, "the Kurdish Hoja".[5] In fact the order was to offload Bediuzzaman and his students in some isolated spot on the road and to shoot them. However, the officer in charge, Ruhi Bey, was sympathetic and did not carry out the order. Moreover, he ordered their handcuffs to be unfastened at the appropriate time, so they could perform the prayers. One student records that he was expelled from the army in consequence.[6] They travelled as far as Afyon in the lorries in which they had been permitted neither to speak nor to open any window for air, and still handcuffed in pairs and under the bayonets of gendarmes, were transferred to a train. The following morning they arrived at Eskişehir.[7]

Eskişehir Prison

Conditions in the prison were appalling. Bediuzzaman was put in solitary confinement, the others together in a ward. Their number grew from thirty-two to one hundred and twenty as they were joined by more students arrested elsewhere. Once they entered the prison they were not allowed to visit the lavatories. After hours some warders came and dug a hole near the door and inserted a pipe. This is what they would have to use as they were not to be allowed out. With the filth, the bed-bugs, and the cockroaches, it was impossible to sleep at night. For twelve days they were kept without food. The fact was they were considered to be condemned prisoners doomed for the gallows.[8] Notwithstanding

Eskişehir

the conditions, Bediuzzaman continued to write, completing five more treatises in the months he was there. These were the Twenty-Eighth, Twenty-Ninth, and Thirtieth Flashes, and the First and Second Rays. He wrote them very much with his students in mind, suffering so unjustly this first imprisonment. He named prison the School of Joseph (*Medrese-i Yûsufiye*), after Prophet Joseph, the patron of prisoners.

Among those arrested were some that had only the very slightest connection with Bediuzzaman. It was another example of how the government had blown up the case out of all proportion. These were members of the "network of reactionaries" which was threatening the state! A businessman from Bolvadin called Şükrü Şahinler related his own case and two others:

> I had become acquainted with Halil İbrahim Çöllüoğlu in connection with some business. He then wrote me a letter and requested a reply. The reply I sent was enough to send me to Eskişehir Prison and include me among the students of the *Risale-i Nur*. Also in that way I was able to see Bediuzzaman in Eskişehir and visit him.
>
> There was an optician in Aydın called Şevket Gözaçan. Because he had treated the eyes of one of Bediuzzaman's students, Bediuzzaman wrote him a short note to thank him three or four lines long. They sent Şevket Bey to Eskişehir Prison because of this.
>
> And again, a student called Ahmed Feyzi Kul had written Bediuzzaman a letter in Barla and signed it "The Müftü of Aydın" [by way of a joke, *aydın* means enlightened, as well as being a place-name]. When the affair erupted, they sent the real Müftü of Aydın to Eskişehir although he was not connected in any way. Müftü Mustafa Efendi stayed in prison for months together with me. Eskişehir was a mass of crazy mix-ups like this.[9]

Perhaps the most crazy was the case of Bediuzzaman's treatise on the wisdom of fasting in the month of Ramaḍān. When searching the houses of Bediuzzaman and his students for copies of the *Risale-i Nur*, the police had come across this treatise, called in Turkish, *Ramazan'a Ait,* which can mean either Belonging to Ramaḍān, or Concerning Ramaḍān. Besides the holy month of fasting, in Turkey it is a man's name. Thus, the police started searching the villages of Isparta for someone with the name. During the operation it was learnt that the neighbour of a house searched in some remote village was called Ramazan. So they came and clapped handcuffs on the unfortunate villager who knew neither how to read nor write, and sent him to Eskişehir Prison, despite his bewildered protestations of innocence. And there he remained for two months until the authorities admitted their mistake and released him.[10]

"The Prison Became Like a Mosque"

The prison authorities did not neglect to plant an informer in the ward where Bediuzzaman's students were. Postman Kâmil as he was called was doing his military service as a gendarme in Eskişehir when he was assigned to the job. Bediuzzaman sent his students a note one day stuck to the bottom of the teapot warning them not to speak against the government as there was an informer amongst them. In the event, Postman Kâmil was so impressed by Bediuzzaman and these completely innocent people that he himself began to perform the obligatory prayers and in his reports wrote that they were innocent. When describing these days to Necmeddin Şahiner in 1985, he told him:

> While serving in the prison, I was startled by some sudden news: 'Some condemned prisoners are coming, and they are hojas!'... Several days later Hoja Efendi [Bediuzzaman] arrived, and after him, the other *hojas,* his students...

After Kâmil had been instructed to act as informer on the new arrivals, he joined them inside, ostensibly serving the sentence for some crime. He continued:

> Everyone got on well with each other in Eskişehir Prison... They used to perform the prescribed prayers all together, recite the Qur'an, and offer prayers.

They emptied the juveniles' ward for Bediuzzaman and put him in it. His students were somewhere else. The juveniles' ward was large and he stayed in it all alone. They [the authorities] were always speaking ill of him to us so that unavoidably I was influenced by what they said. Then one day I went and kissed his hand. He was a saintly old man, frail, and his hair quite long. His beard had grown a bit, since it had not been shaved. On my being cordial, he embraced me. I was very touched and started to weep. He began to tell me about his life...He said: "I only want the *Risale-i Nur*. I won't give up these works of mine." I was very moved and affected by his terse words, and was sorry at the injustice done to such a great person. I wondered to myself: "Why do they bother this elderly man so much?" Without letting it be known to anyone I kept on visiting him. One time Hoja Efendi drew two fingers over my forehead, and said to me: "Repent and seek forgiveness; provide food for sixty people and pay the blood-money." This was extraordinary. I hadn't said I had killed someone, but with his saintly powers, he knew what I'd done. He was a great saint...

I stayed in the Hoja's students' ward, so of course I was in close contact with them. It was not possible to think of anything else in those cramped quarters. They held good talks there, the prayers were performed, and the Qur'an recited...

That dark prison ward shone with the lights of the Qur'an. Everyone would rise early for the prayers, and take their sections [a thirtieth part] of the Qur'an then the recitations of the whole Qur'an would begin. After the morning-prayer, the prayer for a complete recitation of the Qur'an would be said. From time to time one of the hojas with a fine voice [Mehmed Gülırmak] would sing a *qaṣīdah*. He used to send us into raptures. Then they would start reciting the Qur'an again. The whole Qur'an was recited several times each day. Those innocent people were saved by the readings of the Qur'an and the prayers. Those were good days. The prison became like a mosque. If only I had been able to be like them. There's another thing I witnessed in Eskişehir Prison which has stayed in my mind these fifty years; I always pray for Hoja Efendi's soul. I had plenty to eat, but he made do with tea and a few olives each day. God's grace was with him; just how great he was, I didn't know.[11]

Eskişehir Court

It is apparent from the overreaction of the Interior Minister, Şükrü Kaya, and the government, the furore started in the press, and the rumours put around both in Isparta and Eskişehir, that the intention was to do away with Bediuzzaman. It is remembered that countless people, and especially men of religion, had fallen prey to the secularizing 'reforms', accused of lesser 'crimes'. The charges were several, and involved the infringement of the principle of secularism and of Article 163 of the Criminal Code through, among other things, exploiting religion for organizing a group which might be harmful to public security. The court was under pressure from the Interior Minister to condemn Bediuzzaman. It was thus a matter of life and death for him and his students, but it was not himself he set about to defend in the court. His defence speeches were for the most part defences of the *Risale-i Nur*. They are masterpieces which demolish with his usual straightforward reasoning the government's baseless suspicions concerning him and the trumped-up charges of the court. The fact was that due to his percipience and foresight, Bediuzzaman succeeded in counteracting the depredations against the Islamic faith of the people of Turkey. And more than this, with his writings, he had started a positive movement of renewal without apparently breaking the new laws. And he was able to prove this to the court.

Thus despite the pressure brought to bear on it, the court cleared him of all the charges, save one, which concerned a short treatise expounding some Qur'anic verses about Islamic dress. A topical subject, it made this the pretext and arbitrarily sentenced Bediuzzaman to twelve months' imprisonment, and fifteen of his students to six months. The remaining one hundred and two were acquitted; three had already been released. Bediuzzaman objected to this, for if they had been found guilty of the crimes of which they had been accused, it would have resulted in his own execution and at least imprisonment with hard labour for his students. He described it as "the sentence for a horse thief" and demanded that they show in accordance with the law that his guilt necessitated either his execution or a hundred and one years' imprisonment, or else give him and his friends and his writings their complete freedom and recover their losses from those who caused them.[12]

Quite apart from the trumped-up charges and arbitrary sentence, Bediuzzaman was also denied his most basic rights when it came to preparing his defence, which he himself wrote and delivered. While it had taken the court three to four months to prepare the case, he was allowed only a few days in which to prepare his whole defence; and for some parts of it only a few hours.[13] Also, when he found writing by hand so laborious, he was denied a scribe. And he was not permitted to speak with anyone for two months.[14] However, he was not intimidated by these injustices; he was prepared to do all he could so that the *Risale-i Nur* be cleared and justice upheld. For he recognised the law and the process of the law, and was absolutely opposed to any activities which usurped it, disturbed public order, and infringed the rights of the majority. Thus, in addition to answering the charges according to the existing laws, Bediuzzaman told the court that copies of his defence were to be sent to the Interior Minister and the Governing Body of the National Assembly.[15] And when, despite proving quite clearly that Article 163 was not applicable to him and his activities, he was found guilty of one charge by the court, he applied for the case to be sent to the Court of Appeal.[16] In the event of the Appeal Court upholding the court's decision he was prepared to send a petition to the highest level of government, the Cabinet.[17]

Bediuzzaman's Defence

One by one Bediuzzaman answered the charges made against him, supporting all his replies with evidence. He told the court that since the best wile was to be without wiles, he had taken truth and honesty as the basis of his defence. Thus, he openly admitted his service to belief and the Qur'an, which being in no way concerned with politics was not contrary to the law, and exposed to the court the plot that had been laid against him because of this service. To involve the legal system in this conspiracy and attempt to realise its aims in the name of the law, was a grave error and brought the law and legal system into disrepute. He was quite undaunted by the manifest purpose of the court, his execution. He was after all the Bediuzzaman who had faced the Court Martial set up after the 31st March Incident in 1909, and won his acquittal. He was also the practised preacher and fine orator who had addressed thousands in Aya Sophia the same year, and thousands in the Umayyad Mosque in Damascus in 1911. Thus, he started off his defence with a skilful move which turned the tables on those judging him. He was answering the main charge of "making a tool of religion with the idea of political reaction, with the intention of undertaking an enterprise which might disturb public order":

> God forbid a hundred thousand times that the sciences of belief with which we are occupied should be a tool for anything apart from Divine pleasure! For sure, just as the sun cannot be a satellite of the moon and follow it, so belief in God, which is the luminous and sacred key to eternal happiness and a sun of the life of the hereafter, cannot be the tool of social life. There is no matter in the universe more important than the mystery of belief, the greatest question and greatest riddle of the creation of this world, that belief can be made the tool of it.
>
> Judges of the Court! If this torturous imprisonment of mine concerned only myself and my life in this world, you can be sure that I would remain silent like I have these last ten years. But since it concerns the eternal life of many, and the *Risale-i Nur*, which reveals and explains the mighty talisman of creation, if I had a hundred heads and each day one were cut off, I would not give up this mighty mystery. Even if I am delivered from your hands, I cannot be saved from the clutches of the appointed hour. I am old and at the door of the grave. Consider only this mystery of belief concerning the appointed hour and the grave, which will come to everyone, one of the hundreds of matters the *Risale-i Nur* discloses...

> Can all the weighty political questions of the world loom larger than death for someone who is certain of death, so that he can make it the tool of those questions. For the time of its coming is not known. The appointed hour, which may come at any time to cut off your head, may be either eternal extinction or the despatch papers to go to a better world. The ever-open grave is either the door to a pit of non-being and eternal darkness, or the gate onto a world more permanent and full of light than this world....
>
> Thus, Respected Sirs, is it at all fair, is it at all reasonable, to consider the *Risale-i Nur*, which uncovers and explains hundreds of questions of belief like this, to be a harmful, biased work that exploits political currents? What law requires this?... Also, since the secular republic remains impartial according to the principle of secularism and does not interfere with those without religion, of course it also should not interfere with religious people on whatever pretext.[18]

Thus, Bediuzzaman established that it was the cause of belief and the *Risale-i Nur* that he was going to defend, and then went on to rebut the charges concerning his exploiting religion for political ends. The important questions of political reaction and secularism shall be discussed later.

After pointing out that he had refused Mustafa Kemal's offers to work alongside the new regime in 1923 because he had already withdrawn from the world and politics, Bediuzzaman described to the court five "Pointers" showing that he had not "interfered in the state's business".

Firstly, for thirteen years he had not so much as opened a newspaper, newspapers being "the tongue of politics", which everyone he knew could testify to. Then, for the ten years he had been in the province of Isparta there was not the slightest hint to suggest he had made any attempt "to be involved in politics", despite the great upheavals that were occurring during that time. His house had been raided and searched thoroughly, and all his private papers and books taken. And though these had been studied by both the police and the governor's office, nothing of any political content had been found. Only, in all the works, they had found a few points they were able to raise objections about, but these were mostly scholarly expositions of Qur'anic verses to do with women's dress and inheritance. However, he told the court, these short pieces had been written years before while he was a member of the Darü'l-Hikmeti'l-İslamiye, and he had suppressed them when the new laws were passed, which they might be seen as opposing. But then one copy had been sent to someone by mistake. Furthermore, the fact that he had chosen to remain for nine years in a remote village proved his desire to remain removed from all involvement in social and political matters. In fact he said it was his not applying to the Isparta authorities to be released or transferred elsewhere that had "wounded their pride", so that they had caused the affair to erupt by alarming Ankara. He told the Court:

> All my friends who are in touch with me know that let alone involvement in politics or attempting anything political, even thinking about them is contrary to my basic aim, my mental state, and my sacred duties towards belief. Light (*nūr*) has been given me; the club of politics has not been given me.[19]

So too there was absolutely no evidence to support the charge of disturbing public order by exciting religious emotions. On the contrary, as Bediuzzaman pointed out, the *Risale-i Nur* upheld order:

> The *Risale-i Nur*, which consists of the sciences of belief, establishes and ensures public security and peace. Yes, belief, the source of good characteristics and fine qualities, certainly doesn't disturb public order; it ensures it. It is unbelief that disturbs it, because of its bad character.[20]

Also, not one of Bediuzzaman's students or anyone who read the *Risale-i Nur* had been involved in any of the disturbances which had been given a religious colouring and had occurred since the 'reforms' had been first enacted. In another part of his defence, Bediuzzaman said: "People who receive instruction from the *Risale-i Nur* certainly do not get involved in any public disturbances, which are the cause of the blood of innocents being spilt and their rights being violated."[21] Furthermore, he pointed out that if Article 163 was applicable to them, it was applicable also to the Directorate of Religious Affairs and all the *imams* and preachers whom they employed, since they encouraged religious feelings in the same way.[22]

A further charge and one that Bediuzzaman was to be frequently charged with was with instructing in Sufism, for as was mentioned earlier, Sufism had been outlawed in 1925, and the orders disbanded and their *takiyyahs* closed. This was another baseless charge; as all the *Risale-i Nur* showed, Bediuzzaman was concerned with the truths of belief. He told the court:

"As I have written in numerous treatises, this is not the time of Sufism; it is the time to save belief. There are many who enter Paradise without belonging to a Sufi order, but none who enter it without belief. It is therefore the time to work for belief." There was no one who could come forward and claim he had taught him the Sufi way. What he had taught to a small number of his special students was "not training in Sufism (*tarīqah*), but instruction in the direct way to reality (*ḥaqīqah*)."[23] In connection with this, the court wanted to know what Bediuzzaman lived on. But his extreme frugality was well-known and easily established, as well as his life-long habit of not accepting presents or charity in any form.

Another of the main charges, which was also clearly trumped up, was that Bediuzzaman had set up an organization for political purposes. He was persistently questioned by the court concerning this, and asked where he had secured the funds for it. His reply was in four parts. He began:

> Firstly, I ask those who ask this, what document, what is there to suggest the existence of such a political organization? What evidence, what proof have they found that we have set up an organization with the money they so persistently ask about? For the last ten years I have been in the province of Isparta under strict surveillance. I used to see only one or two assistants and

in ten days one or two travellers. I was alone, a stranger, tired of the world, felt extreme disgust with politics, and had repeatedly witnessed how powerful political movements had been harmful and come to nothing through their reactions. I rejected and took no part in political movements when among my own people and thousands of friends at the most crucial opportunity, and fled from politics as though fleeing from the Devil considering it to be the greatest crime to damage through political partisanship service to true belief, which is most sacred and which it is not permissible to harm by anything...It is not only me, but the province of Isparta and all who know me, and indeed anyone who possesses reason and conscience, will meet with disgust the slanders of those who say, "There is such an organization and you are hatching political plots," and will say to them, "You are accusing him due to your own malicious plans." Bediuzzaman continued:

Our business is belief. Through the brotherhood of belief, we are brothers with ninety-nine per cent of the people of Isparta and this country, whereas a society or organization is the alliance of a minority within the majority. Ninety-nine people do not form a society in the face of one man... He concluded answering this charge by pointing out how unrealistic it was to wonder where someone who had managed to live on a hundred lira in ten years and had worn the same patched cloak for seven years had obtained the money for the organization he was supposed to have formed.[24]

The main point on which the trial rested, however, was the vexed question of secularism, in the cause of which all the radical changes since the establishment of the republic had been brought about. What lay at the base of the accusations against Bediuzzaman was that he had opposed the government and its programme of secularization. While for his part, he denied that he had opposed it, arguing that "the secular republic means the separation of religion from [the matters of] this world",[25] and that "since according to the principle [of secularism] the secular republic remains impartial and does not interfere with those without religion, so too of course it also should not interfere with those with religion on whatever pretext."[26] That is to say, secularism should ensure freedom of conscience, and of expression, and other liberties. This conflict of interpretations over the meaning of secularism and how it should be applied remains unresolved to this day. Thus, Bediuzzaman argued that the *Risale-i Nur* was a scholarly work—and as such should be unrestricted under the secular republic—which silenced materialism and naturalism and the philosophers of Europe and their attacks on the Qur'an; for more than thirty years his attention had been directed towards their attacks. The internal problems of the country he saw as a result of their corrupting influence.[27] The *Risale-i Nur* dealt "powerful blows" at them and at the atheists who furthered their interests and plots in the country[28] under the cover of secularization. It was these "intriguers" and "their irreligious committees" that Bediuzzaman opposed, not the government. He differentiated between the Government and these committees or secret societies working for the cause of irreligion, and warned about their infiltrating the government and deceiving it. It was they who raised the outcries of "political reaction" and "exploiting religion for political ends."[29]

Such accusations levelled at people who supported religion were not new, of course. Much use had been made of them after the Constitutional Revolution of 1908, when the debate between those who favoured secularization and westernization and those who did not was often most virulent, as was described in an earlier chapter. At that time, Bediuzzaman told the court martial set up after the 31st March Incident: "Certain people who make politics the tool of irreligion accuse others of political reaction and exploiting religion for the sake of politics in order to conceal their own misdeeds."[30] Under the republic, the same slogans were used for the same ends: to blacken the names of Muslims and reduce their standing in the eyes of the population, and so by frightening the people away from Islam, to pave the way for the spreading of irreligious ideas. The Menemen Incident was a classic example, and part of the charge against Bediuzzaman was that he had attempted "to imitate" that revolt. It had been a minor incident which occurred in response to provocation, and, amid great storms in the press, had been suppressed brutally as a "reactionary movement". Thirty-three people had been executed in the wake of it and in numerous places repressive measures taken against people known to work for the cause of religion. Reprisals had also been taken against Bediuzzaman, although he had absolutely no connection with it.[31] He explained to the court how forces representing the same interests had attempted to provoke a similar incident in Isparta and having failed were now trying to deceive the judiciary. Saying also that the matter had to be seen in the light of the perpetual struggle between belief and unbelief, religion and irreligion, and that "everyone who is aware of the heart of this matter knows that these attacks on us are an assault on religion directly on behalf of irreligion."[32]

Thus, Bediuzzaman demanded a fair trial from the court. He told it: "Among the branches of government, it is the court that is charged more than any other with preserving its independence, and, remaining free of outside influences, with considering matters impartially and without emotion." Nevertheless, irregularities had taken place. For example, while his name was Said Nursi, in his questioning Bediuzzaman was always referred to as "Said-i Kurdi" and "the Kurd" in a way which would inevitably produce biased opinions.[33] Indeed, the intention was to link Bediuzzaman with the constant opposition to the government and rebellions in eastern Turkey, as is shown clearly from the slanderous campaigns orchestrated against him in the press at the same time. So also, despite his correcting them in all his statements, the dates his works were written were deliberately confused with the dates they were copied out and pieces written over a period of twenty years were shown as having been written in one year.[34]

It was due to his "scholarly defence" of a few Qur'anic verses concerning women's dress and inheritance, written before the foundation of the Republic and adoption of the new Civil Code, "against the objections and attacks of European philosophers",[35] part of which had been included in the *Risale-i Nur* as the Twenty-Fourth Flash, that the court finally convicted Bediuzzaman and sentenced him in entirely arbitrary fashion to one year's imprisonment followed by one year's compulsory residence in Kastamonu under house-arrest, and as mentioned, fifteen of his students to six months. Sentence was passed on 19 August, 1935.[36] He served eleven months and was released the following March.

An extraordinary event occurred while Bediuzzaman was being held in the prison, occasions similar to which were recorded while he was in Denizli Prison. One day, the Eskişehir Public Prosecutor saw him in the market. Overcome with surprise he went immediately to the Prison Governor and asked him why he had allowed Bediuzzaman out of the prison. The Governor assured him Bediuzzaman was being held in solitary confinement inside the prison. They went and looked, and sure enough he was in his cell. The event became well-known, though the authorities had to admit they were at a loss to understand it.[37]

Notes

1. Süleyman Rüşdü Çakın, in *Son Şahitler*, iv, 141.
2. Mehmed Sözer, in *Son Şahitler*, ii, 213-4.
3. *Tarihçe*, 192.
4. Halil İbrahim Çöllüoğlu, in *Son Şahitler*, iv, 121.
5. İsmail Karaman, in *Son Şahitler*, ii, 86-7.
6. Mehmed Gülırmak, in *Son Şahitler*, i, 84.
7. Halil İbrahim Çöllüoğlu, in *Son Şahitler*, iv, 121-3.
8. Mehmed Gülırmak, in *Son Şahitler*, i, 85; Şahiner, *Said Nursi*, 315.
9. Şükrü Şahinler, in *Son Şahitler*, i, 88.
10. Şahiner, *Said Nursi*, 318-19.
11. Postacı Kâmil, in *Son Şahitler*, iv, 147-50.
12. *Tarihçe*, 229.
13. Nursi, *Lem'alar* (Ott. edn.), 541 and 603.
14. *Ibid.*, 563; *Tarihçe*, 205.
15. Nursi, *Lem'alar* (Ott. edn.), 542.
16. *Ibid.*, 615.

17. *Ibid.*, 624-32; *Tarihçe*, 229-32.
18. *Tarihçe*, 194-5.
19. *Ibid.*, 194-6.
20. *Ibid.*, 198.
21. *Ibid.*, 207.
22. *Ibid.*, 218.
23. *Ibid.*, 199.
24. *Ibid.*, 201-2.
25. *Ibid.*, 205.
26. *Ibid.*, 195.
27. *Ibid.*, 198-9.
28. *Ibid.*, 221.
29. *Ibid.*, 214.
30. Nursi, *Divan-ı Harb-i Örfî*, 12.
31. Nursi, *Mektûbat*, 60 (Eng. tr.: *Letters*, 87).
32. *Tarihçe*, 214-5.
33. *Tarihçe*, 203.
34. *Ibid.*, 227.
35. *Ibid.*, 222.
36. Şahiner, *Said Nursi*, 308.
37. *Tarihçe*, 192-3.

14
Kastamonu

Life in Kastamonu

Bediuzzaman was released from Eskişehir Prison in March 1936 and was sent to Kastamonu in the Ilgaz Mountains to the south of the Black Sea. His enforced residence in this, the major town of the province of Kastamonu, was to last seven and a half years. Under constant surveillance, his movements were more restricted than in Barla, and the harassment and persecution continued. He wrote further additions to the *Risale-i Nur* while here, including one of its most important treatises, *The Supreme Sign*. He attracted new students in Kastamonu and particularly the town of İnebolu on the Black Sea which earned the name of "the second Isparta" as a centre from which the *Risale-i Nur* spread. Bediuzzaman kept up continuous correspondence with his students in Isparta and elsewhere and these letters were gathered together to form the *Kastamonu Lahikası*, or Kastamonu Letters. They are an important source of information about the matters with which Bediuzzaman was concerned at this time, and most of the subjects they discuss will be touched on in the course of this chapter. They were a source of great enlightenment, instruction, and encouragement for Bediuzzaman's students, now parted from him, and were conveyed secretly from town to town and village to village by Nur Postmen with copies being made of them on the way, since it was very often not possible for them to be sent by post.

For the first three months he was in Kastamonu Bediuzzaman stayed "as a guest" in the police station. He describes what a trying time this was for him as someone who preferred a life of solitude, and also could not abide the compulsory changes in dress.[1] His refusal to abandon his Islamic *jubbah* and turban were doubtless made the pretext for the harassment he received there. Following this he was moved to a rented house immediately opposite the police station. On two floors, it was a traditional wooden house with the ground floor used as a store for logs and an outside staircase leading to the two upstairs rooms. Bediuzzaman remained here for the seven years he was in Kastamonu.

It was during his first weeks in Kastamonu that he attracted the first of those who were to be his closest students here, Çaycı Emin. He was an exile like Bediuzzaman. A Kurdish tribal chief, he had been exiled to Kastamonu some ten years previously and now made his livelihood by running a tea-stall in the courtyard of the Nasrullah Mosque. It was here that he first saw Bediuzzaman. Bediuzzaman won his heart when he warned him against approaching him, but Çaycı Emin was not one to be deterred by any possible harm from officialdom and thereafter did all he could to assist him.[2] Of Bediuzzaman's other close students in the town of Kastamonu was Mehmed Feyzi,[3] who had a scholarly background. These two most constantly attended Bediuzzaman— as far as they were able, securing his daily needs, and Mehmed Feyzi in particular acting as his scribe and assistant with the *Risale-i Nur*.

Bediuzzaman was virtually confined to his house, going out only once or twice a week either up into the surrounding mountains or climbing up to the citadel which dominates the town. He spent his time either writing the *Risale-i Nur* or correcting the handwritten copies of existing parts, or in worship, prayer and supplication, or in contemplation. The nights he spent in prayer. He was busy with the same activities when he went out into the mountains; he never passed an idle moment. Mehmed Feyzi tells how when accompanying him, Bediuzzaman on horseback would be correcting copies of the *Risale-i Nur* or listening to himself reading them out, or else teaching him and Çaycı Emin and any other of his students who were present. Although Bediuzzaman corrected the copies with the greatest care, he never consulted the originals; they were all in his head.

The high altitude of Kastamonu makes the winters very cold. In several letters Bediuzzaman mentions the bitter cold together with the illnesses he suffered. He was afflicted with chronic lumbago and rheumatism, in addition to which he was poisoned on several occasions. He writes that despite suffering these tribulations in addition to all his other hardships, "I offer endless thanks to my Creator that He has sent me belief, the most sacred remedy for every ill, and the medicine of resignation to the Divine Decree, which results from belief in Divine Determining; it has afforded me complete patience and caused me to offer thanks."[4]

Bediuzzaman's indefatigable endurance is illustrated by the following memory of Çaycı Emin:

> I used to go to Bediuzzaman's house early to light his stove. One day I went it was extremely cold, and without realizing it I had gone two hours before the call to prayer. He was rapt in worship on his prayer-rug. In candlelight in the pre-dawn cold, he was praying in a sad and touching voice, he was pleading, beseeching. Agitated, I waited on my feet for a full one and a half hours. Shivering and trembling, I watched this elevated sight. Finally the sound of the call to prayer began to come from afar, but the Turkish call to prayer of that time. He turned to me and said:
>
> "Emin, you made a great mistake! I swear that I have certain times that should the angels come even, I would not receive them." Çaycı Emin apologised saying he had been misled by the light of the bright moon and said he would not come again before the call to prayer.[5]

Bediuzzaman was subject to constant harassment. Ankara appointed governors to the province whom they knew would keep up the pressure on him. These were the most oppressive days of the Republican People's Party's rule, when it was pursuing its Westernization programme and struggle against Islam with all its resources. Governor Avni Doğan was appointed in September of the year Bediuzzaman was sent to Kastamonu. He was the epitome of the new breed of officials raised up under RPP rule. An avowed enemy of Islam, he did all he could to inflict torment on Bediuzzaman and his students. He remained in this post for nearly four years and was succeeded in 1940 by Mithat Altıok, whose attitude was somewhat more conciliatory. Bediuzzaman, however, endured all that was inflicted on him by these officials, even on one occasion preventing harm coming to Avni Doğan, and incidentally gaining for himself an important student in the process.

Briefly, in response to the destruction of the mosques and Sufi *takiyyahs* and tombs of saints which was carried out with greater ferocity and efficiency in Kastamonu after Avni Doğan was appointed Governor, one of the town's shaykhs, Hilmi Bey, known as the Little Shaykh, in order to try and put a stop to the destruction, vowed to kill the Governor. He obtained a rifle and laid the plans. Then when all was ready, he was walking plunged in thought before Bediuzzaman's house when there was a tap at the window, and Bediuzzaman beckoned to him. Wondering what this elderly *hoja* wanted, he climbed the stairs up to the house. But Bediuzzaman merely gave him a copy of a prayer called the *Tahmidiye*, and asked him to write out copies of it. Hilmi Bey agreed, and on returning home, sat down immediately and started to write it out. He continued far into the night. When he had finished, his mind had been changed completely and he had given up all idea of his projected crime. Thereafter, he became a devoted student of Bediuzzaman, dedicating himself to writing out the *Risale-i Nur* and serving its author.[6]

At Avni Doğan's instigation, Bediuzzaman's house was frequently searched by the police for copies of the *Risale-i Nur*, and they had to hide them in whatever unlikely places they could find. However some of the police officers charged with plaguing him paid for it. One called Hafız Nuri would come every few days and go through Bediuzzaman's house with a tooth-comb; he was finally struck down by a mysterious illness and died. Another called Safvet in Mithat Altıok's time also came to a sorry end. Bediuzzaman wished them no ill; as he told Hafız Nuri's family who came to plead for him, they received these blows from the Qur'an.[7]

Another of Bediuzzaman's students was Taşköprülü Sadık Bey,[8] the local *ağa* or lord. The grandson of Sadık Pasha, one of the heroes of Plevne and educated in the Military Academy in Istanbul, he cast aside his rank and position and devoted himself to serving Bediuzzaman and the *Risale-i Nur*. His village of Taşköprü became a centre for the writing out of the *Risale-i Nur*, as did the town of İnebolu. The *Risale-i Nur* was introduced into İnebolu by two other important students, Nazif and Selahaddin Çelebi, who were father and son. Selahaddin recounted this while describing his first visit to Bediuzzaman, when he took to be corrected a copy of the Fourth Ray which his father had written:

> I climbed the mountain...under a tree a person dressed in white was performing the prayers. "This must be him", I said to myself. After finishing them, he motioned with his head for me to sit. I knelt down and said 'Amen' to his supplications; in a touching voice he was beseeching Almighty God for the peace and happiness in this world and the next of humanity and the Islamic world. Finally I gave him the book I had brought. "Welcome, my brother", he said. "Let's correct it." It took half an hour. I studied the Hoja Efendi carefully, whom I was seeing for the first time. He was correcting it with great attention, even correcting wrong points and letters in the words. He asked me: 'Do you know this [Ottoman] writing?', and got me to write a sentence.
>
> "*Mā shā' Allāh!* You write very well", he said. "Will you write out a treatise if I give you one?" When I said I would with pleasure, he gave me around nine of *The Short Words*. And he gave me the Eleventh and Twelfth Words for my father. "They

must be written out exactly", he said. I asked his permission, and left him.

The *Risale-i Nur* was introduced into İnebolu in this way. Subsequently, hundreds of hands started to write it out, for five years their pens worked like a printing press. The Nur Postmen were organised between Kastamonu and İnebolu. And the various treatises of the *Risale-i Nur* were sent to Anatolia [by sea] from the port of İnebolu....This work was being carried on unceasingly in this way when I saw a duplicating machine in a shop in Istanbul. On learning that it duplicated at the rate of a hundred pages a minute, I bought it immediately and took it to İnebolu. First of all we duplicated the Seventh Ray, *The Supreme Sign*. When I took the first copy to Ustādh, he was tremendously pleased. He expressed his feelings at the end of the work with these words:

"Oh God, grant happiness in Paradise to Nazif Çelebi and his blessed helpers, who have written five hundred copies with one pen!"[9]

In the villages of Isparta the treatises of the *Risale-i Nur* were being written out by hand unceasingly. Bedre, İlema, Kuleönü, İslamköy, Sav, and Atabey; hundreds of people in these villages devoted themselves entirely to writing out the *Risale-i Nur*. 'Nur Exchange' Sabri, the 'Jetty Official', in the village of Bedre. The parts of the *Risale* and Bediuzzaman's letters would come to him. He would make copies immediately and send them by means of Nur Postmen to Eğridir, and from there they would be taken to Hafız Ali in İslamköy. All were aware of the urgency of the task. In the village of Sav, and elsewhere, the women dedicated themselves with great devotion to this work, while the shepherds acted as carriers for the written pieces.[10] We learn from one of Bediuzzaman's letters that his student Hüsrev, "one of the heroes of the *Risale-i Nur*", wrote out in his exceptionally fine handwriting four hundred copies of various parts of the *Risale-i Nur* over a period of nine to ten years, as well as three copies of the Qur'an which contained clear examples of the coinciding of Divine Name of Allah.[11]

Bediuzzaman's letters to his students, which, like the *Risale-i Nur*, have a warmth and directness which address all who read them, concern mostly the aims, purpose, and way of the *Risale-i Nur* and the position its students should take in the face of the political and social conditions of the time. They stress the caution they should practice in the face of their numerous enemies. They emphasise too the importance of obtaining sincerity and selflessness in their task of serving the Qur'an so as to be able to form strong bonds of brotherhood with their fellows and develop the collective personality necessary to combat the joint attacks of those who were inimical to Islam. Many of the letters also describe the importance of the role the *Risale-i Nur* and its students had to play, and also the great blessings and benefits associated with it. Bediuzzaman often expresses his gratitude for the students who had been drawn to the *Risale-i Nur* and their self-sacrificing service; it was a major source of consolation for him in the face of the oppressive conditions under which he had to live and work. Before examining some of the letters concerning the *Risale-i Nur*, included here are one or two examples illustrating this:

"My Dear and Loyal Blessed Brothers and Sincere, Vigorous, and Renowned Comrades in the Service of the Qur'an and Belief!

I offer endless thanks and praise to Almighty God that He has affirmed the hopes expressed in the Treatise for the Elderly and proved true the claims in the treatise containing my defence speeches. Yes...He has bestowed on the *Risale-i Nur* through you thirty Abdurrahmans who are the equivalent of thirty thousand, rather, He has bestowed one hundred and thirty or one thousand one hundred and thirty Abdurrahmans."[12] And another example:

"My Dear and Absolutely Loyal Brothers!

You are my consolation and means of joy in this world. If it hadn't been for you, I wouldn't have been able to endure these past four years of torment. Your persistence and fortitude have afforded me a powerful patience and endurance."[13] And again:

"My Dear and Loyal Brothers!

> I was happier at your letters than I can describe. Especially Hüsrev's two most valuable letters saying that the *Risale-i Nur* is spreading in extraordinary fashion in Haji Hafiz's village—they have been kept like copies of the *Risale-i Nur* and clear proofs, and are being shown to the *Risale-i Nur* students in this area as a spur and encouragement."[14]

The Way of the *Risale-i Nur* and its Function

Bediuzzaman wrote to his students that the *Risale-i Nur's* function was to save and strengthen belief in the face of the concerted attacks against it at the present time.[15] Besides those briefly described in the preceding chapters, he explained also that what was being suffered at that time was the accumulated objections and doubts levelled against belief and the Qur'an by the European [Western] philosophers over a period of some thousand years. Their aim was to shake the pillars of belief, which are the foundation and key of eternal life and everlasting happiness. Thus, what was essential was to strengthen belief and transform it from "imitative belief" into "certain belief".[16],[17] In one letter he described the enormity of the *Risale-i Nur's* role like this:

> The *Risale-i Nur* is not only repairing some minor damage or some small house; it is repairing vast damage and the all-embracing citadel which contains Islam, the stones of which are the size of mountains. And it is not striving to reform only a private heart and an individual conscience; it is striving to cure with the medicines of the Qur'an and belief and the Qur'an's miraculousness the collective heart and generally-held ideas, which have been breached in awesome fashion by the tools of corruption prepared and stored up over a thousand years, and the general conscience, which is facing corruption through the destruction of the foundations, currents, and marks of Islam which are the refuge of all and particularly the mass of believers.
>
> Certainly, for such universal breaches and awesome wounds, proofs and equipment of the utmost certitude and the strength of mountains, and well-proven medicines and numberless drugs of the effectiveness of a thousand remedies are

necessary. Emerging at this time from the miraculousness of the Qur'an of Miraculous Exposition, the *Risale-i Nur* performs this function, and is also the means of advancing and progressing through the infinite degrees of belief.[18]

Thus, in the course of time the belief of the mass of believers in the fundamentals of Islam had lost its vitality, primarily as a result of the doubts and scepticism planted in the common mind by philosophies of Western origin. This process had received a powerful impetus with the deliberate policy of Westernization favoured since the establishment of the Republic. It was the *Risale-i Nur* with its concentration on developing belief from being merely imitative into "certain" belief, and into the degrees beyond this, that had the ability to reverse the decline and help rebuild the structure of Islam. While in Kastamonu Bediuzzaman wrote *The Supreme Sign*, to which he attached great importance as one of the parts of the *Risale-i Nur* most effective at developing "certain belief". We can look at it briefly in order to learn both what Bediuzzaman meant by belief of this kind, and the new method he put forward in the *Risale-i Nur* by which it could be attained.

The Supreme Sign

The Supreme Sign is a key to understanding Bediuzzaman's view of existence and his way of worshipping, for he said of it that he wrote it for himself according to his own understanding.[19] The treatise comprises "the observations of a traveller questioning the universe about his Maker", and describes a journey in the mind through the universe made by a traveller most curious to learn about and become acquainted with "the Owner of this fine guesthouse, the Author of this vast book, the Monarch of this mighty realm." He questions first the heavens with their suns and stars and heavenly bodies, then the atmosphere with its thunder and lightning, winds, clouds and rain, then the earth, and so on, each of which proves the necessary existence and unity of its Maker. With the "thirty-three degrees in the necessary existence and Unity of the Creator" proclaimed by these "thirty-three universal tongues", it forms thirty-three degrees of belief. That is to say, as the traveller travels through the universe questioning each of its realms and learning of their testimony to the Divine existence and Unity, his belief gains universality and strength with each degree, and passes from being "imitative belief" to the degree of "certain and true belief", and beyond.

One of the central features in this new way which the *Risale-i Nur* opened up to renew and strengthen belief in God, is that it "blends" the heart and the mind. That is, both the reasoning faculty and the subtle inner senses are utilised in reaching the truth and in the process are illuminated with the knowledge obtained. We can look at the first of these, the mind or reason.

It will be recalled that on realizing the severe nature of the threats to the Qur'an and Islam way back at the beginning of the century, Bediuzzaman set for himself the task of learning modern science, for he understood that they could be truly defended in the modern age only through a combination of modern science and the Islamic sciences. So he mastered the physical sciences and they became "the steps by which to understand the Qur'an and prove its truths."[20] The Old Said had striven to find a short path to the truth which would combine science and religion, and to found the Medresetü'z-Zehra where they would be taught in combined form, but it was not till the New Said and the writing of the *Risale-i Nur* that this aim was realised. Yes, the evidence of Bediuzzaman's knowledge of modern science is to be found on almost every page of the *Risale-i Nur*. The physical sciences uncover and describe the order in the universe and its functioning. Each branch, such as astronomy, geography, geology, and biology, describes the order in a particular area. Thus, since the Qur'an was being attacked in the name of science, and science and philosophy were being put forward as alternatives to religion and concepts such as 'nature' taking the place of the Creator, benefiting from his knowledge of science, Bediuzzaman also described the universe. He showed that, through its order and the infinite wisdom and other attributes manifested in it, it demonstrated the existence and Unity of a Single Maker. It may be seen from this how the *Risale-i Nur* addresses reason; the evidence for the reasoned proofs its puts forward for the truths of belief is taken from the functioning universe as described by science. For an example of this, we can return to *The Supreme Sign*:

> Then [the traveller] looks at the rain and sees that within it are contained benefits as numerous as the raindrops, and manifestations of the Most Merciful One as multiple as the particles of rain, and instances of wisdom as plentiful as its atoms. Those sweet, delicate, and blessed drops are moreover created in so beautiful and ordered a fashion, that particularly the rain sent in the summertime, is despatched and caused to fall with such balance and regularity that not even stormy winds that cause large objects to collide can destroy its equilibrium and order; the drops do not collide with each other or merge in such fashion as to become harmful masses of water. Water, composed of two simple elements like hydrogen and oxygen, is employed in hundreds of thousands of other wise, purposeful tasks and arts, particularly in animate beings; although it is itself inanimate and unconscious. Rain which is then the very embodiment of divine mercy can only be manufactured in the unseen treasury of mercy of One Most Compassionate and Merciful, and on its descent expounds in physical form the verse: *And He it is Who sends down rain after men have despaired, and thus spreads out His mercy* [21],[22]

An important element of the *Risale-i Nur's* method which is related to the mind is reflection or meditation (*tafakkur*). In one of his letters to his students, Bediuzzaman writes that because he took the path of reflection at the time the Old Said was being transformed into the New Said, he sought the true meaning of the Ḥadīth, "An hour's reflection is better than a year's [voluntary] worship." After twenty years this meaning had found, after *The Supreme Sign*, its final form in a collection of Arabic pieces which included the well-known *al-Jawshan al-Kabīr*, and a summarized extract of *The Supreme Sign*, called *Khulāṣah al-Khulāṣah*.[23] This reflection entails pondering over the beings in the universe in the manner of the traveller in *The Supreme Sign* and "reading their tongues", which proclaim the Unity of their Maker and point to the other Divine Names and attributes. Bediuzzaman described how this form of reflection illuminates the whole universe, on the one hand displaying the baselessness of concepts such as nature on which unbelief is based, and on the other, resulting in a level of belief that leads to an awareness of the universal Divine presence and universal worship:

> In the *Hizbü'l-Nuri* there is both the meaning of "*An hour's reflection,*" and universal worship...I saw that the *Jawshan al-Kabīr*, the *Risale-i Nur*, and the *Hizbü'l-Nuri* illuminate the universe from top to bottom; they disperse the darknesses; they destroy heedlessness and 'nature'; and they rend the veils under which the people of heedlessness and misguidance want to hide. I observed that they card the universe and all its beings like cotton, and comb them out. They show the lights of Divine Unity behind the furthest and broadest veils of the universe in which the people of misguidance have become submerged...
> And they show in such a way that from top to bottom the universe reflects the manifestations of the Divine Names like mirrors that no possibility remains for heedlessness. Nothing becomes an obstacle to the Divine presence. I saw that rather than banishing or forgetting or not recalling the universe like the Sufis and mystics [*ahl al-ṭarīqah wa al-ḥaqīqah*] in order to gain permanent access to the Divine presence, it gains a level of the Divine presence as broad as the universe, and that a sphere of worship opens up as broad, universal and permanent as the universe.[24]

Very often when explaining the way of the *Risale-i Nur*, Bediuzzaman compares it with Sufism, as in the above piece. Founding a new *ṭarīqah* was something he was frequently accused of in Eskişehir Court. Many of his students were familiar with it. These comparisons show clearly the differences between them:

besides seeing and learning to 'read' the universe as a means to knowledge of God rather than casting it into oblivion, the main difference is that while in Sufism it is the heart that is the means to reaching reality through illumination and wonder-working, the *Risale-i Nur* addresses reason as well as the heart and other subtle faculties. The conditions of the time demand this. With its proofs based on the modern understanding of the universe, it saves belief and raises it to a level of certainty whereby it can withstand all the doubts and assaults made against belief and religion at the present time. So also, Bediuzzaman writes, the *Risale-i Nur* does not only teach "with the feet of reason" like the works of the *'ulamā'*, the religious scholars, "...rather, proceeding with the feet of the combining of reason and the heart, and the mutual assistance of the spirit and other subtle faculties, it flies to the highest peaks; it ascends to where not the feet, but the eyes even of philosophy which attacks [religion] cannot reach; and it shows the truths of belief to eyes that are blind."[25]

Bediuzzaman found that *The Supreme Sign* with its thirty-three degrees proving the Divine existence and unity and *Hizbü'l-Nuriye* in particular illuminated the heart and other inner faculties. He wrote that when he read them, his "spirit, imagination, and heart expanded and unfolded to such a degree that when I gave the testimony 'There is no god but God' that each degree declares, I was aware of the Divine Unity on a vast scale as though that universal tongue was mine. Thus, *The Supreme Sign* can impart lights of belief to the spirit as brilliant as the sun. I formed this unshakeable conviction, and I witnessed it."[26]

'Regenerator of Religion'

In connection with its unparalleled role in strengthening and revitalizing belief in this century of severe attacks on religion, Bediuzzaman and the *Risale-i Nur* came to be recognised by many as fulfilling the requirements of Regenerator of Religion, promised by Prophet Muḥammad (ṣ) in the well-known Ḥadīth:

"At the start of each century Almighty God will send someone to this community [*ummah*] to renew its religion."²⁷ In addition to Bediuzzaman's students recognizing the *Risale-i Nur* as such, many established *'ulamā'* and religious scholars also did not hesitate to speak out in its defence, recommending it in fulsome terms. Three may be mentioned. The first and most important was one of the highest of the Istanbul *'ulamā'* and former head of the office for issuing *fatwās*, Fatwā Emini, Ali Rıza Efendi. He said after studying *The Supreme Sign* and the Twenty-Fifth Word on the Miraculousness of the Qur'an, and other parts of the *Risale-i Nur*:

> Bediuzzaman has performed the greatest service to the religion of Islam at this time. His works are absolutely correct, and no one else sacrificed themselves to this extent at this time, that is, given up the world and produced such a work. He is altogether worthy of congratulations. The *Risale-i Nur* is the Regenerator of Religion; may Almighty God grant him every success and blessing.²⁸

Another was Haji Hafız Hasan Sarıkaya, known as 'the Golden Voiced Hafız'. He had led the morning prayers for Sultan Abdulhamid II in Yıldız Palace before the Sultan's dethronement, and had known Bediuzzaman at that time. After the founding of the Republic and closure of the *madrasahs* he had persisted in teaching religion and the Qur'an, and had raised many hundreds of students. He told his son:

> Bediuzzaman is the *Imam* and Renewer of this century....He is not merely a scholar. Every century has its Renewer, and he is the Renewer of this century.²⁹

A third example is the Mufti of Karamanmaraş, Hafız Ali Efendi. He told Mustafa Ramazanoğlu, one of Bediuzzaman's students, in the 1950's:

> Such a work has not appeared for two hundred years; and it is not clear whether one will appear again in the future [that is, another will not appear]. I have no doubt that he is the Regenerator of Religion.³⁰

It is also recorded that Bediuzzaman's mission as Renewer was foretold in the year of his birth, and this was not by someone in his native East, but by one of the leading figures of the Naqshbandī *ṭarīqah* in the region of Isparta, Beşkazalızade Osman Halidi. The shaykh gave certain news in the year of his death, 1293, that is, 1876 or 7, or possibly the previous year, that "A Renewer who will save belief in God will appear, and he was born this year." He added that one of his four sons would have the honour of seeing him. And indeed, some fifty years later Bediuzzaman was exiled to the province of Isparta, and his youngest son, Ahmed Efendi, met him. And it was here that Bediuzzaman wrote the greater part of the *Risale-i Nur* and from this centre it was spread.[31]

Mawlānā Khālid Baghdādī's *Jubbah*

Probably in 1940, Asiye Hanım, the wife of the Governor of Kastamonu Prison, brought a hundred-year-old *jubbah*, that is, the gown worn by religious scholars, to give to Bediuzzaman. Knowing that he would not accept it as a gift, she consulted Mehmed Feyzi, and they decided on presenting it to him as a trust. Bediuzzaman however accepted it readily as though receiving his own property.

Asiye Hanım had inherited the *jubbah* from her father, who in turn had received it from his father, Shaykh Muḥammad ibn Abdullāh al-Khālidī, well-known by the name Küçük Aşık. From Afyonkarahisar, he had made his way to Baghdad when still of tender years to study under the famous founder of the Naqshbandī/Khālidī order, Mawlānā Khālid Baghdādī. On completing his studies he was sent by the Master as a *khalīfah* to Anatolia, who gave him the *jubbah* as a gift. Küçük Aşık later went on to Egypt where he died in 1884. His family preserved the *jubbah*, and even when they were forced to abandon their home in Afyon in the face of the Greek invasion during the War of Independence, this was the first thing they took with them. Finally Asiye Hanım married an official called Tahir Bey. On his being posted to Kastamonu as Governor of the Prison, Asiye Hanım came to know of Bediuzzaman, and realised that the *jubbah* they had so carefully guarded all these years as a trust had found its true owner, and she handed it over to him.³² Bediuzzaman recalled in a letter that when he had received his diploma on completing his studies, he had been too young to don the scholar's gown and turban. Now fifty-six years later Mawlānā Khālid had dressed him in his own *jubbah* over a hundred year distance.³³

Mawlānā Khālid was the most important figure in Naqshbandī sufism after Shaykh Ahmad Sirhindī, Imam Rabbānī, Bediuzzaman's spiritual link with whom has been mentioned in several contexts. Born a hundred or so years later than Imam Rabbānī, who was known the Regenerator of the Second Millennium, Mawlānā Khālid was recognised by many as the Regenerator or Renewer of the following century.³⁴ The movement he started was one of renewal and became very influential in the eastern Ottoman Empire.³⁵ In a short piece, one of Bediuzzaman's students, Şamlı Hafız, pointed out some of the parallels, and differences, between Bediuzzaman and Mawlānā Khālid, which show that indeed the *jubbah* had found its true owner. The main ones are as follows. The dates are according to the Rumi calendar:

> Mawlānā Khālid was born in 1193, in 1224 went to the capital of India, Jihanabad, where he entered the Naqshi Order and its revivalist (*mujaddidī*) branch in particular. In 1238 "he attracted the attention of the politicians" and had to migrate to Damascus. Descended from 'Uthmān, the third Caliph of Islam, he was brilliant and highly gifted and before reaching the age of twenty became the foremost scholar of his time. These points coincide with corresponding dates in Bediuzzaman's life in a way that cannot be attributed to chance. Bediuzzaman was born in 1293,³⁶ in 1224 he went to Istanbul, the capital of the Ottoman Empire, where he prepared for his struggle in the way of Islam. In 1238 he went to Ankara, saw that he could not work alongside the new leaders, and withdrew to Van, from where as a result of the baseless suspicions of the politicians, he was sent into exile. So too at the extraordinarily early age of fourteen Bediuzzaman

received his diploma and started to teach. When it comes to the differences, the most important are that while Mawlānā Khālid's person was the 'pole' and guide, Bediuzzaman "dismissed his own person, and showed only the *Risale-i Nur*", and while together with attaching great importance to and strengthening the Prophet's Sunnah, Mawlānā Khālid's way was that of Sufism (*'ilm al-ṭarīqah*), Bediuzzaman, "due to the requirements of this fearsome age, favoured the science of reality (*'ilm al-ḥaqīqah*) and the way of the truths of belief, and considered Sufism to be third in importance."³⁷

More on the *Risale-i Nur's* Function and Bediuzzaman's Advice to his Students Concerning This

While explaining the *Risale-i Nur's* functions and duties in his letters to his students, Bediuzzaman frequently stresses that they are concerned with belief and the strengthening and saving of it, and advises them, in the particular conditions of that time, to concentrate all their attention on matters related to these and not to become involved in any degree with political, social, and worldly matters.

This included the Second World War, which although Turkey did not take part in it, was the cause of great dissension in the country. Various reasons for this emerge from the letters like the preservation of absolute sincerity and the harm to service to religion of political bias, and although not expressed, this attitude was demanded by the political conditions of the times and the despotic regime's persecution of those who worked openly for the cause of Islam. However, in mentioning some of these points, a further underlying reason emerges for Bediuzzaman's insistence on his students remaining aloof from politics and working solely for belief, and this was in connection with the *Risale-i Nur's* function as Renewer of Religion, which he saw in the long term view of the future. It can be understood from his letters that during these years he was concerned with 'the end of time', and related the War and dreadful events of this century to those foretold to occur at that time. He placed the *Risale-i Nur* and its mission within this perspective. This becomes clear particularly from his replies to questions put to him concerning the Mahdī, who is to appear at that time. The following letter makes this clearer. It was written by a number of Bediuzzaman's students to a *hoja* who had written to him on the subject:

> Our Master says: Yes, at this time both belief and religion, and social life and the Sharī'ah, and public law and Islamic politics, are all in need of a renewer of great stature. But the duty of renewal in regard to saving the truths of belief is the most important, the most sacred, and the greatest. The spheres of the Sharī'ah, social life, and politics take second, third, and fourth places in relation to it. Also, the greatest importance in Hadīths about the renewal of religion is in regard to renewal in the truths of belief. But since in the view of public opinion and those caught up in this life Islamic social life and the politics of religion, which are attractive in that they are apparently far-reaching and predominant, appear to be of greater importance, they look from that point of view, through that lens; they give it that meaning.
>
> In addition, it does not appear to be possible for these three duties to be performed together perfectly by one person or community at this time, and for them not to damage one another. They can only be brought together at the end of time by the Mahdī and the collective personality of his community, which represents the luminous community of the Prophet's Family. Endless thanks be to Almighty God that in this century He has given the duty of renewal and the preservation of the truths of belief to the *Risale-i Nur* and to the collective personality of its students.[38]

In stressing the paramount importance of belief and its strengthening Bediuzzaman writes in another letter that it is not possible to change all these matters together at this time, so that even if the Mahdī was to come now, he would concentrate on the question of belief:

> At this time there are currents so overwhelming that they draw everything to their own account. So even if the true awaited

person, who will come next century, were to come now, my conjecture is that he would forego the political world and change his goal and not let his movement be carried away on those currents.

Also, there are three matters: one is life, another is the Sharī'ah, and another is belief. In the view of reality, the most important and the greatest is the question of belief. But in the view of most people at this time, compelled by the world situation, the most important appear to be life and the Sharī'ah. And so, even if he were to come now, since to change these three matters altogether throughout the world is not in keeping with the Divine laws in force in humankind, he would surely take the greatest matter as the basis and not the others, so that the service of belief would not be tainted in the general view and so that he would not let that service appear to ordinary people, who are easily deceived, to be exploited for other ends.[39]

Thus, it is in this perspective that Bediuzzaman establishes the *Risale-i Nur*'s primary function of renewing and strengthening belief, and it is with this view in mind that he guides his students in its service. For the sake of completeness, included at this point are examples of letters illustrating some of the main points he made in advising his students in this service. Firstly are examples of those mentioned above, advising them to disregard political and worldly matters. These are followed by examples of some of those warning the students to be above all cautious and circumspect in the face of the plots and intrigues hatched against them by their many enemies. And finally are examples of letters guiding them towards developing complete sincerity (*ikhlāṣ*) in their service and selflessness before their fellow *Risale-i Nur* students, so that the collective personality necessary to fulfil the *Risale-i Nur*'s unique functions could emerge. This consciousness of a joint or corporate personality is one of the distinguishing marks of the *Risale-i Nur* and its students, and Bediuzzaman himself offered the finest example in his total sincerity and selflessness, always putting this collective personality before himself.

Aloofness from Political Life

Bediuzzaman saw the modern world as having captured man's soul and plunged him into the life of this world and pointed out that the way to be saved from this abyss was through following the teachings of the *Risale-i Nur*. One aspect of this was life and the living of it. He wrote that this vein had become so wounded due to the burdens of inessential needs, wastefulness and greed that it attracted and held all the attention of the misguided, so that the least worldly need took preference over the greatest matter of religion. As "the dispenser of the healing remedies of the Qur'an", the *Risale-i Nur* "was able to withstand this strange sickness of this strange age", and "its resolute, unshakeable, constant, sincere, loyal, and self-sacrificing students were able to resist it."[40] Also the modern world has infected people with a senseless curiosity about "the chess-games" of politics and diplomacy, the most harmful result of which was division in society along political lines.

> Although before everything the truths of belief should come first at this time and other things remain in second, third, and fourth place, and serving them through the *Risale-i Nur* should be the prime duty and point of curiosity and main aim, the state of the world has stimulated to a high degree the veins of worldly life, and especially of social life, and of political life, and more than anything of partisanship in regard to the World War, which is a manifestation Divine Wrath in punishment for the vice and misguidance of civilization; this inauspicious age has injected those harmful, passing desires into the very centre of the heart, even as the diamonds of the truths of belief.

Bediuzzaman continues that this age has implanted these to such a degree that they are the cause of difference and disunity among even the religious. Some religious scholars, for example, give only secondary, or less, importance to matters of belief because of those political and social matters and love an enemy of religion who shares the same view and while nurturing enmity for followers of the Sufi path who oppose them. Thus, he himself completely disregarded current events "in the face of this fearsome danger of this age", and he urged his students not to allow the chess-games of tyrants to distract them from their sacred duty, nor let them taint their minds.⁴¹

The prevailing note in many of these letters is one of encouragement, even cajoling. Bediuzzaman frequently points out the great profit and benefits that the *Risale-i Nur* had brought with the new and direct way it had opened up in gaining 'certain belief', and urges his students to be steadfast and unwavering in their service of it. For the *Nur* movement was still hardly established when the students met with considerable opposition from both the *hojas* and religious scholars, and from the Sufis and followers of the *tarīqahs*, who saw the movement in terms of rivalry, as well as from the enemies of religion. It is in this light that his frequently pointing out the special instances of Divine Favour associated with the *Risale-i Nur* should be seen. This hostility was on occasion fanned and exploited by the enemies of religion. Thus, Bediuzzaman always urged his students to act tolerantly and peaceably towards followers of other paths and to return any criticism or aggression with good will, above all not allowing political differences to cause disunity and thus aid irreligion. Religion should be adhered to as the point of unity:

> Beware! Don't let worldly currents, and particularly political currents, and currents which look outside the country sow discord among you. Don't let the parties of misguidance unified before you cast you into confusion. Don't let the satanic principle of 'love for the sake of politics, enmity for the sake of politics' take the place of the principle of the Most Merciful, 'Love for God's sake; enmity for God's sake'. Don't agree to the tyranny of displaying hatred for your brother and love and support for a satanic political colleague, and so in effect share in his crime.⁴²

Bediuzzaman often also insists that politics should be avoided since the truths of belief and the Qur'an can be made a tool for nothing:

The three supreme matters in the worlds of humanity and Islam are belief, the Sharī'ah, and life. Since the truths of belief are the greatest of these, the *Risale-i Nur's* select and loyal students avoid politics with abhorrence so that they should not be made the tool to other currents and subject to other forces, and those diamond-like Qur'anic truths not reduced to fragments of glass in the view of those who sell or exploit religion for the world, and so that they can carry out to the letter the duty of saving belief, the greatest duty.[43]

In regard to the Second World War, Bediuzzaman wrote that the feelings of partisanship that the War had given rise to required his students not to concern themselves with it, because "just as consent to unbelief is unbelief, so too consent to tyranny is tyranny. In this duel, tyranny and destruction so ghastly are occurring that they make the heavens weep…it has given rise to such fearsome wrongdoing that in its barbarism it is unprecedented." It was inappropriate for people occupied with the truths of the Qur'an to follow those events unnecessarily as though applauding the destruction of those tyrants.[44]

The war years in Turkey saw a worsening of economic conditions, which had in any case been severe throughout the 1930's, and there were serious shortages in many basic essentials. Together with this there had been a decline in moral standards during the years of the republic as the regime chipped away at the Islamic cement binding society. These severe conditions are reflected in various contexts in Bediuzzaman's letters. On the one hand, they were exploited by the authorities to try to distance from religion those who were not well-off, like the majority of the *Risale-i Nur* students, through their struggles to secure a livelihood, and on the other, to sow discord among the students in order to break their solidarity. He continually warned them to be vigilant, and not allow themselves to be shaken in the face of this often extreme hardship, and their unity harmed. He urged them to respond with the principles of "frugality and contentment."[45]

In regard to the decline in moral standards, Bediuzzaman urged his students to adopt the Qur'anic concept of *taqwā*, fear of God or piety, as the basis of their actions in the face of the corruption and destruction of that time. In a letter marked "extremely important", he defined it as "avoiding sins and what is forbidden," while good works was "acting within the sphere of the obligatory good works", and said that in those severe conditions a few good deeds became like many; those who fulfilled their obligations and did not commit serious sins would be saved. The *Risale-i Nur* was a "repairer" resisting destruction. "With the shaking of the ramparts of the Qur'an,…a dark anarchy and irreligion more fearsome than Gog and Magog have begun to corrupt morality and life." Righteous action even to a small degree on the part of the *Risale-i Nur* students would have extremely positive results. Bediuzzaman concluded this letter by telling them that their greatest strength lay in strengthening each other's *taqwā*:

> After sincerity (*ikhlāṣ*), our greatest strength at such a time in the face of these fearsome events is, in accordance with the principle of 'sharing the works of the hereafter', for each of us to write good deeds into 'the righteous-act books' of the others with our pens, and with our tongues, to send reinforcements and assistance to the 'forts' of the others' *taqwā*.[46]

Sincerity and the Collective Personality of the Students of the *Risale-i Nur*

As mentioned in the letter above, Bediuzzaman considered their greatest strength to be sincerity. In another letter he described the way of the *Risale-i Nur* as being "based on the mystery of sincerity."[47] While still in Barla and Isparta, he had explained this principle in detail in two treatises, the Twentieth and Twenty-First Flashes, and the points he makes in the Kastamonu letters are by way of reminders. Just as the acquisition of sincerity was essential to form a 'collective personality', so was it necessary in order to prevent the enemies of religion taking advantage of differences among the followers of different paths and ways.

> Since our way is based on the mystery of sincerity and is the truths of belief, we are compelled by our way not to get involved in worldly and social life unless forced to, and to avoid situations which lead to rivalry, partisanship, and dispute. It is to be regretted a thousand times over that now while subject to the assaults of terrible serpents, unfortunate religious scholars and the people of religion make an excuse of minor faults like mosquito bites, and assist in the destruction of serpents and atheistic dissemblers and kill themselves with their own hands.[48]

The secret of the *Risale-i Nur*'s success in combating the destruction of atheism lay in this sincerity:

> "The *Risale-i Nur*'s victorious resistance against so many fearsome and obdurate deniers arises from the mystery of sincerity, and being a tool for nothing, and looking directly to eternal happiness, and following no aim apart from the service of belief, and attaching no importance to the personal illuminations and wonder-working that some followers of the *ṭarīqahs* consider important, and in accordance with the mystery of the legacy of prophethood, only disseminating the lights of belief and saving the faith of the believers, like the Companions of the Prophet, who possessed supreme sainthood…And they do not interfere in anything outside their own duties such as being successful or not, which is God's duty, or making the people accept or demand [their service], or making it to prevail or receiving the fame, illuminations, or Divine favours they deserve. They work with pure, total sincerity, saying: 'Our duty is to serve. That is sufficient.'"[49] "The true students of the *Risale-i Nur* see the service of belief as superior to everything; should they be accorded the rank of spiritual pole even, out of sincerity, they would prefer that of service."[50]

It was in order to develop a collective personality, a characteristic of the modern age, that the students of the *Risale-i Nur* had to renounce all the demands of the ego; to "transform the 'I' into 'We', that is, give up egotism, and work on account of the collective personality of the *Risale-i Nur*."[51]

Kastamonu

> The present is not the time for egotism and the personality for those who follow the path of reality; it is the time of the community. A collective personality emerging from the community rules, and may persist. In order to have a large pool, the ego and personality, which are like blocks of ice, have to be cast into the pool and melted.[52]

While in the past, the age of individuality, individuals of great stature like 'Abd al-Qādir al-Jīlānī, Imam Ghazālī, and Imam Rabbānī had been sent to guide the Muslim community in accordance with Divine wisdom, the unprecedented difficulties and conditions of the present time demanded a collective personality to undertake such duties.[53]

More Glimpses of Bediuzzaman's Life in Kastamonu

Despite the harassment Bediuzzaman received at the hands of officials and his being under constant surveillance, he was held in great respect by the majority of the inhabitants of the town, and a number used to visit him as far as they were permitted. We learn from one of his students, Tahsin Aydın, that among these was the Head of the Town Council. He also tells of an occasion when Bediuzzaman refused the offer of money for his students, even though sent by one of the heroes of the War of Independence.[54] He never broke this fundamental rule of his life, that of never accepting money under any circumstance, even though his situation was so difficult at one point in Kastamonu that he was forced to sell his quilt to pay the rent.[55]

Bediuzzaman also concerned himself with others in difficulties. Also there were many drunkards and people who had fallen foul of the law that he saved. An example of the former was a family who had been deported from eastern Anatolia after one of the disturbances, one member of which was a thirteen-year-old boy who used to run errands for Bediuzzaman. Necmeddin Şahiner has recorded his account of those days. Since he was a child, he could come and go unquestioned, and relates how besides performing such vital jobs as sending Bediuzzaman's letters, he would also "prepare the ground" for people wanting to visit him by conducting them on roundabout routes to avoid being spotted from the police-station opposite his house. He also mentions that on Bediuzzaman's recommendation his family were able to move to a house which Bediuzzaman had originally been going to live in, but had not been able to since it was in a quiet and secluded spot. The house was still empty and they lived there for nine years without paying any rent. Bediuzzaman helped out this family in numerous ways. On one occasion an unjust complaint was lodged against them by a neighbour, a retired police superintendent called Süleyman. Being complete strangers in the town, they were understandably very perturbed. The boy, Nadir, ran to Bediuzzaman to explain, and he sorted out the matter in no time. Since it illustrates the authority Bediuzzaman wielded, despite his position, as well as his concern for the downtrodden, a few lines are quoted in full:

> ...When I got there, Ustādh met me at the door. On my explaining the situation to him, he said to me: "I understood that you were upset. Go and tell the headman of the quarter, Çarıkçı İhsan Efendi, to come here." I went and told him and he said he would go immediately with pleasure. He went at once. Ustādh told him: "Go and tell Süleyman not to bother these people!" So İhsan Efendi went to Süleyman and repeated this. From there he came to us and consoled us, saying: "Relax! No one is going to bother you. If you have any difficulties, I'm here!' And so the problem was solved."[56]

Well-known in Kastamonu was the story of how Bediuzzaman saved Araçlı Deli Mu'min. Deli Mu'min had not been aptly named and was one of the roughs and rowdies of the district notorious for his acts of banditry. Drink and gambling were his normal pursuits. He had even killed a few people. Then one day, Çaycı Emin went in the darkness just before dawn to Bediuzzaman's house, to light his stove. Going to open the door, he made out a figure slumped on the doorstep. He drew closer and peered at it; it was Araçlı Deli

Mu'min. He said to him: "What do you want here? You're drunk again. Do you know whose doorstep you're on?" Deli Mu'min knew where he was. He started pleading: "I've repented! Pray for me! Accept me as your student!" Çaycı Emin went up and told Bediuzzaman. And Bediuzzaman did not turn him away. He said: "Yes, my brother", and received the drunk bandit. But from then on Araçlı Deli Mu'min was saved from drink, from banditry, from crime. Now he lived up to his name, he was a believer. And this is just one example of many.[57]

The *Risale-i Nur* becomes Established

During these years the *Risale-i Nur* became firmly rooted in Turkish society, and Bediuzzaman wrote that now it was certain to continue into the future. He felt certain of this as women and children responded to it so enthusiastically, both in the region of Isparta, and in Kastamonu, and so too it began to have readers among schoolboys in Kastamonu. He mentions this in a number of letters, expressing his extreme pleasure at the large numbers of parts of the *Risale-i Nur* written out by children, women, and the elderly. In one letter he writes:

> My Dear and Loyal Brothers!
> Copies written out by fifty to sixty of the *Risale-i Nur's* young and innocent students have been sent to us, and we have collected them into three volumes. We have noted down some of their names: Ömer 15 years old, Bekir 9 years old, Hüseyin 11 years old...Their serious efforts at this time show that...the *Risale-i Nur* provides a greater pleasure, joy, and eagerness than the various amusements and incentives they have created to entice children to study in the new schools. It also shows that the *Risale-i Nur* is taking root. God willing, nothing will be able to eradicate it and it will continue down the generations.

In the same letter he writes that they had gathered together the forty or fifty pieces written by the illiterate elderly, who had learnt to write after the age of fifty. So too "harvesters, farmers, shepherds, and nomads" were all putting aside their own pursuits and working for the *Risale-i Nur*. He goes on to mention that the difficulties in correcting all these copies were compensated for by the fact that he was compelled to read them slowly and carefully, and by the pleasure he received from hearing the *Risale-i Nur's* lessons from "their sincere and innocent tongues."[58]

In other letters, which encourage these Nur students so tactfully and kindly, Bediuzzaman mentions that they had made up five and seven volumes of these pieces, one of which included pieces written out by children that illustrated examples of the coinciding of letters.[59] Women too, he said, had a close affinity with the *Risale-i Nur* and he had long expected them to respond warmly to it. He wrote:

> In fact, since the chief foundation of the way of the *Risale-i Nur* is compassion, and women are mines of compassion, I had long expected the *Risale-i Nur's* true nature to be understood in the world of women. Thanks be to God, the women here are more active and work with greater enthusiasm than the men hereabouts...These two manifestations are an auspicious sign that [in the future] the *Risale-i Nur* will shine and make many conquests in those mines of compassion.[60]

Although it was while in the Darü'l-Hikmeti'l-İslamiye that Bediuzzaman had written the treatise on the wisdom in Islamic dress for women, which he renamed the Twenty-Fourth Flash while still in Barla, it was only during these years that he consented to receive women from time to time for the purpose of teaching them from the *Risale-i Nur*. It was also at this time that some of the pieces that were later to be made into the collection published under the name of *A Guide for Women* were written.[61] These most probably formed the basis of his guidance to these visitors.

Bediuzzaman was also concerned with the youth, as those most susceptible to the materialist ideologies being propagated with such fury. In 1940 or '41, some high school boys started to visit Bediuzzaman, one of which was Abdullah Yeğin, who from that time on was a devoted student of his and the *Risale-i Nur*, and in future years was one of his most active students. Some of the replies to the questions they asked became the basis of various parts of the *Risale-i Nur,* and it was for them that Bediuzzaman compiled the pieces finally published under the name of *A Guide for Youth.* It was also because of them that Bediuzzaman first gave permission for the *Risale-i Nur* to be written in the Latin alphabet, thus becoming immediately accessible to the younger generation. Some of the young schoolboy's impressions are as follows:

> I was in the second class of the middle section of Kastamonu High School, in 1940-1. On hearing Ustādh's landlord and some others who visited us speak praisingly of him, it awoke in me the desire to go and see him. What I heard about him was that he was an important person, did not accept presents, and did not receive everyone.
>
> One day during the break in school I broached the subject with my bench-mate, Rıfat. When I told him there was a famous hoca here worth seeing, he replied: 'Yes, I know, his house is opposite ours. He's a very good person, let's go together. I sometimes visit him.'
>
> We went together at a convenient time. We knocked at the door and it was opened. We went upstairs, and entered his room by the door on the right. First Rıfat and then I kissed his hand and we sat down. He was seated on a high platform like a bed, with a quilt drawn up over his knees and leaning against the back. He was holding a book. His hair came down to his ears. Looking at us over his fine spectacles, he said to us: 'Welcome!' He asked my friend about me, and he introduced me as his school friend. He asked my name and was very kind. He spoke to us about Islam, the beauty of belief in God, death, and the hereafter. We sat for a while then we left.
>
> One day when I went to visit him, I saw Ustādh to be very profound and humble. It was because of this humility that I wondered if he knew anything—because he always came down to our level and spoke of things that we knew. I even asked Mehmet Feyzi Efendi one day if he knew Arabic. Of course Feyzi Efendi just laughed.
>
> Ustādh's modesty and humility, and affection and interest in us bound us to him. From time to time I would take other friends to him. He always gave excellent answers to the

questions we asked him. I lost the negative ideas about religion I had acquired from some of the teachers at school when I visited Ustādh.

Another time I visited him, I asked: "Our teachers don't speak about God. Tell us about our Creator." Ustādh explained at great length about this subject. I can't exactly remember when the answer to our question was written down. When we visited him, Mehmed Feyzi Pamukçu used to read from *The Supreme Sign* or *The Short Words* and we would write them down in our notebooks in the new letters...

One day at school it was the geography lesson and the teacher asked the class: 'Who's been to that reactionary *hoja* they call Bediuzzaman?' Six people raised their hands. He asked why we'd gone, and said that Ustādh was an enemy of the reforms and didn't like Ataturk. He sent us to the Disciplinary Council. They asked various questions. As a result, a friend called Suat and myself were banned from school for six days, and the others were given warnings. We said in the statements we gave that we had gone because we wanted to learn about our religion, no one had said anything against anyone, and that we were religious and liked performing our worship. A few days later the police raided the house where I was staying and went through it with a tooth-comb. My statement was taken by the police. I described what had happened to me. The Prosecutor asked: 'There's the Mufti and lots of *hojas*. Why don't you go to them?' I said I didn't know the Mufti...

The reason I had first visited Ustādh was this: he did not accept presents from anyone!

I saw the way he lived; he was really and truly poor! In one of his rooms was a woven rug and a few cloth prayer-mats. The other was completely bare. If the well-to-do people in the town brought him anything, he would most kindly and graciously refuse it. He did not want to offend anyone. He absolutely would not take anything or eat anything without giving something in return. He really lived what he wrote. The only thing he spoke about was the *Risale-i Nur*. The way he acted was like a repetition of what it teaches.[62]

Abdullah Yeğin notes also another side of Bediuzzaman's character, his refusal to compromise his beliefs in any way in the face of threat or tyranny, which was a powerful source of strength and inspiration for others in those dark days:

> Like his speech, Ustādh's manner was unique, and everyone used to look at him in amazement. For his dress, his manner, and his actions resembled no one else's...I'll never forget the way in that time of repression when the police and gendarmes were much feared, Ustādh walking with firm and resolute steps towards the governor's residence escorted by the police, in exactly the same dress he had always worn and the way the onlookers stared at him in wonder, a shiver passing over the crowd watching him.[63]

Parts of the *Risale-i Nur* Written in Kastamonu

Between his arrival in Kastamonu in March 1936 and probably 1940 Bediuzzaman wrote from the Third to the Ninth Rays inclusive.[64] Of these, the Seventh Ray, *The Supreme Sign*, was written in Ramaḍān of 1938 or '39.[65] It was followed immediately by the Eighth Ray,[66] and the summary of the Arabic Twenty-Ninth Flash, *Ḥizb al-Akbar al-Nūrī*.[67] Bediuzzaman sent numerous letters to his students in Isparta, and also while in Kastamonu, he prepared the final drafts of the First and Second Rays, which had been written in Eskişehir Prison. The second part of the Index, which included the parts of *Lem'alar* (The Flashes) subsequent to the Fifteenth Flash—the Fifteenth Flash forms the Index for all the Words, Letters, and the First to the Fourteenth Flashes—was also written at this time by some of Bediuzzaman's students in Isparta.[68] There followed after 1940 a period of cessation as far as writing new works was concerned.[69]

As the *Risale-i Nur* spread and became established Bediuzzaman had some of its parts put together in the form of collections, and some of these he had typed out in the new letters. This was in 1942 and 1943. One was a collection of four pieces for the High School boys.[70] Abdullah Yeğin mentions above their writing out pieces in the new Latin script. There were other collections for which he suggested various titles, including what was later published as *A Guide for Youth*, and another called *The Ratifying Stamp of the Unseen*.[71] Bediuzzaman also put together other pieces on the resurrection of the dead to be included as addenda to the Tenth Word.[72] In 1943 Tahiri Mutlu, from the village of Atabey near Isparta, had *The Supreme Sign* published in Istanbul. Although it was only during Bediuzzaman's Kastamonu years that he had come to know the *Risale-i Nur*, Tahiri Mutlu was to be one of its most important students. It was also through his enterprise that handwritten copies of the *Ḥizb al-Qur'ān* and *Ḥizb al-Nūrī* were printed photographically at this time. Also in 1943, the Fifth Ray about Ḥadīths alluding to the signs of the end of the world and resurrection and the fearsome individuals or antichrists who were to appear at the end of time, began to be sought after. The final draft of this treatise had been made in 1938 from a first draft made while Bediuzzaman was a member of the Darü'l-Hikmet from pieces some of which were taken from *Muhâkemat*, published in 1909. This Fifth Ray was to be the main cause of his, and a number of his students' arrest in August of 1943 and their second sojourn in prison.

Increased Harassment and Arrest

Both Bediuzzaman and his students in Kastamonu, and the *Risale-i Nur* students in the region of Isparta and other places were under constant pressure from the authorities. This increased as time passed, culminating in widespread arrests and the Denizli trials and imprisonment in 1943-4. On several occasions previous to this copies of the *Risale-i Nur* were seized after searches, students arrested and then subsequently acquitted and the copies of the *Risale-i Nur* returned. It was the Fifth Ray in particular that was being searched for. In 1940, thirty to forty were arrested then released. Towards the end of 1941, there was another incident in Isparta involving a *Risale-i Nur* student called Mehmet Zühtü Efendi, and this was followed by a third incident.[73] The closeness of the surveillance under which Bediuzzaman was held, and the pressure on him, also increased. These incidents are reflected in Bediuzzaman's letters together with repeated warnings to his students to observe the utmost caution and discretion and to guard against the plans and plots that were being hatched against them. These have been mentioned in part above; their principle aim was to break the solidarity of the *Risale-i Nur* students by sowing conflict among them, and to distract, tempt, or scare them away from their service to the *Risale-i Nur*. It was a serious, planned attempt to stop the spread of the *Risale-i Nur*.

This series of arrests occurred in Isparta and Bediuzzaman was not actually taken into custody. However, the authorities attempted to solve their problem by more dastardly means: they had him poisoned on several occasions. Çaycı Emin stated that from time to time Bediuzzaman suffered severe bouts of illness as a result of being poisoned.[74] He also described an occasion when Bediuzzaman was poisoned when alone in the mountains having bought some fruit on the way. Mehmed Feyzi also describes it, as it was he who received word from some unknown source and went up into the mountains and found him in a semi-conscious state. Bediuzzaman had known the grocer he had bought the fruit from, since he very often got something from him on his way. The wretch had evidently been persuaded by the agents who followed Bediuzzaman wherever he went to give him pieces they had injected with poison. Mehmed Feyzi had taken the horse Bediuzzaman had been riding, which had made its own way back to the town when he was overcome by the effect of the poison, back up the mountain and brought Bediuzzaman back on it. Bediuzzaman was ill for some time following this, which occurred shortly before the final events before his arrest and another attempt to poison him. This time it was certified by the doctor who attended him.[75]

In early August 1943, a *Risale-i Nur* student who was active in the Denizli region was arrested along with several others. He had been informed on by the local Mufti as a result of which extensive searches were carried out in the area and handwritten copies of the *Risale-i Nur* were seized.[76] As with the Eskişehir affair, the matter was taken up by Ankara and blown up out of all proportion. President İsmet İnönü, Prime Minister Şükrü Saraçoğlu, and Education Minister Hasan Ali Yücel were directly concerned. Instructions were sent to Isparta and Kastamonu, and the houses of numerous *Nur* students searched. Then the arrests started in Isparta.

Bediuzzaman is Arrested

Meanwhile Bediuzzaman's house in Kastamonu was searched three times in succession. When after the first time they were unable to find what they were searching for, the Fifth Ray, they determined to do away with Bediuzzaman and succeeded in poisoning him again. This was verified by a doctor and when seriously ill with the effects of it and running a temperature of over 40°, his house was searched a second time. This coincided with the start of Ramaḍān, which in 1943 began on 2 September. This was followed by a third and most rigorous search directed by a number of high-ranking police and officials.[77] On this occasion they found some parts of the *Risale-i Nur* hidden in a strong-box under the coal and fire-wood. They included the Fifth Ray, the collection called *The Ratifying Stamp of the Unseen*,[78] the treatise on Islamic dress for women which had been the pretext of Bediuzzaman being convicted by Eskişehir Court, and another called *Hücumat-i Sitte*.[79] Bediuzzaman was then arrested and held in Kastamonu police station for some two to three weeks.

In the spring of that year Bediuzzaman had had a premonition that he would not remain much longer in Kastamonu. He expressed this to the schoolboy Abdullah Yeğin before he went away for the long summer holiday. And Abdullah Yeğin returned to see Bediuzzaman being driven away by the police. He described it like this:

It was in the spring of 1943. It was going to be the school holidays and we went to visit him again. I'll never forget these words he said to us after giving us lengthy instruction on matters to do with belief and morality:

"My brothers! For a long time I've never stayed more than eight years in one place. It's now eight years since I came here, so this year I'll either die or go somewhere else. Perhaps we won't meet again. A time will come when there will be *Risale-i Nur* students everywhere. Don't part from one another or from the *Risale-i Nur*."

His speaking in this way affected me greatly and I was very upset. When he saw this, he said:

"Don't worry. We'll meet again, God willing."

Three months later the holidays came to an end and we returned to Kastamonu from Araç. I wanted to go and visit him. Then he warned Çaycı Emin Bey, 'They are following me. Don't let anyone come.' For this reason we could not go to him.

Then one day we were in the playground of Kastamonu High School for the break. They were taking him in a light open carriage along the street. He had a wicker-work basket, a tea-pot, ewer, and a few possessions with him. Then the carriage stopped and they got out. There were a gendarme sergeant and a few policemen with him. A crowd gathered. He was wearing a black turban and a long gown, also black. It was impossible to go out dressed in such clothes at that time, above all with the police.

In the school the others saw me watching him and called me "Bediuzzaman follower". Then the bell rang and we went into class.

How many days passed after this I don't know, but one night around midnight our house began shaking. The earthquakes had started. The tremors continued in this way for about two weeks. The people said: "Hoja Efendi was a good man. They harassed him, treated him badly, and slandered him so there were earthquakes."[80]

Nadir Baysal, some of whose reminiscences were given above, described the air of terror that descended on the town after Bediuzzaman was arrested. He says also that Bediuzzaman was not held in the prison but in his house:

It was Ramaḍān in 1943. I was going towards Ustādh's house when in the Shoemakers' Market I saw them taking him, still with a turban on his head, in a phaeton to the Law Courts. Çaycı Emin, Mehmet Feyzi and altogether twenty-two people were kept for about two weeks in the prison. Ustādh did not stay inside but was sent back to his house under police supervision. Two weeks later they transferred them all to Denizli Court. Such an air of terror overwhelmed the town at that time that it was as though anyone who had met with Ustādh had committed a crime. Some people did not dare to go out of their houses...

While Ustādh was leaving Kastamonu, the leaves of the calendar showed 1943. A short while later the earthquakes started. A great stone rolled down from the citadel and seven people were killed in the house on which it fell. In the region of Tosya between six and seven hundred people died.[81]

Kastamonu-Ankara-Isparta

On the Night of Power, which in Turkey is generally considered to be 25-26 Ramaḍān, and was thus probably 27 September, Bediuzzaman was taken from the police station opposite his house in Kastamonu and put on the bus for Ankara, some 271 kilometres to the south. He is reported to have told the police there:

> Tell that Midhat [the Governor of Kastamonu] to send my defence speeches in both the new and old letters on after me![82]

This, reported by Selahaddin Çelebi, referred to Bediuzzaman's defence from Eskişehir Court which he had given to the officials and police while they had been searching his house for the Fifth Ray and other treatises.[83]

Also present in the bus was an official from İnebolu called Ziya Dilek, who was also later arrested and sent to Denizli. His account of the journey was recorded by Necmeddin Şahiner:

> I had got on the bus to go to my job at Ilgaz. It was stopped by police and gendarmes at Olukbaşı [where the police station was] and space for three people cleared at the back. They put Bediuzzaman Hoja Efendi there. When the bus moved off Hoja Efendi felt unwell; he was seventy years old and ill. He

said: "They count me as a political prisoner, so I should be sent by a private taxi." Whereupon a soldier sitting next to me got up and offered his seat to the *hoja*, and they changed places. I was very scared and could not do anything to help him. When he sat down beside me he asked me my name. On my saying Ziya Dilek, he said. "Are you our Ziya? Did you come to see me off on behalf of the people of Kastamonu?" Turning to the policeman Safvet behind him, who had brought him, he said; "Safvet! Where is the Qur'an was I reading when you raided my house?" And asking for a piece of paper, got me to write down the verse, "So bear in patience the command of your Sustainer for you are in Our sight, and offer praise and glory"(Qur'an, 52:48). Then asking, "Wasn't I reading this verse?", he showed it to Safvet and the others. Then he said to me:

"Ziya, tell your friends not to worry. We won't be convicted. They'll either make a truce or give an amnesty." He was sending through me greetings and the good news to his friends who had been arrested. But I was not going there and I had not been arrested.

Later he said: "Would you tell the driver to please stop the bus. There's no compulsion in religion. I have a few words of advice for the passengers." So the driver stopped the bus and Hoja Efendi immediately started to address the passengers:

"Tonight is most likely the Night of Power. When recited on other days each letter of the Qur'an yields ten rewards, in Ramaḍān a thousand rewards, and on the Night of Power thirty thousand. If you were told you would be given five gold liras in return for doing something, wouldn't you want to obtain them?" The passengers replied that they would, so the *hoja* continued: "You spend all your strength and energy to gain five gold liras for this transitory life, don't you want to prepare some provisions for your provisions-bag for eternal life?" Again the passengers replied in the affirmative. So Bediuzzaman said: "In that case, if a Muslim recites Sūrah al-Ikhlāṣ three times, Sūrah al-Fātiḥah once, and Āyah al-Kursī once, he will have prepared some provisions for his bag for eternal life."

The driver, Rizeli Lütfü, and the passengers thanked Bediuzzaman, and soon afterwards it was time to break the fast. He stopped the bus at a famous spring in the pine forests in the

Ilgaz Mountains for a break. There, Hoja Efendi gave me the food given to him by the Town Council and I gave him mine, and we broke the fast in that way. We performed the evening prayers together. In Ilgaz I left Hoja Efendi and went to work, but a while later they arrested me and sent me to Denizli. They still had not brought Hoja Efendi there when I arrived. When the friends in the prison asked me anxiously if I had seen Ustādh Hazretleri, I remembered the verse he had got me to write in the bus on the way to Ilgaz. I got it out and read it to them and related what had happened on the journey. It was a powerful consolation for them and they were very pleased.[84]

Assigned to accompany Bediuzzaman from Kastamonu to Isparta was a non-commissioned gendarme officer called İsmail Tunçdoğan. He noted that on reaching Ankara, he and Bediuzzaman put up at a hotel in the Samanpazarı district.[85] Soon after arriving, in a manner entirely outside the normal course of events, Bediuzzaman was summoned by the Governor of Ankara, Nevzat Tandoğan. There followed an incident which if it had not been for the appalling disrespect shown to Bediuzzaman, would have been quite simply ludicrous. This unhappy man, who was one of the notables of the Republican People's Party and for seventeen years was Governor of Ankara, had summoned Bediuzzaman in order to force him to take off his turban and put on the 'official' peaked cap. Needless to say, he was not successful. Bediuzzaman told him: "This turban only comes off with this head!"[86] In addition to the gendarme officer, who noted that Bediuzzaman came out of the office carrying a peaked cap, the incident was witnessed by Bediuzzaman's student from İnebolu, Selahaddin Çelebi, who had been arrested in Ankara some days previously, and was taken after Bediuzzaman to the Government Building. He described it like this:

> It was a hot day towards the end of Ramaḍān. I was at the door of Nevzat Bey's office. The officials brought Bediuzzaman and went into the governor's office together. Then the officials came out and the door was closed. The sound of angry voices came from inside. Then a bell rang and a servant went in and then

came out again. At that point, Bediuzzaman said angrily to Tandoğan: "I represent your forefathers. I live in seclusion. The dress laws may not be enforced against those living in isolation. I don't go out. You brought me out by force. I hope you pay for it!" The servant then returned carrying a twenty-five kuruş peaked cap and went into the governor's office.[87]

According to one account the governor himself actually physically put this cap on Bediuzzaman's head, and according to another, he tried to, but could not. In any event, some three years later he came to a sorry end, by committing suicide by putting a bullet through his own head.[88] Bediuzzaman was then taken to the station and put on the train for Isparta. Governor Tandoğan however did not give up at this point and went also to the station together with some police with the intention of catching Bediuzzaman red-handed. But the moment they were going to seize him, Bediuzzaman whipped off his turban and climbed into the train. They stopped in amazement, how had he known they were there and what they intended to do? Bediuzzaman later said that they had been defeated by a flea. For just as he was about to board the train, a flea alighted on his head, and he had taken off his turban to scratch it! So they could do nothing. Bediuzzaman said it had been an instance not of his own but the *Risale-i Nur's karāmah*.[89]

According to the gendarme İsmail Tunçdoğan, a large crowd gathered to greet Bediuzzaman at Isparta. Also on the train was one of his students from his days in Barla, Çaprazzade Abdullah. He had come and spoken with Bediuzzaman on the journey and as a result was held for questioning for two days in Isparta on arrival.[90] Bediuzzaman was taken from the station to the prison, where *Risale-i Nur* students from a number of regions had already been brought. As in all his stays in prison, Bediuzzaman was put into solitary confinement. Then he and the other students were subject to intense questioning and interrogation. They were to remain less than a month in Isparta before being transferred to Denizli Prison for the trials. The Ministry of Justice in Ankara specified Denizli, since it was where the first arrests had taken place.

Notes

1. Nursi, *Lem'alar*, 251 (Eng. tr.: *Flashes*, 333).
2. See, Çaycı Emin Bey, in Şahiner, *Nurs Yolu*, 100-3; and, *Son Şahitler*, i, 108-116.
3. Mehmed Feyzi Pamukçu, in *Son Şahitler*, ii, 158-164.
4. Nursi, *Kastamonu Lahikası*, 12.
5. Çaycı Emin Çayir, in *Son Şahitler*, i, 112.
6. Hilmi Semâ, in *Son Şahitler*, v, 202-3.
7. See, Çaycı Emin, in *Son Şahitler*, i, 110-111; and, Mehmed Münip Yalaz, in *Son Şahitler*, ii, 188.
8. Sadık Demirelli, in *Son Şahitler*, ii, 135-157.
9. Selahaddin Çelebi, in *Son Şahitler*, i, 138.
10. Nursi, *Kastamonu Lahikası*, 62.
11. *Ibid.*, 72.
12. *Ibid.*, 5.
13. *Ibid.*, 10.
14. *Ibid.*, 53.
15. *Ibid.*, 48, and, 10.
16. Nursi, *Şualar*, 140 (Eng. tr.: *Rays*, 188).
17. A closer translation of "certain belief", in Turkish *tahkikî*, or according to its Arabic transliteration, *tahqīqī, iman*, would be 'verified', 'ascertained through enquiry', 'resulting from investigation', or 'confirmatory'.
18. Nursi, *Kastamonu Lahikası*, 25.
19. Nursi, *Şualar*, 82 (Eng. tr.: *Rays*, 123).
20. Nursi, *Sikke-i Tasdik-i Gaybî*, 76.
21. Qur'an, 42:28.
22. *Şualar*, 91 (Eng. tr.: *Rays*, 133-4).
23. Nursi, *Kastamonu Lahikası*, 171.
24. *Ibid.*, 174-5.
25. *Ibid.*, 10.
26. Nursi, *Emirdağ Lahikası*, i, 68.
27. For example, in al-Ḥākim's *Mustadrak*, the *Kitāb al-Sunan* of Abū Dāwūd, and Bayhaqī's *Shuʿab al-Īmān*, quoted in Nursi, *Sikke-i Tasdik-i Gaybî*, 14.
28. Nursi, *Kastamonu Lahikası*, 143.
29. Haji Hasan Sarıkaya, in *Son Şahitler*, iv, 357-8.
30. Mustafa Ramazanoğlu, in *Son Şahitler*, iv, 225, 229.
31. See, Nursi, *Sikke-i Tasdik-i Gaybi*, 41-2.
32. Şahiner, *Son Şahitler*, i, 234-5; iv, 351-4; *Nurs Yolu*, 111-3.
33. Nursi, *Kastamonu Lahikası*, 63.
34. In *Şualar*, a Renewer (*mujaddid*) is defined in this way: "The high servants of religion who are described in Ḥadīths as coming at the

start of every century are not innovators; they are followers. That is to say, they do not create anything new themselves, they do not bring any new ordinances; they adjust and strengthen religion by way of following to the letter the fundamentals and ordinances of religion and the Sunnah of the Prophet Muḥammad (ṣ); they proclaim the true and original meaning of religion; they remove and render null and void the baseless matters which have been mixed up with it; they reject and destroy the attacks made on religion; they establish the Divine commands, and proclaim and make known the nobility and exaltedness of the Divine ordinances. Only, without spoiling the basic position or damaging the original spirit, they carry out their duties through new methods of persuasion appropriate to the understanding of the age, and in new ways and with new details." *Şualar*, 563 (Eng. tr.: *Rays*, 635).

35. Şerif Mardin. *Religion and Social Change in Modern Turkey: The Case of Bediüzzaman Said Nursi*, 57-9, 149.
36. Şamlı Hafız gives this as Hijrī; in fact, according to most documents, the year of Bediuzzaman's birth was 1293 Rumi, 1877.
37. Nursi, *Sikke-i Tasdik-i Gaybî*, 14-16.
38. Nursi, *Kastamonu Lahikası*, 139.
39. *Ibid.*, 57-8.
40. Nursi, *Kastamonu Lahikası*, 69-71; 73-4.
41. *Ibid.*, 80-1.
42. *Ibid.*, 84.
43. *Ibid.*, 104.
44. *Ibid.*, 31.
45. *Ibid.*, 167; also, 99, 111, 148, 176-7.
46. *Ibid.*, 106-7.
47. *Ibid.*, 186.
48. *Ibid.*, 186.
49. *Ibid.*, 200.
50. *Ibid.*, 190.
51. *Ibid.*, 135.
52. *Ibid.*, 102.
53. *Ibid.*, 6-7.
54. Tahsin Aydın, in *Son Şahitler*, iii, 104-5.
55. *Tarihçe*, 284.
56. Nadir Baysal, in *Son Şahitler*, iv, 282-6.
57. Şahiner, *Son Şahitler*, ii, 193-5.
58. *Tarihçe*, 278-9.
59. Nursi, *Kastamonu Lahikası*, 82-3.
60. *Ibid.*, 62.
61. For example, Nursi, *Kastamonu Lahikası*, 85.

62. Abdullah Yeğin, in *Son Şahitler*, i, 370-1.
63. *Ibid.*, 380.
64. Şahiner, *Said Nursi*, 309-10; Nursi, *Kastamonu Lahikası*, 157.
65. *Ibid.*, 26-7.
66. *Şualar*, 611, 625.
67. Nursi, *Kastamonu Lahikası*, 25-6.
68. Nursi, *Müdâfaalar*, 156.
69. Nursi, *Kastamonu Lahikası*, 157.
70. *Ibid.*, 106.
71. *Ibid.*, 166-7.
72. *Ibid.*, 74.
73. Nursi, *Sikke-i Tasdik-i Gaybî*, 171.
74. Çaycı Emin Çayır, in *Son Şahitler*, i, 113-4.
75. *Ibid.*, 114-5; Mehmed Feyzi Pamukçu, in *Son Şahitler*, ii, 161; *Tarihçe*, 288.
76. Nursi, *Müdâfaalar*, 97.
77. Nursi, *Kastamonu Lahikası*, 203-4.
78. Nursi, *Lem'alar*, 251 (Eng. tr.: *Flashes*, 333).
79. *Tarihçe*, 358.
80. Şahiner, *Said Nursi*, 335-6.
81. Nadir Baysal, in *Son Şahitler*, iv, 285-6.
82. Şahiner, *Said Nursi*, 338.
83. See, Nursi, *Kastamonu Lahikası*, 203-4.
84. Şahiner, *Said Nursi*, 338-340.
85. İsmail Tunçdoğan, in *Son Şahitler*, iii, 101.
86. Nursi, *Emirdağ Lahikası*, ii, 19.
87. Şahiner, *Said Nursi*, 340-1.
88. *Ibid.*, 340.
89. Bayram Yüksel, in *Son Şahitler*, i, 446.
90. Çaprazzade Abdullah, in *Son Şahitler*, ii, 116; Şahiner, *Said Nursi*, 341.

15
Denizli

Introduction

Bediuzzaman was still weak and ill from the effects of the poison. It was now the end of Ramaḍān. He was most grieved and saddened at this blow to the *Risale-i Nur*. Virtually all its leading students had been arrested in addition to himself. As for the students, they had been rounded up and taken from their homes and villages in the province of Isparta and elsewhere and their families were left without support or protection. What the outcome would be was anything but certain. If conditions had been bad in Eskişehir Prison, in Denizli they were worse. Bediuzzaman said he suffered in one day in Denizli the distress he suffered in a month in Eskişehir. But again it resulted in a victory for right; the truth prevailed over falsehood and the *Risale-i Nur* over its enemies. While at first it seemed as though a crippling blow had been dealt to the *Risale-i Nur* and its dissemination, in the event the Denizli trials and imprisonment, like Eskişehir before and Afyon afterwards, served the cause of the *Risale-i Nur* in ways no one expected.

Firstly was the positive report by the committee of experts in Ankara and the acquittal. Then it was the cause of many officials and others reading *The Supreme Sign* and other parts of the *Risale-i Nur* with favourable results. Also the court case and imprisonment publicised the *Risale-i Nur* and aroused a lot of sympathy towards Bediuzzaman and his students and interest in the *Risale-i Nur*, which counteracted the propaganda campaign against them orchestrated by members of the government.

A factor that contributed to their acquittal was also the extraordinary change that came about in the majority of the other prisoners through the influence of Bediuzzaman and his students. The same had been true to an extent in Eskişehir, but in Denizli Prison hardened criminals even learned how to perform the prayers and recite the Qur'an, and some to assist the students in writing out copies of the *Risale-i Nur*. Bediuzzaman was kept in solitary confinement in a minute damp, dark cell. He was again poisoned on several occasions. Undoubtedly the intention was to do away with him, as well as the most important of his students. Two in fact died during the nine months they were held, one of which was Hafız Ali from the village of İslamköy near Isparta. It was widely believed he had been poisoned. Nevertheless, Bediuzzaman relentlessly continued his struggle. His students were forbidden to visit or speak with him, so he wrote them numerous notes and letters encouraging and consoling them, guiding them, and directing the writing-out and copying of these and the *Risale-i Nur*. Then he wrote the Eleventh Ray, *The Fruits of Belief*. And he also wrote his petitions and defence speeches. Since he and his students were charged with virtually the same 'crimes' as in Eskişehir and he offered the same defence in Afyon Court some four years later in 1948-9, it shall be described only briefly in this chapter.

Life in Denizli Prison

The students who had been gathered together in Isparta were transported to Denizli by train. Handcuffed in pairs, they were packed into windowless coal and straw wagons. Bediuzzaman was handcuffed to a ninety-year-old villager called Hasan Dayı from the village of Sav near Isparta who was so weak he virtually had to carry him.[1] Their handcuffs were not unfastened during the journey. Of the one hundred and twenty-six *Risale-i Nur* students who were taken to Denizli[2] from all over Turkey, in all seventy-three entered the prison and the remainder were released.³ The students from Kastamonu, İnebolu, and Istanbul were brought some two months later. They were then put in with the long-term and condemned prisoners.

The prison was new and outside the town, yet despite this it was more cramped and insalubrious than older buildings. It was built of concrete and was damp, dank and airless. With its tiny heavily barred and high windows, the cells and dormitories were in perpetual gloom. The electricity was of a very low voltage and on only a few hours each day. It was also infested with lice and mosquitoes. At night bed-bugs and mosquitoes descended on the prisoners from the ceilings "like a fine rain". Bediuzzaman was put in a cell so small a bed could scarcely fit in it. According to Selahaddin Çelebi who was sent by the prison Governor on one occasion to write out Bediuzzaman's defence speech for him, it was airless and closed like a cave, and so damp the human body could scarcely withstand it. They had to work by the light of a candle. After one hour of writing down what Bediuzzaman dictated, he was completely exhausted.⁴ The cell had one small window which overlooked the long-term prisoners' exercise yard. Since Bediuzzaman was in total isolation and his students and all the prisoners were forbidden to speak or communicate with him on pain of being beaten, he used to throw the notes, letters, and pieces he wrote out of this window to them. They were most often written on scraps of paper folded up inside match-boxes. When this was discovered by the prison authorities, they boarded up the window for a time. He also sent them by means of a go-between called Arnavut Adem Ağa. When they received them, the students would start writing out copies. The cell was also next to the juveniles' ward, and the delinquents were encouraged by the warders to disturb Bediuzzaman, who was extremely sensitive to noise, and to strike up a din particularly while he was praying or performing his worship.

When Selahaddin Çelebi, Mehmet Feyzi, and the other students from Kastamonu arrived, they were put in with the long-term and condemned prisoners. Among these was the prisoners' spokesman and leader, Süleyman Hünkâr, a person of considerable power and influence in the day to day affairs of the prison. Süleyman Efe as he was known both 'reformed' and giving up his former bad ways, became a loyal student of Bediuzzaman, and he struck up a close friendship with Taşköprülü Sadık Bey. Sadık Bey also had followed the fast life of a *derebey* till Bediuzzaman came to Kastamonu and he had become his student. Although all Bediuzzaman's students and some of the prisoners worked continuously in those appalling conditions for the cause of religion and the *Risale-i Nur*, it was really through these two that it was possible to organise it.

İbrahim Fakazlı from İnebolu described how the prisoners started to reform and perform the prayers. It had happened soon after the others had arrived and before they had come. When Bediuzzaman had gone to take ablutions the prisoners had crowded at a window wanting him to speak to them. This happened three times and he ignored them. Then the third time, he told them: "Go and wash!" So Süleyman Efe gathered together seventy to eighty of the prisoners and asking them, "Which of you is dirty?" harangued them and ordered them to take baths. Then the prisoners again asked Bediuzzaman to speak to them, so this time he told them to perform the prayers. When they said they did not know how to, he said he would send his students to teach them.[5] In this way the greater part of the prisoners began to give up their former ways and to perform the five daily prayers. Bediuzzaman's students also taught them the basic rules of religion and how to read and recite the Qur'an. Together with the Kastamonu prisoners were a number of well-known *hojas* from Istanbul, one of whom was Gönenli Mehmed Efendi, one of Turkey's best known Qur'an *hojas*. He also taught the prisoners the Qur'an. One called Mehmed, who had murdered four people, learnt to read the whole Qur'an and memorised the last twenty-two sūrahs, thus earning the right to lead the others in prayer.[6]

Others were taken away to be hanged while reading the Qur'an or performing the prayers, having been saved from every kind of vice and evil-living. What a lesson for secular and humanist sociologists and reformers!

When the students from Kastamonu and İnebolu arrived at the prison, Sadık Bey immediately established good relations with the other prisoners, who according to Süleyman Efe were all "his men". Bold-spirited and generous, he won their respect and soon formed a team to carry out the necessary jobs for continuing the work of the *Risale-i Nur*. Through them it was possible for Bediuzzaman's writings to be distributed round the prison, and be smuggled in and out of it. Süleyman Efe also secured a typewriter, and Sadık Bey and his team used to write out his defence speeches and other writings in the new letters and then have copies sent to various government departments in Ankara or wherever required. He won Bediuzzaman's admiration and gratitude with this unparalleled service, which was reflected in the notes and letters he wrote him, and in his accepting Sadık Bey's soup. Bediuzzaman, who would accept nothing from anyone without giving something in return, was happy to live on the soups Sadık Bey cooked for him.[7] It has also been recorded that the *Risale-i Nur* was smuggled in and out of the prison by a gendarme stationed there who came from the village of Kuleönü near Isparta. He would take the pieces copied out in the village of Sav for Bediuzzaman to correct, and the presents his students sent him, such as the area's famous rose oil.[8]

Besides Bediuzzaman's letters and defence speeches, and indeed the students' own defences, which had to be composed and written out, it was mostly *The Fruits of Belief* that copies were made of in the prison. This, the Eleventh Ray, which Bediuzzaman described as "a fruit and memento of Denizli Prison and the product of two Fridays", consists of eleven pieces or Topics, the last two of which were written in Emirdağ after he was released. Addressing the prisoners, each Topic explains some matter of belief such as knowledge of God, resurrection and the hereafter, and particularly relevant to that situation, the question of death. It also forms a summary of the truths of the *Risale-i Nur*. The concluding part of the Eighth Topic was written during the *Kurban Bayramı*[9] or *'Īd al-Aḍḥā*, the Feast of the Sacrifices, which in 1943 began on 8 December. Numerous copies of this most important part of the *Risale-i Nur* were made by Bediuzzaman's students and the other prisoners in Denizli, and it was the effect of this more than anything that led to the extraordinary reform of the prisoners. So much so that while at first it was written out and smuggled around the prison in the greatest secrecy, when this improvement in conduct was noted by the prison authorities, they permitted copies to be made without restriction. It was also sent to the Appeal Court and relevant departments in Ankara as a defence of the *Risale-i Nur* and was instrumental in securing their acquittal.[10]

Denizli Court

The same charges were made against Bediuzzaman and his students in Denizli Court as in Eskişehir. They included creating a new Sufi *ṭarīqah*, organizing a political society, opposing the reforms, and exploiting religious feelings in a way that might disturb public security. The Fifth Ray on Ḥadīths about the end of time, the treatise that had led to the arrests, was the prosecution's main evidence for their exploiting religion on the grounds it identified Mustafa Kemal as the Dajjāl, or Antichrist. Thus, on Bediuzzaman and his students being transferred from Isparta to Denizli, they were again questioned and the Denizli prosecutor set up a committee to study the *Risale-i Nur* and produce a report for the court. Composed of two local school teachers entirely unqualified to undertake such a job, they produced the report the prosecutor wished of them in a few days and the case was put before the Criminal Court. Their report was superficial to a degree and contained the most shameful misrepresentations. Bediuzzaman objected to it vigorously and setting out the errors and his corrections, presented them to the court together with a request for a committee of qualified scholars to be set up in order to examine the *Risale-i Nur*. After some delay, his request was accepted and on 9 March 1944, all the material of the case was sent to the First Ankara Criminal Court. A committee of three established scholars was then appointed under the chief judge of the court, Emin Böke, and it set about studying in detail the entire *Risale-i Nur* and all Bediuzzaman's letters and those of his students.

In the meantime the court hearings continued in Denizli. Bediuzzaman offered his defence and answered all the charges. His students too presented their defences. Mehmet Feyzi noted that Bediuzzaman sent a petition to the court seeking permission not to attend on the grounds of illness, but when he saw the positive attitude of the chief judge, Ali Rıza Balaban, who had the courtroom arranged like an amphitheatre, he took it back. And the judge did prove to be fair, both in the final outcome of the case, and in allowing Bediuzzaman to sit while the court was in session despite the objections of the prosecutor.[11] They walked from the prison to the court, a line of seventy handcuffed in pairs. It was the only time the students from the various parts of the prison could meet. They handcuffed Bediuzzaman to a different person each time. Accompanied by more than thirty gendarmes with fixed bayonets, the people of Denizli lined their route and expressed their sorrow and sympathy.[12]

Extracts from Bediuzzaman's Defence

In His Name, be He be glorified!

Sirs!
I tell you with certainty that apart from those here who have no connection or little connection with us and the *Risale-i Nur*, I have as many true brothers and loyal friends on the way of truth as you could wish. Through the certain discoveries of the *Risale-i Nur*, we know with the unshakeable certainty of twice two equalling four that through the mystery of the Qur'an for us death has been transformed from eternal extinction into a

discharge from duties, and that for those who oppose us and follow misguidance certain death is either eternal extinction (if they do not have certain belief in the hereafter), or everlasting, dark solitary confinement (if they believe in the hereafter and take the way of vice and misguidance). Is there a greater or more important question for man in this world that it can be a tool for it? I ask you! Since there is not and cannot be, why do you strive against us? In the face of your greatest penalty we receive our discharge papers to go to the world of light, so we await it in complete steadfastness. But we know as clearly as seeing it, like we see you in this court, that those who reject us and condemn us on behalf of misguidance will in a very short time be condemned to eternal extinction and solitary confinement and will suffer that awesome punishment, and by virtue of our humanity we earnestly pity them. I am ready to prove this certain and important fact and to silence the most stubborn of them. If I were unable to prove it as clearly as daylight, not to that unscholarly, prejudiced committee of scholars who knew nothing of spiritual and moral matters, but to the greatest scholars and philosophers, I would be content with any punishment!

As an example, I offer the treatise, *The Fruits of Belief*, which was written for the prisoners on two Fridays, and explaining the principles and bases of the *Risale-i Nur*, and is like a defence of it. We are working secretly under great difficulties to have this written out in the new letters so as to give it to the departments of government in Ankara. So read and study it carefully! If your heart (I cannot speak for your soul) does not affirm me, I shall remain silent in the face of whatever insults and torment you inflict on me in the solitary confinement in which I now am!

In Short: either allow the *Risale-i Nur* complete freedom, or smash this powerful and irrefutable truth if you can! Up to now, I have not thought of you and your world. And I was not going to think of it, but you forced me. Perhaps Divine Determining sent us here in order to warn you. As for us, we are resolved to take as our guide the sacred rule, 'Whoever believes in Divine Determining is safe from grief' and to meet all our difficulties with patience.

Prisoner Said Nursi[13]

In His Name, be He glorified!

Sirs!
I have formed the certain opinion due to numerous indications that we have been attacked on behalf of the government not for disturbing public order by exploiting religious feelings but, behind a tissue of lies, on behalf of atheism, because of our belief and our service to belief and public order. One proof of this out of many is that despite twenty thousand people reading and accepting the twenty thousand copies of the parts of the *Risale-i Nur* over twenty years, public order has not been disturbed by students of the *Risale-i Nur* on any occasion whatsoever, and no such incident has been recorded by the government, and neither the former nor the present courts have discovered such an incident. But such widespread propaganda would have brought it to light within twenty days. That is to say, contrary to the principle of freedom of conscience, Article 163 of this ambiguous law, which embraces all who give religious counsel, is a bogus mask. Atheists deceive certain members of the government, confuse the legal establishment, and want to crush us whatever happens.

Since the reality of the matter is this, we declare with all our strength: O wretches who sell religion for the world and have fallen into absolute unbelief! Do whatever you can! Your world will be the end of you! Let our heads be sacrificed for a truth for which hundreds of millions of heads have been sacrificed! We are ready for any penalty and for our execution! In this situation, being outside prison is a hundred times worse than being inside it. Since there is no freedom at all—neither religious freedom, nor freedom of conscience, nor scholarly freedom—under the absolute despotism that confronts us, for those with honour, the people of religion, and supporters of freedom there is no solution apart from death or entering prison. We say, *We belong to God and our return is to Him,* and we trust in God.

Prisoner Said Nursi[14]

In His Name, be He glorified!

Sirs!
The Ankara committee of experts has confirmed our decisive reply to the charge of organizing a political society insistently put forward by you as a pretext for our conviction, which you have

decided upon [as may be deduced from] the course followed by the prosecution. While feeling amazed and astonished at your insisting on this point to this degree, the following occurred to me: friendship, fraternal communities, gathering together, sincere associations pertaining to the hereafter and brotherhood are all foundation stones of social life, an essential need of human nature, and the ties binding together all life from family life to the life of tribe, nation, Islam, and humanity, and points of support and means of consolation in the face of the assaults of the material and immaterial things which cause harm and alarm and which each person encounters in the universe and cannot combat on his own, and prevent him carrying out his human and Islamic duties. Now some people hang the name of "political society", although it has no political front, to the gathering together of the students of the *Risale-i Nur* around the teachings of belief, which is most praiseworthy and is a sincere friendship [centred] on the teachings of belief and the Qur'an; and is a certain means to happiness in this world, in religion, and in the hereafter, and is a companionship on the way of truth; and co-operation and solidarity in the face of things harmful to the country and the nation. Most certainly and without doubt, therefore, either they have been deceived in some appalling manner, or they are extremely vicious anarchists who are both barbarously inimical to humanity, and tyrannically hostile to Islam, and harbour enmity towards social life in the utterly corrupt and depraved manner of anarchy, and strive obdurately and intractably as apostates against this country and nation, the sovereignty of Islam and sacred things of religion. Or they are satanic atheists who, working on behalf of foreigners to cut and destroy the life-giving arteries of this nation, are deceiving the government and confusing the judiciary in order to destroy or turn against our brothers and our country the immaterial weapons which up to now we have used against them—those satans, pharaohs, and anarchists.

Prisoner Said Nursi[15]

The 'Fifth Ray'

In regard to the Fifth Ray, since it played a prominent part in the Afyon trials in 1948-9, a more detailed discussion of it will be left to then, and here only one or two points will be mentioned briefly. Firstly, as noted above and Bediuzzaman told the court, the original of this treatise, in which they alleged Ḥadīths were used to prove Mustafa Kemal was the Sufyan or Islamic Dajjāl, that is, the Antichrist who is to appear at the end of time, had been written when Bediuzzaman first came to Istanbul in 1907, long before Mustafa Kemal rose to prominence. And its rough draft had been made some twenty-five years earlier while Bediuzzaman was a member of the Darü'l-Hikmeti'l-İslamiye, in order to "save from denial allegorical Ḥadīths and strengthen the belief of those whose belief was weak."[16] Furthermore, Bediuzzaman had not allowed it to be published, and in the eight years he had been in Kastamonu only two copies had come into his hands, and these he had disposed of. The affair had started when some "rivals", that is, the Mufti and preacher who had informed on Atıf Egemen in the province of Denizli in July 1943, had obtained a copy of it. At the same time, without Bediuzzaman's agreement, *The Supreme Sign* had been printed in Istanbul. The authorities, who had been informed of this, then confused this, the Seventh Ray with the Fifth Ray. The matter was then blown up out of all proportion by their enemies, and resulted in the mass arrests and Denizli trials.[17] In any event, it was cleared by the court at Denizli along with the rest of the *Risale-i Nur*; if the committee of scholars set up in Ankara raised a number of objections concerning it, Bediuzzaman pointed out these to be in error along with other points they raised.[18] In fact, Bediuzzaman had wanted *The Key to Belief Collection* to be printed rather than *The Supreme Sign*,[19] but he wrote in a letter than he was "profoundly happy" with the student who had had it printed, Tahiri Mutlu's, other great service to the *Risale-i Nur*, and "expected from divine mercy" that the attention drawn to *The Supreme Sign* in this way would in the future result in the victories it deserved.[20]

The True Nature of the Case

These months of the trial in Denizli Prison were truly a great test for Bediuzzaman and his students. In addition to the physical distress and hardship, it was clear certain forces within the Government were working for Bediuzzaman's execution as well as that of a number of his leading students. Their situation was one of extreme uncertainty. Besides the severe criticism of the first committee set up to examine the *Risale-i Nur*, Bediuzzaman mentions the attacks made on them by the Education Minister Hasan Ali Yücel and his publishing a manifesto against them.[21] The Prime Minister, Şükrü Saraçoğlu, was also directly concerned with the case. Furthermore, since it was really the *Risale-i Nur* that was on trial, both Bediuzzaman's defence and those of his students were defences of the *Risale-i Nur*. And so, while for the most part Bediuzzaman's tone in his defence was mild and reasoning, when it came to exposing the plots against the *Risale-i Nur*, which were the cause of the trial, his words were anything but mild, despite the precariousness of their own position.

It was this external pressure brought to bear on the case and the fact that the law was clearly being used as a shield and a means of suppressing religion by forces whose aim it was to establish communism in Turkey that led Bediuzzaman to inform his students in a letter that "the real cause of the widespread and significant assault and aggression" against them was not the Fifth Ray, but *The Key to Belief* and *Hüccetü'l-Baliğa* (The Eloquent Proof) and *Ḥizb al-Nūrī*. These works with their convincing proofs of the truths of belief had defeated irreligion. Thus, "because the atheists had been unable to defend their way of absolute unbelief against the blows of these two keen diamond swords", they had presented the Fifth Ray as an apparent reason and deceived the Government into moving against them.[22]

Bediuzzaman's response to these covert moves to subvert the course of justice show what a brilliant tactician he was, and also his extraordinary grasp of the situation, although he had been for several months in total isolation in the prison. He took them by storm. He had sent to seven departments of government copies in the new letters of *The Fruits of Belief* and the defence speeches,

Denizli

and all the parts of the *Risale-i Nur* to the Ministry of Justice.[23] And then, when the Education Minister launched his attack on them, Bediuzzaman sensed that this was out of fear and had sent to that ministry four boxes of various parts of the *Risale-i Nur*.[24] In another letter, urging his students to contain themselves in patience during these long drawn out proceedings, he pointed out what an event it was, the *Risale-i Nur* being read by those who most fervently supported the regime, at that time when "love for that fearsome dead man was being inculcated into the people, in all schools and departments", which would have had grim consequences for the Islamic world. At the very least, the *Risale-i Nur* would moderate their absolute unbelief and so lessen the attacks on them.[25]

The Acquittal

Then, when the situation of Bediuzzaman and his students seemed most grim and they were expecting Ankara to act most severely towards them, Bediuzzaman's move proved successful and a relatively soft and even conciliatory position was taken.[26] On 22 April 1944, the committee set up to examine the *Risale-i Nur* presented their unanimous report to the Ankara Criminal Court. Their findings were positive to a degree far exceeding all expectations. They were forwarded to Denizli and a copy of the report reached Bediuzzaman.

The report stated that 90% of the *Risale-i Nur* was formed of scholarly explanations of the truths of belief, and that these parts "did not part at all from the way of scholarship and principles of religion." There was nothing in these to suggest the exploitation of religion, the founding of a society, or that there was a movement that would disturb public order.[27] Bediuzzaman wrote in a letter to his students:

> It is a manifestation of dominical favour and instance of divine succour and preservation that as I have heard, the committee of experts in Ankara has been defeated in the face of the truths of

the *Risale-i Nur*, and that while there were numerous reasons for their severe criticisms and objections they have quite simply given the decision for its acquittal.[28]

Almost as though to placate those in high places opposing the *Risale-i Nur*, the committee stated that the treatises marked as confidential, which they described as being "unscholarly", had in part been written when Bediuzzaman was in a state of "mental excitement, ecstasy, or spiritual turmoil", and that he should not therefore be held responsible for them. They wrote also that "there was a possibility he suffered from hallucinations in regard to hearing and sight." As Bediuzzaman pointed out in the letter he described these to his students, the rest of the *Risale-i Nur* was sufficient to refute such allegations. They showed as evidence titles like *The Thirty-Three Windows* (The Thirty-Third Letter), the fact that Bediuzzaman heard his cat reciting the divine name, "Most Compassionate One!", and that in another treatise he saw himself as a gravestone![29]

In addition, the committee put forward fifteen objections on scholarly grounds. These Bediuzzaman answered and showed to be errors on the part of the committee.[30] The final and longest answers and corrections he presented to the court on 31 May 1944, the day the prosecutor made his final observations and summing-up, and put forward his requests for the sentences.

On 16 June 1944, the court reached its decision, Number 199-136. Largely on the strength of the committee's report, it announced its unanimous decision for the acquittal of all the prisoners and their immediate release. The prosecutor insisted on the sentences he was demanding, and so the case was sent to the Appeal Court in Ankara. The request was denied and on 30 December 1944, it confirmed the verdict of the Denizli Court.[31]

The Şehir Hotel

When Bediuzzaman and his students emerged from the court, the people of Denizli greeted them with cheers and cries of "Long live justice!", and accompanied them to the prison where they collected their belongings. The area outside the prison was like a festival. A string of phaetons came from the town to collect them. They were the guests of Denizli. The people took them into their houses in small groups and offered them the best of whatever they had. A merchant called Haji Mustafa Kocayaka, chosen by the people, had a large sum of money to distribute among Bediuzzaman's students, but none was accepted. And when they went to the station, he and many of the town's notables came to assist them and see them off onto their trains. Bediuzzaman and the *Risale-i Nur* had conquered the town.[32]

On leaving the prison, Bediuzzaman moved to a room with fine views on the top floor of the Şehir Hotel in the town, where he was to remain for one and a half months. Within one or two days, all his students had dispersed, returning to their home towns and villages. As soon as he was settled, vast numbers of people came to visit him, five hundred or so daily to start with. Some of them continued their visits. Ankara was notified of their names. One was a teacher from Erzurum, called Nureddin Topçu, who had drawn the wrath of the Education Minister on himself with some writings and had been posted to Denizli by way of a punishment. Part of his interesting account of his visits to Bediuzzaman in the Şehir Hotel is as follows:

> His name was to be heard everywhere in the town; everyone was talking about him...After the acquittal, he settled in a room on the top floor of the Şehir Hotel. He was under very close surveillance. All those who visited him were followed in the same way and their names were taken. They could only visit him for a very short time and had to leave immediately." Nureddin Topçu used to visit him during the time of the evening meal when there was no one about and he could stay half an hour or so. He also knew the two teachers who had been appointed to produce the first 'experts' report for Denizli Court. Evidently they were completely without religion and most undesirable characters. He was impressed by Bediuzzaman's forgiving them, and offering to call them to religion:

Bediuzzaman was a truly great person; he said that he forgave them. It was a great virtue to be able to forgive people who had worked against him in a way that could have led to his execution.

He was a man of action, enterprising. He used to talk to everybody. He would explain his cause. He wasn't one for diffidence or hanging back...

They brought the evening meal; it was a lavish spread. He returned it to the waiter who brought it and told him to give it to the poor. He had some olives with him, and ate them and some bread. He said: 'One loaf lasts me two weeks.' He had a samovar he used to make tea with and he would offer me some. He had just been released from prison. There was nothing in his room by way of belongings, only his works, both handwritten and in the form of proofs. Thousands of his handwritten books were being passed around from hand to hand. They were being written everywhere, in the villages and towns; everywhere copies of the *Risale-i Nur* were being written out. That was a heartening time; like the time the sun rises.

Around that time I went to the village of Güveçli near Denizli. His works were being written out in every house, in all the villages around, tens of thousands of pages, such was the eagerness and zeal.

He had a very manly and bold manner. His courage and excellence were immense. Then the things his brilliant mind discovered were extraordinary. He met disasters with patience and resignation. He had given himself to Allah, as a matter of a fact those works of his were all the product of these things. All Denizli was filled with an eagerness and enthusiasm. Friend and foe alike were struck with admiration for him. Denizli's night had turned into day. He had conquered it.[33]

Nevertheless Bediuzzaman felt keenly his being parted from his students and brothers. Above all Hafız Ali's death in prison had caused him great sorrow. The first thing he did on being released was to visit his grave. Selahaddin Çelebi was also present and he recalled how after recitation of the Qur'an Bediuzzaman offered a sad prayer then raised his hand and said: "This martyr was a star." Involuntarily all those present raised their heads and in the sky a single star was shining.³⁴

Bediuzzaman described his state of mind as follows in the Tenth Topic of *The Fruits of Belief*:

> After our release from Denizli Prison, I was staying on the top floor of the famous Şehir Hotel. The graceful dancing of the leaves, branches and trunks of the many poplar trees in the fine gardens opposite me, each with a rapturous and ecstatic motion like a circle of dervishes at the touch of the breeze, pained my heart, sorrowful and melancholy at being parted from my brothers and remaining alone. Suddenly the seasons of autumn and winter came to mind and a heedlessness overcame me. I so pitied those graceful poplars and living creatures swaying with perfect joyousness that my eyes filled with tears. With this reminder of the separations and non-being beneath the ornamented veil of the universe, the grief at a world-full of deaths and separations pressed down on me. Then suddenly, the light the Muhammadan reality had brought came to my assistance and transformed my grief and sorrow into joy... Just when they had turned the world into a sort of hell and the reason into an instrument of torture, the light Muḥammad (ṣ) had brought as a gift for mankind raised the veil; it showed in place of extinction, non-being, nothingness, purposeless, futility, and separations, meanings and instances of wisdom to the number of the leaves of the poplars, and as is proved in the *Risale-i Nur*, results and duties which may be divided into three sorts...³⁵

Notes

1. Osman Yıldırımkaya, in *Son Şahitler*, ii, 209.
2. Şahiner, *Said Nursi*, 341.
3. Sadık Demirelli, in *Son Şahitler*, ii, 146.
4. Selahaddin Çelebi, in *Son Şahitler*, i, 145.
5. İbrahim Fakazlı, in *Son Şahitler*, i, 178.
6. Selahaddin Çelebi, *ibid.*, 144.
7. See, Süleyman Hünkâr, in *Son Şahitler*, i, 183-8; Sadık Demirelli, in *Son Sahitler*, ii, 135-57.

8. Mustafa Gül, in *Son Şahitler*, iv, 328.
9. Nursi, *Şualar*, 196 (Eng. tr.: *Rays*, 253).
10. *Tarihçe*, 377.
11. Mehmed Feyzi Pamukçu, in *Son Şahitler*, ii, 163.
12. Selahaddin Çelebi, in *Son Şahitler*, i, 145.
13. Nursi, *Şualar*, 235-6 (Eng. tr.: *Rays*, 298-9).
14. *Ibid.*, 236-7; *Tarihçe*, 356.
15. Nursi, *Şualar*, 242-3 (Eng. tr.: *Rays*, 312-13); *Tarihçe*, 362.
16. Nursi, *Müdâfaalar*, 97.
17. *Op. cit.*
18. *Ibid.*, 130.
19. *Şualar*, 249 (Eng. tr.: *Rays*, 321).
20. *Ibid.*, 250.
21. Nursi, *Lem'alar*, 252 (Eng. tr.: *Flashes*, 334).
22. Nursi, *Şualar*, 265 (Eng. tr.: *Rays*, 340).
23. Nursi, *Lem'alar*, 252 (Eng. tr.: *Flashes*, 334).
24. Nursi, *Şualar*, 280-1 (Eng. tr.: *Rays*, 258-9).
25. *Ibid.*, 284 (Eng. tr.: *Rays*, 362).
26. *Ibid.*, 286 (Eng. tr.: *Rays*, 365).
27. Nursi, *Müdâfaalar*, 151.
28. Nursi, *Şualar*, 287 (Eng. tr.: *Rays*, 365).
29. *Ibid.*, 288 (Eng. tr.: *Rays*, 367).
30. Nursi, *Müdâfaalar*, 123-32.
31. *Tarihçe*, 348.
32. See, Selahaddin Çelebi, in *Son Şahitler*, i, 146; and İbrahim Fakazlı, in *Son Şahitler*, i, 179.
33. Şahiner, *Nurs Yolu*, 123-7.
34. Selahaddin Çelebi, in *Son Şahitler*, i, 148.
35. *Şualar*, 213-4 (Eng. tr: *Rays*, 272-3).

16
Emirdağ

Emirdağ

Bediuzzaman had been a month and a half in the Şehir Hotel in Denizli when the order came from Ankara that he was to reside in the province of Afyon, still in western Anatolia, to the north-east of Denizli. A letter dated 31 July 1944 written by the Denizli businessman, Hafız Mustafa Kocayaka to Sadık Demirelli, who had sent Bediuzzaman some Kastamonu rice, states that Bediuzzaman had left that day in the company of a police inspector. He was in good health and content at the prospect of the move. The Government had ordered that he be given the generous travelling allowance of four hundred liras.[1] Bediuzzaman was put up in the Ankara Hotel in Afyon for two to three weeks and then ordered to settle in Emirdağ. Thus, he arrived in this small provincial town set in high rolling hills in the second half of August 1944. It was to be his place of residence for the next seven years, till October 1951, with the break of twenty months in Afyon Prison from January 1948 to September 1949. Since it was in the month of Shaʿbān that he arrived in Emirdağ, it was before 21 August, the day on which the month of Ramaḍān began that year.

Introduction

The first three and a half years of Bediuzzaman's stay in Emirdağ saw an intensification of his struggle with the forces of irreligion, which up to this time had felt themselves to be in an unassailable position in Turkey. The acquittal in Denizli had taken them entirely by surprise, in the words of one writer, exploding like a bomb-shell so that they did not know what hit them. It was a clear victory for the *Risale-i Nur* and religion, and a forerunner of its future victories. The fruits of Bediuzzaman's twenty years of silent struggle were starting to show.

Contrary to the intentions of those who had instigated the case, the widespread publicity of the Denizli trials and imprisonment of Bediuzzaman and the *Risale-i Nur* students led directly to a considerable expansion in activities connected with the *Risale-i Nur*. While up to this time, activity had been mainly concentrated in two or three areas, now many thousands of people in different areas of Turkey became its students and began to serve it and the cause of the Qur'an in various ways. In addition to this, in 1946 or '47 two of the first duplicating machines to come to Turkey were bought by his students and one set up in Isparta and the other in İnebolu, with the result that copies of the *Risale-i Nur* were now available on a far wider scale than before. This greatly increased the spread of the *Risale-i Nur*. The acquittals further infuriated the enemies of religion and drove them to embark on a series of plots and plans in their attempts to stop it. The basic aim of these was to make both the local government and Ankara feel sufficiently apprehensive about Bediuzzaman and the *Risale-i Nur* movement and act against them once again. One result of this was that all the attention was focussed on Bediuzzaman himself and constraints on him increased. Thus, despite the fact that he had been acquitted by the Denizli Court and the *Risale-i Nur* had been cleared, the surveillance under which he was held was even stricter than before, and the illegal harassment and ill-treatment more severe. However, he wrote to his students that he accepted this "with pride" as it meant it was his person that was concentrated on and harassed rather than the *Risale-i Nur* or its other students; it allowed them to continue their service of it relatively unmolested.[2]

A further reason for this intensification of the ideological battle between belief and unbelief at this time, culminating in Bediuzzaman's and a number of his students's arrest and detention in Afyon Prison, was related to the changing conditions in Turkey. This may be attributed to the fact that, with increased American influence after the end of the Second World War and moves towards democracy and more religious freedom, those working for the cause of irreligion increased their attacks as they felt the ground slipping away from under their feet.

Thus, the struggle was pursued with greatly increased publication and dissemination of the *Risale-i Nur*. Also Bediuzzaman followed up the advantage he had gained by the Denizli acquittals by sending petitions to various high officials and members of the Government informing them of the real nature of this struggle and the vital role the *Risale-i Nur* had to play. The aim was to save the country from the anarchy into which it was being pushed by forces working for the causes of communism, freemasonry, and zionism, and also informing them of the illegal treatment he was suffering at the hands of some officials.

Arrival in Emirdağ

Bediuzzaman arrived in Emirdağ on a hot August evening, shortly before sunset. A small group of people were sitting drinking tea in front of the government building when a bus arrived in a cloud of dust from the direction of Afyon. Among them was the government doctor, who also acted as District Settlement Officer, Dr Tahir Barçın. He saw the unusual sight of someone wearing a turban and gown alight, escorted by two gendarmes. And even stranger, this elderly person in his seventies set about looking for a suitable spot, and on learning the direction of the *qiblah*, spread out the prayer-mat he was carrying, and performed the afternoon prayers, something unheard of at that time of religious persecution. It was a happy moment for the doctor, who as a young *madrasah* student in Istanbul in 1922, had seen Bediuzzaman in

Fatih Mosque. He became his close student in Emirdağ, and when posted to Bitlis in eastern Turkey in 1945 for a year, played an important role in introducing the *Risale-i Nur* to Bediuzzaman's native region, where many people thought he had not survived his exile.[3]

As in each place he was sent, Bediuzzaman attracted students who served him loyally, unhesitatingly sacrificing themselves and their property and position for him and the *Risale-i Nur*. In Emirdağ it was the Çalışkan family who took it upon themselves to see to his needs and assist him. One of these six brothers, Hasan, was his first visitor in Emirdağ. Thereafter, they and their families attended to all his personal needs, such as sending his food, for which he always paid, as well as doing everything necessary for the work of the *Risale-i Nur* to continue. In 1945, Bediuzzaman adopted as his spiritual son, Ceylan, the exceptionally intelligent twelve-year-old son of Mehmed Çalışkan. He remained with him, and in future years became one of the leading students of the *Risale-i Nur*.[4]

The house that was found for Bediuzzaman was in the centre of town, on a busy street near the police station and Municipal Buildings. With guards posted permanently at his door and windows, it was extremely difficult to visit him. At one point when even the boy Ceylan was forbidden to assist him, the Çalışkan's made a hole into his house from the neighbouring shop, in order to reach him. One of the immediate reasons for the renewed vigour of the repressive measures was that Bediuzzaman refused the offers of a pension that the Government now made for him. On the acquittals, initially they had planned to follow a new line in order to silence him; they planned to buy him off by offering him a regular pension, to build him a house according to his own specifications and also sent him the travelling allowance mentioned above. After due consideration, Bediuzzaman wrote by way of consulting his students, that in order not to break his life-long rule, and also to preserve sincerity, he had refused these offers. The authorities were annoyed at this, and stepped up their harassment as a result.[5] Life became so hard for him that he also wrote that he suffered in one day in Emirdağ what he had suffered in a month in Denizli Prison.

As far as he was able, Ceylan attended to Bediuzzaman's needs in the house, such as making his tea and writing out his letters. As ever Bediuzzaman liked to spend as much time as possible in the countryside, particularly in the spring and summer, and would walk out into the open stone-wall country around Emirdağ taking copies of the *Risale-i Nur* to be corrected with him. He was always followed and watched by a number of gendarmes. Later when the burden of work became too heavy, the Çalışkan's eventually found a light horse-drawn carriage for him, called a phaeton, which he then travelled in, usually taking just one student with him as the driver. It became a familiar sight in the area. Despite his preoccupation and the efforts to isolate him, Bediuzzaman always concerned himself with all those he encountered. The children of Emirdağ and surrounding villages would flock round him and run after the phaeton whenever they saw it, shouting: "Hoja Dede!" "Grandpa Hoja!"[6] Bediuzzaman always acted very kindly towards them, saying that they were the *Risale-i Nur* students of the future. And just as he captivated them, so too he drew the people from every class that he met while driving round the country. He would tell the shepherds, workers, farmers, or whomever he met: "This work you do is of great service to others; so long as you perform the prescribed prayers five times a day, all of your work will become worship and benefit you in the hereafter."[7]

The guidance and close concern Bediuzzaman offered these people had considerable effect, for large numbers of those children did become students of the *Risale-i Nur* in the future and serve the cause of religion and the Qur'an. And besides the people in the countryside who benefited, in Emirdağ itself the honesty and uprightness of the shopkeepers, traders, and craftsmen became well-known. A plainclothes policeman sent to spy on Bediuzzaman in 1947 remarked on this when, while buying some butter, he saw the shopkeeper weigh the paper separately. In his words, "It was Bediuzzaman that made Emirdağ like this!"[8]

The *Risale-i Nur*

If Hafız Mustafa had written to Sadık Bey from Denizli that Bediuzzaman had left in good health, Bediuzzaman described himself as being extremely ill, weak and wretched when a short time later he was settled in his house in Emirdağ in the month of Ramaḍān. It was poison that caused him to write to his students in Isparta, whom he so loved, his first letter from Emirdağ, saying that it was only their prayers that had saved him from "the severe illness" he had suffered.[9] Notwithstanding his wretched state—indeed perhaps because of it, since many parts of the *Risale-i Nur* were written when Bediuzzaman was afflicted with severe illness or distress—he wrote the Tenth Matter of *The Fruits of Belief*, the first nine of which had been written in Denizli Prison. "An extremely powerful reply to objections raised about repetitions in the Qur'an", he wrote that he reckoned he had been inspired to write it because of "dissemblers, who, like silly children trying to extinguish the sun of the Qur'an by blowing at it", were attempting to have the Qur'an translated in order to discredit it, having "taken lessons" from "a most dreadful and obdurate atheist".[10] Bediuzzaman wrote also in the above-mentioned letter that he was sending them this Tenth Matter.

When writing to his students in Isparta at the end of March the following year, Bediuzzaman told them that he was sending them "a further part of 'The Fruit' about the Angels." This was the Eleventh and final part of the Eleventh Ray, *The Fruits of Belief*.[11] The *Risale-i Nur* was approaching its completion at this time. With the exception of *Elhüccetü'z-Zehra*, written in Afyon Prison, *The Fruits of Belief* was the last main piece to be written, and subsequent to this it was largely published in the form of collections.

At this time, the battle against atheism and unbelief was for the main part carried out with two collections, *The Staff of Moses* (*Asâ-yı Mûsa*) and *Zülfikar*. The first part of *The Staff of Moses* consisted of the eleven parts of *The Fruits of Belief*, and the second, of eleven pieces from various parts of the *Risale-i Nur*, including the First Station of *The Supreme Sign* and the *Treatise on Nature*. *Zülfikar* consisted of the Nineteenth Letter, *The Miracles of Muhammad*, and the Twenty-Fifth Word, *The Miraculousness of the Qur'an*. Also, printed in 1947 in Eskişehir was *A Guide for Youth*, the collection mentioned in a previous chapter made up largely of pieces written originally for the schoolboys who became Bediuzzaman's students in Kastamonu.

The case of Bediuzzaman and his students at Denizli had been sent to the Appeal Court in Ankara on the prosecutor's demanding the acquittals be quashed. The Appeal Court however had upheld the decision of the Denizli judges, reaching its unanimous decision on 30 December 1944. This decision was announced on 15 February 1945. With all these legal delays it was not till 29 June 1945, that the Denizli lawyer acting for Bediuzzaman, Ziya Sönmez, was able to collect Bediuzzaman's books and copies of the *Risale-i Nur*. Hafız Mustafa then brought them to Emirdağ to hand over to Bediuzzaman.[12]

Legally there was no obstacle now for the publication and free distribution of the *Risale-i Nur*. In addition, since the Denizli trials, the demand for it had greatly increased. All over Turkey people were seeking the *Risale-i Nur*. It was at this point while students in the Isparta and Kastamonu areas, Denizli and other places were writing out by hand copies of *The Staff of Moses* and *Zülfikar*, and other parts of the *Risale-i Nur*, that in 1946 or '47 the Çelebi's and other *Risale-i Nur* students in İnebolu bought one of the first duplicating machines to come to Turkey. When it was seen that this was successful, Tahiri Mutlu came from Isparta to see it and then returned there via Istanbul, where he bought a second one. These two machines greatly facilitated the spread of the *Risale-i Nur*. They were bought and run by the students, who with considerable sacrifice, pooled their resources, and were later financed from the sale of the books produced. They were used for the one and a half to two years till the arrests preceding the Afyon trials and imprisonment at the start of 1948.

The main parts of the *Risale-i Nur* to be duplicated on these machines by the students were: *The Staff of Moses, Zülfikar, The Illuminating Lamp, The Ratifying Stamp of the Unseen, A Guide for Youth*, and *The Short Words*. In addition to these collections were thousands of copies of other parts of the *Risale-i Nur* and the numerous letters Bediuzzaman wrote his students at this time directing these activities and on various subjects. At the same time, the writing out by hand of both of these collections, other parts of the *Risale-i Nur* and Bediuzzaman's letters continued at full pace. Certain collections, mainly *A Guide for Youth* and *The Staff of Moses* were now reproduced for the first time in the new Latin alphabet in order to make them immediately available to the younger generation. However, "Since an important function of the *Risale-i Nur*" was "the preservation of the Arabic script, the script of the vast majority of the Islamic world",[13] for the greater part it continued to be reproduced in that alphabet.

This much expanded activity was to have far-reaching results, for now the *Risale-i Nur* found new students among the younger generation who were to be important figures in the Nur movement in later years. That the *Risale-i Nur* answers in particular the needs of people whose ideas have been influenced by materialist philosophy was proven by the fact that it now began to draw university students and teachers, and others who had been through the educational system of the Republic. Among these was the teacher in a Village Institute, Mustafa Sungur, who became one of Bediuzzaman's closest and most influential students, and his "spiritual son". Another was Mustafa Ramazanoğlu, a university student, and Zübeyir Gündüzalp, a Post Office official who first visited him in 1946. Although Bediuzzaman appointed

Emirdağ 359

no successor, since, as he said, the true 'üstadh' of the *Risale-i Nur* movement was its collective personality, Zübeyir Gündüzalp was to emerge as one of its leaders after 1960.

Moreover, at this time the *Risale-i Nur* began slowly to spread to the Islamic world. This was assisted when after 1947 it became possible to go on the Hajj. Copies of some of the collections were sent to al-Azhar in Egypt, to Damascus, and Madīnah,[14] and some were given to a Kashmiri religious scholar who agreed to convey them to the Indian *'ulamā'*.[15]

So also Salahaddin Çelebi in İnebolu—Bediuzzaman called him Abdurrahman Salahaddin—struck up relations with some American missionaries and over a period of months read them *The Staff of Moses* and *Zülfikar* Collections, and gave them copies.[16]

In connection with this, in the face of the growing threat of communism described in the following section, with his extraordinarily clear-sighted view of the future, in accordance with certain Ḥadīth, Bediuzzaman advocated co-operation between truly religious Christians against this threat. He wrote: "In connection with Selahaddin giving the American *The Staff of Moses*, we say this:

> It is essential that missionaries and Christian clergy as well as Nurjus are extremely careful, for certainly, with the idea of defending itself against the attacks of the religions of Islam and Christianity, the current from the North will try to destroy the accord of Islam and the missionaries."[17],[18]

Conditions

The writing of the *Risale-i Nur*, then, was virtually complete within a few months of Bediuzzaman's coming to Emirdağ, and a large part of his time here was spent in correcting the copies sent to him of the *Risale-i Nur*, both handwritten and duplicated—this work even sometimes taking part of the time he set apart each day for worship and contemplation. In many of his letters directing his students' activities, together with encouraging them and insisting on the continued importance of the handwritten copies, he urged them to pay attention to writing out the pieces accurately, so as to assist him in this laborious and time-consuming task. He constantly urged caution on them, and to act circumspectly, aware that their enemies were always seeking ways of halting their work.

Bediuzzaman's three and a half years in Emirdağ were truly torturous for him. This is clear from his letters. The people of Emirdağ and his students testified to the entirely unlawful and vindictive treatment and harassment he received. He was approaching seventy years of age when he arrived and suffered perpetual ill-health, largely due to his periods in prison, the frequent times he had been poisoned, and his long years of exile and deprivation.

The aim on the one hand was to keep him under a cloud of suspicion and guilt so as to destroy his influence over the people. The isolation in which he was held and constant and oppressive surveillance were to this end, in addition to numerous incidents intended to belittle him in the eyes of the people. And when after Bediuzzaman had been in Emirdağ a short time, he started to draw the people to him like in Denizli—in his words: "With the same situation starting here as in Denizli where on account of the *Risale-i Nur*, the people showed me regard far greater than was my due"[19]—they increased the pressure on him and used official influence to conduct a propaganda campaign against him, so as to frighten the people off and keep them away from him.

Secondly, "the dissemblers" employed various plans and stratagems in order to provoke "an incident", so that Bediuzzaman could be accused of "causing a disturbance and upsetting public order" and the authorities could be made to come down on him with excessive force. The constant pressure under which he was held, the assaults on his person, in particular on the pretext of his dress, and the raids on his house were to this end. In essence, these methods were no different than previous ones, which also failed. What was different in Emirdağ were their frequency and severity.

The underlying reasons for the intensification of Bediuzzaman's struggle against irreligion and the increase in the attempts to silence him and halt the spread of the *Risale-i Nur* may be found again in Bediuzzaman's letters, and from looking at his life.

In 1945, after the acquittals had been ratified and the confiscated copies of the *Risale-i Nur* returned, and before the duplicating machines were obtained, efforts were made to have more parts of the *Risale-i Nur* printed, like *The Supreme Sign*. The debate was now over the alphabet to be used, the old or the new. In consultation with his students in Isparta, Bediuzzaman decided to send Tahiri Mutlu to Istanbul, to have *The Staff of Moses* printed in the new letters, and *Zülfikar* in the old.[20] However, their enemies got wind of this and prompted various authorities to move against them and seize copies of the *Risale-i Nur*. For this reason, these two collections were not printed at that time. In a subsequent letter, Bediuzzaman explained "an important reason" for their decision to print part of the *Risale-i Nur* in the new letters, although contrary to their intention, to do so "as though put the *Risale-i Nur* in an offensive position."

He wrote that the time had come to print the *Risale-i Nur* on a large scale, "in order to repulse two fearsome calamities which were threatening the country, of which it was "a sort of saviour".

One of these calamities was communism, against the racing tide of which the *Risale-i Nur* "could perform the function of a Qur'anic barrier", while the second was "the severe objections" levelled at the Turkish people by the Islamic world, from which since the founding of the Republic, it had drawn away; The *Risale-i Nur* was "a miracle of the Qur'an" that could be the means of restoring previous love and feelings of brotherhood.[21]

Bediuzzaman believed the threat to the Turkish nation of these "calamities" to be so real that "patriotic politicians" should have it published officially in order to counter the threat. He wrote letters and petitions to high government officials describing their nature and severity, and possible dire consequences, and urged them to counter them by returning to Islam and publishing the *Risale-i Nur*.

In essence this was a continuation of the same struggle he had been pursuing since his youth, for Islam and the Qur'an to be accepted by the country's rulers as the source of true progress and civilization, rather than the West and its philosophy. On coming to power after the War of Independence, the new leaders had adopted the path of Westernization, which had already been followed to some degree for over a century. Only, their aim was total Westernization, and demanded complete secularization and that Islam was rendered ineffectual, as we have seen. What emerged was a battle between belief and unbelief. Up to this time during his years of exile, his role in this battle had been "defensive"; he had written numbers of treatises explaining and proving the basic truths of belief which were then subject to fierce attacks in the name of science, philosophy, and atheism. He had sought to defend Islam and belief against these orchestrated onslaughts which had been conducted on many fronts: the press, publications of all sorts, education in schools, adult education programmes, and so on. In a very low key and unobtrusive manner the *Risale-i Nur* had been passed from hand to hand among the ordinary people, had been copied out by hand, and by degrees, had spread till by 1945 he and the *Risale-i Nur* had many thousands of followers all over Turkey.

Now, in 1945, because of the path that had been taken, Bediuzzaman saw that the Turkish nation was in great danger: having been broken off from its natural support of the Islamic world in addition to being divorced and alienated from its own true identity of Islam. It would now be unable to withstand and counter what he saw as the devious plans of the forces of unbelief, which step by step were being put into practice and would finally destroy it. The Turkish nation could only withstand these designs on it through the strength of the Qur'an. It was at this point therefore that Bediuzzaman took on a role that could be interpreted as "offensive", by attempting to publish the *Risale-i Nur* in the new alphabet and on a larger scale.

At the same time Bediuzzaman was not working against the government and the established order. On the contrary, it was stability and social order that he was aiming to preserve in the face of the two outside currents or "calamities" mentioned above and those working for them within the country that were seeking to destroy public order, destabilise the country and create anarchy. And he wrote a number of open letters and petitions to various members of the government in order to alert them to the dangers.

One such letter was to Hilmi Uran, Interior Minister until October 1946 then General Secretary of the Republican People's Party. In it Bediuzzaman described the two currents, pointing out the inseparable nature of Islam and the Turkish nation and the grave error in trying to replace Islam by "civilization", that is, uprooting religion and imposing philosophy in the form of positivism and nationalism. One of these currents was composed of the forces seeking to split up and divide the Islamic world. Through what Bediuzzaman describes as "atheistic committees" (*zındıka komitesi*), "secret organizations", and "the forces of corruption", it was seeking to establish "absolute unbelief" in order to create enmity towards the Turkish nation, "the heroic brother and commander of the Islamic world", and for relations to be cut between them. Bediuzzaman told Hilmi Uran that "if in place of the propaganda of civilization to the detriment of religion, you do not work to spread directly the truths of belief and the Qur'an", the Turkish nation would fall prey to the anarchy underlying that absolute unbelief; it would fall apart and disintegrate, and would be "overwhelmed by the fearsome monster that has emerged in the North."

Communism, the other current, formed a real threat at that time. Having overrun all Eastern Europe, its overwhelming presence to the North and aggressive stance towards Turkey pushed it to join the West. Within Turkey, since the establishment of the Republic, Moscow and its agents and sympathizers had been working for communism's spread. This other "destructive" current of unbelief was also trying to create anarchy. Bediuzzaman pointed out in the above letter that it would only be halted by the Qur'an and the Turkish nation which was "fused with Islam and was at one with it."[22]

It was with these covert forces working on behalf of the first current above, "the secret committees" and "atheistic organization whose roots are abroad", that Bediuzzaman had been struggling with since before the setting up of the Republic, even since the days of the Constitutional Revolution. Seeing him as an obstacle to spreading irreligion in Turkey and corrupting its people, they had employed every device and stratagem to have him silenced. Some of these had resulted in trials and imprisonment. Others were the attempts to poison him. Now in Emirdağ, their plans included mobilizing government influence against Bediuzzaman by means of certain officials.[23]

With regard to communism, in addition to the external threat, it had gained considerable strength within the country since İnönü came to power on Ataturk's death in 1938. The policies he followed favoured its spread, and through such means as the setting up in 1940 of village institutes for the training of teachers, foresaw its eventual establishment. He had ties with Soviet Russia and in addition appointed communist sympathizers to high office, such as Şükrü Saraçoğlu, Prime Minister from 9 July 1943 to 5 August 1946, and Hasan Ali Yücel, the Education Minister. The two were personally involved in Bediuzzaman's and his students' arrest prior to the Denizli trials. The Kaymakam, Abdülkadir Uraz, specially appointed to Emirdağ by the Interior Minister in 1945 in order to exert pressure on Bediuzzaman was a socialist. When forced by the threat of Russian aggression to turn to the West, İnönü was obliged to take the path of democracy and liberalization, leading to greater religious freedom; this also drove those secretly working for this cause to increase their efforts to silence Bediuzzaman and halt the spread of the *Risale-i Nur*.

Together with the problems and moral decline these two currents had already caused in Turkey, Bediuzzaman saw the real dangers to lie in the future. Twenty years previously he anticipated the present situation and withdrew entirely from politics in order to find a solution to this "calamity" that he saw would occur. He described this in a letter to "the Minister of Justice and Judges of the Courts concerned with the *Risale-i Nur*", urging them "to protect the *Risale-i Nur* and its students" instead of striving against them, as the solution lay there. He pointed out to them that just as the results of "the libertarians" of some thirty years previously advocating a loosening of the constraints of religion and its morality were now apparent, so too that present situation would result in fifty years' time in a fearful moral degeneration and dissolution of society. For, "Muslims do not resemble others; a Muslim who abandons religion and departs from the high moral character of Islam falls into absolute unbelief, becomes an anarchist and can no longer be governed."[24]

Bediuzzaman argued that the "moral and spiritual" (*ma'nawī*) destruction of these forces could only be halted and countered by the truths of the Qur'an and belief. Issuing from the Qur'an, the *Risale-i Nur* was "a repairer of the strength of an atom bomb" and "a Qur'anic barrier" before those forces. The law and processes of justice could not arrest them with their "material" penalties.[25] Neither could politics or diplomacy. Thus, in his letters both to his students and departments of government, Bediuzzaman stressed the importance of "politicians and patriots embracing the *Risale-i Nur*." Similarly, he frequently pointed out that it was these forces that were themselves attempting to destroy order and create anarchy and thus were conspiring against the country. The *Risale-i Nur* and its students protected the bases of public order, preserved security and prevented subversion and sedition.[26] And he wrote to the Afyon police headquarters: "In the near future, this country and its government will have intense need of works like the *Risale-i Nur*."[27]

Increased Harassment and Prelude to Afyon

The swift spread of the *Risale-i Nur* over the three and a half years from 1944 to the beginning of 1948, together with Bediuzzaman intensifying his struggle against the forces working against them drove their enemies to increase their pressure on him and the other *Risale-i Nur* students as part of a wider plan to halt their activities. This culminated in the third and worst large-scale imprisonment of Bediuzzaman and his students.

Sometime towards the end of 1947, the President, İsmet İnönü, visited Afyon and gave a speech, following which the pressure and harassment on Bediuzzaman were increased.[28] He was reported to have said during his visit that "it is reckoned a disturbance connected with religion will break out in this province." Bediuzzaman wrote in a letter that this pointed to the large scale of the conspiracy against them, and that—as previously—the aim of the harassment inflicted on him was "to provoke an incident and disturbance."[29]

Following this, the police moved against *Risale-i Nur* students in the provinces of Isparta, Kastamonu, Konya, and many other places. Houses were searched, enquiries were made.[30]

At the same time, Bediuzzaman was subjected to a series of entirely unlawful raids, assaults, and harassment. It is clear by this "making numerous mountains out of one molehill" that it was leading up to further arrests. On the orders of the Interior Minister, the governor of Afyon and chief of police came to Emirdağ at night with the intention of searching Bediuzzaman's house. When the public prosecutor did not endorse this, they waited till the morning then appointed two men to break the lock on the door and made a forcible entrance.[31] These two officials, that is, the governor and police chief came five times over a period of ten days. On searching Bediuzzaman's house they found nothing, but took his Qur'an and some sheets written in the Arabic script. Two gendarmes were ordered to take Bediuzzaman to the police station. Having failed to anger him by raiding his house, they now tried again to provoke an incident by attempting to make a spectacle of Bediuzzaman by trying to remove his turban by force and make him wear a hat in public when taking him to give his statement. They again failed. Bediuzzaman wrote:

> Endless thanks be to Almighty God for He bestowed on me a state of mind whereby I would have sacrificed my self-respect and dignity a thousand times for the unfortunate people of this country, and repulsed calamities from them; I decided to endure what they did and the insults and abuse they intended. I am ready to sacrifice my life and dignity a thousand times over for the security of this nation, and the worldly tranquillity and happiness in the next life of particularly innocent children, respected elderly, and the unfortunate ill and poor...

That day and the following day when Bediuzzaman went out in his phaeton into the country surrounding Emirdağ, he was followed by five aircraft.[32] It may be imagined how all this intimidated the people of the town.

Now, at the beginning of 1948, Bediuzzaman was repeatedly summoned to the police station and government offices to give statements and in such a way as to insult and degrade him. On one occasion, although ill and over seventy years old, he was kept standing for four hours while being asked facile and meaningless questions. As during the Denizli episode, that night there were four severe earth tremors, the epicentre of which was Emirdağ. [33,34]

As part of the build-up of this plan to halt the spread of the *Risale-i Nur*, three plainclothes police were sent to Emirdağ from Afyon to watch Bediuzzaman, establish who his students were, and learn their activities.[35] The senior policeman of the group, Abdurrahman Akgül, later related his experiences in some detail. A summary is as follows:

The three were briefed carefully, given false identities, and were to go entirely incognito with not even their families knowing where they were. Abdurrahman was warned by the police chief not to annoy Bediuzzaman, for if he did, he would meet with trouble. The three arrived in Emirdağ on 13 December, 1947. Only the gendarme chief there and Kaymakam knew who they were.

Having been shown where Bediuzzaman's house was, the three sat down in a cafe opposite and started to watch it. A short while later Bediuzzaman appeared at the door and some of his students came out. Abdurrahman commented on their youth. The students then came towards the cafe, spoke with the proprietor, and approached them. They told the three:

"Ustādh sends you his greetings and wants to meet you."

The three police were dumbfounded, and trying to cover it up, pretended ignorance. Eventually Abdurrahman sent one of the other two, Hasan, with them. A while later he returned and told them what had passed between them.

Bediuzzaman first asked him his name. Hasan replied:

"Ahmed."

To which Bediuzzaman said: "Look here, Ahmed. Promise me you'll tell the truth."

"I promise." Bediuzzaman continued:

"I received news that three police are being sent in order to investigate me. I have many students and friends. If you are those three police, say so, and I'll warn them so no harm comes to you."

Hasan remonstrated, insisting that they were not police.

The following day, the same thing happened. Only this time, Abdurrahman sent both the others. Bediuzzaman spoke to them concerning belief and the Qur'an, then offered them some *lokum*, Turkish Delight, and gave them handwritten copies of *The Staff of Moses* and *A Guide for Youth*.

Abdurrahman related how the third policeman, Salih, had written out a memo stating that "Said Nursi got one of his students to buy some liquor from the grocer", but could get no one to sign it.[36] Salih received his deserts for this: that night he himself drank too much, got into a fight and was beaten up. He was found unconscious lying in the gutter, with his revolver stolen. As a punishment, his superiors fined him three times the cost of the revolver, demoted him, and sent him elsewhere.

When it came to Bediuzzaman and his students being arrested, Abdurrahman described it like this:

> Whenever Bediuzzaman went out in Emirdağ, all the people used to wait for him along his way, and he would greet them smiling. While we were there, the governor and public prosecutor came to Emirdağ five or six times, and carried out searches. Finally one evening they gathered up ten people from their homes, and the [five] others from their places of work. They collected Bediuzzaman the following morning then took them altogether in the police bus to Afyon. We returned to Afyon the same day, that is, on 17 January 1948. They stayed three days in the Emniyet Hotel in Afyon, and their statements were taken. Large crowds gathered in the vicinity during these three days. Then all the police surrounded the hotel and lined the route to the prison. The chief of police said that I was to take Bediuzzaman from the hotel. I put on my uniform then I said to him:
>
> "How can I? He knows me. It will be terribly impolite."
>
> "So be it. Everything's out in the open now", he replied.
>
> I went to the hotel with a number of police. They went inside and I waited at the door. When Bediuzzaman came out, he saw me at the top of the steps, and smiling, exclaimed: 'Abdurrahman!' Then he patted my back, and said:
>
> "I still like you, because you do your duty."
>
> We took Bediuzzaman by way of empty streets to the prison and his students by the route along which the people were waiting. The court hearings continued for a long time. I too gave my statement and said I had seen Bediuzzaman do nothing that was at all harmful.[37]

Although Abdurrahman Akgül states above that Bediuzzaman and his students remained three days in the hotel, since it was 23 January when they were officially arrested and put in Afyon Prison, it was a week that the fifteen or so of them stayed there. During this time students were rounded up in Isparta, Denizli, Afyon, Kastamonu and other places and brought to Afyon, making a total of fifty-four who underwent the preliminary questioning. This coincided with a spell of cold weather rarely experienced even in Afyon,[38] which has its own micro-climate and where the temperature frequently drops lower than in other places.

Notes

1. Sadık Demirelli, in *Son Şahitler*, ii, 143-4.
2. Nursi, *Emirdağ Lahikası*, i, 93.
3. Tahir Barçın, in *Son Şahitler*, ii, 125-7; Şahiner, *Said Nursi*, 352-3.
4. See, Emirdağ, Çalışkanlar Hanedanı ve Ceylan, in *Son Şahitler*, iv, 41-114.
5. Nursi, *Emirdağ Lahikası*, i, 23; 36.
6. Mehmed Çalışkan, in *Son Şahitler*, iv, 54-5.
7. *Tarihçe*, 403-6.
8. Abdurrahman Akgül, in *Son Şahitler*, i, 13.
9. Nursi, *Emirdag Lahikası* (handwritten original), 6.
10. Nursi, *Şualar*, 204, 213 (Eng. tr.: *Rays*, 262, 272).
11. Nursi, *Emirdağ Lahikası*, i, 24.
12. Ziya Sönmez, in *Son Şahitler*, ii, 183.
13. Nursi, *Emirdağ Lahikası*, i, 81.
14. *Ibid.*, 234-6.
15. *Ibid.*, 269.
16. *Ibid.*, 154; 179.
17. *Ibid.*, 156.
18. Also in this connection, it is worth noting that in a footnote to the Twentieth Flash, *On Sincerity*, written in 1934, Bediuzzaman spoke of this co-operation. He wrote: "It is even recorded in authentic traditions of the Prophet that at the end of time the truly pious among the Christians will unite with the people of the Qur'an and fight their common enemy, irreligion. The people of religion and truth will sincerely unite not only with their own brothers and fellow-believers but also with the truly pious clergy of the Christians, refraining from the discussion and debate of points of difference in order to combat their joint enemy—aggressive atheism." *Lem'alar*, 146 (Eng. tr.: *Flashes*, 203-4 fn 8).
19. Nursi, *Emirdağ Lahikası*, i, 36.
20. *Ibid.*, 80-1.
21. *Ibid.*, 101.
22. *Ibid.*, 214-5.
23. *Ibid.*, 189-90.
24. Nursi, *Emirdağ Lahikası*, i, 20-1.
25. Nursi, *Emirdağ Lahikası*, ii, 71, 164.

26. For example, Nursi, *Emirdağ Lahikası*, i, 29, 75-6.
27. *Ibid.*, 77.
28. Mustafa Bilal, in *Son Şahitler*, iv, 20.
29. Nursi, *Emirdağ Lahikası*, i, 156.
30. *Tarihçe*, 473-4.
31. Nursi, *Emirdağ Lahikası*, i, 270.
32. *Ibid.*, 29-30; *Tarihçe*, 460.
33. Nursi, *Emirdağ Lahikası*, i, 168, 170, 277.
34. This close connection between the *Risale-i Nur* and the universe and the creatures within it manifested as *tevâfukat*, or 'coincidings', has been mentioned in various places in previous chapters, in both 'negative' and 'positive' contexts. There were numerous examples in Emirdağ of both, of which the above earthquakes were just one. Instances of 'positive' contexts mostly involved birds of different varieties either acting as heralds of good news or entering a room in a manner quite out of the ordinary and remaining over a period of time while the *Risale-i Nur* or Bediuzzaman's letters were read, for example. See, Nursi, *Emirdağ Lahikası*, i, 46-7, 67, 86, etc.
35. *Tarihçe*, 437.
36. Bediuzzaman refers to this in several places, which was part of a campaign of slander that "no devil could in any way deceive anyone with", which showed that no other weapon remained with them which they could use against the *Risale-i Nur*. See, Nursi, *Emirdağ Lahikası*, i, 257; also, *Lem'alar*, 246-7 (Eng. tr.: *Flashes*, 327).
37. Abdurrahman Akgül, in *Son Şahitler*, i, 11-18.
38. Şahiner, *Said Nursi*, 364-5.

17
Afyon

Afyon Prison

Thus, Bediuzzaman and the *Risale-i Nur* students entered their third School of Joseph (*Medrese-i Yûsufiye*). And as before they transformed it into a 'school' by persisting in writing out copies of the *Risale-i Nur* and the long piece Bediuzzaman wrote, *Elhüccetü'z-Zehra*. And they studied and instructed other prisoners, despite the conditions, which in their harshness, far exceeded what they had experienced in Eskişehir and Denizli.

The years of despotic Republican People's Party rule were drawing to an end; already in 1946 the Democrat Party had been founded. As if to have a final strike at religion and Islam, to which they were now having to make concessions, they inflicted on Bediuzzaman twenty months of the most terrible imprisonment. But he survived the inhuman conditions and lived to see the virtually free printing of the *Risale-i Nur* under the Democrat Party and the consolidation of his students into a powerful movement.

It is clear that their imprisonment and conviction were a foregone conclusion. After the previous acquittals their enemies determined to have them convicted come what may, although this meant "being disrespectful to three major courts, slighting their honour and justice, and even insulting them."[1] The charges were the same. There are a number of things which point to this. Firstly, it was stated "by a Prime Minister" in the Grand

Afyon

National Assembly during the debates on changes to the "elastic" Article 163 of the Criminal Code with a view to making it more comprehensive and carrying heavier penalties, that this would be applied directly against Said Nursi and his students.[2]

Secondly, the following account of the governor of Afyon Prison, Mehmet Kayihan, shows that it was a foregone conclusion that Bediuzzaman would be imprisoned:

> Since it had been established by the government that Said Nursi was spreading religious propaganda, a policeman called Sabri Banazlı and some others were sent to Emirdağ in civil clothes. One day Banazlı came to the prison and said to me, 'We'll be bringing you someone called Bediuzzaman soon.' Then some time after this they brought Said Nursi to the prison.[3]

That is, he was informing the governor that Bediuzzaman was going to be sent to the prison before there having been any court proceedings or other formalities.

Then once inside the prison, Bediuzzaman was kept in strict isolation. Rules benefiting prisoners were not applied to him. He was allowed no visitors. He was denied assistance with and information about the court proceedings, and to hinder his defence, the public prosecutor held up giving him the Ankara Experts' report for six or seven months, on which his own forty-six-page indictment was in part based.[4]

In addition, the prosecutor abused his office in various ways in order to indict Bediuzzaman and his students, and drag out the proceedings. For instance, it is said he was involved in the creation of disturbances within the prison by means of various prisoners in the hope of implicating the *Risale-i Nur* students. There was a revolt while they were there, but none of the students were involved.[5] And he repeatedly delayed the proceedings by delaying the sending of all the documents of the case to the Appeal Court for three months.

After the preliminary proceedings, the hearings of the case began some four months after their arrest and continued for six and a half months. Thirty of the students were tried not under arrest, and a fluctuating number, nineteen at one point including Bediuzzaman were inside the prison. The decision reached by the court finding Bediuzzaman guilty on some of the charges in the face of all the evidence showed clearly its purpose. Although the previous 'committee of experts' had declared the *Risale-i Nur* innocent of anything legally reprehensible, this time the committee set up the Directorate of Religious Affairs which contained a number of negative points, also probably due to external pressure, which the prosecution in Afyon was able to utilise against Bediuzzaman and his students.

Life in Afyon Prison

Bediuzzaman was in Afyon Prison for twenty months, and his students for periods varying from a few days to eighteen months; the majority were there six months, one group before the court passed sentence, and others after it. Although summer months intervened in this time, many of the accounts speak of the intense cold.

As in Emirdağ, so now in the trial and in the prison, it was Bediuzzaman's person that was focussed on and made the object of attack. And again unwittingly his enemies engineered their own defeat. For his sincerity and qualities were such that he willingly endured the extreme conditions and appalling distress he suffered for the sake of the *Risale-i Nur* and its students. He not only survived the conditions, he conquered them. Over seventy years of age, petrified from cold, weakened from lack of food, on several occasions on the point of death from poison, alone, untended, suffering distress it is difficult to imagine, Bediuzzaman continued to write for the guidance of his students and the other prisoners. He spent his nights in prayer and contemplation, and compose not only his own defence, but directed a publicity campaign of his and his students' defences, in order to make known the reality of the case and defended the *Risale-i Nur* against this latest attack. With his indomitable spirit, he utterly defeated his enemies.

The prison consisted of six wards or dormitories. On arrival Bediuzzaman was put in solitary confinement in a seventy-person ward on an upper floor which was in an advanced state of decay. It had forty small windows of which only fifteen had intact glass. Ill with fever, he was left entirely alone in this huge, draughty room in sub-zero temperatures with no stove or heating.[6] Later, if he was given a stove, we learn from one of his defence speeches that after three and a half months in total isolation, the public prosecutor had still not permitted his books to be given to him.[7]

It was the prosecutor and the governor of the prison whom Selahaddin Çelebi described as a Gestapo chief that prohibited Bediuzzaman's students from visiting him,[8] even penalizing warders that were slack. Nevertheless, his students found ways of circumventing them and would go and assist him. If caught they were beaten.

Bediuzzaman's students willingly endured the appalling primitive conditions in the crowded wards in the way of serving the cause of the Qur'an and belief through the *Risale-i Nur*, facing also with equanimity the abuse and ill-treatment they frequently received. Their Ustādh was a perpetual source of strength and consolation for them. Some tell of how the sound of his supplications at night would console them.[9] They all tell of his kindness, even tenderness towards them in prison. They would see him watching them from his ward on the upper floor when out for their exercise in the yard. He would drop down notes to them to cheer them up and enquire if anything appeared to be wrong.[10]

During these twenty months, Bediuzzaman also wrote numerous letters, mostly short, to his students in the prison, in addition to notes such as those mentioned above. These are about various matters concerning their life in the prison, like his letters in Denizli Prison. Most importantly they urged the students to look on their imprisonment in positive terms in the light of Divine wisdom, as a trial and test, which presented new possibilities for service to the Qur'an through the *Risale-i Nur*. Especially when the trial dragged on and they were held for months in those conditions, Bediuzzaman frequently pointed out the benefits in this, since it "expanded the field of the *Risale-i Nur*", and urged patience on them. Some of the letters concern the trial and direct the writing out of copies of the defence speeches and their being sent to various government offices and departments, and other aspects of the students' "service". Others warn them of informers and spies, and efforts to sow discord between them in order to break their solidarity. Also Bediuzzaman saw an important aspect of their "service" in prison to be the reform of the other prisoners, and a number of his letters address them. Again these showed their effect, for many of the prisoners did reform. These included hardened murderers like the famous Butcher Tahir.[11]

As for the students, they constantly sought ways of visiting Bediuzzaman, and they found various means of exchanging letters. The students were dispersed through a number of wards. Each group formed its own '*madrasah*' to study together the *Risale-i Nur* and give instruction to any of the other prisoners who wished. The students continuously wrote out various parts of the *Risale-i Nur*. A student called Mustafa Acet is a good example of someone who benefited from this *Medrese-i Yûsufiye*. A relative of the Çalışkan's from Emirdağ, his arrest had been a case of mistaken identity. He was arrested in place of someone called Terzi Mustafa. But during the eleven months this entirely innocent person spent in Afyon Prison, he learnt from the *Risale-i Nur* students not only how to write the Qur'anic script, so that in subsequent years he was employed as a calligrapher by the Department of Religious Affairs, but also how to recite it, so that for ten years subsequent to being released from the prison he acted as imam in a mosque in Emirdağ![12]

On the ground floor, the stone-floored wards measured twenty to twenty-five metres by eight to ten metres, with three lavatories opening onto the ward. If anyone wanted a bath, they had to find a can of water and take it in these latrines. There were usually seventy to eighty prisoners in any one of these wards. Some food was distributed by the prison, but this had to be paid for. Since the great majority of prisoners were local, they had their food sent and laundry done by relatives outside. But since the *Risale-i Nur* students were from other areas and mostly had little money, they subsisted on the very meagerest of rations. İbrahim Fakazlı describes the *tarhana* (dried yogurt) soup that he subsisted on. The prisoners used to cook this soup on little braziers made of old tin cans. It was made with oil of such low quality that it was inedible if not first scalded. The *tarhana* was then added to this. He described how the stench of the scalded oil together with that of the latrines was so powerful, it almost knocked him unconscious when he first arrived. He grew accustomed to it after two or three days.[13] Part of the time, Bediuzzaman's food was prepared by his students, and sent from the Sixth Ward, where Mehmet Feyzi, Hüsrev, Ceylan, and others were. Bediuzzaman would not eat the bread provided by the prison. Nevertheless he was poisoned on at least three occasions in the prison. There are heart-rending descriptions of him on these occasions. And also his own description in letters, one of which is as follows. It is taken from one of two personal notebooks which Zübeyir Gündüzalp kept in prison:

> My Brother!
> My life is in danger, the torments and terrible oppression they are torturing me with on account of freemasonry and communism in a way which is beyond my endurance and entirely outside the law and contrary to prison regulations, compels us to transfer our case to another court. You must try with all your strength to inform both the lawyers here, and by telegraph our friends in Istanbul, and Hulûsi in Ankara that my life is in danger. I can no longer endure it, due to being poisoned as part of a conspiracy, and illness, and old age, and solitary confinement, and even [being forbidden] to look at or speak with whoever brings my food to the hatch. And now for the third time was yesterday's incident, a plot. On visiting day,

Ceylan is to inform Zübeyir of this and my pitiful condition, and let him do whatever is possible. In my opinion those two men are trying on account of the Masons to force me into making a muddle of things. It is essential in the name of the law to attempt to make the Appeal Court deliver us, in the name of the country and nation, from their extreme oppression and injustice.[14]

In his account of Afyon, İbrahim Fakazlı mentions Bediuzzaman's pitiful condition either on this or a similar occasion and goes on to describe the extreme cold, and how the prison authorities finally moved Bediuzzaman temporarily to another crowded ward:

> If we didn't see Ustādh at the window, we would be very worried and wonder as to the reason. Whatever the price, we would find an opportunity to go up to him and see. One bitterly cold winter's day, I slipped up to him [secretly] without being seen. Ustādh was very ill. He stretched out his hand to me and told me to take it. I took it and kissed it. It was burning and he could not stand the heat of my hand. He said: 'İbrahim, I am extremely ill. I'm about to die. But I feel comforted since you're here.' At that point Ceylan came. He repeated the same things to him. We wept in bewilderment. Ustādh was weeping as well. We were completely at a loss as to what to do. He embraced both of us and bade us farewell, then he recited a lot of prayers for us and sent us away. On returning to the ward, we explained the situation to the brothers, and we recited a lot of prayers and read *Jaushan*.[15] Later we realised that Ustādh had been poisoned.
>
> It was winter. Everywhere in Afyon was frozen and communications were cut from its surroundings. The railway was closed. For fifteen to twenty days no food or fuel could reach the town, and there was no running water. It wasn't possible to heat Bediuzzaman's ward with its broken windows and gaping floor-boards. That day, I saw Hazret-i Ustādh under two blankets double-folded with an oil-can in front of him in which was a little bit of charcoal and a kettle and tea-pot.

While the innocent, elderly, and ill Bediuzzaman was freezing to death in his empty ward virtually open to the elements, the ward opposite was in a good state of repair, with a cast-iron stove and hot water. Its inmates were a young man serving a life-sentence for communism, a doctor convicted of rape, and a political prisoner. They received every sort of privilege, the communist even being allowed out into the town in the company of a guard.

The *Risale-i Nur* students sent petitions to the prison authorities for coal and a proper stove for Bediuzzaman, but as a consequence they forcibly moved him to the Fifth Ward, the ward for pickpockets, thieves, and vagrants. It was as though they had taken pity on him, but alas, more in keeping with them, they knew he could not abide the crowded, filthy conditions and the noise, and that it would be even greater torment for him. However, the prisoners turned out to be more sympathetic: they divided off a portion of the ward with blankets, set up a stove in it, placed Bediuzzaman in it, and themselves did not make a sound outside. It became the warmest place in the prison, and it was here that Bediuzzaman wrote *Elhüccetü'z-Zehra*.[16]

The seriously ill and extremely weak Bediuzzaman wrote that it occurred to him there that since there were *Risale-i Nur* students in all the other wards, it was only in this Fifth Ward that the inmates were deprived of the lessons of the *Risale-i Nur*, so saying *"Bismillah"* he began to teach the youths there in particular, explaining eleven brief proofs of the Divine existence and unity.[17] As for the prisoners, they began to compete with each other as to who could do the most to assist Bediuzzaman and many of them began to perform the five daily prayers.

Bediuzzaman was at first distressed at being moved to the crowd and din of the fifth ward, although "it later turned into a mercy", and said by way of a warning to the prison authorities that they would suffer for it and that the cold would become even more intense. One of the prisoners who did much to assist him in the prison, a bookseller by profession, described how following this the temperature plummeted even further so that all the drains also became completely frozen. And the people in the town said that "they must have done something to the *Hoja* again." At that point he and some others set up a stove in Bediuzzaman's old ward and made it more inhabitable, and Bediuzzaman moved back there. A while later, a warm wind began to blow and the temperature rose and the ice began to thaw, whereupon the drain pipes began to split and burst and the whole town, including the prison, was flooded by filth and water from the drains. It took days to clean everywhere and rid it of the stench. In this way, Bediuzzaman's prediction was fulfilled.

Bediuzzaman then wrote the Second Station of *Elhüccetü'z-Zehra*, and this same prisoner, Kemal Bayraklı, describes how he would convey the parts of it as they were written to Hüsrev. He and the other *Risale-i Nur* students would then immediately write out copies. When complete, these would be returned to Kemal Bayraklı, who being allowed his professional tools in the prison, would bind them into book form.[18] This was all carried out in the greatest secrecy. Thus, the work of the *Risale-i Nur* was continued even in the conditions of Afyon Prison.

A final point that may be mentioned in connection with this is a strange event also described by the same prisoner, and associated with the torments suffered by Bediuzzaman. It was also recalled by Necati Müftüoğlu, who acted as chief clerk in Afyon Court in 1948.[19] Kemal Bayraklı said: "One strange day that strange winter, it was as though there was a growl in the sky. Everybody heard it. When it came to morning, there were waves of stains [on the snow] in the yard. They were blood-coloured. On watching the snow, we saw that it snowed like that all morning, covering up the stains and then the stains appearing again."[20]

Bediuzzaman is Seen Outside the Prison

As in Eskişehir[21] and Denizli Prisons, on several occasions while in Afyon Bediuzzaman was seen outside the prison in a number of mosques. As was usual with his extraordinary powers and miracles, for want of a better word,[22] he always virtually discounted them in regard to himself, concealing his own powers and attributing them to the Qur'an or *Risale-i Nur*. There are two accounts of his being seen in mosques in the town, one by a prison warder, Hasan Değirmenci, and one by a local inhabitant. The warder said:

> Although Bediuzzaman was inside the prison, rumours started up that he was being seen in the mosques and in the marketplace. I did an ignorant thing at that time: I thoroughly cleaned and polished his shoes to see if they would get dirty or dusty. If they had got dusty, I would have proved that he had really gone. That's youth and ignorance for you![23]

Hilmi Pancaroğlu, who lived in Afyon and visited Bediuzzaman when he was staying in the town after being released from the prison, gave this account:

> While in the prison, Bediuzzaman asked permission to attend the Friday Prayers, but he was refused it. Then, when the warders looked into his ward, they could not see him. In a panic, they started to search the mosques. Police went to various mosques, and different groups of them saw him performing the prayers simultaneously in the İmarat, Otpazarı, and Mısırlı Mosques. Only, when everyone came out after the prayers, they could in no way find him. Then, on returning to the prison, what did they see, but Ustādh in his ward. Most of the people of Afyon know of this event.[24]

Evidently in reply to a question on this matter, Bediuzzaman confirmed that it had occurred, but as was mentioned above, considered it to be unimportant and wanted attention to be directed away from himself towards the *Risale-i Nur*. He wrote:

> One time a famous scholar was seen on numerous fronts in the War by those who had gone to the *jihād*. They said to him... And he replied: 'Certain saints are doing this in my place in order to gain reward for me and allow the people of belief to benefit from my teaching.' In exactly the same way, in Denizli it was even made known officially that I had been seen in mosques there, and the governor and warders were informed. Some of them became alarmed, saying, 'Who opened the prison gates for him?' And exactly the same thing happened here. But rather than attributing a very minor wonder to my own very faulty and unimportant self, *The Ratifying Stamp of the Unseen Collection*,

which proves and demonstrates the *Risale-i Nur's* wonders, wins confidence in the *Risale* a hundred or rather a thousand times more, and ratifies its acceptance. And the heroic students of the *Risale-i Nur* in particular ratify it with their pens and states, which are truly wonders.[25]

The Flag Incident

One Republic Day, that is, 29 October, while Bediuzzaman was in Afyon Prison, perhaps hoping to provoke an incident, the governor had the national flag, the famous star and crescent, hung on Bediuzzaman's ward, obviously believing that he would be displeased or discomforted by this, and maybe try to have it removed. How little these officials understood Bediuzzaman— who had been "a religious republican" since an early age, and had spent his entire life striving for the good and salvation of the Turkish nation and country, both on the battlefield and with his pen. So he wrote the governor a letter. It went like this:

> Sir!
> I thank you for having the flag of the Independence Holiday hung on my ward. During the National Action in Istanbul, Ankara knew that I had performed the service of maybe a military division through publishing and distributing my work *The Six Steps* against the British and Greeks, for twice Mustafa Kemal notified me in cypher wanting me to go to Ankara. He even said: 'We have to have this heroic *hoja* here!' That is to say, it is *my* right to hang this flag this holiday.
> Said Nursi[26]

Afyon Court

Just as in the prison Bediuzzaman and his students were abused and ill-treated in ways that were entirely unlawful, so too in the trial, the law was subverted and exploited in the clear purpose of the court to convict Bediuzzaman whatever the reality of the case. As the tide was turning against them, the trial and imprisonment were a last, futile attempt to silence Bediuzzaman and stem the flood turning to the Qur'an and Islam due to the teachings of the *Risale-i Nur*. Their desperation was demonstrated by the fact that the same charges that had been cleared by previous courts, on which Bediuzzaman and his students had been declared innocent, were again put forward—he described them as "collecting water from a thousand streams": "exploiting religious feelings in a way that might disturb public order", "founding a secret society for political ends", "forming a new Sufi *ṭarīqah*", "criticizing Mustafa Kemal and his reforms", "spreading ideas opposed to the regime", and again Bediuzzaman was accused of being "a Kurdish nationalist"; a charge so far from the truth that more than anything it shows the lengths the authorities were prepared to go to in order to discredit him.

Two points the Prosecution made much of in regard to "inciting the people in ways that might disturb the peace" concerned firstly the Fifth Ray, which explains a number of Ḥadīths alluding to the Sufyān and Dajjāl and events at the end of time, and which the authorities again interpreted as referring to Mustafa Kemal. It unfortunately received support for this from the Experts' Report. Related to this was the hat question. And secondly, the brief passages in the Twenty-Fifth Word explaining Qur'anic verses about Islamic dress and inheritance were alleged to be inflammatory, as in Eskişehir Court. But once again if there was some sort of conspiracy, it backfired, for rather than arousing hostility towards Bediuzzaman, the *Risale-i Nur* and religion, the widely publicised trial and imprisonment aroused sympathy. In fact, public indignation was such that the heartless, inhuman, and unlawful treatment suffered by the entirely innocent Bediuzzaman and his students that it has been suggested that it contributed to the defeat of RPP in the 1950 elections.

Since the charges were the same as in the Eskişehir and Denizli Courts, Bediuzzaman was able to reuse a part of his former defence merely changing some of the wording. Once again he clearly disproved the charges and demonstrated that neither the

Risale-i Nur nor the activities of himself and his students had contravened the law. The following are some extracts from his defence speeches. Firstly from those refuting the political society and public order charges:

> The one hundred and thirty parts of the *Risale-i Nur* are there for all to see. Understanding that they contained no worldly goal and no aim other than the truths of belief, the Eskişehir Court did not object to them with the exception of one or two of the parts, and the Denizli Court objected to none at all, and despite being under constant surveillance for eight years the large Kastamonu police force could find no one to accuse apart from my two assistants and three others on pretexts. This is a decisive proof that the students of the *Risale-i Nur* are in no way a political society. If what is intended by "society" in the indictment is a community concerned with belief and the hereafter, we say this in reply:
>
> If the name community is given to university students and tradesmen, it may also be applied to us. But if you call us a community that is going to disturb public order by exploiting religious feelings, in response we say:
>
> The fact that in no place over a period of twenty years in these stormy times *Risale-i Nur* students have infringed or disturbed public order, and the fact that no such incident has been recorded by either the government or any court, refutes this accusation. If the name community is given meaning it might harm public security in the future through strengthening religious feelings, we say this:
>
> Firstly, foremost the Directorate of Religious Affairs and all preachers perform the same service.
>
> Secondly, the *Risale-i Nur* students protect the nation from anarchy with all their strength and conviction, and secure public order and security, they do not disturb it...
>
> Yes, we are a community, and our aim and programme is to save firstly ourselves and then our nation from eternal extinction and everlasting solitary confinement in the intermediate realm, and to protect our compatriots from anarchy and lawlessness, and to protect ourselves with the firm truths of the *Risale-i Nur* against atheism, which is a means of destroying our lives in this world and in the next.[27]

Bediuzzaman frequently stressed in his defence speeches that the nature of their service to the Qur'an prohibited them from participating in politics; it was those opposed to the positive and constructive social results of this service who repeatedly accused them of political involvement:

> We students of the *Risale-i Nur* do not make the *Risale-i Nur* a tool for worldly [political] currents, not even for the whole universe. Furthermore, the Qur'an severely prohibits us from politics. For the *Risale-i Nur's* function is to serve the Qur'an through the truths of belief and through extremely powerful and decisive proofs, which in the face of absolute unbelief which destroys eternal life and also transforms the life of this world into a ghastly poison, bring even the most obdurate atheist philosophers to belief. Therefore we may not make the *Risale-i Nur* a tool for anything.
>
> Firstly: We are prohibited from politics lest we give the false idea of political propaganda so reducing to mere glass in the view of the heedless the diamond-like truths of the Qur'an.
>
> Secondly: Compassion, truth and right, and conscience, which are fundamental to the *Risale-i Nur's* way, prohibit us sternly from politics and interfering with government. For dependent on one or two irreligious people fallen into absolute unbelief and deserving of slaps and calamities are seven or eight innocents—children, the sick and the elderly. If slaps and calamities are visited on the one or two, those unfortunates suffer also. The result being thus doubtful, we have been severely prohibited from interfering through politics in social life, which would be detrimental to government and public order.
>
> Thirdly: Five principles are necessary and essential at this strange time in order to save the social life of this country and nation from anarchy: *respect, compassion, refraining from what is prohibited (ḥarām), security, the giving up of lawlessness and obedience [to authority]*. Evidence that when the *Risale-i Nur* looks to social life it establishes and strengthens these five principles in a powerful and sacred fashion and preserves the foundation-stone of public order, is that over the last twenty years it has made one hundred thousand people into harmless, beneficial members of this nation and country. The provinces

of Isparta and Kastamonu bear witness to this. This means that knowingly or unknowingly the great majority of those who object to the *Risale-i Nur* are betraying the country and nation and dominance of Islam on account of anarchy.²⁸

In response to the repeated charge of forming a *ṭarīqah*, Bediuzzaman said:

> The basis and aim of the *Risale-i Nur* is certain belief and the essential reality of the Qur'an. For this reason, three courts of law have acquitted it in regard to being a *ṭarīqah*. Furthermore, not one person has said during these twenty years: 'Said has given me *ṭarīqah* [instruction].' Also, a way to which for a thousand years most of this nation's forefathers have been bound may not be made something for which [the members of the nation] are answerable. Also, those who combat successfully those secret dissemblers who attach the name of *ṭarīqah* to the reality of Islam and attack this nation's religion may not themselves be accused of being a *ṭarīqah*.²⁹

Of all the trumped-up charges, the most obviously false was that of Kurdish nationalism. Bediuzzaman, who as the Old Said had striven to maintain and strengthen the unity of the Ottomans, and as the New Said in his years of exile had again sacrificed himself for the salvation of the Turkish nation. In spite of this, the Court found Bediuzzaman guilty on this charge—"the blood of Kurdish nationalism is still boiling in his veins", and in this clear contempt of justice in the name of the law, the court condemned itself.

"Can any court in the world accuse me of such a thing?... although Said left his native country and relations and sacrificed his spirit and life for the religious Turks and this Muslim nation... [can such a thing be said] of someone who, in the face of twenty-eight years of torment and torture has not been shaken one iota in his sincere brotherhood with the Turks...and whom no court in the world can accuse of this...and who, since racialism has no true reality and is harmful to Islamic brotherhood, has for fifty years said: 'Islamic nationhood is equal to everything', and has supported that nationhood…and who has said: 'Give up racialism and take up Islamic nationhood, which gains for you four hundred million brothers'; and who has always taught this?"[30]

A further matter the court unjustly found Bediuzzaman guilty of concerned his explanations of certain Islamic laws concerning women. In his defence to the Appeal Court, he wrote defending these:

> One reason they showed for punishing me was my commentary on the Qur'an's explicit verses about veiling, inheritance, recitation of the Divine Names, and polygamy, written to silence those who object to them [in the name of] civilization… .
>
> I say this that if there is any justice on the face of the earth, [the Appeal Court] will quash this decision which convicts someone who expounded [Qur'anic verses] which every century for one thousand three hundred and fifty years have been held to be sacred, true Divine principles in the social life of three hundred and fifty million Muslims, and expounded them relying on the consensus and affirmation of three hundred and fifty thousand Qur'anic commentaries and following [what have been] the beliefs of our forefathers for one thousand three hundred years. Is it not denial of Islam and betrayal of our millions of religious, heroic forefathers to convict, because he expounded those verses, someone who according to reason and learning does not accept certain European laws applied temporarily due to certain requirements of the times and who has given up politics and withdrawn from social life, and is it not to insult millions of Qur'anic commentaries?[31]

The Experts' Report

While the preliminary questioning was being carried out by the public prosecutor and examining magistrate after the arrests of Bediuzzaman and his students, the collections of the *Risale-i Nur*, such as *Zülfikar*, *The Staff of Moses*, *The Illuminating Lamp* (*Sirac-ün-Nur*), and *A Guide for Youth*, as well as letters and other documents were all sent to the Directorate of Religious Affairs in Ankara to be scrutinized by another 'committee of experts'.

Although it produced its report in a short time, presenting it to Afyon Court on 16 March, 1948, due to the prosecutor's interference, it was not for several months that Bediuzzaman was able to obtain a copy of it. This committee bowed to pressure from the government, and included two main points that the prosecution was able to use against Bediuzzaman,[32] although only three years before the previous 'experts' had cleared the *Risale-i Nur*. Nevertheless, importantly, they rejected the charges of forming a *ṭarīqah*, organizing a political society, and disturbing public order, and concentrated their objections, which Bediuzzaman described as, "unfair, incorrect, and unjustifiable", on the Fifth Ray.[33] The second point they raised, also entirely unfair and mistaken but one which, out of fear, Bediuzzaman's enemies frequently levelled at him, was being "conceited and vainglorious", by which was meant building up by means of his students' good will towards him, a position of personal prestige and power.

Bediuzzaman answered these objections the committee raised in a "Thank-you Letter", in which he firstly expressed his gratitude to them for exonerating him of the main charges. He then pointed out in scholarly and reasoned fashion the errors in their objections to the Ḥadīths in the Fifth Ray and his interpretation of them. Since together with the few lines on inheritance and Islamic dress this was the one part of the *Risale-i Nur* that was made the pretext for this court case and numerous subsequent cases—since the authorities interpreted it as attacking Ataturk, it is worth mentioning here the history of this extraordinary treatise, which illustrates one reason how Bediuzzaman earned his name, the Wonder of the Age, and also, unfortunately, how this frequently resulted in rivalry and jealousy on the part of other religious scholars.

The Fifth Ray had originated over forty years previously, from when Bediuzzaman came to Istanbul in 1907 before the Constitutional Revolution. At that time, when the "prodigy from the East" had put a notice on his door saying "Here all questions are answered, but none are asked", the Istanbul *'ulamā'* put some questions to him about some allegorical Ḥadīth referring to the end of time, which had been asked them by the visiting Japanese Commander-in-Chief. Then, when a member of the Darü'l-Hikmeti'l-İslamiye after the First World War, in reply to some further questions on the same subject, Bediuzzaman arranged these replies roughly in the form of a treatise, the purpose of which was to save believers from doubts about the allegorical Ḥadīths, which superficially appeared to be unconformable with reason.[34] Then, in 1922 he was invited to Ankara by Mustafa Kemal, and he saw part of what these Ḥadīths foretold "in someone there", and for that reason felt compelled to refuse the offers made to him of various posts, and withdrew from politics and the world to eastern Anatolia in order to work "solely on the way of saving belief." And again on being asked questions on these allegorical Ḥadīths foretelling events at the end of time when in exile in Kastamonu in 1938, Bediuzzaman arranged this treatise in its final form and it was incorporated into the *Risale-i Nur* as the Fifth Ray.[35] That is to say, as time unfolded, the interpretations of some of these Ḥadīths which Bediuzzaman had given as far back as 1907 were realised; what they prophesied was fulfilled.

For example, one of these Ḥadīths says: "A fearsome individual at the end of time will rise in the morning and on his forehead will be written: 'This is a *kāfir*'." In 1907, Bediuzzaman had interpreted this as: "This extraordinary individual will come to lead this nation. He will rise in the morning and put on a hat, and he will make others wear hats."[36] ... "The Sufyān will put on a European hat, and make others wear [similar hats]. But because this will be by compulsion and force of law, the hat will made to prostrate [before God] and God willing will be rightly-guided, and by wearing it—unwillingly—everyone will not become *kāfirs*."[37]

It was for this reason, because of its topicality, that Bediuzzaman had suppressed the treatise and not permitted it to be circulated.

It was only after the entire *Risale-i Nur*, including the Fifth Ray, had been declared legally innocuous by the previous Committee of Experts and Denizli Court that he had allowed it to be duplicated.

Now the present committee of experts levelled criticisms at the Fifth Ray which Bediuzzaman described as "unfair, mistaken, and unjustifiable."[38] These centred on the nature of the Ḥadīths, which they said were either "unsound" or "weak", and on his interpretation of them. In his "Thank-you Letter", Bediuzzaman answered these criticisms with little difficulty.[39] Besides this, he described the criticisms as resulting from jealousy and "a vein of Wahhabism", which points to the reasons for their second point of objection, which was equally mistaken. They criticised the encomia written to Bediuzzaman and the *Risale-i Nur* by some of his students.

Concerning the encomia he pointed out it was a long-standing custom among scholars and literary people to write such pieces about one another's work, and for these to be included at the end of the works when they first appeared. If they had been directed towards himself, Bediuzzaman had changed them to refer to the *Risale-i Nur*. In any event, time was proving what was written about the *Risale-i Nur* to be true. And even if what they wrote had been excessively exaggerated or even wrong, it would still only have been a scholarly error, and everyone was entitled to his own opinion. He went on to gently put three questions to the 'experts' from the Directorate of Religious Affairs, suggesting that they were busying themselves with trifles while religion and the Qur'an were suffering the awesome attacks of that period, or even assisting them.[40]

Nevertheless, despite the unfair criticisms in the report and their consequences, Bediuzzaman maintained a positive attitude towards the Directorate of Religious Affairs, marked by the "Thank-you Letter" above and the fact that in addition to other government departments, he arranged for copies of the defence speeches to also be sent to them.[41] In fact, previous to their arrests, and subsequently, he sent students to them to seek their co-operation.[42]

The Trial Continues

Another fact supporting the claim that the trial was an officially-backed conspiracy against Bediuzzaman and the *Risale-i Nur* movement was that he was denied all sorts of legal rights in the trial. In addition to being denied access to such important documents as the report, he was even frequently denied the right to speak in the court itself. His being totally isolated for the first eleven months of his imprisonment, during the trial, was clearly both to prevent him from receiving information and assisting his students. Thus, he was also often not allowed anyone to assist him with the writing out of his defence. Of course, Bediuzzaman never used the Latin alphabet, so he was dependent on his students or others for the reading of all official documents, and also the writing of any document or letter that had to be presented to the court or authorities. As with his dress, he refused to compromise. Since the Ottoman script was now illegal and invalid, when his signature was necessary on official papers, they used either his finger-print or a rubber-stamp with his name on it in the new letters.

Nevertheless, Bediuzzaman and his students were not in any way intimidated by the wrongs and injustices they suffered. A gendarme who served both in Emirdağ and Afyon Court, called İbrahim Mengüverli, described how on one occasion Bediuzzaman rose to speak in court, and continued for two hours. Then, when the Judge told him that was enough, Bediuzzaman grew exceedingly angry, traced a circle in the air with his hand and jabbed his forefinger at the Judge, saying:

> I have the right to speak for eight hours. I'll speak for as long as I want.[43]

There were three lawyers who acted as defence lawyers for Bediuzzaman and his students at Afyon. One of these, Ahmet Hikmet Gönen, also a student of Bediuzzaman described the defence speeches of the *Risale-i Nur* students. They all gave their own defences in the court, as well as writing petitions. Two were particularly noteworthy, Zübeyir Gündüzalp's and Ahmet Feyzi Kul's. The latter's, which continued for a full eight and a half hours, earned him the name of 'the *Risale-i Nur* Lawyer' from Bediuzzaman.[44]

Bediuzzaman also insisted on his right to perform the prayers at the appropriate times when the court was in session. Several witnesses have described such occasions in their accounts. One was the above lawyer. Another was Mustafa Acet from Emirdağ. He described how during one hearing, the time for the prayers was passing, so presumably not having been allowed to leave the court earlier for five minutes, Bediuzzaman said angrily to the prosecutor:

> "We're here in order to protect the rights of the prayers. We are not guilty of anything else!" And he immediately got up and walked out. The usher hurried out after him, and he performed the prayers in the secretary's office.[45]

The trials aroused great interest country-wide, and numbers of people flocked to Afyon from all over.[46] One of Bediuzzaman's students tells of one occasion when Bediuzzaman emerged from the court, a great mass of people moved forward to kiss his hand, then in turn they started to kiss it. At that point the public prosecutor came out, and unable to stomach such a situation, roared at the police and gendarmes: "Why are you permitting this?" Bediuzzaman was exceedingly angry at this, and said in a loud voice:

> "What's this? What's this? I'll meet with my brothers if I want!" And he grew so excited his turban fell off. We picked it up off the ground and put it back on his head. Scared out of his wits, the prosecutor made off without looking behind him, but

in order to provoke an incident, kicked somebody's leg. This brother felt no pain. But we looked at his leg later, and it was all purple and bruised.[47]

At the same time Bediuzzaman was not content to allow the injustices of the trial to pass unnoticed. As in Denizli, he arranged through his students for copies of his defence speeches, and also those of his students and copies of his table of the ninety errors in the indictment and his answers, to departments of government in Ankara, in order to make known the reality of the case. Only here in Afyon, he endeavoured to organise it on a larger scale, sending copies also to Isparta—for his students there to duplicate, to be shown to the public prosecutor, and also to Denizli and Istanbul. These were also made into book form and distributed. He also instructed them to send copies to the Directorate of Religious Affairs in Ankara.[48]

This operation had to be organised in secrecy and under the difficult conditions of the prison. The copies which Bediuzzaman wanted produced in the new letters had to be typed out on typewriters, which unlike in Denizli, they were not permitted. Their lawyer, Ahmed Bey, assisted them with this—Bediuzzaman stressing in his letters the need for accuracy. A soldier stationed in Afyon called Nihad Bozkurt, who used to visit a friend in the prison twice a week, also typed out the defence speeches for them.[49]

At one point even, the court had reproduced parts of the indictment "which they imagined were against" Bediuzzaman and his students. In response to this propaganda campaign, which was undoubtedly an abuse of the court's powers and was aimed at turning public opinion against them, Bediuzzaman had duplicated copies of his table of the errors in the indictment, which were little more than slander, in order to have them distributed, and also additional copies of their defences so as to inform people of the truth of the matter.[50]

The Court's Verdict

With all the delays and hold-ups, the court finally announced its verdict on 6 December, 1948. Disregarding all the evidence, it found Bediuzzaman guilty under Article 163 of the Criminal Code in various respects, "exploiting religious feelings and inciting the people against the government." That a court of law should have allowed itself to be used in this blatant miscarriage of justice was a denigration of the law itself and a disgraceful episode in Turkish legal history.[51] It sentenced Bediuzzaman to two years' "penal servitude", which was reduced to twenty months due to his age. Ahmet Feyzi Kul, who had made the long defence, was sentenced to eighteen months, and twenty others of Bediuzzaman's students to six months each. Some of these had already been inside the prison for eleven months, others for less. Some who had served their terms were released, others who had been tried not under arrest were arrested and put inside.

Then began a long drawn-out legal wrangle that did not reach a final conclusion until 1956. On the court's passing sentence, the case was immediately sent to the Appeal Court in Ankara, but as mentioned earlier, the prosecutor delayed the sending of the documents, only sending them on the intervention of the three lawyers.[52] In the prison also the injustices against Bediuzzaman continued, or were even increased, for it was at this time that the weather became so cold and he was forcibly moved to another ward.[53] Both he and his students wrote further defences and pieces to be sent to the Appeal Court. The lawyers gave the defence in the Appeal Court, which gave its decision on 4 June 1949: since Said Nursi had been acquitted on the same charges by the Denizli Court, and this decision had been confirmed by the Appeal Court, it quashed the decision of the Afyon Court.

Although Bediuzzaman and his students should have been released at this point, the Afyon Court reassembled on the case being referred back to it. They were asked what they wanted. On their replying that they wanted the Appeal Court's decision to be applied, the court withdrew for prolonged consideration. Finally, it had no choice but to agree. But then, on 31 August, 1949, the decision was taken to retry the case, and hearings began once again. In this way, with continual postponements and delays, in an entirely unlawful manner, Bediuzzaman was made to serve the full twenty months the court had originally sentenced him to. Only when he had completed this term did they release him. His students also were released on completing their sentences. In this way, the tyrannical and obdurate prosecutor perpetrated what was no less than a crime on these innocent people right up to the very last moment he was able. And when it came to releasing Bediuzzaman, they did not permit him to leave the prison at the normal hour, but just before dawn.

The story of the Afyon Court does not finish here; the hearings continued with the accused in absentia, until the general amnesty announced after the victory of the Democrat Party in the 1950 general elections. But even then the prosecutor would not let the matter rest; he insisted on the works in question—the *Risale-i Nur*—being separated from the criminal proceedings, and the continuation of the case. Thus, the trial of the *Risale-i Nur* continued.

The court finally reached a decision that copies of the *Risale-i Nur* should be confiscated. The case was sent to the Appeal Court. The Appeal Court again quashed the Afyon Court's decision. The Afyon Court had no choice now but to comply with the Appeal Court's judgement and acquit the *Risale-i Nur*. But the prosecutor would not accept this, and he sent this decision before the Appeal Court. This time, the Appeal Court quashed the Afyon Court's latest decision due to some technicalities. The case continued. Then the Afyon Court ruled that the *Risale-i Nur* should be acquitted and copies returned to their owners, whereupon the prosecutor again sent the case to the Appeal Court.

This time the Appeal Court decided that the entire *Risale-i Nur* should be rescrutinized by a committee of experts and the

Directorate of Religious Affairs was directed to set one up. A new committee produced a report. And finally, relying on this report, in June, 1956, the Afyon Court cleared the *Risale-i Nur* and ruled that all the confiscated copies should be returned to their owners. This time the prosecutor admitted his defeat, and the decision was made final.[54]

Notes

1. Nursi, *Şualar*, 291 (Eng. tr.: *Rays*, 370).
2. İbrahim Fakazli, in *Son Şahitler*, v, 23.
3. Mehmet Kayıhan, in *Son Şahitler*, i, 19.
4. Nursi, *Şualar*, 339, 433 (Eng. tr.: *Rays*, 425, 514).
5. *Ibid.*, 423 (Eng. tr.: *Rays*, 507-8).
6. Nursi, *Lem'alar*, 246-7 (Eng. tr.: *Flashes*, 327).
7. Nursi, *Şualar*, 322 (Eng. tr.: *Rays*, 405).
8. Selahaddin Çelebi, in *Son Şahitler*, i, 148.
9. İbrahim Fakazli, in *Son Şahitler*, v, 30.
10. *Ibid.*; also Mustafa Sungur, in Şahiner, *Aydınlar Konuşuyor*, 382.
11. See, H. Pancaroğlu, in *Son Şahitler*, iii, 170; Şahiner, *Nurs Yolu*, 54-6.
12. Mustafa Acet, in *Son Şahitler*, i, 27-9.
13. İbrahim Fakazlı, in *Son Şahitler*, v, 33-4.
14. Şahiner, *Son Şahitler*, i, 24.
15. The *Jaushan al-Kabīr* is the famous supplication revealed to Prophet Muhammed (ṣ) which, comprising the divine names, is said to possess many merits.
16. İbrahim Fakazlı, *Son Şahitler*, v, 35-6.
17. Nursi, *Şualar*, 502-3 (Eng. tr.: *Rays*, 570).
18. Kemal Bayraklı, in *Son Şahitler*, iv, 288-9.
19. Necati Müftüoğlu, in *Son Şahitler*, v, 82.
20. Kemal Bayraklı, in *Son Şahitler*, iv, 289.
21. *Tarihçe*, 193.
22. Miracles (*mu'jizāt*) are particular to prophets, while in saints and others such 'wonder-working' is known as *karāmah*.
23. Hasan Değirmenci, in *Son Şahitler*, i, 31.
24. Hilmi Pancaroğlu, in *Son Şahitler*, iii, 169-70.
25. Nursi, *Şualar*, 409 (Eng. tr.: *Rays*, 481).
26. Nursi, *Şualar*, 455 (Eng. tr.: *Rays*, 533); Şahiner, *Said Nursi*, 366-8.
27. Nursi, *Şualar*, 305 (Eng. tr.: *Rays*, 387).
28. *Ibid.*, 292-3 (Eng. tr.: *Rays*, 372).

29. *Ibid.*, 313 (Eng. tr.: *Rays*, 395 fn 16).
30. Nursi, *Müdâfaalar*, 464.
31. Nursi, *Şualar*, 378-9 (Eng. tr.: *Rays*, 445).
32. Bediuzzaman had surmised that the Experts' Report had arrived some time previously, because some of the answers in a table he had made out of ninety errors and factual inaccuracies in the indictments and his answers to them corresponded exactly to the Report. In other words, the indictment was in part based on the report (*Şualar*, 433; *Rays*, 510.) For the table, see Nursi, *Şualar*, 342-361.
33. Nursi, *Şualar*, 437 (Eng. tr.: *Rays*, 515).
34. *Ibid.*, 296, 383 (Eng. tr.: *Rays*, 376-7, 451).
35. *Ibid.*, 300-1 (Eng. tr.: *Rays*, 380-2).
36. *Ibid.*, 300 (Eng. tr.: *Rays*, 381).
37. *Ibid.*, 490 (Eng. tr.: *Rays*, 103).
38. *Ibid.*, 437 (Eng. tr.: *Rays*, 515).
39. *Ibid.*, 338-9 (Eng. tr.: *Rays*, 423-4).
40. *Ibid.*, 338-341 (Eng. tr.: *Rays*, 423-7).
41. *Ibid.*, 409 (Eng. tr.: *Rays*, 482).
42. Nursi, *Emirdağ Lahikası*, i, 232-3; ii, 6, 9.
43. İbrahim Mengüverli, in *Son Şahitler*, iii, 123.
44. Ahmet Hikmet Gönen, in *Son Şahitler*, iii, 178-9.
45. Mustafa Acet, in *Son Şahitler*, i, 28.
46. İbrahim Mengüverli, in *Son Şahitler*, iii, 123.
47. Mustafa Ezener, in *Son Şahitler*, iv, 180.
48. Nursi, *Şualar*, 409, 412 (Eng. tr.: *Rays*, 482, 486).
49. Nihad Bozkurt, in *Son Şahitler*, iv, 248-9.
50. Nursi, *Şualar*, 453 (Eng. tr.: *Rays*, 531).
51. This is further proved by the fact that subsequently to 1949 the *Risale-i Nur* and Fifth Ray in particular, which was made the main pretext of the Afyon judges' decision, have been acquitted more than 1500 times in Turkish courts of law.
52. Nursi, *Şualar*, 454 (Eng. tr.: *Rays*, 532).
53. *Ibid.*, 502 (Eng. tr.: *Rays*, 570).
54. *Tarihçe*, 475-7, 539.

Part III
The Third Said

18
The Third Said

Introduction

We come now to the last ten years of Bediuzzaman's life and the last of its three main stages, in Bediuzzaman's own words, that of the Third Said. The Third Said is generally defined in terms of changes Bediuzzaman made in the way he had patterned his life over many years, the expansion of activities associated with the *Risale-i Nur*, and his involving himself more closely with social and political developments.

The emergence of the Third Said roughly coincided with the defeat of the Republican People's Party in the general elections of May, 1950, and coming to power of the Democrat Party under Adnan Menderes, although while still in Afyon Prison Bediuzzaman wrote that he "surmised" that "a Third Said" would emerge.[1] With the end of RPP rule the restrictions on his movements were lifted and he spent these years largely in Emirdağ and Isparta, with visits to Istanbul, Ankara and other places as was required by either the ever-expanding activities connected with the *Risale-i Nur*, or to make court appearances. Despite the new government, the bureaucracy and governing structure of the country were still largely in the hands of supporters of the former regime. Thus, copies of the *Risale-i Nur* continued to be seized, Bediuzzaman and his students continued to suffer repression and the court cases continued.

In the early fifties, in numerous villages and towns in many regions of Turkey *Risale-i Nur* students continued to write out copies by hand and distribute and read them, while in Isparta and Inebolu it was reproduced on the duplicating machines and distributed in the form of collections. Then, in 1956, on the Afyon Court reaching a final decision and lifting all legal restrictions on the *Risale-i Nur*, a new generation of young students set about printing and publishing the entire collection on modern presses in the new letters. This further expanded the number of its readers and students so that they now ran into many hundreds of thousands.

Together with these developments the *Risale-i Nur* movement itself became established as a cohesive movement and some of the changes in Bediuzzaman's life can be seen to be directed towards training the new generation of students who would lead it after he himself would be no longer there to do so. Of these, a number had visited Bediuzzaman and became involved with the work of the *Risale-i Nur* in the 1940's and as a consequence had served terms in Afyon Prison along with him. Following this, which served as a crucible refining this new generation for their work in the cause of the Qur'an, such students as Zübeyir Gündüzalp, Mustafa Sungur and Ceylan Çalışkan devoted themselves entirely to the *Risale-i Nur*, and, among others, it was for them that Bediuzzaman changed a number of his habitual practices. For example, after 1953, he had them living in the same house as himself, whereas previously he had lived alone allowing no one into his presence from the time of the evening prayers to the following morning.

Afyon served the cause of the *Risale-i Nur* in other ways too, as had Eskişehir and Denizli before it, one of which was that it was a means of unifying the *Nur* movement. For on the days of the court hearings, *Risale-i Nur* students from all over Turkey flocked to Afyon to observe the proceedings and give moral support to their fellows being tried, and in this way they both got to know each other and establish firm relations. They also become better informed about Bediuzzaman and the *Risale-i Nur* and its method

The Third Said

of service. Afyon thus formed an important step in consolidating the movement.[2]

The main change in Bediuzzaman, due to which this period of his life is known as that of the Third Said, was a closer involvement with social and political life. This aspect of the Third Said was directly connected with the coming to power of the Democrat Party in 1950. However, his involvement took the form of support and guidance for the Democrats, which he described as "the lesser of two evils", and supported it in order to prevent the RPP returning to power. He also did not permit his students to engage in active or power politics in the name of the *Nur* movement. If any wished, they did so in their own names.

While in Emirdağ before being sent to Afyon in 1948, Bediuzzaman had written letters to members of the government explaining the nature and seriousness of the dangers facing the country from communism. He urged them to restore the Qur'an and truths of belief as the ideological basis of the state in place of the imposed philosophy and irreligion, as the sole means of saving it from these threats. Now, with the coming to power of the Democrat Party, Turkey had a government that was to take a firm stand against communism and was sympathetic towards Islam and religion; it intended to reflect the will of the nation and redress the wrongs of the twenty-five years of RPP rule. Thus Bediuzzaman concerned himself to a greater degree with political developments; he offered guidance to the new government primarily by means of letters, his students, and some personal relations with Democrat deputies, pointing out where the dangers lay and how, by adopting policies based on Islamic principles, they could overcome them, and encouraging them in any moves in this direction. He gave them his moral support and urged his students to support them, openly giving them his vote in the elections of 1957, so that the support of the *Risale-i Nur* movement was of no mean importance for the Democrats, especially as their popularity waned. Bediuzzaman saw the Democrats as "assisting" the *Risale-i*

Nur students in their struggle against communism and irreligion, in forming a barrier against these threats and righting the "moral and spiritual damage" they had caused.

Thus, when Bediuzzaman considered political matters, he did so with the eye of making them serve religion. He wrote to the new President, Celâl Bayar: "In the face of those who have ill-treated us making politics the tool of irreligion in a fanatical manner, we work for this country and nation's well-being by making politics the tool and friend of religion."[3]

The introduction of policies favouring Islam and the strengthening of religion would also heal the breach between Turkey and the Islamic world. Bediuzzaman impressed on the government the need to re-establish relations, for this "would gain [for the country] a reserve force within the sphere of Islamic Unity of three hundred and fifty million through the brotherhood of Islam."[4] He also supported the signing of the Baghdad Pact in 1955 as an important step in establishing peace in the area. In connection with this he strongly urged the government to give a religious base to the Eastern University that was being planned, which he saw as potentially playing the central and conciliatory role in the area of his Medresetü'z-Zehra, which he had worked for in eastern Turkey for so many years. He was essentially urging the Democrats to strengthen feelings of "Islamic nationhood" in place of the divisive racialist nationalism of the former regime.

Bediuzzaman's attitude towards the West also changed following the Second World War, for such countries as Britain, France, and America should no longer be opposed to Islamic Unity; in the face of the anarchy arising from communism and atheism, they were now in need of it.[5] He particularly regarded post-war America, which he saw as working for religion in a serious manner, in friendly terms.[6] With a number of Islamic countries gaining their independence from the colonial powers in the late 1940's and the 50's, and new Islamic states being formed, together with other indications, he once again started to speak of the forthcoming ascendancy of the Qur'an and Islam, which he had foretold in the early years of the century. He even foresaw the Islamic countries as a federation, "the United Islamic States".[7]

On occasion Bediuzzaman called the Democrats "Ahrarlar," sometimes translated as liberals, by which he meant supporters of *hürriyet-i şer'iye*, the "freedom in accordance with the Sharī'ah" the establishment for which he had worked during the Constitutional Period in the early decades of the century, and which path he hoped they would take. Bediuzzaman supported gradual change and the gradual achievement of what he believed was the inevitable future supremacy of Islam and the Qur'an. He saw democracy as a licit means of achieving this, and attached the greatest importance to the maintenance of public order and security. As he frequently pointed out, despite all the provocation and attempts to implicate and involve *Risale-i Nur* students in disturbances by those who made it their business to disrupt order, none had been recorded. The way of the *Risale-i Nur* and its students was service to belief and the Qur'an by peaceful means and "positive action". It was peaceful struggle or "*jihād* of the word" (*jihād-ı ma'nawī*) in the face of the moral and spiritual depradations of atheism and unbelief, to instil certain belief in hearts and minds. While in many Muslim countries violent change had been brought about by revolution in which thousands of innocents were killed, the *Risale-i Nur*'s method was "the positive service of belief which results in the preservation of public order and stability." The destruction caused by atheism and unbelief was of a moral, spiritual or non-material nature (*ma'nawī*), so internal *jihād* against it had to be of the same nature; it was to work for the spread and strengthening of belief with sincerity and "not to interfere in God's business" that is, not to be precipitate and expect immediate results; leave the results to Almighty God.[8]

Emirdağ

On being released from Afyon Prison in the early morning of 20 September, 1949, Bediuzzaman was escorted by two police officers to a house in the town which had been rented by some of his students, released earlier than himself. Among these were Hüsrev and Zübeyir Gündüzalp. Again under close surveillance, with two or three policemen permanently posted at the house who took down the names of all visitors, Bediuzzaman remained there around two months before moving back to his former house in Emirdağ.⁹

Back in Emirdağ among his many students, Bediuzzaman took up where he had left off two years earlier when he had been arrested and sent to Afyon. In one of his first letters to his students in Isparta, he asks for one of them to go to Ankara to the Directorate of Religious Affairs to inform the Director, Ahmed Hamdi Akseki, that despite illness from poisoning, he was struggling to correct the entire set of the *Risale-i Nur* they had requested two years earlier and would present it when completed. In return he requested the Director to do all he could for the *Risale-i Nur*'s free circulation, and also to print photographically the 'miraculous' Qur'an Hüsrev had written showing the coincidings in the word Allah, and other Divine Names.¹⁰ Thus, Bediuzzaman overlooked the harm caused to himself and the *Risale-i Nur* by the negative report of the Committee of Experts set up by the Directorate for Afyon Court, and the first thing he did on being released was to renew his efforts to persuade them—and through them the muftis and *hojas*—of the extreme value of the *Risale-i Nur* as a commentary on the Qur'an, to use their influence to get the legal restrictions lifted, and even to publish it officially themselves. Although Ahmed Hamdi agreed in principle to publish the *Risale-i Nur*, this never came to fruition. In 1956 after the *Risale-i Nur* had been cleared by the Afyon Court, the new Director, Eyüp Sabri Hayırlıoğlu, was again approached on the subject, this time on the recommendation of the Prime Minister, Menderes, but the attempt again came to nothing.¹¹

In Emirdağ Bediuzzaman continued his life as before, but some of his students there noted certain changes. For instance,

The Third Said

Mehmet Çalışkan remarked how following Afyon, Bediuzzaman's food was prepared by his students who accompanied him, rather than the Çalışkan family, and that he now had read to him two or three newspapers daily. Mehmet Çalışkan describes also how they would collect the papers from the newsagent, then slipping them into an inner pocket take them to Bediuzzaman, read him the appropriate parts, and later return them to the newspaper seller.[12] With the coming to power of the Democrat Party some six months after Bediuzzaman returned to Emirdağ, the restrictions on his movements were theoretically lifted, and that year, in addition to sharing the joy of the whole country on the ban on the Arabic call to prayer being lifted, he was able to join the congregation in the Çarşı Mosque for the *tarāwīḥ* prayers each of the thirty nights of Ramaḍān.[13]

On the Democrats winning the elections on 14 May, 1950, Bediuzzaman sent the following telegram to the new President, Celâl Bayar:

> To: Celâl Bayar, President of the Republic.
> We offer our congratulations. May Almighty God afford you every success in the service of Islam, and the country and nation.
>
> In the name of the students of the *Risale-i Nur*, and one of them,
>
> Said Nursi

To which he received this reply:

> To: Bediuzzaman Said Nursi, Emirdağ.
> I was exceedingly touched at your cordial congratulations and offer my thanks.
>
> Celâl Bayar[14]

Since his days in Kastamonu Bediuzzaman had attached the greatest importance to guiding the young and the numbers of *Risale-i Nur* students in their youth. Then in the early 1950's there was a striking increase in their numbers—and in the importance of the role they played in the work of the *Risale-i Nur*. In fact, in many respects these last ten years of Bediuzzaman's life may be seen as directing and training these young students and preparing some of them to lead the *Nur* movement in later years. It may also perhaps be seen as symbolic that while Bediuzzaman had written to his leading students of the older generation in Isparta wanting one of them to go to Ankara to the Directorate of Religious Affairs as described above, in the event it was the young Mustafa Sungur who deputized for him, both on this occasion and many subsequent occasions.

In Istanbul and Ankara in particular, young and enterprising *Risale-i Nur* students, many of whom were university students, devoted themselves to working for the *Risale-i Nur* and the cause of religion. In Ankara they were active among the deputies in the National Assembly, writing letters and circulars publicizing Bediuzzaman's views and the case of the *Risale-i Nur*, meeting with deputies, particularly one's known to be sympathetic towards Islam, and pointing out and warning about various stratagems of the Republican People's Party (RPP) supporters who had infiltrated the Democrat Party.

One such case concerned the destruction of one hundred and seventy copies of the large collections, *The Staff of Moses* and *Zülfikar*, seized by the authorities in Isparta. This was despite their having been cleared by the Democrat Justice Minister and was evidently part of a plan of RPP supporters to arouse antagonism among the *Risale-i Nur* students towards the Democrats, for whom they formed an important body of support.[15]

This fanatical partisanship, which Bediuzzaman had alluded to in the letter he wrote to the new President, and warned against on other occasions, was an additional element in the harassment and oppression which he and his students continued to receive from certain sections of officialdom. These officials were supporters of the RPP, and they continuously hatched plots by which to divide the forces working for religion and prevent them from uniting. Thus, since the governing structure of the country was still largely in the hands of supporters of the RPP, the repression of

Bediuzzaman and the *Risale-i Nur* students continued throughout these ten years, as did the court cases. Besides the Afyon Court decision to confiscate copies of the *Risale-i Nur*, on other occasions copies were seized illegally. Often Bediuzzaman was harassed and threatened on account of his dress, even being sent before the court in Emirdağ in the summer of 1951 for refusing to wear a European-style hat. In early 1952, a case was brought against him and a young *Risale-i Nur* student who had had *A Guide for Youth* published in Istanbul; it resulted in acquittals. And the following year a case was opened in Samsun on the Black Sea, which Bediuzzaman could not attend due to ill health, but Mustafa Sungur stood trial; it also ended in acquittals. And in 1956, a case was brought against Bediuzzaman and eighty-nine *Risale-i Nur* students in Isparta for "forming a secret society", which was dismissed as not being proven. Then in Ankara, Isparta, and many other places were further cases against *Risale-i Nur* students, all of which ended in acquittals. In the face of the confiscations and the Afyon Court proceedings in the early 1950's, Bediuzzaman wrote a number of petitions to the president and other ministers, and for the Appeal Court and to be distributed by his students among "religious deputies" of the National Assembly, pointing out the realities of the case.[16]

Korea

Bediuzzaman supported the decision to send Turkish troops to Korea to fight the communist invasion from the north, and was delighted when his close student Bayram Yüksel was to be sent there in 1951 during his military service, saying; "I wanted to send a *Risale-i Nur* student to Korea and was thinking of either you or Ceylan. The atheism there has to be combated." Bediuzzaman also supported Turkey's joining NATO. He gave Bayram Yüksel his own *Jawshan al-Kabīr* prayer book and some parts of the *Risale-i Nur* to give to the commander-in-chief of the Japanese army whom he knew from when he first came to Istanbul in

1907. Bayram Yüksel went to Korea with Bediuzzaman's blessing, and fighting in some of the fiercest battles of the war, came out unscathed. He also visited Japan, and gave the parts of the *Risale-i Nur* to the National Library in Tokyo, since the commander-in-chief had departed this life some years previously.[17]

Eskişehir and Isparta

After years of being confined to his place of exile, very often not even being allowed to attend the mosque or walk out to take exercise, Bediuzzaman was now free to move about as he wished. In October of 1951 he went to Eskişehir, where he stayed in the Yıldız Hotel. He met there with many of his students, of all classes, the young in particular. Members of the armed forces also visited him, with airmen being in the majority. After a month or so, Bediuzzaman moved on to Isparta, where he stayed for some two months, until summoned to Istanbul to stand trial together with one of his students at Istanbul University, Muhsin Alev, who had printed *A Guide for Youth*.

While in Isparta and Istanbul Bediuzzaman wrote a number of letters which he subsequently put together in a booklet and published under the title, *A Key to the World of the Risale-i Nur*.[18] Before describing the *Guide for Youth* trial in Istanbul, it is worth mentioning these letters, since the small collection they form was the last piece to be added to the *Risale-i Nur*. By relating science to the truths of belief, and showing that rather than their conflicting in any way, if considered in the light of the Qur'an, science may be seen to broaden and strengthen belief. One of the pieces was inspired by the radio. The radio, which he listened to from time to time, inspired him to write an interesting exposition of the element of air. Its "duties" proved Divine Unity so decisively while disproving that nature or chance could have had any hand in its creation. Indeed, Bediuzzaman was most concerned to convey such explanations of Divine Unity and the other truths of belief related to science and technology to the young and his students among university and school students. To mention these letters here also redresses the balance somewhat, for while in the last ten years of his life he concerned himself to a greater degree with social and political matters, his purpose and aim was still to serve the Qur'an and belief through the publication and spreading of the *Risale-i Nur*.

The 'Guide for Youth' Trial—1952

In January 1952, Bediuzzaman went to Istanbul. It was his first visit there since he had stayed there on his way to exile twenty-seven years earlier. The previous year a number of his students at Istanbul University had had printed two thousand copies of *A Guide for Youth* in the new letters, as a result of which the public prosecutor had opened a case against Bediuzzaman. The summons came for him to attend Istanbul First Criminal Court in January, 1952. The charges, under the 'elastic' Article 163 of the Criminal Code, were that *A Guide for Youth* was "religious propaganda, which, contrary to the principle of secularism, had been written for the purpose of adapting the state system to religious principles."[19]

Coming from Isparta, Bediuzzaman was in court for the first hearing on 22 January, 1952. It took place on an upper floor of the Court House, which now serves as the Main Post Office. For the two months or so he was in Istanbul, Bediuzzaman stayed first in the Akşehir Palas Hotel, close to the court in Sirkeci then he moved to the Reşadiye Hotel in the Fatih district. During his stay he was visited by a constant flood of visitors; hundreds of old friends and acquaintances, *Risale-i Nur* students, some well-known figures, and many others, including large numbers of young people. The three court hearings—and particularly the second and third—attracted literally thousands. Once again the trial served to publicise Bediuzzaman and the *Risale-i Nur* movement in a way those who had instigated it can hardly have wished.

The courtroom and corridors were filled to overflowing for the first hearing. The indictment and experts' report were read then Bediuzzaman was questioned. The matters with which he was accused by the report in regard to *A Guide for Youth* demanded a prison sentence of five years and included matters additional to exploiting religion for political purposes, such as, "supporting religious education", "encouraging Islamic dress and conduct for women", and "attempting to acquire personal prestige and influence."[20] Three Istanbul lawyers undertook Bediuzzaman's defence for the trial. Following his reply, the court was adjourned till 19 February at 2 o'clock.

In addition to this trial, Bediuzzaman was questioned concerning a part of *A Guide for Youth* that appeared in the magazine *Volkan*, but since the work had been acquitted by the Denizli Court in 1943, in this case the decision was taken that retrial was not permissible.[21]

The news had got around about 19 February and from an early hour hundreds of well-wishers and Bediuzzaman's students started to fill the court building in order to see him and follow the proceedings. By the time he and the lawyers and judges arrived the crowd was so dense inside the court that in the courtroom itself, the spectators had occupied even the space round the judges' bench, while outside the building the buses could not pass for the throng and were re-routed.[22] In the court the police seemed incapable of doing anything, nor was any attention paid to the judge when he ordered the crowd out. It was not till at the judge's request, Bediuzzaman turned and made a sign that the crowd moved back out of the room and the trial could begin.[23]

First heard were the statements of the printer who had printed *A Guide for Youth* and the police, then Bediuzzaman's objections to the Experts Report. The defence lawyers criticised it in severe terms and at length. Then, on Bediuzzaman requesting permission to perform the afternoon prayers as the time was growing short, the Court was adjourned till 5 March. He left amid cheers and applause and was driven to the Sultan Ahmed Mosque.

When it came to 5 March the police were out in force to prevent crowds forming in the court building. Nevertheless the court was packed to hear first Muhsin Alev, the student who had had the work printed, then the defence speeches of Bediuzzaman, then his three lawyers.

Once again Bediuzzaman pointed out that what he was, and had been, accused of principally was "opposing the regime", but on condition public order was not disturbed in any way, to do so could not be considered a crime. On the contrary, to oppose wrong, oppression, and unlawfulness was licit and a genuine element of justice. Secondly was the charge of disturbing public security, but six courts in six provinces having been unable to produce any evidence for this proved that Nurju's—*Risale-i Nur* students—were preservers of the peace. As for exploiting religion for political ends, again the courts had cleared him of this and to accuse someone of over eighty years of age who was "at the door of the grave" and owned nothing in the world was entirely unjust and wrong. Bediuzzaman concluded his speech by saying:

> Respected judges, for twenty-eight years they have oppressed and wronged me and my students in this way. The prosecutors in the courts did not hold back from insulting us. We met it all with patience and continued on the way of serving belief and the Qur'an. We forgave the officials of the former regime for their tyranny and oppression, for they met the end they deserved, while we gained our rights and our freedom. We thank Almighty God for giving us this opportunity to speak these words before just and believing judges like yourselves.[24]

Bediuzzaman's three lawyers then presented their defences[25] and the judges withdrew to deliberate. Their unanimous decision was announced; once again, acquittal. The announcement met with resounding applause from Bediuzzaman's students and the spectators.[26] In later years the chief judge of the case said of that day:

> He was an intelligent person; he foresaw the result of the trial from the way it was going. He did not display the slightest trace

of anxiety or excitement, and was relaxed and at ease as though speaking with his friends in his own house. He spoke with an Eastern accent.[27]

Akşehir Palas and Reşadiye Hotels

There are numerous accounts of visits to Bediuzzaman in the Akşehir Palas and Reşadiye Hotels from among the many different people who visited him during his brief stay of two to three months. Also there are descriptions by those of his close students who remained with him and attended to his needs. One of these was Muhsin Alev, Bediuzzaman's fellow-accused in the trial. He wrote: "When Ustādh came to Istanbul, it was as though its entire populace poured into the Akşehir Palas Hotel. Every day hundreds of people visited him. Among them were many well-known people." Muhsin Alev goes on to describe visits by the famous poet and writer and producer of *Büyük Doğu* magazine, Necip Fazıl Kısakürek,[28] and then, in the Reşadiye Hotel, Osman Yüksel Serdengeçti, who wrote for and published *Serdengeçti* magazine.[29] In fact, it was articles appearing in these and other publications of the Islamic press such as Eşref Edip's *Sebilürreşad* that had contributed to informing the young educated classes about Bediuzzaman and the *Risale-i Nur*, and continued to do so. Muhsin Alev himself had been active in this field. One of the most descriptive of these accounts is by one of three youths, then students at Galatasaray Lycée, who had benefited from these publications. The student in question, Mehmet Şevket Eygi, went on to bring out various newspapers and publications in later years. These three friends, who secretly read handwritten duplicated copies of the *Risale-i Nur* in school, decided to visit him. His description shows the modest conditions Bediuzzaman chose, even when staying in a hotel, together with the interest he showed in these boys.

> We entered the small room in which Bediuzzaman was staying on the top floor of the hotel. It had a low ceiling and small

windows. Ustādh was sitting cross-legged on the bed, and was wearing something like a scarf of coloured material as a turban. There was a small radio made of baccalite on a shelf on the wall. There wasn't anything else. We sat on the floor.

Ustādh spoke Turkish with an Eastern accent...He was pleased we were Galatasaray students, and spoke to us giving us advice. He dwelt particularly on the dangers of Bolshevism. Communism was not all that widespread in Turkey at that time...and it was truly great far-sightedness that he would perceive that it would be such a problem for Turkey in the future.[30]

Just as visits such as this led directly to increased coverage and support of Bediuzzaman and the *Nur* movement in the Islamic press, so too at this time Bediuzzaman's Istanbul visit afforded the opportunity for a number of young *Risale-i Nur* students to visit Bediuzzaman for the first time.

In his account, Muhsin Alev also describes Bediuzzaman's trips around the city of Istanbul visiting places he had frequented in earlier days, such as the old War Ministry which now housed Istanbul University, where he faced the wrathful pashas in the Court Martial set up after the 31st March Incident in 1909.[31] Another student who went to visit Bediuzzaman in the Reşadiye Hotel describes the sprightly way he walked, stepping lightly up onto the pavement opposite the hotel "like a youth of twenty", and how, when he emerged from the great Fatih Mosque after attending the prayers, he was mobbed by such a large and enthusiastic crowd, all wanting to kiss his hand, that he could only be saved by jumping into a taxi.[32]

Nevertheless, as ever, Bediuzzaman's enemies were not idle and a further attempt to poison him was made while staying at the Akşehir Palas Hotel in Sirkeci. The incident was described by İbrahim Fakazlı, one of Bediuzzaman's students from İnebolu, who had taken over the night in question from Muhsin, Zübeyir, and Ziya Arun. Poison was thrown in Bediuzzaman's food, which he had left outside the window to cool. When he understood what had happened, he alerted the hotel staff, and it was learnt that among the occupants of the adjacent room was an Armenian Taşnak militant. He was caught and confessed to Bediuzzaman that he had come that day from Edirne with the intention of carrying out the cowardly crime. İbrahim Fakazlı witnessed this.[33]

Emirdağ

Bediuzzaman returned to Emirdağ soon after the acquittals in March of 1952, writing in a letter that much as he wanted to meet with his many friends who wished to visit him, due to his age, ill health and weakness from poison, so long as it was not essential, he no longer had the strength and could not speak much. "However", he wrote,

> I tell you certainly that each part of the *Risale-i Nur* is a Said. Whichever part you look at you will benefit ten times more than meeting me in person, and also you will have truly met with me.[34]

Again on his return to Emirdağ Bediuzzaman was subject to unlawful harassment, which led to a further court case. This time it was at the hands of some gendarmes and concerned his dress. One day in the month of Ramaḍān, which in 1952 began towards the end of May, Bediuzzaman went out of the town into the surrounding country to take some exercise. Though alone, he was followed by three gendarmes and a sergeant, who, when he was sitting alone in the hills, approached him and told him to remove his turban and put on a hat. They then forcibly took him back to Emirdağ to the police station.

As a result of this entirely arbitrary infringement of his liberty, Bediuzzaman wrote a petition to the Justice and Interior Ministries in Ankara by way of a complaint, wanting his students in Ankara to give copies to sympathetic deputies. One of his students there sent a copy also to a newspaper printed in Samsun called *Büyük Cihad*. Upon the newspaper printing the petition, the Samsun public prosecutor opened proceedings against Bediuzzaman, and a summons arrived in Emirdağ ordering him to appear in Samsun Criminal Court. Bediuzzaman wrote a reply referring them to his lengthy and unrefuted defences of five previous cases since they were repeating the same old charges.[35] He also obtained medical reports stating he was unfit to travel. In the meantime, on 22 November 1952, the Malatya Incident occurred, in which an attempt was made on the life of a well-known journalist, Ahmet Emin Yalman. It was blown up out of all proportion by the leftist press, and finally the government bowed to pressure and closed down Islamic newspapers and arrested many supporters of religion. Among these were the *Büyük Cihad* and its owner, and also Bediuzzaman's close student Mustafa Sungur, who was in Samsun and had also had an article published in the paper. Mustafa Sungur was held in Samsun Prison and first convicted and sentenced to one and a half years, much to Bediuzzaman's wrath,[36] but the Appeal Court subsequently reversed the decision, and on the court reconvening, was acquitted.[37]

The Samsun public prosecutor insisted on Bediuzzaman's attending the court to answer the charges against him, so finally the seventy-five-year-old Bediuzzaman decided to make the journey. He reached Istanbul, but here was taken ill and obtaining further medical reports requested to be permitted to give his defence in Istanbul Criminal Court. Once again the case resulted in acquittal. However, it served as a cause to bring him to Istanbul a second time, and on this occasion he stayed three months.

The Pakistan Deputy Education Minister's Visit

Before describing Bediuzzaman's stay in Istanbul, there are one or two events which occurred previously and should not go unmentioned. One of these was the unofficial visit to Bediuzzaman of the Deputy Education Minister in the Pakistan government, Sayyid 'Ali Akbar Shah, who was on an official visit to Turkey. The visit was made at the suggestion of the Turkish Education Minister, Tevfik İleri, and occurred according to the student who accompanied him, in 1952. Bediuzzaman describes the visit in a letter congratulating those he was writing to on the occasion of the Prophet's birthday, which that year fell on 28 November.[38]

In Salih Özcan's description of the visit, Bediuzzaman requested him to act as interpreter, since their common language was Arabic.

Bediuzzaman explained the *Risale-i Nur* and its method of service to his visitor, but when the discussion became more complex, Salih Özcan had difficulty in interpreting. "Whereupon", he writes, "Bediuzzaman straightened himself up onto his knees [on the bed on which he sat] and began to speak in the most eloquent Arabic. I had never heard such fluent and eloquent Arabic before."

The Deputy Minister was exceedingly pleased at the visit and expressed his appreciation when they returned to the hotel they had occupied in Emirdağ, wanting to visit Bediuzzaman again in the morning before leaving. Bediuzzaman did not consent to the second visit. However, as the bus they were to take to Ankara was about to leave, he appeared to see the minister off, and travelled in the bus some seven or eight kilometres sitting next to the minister before alighting. 'Ali Akbar Shah was most gratified at this. In Ankara, he addressed a gathering of university students on the subject of Bediuzzaman and the *Risale-i Nur*, and on returning to Pakistan actively publicised them. He had in fact invited Bediuzzaman to Pakistan offering him access to all the media, but Bediuzzaman replied that "the front" was in Turkey since the fundamental sickness had started there.[39] Sayyid 'Ali Akbar Shah was subsequently appointed Rector of Sind University and both kept up a correspondence with the *Risale-i Nur* students in Turkey, and did what he could to spread the *Risale-i Nur*.[40]

During the 1950's the *Risale-i Nur* found numerous new students and readers in different parts of the world, including Pakistan. The last section of Bediuzzaman's official biography, first published during his lifetime in 1958, is devoted to these developments and includes letters from *Risale-i Nur* students from as far afield as Finland and Washington, as well as various Islamic countries. Articles began to appear in such countries as Iraq[41] and Pakistan.[42] Also some of Bediuzzaman's students travelled to foreign countries to introduce the *Risale-i Nur* and establish relations, for example, to the Ḥijāz, Syria, and Iran.[43] In 1954 Bediuzzaman sent his close student Muhsin Alev to Germany,[44] to have the 'miraculous' Qur'an printed there, since repeated attempts to have it printed in Turkey had come to nothing. He remained in Berlin, actively serving the cause of the *Risale-i Nur*. Bediuzzaman previously had sent to Germany the collection, *Zülfikâr*, and other parts of the *Risale-i Nur*, which met with a good reception.[45] Bediuzzaman also received visits from religious scholars and figures from the Islamic world.[46] Links were reforged as one of his ultimate aims began to be realised: the renewal and strengthening of relations between Muslims in Turkey and other parts of the world by means of the *Risale-i Nur*. In fact it was Selahaddin Çelebi from İnebolu who, with Bediuzzaman's permission, in 1950 sent *Zülfikâr* to the Imam of the Berlin Mosque. He also sent copies to al-Azhar in Egypt, the Pakistani ambassador, and to the Pope in Rome. In response to the latter, Bediuzzaman received a letter of thanks from the Vatican dated 22 February, 1951.[47] As has been pointed out previously, although Bediuzzaman always upheld and struggled for the independence of the Islamic world against the West and the maintenance of its cultural integrity, he foresaw the co-operation of Muslims and sincere Christians in the face of aggressive atheism.[48] It is in this light also that Bediuzzaman's visit to the Greek Orthodox Patriarch of Istanbul, Patriarch Athenagoras, should be seen, which he made during his visit to Istanbul in the spring and summer of 1953.[49]

Istanbul

Bediuzzaman came to Istanbul from Emirdağ, probably between the 20th and 25th April, 1953,[50] on his way to Samsun. He stayed first in the Marmara Palas Hotel in Bayezıt then stayed one night in Çamlıca on the Asian side of the Bosphorus, after which he moved to Üsküdar, where he stayed three nights. Finally, on the invitation of one of his young students in Istanbul, Mehmet Fırıncı, Bediuzzaman moved to his house in the Draman district, close to Fatih. The family moved to another house next to their bakery, and being unable to complete his journey, Bediuzzaman stayed three months in their modest but pleasant old wooden house. It was exactly what he had been looking for.[51]

Beside obtaining medical reports and then making his defence in Istanbul Criminal Court,[52] Bediuzzaman attended the celebrations marking the five hundredth anniversary of the conquest of Istanbul by Fatih Sultan Mehmed in 1453 during his stay, received many visitors, and was able to make excursions by bus around Istanbul. He also wrote a number of important letters, one of which on the radio was included in *A Key to the World of the Risale-i Nur*. Another letter, described as a fruit of Bediuzzaman's trips in and around Istanbul, reflects his attitude towards modern life and its encouragement of wastefulness, extravagance, and idleness. Part of it is included here:

> Since modern Western civilization acts contrary to the fundamental laws of the revealed religions, its evils have come to outweigh its good aspects, its errors and harmful aspects its benefits; and general tranquillity and a happy worldly life, the true aims of civilization, have been destroyed. And since wastefulness and extravagance have taken the place of frugality and contentment, and laziness and the desire for ease have overcome endeavour and the sense of service, it has made unfortunate mankind both extremely poor and extremely lazy. In explaining the fundamental law of the revealed Qur'an: "Eat and drink, but waste not in excess" (Qur'an, 7:31), and, "Man possesses naught save that for which he strives" (Qur'an, 53:39), the *Risale-i Nur* says: Man's happiness in this life lies in frugality and endeavour, and it is through them that the rich and poor will be reconciled. I shall here make one or two brief points in accordance with this explanation.

The First: In the nomadic stage, man needed only three or four things, and it was only two out of ten who could not obtain them. But now, through wastefulness, abuse, stimulating the appetites, and such things as custom and addiction, present-day civilization has made inessential needs seem essential, and in place of the four things of which he used to be in need, modern civilized man is now in need of twenty. And it is only two out of twenty who can satisfy those needs in a totally licit way. Eighteen remain in need in some way...

Second Point: Since the wonders of modern civilization are each a dominical bounty, they require real thanks and to be utilised for the benefit of mankind. But now we see that since they have encouraged a significant number of people to be lazy and indulge in vice, and have given them the wish to heed their desires in ease and comfort, they have destroyed their eagerness for effort and endeavour. And by way of dissatisfaction and extravagance, they have driven them to dissipation, wastefulness, tyranny, and what is unlawful.

For example, as it says in *A Key to the World of the Risale-i Nur*, although the radio is a great bounty and demands thanks in the form of being used for the good of mankind, since four fifths of it are used for stimulating desires and unnecessary, meaningless trivia, it has encouraged idleness and depravity, and destroyed the eagerness for work...

In Short: Since modern Western civilization has not truly heeded the revealed religions, it has both impoverished man and increased his needs. It has destroyed the principle of frugality and contentment, and increased wastefulness, greed, and covetousness. It has opened the way to tyranny and what is unlawful. By encouraging people to take advantage of the means of dissipation, it has cast those needy unfortunates into total laziness. It has destroyed the desire for effort and work. It has encouraged depravity and dissipation and wasted their lives on useless things. Furthermore, it has made those needy and lazy people ill. Through abuse and prodigality, it has been the means of spreading a hundred sorts of diseases.[53]

During Bediuzzaman's stay in Istanbul, the famous orientalist Alfred Guillaume came to Istanbul University to give a series of five lectures. Muhsin Alev, who was about to graduate from the

Philosophy Department, and Ziya Arun, attended the first of them. The visiting orientalist proceeded to deny the Qur'anic verses about "seven heavens",[54] saying that today astronomy had made great advances and no seven "layers" have been found in the skies or in space; the verse was therefore contrary to science. On their informing Bediuzzaman, he compiled a letter on the subject, from pieces taken from the *Risale-i Nur*, and the following day they went to the university and distributed copies of it before the lecture. It was read to the orientalist, who is reputed to have cut short his lecture.[55]

That year there were tremendous celebrations for the five hundredth anniversary of the conquest of Istanbul. These reached their climax on 29 May, with the *Mehter* bands, the traditional military bands of the Ottoman armies, marching in traditional dress and playing original instruments from Topkapi at the city walls to Fatih. The population of Istanbul turned out to watch and follow them. The culmination was a ceremony at the great mosque in Fatih where Fatih Sultan Mehmet's tomb is situated. Here a platform had been erected outside the mosque and tiers of benches for the spectators. When Bediuzzaman arrived he was given a seat of honour on the platform next to the governor of Istanbul,[56] from where he followed the proceedings with real pleasure, particularly the *Mehter* bands.[57]

Although Bediuzzaman was now theoretically free to go where he pleased, he was still constantly watched and followed by the police. Mehmet Fırıncı describes how they were alarmed at losing his traces when he first arrived in Istanbul. After Bediuzzaman moved to the house in Draman, a policeman was permanently posted in front of the house. They told Mehmet Fırıncı, who was questioned at length for Bediuzzaman's staying in his house, "We are responsible for him and have to protect him."[58] One of Bediuzzaman's visitors there, the chairman of the local branch of the Millet Party, Hüseyin Cahid Payazağa, relates how a chief inspector had been assigned the job of watching the house and noting down all who visited it. Bediuzzaman was followed by police even when going to the mosque, or when making his excursions. Payazağa also writes that they were frightened of Bediuzzaman's going to Aya Sophia at the time of the Conquest celebrations, for there were rumours that he was going to walk there from Fatih.⁵⁹ In fact, as the writer Münir Çapanoğlu wrote, the reason the authorities perpetually drove Bediuzzaman from exile to exile and prison to prison was that they were frightened of him. "They were frightened of Said Nursi...of his person, of his ideology, of the fact he would raise to life the Islamic cause...from the time of the Constitutional Revolution and ever after."⁶⁰

Hüseyin Payazağa recalls too how in Draman there was a non-Muslim Greek grocer and it was there Bediuzzaman used to do his shopping. Dimitrios as he was called used to show Bediuzzaman great respect. He told Payazağa: "You don't know who this person is. If he was in Greece, they would make him a house out of gold."⁶¹ Muhsin Alev also relates how one day they went to Bakırköy to what was then open countryside to take some air, and there a Christian from Beirut called Suleyman hurried up to Bediuzzaman. Bediuzzaman did not turn the man away, but talked with him for a while, even accepting the coffee he gave him.⁶²

It was the month of Ramaḍān while Bediuzzaman was in Istanbul, and Mehmet Fırıncı notes that he hardly slept for the whole month, spending the nights in worship and prayer while continuing his usual daily activities of reading the *Risale-i Nur* and teaching his students, correcting proofs, receiving visitors, and so on. At night the local people would gather in the house opposite to watch Bediuzzaman, as he continued his worship in bright electric light till the morning. On their finally closing the windows, the people objected saying, "Why have you closed them? We were reciting our prayers and supplications along with the Hojaefendi?"⁶³

Isparta

Bediuzzaman returned to Emirdağ towards the end of July, and after a week moved to the Yıldız Hotel in Eskişehir. In August, towards the end of the month, he travelled to Isparta. Here, after staying a week in the hotel of one of his students, Nuri Benli, he moved to the rented house which, although he continued to return to Emirdağ and Eskişehir for visits, now became his base. Indeed, he loved Isparta above all places and wanted to spend his last years there among his numerous students. The house he took had garden on two sides and was spacious, with rooms for both himself and those of his students who now stayed permanently with him.

Having four or five of his closest students living with him was an important change in the way he had ordered his life over the years. It had also been his unchanging rule to admit no one into his room from sunset, the time of the evening prayers, till the following morning, and had had his door locked on both the outside and the inside. Now his students, most usually Zübeyir Gündüzalp, Tahiri Mutlu, Mustafa Sungur, Bayram Yüksel, and Ceylan Çalışkan saw to his personal needs, and were allowed to enter his room if the need arose. Nevertheless, it was still Bediuzzaman's practice to be constantly occupied, and their room and activities remained separate. Thus, on the one hand they saw to all his needs, for Bediuzzaman was now approaching eighty years of age, and on the other, he was training these students for their important future roles in the *Nur* movement.

It was at this time that Bediuzzaman starting holding readings and study sessions of the *Risale-i Nur* (*dars*) as a group. This practice was followed by *Risale-i Nur* students all over the country and became the hallmark and central feature of the *Risale-i Nur* movement. Bediuzzaman and his students held these readings after the morning prayers and very often they would continue for as much as five or six hours. All present would read out loud in turn from one of the books of the *Risale-i Nur*, and Bediuzzaman would explain and illustrate it. Bayram Yüksel, who has provided the most details of these years, writes that he "had the energy and youth of someone of twenty, growing younger the more he read", while his young students lacked the endurance to keep going for that length of time.⁶⁴

In his account,⁶⁵ Bayram Yüksel gives many personal details about Bediuzzaman, about his food, his dress and his cleanliness, the awe-inspiring manner in which he performed the five daily prayers—always just as the time for each had been entered, how he was never idle, the importance he attached to the prompt and efficient carrying out of any matter in hand, and to the correction of proofs and handwritten copies of the *Risale-i Nur*. He describes his extreme frugality, and also his kindness to animals. In connection with the latter he describes how when going for excursions in the countryside, Bediuzzaman would study "the great book of the universe", and urge them to study it. He had affection for all creatures and extraordinary compassion for them. His interest and compassion extended to all the creatures they encountered from dogs to ants. He also tells of how in the house in Isparta, which was a traditional wooden house, the mice used to eat all the books and papers they put in the loft for safekeeping with the exception of copies of the *Risale-i Nur*. Bediuzzaman used to say that the mice would not harm them, and indeed they did not. Bayram Yüksel goes on to say that he witnessed many things of this nature, but that he did not record them as Bediuzzaman did not wish attention to be drawn to *karāmāt*, or his powers of this sort.

In 1954, Bediuzzaman returned to Barla, his first visit since he had left there twenty years earlier, and wept with emotion as he entered his first *Risale-i Nur Madrasah*, where he had lived for eight years, and saw the mighty plane tree which stands outside it, for it was here and in the gardens and mountains of Barla that the greater part of the *Risale-i Nur* had been written.⁶⁶

With his increasing years these trips became difficult for him, but every day he felt the need to go out into the countryside to take in the fresh air. So finally in 1955 his leading students from Isparta, İnebolu, and Emirdağ clubbed together and bought first a jeep, and then, when it was seen this was too uncomfortable for Bediuzzaman on the rough roads of that time, they exchanged it for a 1953 Chevrolet. This he used for his remaining years.[67]

The Publishing of the *Risale-i Nur* and Other Activities

Prior to the final Afyon Court decision in 1956 to return all the confiscated copies of the *Risale-i Nur*, handwritten copies continued to be reproduced on duplicating machines in Isparta and İnebolu. These were still for the most part in the Ottoman script. In Ankara and other places young *Risale-i Nur* students also reproduced copies, some of which were in the new letters, but this was on a small scale. An important part of the work now was reproduction of the Bediuzzaman's letters—the *Lahika* or Additional Letters. Up to 1953 these were copied out onto waxed paper by Hüsrev in Isparta, and then taken to the village of Sav, where they were duplicated and distributed countrywide. The large collections, also duplicated there, were sent to Istanbul to be bound then returned in book form. The *Risale-i Nur* students, and particularly Hüsrev, were constantly watched by the police. They still had to act with extreme circumspection, always on the alert against possible raids and harassment of other sorts.[68]

Following Bediuzzaman's visit to Istanbul in 1953, young *Risale-i Nur* students including Mehmet Fırıncı in whose house Bediuzzaman had stayed, formed themselves into a group and by degrees undertook similar activities for the publishing and distribution of the *Risale-i Nur* as far as their limited means allowed. Finally they were given the use of a house near the Süleymaniye Mosque where they were able to install duplicating machines, all in the greatest secrecy. This house became the first '*Risale-i Nur* Study Centre' (*dershane*) in Istanbul, and these students also formed the nucleus of *Risale-i Nur* students in Istanbul, holding the communal readings of the *Risale-i Nur* in many places throughout the city and with groups of people from all walks of life.[69]

Bediuzzaman attached the greatest importance to these activities, particularly to the publication, and after they were printed, the proofs. Those in the new letters, he would correct together with one of his students. It often happened that when out in the country he would suddenly decide to return, and he and his students would find one of the Istanbul or Ankara students awaiting him with proofs to be corrected. Bediuzzaman would immediately correct them and do nothing else till they were completed. He also concerned himself with these young students, most of whom were well-educated, reading to them and teaching them from the *Risale-i Nur* and encouraging them to study it.

Bediuzzaman was seeing now the fruition of the labours of thirty years of exile, imprisonment, and torment. Especially after the *Risale-i Nur* began to be printed on modern presses in the new letters in 1957 in Ankara and Istanbul, he declared: "This is the *Risale-i Nur's* festival. My duty is finished. This is the time I have long waited for. Now I can go." He was so filled with joy, he could not stop in one place, wanting to make excursions to Eğridir and its lake, to Barla, and to all the many places of beauty around Isparta, whether by horse, donkey, or car.[70]

Firstly, Bediuzzaman had wanted the Prime Minister, Menderes, to print the *Risale-i Nur* officially, and one of the Isparta deputies, Dr Tahsin Tola, had approached him on the matter. Menderes had great respect for Bediuzzaman and had met the suggestion favourably, telling Dr Tola to organise it through the Directorate of Religious Affairs. The attempt did not get further than that, however, and it was at that point that Bediuzzaman instructed his students to have it printed.[71] Dr Tola was able to secure the paper through the Democrat Government, at a time of shortage, and first of all they had printed *Sözler, The Words*. Taking advantage of his parliamentary immunity, Tahsin Tola supervised the sending of it to Istanbul to be bound. The *Risale-i Nur* students still worked under constant fear of police intervention. Following this, the other main collections of *The Flashes* (*Lem'alar*), and *Letters*

(*Mektûbat*) were printed.⁷² At the same time, the students in Istanbul started printing ten thousand copies of *The Short Words*, two thousand five hundred of which they immediately posted to various places in Anatolia. They also printed five thousand copies of *A Letter to Women*.⁷³

In 1958 some of Bediuzzaman's close students, primarily Mustafa Sungur and Zübeyir, prepared Bediuzzaman's official biography. Wanting attention to be focussed on the *Risale-i Nur*, Bediuzzaman cut out most of the sections describing his personal life and exploits. There was a dispute as to whether or not photographs should be included, and on Bediuzzaman's indication a number were added.⁷⁴

Bediuzzaman gave importance to translations during these years, both from Turkish into Arabic—to further spread the *Risale-i Nur* in the Islamic world, and of the Arabic parts into Turkish. While he himself translated *The Damascus Sermon* into Turkish in 1951, his younger brother Abdülmecid, who was then Mufti of Ürgüp near Kayseri, translated *The Staff of Moses* into Arabic at Bediuzzaman's suggestion. He wanted to interest many quarters in this work.⁷⁵ Later, in 1955 Abdülmecid translated the Qur'anic commentary written during the First World War, *Signs of Miraculousness* (*İşârâtü'l-İ'caz*), and his *Mesnevi-i Nuriye*, from Arabic into Turkish.⁷⁶ The Turkish translation of *İşârâtü'l-İ'caz* was then printed in Ankara in the new letters of the Latin alphabet.

The *Risale-i Nur*'s 'Positive' Method of Service and Relations with the Democrat Government

Even if still under threat of police action, the legal and open printing of the *Risale-i Nur* was a tremendous victory for Bediuzzaman and his students over those who for thirty years had employed every means to eliminate and silence them. The *Risale-i Nur* and its method of "positive action", the patient and silent struggle to save and strengthen belief in God and the other truths of religion by peaceful means—primarily the written word—and non-involvement in politics had prevailed over those who behind the screen of secularization were seeking to eradicate Islam and extinguish belief. The unique function of the *Risale-i Nur* in the renewal of belief and revitalization of Islam demanded this method, which had few counterparts in the Islamic world, where attempts to serve Islam were often by direct, violent, or political methods, which Bediuzzaman called "material" (*māddī*).

As described in the introduction to the present chapter, the *Risale-i Nur* method was peaceful *jihād* or '*jihād* of the word' (*maʿnawī jihād*) in the struggle against aggressive atheism and irreligion. By working solely for the spread and strengthening of belief, it was to work also for the preservation of internal order and peace and stability in society in the face of the moral and spiritual destruction of the forces of irreligion which aimed to destabilise society and create anarchy, and to form "a barrier" against them. Since the Democrat Party also understood the dangers which these posed and took a positive stand against them, and furthermore took steps to strengthen Islam, Bediuzzaman described the Democrats as "assisting" the *Risale-i Nur* students in their struggle and offered them their support. And he himself gave them advice and guidance on these matters from time to time.

Thus, since, unlike many groups and individuals who mistakenly aimed to further the cause of Islam by 'negative' means the *Risale-i Nur* students followed this 'positive' method, the Democrat government took a lenient attitude towards them, permitting the open publication of the *Risale-i Nur* after it had been cleared by Afyon Court in 1956 and not attempting to repress the movement. In view of these facts, Bediuzzaman continued to support the Democrats, and in particular the Prime Minister, Menderes, throughout the ten years they were in power and in the face of the opposition Menderes faced from all quarters including some Islamist groups. Indeed, Menderes and the government had to sustain opposition of the most vengeful and ruthless kind from the ousted Republican People's Party and particularly its leader, İsmet İnönü. This support was despite Bediuzzaman and the *Risale-i Nur* students continuing to be subject to various sorts of harassment at the hands of officials—mostly supporters of the RPP—and to be called up before the law, and also despite the fact that the Democrats were, in Bediuzzaman's words, "the lesser of two evils" and that among them were individuals who could not be considered sympathetic towards religion. In his view Menderes performed great services for the cause of Islam and did much to reverse the harm of the quarter century of RPP rule. Despite the army coup which overthrew him two months after Bediuzzaman's death in 1960, and subsequent coups, the religious freedoms he returned to the Turkish people were not subsequently lost and made possible the future blossoming of Islam, in which the *Risale-i Nur* played such an important part. In fact, Bediuzzaman told Giyaseddin Emre, elected as Independent Deputy for Muş to the National Assembly in 1954, who visited Bediuzzaman on numerous occasions:

> Adnan Menderes is a champion of religion; he has performed great services for religion and will perform [more]. But he won't see the fruits of this that he wishes. I too have performed services for religion, I can't conceal it, and like Adnan Bey, I also won't see the results. The fruits of both will become apparent in the future.[77]

Bediuzzaman's Support for the Baghdad Pact

It is in the light of this positive attitude towards the Democrats of Bediuzzaman and the *Risale-i Nur* movement, and in those often difficult and hostile conditions their always aiming to draw them with advice and guidance towards further, more far-reaching measures favouring Islam and religion that his letter of support for the Baghdad Pact should be seen. Indeed, this method of service enabled the movement to emerge as a significant force within the country, although the *Risale-i Nur* students themselves did not participate in politics. Also Bediuzzaman's support for the pact shows his support of Turkey's and some Islamic countries joining the Western alliance against the threat of communism, in the same way that he sent one of his students to fight in Korea with his blessing.

The Baghdad Pact was first signed in February 1955 between Turkey and Iraq, and was subsequently joined by Pakistan, Iran, and Britain. In connection with this agreement Bediuzzaman wrote a letter of congratulations[78] to Menderes and the President, Celâl Bayar, applauding the move as a necessary first step towards securing peace in the area, and as someone who had studied its problems for some fifty-five years, he pointed out the two solutions he had found.

Bediuzzaman supported Turkey's agreement with Iraq and the other Muslim countries in the Baghdad Pact primarily because it realigned her with the Islamic world and was a step towards re-establishing close relations between Turkey and the Arab world, which had been virtually non-existent since the collapse of the Ottoman Empire after the First World War. Islamic Unity of a non-political nature would be a source of strength for Turkey, particularly against communism and irreligion, and he encouraged Menderes and the Democrats to work for and benefit from in a number of letters.[79]

In his letter about the Pact, Bediuzzaman explained that the greatest danger for the area lay in "negative nationalism" and racialism. Just as it had caused harm to the Muslim peoples in the past, so again at that time there were signs that it was being exploited by "covert atheists" in order to destroy Islamic brotherhood and prevent the Muslim nations from uniting. Whereas the true nationality or nationhood of both Turks and Arabs was Islam; their Arabness and Arab nationality and Turkishness had fused with Islam. The new alliance would repulse the danger of racialism, and besides gaining for the Turkish nation "four hundred million brothers", it would also gain for them the "friendship of eight hundred million Christians." That is to say, Bediuzzaman saw it as an important step towards general peace and reconciliation, of which all were in such need.

The two solutions Bediuzzaman had found on learning of the explicit threats to the Qur'an, Islam, and the Islamic world some sixty years previously had been the *Risale-i Nur* and his Eastern University, the Medresetü'z-Zehra. Both were effective means of establishing Islamic Unity. The *Risale-i Nur* served to develop "the brotherhood of belief"; as it was already demonstrating throughout the Islamic world and beyond. So too it had defeated atheistic philosophy and other means of corruption. Thus, Bediuzzaman called on the President and Prime Minister to use the means at their disposal to make the *Risale-i Nur*, "this manifestation of the Qur'an's miraculousness", better known to the Islamic world.

As for the Medresetü'z-Zehra, Bediuzzaman intended for it to play the central and unifying role in Asia that al-Azhar performs in Africa. Besides combating racialism and nationalism by acting as a centre of learning and attracting students from "Arabia, India, Iran, Caucasia, Turkestan, and Kurdistan" and thus contributing to the development of a sense of "Islamic nationhood", this large Islamic university would also "reconcile the sciences of philosophy and those of religion, and make peace between European civilization and the truths of Islam." In thus unifying secular and religious education, it would be both a modern secular school and a religious school. As has been described in previous chapters, Bediuzzaman received money at various times for its construction, but due to the vicissitudes of the times, the project could not be realised.

Doubtless the main reason Bediuzzaman mentioned the Medresetü'z-Zehra was that the new president, Celâl Bayar, had announced in a speech in Van in 1951 that the Democrat government planned to build a university there in eastern Turkey. Bediuzzaman had met the announcement with gratification, equating it with his Medresetü'z-Zehra, and writing to inform his students of it under the heading "Some Important Good News for *Risale-i Nur* Students".[80] Again in the present letter, he applauded the president's move, both for Turkey as a whole, and the east of the country, and as "a foundation stone of general peace in the

Middle East." Only he stressed that for it to perform this vital function, the sciences of religion should be taken as the basis of the university, for "the destruction" was caused by external forces and was not of a physical nature, but was "moral and spiritual" (ma'nawī). What would counter and reverse the destruction also had to be of a moral and spiritual nature, "as powerful as an atom bomb". As a specialist on these matters of some fifty-five years' standing, Bediuzzaman had the right to speak concerning them.

It may be added that although the government completed the project and the Eastern University was opened in November 1958, it was built in Erzurum, not Van, and given the name, Ataturk University. The campaign the RPP and some newspapers conducted against the government protesting that it was "building Said Nursi's *madrasah*" may have had some bearing on this.

In connection with the Baghdad Pact, it might also be mentioned that Bediuzzaman's students who were with him at the time of the revolution in Iraq, 14 July 1958, have recorded his extreme distress at the events there. This was not only at the brutal killings, many of the victims of which were descendants of the Prophet (ṣ), but also because the revolution "put a bomb to the auspicious developments" of the pact and the moves towards Islamic Unity and co-operation. However it is apparent from a statement Bediuzzaman made on the fourth day after the revolution that he expected unity on a broader scale to result from such actions on the behalf of communism and unbelief, for he said:

> I was expecting Germany, Japan, India, Pakistan, America, and the Islamic world to strike together against absolute unbelief. It means the time has not yet come.[81]

Other Matters on which the Third Said Addressed the Democrats

It was because from time to time Bediuzzaman concerned himself with matters such as the Baghdad Pact that these last ten years of his life are known as the period of the Third Said. The favourable attitude towards Islam of Menderes and a number of Democrats prompted him to put forward to them certain key principles which would counter the destructive moves made by "those who exploited politics for the cause of irreligion" and establish unity and harmony in society and solidarity with the Islamic world. In order to understand this endeavour, and also the opposition he continued to receive from the RPP and the enemies of religion, which demonstrated their fear of him and his penetrating analyses of the situation, it is worth recalling briefly the nature of the struggle.

The basis of the argument that had now been continuing in Turkey for over a century and a half had been over what was necessary firstly to save the Ottoman Empire, and then when the Empire collapsed, to set Turkey on the road to progress and prosperity. Simply, on the one hand, there had been those who had favoured Westernization and adopting 'man-made' philosophy of some sort as the ideological basis of the state and society. On the other, there were those who believed that religion, Islam, was the source of true civilization. Among these some, like Bediuzzaman, stated that it was necessary to take science and technology from the West but nothing else. Thus, in this struggle between 'philosophy' and 'religion', Westernization and Islam, which had turned into a battle between belief and unbelief and had been so bitter in Turkey, he had dedicated his life to proving that Islam and religion were superior to Western philosophy and civilization, and that mankind's happiness and salvation were to be found only in them. In numerous places in the *Risale-i Nur*, he proves and demonstrates this in the context of belief. Now to return to the Third Said, primarily by means of letters to Menderes and the Democrats, Bediuzzaman diagnosed some of the ills in the socio-political situation of that time, pointed out both their source and origin in philosophy, and their possible dire consequences, and at the same time, the remedies, which were in the form of basic principles taken from the Qur'an or Ḥadīths. The following is a brief example.

The "fundamental law", as he called these basic Islamic principles, that he most often put forward was the Qur'anic verse: "*No bearer of burdens can bear the burden of another*,"[82] which he used in its meaning of "No one is answerable for another's faults or errors."[83] He frequently used this principle in different contexts as the solution for various ills in society resulting from the adoption of Western principles.

In one letter, he wrote that the reason he had altogether given up politics for nearly forty years was that contrary to the basic principle of the above-mentioned verse, one of the most basic principles of "human politics", that is, politics and diplomacy based on principles taken from "philosophy" of some sort rather than divinely revealed religion, was, "Individuals may be sacrificed for the good of the nation and society. Everything may be sacrificed for the sake of the country." This "fundamental human law" had resulted in appalling crimes throughout history, including the two World Wars this century, which had "overturned a thousand years of human progress", and had given the licence for the annihilation of ninety innocents on account of ten criminals. The verse taught the principle that no one was responsible for another's crimes, and no innocent person could be sacrificed without his consent, even for the whole of humanity. It establishes true justice for man.[84]

The main context in which he advises the adoption of the "fundamental law", "*No bearer of burdens can bear the burdens of another*," is in connection with the extreme partisanship among supporters of the various political parties which was then being "implanted" in Turkish life. He describes the dire social consequences of this partisanship as firstly destroying love and brotherhood, the foundations of unity and consensus. Moreover, through such clashes, the three or four opposing forces or parties lose their power, so that the power that remains is insufficient to secure what is beneficial to the country and maintain internal order and security. This partisanship could even therefore allow the seeds of revolution to become established. So too the resulting weakness prepares the ground for foreign intervention. With its meaning, "No one is responsible for the mistakes of another. Even if it is his brother, or tribe, or group, or party, one cannot be considered guilty because of another's crime. Even if he gives it his moral support, he will only be answerable in the hereafter, not in this world", the above-mentioned Qur'anic principle prevents extreme partisanship. It should be taken as the rule of conduct along with other "basic principles", such as "Indeed, the believers are brothers" (Qur'an, 49:10), and, "Hold firm to God's rope, all together, and be not divided among yourselves" (Qur'an, 3:103).

Bediuzzaman also examined this same question in connection with "the accusation of [political] reaction (*irtijā'*)", which ever since the 31st March Incident in 1909 had been a favourite means of attacking religion by "those who make politics the tool of irreligion." It was continually used against Menderes and the Democrats throughout their ten years in power by the RPP and İnönü in particular. It will be recalled how an outcry of "reaction" was raised against Bediuzzaman and his students by the RPP in 1934 before the Eskişehir trials. The newspapers were the usual means of these campaigns being carried out. In connection with the matter in question, Bediuzzaman points out that the truth had been turned on its head, for those who attack religion in the name of civilization by making accusations of political reaction are in reality the reactionaries. Because, for example, the 'human' principle which allows individuals to be sacrificed for the good of society, permits minor wrongs when it comes to the good of the state, and has led to whole villages being wiped out on account of one criminal, and so on. And in the First World War, thirty million unfortunates perished on account of the criminal political mistakes of three thousand. Those who supported a barbaric principle which thus destroys the well-being, justice, and peace of mankind are retrogressing to a barbarism of former times. Yet, these true reactionaries pose as patriots and accuse of political reaction those who work to secure unity and brotherhood through

Qur'anic principles such as those mentioned above, which are the means to true justice and progress.[85]

Another "fundamental Islamic law" which Bediuzzaman advised Menderes and the Democrats to adopt was taken from the Ḥadīth, "A nation's ruler is its servant." Because, Bediuzzaman wrote, "At this time, due to the lack of Islamic training and weakness in worship, egotism has been strengthened and tin-pot dictators have multiplied." That is to say, under the former regime, which aimed to substitute Western civilization for Islam, as a bribe to its supporters, positions in government and the administration ceased being about service and became a means of domination and despotism. Everyone's rights were trampled on and justice was completely destroyed.[86] As early as 1952 Bediuzzaman warned Menderes that these discountenanced officials, many of whom remained in their positions after 1950 but were compelled by the Democrats to serve the nation rather than oppressing and exploiting it, formed a current of opposition ready to attack the Democrats. A second current was the racialist nationalists.[87] In fact, both played an important role in the Democrats' overthrow.

Further Victories and the Struggle Continues

The struggle between these various forces continued. Rather, it grew fiercer and more intense. The opposition of İnönü and the RPP towards Menderes grew fiercer the longer the Democrat Party remained in power; with the spread and successes of the *Risale-i Nur*, supporters of the former regime, still powerful in the police, judiciary, and administrative structure, used their positions to increase pressure on the *Risale-i Nur* students. There were further court cases, a campaign of vilification in the press against Bediuzzaman and his students, and Bediuzzaman himself was held under closer surveillance.

Following the general elections of October 1957, which the Democrats again won though with a decreased majority, the opposition stepped up its campaign against the government. By

1959 this had degenerated into the open incitement of disturbances throughout the country.[88] In order to prevent the RPP returning to power in the face of the difficulties the Democrats were facing, Bediuzzaman openly gave the Democrats his vote in the elections,[89] and urged all the *Risale-i Nur* students to do likewise. As a result, the RPP, who had expected to win the elections, held Bediuzzaman responsible for their defeat. İnönü is even reported to have declared that it was the Nurju's (*Risale-i Nur* students) who defeated him.[90] This was an added element in the pressure RPP supporters now endeavoured to bring to bear on the *Risale-i Nur* students.

At the same time, with the officially free publication of the *Risale-i Nur*, as well as the freedoms that had been gained with the Democrat government, the *Nur* movement had been greatly strengthened and expanded. *Risale-i Nur* study-centres (*dershane*) were opened in every part of the country. It was the custom to bring the key of each as it was newly opened to Bediuzzaman, who would offer prayers for its success. In eastern Turkey also, through the endeavours of old students such as Hulûsi Bey and Çaycı Emin, the *Risale-i Nur* spread rapidly at this time, so that from one letter we learn that there were around two hundred *dershanes* in Diyarbakır and the east, including four or five specifically for women in Diyarbakır itself.[91] On occasion as many as a thousand people would attend the *dars*, the readings of the *Risale-i Nur*. In Ankara, Istanbul, Eskişehir, and all the main centres in Anatolia, the *Risale-i Nur* and its associated activities flourished.

The corollary of these successes was increased pressure and harassment. Bediuzzaman told Hulûsi Bey when he visited him in Emirdağ in 1957 that in the face of the threats he had been forced to take further precautions to protect himself. Another attempt had been made on his life, when an unknown person had entered his house by way of the roof and thrown poison in his water jug.[92] Then in April, 1958, RPP supporters in Nazıllı in western Anatolia hatched a plot against the local *Risale-i Nur* students, two of whom were arrested. In concert with them, the newspapers started a furore describing the Nurcus as "enemies of the reforms".[93] In response the *Risale-i Nur* students in Ankara wrote and published a letter answering their misrepresentations and lies, whereupon eleven of the leading students were arrested and held in Ankara Prison. This was the first case the lawyer Bekir Berk undertook for the *Risale-i Nur* students, who were all acquitted.[94] Bekir Berk, subsequently famous as "the Muslims' lawyer" was also appointed by Bediuzzaman as his attorney.[95] In Konya too, where the *Risale-i Nur* students were active, there were arrests and court cases[96]. At the same time the country-wide press campaign against Bediuzzaman and the *Nur* movement continued unabated, with blatant misreporting and misrepresentations. Bediuzzaman and his students did not let these attacks remain unanswered and published replies, a number of which are included in the second volume of *Emirdağ Lahikası*.[97] This wide press coverage of all of Bediuzzaman's movements and activities continued right up to the time of his death, and particularly during December 1959 and January 1960, when he made a number of journeys to Konya, Ankara, and Istanbul. The criminal charges made against the *Risale-i Nur* students were mostly under Article 163 and involved the infringement of the principle of secularism and exploitation of religion for political ends in some respect, so too the supporters of the RPP, the press, and Bediuzzaman's enemies still persisted in accusing him of pursuing political ends. That is to say, although Bediuzzaman and his students had been acquitted by courts of law on such charges on numerous occasions, in this continuing and bitter struggle, their enemies could find no other weapon with which to attack them.

Sincerity and Bediuzzaman's Health and State of Mind

As we approach the end of Bediuzzaman's life, just how baseless and far from the truth such accusations were may be further illustrated by descriptions of Bediuzzaman's health and state of mind during these last years, both by himself and his students who were constantly with him. As has been mentioned in other contexts, the basis of the *Risale-i Nur's* way is sincerity (*ikhlāṣ*), which was the secret of its successes and victories. That is, to follow no aim other than God's pleasure in the service of belief and the Qur'an, and to make such service the tool of nothing. The preservation of this sincerity precluded participation in politics or the following of personal benefits of any kind. Bediuzzaman embodied sincerity in all its aspects to the highest degree. The letters and statements describing his health at this time point out how, just as throughout his life he had inclined towards and chosen solitude and especially for the last thirty or so years, had avoided inessential social intercourse and conversation. And a second rule of his had been never to accept unreciprocated gifts, alms or charity and he had always practised absolute self-sufficiency. Now that Bediuzzaman was over eighty years of age and in need of others and their assistance two illness had been visited on him so that he could preserve his total sincerity.

The first of these illnesses was that he was very often unable to speak; after speaking for two or three minutes, he would be overcome by a terrific thirst. He wrote in a letter that at a time when enemies even were being transformed into friends, by preventing unnecessary conversation, this helped maintain maximum sincerity.[98] And the second illness was that now gifts, both material and immaterial, caused him to become ill. So much as a mouthful of food, if it was an unreciprocated gift, and even if it was from one of his closest students, would make him ill.[99] So too, Bediuzzaman defined the visits paid to him by the thousands wanting to see and speak with him as "immaterial gifts" which he was unable to repay. Then at that time when the *Risale-i Nur* was spreading so rapidly and finding so many new readers, he had been given a state of mind, like an illness, whereby he was severely discomforted by the often excessive respect and veneration shown him and by conversing and shaking hands with his visitors, again so that he could preserve the maximum sincerity.[100]

Thus, Bediuzzaman was able to receive a very few of all those who came from all over Turkey and beyond to visit him. He published letters explaining this: due to these illnesses, it was his wish to meet only those concerned with the publication of the *Risale-i Nur*. In a letter written by his students explaining this state of mind to those who came to visit him and had to return without seeing him, they wrote:

> On numerous occasions we have understood that to shake hands and have his hand kissed is as distressing for Ustādh's spirit as receiving a blow. Also he is severely distressed at being looked at and being studied. Even we may not look at him, although we attend to his needs, unless it is essential. We have understood the meaning and wisdom of this to be as follows:
>
> Since the fundamental way of the *Risale-i Nur* is true sincerity, the occurrences of the present time—speaking with people and being shown excessive respect—affect him adversely and severely, because in this age of egotism they are signs of self-worship, hypocrisy, and artificiality. For he says, if those who want to meet with him want to do so for the *Risale-i Nur* and for the hereafter, the *Risale-i Nur* leaves no need for him; each of its millions of copies is as beneficial as ten Said's. If they want to meet with him in respect of this world and worldly matters, then since he has earnestly given up the world, he suffers serious discomfort, because things concerning it are trivial and a waste of time. And if it is concerning the service and publication of the *Risale-i Nur*, it is sufficient for them to meet with his true, self-sacrificing students who serve him, his spiritual sons and brothers, in his place. He says that no need remains for him.[101]

In a letter Bediuzzaman wrote, he interprets his thirty years or so of exile, imprisonment and oppression as continual Divine warnings not to make his service to religion the means to personal benefits of any kind, thereby preserving this absolute sincerity. The oppression and tyranny he suffered due to the entirely false and unjust accusations of "exploiting religion for political ends" acted as a sort of "obstacle" preventing him from succumbing to "the great danger in the service of belief in this egotistical age", which was to make that service the means to his own spiritual progress and advancement, and to salvation from Hell and earning Paradise. Bediuzzaman had been aware that something had prevented him and it was only now that he understood the real cause. For although to work for these things was perfectly licit, at the present time in the face of the collective personality of misguidance and irreligion, the truths of the Qur'an and belief had to be taught in an effective and convincing way in order to refute and smash unbelief. And that was through such teaching being the tool of nothing. "So that those needy for belief would understand that it is only truth and reality which speaks, and the doubts of the soul and wiles of Satan would be silenced."

Bediuzzaman wrote that the secret of the *Risale-i Nur's* success in halting and defeating absolute unbelief in those difficult conditions in Turkey at that time where others had failed lay in this fact. He himself was perfectly resigned to all the torments and oppression he had suffered, forgiving those who had perpetrated them. If he had not sacrificed everything, this extraordinary power of the *Risale-i Nur* would have been lost whereas the belief of some people had been saved by only a single one of its pages.[102]

It was through this sincerity that the collective personality of the *Risale-i Nur* was formed, which Bediuzzaman described as a sort of Renewer or Regenerator of Religion (*mujaddid*). For just as a Renewer was sent each century who would serve religion and belief in exactly the required way, in the present age of the assaults of secret organizations and the collective personality of misguidance, the Renewer of Religion has to be in the form of a collective personality. Just such a collective personality was that of the *Risale-i Nur*, formed through the self-sacrificing sincerity of Bediuzzaman and his students. Indeed, Bediuzzaman described his life as a seed out of which in His mercy, Almighty God had created the valuable, fruit-bearing tree of the *Risale-i Nur*. "I was a seed; I rotted away and disappeared. All the value pertains to the *Risale-i Nur*, which is a true and faithful commentary on the Qur'an, and is its meaning."[103]

Bediuzzaman's Will and His Wish for an Unknown Grave

It was for the same reason, to preserve this "maximum sincerity" wherein lay the *Risale-Nur's* power and the secret of its success. On numerous occasions Bediuzzaman stated that he wanted the location of his grave to remain secret, known only by one or two of his closest students. He also had this written in his will.

Bediuzzaman made his will on a number of occasions, the first being in Emirdağ before being sent to Afyon in January 1948. Pointing out that it was a Sunnah of the Prophet (ṣ) to make a will since the appointed hour was unknown he named a committee of his students to which he wished his personal effects and finest volumes of the *Risale-i Nur* to be left.[104] In his later wills, he stipulates two points, one of which is the question of his grave being secret and the other, the payment of allowances to those of the *Risale-i Nur* students who worked solely for the *Risale-i Nur* and had no other means of subsistence.

Bediuzzaman stated that those who wished to visit his grave should do so only in the spirit and recite the *Fātiḥah* for his soul from afar. For, "Like in olden times, out of the desire for fame and renown, the Pharaohs turned the attention of people to themselves by means of statues, pictures and mummies, so in this fearsome age, through the heedlessness it produces, egotism directs all attention to this world by means of statues, portraits, and newspapers, and the worldly attach more importance to the worldly fame and renown of the deceased through the worldly future they imagine has thus been obtained for them. They visit the deceased in this way, rather than visiting them for God's pleasure alone and their future in the hereafter. In order not to spoil the maximum sincerity of the *Risale-i Nur* and through the mystery of that sincerity, I enjoin that my grave is not made known."[105] Just as he did not wish to receive visitors in this world, so he did not want his grave to be visited.

At various times Bediuzzaman stated where he wished to be buried. In one letter he said that he would prefer the graveyard in the village of Sav near Isparta to Barla,[106] and in one of his wills that if he died in Emirdağ, his students should bury him in the 'upper graveyard', and if in Isparta, in the 'middle graveyard'.[107] He also said he would like to die in Urfa in south-eastern Turkey, where the Patriarch Abraham lies, and which is where in fact he did die. He told this to Salih Özcan, who recounted it like this:

> It was in 1954. In Emirdağ, Mustafa Acet, Sadık and myself went up into the hills with Ustādh. When we came to a tree, Ustādh stopped at it for half an hour, deep in contemplation. Then he called us to him and said:
> "Keçeli! Keçeli! No one will know my grave. You won't know it either. I want to die in your home region [Urfa]. I want to die near the Friend of the Most Merciful [Abraham]."[108]

In 1950 Bediuzzaman had sent some of personal belongings to Urfa with one of his students saying that he himself would be going there. These included Mawlānā Khālid al-Baghdādī's gown, given to him in Kastamonu. The student later handed them over to Abdullah Yeğin,[109] Bediuzzaman's close student since his schooldays, who stayed some eight years in Urfa. He opened a *dershane* there which became an important centre of *Risale-i Nur* activities. Bediuzzaman was unable to visit it until the time of his death.

He also wrote three additional wills directing his closest students to continue his practice of paying an allowance to those *Risale-i Nur* students who had dedicated themselves to its service and who could not otherwise provide for themselves. These were probably written in 1959. It had been the Old Said's practice to provide for his students. He describes how through "the abundance resulting from frugality and contentment", he had been able to provide for the needs of twenty, thirty, and sometimes sixty students without breaking his principle of self-sufficiency. Now, the *Risale-i Nur* had begun to produce sufficient profit to do likewise. One fifth of the money obtained from selling copies of it was sufficient to pay an allowance to fifty or sixty students.

Bediuzzaman wrote that he was making plain these wishes of his in a will because, "Personally I no longer have the strength to

The Third Said

carry out the duties connected with the *Risale-i Nur*. And perhaps no need remains for me to do so. It is as though, due to being poisoned many times and because of extreme old age and illness, I do not have the endurance to continue living. Even if death, which I so long for, does not come to me, it is as though I have died outwardly." "Since I am no longer needed at all in regard to the *Risale-i Nur*, to go to the Intermediate Realm [beyond the grave] is a source of joy for me. As for you, do not be sad. Congratulate me, rather, for I am going from hardship and difficulties to mercy."[110]

Bediuzzaman's Trips to Ankara, Istanbul, and Konya

In December 1959 and January 1960, Bediuzzaman embarked on a series of trips to Ankara, Konya, and Istanbul, which in the light of the above descriptions of his health and state of mind show more than anything his extraordinary perseverance and self-sacrifice in continuing to uphold the cause of the *Risale-i Nur* in the midst of all the difficulties it was facing. To visit his students and the *Risale-i Nur* study centres (*dershane*), which was his immediate reason for the trips, when not only meeting with people and being held in esteem was such torment for him, but also his health was so poor, was truly a feat of endurance which only someone of the will and determination of Bediuzzaman could have achieved.

Bediuzzaman was now receiving repeated and insistent invitations from his students all over Turkey for him to visit them, and his trips were in response to these. At the same time they had the character of farewell visits. Ankara and Istanbul were the main centres of publication, and Konya was both an important centre of activity and where his brother, Abdülmecid, now lived, whom he had seen only once in forty years. He visited Istanbul once during these two months, Konya, three times, and Ankara, four times. His trips to Ankara had a further important purpose; he wanted to warn Menderes and the Democrats of the dangers looming before them and to suggest ways of averting them.

The clouds of disaster and revolution were gathering in Turkey. A coup attempt had already been uncovered and forestalled in 1958.[111] Unable to abide the liberalism, religious freedoms, and resurgence of Islam which were the fruits of Democrat rule, supporters of the former regime, now represented by İnönü and the RPP, were preparing to regain power by force. They could not do so by the vote or legal means. Mentioned above was Bediuzzaman's warning to Menderes in 1952 of "the possible attack" of the two currents within the opposition whose interests were most harmed by Democrat policies. Now the danger was imminent and he was anxious above everything to warn them of this. For it was not only a question of saving the Democrats, it was a question of saving the country from the consequences of once again coming under the rule of forces hostile to Islam and favourable to irreligion. However, this was only one reason for the journeys, which as a citizen Bediuzzaman had a perfect right to make, just as he had the right to offer advice to politicians. Nevertheless, İnönü and the RPP seized on them as a means of further attacking and weakening the government; besides İnönü making a series of inflammatory statements, they prompted the press to create a sensation and furore over the journeys, which resulted in over-reaction by the police and their taking extraordinary measures against Bediuzzaman wherever he visited.

Bediuzzaman's urgent advice to Menderes and the Democrat deputies who visited him in Ankara was to re-open Aya Sophia as a place of worship[112] and to make an official announcement stating that the *Risale-i Nur* was not subject to any restrictions.[113] That is to say, he saw that the only way the Democrats could now save themselves, having fallen into a position of weakness and disadvantage before İnönü and the RPP, was to stand up and make bold statements concerning the principles in which they believed, and in the service to which their former successes and popularity lay. However, for whatever reasons, Menderes did not have the will or courage to respond to these urgent suggestions and within less than six months was overthrown by the coup Bediuzzaman had foreseen, and the country was back in the hands of its former rulers. As for Bediuzzaman, when he saw that his advice evoked no response from Menderes, he complied with the wish of the authorities and remained in Emirdağ, then Isparta, making his final journey to Urfa some two months later in March.

All of Bediuzzaman's journeys were made in the Chevrolet his students had bought him. His first trip was to Ankara on 2 December 1959. Accompanied by Zübeyir, he stayed one night in the Beyrut Palas Hotel then returned to Emirdağ the following day.[114] He continued to Isparta, where he remained for two weeks, then returned to Emirdağ. On 19 December he went to Konya on the invitation of his brother, Abdülmecid. It should also be mentioned that due to his various indispositions, Bediuzzaman could not remain in one place and felt the continual need for a change of air and scene.[115]

On this occasion, in addition to Zübeyir, he was accompanied by two of his most active Ankara students, Atıf Ural and Said Özdemir. The latter described the visit. On Bediuzzaman's car stopping in the middle of Konya, it was surrounded by a large crowd. Abdülmecid arrived and spoke with this elder brother through the open window of the car. Then the police arrived on the scene and started to break up the growing crowd by force, upon which Bediuzzaman stated his wish to perform the prayers and visit the tomb of Mawlānā Jalāl al-Dīn al-Rūmī. The Director of the Museum opened the tomb especially for Bediuzzaman since it was closed that day. Taking off his shoes, he entered the tomb and offered some prayers; he was weeping. He was surrounded by people and police even in the tomb. On emerging, he told the police:

"Thank you! It is torment for me to have my hands kissed, and you prevented it. For twenty-eight years I have served this country's peace and security and have suffered imprisonment, torment, detention, and oppression. You serve its order and security physically, while I serve it in a non-material way. We have served it as much as a thousand public prosecutors and police chiefs, so look upon us as fellow-officials, not in any other way. And tell your fellow police." Bediuzzaman then returned to Emirdağ,[116] or more likely, Isparta.

That night Bediuzzaman set out again for Konya, and arriving at four o'clock in the morning was able to visit his brother's house. After speaking with Abdülmecid for a while, who was then a teacher in Konya Imam Hatip School, they performed the morning prayers together then Bediuzzaman left for Emirdağ.

On the morning of 30 December he arrived in Ankara for a second time, and again stayed in the Beyrut Palas Hotel. His visit was greeted with sensational headlines in the newspapers: "The Said Nursi Event is growing" (*Cumhuriyet*) "Said Nursi has again come to Ankara…"(*Milliyet*) "Said Nursi's eventful visit to Konya…Thousands of Nurcus poured onto the streets to greet him: the police were compelled to break up the crowd…" He received numerous visitors in the hotel: politicians and officials, including three Democrat deputies, *Risale-i Nur* students and ordinary people. The police again over-reacted and the hotel was both held in a cordon of police and gendarmes, and the inside was filled with them. That evening, Bediuzzaman gave a farewell *dars*, which among various subjects, impressed once again on the *Risale-i Nur* students that the way of the *Risale-i Nur* was that of "positive action" and the maintenance of public order and security.[117]

Before Bediuzzaman's arrival in Ankara, the police had seized copies of *The Ratifying Stamp of the Unseen Collection* in the press while Said Özdemir and others were having it printed. In connection with this, Bediuzzaman received a request from Bekir Berk in Istanbul for a signature. At the same time he was receiving invitations from his students there. The following day he set off in his car for Istanbul.

It was the first day of January 1960. The newspapers had gotten wind of his visit and by the time he and his students had reached the Piyer Loti Hotel where he was to stay, there was such a thronging crowd that it was only with the greatest difficulty that they could mount the steps to enter it. Bediuzzaman had to be shielded against the barrage of flashing cameras with an umbrella. Police had taken over the inside of the hotel, and the press had set up a headquarters there. Nevertheless, that evening, with astonishing energy, he gave a long *dars* to his students gathered in Istanbul.[118] He was to have stayed several days but the following day, 2 January, a newspaper reporter climbed onto the back balcony of his room and photographed him performing the midday prayers. He was exceedingly angry at this and decided to cut short his visit and return to Ankara. On this occasion he stayed three days, and not in the hotel but in a rented house in Bahçelievler. However, the police still did not leave him in peace.[119]

Bediuzzaman again received visitors during this stay. Three Democrat deputies have given accounts of visits although it is not absolutely clear during which of his stays they occurred. Said Köker, the deputy for Bingöl, says he paid him three visits and that he told him and the deputies with him explicitly of the 27 May military coup, which he said would occur shortly. Bediuzzaman also said he had no connection with political parties and that "he only liked Menderes."[120] Other accounts are by Giyaseddin Emre, the deputy for Muş,[121] and Dr Tahsin Tola, former Isparta deputy. Dr Tola, who had contributed so much to the publication of the *Risale-i Nur*, was in constant touch with Bediuzzaman in Ankara. He describes Bediuzzaman's anxiety at the forthcoming calamity, and how he related his urgent message to the government concerning Aya Sophia and the *Risale-i Nur*.[122] Bediuzzaman also stated in a letter that "an important reason" for his going to Ankara was to urge Menderes and the government to clean up Aya Sophia and make it once more into a place of worship.[123] It may also have been during this stay that he gave his last *dars* to his students in Ankara.

Bediuzzaman left Ankara on 6 January and went once again to Konya. On 5 January he had given a long statement to the Time correspondent, who had wanted to accompany him on the journey, but Bediuzzaman had not consented, since his trip to

Konya was "a personal trip".[124] Yet despite this being the case—Bediuzzaman went to his brother's house then again visited the tomb of Mawlānā Jalāl al-Dīn al-Rūmī—he was met by a huge police presence and followed by police cars wherever he went. He stayed only two hours then returned to Emirdağ.

On 1 January, Bediuzzaman set out once again for Ankara. But now the government had bowed to the pressure of the opposition and he was not permitted to enter the city. His car was stopped by police outside the city and he was told of the cabinet decision "advising" him "to rest" in Emirdağ. That is, henceforth Emirdağ was his place of compulsory residence. Bediuzzaman had already heard the decision, which had been broadcast over the radio, and complied with the request on the car being stopped by the police barricades. He returned to Emirdağ.[125]

He later wrote a statement to the newspapers saying that firstly, because of his illnesses and the fact he very often could not speak, it was a Divine mercy to be requested by the government to remain in Emirdağ. He hoped his students would not be offended at his not being able to respond to their invitations. Secondly, a proof that his journeys were nothing to do with politics was that among other things, due to the rule taken from the Qur'an, "*No bearer of burdens can bear the burden of another*," meaning, "to disturb public order is to wrong ninety innocents on account of five criminals", their service was extremely beneficial for the country and public security. For that reason he forgave the police who had caused him difficulties. And thirdly, because the *Risale-i Nur* had spread everywhere and was so sought after, he had received invitations from twenty provinces, of which he had only been able to visit three. Now he was happy to be in Emirdağ, but wanted to go to Isparta.[126]

Bediuzzaman's Last Days[127]

On returning to Emirdağ, Bediuzzaman apparently no longer concerned himself with the plight of Menderes and the

The Third Said

government. He had done whatever he could to warn them, and now, through their own intervention, he was able to do no more. In fact, his student Said Özdemir reported Bediuzzaman as saying at this point: "Menderes did not understand me. I shall depart soon. And they too will go—overturned, head over heels."[128] The government had indeed lost its credibility by then in the face of İnönü's attacks and the continual incidents provoked throughout the country, and its grip on the country's affairs continued to decline from this time onwards. İnönü was visited in his house by leading members of the military. The plans were laid for the coup. Menderes survived only two months after Bediuzzaman's death. The increased surveillance under which Bediuzzaman was now held continued right up to the time of his death.

He remained in Emirdağ for some eight days then, in accordance with the wish he had stated to the press, on 20 January he went to Isparta. Here he stayed in his rented house till 17 March, when he returned to Emirdağ for two days. The month of Ramaḍān began that year on 26 February. Thus it was 19 Ramaḍān 1379 when Bediuzzaman set off for Emirdağ in his car together with Zübeyir, Mustafa Sungur, and Hüsnü Bayram, who acted as the driver. His health had deteriorated considerably. Until 15 Ramaḍān, he had even been able to perform the *tarāwīḥ* prayers then he had started to fail. The following day in Emirdağ, Bediuzzaman's students called the doctor, Tahir Barçın, himself one of Bediuzzaman's students, for Bediuzzaman was now seriously ill.

According to Dr Barçın, who answered their call immediately, Bediuzzaman's temperature was 38° and his condition was serious: he had caught double pneumonia. He gave him an injection of penicillin then Bediuzzaman dozed off. A short while later, he smiled, opened his eyes and said to those present:

> My brothers! The *Risale-i Nur* now prevails over this country. It has broken the backs of the Masons and communists. You will suffer some difficulties, but the end will be truly good.[129]

In the morning his condition was easier and he announced that they were returning to Isparta. The preparations were made and unlike previous occasions when Bediuzzaman had left for somewhere else, this time he bade a sorrowful farewell to the faithful Çalışkans and all his students in Emirdağ. Still, the doctor wrote, it did not occur to them that he was going to die. It was only when they later heard the news from Urfa that they realised that he had been bidding them farewell for the last time.[130]

Later in the afternoon of 19 March, Bediuzzaman arrived back in Isparta. His students Tahiri Mutlu and Bayram Yüksel were waiting for him. An hour previously the police had come searching for him saying that they had left Emirdağ. The account is now Bayram Yüksel's.[131] He states that it was with great difficulty that they got Bediuzzaman out of the back seat of the car, where he lay, and up the stairs to the house. He was running a high temperature and could not be left. That night at around two o'clock Bayram and Zübeyir were with him when Bediuzzaman suddenly said: "We're going!" On their asking where, he replied: "Urfa... Diyarbakır." They thought he was feverish. He kept on repeating, "Urfa. We're going to Urfa." The car tyres needed repairing, but he insisted, even if it means hiring another car, they would go. Finally, the repairs were done, the back of the car was made up as a bed and at exactly 9 o'clock on 20 March they were ready for the road. Two police were watching the house. Tahiri Ağabey was to remain to watch the house; he was not to open the door to the police. Bediuzzaman said good-bye to the landlady, Fıtnat Hanım, she also would say nothing to the police of their destination; and they set off.

It was raining. The rain grew harder and they were not seen as they passed through Eğridir. Before Şarkîkaraağaç they daubed the number-plate in mud, and after it, Bediuzzaman recovered a little, got out of the car and renewed his ablutions at a spring by the side of the road and performed the prayers on a flat rock. Later his condition again worsened and he could not speak. On entering

The Third Said

Konya they stopped and bought cheese and olives with which to break the Ramaḍān fast. They had all been reciting Āyah al-Kursī since leaving Isparta against the evil intentions of the governor of Konya, whose vow to "rip up the Nurcus by the roots" had made the headlines in all the newspapers. Through Divine grace, they passed unspotted through Konya, skirting the mosque of Mawlānā Jalāl al-Dīn.

They continued. Karapınar. Ereğli. Now Bediuzzaman could not get out of the car to pray. At sunset they were at Ulukışla. It grew very cold. Bediuzzaman could eat nothing. They passed through Adana in the dark, and reached Ceyhan, where they performed the evening prayers and Hüsnü, the driver, slept for an hour. At the time to eat *saḥūr*, they were at Osmaniye. Here they filled up the tank with petrol. Bediuzzaman again ate nothing. At around 7.30 on the morning of 21 March, they reached Gaziantep. They continued. The road was now very rough, churned up with a mixture of snow and mud, but they passed along it without mishap. Finally they reached Urfa at exactly 11 o'clock that morning, which was Monday.

Urfa

On arriving in Urfa,[132] the first place they went was the Kadıoğlu Mosque, where Abdullah Yeğin stayed. Bediuzzaman's student since a schoolboy in Kastamonu, he had spent nearly ten years in Urfa, helping to build it up as an important centre of *Risale-i Nur* activity. They discovered the best hotel, the İpek Palas, and took Bediuzzaman there. He was now in a very poor state. His students had to virtually carry him up to the room they took, Number 27 on the third floor. Then followed the most extraordinary tussle between the police and government representatives on the one hand, who on the orders of the Interior Minister in Ankara, tried to compel Bediuzzaman to return to Isparta, and his students, the people of Urfa and some officials on the other, who categorically refused to allow the extremely ill and weak Bediuzzaman to be moved anywhere.

Bediuzzaman had a joyous reception from the people of Urfa, who began to gather outside the hotel and visit him in an unending stream. Bayram Yüksel writes that he had to hold Bediuzzaman's hands for the people to kiss. Yet despite his extreme weakness and contrary to his previous practice, he received all who came. And all did come: tradesmen, army officers, soldiers, police, officials, ordinary people; they came in their hundreds. Bediuzzaman explained to Abdullah Yeğin the importance of Urfa, speaking of the service to Islam of its people, who, being Turkish, Arab, and Kurdish, would be a means to unity and Islamic brotherhood. He managed to keep going and receive all the people who kept coming.

Suddenly two plain-clothes police arrived and told Bediuzzaman's students that they had to get ready to leave and return to Isparta. These were joined by eleven or so others. They informed Bediuzzaman, who declared:

> How strange! I came here to die, and perhaps I will die. You can see my condition, you defend me!

They replied that they had their orders and brought Hüsnü together with the car round to the front of the hotel. The hotel manager began protesting at his guest being treated in this way. The crowd became excited, and started shouting and protesting. The situation became very tense. The police could no longer enter the hotel. Then the car disappeared and the crowd calmed down a little. The people continued to visit Bediuzzaman.

The police insisted, saying the order came directly from the Interior Minister in Ankara, Namık Gedik, and was final. Bediuzzaman would be sent by ambulance if they did not take him by car. His students said it simply was not possible, and in any event, it was not up to them to relay police orders to him. The heated exchanges continued in this vein. Telegrams were sent to Menderes. Hundreds of telegrams passed between Ankara and Urfa that day. The people declared they would not let Bediuzzaman go.

The news spread that Bediuzzaman was going to be expelled from Urfa. The president of the Urfa branch of the Democrat Party heard, and going straight to the police headquarters, told the police chief in the strongest terms that Bediuzzaman was their honoured guest and that there was no question of his being treated in this way. The argument continued and the Democrat Party president banged his revolver down on the police chief's desk, making it plain that if they were to resort to force, the police would have to dispose of him first.

Meanwhile a crowd of five or six thousand gathered outside the hotel. The Democrat Party president brought the government doctor, who examined Bediuzzaman. He had a temperature of 40°. The doctor pronounced him unfit to travel, and said a general report would be made out the following day.

It was now Tuesday evening. Bediuzzaman's students were taking turns to remain with him. They were all exhausted. Bayram slept for two hours, then Zübeyir woke him up; he could not keep going any longer. Then Hüsnü went and joined Zübeyir and Abdullah Yeğin. Only Bayram was left. He stayed with Bediuzzaman. The door was locked against any possible intrusion. Bediuzzaman was running a high temperature and was feverish. He could no longer speak. He had wanted some ice during the day, but they had been unable to find any. Later they found some, but he had not wanted it. His lips were parched. Bayram wiped them with a damp handkerchief. This elevated degree of fever was new. At two thirty in the morning Bayram kept pulling up the covers, which Bediuzzaman kept throwing off. He draped a cloth over the light to reduce its brightness. Then suddenly Bediuzzaman reached up with his hand and touched Bayram's neck; he was massaging Bediuzzaman's arms. Bediuzzaman put his hands on his chest and slept. Or so Bayram thought. But Bediuzzaman had not fallen asleep, he had departed this life and his spirit had flown to the eternal realm. It was three o'clock in the morning of Wednesday, 23 March 1960; 25 Ramaḍān 1379.

Bediuzzaman is Buried in the *Halilürrahman Dergah*

Bayram lit the stove so that Bediuzzaman would not get cold, for he thought he was sleeping. A while later Zübeyir and the others came. Bediuzzaman's body was hot, but no sound came from him. It was not till they sent for Vaiz Ömer Efendi, a well-known religious figure who was visiting Urfa, who as soon as he entered the room, uttered the words, "*To God do we belong, and to Him we shall return,*" that they could accept that Bediuzzaman had died.

The news spread instantly around Urfa. Zübeyir, Hüsnü, and Abdullah went to telephone and telegraph *Risale-i Nur* students in Emirdağ, Isparta, Istanbul, and all over Turkey. The hotel owner came to the door, and started wailing when he saw what had happened. He met the police chief on the stairs and told him the news. The police chief had come to the hotel together with a troop of gendarmes to take Bediuzzaman by force back to Isparta; they returned to the police headquarters. The police sent a doctor to make out a report. But the doctor felt doubtful and only later wrote his report, for the body was so hot; it did not resemble the normal state of death. He did not want him to be buried immediately.

Then the estate lawyer came; he noted down Bediuzzaman's personal effects and fixed their value. According to the report in the newspaper, *Akşam*, this was 551 liras 50 kuruş. That is to say, apart from his watch, gown, prayer-mat, tea-pot and glasses, and a few odds and ends, Bediuzzaman owned nothing in the world. On the request of his students, Bediuzzaman's only surviving brother, Abdülmecid, was made the sole heir to these.

As the news spread, thousands of people started to pour into Urfa. It was decided that Bediuzzaman's body would be washed and buried in the *Dergah*, where the Patriarch Abraham lies. He was taken there after the midday prayers. The people of Urfa closed all the shops and filled the streets. While the body was washed and wrapped in its shroud on Wednesday afternoon thousands of white-winged pigeons and birds other sorts flocked and flew in the air above the *Dergah*. It was raining gently. Bediuzzaman's body was washed by Mullah Abdulhamid Efendi. Also present were Zübeyir, Bayram, Hüsnü, and Abdullah, and also the *Risale-i Nur's* "first student", Hulûsi Bey. Bediuzzaman's body was then taken to the Ulu Mosque, where it was to rest till it was buried. The Qur'an was read continuously and prayers were recited. The mosque was filled.

The burial was to have taken place on Friday, but the numbers of people crowding into Urfa from all over Turkey and beyond became so great, the governor called Bediuzzaman's students and said that he would have to be buried on Thursday following the afternoon prayers. They had no option but to agree. It was announced over loudspeakers.

The funeral prayers were performed in the courtyard of the Ulu Mosque then the bier holding the body was raised up and carried on the hands of the crowd. The governor of Urfa, the mayor, the local garrison commander, the people of Urfa, those of the *Risale-i Nur* students who had been able to reach Urfa in time for the burial, thousands of people crowded in and around the mosque then moved in a thronging mass to carry the body the short distance to the *Dergah*. Everyone wanted to touch the bier, and it was passed from hand to hand as is the custom; after close to two hours it was only with the assistance of soldiers and police, who opened up the way, that it was finally brought to the *Dergah* and buried.

It was still raining. That night the recitations of the Qur'an continued unceasingly over the grave. Bediuzzaman was now resting near the Patriarch Abraham, the Friend of the Most Merciful. The tomb in which he had been laid had been built in 1954 by a local shaykh called Shaykh Muslim, while repairs were being made to the *Dergah*. He dreamt three times that he was told that the tomb belonged to another, as a result of which he ordered that on his death he be buried in the general graveyard. And so they buried Bediuzzaman in the tomb, but it was to be only a temporary resting-place for him.

The Military Junta Orders the Removal of Bediuzzaman's Remains to an Unknown Spot

The military coup Bediuzzaman had foretold occurred on 27 May 1960. Foremost Menderes and leading members of his government, and Democrat deputies, officials, and sympathizers were all rounded up and sent to various camps and prisons. A campaign was started against the *Risale-i Nur* students and movement. Once again the searches, confiscations, arrests, imprisonment, and court cases began. Hundreds of *Risale-i Nur* students were subject to this new wave of vengeful repression. The country was now governed by the so-called National Unity Committee, and the decision was taken to move Bediuzzaman's remains to an unknown spot. They could not even leave him in peace in his grave, just as they had hounded and harassed him up to his last moments in this world. His brother writes:

> It was in early July and three and a half months since my elder brother's death. I had performed the midday prayers on time in the house I rented near Mawlānā's tomb in Konya when the Special Branch chief, whose name I learnt was İbrahim Yüksel, came. He told me that the governor wanted me. Together we went to the governor's office. On our entering, there were three generals. One was Cemal Tural, and one was Refik Tulga. Refik Tulga was at that time the Second Army commander and temporary governor of Konya.
>
> Cemal Tural said to me: 'The people in the east and from beyond our southern borders are coming and visiting your brother's grave illegally. The times are sensitive. With your co-operation, we're going to move his grave to inner Anatolia. Please sign this paper.'
>
> He handed me a petition written as though by myself. I read it and said: "I have no such wish. At least leave him in peace in his grave." But they told me:
>
> "You have to sign it. Don't put us in a difficult position."
>
> We climbed into the vehicle that was to take us to the airfield after signing the petition...Finally we boarded the aeroplane. My family and children knew nothing of this. Of course they were all anxious and frightened.

We reached Diyarbakır. After a brief rest we boarded a different plane and took off for Urfa. They took me in a military vehicle to an army building. They offered me some food, but I didn't want it; I was exhausted. We had landed at Urfa in the afternoon. After nightfall they took me in a jeep together with a captain and some soldiers to the *Halilürrahman Dergah*. There were two coffins in the courtyard of the mosque. There were a number of soldiers wandering about.[133]

From other accounts we learn that this was the night of 12 July 1960. The town had been taken over by the army. There was a strict curfew and no one was allowed on the streets. Tanks and armoured vehicles had been positioned at all key points in the town. The *Dergah* was surrounded by a tight cordon of soldiers. Acting on the orders they had received, soldiers entered the twin-domed building containing Bediuzzaman's tomb, not by the door, but by breaking the iron grill on the windows. They then began to smash the marble slabs of the tomb with hammers.[134]

Abdülmecid continues: A doctor came up to me and said: "Don't be too anxious and upset. We're moving Ustādh to Anatolia. That's why they have brought you here." I completely broke down on hearing these words and I started to weep.

The doctor told the soldiers: "Open that coffin and take Ustādh out of it and put him in this one." But the soldiers held back and were frightened, "We can't do it. We'll be struck down", they said. But the doctor told them: "My brothers, we have our orders. We have to do it." We opened the coffin altogether. I was saying to myself, "Seyda's bones will be all mixed up together." But on touching the shroud with my hand, it felt as though he had only just died. Only the shroud had discoloured slightly round its opening. And on the outside was a stain like from a drop of water. The doctor opened the shroud. I looked at his face; he was smiling. Again altogether we embraced the great and wronged Ustādh and placed him in the large, extremely heavy coffin the soldiers had brought.[135] They filled the empty space in the coffin with grasses and herbs. When everything was completed, we climbed into an army truck and went straight to the airfield. The streets were all being patrolled by soldiers with bayonets fixed.

> The coffin would not fit in the first plane. [Hours later] a second plane arrived. We put the coffin in it, and I sat beside it. I was utterly sorrowful and my eyes full of tears.[136]

And to continue from another account by Abdülmecid which is more detailed:

> I reckon the journey was six to seven hours. We landed at Afyon near mid-afternoon. Of course, it was they who said it was Afyon. After landing, they unloaded the coffin and placed it in an army lorry. I again sat in the driver's cab. Behind us were two jeeps and small trucks. We set off. It was a mountainous region. I don't know where we went and in what direction, and I didn't ask. I was as though dazed by the situation.
>
> We travelled slowly for I reckon about seven hours, in the late hours of the night we arrived somewhere and stopped. There were several soldiers and non-commissioned officers. They had dug a grave and were awaiting us. They immediately and hastily unloaded the coffin, put it in the waiting grave, and covered it with earth. While they were doing this, I looked around, and although I could not see very well, the place resembled a mountain-side. There was a wall about a metre in height. I climbed onto it and looked around; there was not a light to be seen. Everywhere was in complete darkness.
>
> They buried the coffin. The work was finished. An N.C.O. said to me: "Do you want to stay here tonight, *Hoja*, or do you want to return home?" I thought, what shall I do if I stay here. A short time later a black car arrived. The driver was a soldier. I got in and it set off. After travelling for about one and a half hours we approached a town with lights. I asked the driver where the lights were, what town. He replied, "Eğridir." We continued on our way and I returned to my house in Konya at eight or nine o'clock.

Thus, due to this barbaric act, Bediuzzaman found his final resting-place in his beloved Isparta in accordance with his wishes, and so too, with the exception of two or three of his closest students and a small number of officials bound to secrecy by oath, the location of his grave remains unknown.

Finally, in some couplets entitled *Eddâi* (The Supplicant), included in the introduction to *Leme'ât*, a sizeable collection of pieces written in semi-verse and first published in 1921, Bediuzzaman foretold both the year of his death and that his grave would be demolished. A literal translation is as follows:

> My demolished grave in which is heaped up*
> Seventy-nine dead Said's** with his sins and sorrows.
> The eightieth is a gravestone to a grave;
> Altogether they weep*** at Islam's decline.
>
> Together with my gravestone and moaning grave of dead Said's
> I go forward to the field of tomorrow's future.
>
> I am certain that the skies of the future and Asia
> Will together surrender to Islam's clean, shining hand.
>
> For it promises the prosperity of belief;
> It affords peace and security to mankind.

Bediuzzaman's footnotes are as follows; the second and third he added in the 1950's:

* This line is his signature.

** Since the body is renewed twice every year, it means that [each year] two Said's have died. Also, this year Said is in his seventy-ninth year. It means one Said has died every year, so that he will live to this date. [Bediuzzaman died in 1379 according to the Hijrī calendar, and his grave was demolished and moved in 1380.]

*** With a premonition of the future, he perceived its present state, twenty years later.

Notes

1. Nursi, *Şualar*, 446 (Eng. tr.: *Rays*, 523).
2. *Tarihçe*, 537.
3. Nursi, *Emirdag Lahikası*, ii, 17.
4. Ibid., 56.

5. *Ibid.*, 24,
6. *Ibid.*, 178.
7. *Ibid.*, 83, 76, 100.
8. *Ibid.*, 213-4.
9. *Tarihçe*, 537-8; Hilmi Pancaroğlu, in *Son Şahitler*, iii, 169.
10. Nursi, *Emirdağ Lahikası*, ii, 6-7.
11. Şahiner, *Said Nursi*, 414-5; Tahsin Tola, in *Son Şahitler*, i, 158.
12. Mehmet Çalışkan, in *Son Şahitler*, iv, 57; 59.
13. Hafız Nuri Güven, in *Son Şahitler*, iv, 37.
14. Nursi, *Emirdağ Lahikası*, ii, 16; Şahiner, *Said Nursi*, 381.
15. Nursi, *Emirdağ Lahikası*, ii, 29.
16. *Ibid.*, 53-4; 23-4.
17. Bayram Yüksel, in *Son Şahitler*, i, 392-6; Şahiner, *Said Nursi*, 383-4.
18. *Tarihçe*, 569.
19. *Ibid.*, 570; Eşref Edip, *Said Nursi, Hayatı, Eserleri, Mesleği*, 119.
20. Nursi, *Müdâfaalar*, 477-80.
21. Eşref Edip, *Said Nursi*, 123.
22. M. Emin Birinci, in *Son Şahitler*, i, 258.
23. See also, Muhiddin Yürüten, in *Son Şahitler*, iii, 80-1; Dr Alaeddin Yılmaztürk, in *Son Şahitler*, ii, 45-6.
24. *Tarihçe*, 575; Eşref Edip, *Said Nursi*, 125-130; Nursi, *Emirdağ Lahikası*, ii, 127-8.
25. Eşref Edip, *Said Nursi*, 130-152.
26. *Tarihçe*, 583.
27. Şahiner, *Said Nursi*, 396.
28. See also, Avni Toktor, in *Son Şahitler*, iv, 191.
29. Muhsin Alev, in *Son Şahitler*, i, 220-1; Osman Yüksel Serdengeçti, in *Son Şahitler*, ii, 61-9.
30. Mehmet Şevket Eygi, in *Son Şahitler*, v, 218-9.
31. Muhsin Alev, in *Son Şahitler*, i, 221.
32. Mustafa Ramazanoğlu, in *Son Şahitler*, iv, 223-4.
33. İbrahim Fakazlı, in *Son Şahitler*, v, 21.
34. Eşref Edip, *Said Nursi*, 90.
35. Nursi, *Emirdağ Lahikası*, ii, 146-7.
36. Mehmet Fırıncı, in *Son Şahitler*, iii, 234.
37. For a description, see also, M. Emin Birinci, in *Son Şahitler*, i, 257.
38. Nursi, *Emirdağ Lahikası*, ii, 55.
39. Salih Özcan, in *Son Şahitler*, iii, 130-1.
40. *Tarihçe*, 624; 626.
41. Nursi, *Emirdağ Lahikası*, ii, 138-40.
42. *Ibid.*, 148-50.
43. *Ibid.*, 63; Kâmil Acar, in *Son Şahitler*, ii, 251-2.
44. Hakkı Yavuztürk, in *Son Şahitler*, ii, 269-70.

45. Kâmil Acar, in *Son Şahitler*, ii, 250; Nursi, *Emirdağ Lahikası*, ii, 55.
46. For example, Ömer Adil Mehalifçi, in *Son Şahitler*, v, 122-3.
47. Nursi, *Emirdağ Lahikası*, ii, 62; Şahiner, *Said Nursi*, 384.
48. It may be noted here that only ten years subsequent to the sending of *Zülfikar*, which in particular puts forward proofs of the Prophethood of Muḥammad (ṣ) and the Qur'an being the Word of God, Islam was recognised by the Second Vatican Council as a genuine revealed religion and means of salvation.
49. Şahiner, *Said Nursi*, 405.
50. Mehmet Fırıncı, in *Son Şahitler*, iii, 218.
51. *Ibid.*, 218-38.
52. See, Nursi, *Emirdağ Lahikası*, ii, 135-7.
53. Nursi, *Emirdağ Lahikası*, ii, 97-99.
54. Qur'an, 2:29, 67:3, 71:15.
55. Mehmet Fırıncı, in *Son Şahitler*, iii, 226-7.
56. The governor was Fahreddin Gökay, a co-founder with Bediuzzaman of the Green Crescent Society in May, 1920.
57. Muhsin Alev, in *Son Şahitler*, i, 223; Mehmet Fırıncı, in *Son Şahitler*, iii, 234.
58. *Ibid.*, 221.
59. Hüseyin Cahid Payazağa, in *Son Şahitler*, v, 269-70.
60. Münir Çapanoğlu, in Şahiner, *Nurs Yolu*, 131.
61. Hüseyin Cahid Payazağa, *Ibid.*, 270.
62. Muhsin Alev, in *Son Şahitler*, i, 226.
63. Mehmet Fırıncı, in *Son Şahitler*, iii, 235.
64. Bayram Yüksel, in *Son Şahitler*, i, 398; 406.
65. *Ibid.*, 386-461.
66. *Tarihçe*, 596-8; Şahiner, *Said Nursi*, 410-11.
67. Mahmud Çalışkan, in *Son Şahitler*, iv, 68-9; Bayram Yüksel, in *Son Şahitler*, i, 409-10.
68. *Ibid.*, 414.
69. See, Mehmet Fırıncı, in *Son Şahitler*, iii, 239-43; M. Emin Birinci, in *Son Şahitler*, i, 264-6; Hakkı Yavuztürk, in *Son Şahitler*, ii, 267-73.
70. Bayram Yüksel, in *Son Şahitler*, i, 406-7.
71. Şahiner, *Said Nursi*, 413-5.
72. Said Özdemir, in *Son Şahitler*, v, 49-50; M. Emin Birinci, in *Son Şahitler*, i, 266-7.
73. Mehmet Fırıncı, in *Son Şahitler*, iii, 244.
74. M. Emin Birinci, in *Son Şahitler*, i, 284.
75. Nursi, *Emirdağ Lahikası*, ii, 36-7.
76. See, Ahmed Gümüş, in *Son Şahitler*, i, 319.
77. Giyaseddin Emre, in *Son Şahitler*, ii, 56.
78. Nursi, *Emirdağ Lahikası*, ii, 194-7.

79. See, Nursi, *Emirdağ Lahikası*, ii, 24; 56.
80. *Ibid.*, 35.
81. Mustafa Sungur, in *Nur—The Light*, Vol. V, No. 57, September 1990, 2-4.
82. Qur'an, 6:164, 17:15 etc.
83. Nursi, *Emirdağ Lahikası*, ii, 82.
84. *Ibid.*, 97-8.
85. Nursi, *Emirdağ Lahikası*, ii, 81-3.
86. *Ibid.*, 132, 143.
87. *Ibid.*, 143.
88. *Türkiye Tarihi*, iv, 186.
89. Şahiner, *Said Nursi*, 415-6.
90. Ali Tayyar, in *Son Şahitler*, v, 112.
91. Nursi, *Emirdağ Lahikası*, ii, 203.
92. Hulûsi Yahyagil, in *Son Şahitler*, i, 40; Nursi, *Emirdağ Lahikası*, ii, 14.
93. See, *Son Şahitler*, iv, 307-316.
94. See, M. Emin Birinci, in *Son Şahitler*, i, 267-7; Mustafa Türkmenoğlu, in *Son Şahitler*, iv, 110-12.
95. Şahiner, *Said Nursi*, 419-20.
96. Ali Tayyar, in *Son Şahitler*, v, 110-14.
97. See, pp. 153-4, 162-3, 163-6, 189-91, 202.
98. Nursi, *Emirdağ Lahikası*, ii, 198-9.
99. *Ibid.*, 172.
100. *Ibid.*, 172-3, 155.
101. *Ibid.*, 183.
102. *Ibid.*, 102-4.
103. *Ibid.*, 120-1.
104. Nursi, *Emirdağ Lahikası*, i, 132-3.
105. Nursi, *Emirdağ Lahikası*, ii, 173.
106. Nursi, *Emirdağ Lahikası*, i, 166.
107. Kâmil Acar, in *Son Şahitler*, ii, 256.
108. Salih Özcan, in *Son Şahitler*, iii, 131-2.
109. Vahdi Gayberi, in *Son Şahitler*, iv, 12-13.
110. Nursi, *Emirdağ Lahikası*, ii, 187-8, 204-5, 206.
111. *Türkiye Tarihi*, iv, 184-5.
112. Transformed into a mosque by Fatih Sultan Mehmet on his conquering Istanbul in 1453, for nearly 500 years Aya Sophia had been the symbol of Islamic supremacy over Christianity. It was made into a museum by secret Cabinet decision in October, 1934, and closed to worship. On the pretext of repairs, it has remained as such, having been opened to worship only partially in 1991. See, Eyice,

The Third Said 465

Semavi, "Ayasofya," in *İslam Ansiklopedisi*, iv, 206-10; "Ayasofya Zulmü," in *Yakın Tarih Ansiklopedisi*, vii, 6-104.
113. Tahsin Tola, in *Son Şahitler*, i, 160.
114. Şahiner, *Said Nursi*, 421.
115. Nursi, *Emirdağ Lahikası*, ii, 193.
116. Said Özdemir, in *Son Şahitler*, v, 53-4; Şahiner, *Said Nursi*, 421.
117. See, Nursi, *Emirdağ Lahikası*, ii, 213-9.
118. See, Mehmet Fırıncı, in *Son Şahitler*, iii, 248-9.
119. Said Özdemir, in *Son Şahitler*, v, 55.
120. Said Köker, in *Son Şahitler*, v, 151.
121. Giyaseddin Emre, in *Son Şahitler*, ii, 57-8.
122. Tahsin Tola, in *Son Şahitler*, i, 160-1.
123. Nursi, *Emirdağ Lahikası*, ii, 208-9.
124. Fehmi Yılmaz, in *Son Şahitler*, i, 245.
125. For an account, see, Re'fet Kavukçu, in *Son Şahitler*, ii, 231-8. It includes some newspaper cuttings, one of which describes "the battle of words" in the National Assembly between Menderes and İnönü on the subject of Said Nursi.
126. Nursi, *Emirdağ Lahikası*, ii, 211-12.
127. Said Özdemir, in *Son Şahitler*, v, 55.
128. Şahiner, *Said Nursi*, 436.
129. Tahir Barçın, in *Son Şahitler*, ii, 133.
130. Bayram Yüksel, in *Son Şahitler*, i, 429-34.
131. The following account is taken from Şahiner, *Said Nursi*, 440-51; Abdullah Yeğin, in *Son Şahitler*, i, 373-8; Bayram Yüksel, in *Son Şahitler*, i, 434-40.
132. Şahiner, *Said Nursi*, 461-3.
133. *Ibid.*, 456-7.
134. As Abdülmecid had mentioned, there were two coffins: one of galvanised metal, which was placed inside a large second coffin of zinc. They were sealed with solder on Bediuzzaman's body being placed in them, after being treated with chemicals.
135. N. Şahiner, *Said Nursi*, 463-4.
136. *Ibid.*, 466-7; Nursi, *Sözler*, 647 (Eng. tr.: *Words*, 727).

Conclusion

Bediuzzaman Said Nursi emerges from these pages as a unique figure whose service to the Qur'an and belief this century is without equal. The child prodigy from Nurs who at the age of fourteen silenced in debate all the *'ulamā'* of the region and from an even earlier age displayed an instinctive dissatisfaction with the existing educational system went on in his maturity as the New Said to open up a new way of relating the Qur'anic truths which would be the means of reinvigorating the belief of millions of Muslims within the framework of Orthodox Sunni Islam.

Bediuzzaman was born at a time when the fortunes of the Islamic world were at their lowest ebb, yet it was his unwavering conviction that the Qur'an and Islamic civilization would dominate the future and be the means of mankind's salvation, as the lines quoted above foretelling the year of his death illustrate. Foregoing every sort of comfort and personal benefit and undertaking every difficulty, he sacrificed himself to this end, chiefly serving it through his learning, but also as the Old Said through energetic participation in social and political life and in the wars and movements of that time. Realizing at an early age that science also would dominate the future, contrary to other religious scholars, and indeed he received opposition because of it, Bediuzzaman studied and mastered most of the modern physical and mathematical sciences. He also took up the study of philosophy in the belief that it could be made to serve Islam.

And while his wide knowledge of both of these was reflected in his Qur'anic commentary and "fruit" of his life, the *Risale-i Nur*, it was his inner struggle to free himself from philosophy which made way for the emergence of the New Said, who took the Holy Qur'an as his "sole guide."

Bediuzzaman's study of science and involvement with philosophy should be seen in the context of the increasing Western influence in the Ottoman Empire at the end of the 19th and early 20th centuries and the attacks which were being made on the Qur'an and Islam in the name of science and materialism and Positivist philosophy in particular; he studied them so as to be able to answer these attacks. On the founding of the Republic, the drive for Westernization received a strong impetus and philosophy was progressively inculcated into the Turkish people at the expense of Islam. In keeping with the extraordinary perspicacity and farsightedness that he displayed at every stage of his life, Bediuzzaman had perceived these designs of the new regime at the outset and understanding that it was not to be combated in the realm of politics, had withdrawn from social and political life. Within a short time he was proved right, for as he later wrote, in modern states, where freedom of conscience is accepted as a fundamental principle, internal *jihād* has to be on the level of ideas and learning. Struggle with weapons and the sword in the way of religion has made way for "religious striving of an immaterial nature with the sword of true and certain belief." Thus, when he was sent into exile in western Anatolia, with his learning in science and philosophy as well as the religious sciences he was uniquely well-fitted to pursue this goal.

In his exile which was little better than captivity, Bediuzzaman started writing treatises which demonstrate all the truths of belief by means of powerful proofs. Using logical proofs and reasoned argument and frequently comparing Qur'anic teaching and civilization with those of philosophy, they specifically answer the questions and doubts raised by philosophy and the scepticism it causes. This method, which shows these truths in an unprecedented way, as well as solving and explaining with convincing proofs many mysteries of religion, indeed resulted in large numbers of people attaining certain belief, and had unparalleled success under the repressive conditions of those times, spreading throughout Turkey. Furthermore, since Westernization is a universal phenomenon and Western materialist philosophy has permeated the Islamic world, the success of these writings, the *Risale-i Nur*, in saving and strengthening belief has continued to grow, and is now to be witnessed throughout the Islamic world.

Other aspects of the *Risale-i Nur* have been described, so suffice it to say here that through the inspiration of the Qur'an, with the *Risale-i Nur*, Bediuzzaman opened up a "direct way to the truth" whereby firm belief in the truths of religion may be gained in a short period of time. The essential teachings of theology and knowledge of God that formerly took many years to master and acquire are presented to "the fast-travelling sons of this age" in a manner appropriate to their mentality and which answers their needs.

Bediuzzaman saw this century and its events and the rise of materialism and communism in the context of the end of time and insisted above all else that what took precedence in the struggle against these was the saving and strengthening of belief. It is also in this context that his insistence on the way of positive action and peaceful *jihād* or *jihād* of the word (*ma'nawī jihād*) for the *Risale-i Nur* students should be seen. Another of the unique features of the *Nur* movement, it may be seen as an important factor in both its survival and growth during the twenty-five years of single-party rule, and continued growth ever since.

Bediuzzaman stated that the aim of those working to impose materialist philosophy was destruction of a moral, immaterial nature. Thus, the prime duty of the *Risale-i Nur* students was "the service to belief which resulted in the preservation of public order and security." Their service had to be of a constructive nature, repairing the damage, and acting as a barrier against it. It was in the cause of this positive action that Bediuzzaman, who had bowed before no one as the Old Said, as the New Said bore with patience all the insults, injustice, and torments meted out to him. Moreover, despite the fact that they were utilised against him, he accepted the law and state institutions rather than challenging them; his battle was with the small number who, concealing their true faces, were the moving force behind the destruction that was being wrought. It was a covert battle, and it was due to Bediuzzaman and his students responding positively to the provocation, subversion of the law, and other illegal attempts of this "5%" to silence and eliminate them, that they prevailed over them. Although they fell from power, the struggle between those working to establish materialist philosophy of some form under the guise of Westernization or modernization and those striving in the way of Islam and religion continued in essentially the same form. Thus, the last time Bediuzzaman addressed his students before his death, the point he stressed above all others was this question of positive action and peaceful *jihād*. And this is the path the movement had taken.

Turkey had been virtually broken off from the Islamic world during the years of single-party rule. Upon the Democrats gaining power in 1950, one of Bediuzzaman's endeavours was to have the *Risale-i Nur* translated into Arabic so that it could show the effectiveness in the strengthening and renewal of belief it had demonstrated in Turkey on a wider scale. As many Islamic countries were gaining their independence he saw this as a means to Islamic Unity; unity based on the "brotherhood of belief" from which would spring co-operation in many fields. Indeed, it was at this time that he translated (from Arabic into Turkish) the text of his Damascus Sermon of 1911, and had it published with alterations, which deals with this question and foresees the supremacy of Islam that he once again started to speak of at that time.

Also connected with the Islamic world was Bediuzzaman's Eastern University, the Medresetü'z-Zehra, concerning which he addressed the President and Prime Minister in 1955 in connection with the setting up of the Baghdad Pact. He judged that an educational establishment which combined the religious and modern sciences and was of sufficient stature to attract students from the eastern Islamic world would both bring together the Muslims of those countries, and besides encouraging unity and reconciliation in that troubled region, would combat communist influence and its depradations. The forces that aimed to divide the Islamic world, and the moral decay, dissension, and disunity they caused had to be combated through the positive means of learning, knowledge and religion. Such a university, he stated, would be "the foundation-stone and chief citadel" of peace in that area and the Middle East.

As time passes, Bediuzzaman's statements and predictions concerning the future become realised, his judgements as to which course of action should be taken are proved correct, and his importance become clearer. At a time that the Islamic world was apparently crushed beneath the heel of Europe, he foretold its rise and saw the Qur'an holding sway over the future, the age of science and reason. While the part he played through the *Risale-i Nur* in this rise is now indisputable, in the future it will undoubtedly be universally accepted. For in his refuting Naturalism and the other materialist philosophies which are the mainstays of atheism and unbelief and chief means of attacking religion in modern times, and in demonstrating in pure form in the *Risale-i Nur* the Qur'anic message in a way that addresses modern man's mentality, that is, in expounding and explaining the face of the Qur'an that looks to this age, he performed a service to Islam which is without equal. Just as the *Risale-i Nur* continues to save and strengthen the belief of increasing numbers of Muslims throughout the Islamic world, so is it the means of increasing numbers of non-Muslims entering Islam. That he and the *Risale-i Nur* are the Regenerators of Religion promised each century in the Ḥadīths of the Prophet (ṣ) cannot be doubted. Indeed, in this age of tumult and upheaval when darkness has threatened to engulf mankind, the Light which Muḥammad (ṣ) brought, the Light of Divine Revelation and true knowledge, has found a worthy vessel in the *Risale-i Nur*, through which it is reflected into the hearts and minds of millions of believers, and through which, God willing, it will illuminate the future.

Addendum
Selections from the *Risale-i Nur*

1. The Order in the Universe

While the reasoning from work to author, like the evidence of fire to smoke, is known as the argument from material cause to material effect, the reasoning from material effect to material cause, like the evidence of smoke to fire, is known as argument *a posteriori*. The latter is sounder and freer from doubt.

One of the proofs of the above-mentioned verses [Qur'an, 2:21-22] indicating the Maker's existence and unity is the proof of divine providence (*dalīl ināyatī*). This proof consists of the order and regularity which preserves the universe and all its parts from disturbance, difference, and being dispersed, and which, taking all its particulars under order, gives it life. It is the source of all good things, instances of wisdom, benefits, and advantages. All the verses of the Qur'an which speak of benefits and advantages proceed on this order and manifest it. Therefore, just as order, which is the source of all things good, beneficial, and useful, most certainly points to the existence of an orderer, by also pointing to the orderer's purpose and wisdom, it repulses the delusion of blind chance.

O man! If your mind and view are powerless to find this elevated order and you are not capable of reaching it through inductive reasoning, that is, through general investigation, consider the universe by means of the sciences, which have arisen from the meeting of minds—called the conjunction of ideas—and are like the senses of humankind; read its pages so that you may see this elevated order, which leaves minds in amazement.

Indeed, sciences have been formulated that study each part of the universe, or they will be formulated. As for the sciences, they consist of universal laws. And the universality of laws indicates the excellence of the order and its beauty. For that which lacks order can have no universality. For example, there is a white turban on the head of each religious scholar. This statement, which may be made due to universality, reflects the existence of order in the scholar class. Since this is so, by virtue of the universality of its laws, each of the physical sciences, the result of general investigation, is a proof of the existence of an elevated order in the universe. Each science is a light-giving proof which, by showing the fruits of the benefits which hang like bunches of grapes from the chains of beings and the advantages concealed in their changing states, proclaims the purpose and wisdom of the Maker. Quite simply, each science is a shining star piercing the darkness and repulsing the satans of delusion and doubt. That is, each is a star that pierces and destroys those vain, absurd doubts.

Friend! Rather than investigating the whole universe in order to find the order, study the following example carefully and your goal will be achieved.

Despite its smallness, a microbe or organism invisible to the eye comprises an extremely fine and wonderful divine machine. Since it is a contingent being, its existence and non-existence are equally possible. Its coming into existence without a cause is impossible; its coming into existence from a cause is necessary. As for the cause, it could not be natural causes, because the fine order of the machine is the work of knowledge and consciousness, and natural causes are lifeless things without knowledge or intelligence. The person who claims that such a fine machine, which leaves minds in astonishment, arises from natural causes, together with attributing the consciousness of Plato and wisdom of Galen to each minute particle of the causes, has to believe that there is communication between the particles. And this is a nonsense and superstition that puts to shame even the famous Sophists.

Furthermore, the coming together in indivisible particulars of the forces of attraction and repulsion has been chosen, which are held to be the basis of material causes. But their coming together is not permissible since they are opposed to one another. But if what is meant by the laws of attraction and repulsion is the divine laws, known as *ādātullāh*, and the Sharī'ah of Creation, which is called nature, it is permissible. Their coming together is acceptable on condition they are not shown to be nature despite their being merely laws, nor thought to have external existence although they exist only in the mind, nor to be actual matters despite being theoretical matters, nor to being effective although they are only instruments. That is not permissible.

Friend! If you have seen with your mind the order and regularity in the microscopic animal's, that is, the microbe's, large factory, which I have given as an example, raise your head and look at the universe! You will see and read that elevated order which is written in clear and legible fashion on the pages of the universe, for it is as clear and obvious as the universe itself.

From *Signs of Miraculousness*.

2. Part of Bediuzzaman's Refutation of Nature

In Short: The imaginary and insubstantial thing Naturalists call Nature, if it has an external reality, can at the very most be a work of art; it cannot be the Artist. It is an embroidery, and cannot be the Embroiderer. It is a set of decrees; it cannot be the Issuer of the decrees. It is a body of the laws of creation, and cannot be the Lawgiver. It is but a created screen to the dignity of God, and cannot be the Creator. It is passive and created, and cannot be a Creative Maker. It is a law, not a power, and cannot possess power. It is the recipient, and cannot be the source.

To Conclude: Since beings exist, and as was stated at the beginning of this treatise, reason cannot think of a way to explain the existence of beings apart from the four mentioned, three of which were each decisively proved through three clear Impossibilities to be invalid and absurd, then necessarily and self-evidently the way of Divine Unity, which is the fourth way, is proved in a conclusive manner. The fourth way, in accordance with the verse quoted at the beginning:

"Is there any doubt about God, Creator of the heavens and the earth?" (Qur'an, 14:10) demonstrates clearly so that there can be no doubt or hesitation the Divinity of the Necessarily Existent One, and that all things issue directly from the hand of His power, and that the heavens and the earth are under His sway.

O you unfortunate worshipper of causes and Nature! Since the nature of each thing, like all things, is created, for it is full of art and is being constantly renewed, and, like the effect, the apparent cause of each thing is also created; and since for each thing to exist there is need for much equipment and many tools, there must exist a Possessor of Absolute Power Who creates the nature and bring the cause into existence. And that Absolutely Powerful One is in no need of impotent intermediaries to share in His Dominicality and creation. God forbid! Rather, He creates cause and effect together directly. And in order to demonstrate His wisdom and the manifestation of His Names, by establishing an apparent causal relationship and connection through order and sequence, He makes causes and Nature a veil to the hand of His power so that the apparent faults and defects in things should be ascribed to them, and in this way His dignity be preserved.

Is it easier for a watch-maker to make the cog-wheels of a clock, and then arrange them and put them in order to form the clock? Or is it easier for him to make a wonderful machine in each of the cog-wheels, and then leave the making of the clock to the lifeless hands those machines? Is that not beyond the bounds of possibility? Come on, you judge with your unfair reason, and say!

And is it easier for a scribe to collect ink, pen, and paper, and then using them proceed to write out a book himself? Or is it easier for him to create in the paper, pen, and ink a writing-machine that requires more art and trouble than the book, and can be used only for that book, and then say to the unconscious machine, "Come on, you write it!", and himself not interfere? Is that not a hundred times more difficult than writing it himself?

If you ask: Yes, it is a hundred times more difficult to create a machine that writes a book rather than writing it out oneself. But isn't it in a way easier, because the machine is the means for producing numerous copies of the same book?

We would reply: Through His limitless power, the Pre-Eternal Inscriber continuously renews the infinite manifestations of His Names so as to display them in ever-differing ways. And through this constant renewal, He creates the identities and special features in things in such a manner that no missive of the Eternally Besought One or dominical book can be the same as any other book. In any case, each will have different features in order to express different meanings.

If you have eyes, look at the human face. You will see that from the time of Adam until today, indeed, until post-eternity, together with the conformity of their essential organs, each face has a distinguishing mark in relation to all the other faces; this is a definite fact. Therefore, each face may be thought of as a different book. Only, for the artwork to be set out, a different writing-set, arrangement and composition is required. And in order to both collect and situate the materials, and to include everything that is necessary for its existence, a completely different workshop will be required for each.

Now, knowing it to be impossible, we thought of Nature as a printing-press. But apart from the composition and printing, which concern the printing-press, that is, setting up the type in a specific order, the substances that form an animate being's body, the creation of which is a hundred times more difficult than that of the composition and ordering, must be created in specific proportions and particular order, brought from the furthest corners of the cosmos, and placed in the hands of the printing-press. But in order to do all these things, there is still need for the power and will of the Absolutely Powerful One, Who creates the printing-press. That is to say, this hypothesis of the printing-press is a totally meaningless superstition.

Thus, like these comparisons of the clock and book, the All-Glorious Maker, Who is powerful over all things, has created causes, and so too does He create the effects. Through His wisdom, He ties the effect to the cause. Through His will, He has determined a manifestation of the Greater Shari'ah, the Shari'ah of Creation, which consists of the Divine laws concerning the order of all motion in the universe, and determined the nature of beings, which is only to be a mirror to that manifestation in things and to be a reflection of it. And through His power, He has created the face of that nature which has received external existence, and has created things on that nature, and has mixed them one with the other.

Is it easier to accept this fact, which is the conclusion of innumerable most rational proofs—in fact, is one not compelled to accept it?—or is it easier to get the physical beings that you call causes and Nature, which are lifeless, unconscious, created, fashioned, and simple, to provide the numberless tools and equipment necessary for the existence of each thing and to carry out those matters, which are performed wisely and discerningly? Is that not utterly beyond the bounds of possibility? We leave it to you to decide, with your unreasonable mind.

The unbelieving Nature-worshipper replied: "Since you are asking me to be fair and reasonable, I have to confess that the mistaken way I have followed up to now is both a compounded impossibility, and extremely harmful and ugly. Anyone with even a grain of intelligence would understand from your analyses above that to attribute the act of creation to causes and Nature is precluded and impossible. And that to attribute all things directly to the Necessarily Existent One is imperative and necessary. I say:

'All praise be to God for belief,' and I believe in Him. Only, I do have one doubt...."

From *Nature: Cause or Effect*

3. Proofs of Divine Unity

The second phrase: 'He is One.'

This phrase demonstrates an explicit degree in the profession of Divine Unity. A convincing argument which proves this degree comprehensively is as follows:

When we open our eyes, when the universe fastens our gaze on its face, the first thing that attracts our eyes is a universal and perfect order; we see that there is a comprehensive and sensitive equilibrium. Everything exists within a precise order and delicate balance and measure.

If we look a little more carefully, a continual ordering and balancing strikes our eye. That is to say, someone is changing the order with regularity and renewing the balance with measuredness. Everything is a model and is clothed in a great many well-ordered and balanced forms.

And when we study it even more closely, a wisdom and justice appear behind the ordering and balancing. A purpose and benefit is considered, a truth, a usefulness is followed in the motion of everything, even the minutest particles.

And when we study it with even greater attention, what strikes the gaze of our consciousness is the demonstration of a power within an extremely wise activity, and the manifestation of a most comprehensive knowledge which encompasses all functions of all things.

That is to say, the order and balance that are in all beings show us plainly a universal ordering and balancing, and the ordering and balancing, a universal wisdom and justice; and the wisdom and justice in turn show us a power and knowledge. That is to say, One Powerful over all things and Knowledgeable of all things reveals Himself to the mind behind these veils.

Furthermore, we look to the beginning and end of all things, and particularly in animate creatures we see that their beginnings, origins, and roots are such that it is as if their seeds contain all the systems and members of those creatures, each in the form of an instruction sheet and timetable. And again, their fruits and results are such that the meanings of those animate creatures are filtered and concentrated in them; they bequeath their life histories to them. It is as if their seeds are collections of the principles according to which they are created, and their fruits and results a sort of index of the commands of their creation. Then we look to the outer and inner faces of those animate creatures. The free disposal of an utterly wise power and the fashioning and ordering of an utterly effective will is apparent. That is, a strength and power creates; a command and will clothes with form.

Thus, when we study all beings carefully, we observe that their beginnings are instruction sheets prepared by One Possessing Knowledge, and that their ends are plans and manifestos of a Maker; that their outer faces are most skilful and beautifully proportioned dresses of artistry devised by One Who Chooses and Wills, and their inner faces, the most well-ordered machines of an All-Powerful One.

This situation and state, therefore, necessarily and self-evidently proclaims that no time and no place, absolutely nothing, can be outside the grip of power of one single Glorious Maker. Each thing and all things, together with all of their functions, are organised and directed within the grip of power of an All-Powerful Possessor of Will; and they are made beautiful with the ordering and graciousness of a Merciful and Compassionate One; and they are embellished through the adorning of a Loving Benefactor. Indeed, for anyone who is conscious and has eyes in his head, the order and equilibrium, and ordering and adorning that there are in the universe and in the beings within it demonstrate at the degree of unity One Who is Single, Sole, Solitary, Unique, All-Powerful, Possessing of Will, All-Knowing and All-Wise.

Assuredly, there is a unity in everything; and as for unity it points to one. For example, this whole world is illuminated by one lamp, the sun; in which case, the world's Owner is also One. And, for example, all the animate creatures on the earth are served by air, fire, and water, each of which is one and the same. So the One Who employs them and subjugates them to us is also One.

From the *Twentieth Letter*.

4. An Explanation of Divine Oneness

The Manifestation of Oneness, which is the Third Source: That is, because the Glorious Maker is not physical or corporeal, time and space cannot restrict Him. Creation and space cannot obtrude on His presence and witnessing. Means and mass cannot veil His actions. There is no fragmentation or division in His regarding and acting towards creation. One thing cannot be an obstacle to another. He performs innumerable acts as though they were one act. It is for this reason that in the same way that, as far as its meaning is concerned, a huge tree can be encapsulated in a seed, a world also can be contained within a single individual. And like a single individual, the whole world may be encompassed in the Hand of Power.

We have explained this mystery in *The Words* like this: the sun is, to some degree, unrestricted with regard to its luminosity, thus its image is reflected in every burnished and shining object. If thousands and millions of mirrors are exposed to its light, the reflection of the sun's manifestation itself will be found in each one of them without being divided, as though they were a single mirror. If the capacity of the mirror were such, the sun would be able to demonstrate its effects in it in all its magnitude. One thing cannot be an obstacle to another. Thousands of things enter thousands of places with the ease of one thing entering one place. Each place displays the manifestation of the sun as much as thousands of places display it.

Thus, "And God's is the highest similitude" (Qur'an, 16:60), the manifestation of the All-Glorious Maker of the universe is such, with His attributes which are light and with all His Names which are luminous that, through the mystery of the functioning of Oneness, although He is not in any place, He is all-present and all-seeing in all places. There is no division in His regarding and acting towards the creation. He performs every task at the same time, in all places, without difficulty, without hindrance.

Thus, it is through these mysteries of the Assistance of Unity, Facility of Unity and Manifestation of Oneness that when all beings are attributed to a single Maker, the creation of all of them becomes as simple and easy as that of a single being. And each being can be as valuable as all beings as regards the fineness of its art. This truth is demonstrated by the fact that, within the boundless plenitude of beings, there are endless subtleties of art in every individual. If the beings are not attributed directly to a single Maker, then each becomes as problematical as all beings and the value of all beings decreases; it falls to that of a single being. Should this be the case, either nothing would come into existence, or if it did, it would be without value, worthless.

Thus, this mystery led the Sophists, who were the most advanced of the people of philosophy, to realise that the path of associating partners with God was hundreds of thousands of times more difficult than the way of truth and path of affirming Divine Unity; that it was irrational to the utmost degree. So, because they had averted their faces from the way of truth and looked to that of unbelief and misguidance, they were compelled to renounce their reasons and deny the existence of everything.

From the *Twentieth Letter*.

5. The Renewal of Belief and the Highway of the Qur'an

You ask concerning the wisdom contained in the saying: "Renew your belief by means of 'There is no god but God.'" The wisdom in it has been mentioned in many of *The Words* and one aspect of it is as follows:

Since man himself and the world in which he lives are being continuously renewed, he needs constantly to renew his belief. For in reality each individual human being consists of many individuals. He may be considered as a different individual due to the number of the years of his life, or rather to the number of days or even hours of his life. For since a person is subject to time, he is like a model and each passing day clothes him in the form of another individual.

Furthermore, just as there is within man this plurality and renewal, so also is the world in which he lives in motion. It goes and is replaced by another. It varies constantly. Every day opens the door of another world. As for belief, it is both the light of the life of each individual in that person, and it is the light of the world in which he lives. And as for 'There is no god but God,' it is a key with which to turn on the light.

And the instinctual soul, desire, doubts, and Satan exercise great influence over man. In order to damage his belief, they are much of the time able to benefit from his negligence, to trick him with their wiles, and thus to extinguish the light of belief with doubts and uncertainty. And someone who opposes the externals of the Sharī'ah may speak and act in a way that in the view of some religious leaders has an effect no less than absolute unbelief. Therefore, there is a need to renew belief all the time, every hour, every day.

Question: The masters of scholastic theology wrapped up the world in the abbreviated concepts of contingency and createdness and having disposed of it, so to speak, proved Divine Unity. And one school of Sufis, in order to experience God's presence and affirm His Unity fully, said: "Nothing is observed but Him." They thus forgot the universe and drew the veil of oblivion over it, and then fully experienced the Divine presence. Another school of Sufis, in order to truly affirm Divine Unity and enter

God's presence at the highest degree, said: "There is no existent but Him." They relegated the universe to the level of imagination and cast it into non-existence, and then fully entered the Divine presence. But you point out that in the Qur'an is a mighty highway besides these three ways. And you say that its mark is the phrases: "There is nothing sought but Him", and, "There is nothing worshipped but Him." Can you provide me with a brief proof of this highway that concerns the affirmation of Divine Unity and point out a short way leading to it?

The Answer: All the *Words* and *Letters* in the *Risale-i Nur* point out that highway. For now, as you wish, we shall concisely indicate an extensive, lengthy and mighty proof of it.

Each thing in the world ascribes every other thing to it own Creator. And each artistically fashioned object in this world demonstrates that all such objects are the works of its own fashioner. And each creative act in the universe proves that all creative acts are the acts of its own author. And each name that is manifest in beings indicates that all names are the names and titles of the one whom it itself signifies. That is to say, each thing is a direct proof of Divine Unity and a window yielding knowledge of God.

Indeed, each object, especially if it is animate, is a miniature specimen of the universe, a seed of the world, and a fruit of the globe of the earth. Since this is so, the one who created the miniature specimen, seed and fruit must also be the one who created the whole universe, for the creator of the fruit cannot be other than the creator of the tree that bears it.

So in the same way that each object ascribes all other objects to its own fashioner, each act also ascribes all other acts to its author. For we see that each creative act appears as the tip of a law of creativity that is so extensive as to encompass most other creatures, and so long as to reach from particles to galaxies. That is to say, whoever performs the creative act must be the author of all the creative acts which are tied to the universal law that encompasses those beings and stretches from particles to galaxies.

For sure, one who gives life to a fly must the one who creates all insects and animals and who gives life to the earth. And whoever spins particles as though they were Mawlawī dervishes must be the one who sets successive beings in motion as far as the sun travelling through the skies with its planets, for the law is a chain and creative acts are tied to it.

That is to say, just as each object ascribes all other objects to its fashioner, and each creative act attributes all acts to its author, in exactly the same way, each Divine Name manifest in the universe ascribes all Names to the One Whom it itself describes and proves that they are His titles. For the Names manifest in the universe are like intersecting circles and blend with one another like the seven colours in light; they assist one another and perfect and adorn one another's works of art.

For example, the instant the Name of Giver of Life is manifested on a thing and life is given, the Name of All-Wise also becomes manifest; it orders the body which is that animate creature's dwelling-place with wisdom. At the same time, the Name of Munificent is manifested; it adorns the creature's dwelling-place. So too, the manifestation of the Name of All-Compassionate appears; it presents the body's needs with tenderness. At the same instant, the manifestation of the Name of Provider appears; it supplies the material and spiritual sustenance necessary for the continued existence of the animate creature in unexpected ways. And so on. That means whoever the Name of Giver of Life belongs to, the Name of All-Wise, which is luminous and comprehensive in the universe, is His. Similarly, the Name of All-Compassionate, which nurtures all creatures with tenderness, is His. And the Name of Provider, which sustains all animate creatures with munificence, is His Name and title. And so on.

That is to say, each Name, each act, each object is a proof of Divine Unity. And such a proof that each is a stamp of Divine Unity and each is a seal of Divine Oneness which has been inscribed on the pages of the universe and on the lines of the centuries. Each indicates that all the words of the universe, which are called beings, are inscriptions traced by the pen of its own scribe.

From the *Twenty-Sixth Letter*.

6. The Three Faces of the World

The representative of the people of misguidance said next: "The world is execrated in your Ḥadīths and called 'carrion'. Also, all the saints and people of truth have contempt for the world; they say that it is pernicious and unclean. But you say that it is the means and proof of all the Divine Perfections and you speak of it rapturously?"

The Answer: The world has three faces.

Its First Face looks to God Almighty's Names, and displays their impressions. It is a mirror to them, reflecting their meanings. This face of the world consists of innumerable letters or missives describing the Eternally Besought One. This face is utterly beautiful. It is worthy of love, not loathing.

Its Second Face looks to the hereafter. It is the seed-bed of the hereafter, the arable field of Paradise, and the flower-bed of Mercy. This face is also beautiful like the first one and is deserving of love not contempt.

Its Third Face looks to man's base appetites. It is a veil of neglect and a plaything for satisfying the desires of the worldly. This face is ugly because it is transient and mortal; it is full of pain and it deceives. The contempt described in the Ḥadīths and the loathing of the people of truth, then, is for this face.

The importance and approbation which the All-Wise Qur'an demonstrates in speaking of the universe and beings, is towards the first two faces. It is the first two faces of the world that the Companions of the Prophet (upon whom be blessings and peace) and other people of God seek.

From the *Thirty-Second Word*.

7. Philosophy and the Qur'an

First principle: Look through the telescope of the following story which is in the form of a comparison, and see the differences between Qur'anic wisdom and that of philosophy and science:

One time, a renowned Ruler who was both religious and a fine craftsman wanted to write the All-Wise Qur'an in a script worthy of the sacredness of its meaning and the miraculousness of its words, so that its marvel-displaying stature would be arrayed in wondrous apparel. So the artist-King wrote the Qur'an in a truly wonderful fashion. He used all his precious jewels in its writing. In order to point to the great variety of its truths, he wrote some of its embodied letters in diamonds and emeralds, and some in rubies and agate, and other sorts in brilliants and coral, while others he inscribed with silver and gold. And he adorned and decorated it in such a way that everyone, those who knew how to read and those who did not, were full of admiration and astonishment when they beheld it. Especially in the view of the people of truth, since the outer beauty was an indication of the brilliant beauty and striking adornment in its meaning, it became a truly precious antique.

Then the Ruler showed the artistically wrought and bejewelled Qur'an to a European philosopher and to a Muslim scholar. In order to test them and for reward, he commanded them: "Each of you write a work about the wisdom of this!" First the philosopher, then the scholar composed a book about it. However, the philosopher's book discussed only the decorations of the letters and their relationships and conditions, and the properties of the jewels, and described them. He did not touch on their meaning at all, for the European had no knowledge of the Arabic script. He did not even know that the embellished Qur'an was a book and a writing expressing a meaning. He rather looked on it as an ornamented antique. He did not know any Arabic, but he was a very good engineer, and he described things very well, and he was a skilful chemist, and an ingenious jeweller. And so this man wrote his work according to those crafts.

As for the Muslim scholar, when he looked at the Qur'an, he understood that it was the Perspicuous Book, the All-Wise Qur'an. This truth-loving person neither attached importance to the external adornments, nor busied himself with the ornamented letters. He became preoccupied with something that was a million times higher, more elevated, more subtle, more noble, more beneficial, and more comprehensive than the matters with which the other man had busied himself. For discussing the sacred truths and lights of the mysteries beneath the veil of the decorations, he wrote a truly fine commentary. Then the two of them took their works and presented them to the Illustrious Ruler. The Ruler first took the philosopher's work. He looked at it and saw that the self-centred and nature-worshipping man had worked very hard, but he had written nothing of true wisdom. He had understood nothing of its meaning. Indeed, he had confused it and been disrespectful towards it and ill-mannered even. For supposing that source of truths, the Qur'an, to be meaningless decoration, he had insulted it as being without value in regard to its meaning. So the Wise Ruler hit him over the head with his work and expelled him from his presence.

Then he looked at the work of the other, the truth-loving, scrupulous scholar, and saw that it was an extremely fine and beneficial commentary, a most wise composition full of guidance. "Congratulations! May God bless you!" he said. Thus, wisdom is this and they call those who possess it knowledgeable and wise. As for the other man, he was a craftsman who had exceeded his mark. Then in reward for the scholar's work, he commanded that in return for each letter ten gold pieces should be given to him from his inexhaustible treasury.

And so, if you have understood the comparison, look at its reality and see this:

The ornamented Qur'an is this artistically fashioned universe. And the Ruler is the Pre-Eternal All-Wise One. As for the two men, one—the European—represents philosophy and its philosophers, and the other, the Qur'an and its students. Yes, the All-Wise Qur'an is a most elevated expounder, a most eloquent translator of the Mighty Qur'an of the Universe. Yes, it is the Criterion of Truth and Falsehood which instructs man and the jinn concerning the signs of creation inscribed by the pen of power on the pages of the universe and on the leaves of time. And it looks at beings, each of which is a meaningful letter, as bearing the meaning of another, that is, it looks at them on account of their Maker. It says, "How beautifully they have been made! How exquisitely they point to the beauty of their Maker!" and thus shows the universe's true beauty. But the philosophy they call natural philosophy or science has plunged into the decorations of the letters of beings and into their relationships, and has become bewildered; it has confused the way of reality. While the letters of this mighty book should be looked at as bearing the meaning of another, that is, on account of God, they have not done this; they have looked at beings as signifying themselves. That is, they have looked at beings on account of beings, and have discussed them in that way. Instead of saying, "How beautifully they have been made," they say "How beautiful they are," and have made them ugly. In doing this they have insulted the universe, and made it complain about them. Indeed, *philosophy without religion is a sophistry divorced from reality and an insult to the universe.*

From the Twelfth Word.

8. On The Nature Of Man

Thirty-First Window

"We have created man in the best of forms" (Qur'an, 95:4) "And in the earth there are signs for those who are certain* And in your own selves; will you then not see?" (Qur'an, 51:20-1)

This Window is the Window of man and it is concerned with man's self. For more elaborate discussions of it in this respect, we refer you to the detailed books of the thousands of learned and scholarly saints, and here only indicate a few principles we have received from the effulgence of the Qur'an. It is like this:

As is explained in the Eleventh Word, "Man is a missive so comprehensive that Almighty God makes perceived to him all His Names through his being." For the details we refer you to the other Words, and here only demonstrate three Points.

First Point: Man is a mirror to the Divine Names in three aspects.

The First Aspect: just as the darkness of the night shows up light, so through his weakness and impotence, his poverty and need, his defects and faults, man makes known the power, strength, riches, and mercy of an All-Powerful One of Glory, and so on...he acts as a mirror to numerous Divine attributes in this way. Even, by searching for a point of support in his infinite impotence and boundless weakness in the face of his innumerable enemies, his conscience perpetually looks to the Necessarily Existent One. And since he is compelled in his utter poverty and endless need to seek a point of assistance in the face of his innumerable aims, his conscience in that respect all the time leans on the Court of an All-Compassionate One of Riches and opens its hands in supplication to Him. That is to say, in regard to this point of support and point of assistance in the conscience, two small windows are opened onto the Court of Mercy of the All-Powerful and All-Compassionate One which may all the time be looked through.

The Second Aspect of being mirror-like is this: through particulars like his partial knowledge, power, senses of sight and hearing, ownership and sovereignty, which are sorts of samples given to him, man acts as a mirror to the knowledge, power, sight, hearing, and sovereignty of dominicality of the Master of the Universe; he understands them and makes them known. For example, he says: "Just as I make this house and know how to make it, and I see it and own it and administer it, so also the mighty palace of the universe has a Maker. The Maker knows it, sees it, makes it, administers it." And so on.

The Third Aspect of being mirror-like: man acts as a mirror to the Divine Names the imprint of which are upon him. There are more than seventy Names the impresses of which are apparent in man's comprehensive nature. These have been described to a degree at the start of the Third Stopping Place of the Thirty-Second Word. For example, through his creation, man shows the Names of Maker and Creator, through his 'finest of forms', the Names of Most Merciful and All-Compassionate, and through the fine way he is nurtured and raised, the Names of All-Generous and Granter of Favours, and so on; he shows the differing impresses of different Names with all his members and faculties, all his organs and substances, all his subtle senses and faculties, all his feelings and emotions. That is to say, just as among the Names there is a Greatest Name, so too among the impresses of those Names there is a greatest impress, and that is man.

O you man who considers himself to be a true man! Read yourself! Otherwise you may become someone who is either animal-like or inanimate!

Second Point: This points to an important mystery of Divine Oneness. It is like this:

The relationship between man's spirit and his body is such that it causes all his members and parts to assist one another. That is, man's spirit is a commanding law from among the laws pertaining to creation—the manifestation of Divine Will—which has been clothed in external existence and is a subtle Dominical faculty. Thus, in administering the parts of the body, and hearing their immaterial voices, and seeing their needs, they do not form obstacles to one another, nor do they confuse the spirit. Near and far are the same in relation to the spirit. They do not veil one another. If the spirit wishes, it can bring the majority to the assistance of one. If it wishes, it can know, perceive, and administer through each part of the body. Even, if it acquires great luminosity, it may see and hear through all the parts.

In the same way, "And God's is the highest similitude" (Qur'an, 16:60), since the spirit, a commanding law of Almighty God's, displays this ability in the body and members of man, who is the microcosm, for sure, the boundless acts, the innumerable voices, the endless supplications, the uncountable matters in the universe, which is the macrocosm, will present no difficulty to the all-embracing Will and absolute Power of the Necessarily Existent One. They will not form obstacles to one another. They will not occupy that All-Glorious Creator, nor confuse Him. He sees them all simultaneously, and hears all their voices simultaneously. Close and distant are the same for Him. If He wishes, He sends all to the assistance of one. He can see everything and hear their voices through everything. He knows everything through everything, and so on.

Third Point: Life has a most important nature and significant function, but since it has been discussed in detail in the Window on Life [the Twenty-Third Window] and in the Eighth Phrase of the Twentieth Letter, we refer you to those, and here only make the following reminder.

The impresses in life, which, intermingled, boil up in the form of emotions, point to numerous Names and essential Divine qualities. They act as mirrors reflecting the essential qualities of the Ever-Living and Self-Subsistent One in most brilliant fashion. But this is not the time to explain this mystery to those who do not recognise God or do not yet fully affirm Him, and so we here close this door.

From the *Thirty-Third Word*.

Bibliography

Abdurrahman, *Bediüzzaman'in Tarihçe-i Hayatı*. Istanbul, Necm-i Istikbal Matbaası, 1335 (1919).
Abdürreşid İbrahim (ed. Mehmed Paksu), *İslam Dünyasi ve Japonya'da İslamiyet*, 2 Vols. Istanbul, 1987.
Akşin, Sina (ed.), *Türkiye Tarihi*, Vol. 4, *Çağdaş Türkiye 1908-1980*. Istanbul, 1989.
Albayrak, Sadık, *Meşrutiyet İslamciliği ve Siyonizm*. Istanbul, 1990.
Albayrak, Sadık, *Son Devrin İslam Akademisi, Dar-ül Hikmet-il İslamiye*. Istanbul, 1973.
Albayrak, Sadık, *31 Mart Vak'asi, Gerici Bir Hareket Mi?* Istanbul, 1977.
Albayrak, Sadık, *Yürüyenler ve Sürünenler* (4th edn.) Istanbul, 1989.
Badıllı, Abdülkadir, *Bediüzzaman Said-i Nursî, Mufassal Tarihçe-i Hayatı*, 3 Vols. Istanbul, 1990.
Bahadıroğlu, Yavuz, *Barla'da Diriliş*. Istanbul, 1990.
Bahadıroğlu, Yavuz, *Bediüzzaman Said Nursî, Hayatı, Tefekkürü, Mücadelesi*, Vol. 1 (1876-1923). Istanbul, 1988.
Bahadıroğlu, Yavuz, *Osmanlı Padişahları Ansiklopedisi*, Vol. 3. Istanbul, 1986.
Bahadıroğlu, Yavuz, *Zindanda Şahlanış*. Istanbul, 1990.
Berk, Bekir, *Türkiye'de Nurculuk Dâvası* (3rd edn.) Istanbul, 1975.
Berkes, Niyazi, *Türkiye'de Çağdaşlaşma*. Istanbul, n.d.
Danişmend, İsmail Hami, *İzahlı Osmanlı Tarihi Kronolojisi*, Vol. 4. Istanbul, 1972.
Düzdağ, M. Ertuğrul (Ed.), *Volkan* Gazetesi, *1908-1909*. Istanbul, 1992.
Edip, Eşref, *Risale-i Nur Müellifi, Said Nursî, Hayatı, Eserleri, Mesleği*. Istanbul, 1958.
Ersoy, Mehmet Akif, *Safahat*. Istanbul, 1987.

Freeman-Grenville, G.S.P., *The Muslim and Christian Calendars.* London, 1977.
Hamza, *Bediüzzaman Saidü'n-Nursî'nin Tercüme-i Halinden Bir Hulasa.*
İnal, İbnülemin Mahmut Kemal, *Son Sadrazamlar*, 4 Vols. (3rd edn.) Istanbul, 1982.
Işik, İhsan, *Bediüzzaman Said Nursî ve Nurculuk.* Istanbul, 1990.
Kara, İsmail, *Türkiye'de İslamcılık Düşüncesi*, 2 Vols. Istanbul, 1986-7.
Kısakürek, Necip Fazıl, *Son Devrin Din Mazlumları* (8th edn.) Istanbul, 1988.
Kocatürk, Vasfı Mahir, *Büyük Türk Edebiyatı Tarihi.* Ankara, 1970.
Kodaman, Bayram, *Sultan II. Abdülhamid'in Doğu Anadolu Politakası.* Istanbul, 1983.
Kutay, Cemal, *[Bediüzzaman] Çağimizda Bir Asr-ı Saadet Müslümanı, Bediüzzaman Said Nursî.* Istanbul, 1980.
Kutay, Cemal, *31 Mart İhtilalinde Sultan İkinci Abdülhamit.* Istanbul, 1977.
Kutay, Cemal, *Tarih Sohbetleri*, Vols. 1-6. Istanbul, 1966-7.
Kutay, Cemal, *Trablusgarb'da Bir Avuç Kahraman.* Istanbul, 1978.
Lewis, Bernard, *The Emergence of Modern Turkey* (2nd edn.) London, 1968.
Mardin, Şerif, and others, *Panel, Bediüzzaman Said Nursî.* Istanbul, 1991.
Mardin, Şerif, *Continuity and Change in the Ideas of the Young Turks.* Istanbul, 1969.
Mardin, Şerif, *Religion and Social Change in Modern Turkey, The Case of Bediüzzaman Said Nursî.* New York, 1989.
Mısıroğlu, Kadir, *Kurtuluş Savaşında Sarıklı Mücahitler.* Istanbul, 1980.
Müftüoğlu, Mustafa, *Her Yönüyle Sultan İkinci Abdülhamid.* Istanbul, 1985.
Mürsel, Safa, *Bediüzzaman Said Nursî Ve Devlet Felsefesi.* Istanbul, n.d.
Mürsel, Safa, *Siyasî Düşünce Tarihi Işığında Bediüzzaman Said Nursî.* Istanbul, 1989.
Nursî, Bediüzzaman Said, *Asar-ı Bediyye.* n.p., n.d.
Nursî, Bediüzzaman Said, *Asâ-yı Mûsa.* Istanbul, Sözler Yayınevi, 1982.
Nursî, Bediüzzaman Said, *Barla Lahikası.* Istanbul, Sinan Matbaası, 1960.
Nursi, Bediuzzaman Said, *Bediuzzaman Said Nursi Letters 1928-1932.* Istanbul, Sözler Publications, 2009.

Nursi, Bediuzzaman Said, *Belief and Man* (trans. Şükran Vahide) Istanbul, Sözler Neşriyat, 1992.

Nursî, Bediüzzaman Said, *Beyanat ve Tenvirler*, Istanbul, Sözler Yayınevi, 1976.

Nursî, Bediüzzaman Said, *Emirdağ Lahikası*. Istanbul, Sinan Matbaası, 1959.

Nursî, Bediüzzaman Said, *Emirdağ Lahikası* (Ott. edn.) n.p., n.d.

Nursi, Bediuzzaman Said, *Fruits From the Tree of Light* (trans. Hamid Algar). El Cerrito, California, 1975.

Nursî, Bediüzzaman Said, *Gençlik Rehberi*. Istanbul, Sözler Yayınevi, 1985.

Nursî, Bediüzzaman Said, *Hanımlar Rehberi*. Istanbul, Sözler Yayınevi, 1981.

Nursî, Bediüzzaman Said, *Hutbe-i Şâmiye*. Istanbul, Sinan Matbaası, 1960.

Nursî, Bediüzzaman Said, *İki Mekteb-i Musibetin Şehadetnamesi veya Divan-ı Harb-i Örfî*. Istanbul, Sözler Yayınevi, 1975.

Nursî, Bediüzzaman Said, *İşârâtü'l-İ'caz*. Istanbul, Sözler Yayınevi, 1978.

Nursî, Bediüzzaman Said, *Kastamonu Lahikası*. Istanbul, Sinan Matbaası, 1960.

Nursî, Bediüzzaman Said, *Lem'alar*. Istanbul, Sözler Yayınevi, 1986.

Nursî, Bediüzzaman Said, *Lem'alar* (Ott. edn.) (Envar Neşriyat).

Nursi, Bediuzzaman Said, *Man and the Universe* (trans. Meryem Weld). Istanbul, Sözler Neşriyat, 1987.

Nursî, Bediüzzaman Said, *Mektûbat*. Istanbul, Sözler Yayınevi, 1981.

Nursî, Bediüzzaman Said, *Mesnevi-i Nuriye*. Istanbul, Sözler Yayınevi, 1980.

Nursî, Bediüzzaman Said, *Müdâfaalar*. Istanbul, Tenvir Neşriyat, 1988.

Nursî, Bediüzzaman Said, *Muhâkemat*. Istanbul, Sözler Yayınevi, 1977.

Nursî, Bediüzzaman Said, *Münâzarat*. Istanbul, Sözler Yayinevi, 1977.

Nursi, Bediuzzaman Said, *Nature: Cause or Effect* (trans. Şükran Vahide). Istanbul, Sözler Neşriyat, 1989.

Nursî, Bediüzzaman Said, *Nur Aleminin Bir Anahtarı*. Istanbul, Sözler Yayınevi, 1977.

Nursî, Bediüzzaman Said, *Nur'un İlk Kapısı*. Istanbul, Sözler Yayınevi, 1977.

Nursi, Bediuzzaman Said, *Resurrection and the Hereafter* (trans. Hamid Algar) Berkeley, California, 1980.

Nursi, Bediuzzaman Said, *Signs of Miraculousness. The Inimitability of the Qur'an's Conciseness.* Istanbul, Sözler Publications, 2004.
Nursî, Bediüzzaman Said, *Sikke-i Tasdik-i Gaybî.* Istanbul, Sinan Matbaası, 1960.
Nursi, Bediuzzaman Said, *Sincerity and Brotherhood* (trans. Hamid Algar). El Cerrito, California, 1976.
Nursî, Bediüzzaman Said, *Sözler.* Istanbul, Sözler Yayınevi, 1980.
Nursî, Bediüzzaman Said, *Şuâlar.* Istanbul, Çeltut Matbaası, 1960.
Nursî, Bediüzzaman Said, *Sünûhat.* Istanbul, Sözler Yayinevi, 1977.
Nursî, Bediüzzaman Said, [*Tarihçe*] *Risale-i Nur Külliyatı Müellifi, Bediüzzaman Said Nursî, Hayatı, Mesleki, Tercüme-i Hâli.* Istanbul, Sözler Yayınevi, 1976.
Nursi, Bediuzzaman Said, *The Damascus Sermon* (trans. Şükran Vahide). Istanbul, Sözler Neşriyat, 1989.
Nursi, Bediuzzaman Said, *The Flashes Collection.* Istanbul, Sözler Publications, 2005.
Nursi, Bediuzzaman Said, *The Key to Belief* (trans. Şükran Vahide). Istanbul, Sözler Neşriyat, 1987.
Nursi, Bediuzzaman Said, *The Miracles of Muhammad* (trans. Risale-i Nur Institute of America). El Cerrito, California, 1976.
Nursi, Bediuzzaman Said, *The Rays Collection.* Istanbul, Sözler Publications, 2004.
Nursi, Bediuzzaman Said, *The Supreme Sign* (trans. Hamid Algar), Berkeley, California, 1979.
Nursi, Bediuzzaman Said, *The Tongues of Reality* (trans. Şükran Vahide). Istanbul, Sözler Neşriyat, 1987.
Nursi, Bediuzzaman Said, *The Words on the Nature and Purposes of Man, Life, and All Things.* Istanbul, Sözler Publications, 2008.
Redhouse, *Yeni Türkçe-İngilizce Sözlük* (3rd edn.) Istanbul, 1979.
Sağman, Ali Rıza, *Mevlit Nasıl Okunur ve Mevlithanlar.* Istanbul, 1951.
Şahiner, Necmeddin, *Bilinmeyen Taraflariyle Bediüzzaman Said Nursî* (5th edn.) Istanbul, 1976; (6th edn.) 1988; (8th edn.) 1990.
Şahiner, Necmeddin, *Nurs Yolu.* Istanbul, 1977.
Şahiner, Necmeddin, *Said Nursî ve Nurculuk Hakkında Aydınlar Konuşuyor* (2nd edn.) Istanbul, 1979.
Şahiner, Necmeddin, *Son Şahitler Bediüzzaman Said Nursî'yi Anlatiyor,* Vol. 1 (2nd edn.) Istanbul, 1980.
Şahiner, Necmeddin, *Son Şahitler Bediüzzaman Said Nursî'yi Anlatiyor,* Vol. 2. Istanbul, 1981.

Şahiner, Necmeddin, *Son Şahitler Bediüzzaman Said Nursî'yi Anlatiyor*, Vol. 3. Istanbul, 1986.
Şahiner, Necmeddin, *Son Şahitler Bediüzzaman Said Nursî'yi Anlatiyor*, Vol. 4. Istanbul, 1988.
Şahiner, Necmeddin, *Son Şahitler Bediüzzaman Said Nursî'yi Anlatiyor*, Vol. 5. Istanbul, 1992.
Şahiner, Necmeddin, *Türk ve Dünya Aydınları Gözüyle Nurculuk Nedir*. Istanbul, 1990.
Shaw, S.J. and Shaw, E.K., *History of the Ottoman Empire and Modern Turkey*, Vol. II, *The Rise of Modern Turkey, 1808-1975*. Cambridge, 1977.
Sungur, Mustafa, *Anarşi, Sebeb ve Çareleri* (5th edn.), Istanbul, 1981.
Tunaya, T.Z. *Türkiye'de Siyasal Partiler*, Vols. 1-3. Istanbul, 1984-9.
Vakkasoğlu, A. Vehbi, *Bediüzzaman Said Nursî'den Siyasî Tesbitler*. Istanbul, 1977.
Yakın Tarih Ansiklopedisi, Vols. 6, 7. Istanbul, Yeni Nesil Gazetesi, 1989.
Yeğin, Abdullah, and others, *Osmanlıca Ansiklopedik Büyük Lûgat*. Istanbul, 1987.
Yeğin, Abdullah, *Yeni Lûgat*. Istanbul, 1975.

Index

'Abd al-Qādir al-Jīlānī, 5, 12, 18, 188, 190, 315
Abdülbaki (son Mufti of Van), 220
Abdülbaki Efendi, 223
Abdulhamid Efendi, Mullah, 457
Abdulhamid II, Sultan, 28, 42, 43, 304
Abdulhamid, Sultan, 23, 28, 36, 42, 49, 64, 78, 92, 95, 102, 130, 181, 304
Abdülkadir Uraz, 364
'Abdullah, Mullah, 9, 13, 14
Abdullah Çavuş, 247
Abdullah Cevdet, 65
Abdullah Enver Efendi, 48
Abdullah Yeğin, 318, 320, 321, 324, 444, 453-455
Abdülmecid, 3, 148, 204, 215, 428, 445, 447, 448, 456, 459, 460
Abdürrahim Zapsu, 152
Abdurrahman Akgül, 367-369
Abdurrahman Salahaddin, 359
Abdurrahman son of Mehmed, 143
'Abdurrahman Tağı, Shaykh, 28
Abraham, Prophet, 444, 456, 457
Adana, 453
ādātullāh, 475
Afghānī, Jamāl al-Dīn al-, 23

Afyon, 154, 275, 276, 305, 333, 334, 342, 351, 353, 356, 358, 365-367, 369, 370, 372-374, 376, 378, 380-382, 388, 391-396, 401-403, 405-407, 409, 426, 429, 443, 460
Afyonkarahisar, 305
ağa(s), 108-110, 295
Ağrı, 224
ahl al-ṭarīqah wa al-ḥaqīqah, 302
Ahmad Khānī, 12
Ahmad Ramiz Efendi, 46
Ahmad Sirhindī, Shaykh, 189, 306
Ahmad-i Cano, Mullah, 217
Ahmed Bey, 393
Ahmed Hamdi Akseki (Director of Religious Affairs), 406
Ahmed Muhtar Pasha, 195
Ahmed Rıza, 65, 78, 95
Ahmedî village, 24
Ahmet Feyzi Kul, 277, 392, 394; *see also Risale-i Nur Lawyer*
Ahmet, Sultan, 102, 159
Aḥrār, 78
akhlāq, 164
Akif, Mehmed, 46, 164, 203
Akşam (newspaper), 456
Akşehir Palas, 411, 414, 415

Al-Azhar, 31, 79, 359, 419, 432
Albania, 127
Albanians, 95
Aleppo, 144
Alfred Guillaume (orientalist), 421
'Ali Akbar, Sayyid, 417, 418
Ali Aras, 146
Ali Çavuş, 146, 221
Ali Himmet Berki, 47
Ali Nihad Tarlan, 169
Ali Rıza Balaban, 339
Ali Rıza Efendi, 140, 304
Ali Suavi Efendi, 23
Allah, Name of, 244, 296
America, 119, 124, 404, 433
American, 136, 161, 353, 359
Anatolia, 8, 13, 28, 31, 34, 44, 46, 48, 96, 106, 107, 110, 112, 135, 136, 141, 143, 145, 161, 168-170, 195, 200, 201, 204, 205, 218, 223, 224, 235, 236, 254, 296, 305, 315, 351, 389, 428, 438, 458, 459, 468
Anatolian, 229
Ankara, 161-164, 169, 195, 198, 203-206, 209, 210, 220, 234-236, 243, 263, 265, 267, 274, 276, 284, 293, 306, 324, 326, 328, 329, 333, 337-341, 343, 345-347, 351, 352, 357, 373, 377, 382, 387, 389, 393, 394, 401, 406, 408, 409, 416, 418, 426-428, 438, 439, 445-450, 453, 454
Ankara National Assembly, 163
Antalya, 160, 205, 224, 227, 275
Antichrist, 338; *see also Dajjāl*
anti-Western, 41
'aqliyāt, 184

Arab(s), 21, 114, 121-123, 128, 147, 162, 431, 454; nationality, 431; states, 162; tribes, 21
Arabia, 223, 432
Arabic, 10, 14, 16, 17, 26, 48, 52, 107, 140, 174, 191, 206, 215, 228, 237, 254-256, 258, 263-265, 301, 319, 321, 358, 366, 407, 418, 428, 470, 487
Araçlı Deli Mu'min, 316, 317
Arif Bey, 204
Aristotle, 192
Armenia, 144, 197
Armenian Taşnak revolutionary, 132
Armenian(s), 42, 60, 111, 112, 132, 136, 137, 141-145, 147, 149, 160, 161, 163, 197, 215, 217, 416
Arnavut Adem Ağa, 335
Arvas, village of, 10
Asaf Dişçi, Dr M., 151
Aşağı Kutis, 143
Asia, 70, 74, 76, 105, 113, 125, 432, 461
Asım Bey, Colonel, 275
Asiye Hanım, 305, 306
Atabey, 296, 322
Ataturk, Kemal, *see* Mustafa Kemal
Ataturk University, 433
atheistic committees, 363
Atıf Efendi, Mehmed, 171
Atıf Egemen, 343
Atıf Ural, 447
Austria, 80, 155
Austrian, 80, 139, 153
Avicenna, 192, 244; *see also* Ibn Sīnā
Avni Doğan, 294

Aya Sophia, 80, 87, 89, 90, 94, 95, 202, 282, 423, 446, 449
Āyah al-Kursī, 327, 453
Ayastefanos, 97
Aydın, 275, 277
Ayyūb, Prophet, 21

Babanzade Ahmed Naim Bey, 169
Badī', 30
Baghdad, 12, 15, 140, 305, 430, 431, 433, 471
Baghdad Pact, 404, 430, 431, 433, 471
Bahçelievler, 449
Bahçeseray, 10; *see also* Müküs
Bakhīt, Shaykh, 79, 80, 119
Bakirköy, 97, 423
Balkan War, 129, 130
Bani Han, 19
Barbaros, 129
Barçın, Dr, 451
Barla, 229-232, 234, 235, 238, 240-243, 246-248, 251-253, 262, 263, 265-267, 269, 270, 277, 291, 313, 318, 329, 425, 427, 444
Başid, 32
Başkâtip, 164
Batum, 105
Bayezit, 10, 11, 99, 102, 174; *see also* Beyazit
Bayram Yüksel, 409, 410, 424, 425, 452, 454-457
Bediuzzaman, family members: 'Abdullah, Mullah (brother), 3, 6, 8, 9, 13, 166, 447, 458; Abdülmecid (brother), 3, 215, 428, 445, 447, 448, 456, 459, 460; Abdurrahman (nephew), 44, 152, 166, 172, 187, 188, 203, 251; Mehmed (brother), 3, 17; Rabia (sister-in-law), 215, 217
Bediuzzaman, titles: Said the Famous, 15, 24, 133, 138; Said the New, 36, 135, 178, 186, 187, 189-191, 211, 215, 216, 218, 228, 240, 242, 267, 268, 300, 301, 386, 467, 468, 470; Said the Old, 14, 132, 189, 190, 211, 216, 219, 240, 242, 268, 301, 386, 444, 467, 470; Said the Third, 399, 401, 403, 433, 434; Said-i Kurdi, 46, 165, 166, 195, 288
Bedre, 252, 296
Beirut, 127, 423
Bekir Berk, 439, 448
Bekir Dikmen, 243
Belkan, 51
Benghazi, 129
Berlin, 135, 149, 160, 419
Beşkazalızade Osman Halidi, 305
Bey, Mehmed, 226
Beyazit, 12, 67; *see also* Bayezit
Beylerbeyi Palace, 130
Beyoğlu, 176
Beyrut Palas Hotel, 447, 448
beys, 109
Beytüşşebab, 32, 51
Bilkan, village of, 4
bilvasita, 186
Binbaşı Asım Bey, 252
Bingöl, 449
Bitlis, 3, 10, 13, 15, 16, 23-28, 34, 44, 45, 55, 105, 131, 135, 136, 141, 145-147, 149, 165, 174-176, 204, 205, 354

Bitlis Incident, 131
Bitlisli Kürt Hakkı, 226
Bitlis-Siirt, 147
Bolshevik Revolution, 154, 160
Bolvadin, 275, 277
Bosnia-Herzogovina, 80
Bosphorus, 176, 188, 199, 420
Britain, 112, 160, 162, 163, 169, 196, 404, 431
British, 35, 91, 96, 106, 112, 160-163, 168-170, 191, 195, 196, 198-204, 220, 382
British Colonial Secretary, 35, 191
Bulanık, 34
Bulgaria, 80
Bulgars, 42, 95
Burdur, 224, 227-229, 266
Butcher Tahir, 376
Büyük Cihad, 416, 417
Byzantine Empire, 161

Çaçuan, 143, 144
Cakalı Hamdi, 197, 198
Çaldiran, 221
Caliphate, 45, 71, 96, 168, 169, 204, 207, 220, 235
Çalışkan family, 354, 407
Çalışkan(s), 354, 355, 376, 407, 424, 452
Çalışkan, Mehmed, 354, 407
Cami, Mullah, 133
Çamlıca, 203, 420
Çanakkale, 129, 139
Çapanoğlu, Münir Süleyman, 82, 423
Çarikçi İhsan Efendi, 316
Carpathian, 139
Çatak, 143
Caucasia, 106, 432

Caucasian, 152, 158, 173
Çaycı Emin, 292, 293, 316, 317, 323, 325, 326, 438
Celâl Bayar, 404, 407, 431, 432
Çelebi, 21, 295, 296, 326, 328, 335, 348, 357, 359, 419
cemaat, 110; see also *jamā'ah*
Cemal Can, 263
Cemal Kutay, 97
Cemal Tural, 458
Cemiyet-i Müderrisîn, 171
Cevdet Bey, 141
Ceyhan, 453
Ceylan Çalışkan, 354, 355, 377, 378, 409, 424
Christian(s), 162, 163, 359, 419, 423, 431
Christianity, 119, 179, 180, 359
Christianization, 163
Church of England, 198
Committee of Union and Progress, 43, 64-66, 77-79, 81, 86-88, 91-96, 99, 101, 102, 111, 129, 130, 160, 200
Constantinople, 161, 163
Constitutional Revolution, 43, 287, 364, 388, 423
Constitutionalism and Freedom, 44
Çoravanis, 146
Court Martial, The, 86, 99
Czar, 28, 152, 153

dahā', 180
Dajjāl, 338, 343, 383; see also Antichrist
dalīl ināyatī, 473
Damascus, 106, 114, 127, 140, 183, 282, 306, 359, 428, 470

Dardanelles, the, 129, 160
dars, 150, 217, 228, 262, 424, 438, 448, 449
Darü'l-Hikmeti'l-İslamiye, 158, 159, 164-169, 173-175, 188, 195, 199, 203, 209, 225, 284, 318, 322, 343, 389
Debates, 22, 107, 124
Değirmenler, 228
Deli Mu'min, 316, 317
Democrat Party, 372, 395, 401, 403, 407, 408, 429, 437, 455
Denizli, 236, 289, 322, 323, 326, 328, 329, 333, 334, 337-339, 343, 345-349, 351-353, 355-357, 360, 364, 367, 369, 372, 375, 380, 381, 383, 384, 390, 393, 394, 402, 412
Dergah, 456, 457, 459
Dersaadet, 45, 158
dershane, 426, 438, 444, 445; see also Risale-i Nur Study Centre
Derviş Vahdetî, 90-92, 94
Dhū al-Qarnayn, 256
Dideban, Mount, 145
Dilo, 143, 144
Divanyolu, 202
Divine Unity, 87, 98, 99, 128, 190, 199, 216, 302, 303, 410, 476, 479, 482-485
Diyarbakır, 108, 227, 438, 452, 459
Documents Sur Les Atrocités Arméno-Russes, 143
Dodacanese Islands, the, 129
Doğu, 10, 174, 414
Doğubayezit, 132
Draman, 420, 422, 423
Dündar, 270
Dürriye, 3

East and Kurdistan Gazette, 50
Eastern University, the, 404, 433
Eddâi, 461
Edirne, 130, 416
Edremit, 129
Efendi, Hoja, 133, 230, 231, 247, 248, 278, 279, 295, 325-328, 423
Eğridir, 229, 230, 232, 234, 241-243, 250, 252, 263, 296, 427, 452, 460
Eğridir, Lake, 229, 230, 234, 241, 242, 252
Egypt, 79, 106, 305, 359, 419
ehl-i hakikat, 190
ehl-i Sünnet, 152
ehl-i tarikat, 190
Elazığ, 250
Elhüccetü'z-Zehra, 356, 372, 379, 380
Emanuel Karaso, 66
Emin Böke, 339
Emin Efendi, Mullah Mehmed, 6, 8, 10, 13
Emin, Shaykh, 10, 15, 16, 28
Emirdağ, 14, 337, 351, 353-357, 359, 360, 364, 366, 367, 369, 373, 374, 376, 391, 392, 401, 403, 405-407, 409, 416-419, 423-425, 438, 439, 443, 444, 447, 448, 450-452, 456
Enver Bey, 43
Enver Pasha, 130, 135, 136, 142, 159, 164
Erciş, 34
Ereğli, 453
Erek, Mount, 215, 218, 221-223, 229, 267
Ertuşi tribes, 51

Erzurum, 10, 136, 137, 141, 174, 224, 225, 347, 433
Eskişehir, 274, 276-280, 289, 291, 302, 321, 324, 326, 333, 334, 338, 357, 372, 380, 383, 384, 402, 410, 423, 424, 436, 438
Eskişehir Court, 280, 302, 324, 326, 383, 384
Eşref Edip, 60, 171, 203, 414
Europe, 32, 35, 41, 64, 66, 70, 71, 74, 79, 80, 119, 129, 162, 167, 179, 264, 287, 363, 471
European(s), 41, 53, 65, 66, 76, 80, 112-115, 118-121, 124, 127, 128, 162, 181, 182, 187, 188, 236, 289, 298, 387, 389, 409, 432, 487, 488; Bosphorus, 176; civilization, 41, 80, 120, 182, 432; literature, 181, 182; Powers 114, 162; science and philosophy, 187
Eyyub Ensari, Shaykh, 21

Fahreddin Kerim Gökay, 171
Fārābī, 192
Fatih, 46, 47, 354, 411, 420, 422, 423; *madrasah*, 46, 48, 49
Fatih Mosque, 49, 354, 415
Fātiḥah, Sūrah al-, 5, 327, 443
Fatin Hoca, the Director of the Observatory, 46
Fatwā Emini, 304
fatwā(s), 31, 95, 140, 161, 167, 169, 170, 183, 304
Fehim, Shaykh, 28
Ferah Theatre, 81
Feraşin, 32
Fethullah Efendi, Mullah, 14, 28
Fettah Bey, 19

fetva emini, 140
Fevzi Çakmak, Marshal, 203, 228
Fevzi Daldal, Mehmed, 269
Fevzi Pasha, 228, 229
Feyzi Efendi, 319
Feyzi, Mehmed, 292, 305, 319, 320, 323, 326, 335, 339, 377
fiqh, 26, 164, 239
Fırıncı, Mehmet, 420, 422, 423, 426
First World War, the, 4, 36, 40, 129, 130, 131, 142, 154, 162, 242, 389, 428, 431, 436
Fıstıklı Bağlar, 176
Fizan, 60
Flashes, 427; *see also Lem'alar*
Franchet Despérey, 160
Freedom and Accord Party, the, 200, 201
French, 66, 78, 143, 160, 161, 163, 237
Friday prayers, 128, 221, 274, 381
Fruits of Belief, 334, 337, 340, 344, 349, 356, 357
Futūḥ al-Ghayb, 156, 188, 190

Galata Bridge, 227
Galatasaray Lycée, 414, 415
Galib, 267
Galician, 139
Gawth al-Aʻẓam, 188, 189; *see also* 'Abd al-Qādir al- Jīlānī
Gazi Ahmet Muhtar Pasha, 195
Gaziantep, 453
Georgia, 105, 149
Gevaş, 10, 141, 142, 223; *see also* Vastan
Ghawth al-Jīlānī, 5, 156; *see also* 'Abd al-Qādir al- Jīlānī

Ghazālī, Imam, 12, 190, 315
ghazis, 205
Giyaseddin Emre, 430, 449
Gog and Magog, 313
Gönenli Mehmed Efendi, 336
Grand Vizier, 82, 130
Great War, the, 137, 154, 175, 195
Greek(s), 42, 95, 112, 160, 161, 163, 180, 184, 200, 205, 305, 382, 419, 423
Green Crescent Society, 170
Guide for Youth, A, 319, 322, 357, 358, 368, 387, 409-412
Gülirmak, Mehmed, 270
Gurbet, 249
Güveçli, 348
Güzeldere, 147

Habib, Mullah, 133, 134, 137, 138, 140, 142
Ḥadīth(s), 12, 25, 26, 49, 56, 72, 81, 98, 115, 184, 131, 260, 301, 303, 308, 322, 338, 343, 359, 383, 388, 389, 390, 434, 437, 472, 486
Hafız Ali, 296, 304, 334, 348
Hafız Efendi, Haji, 49
Hafız Hasan Sarıkaya, Haji, 304
Hafız Mustafa, 351, 356, 357
Hafız Nuri, 295
Haji Abdullah Mosque, 228
Hajj, 183, 359
Hakikat Çekirdekleri, 174
Halil İbrahim Çöllüoğlu, 277
Halil Pasha, 142
Hamdi Kasaboğlu, 228
Hamid, Mullah, 216, 218, 219, 221
Hamidiye regiments, 18, 47
Han, 19, 45, 46, 48, 60

han, 46, 47
Ḥanafī fiqh, 26
Hanım, 3
ḥarām, 385
Harbizade Tavaslı Hasan Efendi, 48
Hasan Ali Yücel, 324, 344, 364
Hasan Bey, 221
Hasan Dayı, 334
Hasan Değirmenci, 381
Hasan Efendi, 48, 223
Hasan Fehmi Başoğlu, 46
Hasan Fehmi Bey, 93
Hasan, Mir, 10
Hasan (of Çalışkan family), 354
Hasan Pasha, 28
Hasankale, 139
Haydar tribe, 51, 224
Haydarizade İbrahim Efendi, 169, 171
Hazret-i Ustādh, 378
Hercules, 128
Ḥijāz, 419
Hilmi Bey, 294
Hilmi Pancaroğlu, 381
Hilmi Uran, 363
History of the Ottoman Empire and Modern Turkey, 136
Hizan, 7, 8, 34, 131, 143, 174-176
Ḥizb al-Nūrī, 321, 322, 344
Ḥizb al-Qurʾān, 322
Hizbü'l-Nuri, 302; see also *Ḥizb al-Nūrī*
hoja(s), 133, 152, 159, 208, 231, 254-256, 278, 279, 294, 308, 311, 320, 327, 336, 382, 406
Horhor, 31, 114, 131, 133, 215
Hubab, 206
Hüccetü'l-Baliğa (The Eloquent Proof), 344

hudā, 180
ḥuffāẓ, 247
Hulûsi Bey, 252, 438, 457
Hulûsi Yahyagil, 250, 252
Hür Adam, 142
hürriyet-i şer'iye, 405
Hurşid Pasha, 100
Hüseyin Cahid, 95, 422
Hüseyin Çelebi Pasha, 21
Hüseyin Payazağa, 423
Hüsnü Bayram, 451, 453-457
Hüsrev, 253, 255, 270, 296, 298, 377, 380, 406, 426
Hüsrev Pasha mosque, 131
Hutuvat-i Sitte, 174

Ibn al-Subkī, 14
Ibn Ḥajar, 12
Ibn Sīnā, 192, 244, 260
İbrahim (Bediuzzaman's friend), 23
İbrahim Fakazlı, 336, 377, 378, 415, 416
İbrahim Hakkı Konyalı, 195
İbrahim Mengüverli, 391
İctihad Publishing House, 46
'Īd al-Aḍḥā, 338
İhsan Efendi, 316
İhsan Üstündağ, 247
Iḥyā' 'Ulūm al-Dīn, 12
ijāzah, 8, 13
ijtihād, 185
İkdam, 92
ikhlāṣ, 309, 313, 440
Ikhlāṣ, Sūrah al-, 327
İki [Mekteb-i], 174
İlema, 296
Ilgaz Mountains, 291, 328
Illuminating Lamp (Sirac-ün-Nur), 387
Illuminist, 12

'ilm al-ḥaqīqah, 307
'ilm al-ṭarīqah, 307
Imam Hatip School, 448
İmarat, 381
India, 106, 306, 432, 433
İnebolu, 105, 257, 291, 295, 296, 326, 328, 335-337, 352, 357, 359, 415, 419, 425, 426
İnönü, 275, 364, 430, 436-438, 446, 451
İpek Palas, 453
Iran, 34, 142, 148, 149, 223, 419, 431, 432
Iraq, 137, 431, 433
İrfan Bey, 148
irtijā', 436
İşârât, 174
İşârâtü'l-İ'caz, 428; see also Signs of Miraculousness
Ishārāt al-I'jāz fī Maẓānn al-Ījāz, 140
Ishrāqiyyūn, see Illuminist
İşkodrali Tahir Pasha, 28
Islamic, rule, 124; Unity, 23, 40, 44, 56, 76, 88, 98, 113, 124, 162, 404, 431-433, 470; world, 22, 23, 29, 31, 35, 40, 41, 44, 52, 53, 59, 72, 83, 89, 99, 106, 107, 110, 111, 113-115, 119, 120, 123-125, 129, 162-164, 168, 183, 191, 196, 205, 209, 235, 239, 295, 345, 358, 359, 361-363, 404, 419, 428, 429, 431-434, 467, 469, 470, 471
İslamköy, 296, 334
İsmail Mahir Pasha, 93
İsmail Perihanoğlu, 217
İsmail Tunçdoğan, 328, 329
İsmet İnönü, 324, 430

Index

İsparit, 6, 143, 174
Isparta, 227-230, 251, 252, 257, 267-270, 275, 278, 280, 283-286, 288, 291, 296, 305, 313, 317, 321-324, 326, 328, 329, 333, 334, 337, 338, 352, 356, 357, 361, 366, 369, 386, 393, 401, 402, 406, 408-411, 423-427, 444, 447-456, 460
isrā'īliyyāt, 184
Istanbul, 10, 23, 28, 36, 40, 44-50, 55, 59, 60, 64, 67, 71, 79-81, 83, 86, 90, 94, 95, 102, 105-107, 119, 127, 129, 130, 135, 140, 142, 149, 155, 156, 158-161, 163, 166-169, 174-176, 181, 186-188, 197-205, 219, 224-226, 236, 243, 295, 296, 304, 306, 322, 335, 336, 343, 353, 357, 361, 377, 382, 388, 389, 393, 401, 408-412, 414, 415, 417, 419-423, 426-428, 438, 439, 445, 448, 449, 456
Istanbul University, 410, 411, 415, 421
Italy, 129, 160
İttihad, (newspaper), 146
İttihad-ı İslam, 88
İttihad-ı Muhammedî (Cemiyeti), 86-88; see also the Society for Muslim Unity
Izhār, 58
Izmir, 127, 160, 161, 224, 227
İznikli Osman, 151

Jabriyyah, 72
Jalālī, Muḥammad, 10-12
Jamʿ al-Jawāmiʿ, 12, 14
jamāʿah, 110
Jami, Mullah, 11

Japan, 410, 433
Japanese, 48, 70, 116, 389, 409; army, 116, 409
Jawshan al-Kabīr, al-, [Bediuzaman's book] 302, 409
Jesus, Prophet, 119
Jews, 42, 160
jihād, 131, 135, 162, 170, 201, 381, 405, 429, 468-470
jihād, maʿnawī 429, 469
jihād-ı maʿnawī, 405
Jihanabad, 306
Jizre, 3, 18-21, 33
Joseph, Prophet, 277
jubbah, 292, 305, 306

kaʿbah, 88
Kaʿbah (in Makkah), 58
Kadıoğlu Mosque, 453
Kadir Mısıroğlu, 169
kāfirs, 389
kalām, 26, 56, 164
kalb, 31
kamet, 263
Kanun-u Şer'i, 71
Karamanmaraş, 304
karāmāt, 218, 425
Karapınar, 453
kasbī, 47
Kashmiri, 359
Kastamonu, 289, 291-294, 296, 299, 306, 315-317, 321, 322, 324-328, 335-337, 343, 351, 357, 366, 369, 384, 386, 389, 407, 444, 453
Kastamonu High School, 319
Kastamonu Letters, 291, 313
Kastamonu Prison, 305
Kayihan, Mehmet, 373

Kaymakam, 364, 367
Kayseri, 428
Kazar Dilo, 143
Kazım Karabekir Pasha, 206, 243
Kazım Orbay, 275
Kazımpaşa Primary School, 147
Kel Ali, 146
Kel Mustafa, 20
kelb tahir-dir, 31
Kemal Bayraklı, 380
Kemal Bey, 23, 248
Kemalism, 237
Kemalist, principles, 237; Revolution, 238
Key to Belief, 343, 344
Key to the World of the Risale-i Nur, A, 410, 420, 421
Khālid Baghdādī, 305-307, 444
Khālidī, 28, 305
Khulāṣah al-Khulāṣah, 302
Khuṭba al-Shāmiyya, al-, 174
Kinyas Kartal, 224
Kızıl Ījāz, 174
Kologrif, 150-152
Konsolidçi Asaf Bey, 197
Konya, 139, 366, 439, 445, 447-450, 453, 458, 460; Kopanisli Mullah Yusuf, 217
Kör Hüseyin Pasha, 220-224
Korea, 409, 410, 431
Kosova, 128, 129
Kosturma, 135, 150, 152, 154, 209
Kubbe-i Hasiye, 17
Küçük Aşık, 305
Küfecizade, 223
Kufrawī, Shaykh Muḥammad, 27, 28
Kuleönlü Mustafa, 252, 255
Kuleönü, 296, 337

Kürd Neşr-i Ma'arif Cemiyeti, 198
Kurd(s), 50, 52, 67, 83, 107, 109, 112, 144, 198, 220, 288
Kurdish, 3, 12, 44, 45, 50, 52, 80, 83, 90, 124, 131, 161, 174, 197, 198, 224, 276, 292, 383, 386, 454; family, 3; saint, 12; tirbes, 124
Kurdish Cavalry Regiment, 158
Kurdistan, 40, 44, 45, 50-52, 55, 58-60, 102, 158, 196, 198, 432
Kürdistan Teâli Cemiyeti, 196
Kursī, Āyah al-, 327
kuruş, 59, 174, 175, 230, 247, 329, 456

Lahika (letter), 426
Lato, 143
Lausanne, Treaty of, 162
Lem'alar, 270, 321, 427
Leme'ât, 166, 174, 181, 461
Libya, 129
Lidvadya, 28
Livar, 143
Lütfi, 253

Macedonia, 66, 127
Macedonians, 95
māddī, 429
Madīnah, 87, 359
Madrasah Teachers' Association, 170, 171
madrasah(s), 4, 6, 8, 10-12, 14, 15, 20, 31, 34, 46-53, 56, 57, 71, 73, 83, 84, 95, 105-107, 114, 131-133, 171, 183, 186, 198, 215, 217, 229, 236, 254-257, 267, 270, 304, 353, 376, 433
Mahallebaşı, 148

Mahdī, 308
Mahey, Mir, 142
Mahmud Şevket Pasha, 95
Mahrec, 164, 165, 175
Makkah, 87
maktab(s), 50, 51, 53, 54, 57
Maktūbāt, 189, 190
Malatya Incident, 417
Malazgirtli Acem Ağa, 33
Mālikī school, 31
ma'nawī, 110, 365, 405, 433
Manyasizade Refik Bey, 64
Maqāmāt al-Ḥarīriyyah, al-, 14
Mardin, 18, 21-23, 40
Masum, Shaykh, 220, 223
Matāli', 26
Mathnawī al-'Arabī al-Nūrī, al-, 191
Mauser rifle, 19
Mawāqif, 12, 26
Mawlawī, 485
mawlid, 87, 89, 90
mecidiye, 132
Medrese-i Yûsufiye, 372, 376, 277; *see also* School of Joseph
Medresetü'l-Kuzat, 47
Medresetü'l-Mütehassisin, 169
Medresetü'z-Zehra, 31, 36, 40, 51-54, 127, 129, 130, 198, 209, 300, 404, 432, 471
Mehter, 422
Mektubat, 251, 427
Memduh, 149
Menderes, Adnan, 401, 406, 427, 429-431, 434, 436, 437, 445-447, 449-451, 454, 458
Menemen, 287
Mercan (Bediuzamman's sister), 3
Mesnevi-i Nuriye, 189, 216, 428

Mevlânzâde, 197, 198
Mezraa-i, 143, 144
Midhat, 326
Mihran, 143
Milas, 275
Military Museum, 195
millah, 111, 171, 175
Millet Party, 422
Milliyet, 448
Ministry of Internal Affairs, 149, 176
Miracles of Muḥammad, 259
Miran tribe, 18, 33
Mirqāt, 26
Mirza Efendi, 33, 158, 175
Misbah, 92
Mısırlı, 202, 381
Mithat Altıok, 294, 295
Mizan, 81, 92
Mizancı Murad Bey, 81
Mosul, 28, 137
Mount Başid, 32
Mount Sübhan, 132, 142
mudarris, 13
Mudros Armistice, 160
mufti(s), 55, 137, 169, 406, 428
Muhajir Hafız Ahmed, 241, 247
Muhâkemat, 174, 175, 183, 322
Muhammad Celali, 174
Muḥammad ibn Abdullāh al-Khālidī, 305
Muḥammad, Prophet, 5, 9, 26, 42, 66, 81, 87-89, 91, 122, 153, 186, 260, 264, 303, 314, 433; birthday of , 87; *see also mawlid*; Companions of, 486; Era of, 101; Sunnah of, 87, 185, 443; *see also sunnah*
Muhsin Alev, 410, 413-415, 419, 421, 423

mujaddid, 303, 304, 442
mujāhidīn, 207
mujtahid(s), 185, 186
Müküs, 10, 144
Müküslü Hamza Efendi, 243
Münâzarat, 22, 52, 107, 127, 174
Münir Bakan, 225
Murad Hudavendigar, Sultan, 128
Murji'ah, 72
mürteci, 275
Muş, 145, 146, 149, 205, 430, 449
Musa Kazim, 165
Musibetin Şehadetnamesi, 174
Muslim(s), 35, 49, 66, 76, 81, 88, 89, 91, 93, 98, 110-113, 115-117, 121-125, 128, 131, 135-137, 139, 144, 145, 148, 151, 154, 161, 163, 164, 166, 169-171, 174, 175, 183, 197, 200, 210, 222, 235, 265, 287, 365, 387, 419, 431, 439, 467, 471; community, 36, 186, 200, 315, 327, 365; countries, 405, 431; groups, 123; morality, 145; nation, 112, 386; non-, 89, 110-113, 116, 423, 471; scholar, 153, 487, 488; Turks, 160, 163
Muslim, Shaykh, 457
Mustafa Acet, 376, 392, 444
Mustafa Ağralı, 224
Mustafa Bolay, 152
Mustafa Efendi, Müftü, 277
Mustafa Kemal, 203, 204, 206, 208-210, 221, 236-238, 283, 320, 338, 343, 364, 382, 383, 388, 389
Mustafa Kocayaka, Haji, 347, 351
Mustafa Pasha, 18-21, 33, 198
Mustafa Ramazanoğlu, 304, 358
Mustafa Sungur, 30, 191, 358, 402, 408, 409, 417, 424, 428, 451
Mustafa Yalçın, 138, 139, 150-152
Mutasarrıf Nadir Bey, 23
Muʻtazilah, 72
Mutkan, 51

Nadir Baysal, 325
Namık Gedik (Interior Minister), 454
Namık Kemal, 22, 41, 42, 60
naqliyāt, 184
Naqshbandī, 5, 7, 28, 249; -Khālidī order, 28, 305; Shaykh, 220; *ṭarīqah*, 5, 249, 305
Naqshi Order, 306
Nasrullah Mosque, 292
National Library of Tokyo, 410
NATO, 409
Nazif Bey, 226, 227
Nazif Çelebi, 296
Nazıllı, 438
Necati Müftüoğlu, 380
Necmeddin Şahiner, 48, 49, 82, 130, 132, 138, 142, 143, 152, 171, 195, 197, 225, 226, 228, 278, 315, 326
Nevzat Tandoğan, 236, 328
Nicholas, Czar, 28
Nicholas, Grand Duke, 136, 209
Nicola Nicolayavich, 152
Nihad Bozkurt, 393
Niyazi Bey, 43
Niyazi Misri, 155
Nokta, 174
Nur Madrasah, 241, 425
Nur movement, 258, 311, 352, 358, 359, 391, 402, 403, 408, 411, 415, 424, 430, 438, 439, 469

Index

Nur Muhammad, Sayyid, 7, 8, 28
Nur Postmen, 291, 296
Nur'un İlk Kapısı, 228
Nurcus, 439, 448, 453
Nureddin Burak, 132
Nureddin Topçu, 347
Nuri Benli, 424
Nuriye Hanım, 3, 7, 175
Nurs, 3, 4, 6-10, 24, 33, 40, 55, 143, 166, 174-176, 467
Nurşin, 8, 131, 215, 216, 221
Nutuk, 78, 83

Olukbaşı, 326
Ömer Efendi, 456
Ömer Pasha, 25-27, 33, 150
Osman Nuri Efendi, 204
Osman Yüksel Serdengeçti, 414
Osmaniye, 453
Otpazarı, 381
Ottoman, army, 131, 136, 162; authority, 196; caliphate, 162; census, 137; Empire, 3, 23, 41, 43, 44, 56, 66, 78, 96, 111, 120, 136, 160, 168, 176, 196-198, 204, 306, 431, 434, 468; records, 143; state, 69, 80, 112, 136, 161, 163, 174, 175
Ottomanism, 79
Ottomans, 23, 41-43, 70, 74, 76, 98, 99, 113, 119, 129, 131, 136, 137, 141, 142, 162, 163, 178, 181, 183, 386

Palulu Sadi, 226, 227
Pan-Islamic, 23, 43
Papşin Han, 147
Paris, 64, 78
Pasinler, 136-139, 141, 150

Patriarch Abraham, *see* Abraham, Prophet
Pirmis, village of, 7
Piyer Loti Hotel, 448
Pontus, 161
Postman Kâmil, 278
Poverty Efendi, 112
Priştina, 128

Qāmūs al-Uqyānūs, 17
qaṣīdah, 279
qiblah, 24, 96, 189, 190, 231, 353
qudsiyyāt, 185

Rabbānī, Imam, 189, 190, 306, 315
rak'ahs, 58, 153
Ramaḍān, 183, 211, 223, 277, 278, 321, 324, 326-328, 333, 351, 356, 407, 416, 423, 451, 453, 455
Ramazan'a Ait, 278
Ratifying Stamp of the Unseen Collection, 381, 448
Re'fet Barutçu, 270
Re'fet Bey, 14, 252, 267, 270, 271
Reddü'l-Evham, 30
Refik Bey, Major, 204
Refik Tulga, 458
Regenerator of Religion; *see mujaddid*
Republican People's Party; *see* RPP
Reşad, Sultan, 128-130
Reşad, Sultan Mehmed, 127, 422
Reşadiye (hotel), 411, 414, 415
Resul, Mullah, 217
Rifat Bey, 197, 198
Risale-i Nur Study Centre, 426
RPP (Republican People's Party), 237, 238, 294, 383, 401, 403, 408, 430, 433, 434, 436-439, 446

Ruhi Bey, 276
Rumelia, 70, 127, 129
Rūmī, Jalāl al-Dīn al-, 190, 447, 450
Rumûz, 174, 199
Russia, 112, 116, 135, 136, 143, 144, 148-150, 154, 160, 186, 364
Russian(s), 28, 105, 106, 112, 132, 135-139, 141-149, 151-155, 158, 159, 165, 175, 215, 364; army, 136; soldiers, 144
Russo-Armenian Army, 137
Rustam, 128
Rüştü, 171, 253

Sabahaddin, prince, 78, 79
Sabri, 171, 252, 296, 373, 406
Sadeddin Pasha, 203
Sadık Albayrak, 173
Sadık Bey, 295, 336, 337, 356
Sadık Demirelli, 351
Sadık Pasha, 295
Sadık, Shaykh, 87
Safvet, 171, 295, 327
Şahiner, 48, 49, 82, 130, 132, 138, 142, 143, 152, 171, 195, 197, 225, 226, 326
şahs-ı ma'nawī, 110
saḥūr, 453
Said Köker, 449
Said, Mullah, 19
Salih Özcan, 418, 444
Şāliḥiyah district, 114
Salonica, 43, 64-67, 77, 86, 94, 95, 128-130
Samanpazarı, 328
Şamlı Hafız Tevfik, 243, 267, 306
Samsun, 409, 416, 417, 419
Santral Sabri, 252

Sanūsī ṭarīqah, 23
Sarikamış, 136
Sarıyer, 173, 176, 188
Şark ve Kürdistan Gazetesi, 92
Şarkîkaraağaç, 452
Sasun, 51
Sav, 257, 296, 334, 337, 426, 444
Savurlu Mehmed Fatih, 23
School of Joseph, 277, 372
Şebab, 266
Sebilürreşad, 60, 203, 414
Şefik Pasha, 59
Şehide Mosque, 21
Şehir Hotel, 346, 347, 349, 351
Şehzadebaşi, 195
Şeker Ağa, 33
Şekerci Han, 45, 46, 48
Selahaddin Çelebi, 295, 326, 328, 335, 348, 375, 419
Selim of Hizan, Shaykh, 131
Selim, Sultan, 23, 56
Serbesti, 92, 93
Serbs, 42, 95
Şevket Bey, 277
Şevket Demiray, 230
Şevket Eygi, Mehmet, 414
Şevket Gözaçan, 277
Sèvres, Treaty of, 149, 161, 196
Şeyhan, 8
Şeyhü'l-İslam, 96, 159, 161, 164, 165, 168-171, 173, 198-200, 225, 226, 235
Seyyid Abdülkadir, 196, 226, 227
Seyyid Sadeddin Pasha, 203
Sha'bān, 351
Shāfi'ī, 14; school, 266; school of law, 174
Sharḥ al-Mawāqif, 12
Sharḥ Shamsī, 13

sharʿī, 239
Sharīʿah, 42, 43, 56, 58, 65-68, 70-74, 76, 77, 82-84, 88, 89, 91, 95-98, 100, 101, 111, 112, 118, 120, 125, 172, 179, 185, 186, 205, 208, 264, 312, 405, 475, 478, 483
Shaw, E.K., 136
Shaw, S.J., 136
shaykhs, 27, 28, 109, 215, 294
shūrah, 54
Sıddık Süleyman, 246
Signs of Miraculousness (*İşârâtü'l-İ'caz*), 428
Siirt, 14, 15, 17, 195, 205
Sikuar, 143
Simek, 147
Sinan Omur, 142
Sind University, 418
Sipkan tribe, 51
Sırat-ı Müstakim, 60
Sirkeci, 225, 411, 415
Şirvan, 13, 16, 17
Şişli, 60
Six Steps, The, 200, 201, 203, 382
Skopjans, 128
Skopje, 128
Society for Muslim Unity, the, 86-92, 100, 102
Sofya, 158
Solomon, Prophet, 119
Sözler, 239, 251, 427
Spanish flu, 167
Staff of Moses, The, 357-359, 361, 368, 387, 408, 428
Şuaat, 174
Sublime Porte, 130
Sufi, 5, 51, 57, 71, 87, 183, 190, 236, 254, 285, 294, 302, 310, 311, 338, 383, 483

Sufi Mirza, 3, 33
Sufism, 5, 192, 285, 302, 303, 306, 307
Sufistic, 33
Sufyān, 383, 389
Süheyl Pasha, 87
Şükrü İçhan, 270
Şükrü Kaya, 275, 276, 280
Şükrü Şahinler, 277
Şükrü Saraçoğlu, 324, 344, 364
Süleyman Efe, 336, 337
Süleyman Hünkâr, 336; see also Süleyman Efe
Süleyman, Mullah, 159, 202, 204
Süleyman Rüşdü, 274
Süleymaniye, 226, 426
Sultan Ahmed Mosque, 412
Sunna, see Sunnah
Sunnah, 87, 185, 186, 266, 307, 443
Sunni, 467
Sünûhat, 168, 174, 178, 185
sunūḥāt, 25
Syria, 419

Taʿlīqāt, 174, 175
tafakkur, 217, 301
tafsīr, 26, 56, 239
Tağ, village, 6, 8
Tağı, Shaykh 8
Tahir Barçın, Dr, 353, 451
Tahir Bey, 305
Tahir (governor of Bitlis), 24, 45
Tahir kelb değildir, 31
Tahir Pasha, 28-35, 44-46, 130, 141
Tahiri Ağabey, 452
Tahiri Mutlu, 322, 343, 357, 361, 424, 452
Tahmidiye, 294
Tahsin Aydın, 315

Tahsin Bey, (the governor of Van), 130, 204, 226, 227
Tahsin Efendi, Hoja, 23
Tahsin Efendi, Müftü, 229
Tahsin Tandoğan, 226
Tahsin Tola, Dr, 427
takiyyahs, 51, 54, 57, 71, 87, 254, 285, 294
Tal'at Bey, 95, 96, 150
Tal'at Pasha, 150
Tandoğan, 226, 236, 328, 329
Tanin, 158, 159, 202
Tanzimat, 41
taqlīd, 54, 184
taqwā, 313
tarāwīḥ, 407, 451
tarhana, 377
ṭarīqah(s), 5, 23, 249, 261, 285, 302, 305, 311, 314, 338, 383, 386, 388
Taşköprü, 295
Taşköprülü Sadık, 295, 336
Tatar(s), 148, 149, 154
Tatvin, 147
tawāfuq, 244
Tenekeci Mehmed, 269, 274
Testimonial of Two Schools of Misfortune, The, 86
tevâfük, 244
Tevfik Demiroğlu, 202-204, 225
Tevfik İleri (Turkish Education Minister), 417
Tevfik Rüştü Aras, Dr, 171
Tevfik Tığlı, 263
Thirty-Three Windows, The, 346
Tiflis, 105, 149, 150, 152
Tigris, 3, 18, 19
Tillo, 17, 18
Tokyo, 410

Topkapi, 422
Toprakkale, 215
Toptaşı, 55
Trabzon, 224, 225
Tripoli, 129, 130
Tripolitanian War, the, 129
Tulu'at, 174
Turk(s), 43, 52, 64, 65, 81, 83, 112, 121, 122, 128, 136, 160, 162, 163, 169, 196, 205, 209, 210, 235, 386, 431
Turkestan, 106, 148, 432
Turkey, 3, 64, 88, 129, 130, 136, 159-162, 164, 169, 200, 225, 235, 237, 238, 242, 250, 258, 275, 278, 280, 288, 307, 312, 326, 334, 336, 344, 352-354, 357, 362-365, 402-404, 409, 415, 417-419, 430-432, 434, 438, 441, 442, 444-446, 456, 457, 469, 470
Turkish, 32, 50, 52, 77, 107, 112, 144, 145, 149, 153, 161, 162, 174, 196, 202, 204, 210, 222, 235, 237, 238, 243, 254-256, 263, 269, 278, 293, 317, 361-364, 368, 382, 386, 394, 409, 415, 417, 428, 430, 431, 435, 454, 468, 470

Ubeyd, Ustādh's nephew, 147
'ulamā', 14, 15, 17, 19, 21, 25, 28, 34, 40, 44-49, 52-57, 73, 79, 80, 98, 114, 128, 130, 140, 158, 161, 164, 168-171, 183, 184, 196, 200, 205, 235, 236, 303, 304, 359, 389, 467
Ulu Mosque, 22, 457
Ulukışla, 453

Index 515

Umayyad Mosque, 114, 119, 282
ummah, 304
United States, 124
Urfa, 108, 444, 447, 452-457, 459
Üsküdar, 420
Ustādh, 146-149, 151, 217, 253, 270, 271, 296, 316, 319-321, 326, 328, 368, 375, 378, 381, 414, 415, 441, 444, 459
'Uthmān, Caliph, 306, 402, 424

Vahdetî, 90-92, 94
Vahideddin, Sultan, 200
Vahiduddin, Mehmed, 165
Vaiz, 456
Van, 3, 10, 28, 29, 31, 33-35, 44, 45, 51, 105, 114, 129, 130, 131, 133, 136, 137, 141, 145, 146, 149, 152, 174, 202, 204, 210, 215-217, 220-225, 229, 267, 275, 306, 432, 433
Van, Lake, 3, 129, 141, 145, 217
Vastan, 10; *see also* Gevaş
Vavink, 143
Veli *madrasah*, 10
Venizelos, 160, 161
Visali Bey, 49
Volga, river, 150, 154, 155, 187
Volkan newspaper, 30, 87, 89, 91, 92, 412

wahbī, 47
Wahhabism, 390
Walking Library, 48
War of 1877-78, 112
War of Independence, 162, 205, 235, 305, 315, 362
Warsaw, 135, 149, 155
waṭan, 22

West, 41, 43, 50, 56, 66, 70, 74, 114, 116, 162, 163, 179, 209, 362-364, 404, 419, 434
World Wars, 435

Yavuz Selim, 56, 169
Yemen, 60
Yeşilköy, 95-97; *see also* Ayastefanos,
Yıldız Hotel, 410, 423
Yıldız Palace, 42, 304
Young Turks, 64, 65, 81
Yukari Adr, 143
Yukari Kutis, 143
Yuşa Tepesi, 188
Yusuf Izzeddin Pasha, 203
Yusuf Pasha Mosque, 108
Yusuf son of Mehmed, 143

zakāh, 9, 182, 183, 199
zāwiyah, 53
Zernabad (river), 216, 218, 223
Zeve, 217
Zeylü'l-Zeyl, 206
Zeyneddin Burak, Nureddin Burak's father, 132
Zeynel Efendi, Kadı, 271
zındıka komitesi, 363; *see also* atheistic committees
Ziya Arun, 415, 422
Ziya Dilek, 326, 327
Ziya, Haji, 105
Ziya Pashas, 60
Ziya Sönmez, 357
Zübeyir Gündüzalp, 358, 359, 377, 392, 402, 406, 415, 424, 428, 447, 451, 452, 455-457
Zühtü Efendi, Mehmet, 322
Zülfikar, 357-359, 361, 387, 408

www.ingramcontent.com/pod-product-compliance
Lightning Source LLC
Chambersburg PA
CBHW022055150426
43195CB00008B/139